W9-BYE-576

Rich Dad's
PLAN FOR
FINANCIAL SUCCESS

Rich Dad POOR DAD
**WHAT THE RICH TEACH THEIR KIDS ABOUT MONEY—
THAT THE POOR AND MIDDLE CLASS DO NOT!**

Rich Dad's CASHFLOW QUADRANT
RICH DAD'S GUIDE TO FINANCIAL FREEDOM

Rich Dad's GUIDE TO INVESTING
**WHAT THE RICH INVEST IN, THAT THE
POOR AND MIDDLE CLASS DO NOT!**

Rich Dad's
PLAN FOR
FINANCIAL SUCCESS

Rich Dad POOR DAD
**WHAT THE RICH TEACH THEIR KIDS ABOUT MONEY—
THAT THE POOR AND MIDDLE CLASS DO NOT!**

Rich Dad's CASHFLOW QUADRANT
RICH DAD'S GUIDE TO FINANCIAL FREEDOM

Rich Dad's GUIDE TO INVESTING
**WHAT THE RICH INVEST IN, THAT THE
POOR AND MIDDLE CLASS DO NOT!**

By ROBERT T. KIYOSAKI
with SHARON L. LECHTER, CPA

**BUSINESS
PLUS**

NEW YORK   BOSTON

Compilation Copyright © 2008 by Robert T. Kiyosaki and Sharon L. Lechter
Rich Dad Poor Dad Copyright © 1997, 1998 by Robert T. Kiyosaki and Sharon L. Lechter
Rich Dad's Cashflow Quadrant Copyright © 1998, 1999 by Robert T. Kiyosaki and Sharon L. Lechter
Rich Dad's Guide to Investing Copyright © 2000 by Robert T. Kiyosaki and Sharon L. Lechter
All rights reserved. Except as permitted under the U.S. Copyright Act of 1976, no part of this publication may be reproduced, distributed, or transmitted in any form or by any means, or stored in a database or retrieval system, without the prior written permission of the publisher.

CASHFLOW, Rich Dad, Rich Dad's Advisors, Rich Dad's Seminars, EBSI, B-I Triangle are registered trademarks of CASHFLOW Technologies, Inc.

E B   E|B   ⬚   ◇   ▲
S I   S|I

Business Plus
Hachette Book Group
237 Park Avenue
New York, NY 10017

Visit our Web sites at www.HachetteBookGroup.com and www.richdad.com.
This 2008 edition published for Barnes and Noble, Inc., by arrangement with Hachette Book Group and The Rich Dad Company.

Trade editions of each title published by Hachette Book Group as follows:
Rich Dad Poor Dad (ISBN 978-0-446-67745-5; $16.95 U.S. / $18.95 CAN)
Rich Dad's Cashflow Quadrant (ISBN 978-0-446-67747-9; $17.95 / $19.95 CAN)
Rich Dad's Guide to Investing (ISBN 978-0-446-67746-2; $19.95 US / $21.95 CAN)

Business Plus is an imprint of Grand Central Publishing.
The Business Plus name and logo are trademarks of Hachette Book Group, Inc.

Printed in the United States of America

First Special Sales Compilation Edition: December 2008

10 9 8 7 6 5 4 3 2 1

ISBN 978-0-446-54857-1

Rich Dad
Poor Dad

What The Rich Teach Their Kids About Money— That The Poor And Middle Class Do Not!

By Robert T. Kiyosaki
with Sharon L. Lechter C.P.A.

**BUSINESS
PLUS**

NEW YORK   BOSTON

*This book is dedicated to all parents everywhere,
a child's most important teachers.*

ACKNOWLEDGEMENTS:

*H*ow does a person say "thank you" when there are so many people to thank? Obviously this book is a thank you to my two fathers who were powerful role models, and to my mom who taught me love and kindness.

Yet, the people most directly responsible for this book becoming a reality include my wife Kim who makes my life complete. Kim is my partner in marriage, business, and in life. Without her I would be lost. To Kim's parents, Winnie and Bill Meyer for raising such a great daughter. I thank Sharon Lechter for picking up the pieces of this book in my computer and putting them together. To Sharon's husband Mike for being a great intellectual property attorney, and their children Phillip, Shelly, and Rick for their participation and cooperation. I thank Keith Cunningham for financial wisdom and inspiration; Larry and Lisa Clark for the gift of friendship and encouragement; Rolf Parta for technical genius; Anne Nevin, Bobbi DePorter and Joe Chapon for insights into learning; DC and John Harrison, Jannie Tay, Sandy Khoo, Richard and Veronica Tan, Peter Johnston and Suzi Dafnis, Jacqueline Seow, Nyhl Henson, Michael and Monette Hamlin, Edwin and Camilla Khoo, K.C. See and Jessica See, for professional support; Kevin and Sara of InSync for brilliant graphics; John and Shari Burley, Bill and Cindy Shopoff, Van Tharp, Diane Kennedy, C.W. Allen, Marilu Deignan, Kim Arries, and Tom Weisenborn, for their financial intelligence. Sam Georges, Anthony Robbins, Enid Vien, Lawrence and Jayne Taylor-West, Alan Wright, Zig Ziglar, for mental clarity; J.W. Wilson, Marty Weber, Randy Craft, Don Mueller, Brad Walker, Blair and Eileen Singer, Wayne and Lynn Morgan, Mimi Brennan, Jerome Summers, Dr. Peter Powers, Will Hepburn, Dr. Enrique Teuscher, Dr. Robert Marin, Betty Oyster, Julie Belden, Jamie Danforth, Cherie Clark, Rick Merica, Joia Jitahide, Jeff Bassett, Dr. Tom Burns, and Bill Galvin for being great friends and supporters of the projects; to the Center Managers and the tens of thousands of graduates of Money and You and The Business School for Entrepreneurs; and to Frank Crerie, Clint Miller, Thomas Allen and Norman Long for being great partners in business.

Table of Contents

There is a Need

*D*oes school prepare children for the real world? "Study hard and get good grades and you will find a high-paying job with great benefits," my parents used to say. Their goal in life was to provide a college education for my older sister and me, so that we would have the greatest chance for success in life. When I finally earned my diploma in 1976—graduating with honors, and near the top of my class, in accounting from Florida State University—my parents had realized their goal. It was the crowning achievement of their lives. In accordance with the "Master Plan," I was hired by a "Big 8" accounting firm, and I looked forward to a long career and retirement at an early age.

My husband, Michael, followed a similar path. We both came from hard-working families, of modest means but with strong work ethics. Michael also graduated with honors, but he did it twice: first as an engineer and then from law school. He was quickly recruited by a prestigious Washington, D.C., law firm that specialized in patent law, and his future seemed bright, career path well-defined and early retirement guaranteed.

Although we have been successful in our careers, they have not turned out quite as we expected. We both have changed positions several times—for all the right reasons—but there are no pension plans vesting on our behalf. Our retirement funds are growing only through our individual contributions.

Michael and I have a wonderful marriage with three great children. As I write this, two are in college and one is just beginning high school. We have spent a fortune making sure our children have received the best education available.

One day in 1996, one of my children came home disillusioned with school. He was bored and tired of studying. "Why should I put time into studying subjects I will never use in real life?" he protested.

Without thinking, I responded, "Because if you don't get good grades, you won't get into college."

"Regardless of whether I go to college," he replied, "I'm going to be rich."

"If you don't graduate from college, you won't get a good job," I responded with a tinge of panic and motherly concern. "And if you don't have a good job, how do you plan to get rich?"

My son smirked and slowly shook his head with mild boredom. We have had this talk many times before. He lowered his head and rolled his eyes. My words of motherly wisdom were falling on deaf ears once again.

Though smart and strong-willed, he has always been a polite and respectful young man.

"Mom," he began. It was my turn to be lectured. "Get with the times! Look around; the richest people didn't get rich because of their educations. Look at Michael Jordan and Madonna. Even Bill Gates, who dropped out of Harvard, founded Microsoft; he is now the richest man in America, and he's still in his 30s. There is a baseball pitcher who makes more than $4 million a year even though he has been labeled 'mentally challenged.' "

There was a long silence between us. It was dawning on me that I was giving my son the same advice my parents had given me. The world around us has changed, but the advice hasn't.

Getting a good education and making good grades no longer ensures success, and nobody seems to have noticed, except our children.

"Mom," he continued, "I don't want to work as hard as you and dad do. You make a lot of money, and we live in a huge house with lots of toys. If I follow your advice, I'll wind up like you, working harder and harder only to pay more taxes and wind up in debt. There is no job security anymore; I know all about downsizing and rightsizing. I also know that college graduates today earn less than you did when you graduated. Look at doctors. They don't make nearly as much money as they used to. I know I can't rely on Social Security or company pensions for retirement. I need new answers."

He was right. He needed new answers, and so did I. My parents' advice may have worked for people born before 1945, but it may be disastrous for those of us born into a rapidly changing world. No longer can I simply say to my children, "Go to school, get good grades, and look for a safe, secure job."

I knew I had to look for new ways to guide my children's education.

As a mother as well as an accountant, I have been concerned by the lack of financial education our children receive in school. Many of today's youth have credit cards before they leave high school, yet they have never had a course in money or how to invest it, let alone understand how compound interest works on credit cards. Simply put, without financial literacy and the knowledge of how money works, they are not prepared to face the world that awaits them, a world in which spending is emphasized over savings.

When my oldest son became hopelessly in debt with his credit cards as a freshman in college, I not only helped him destroy the credit cards, but I also went in search of a program that would help me educate my children on financial matters.

One day last year, my husband called me from his office. "I have someone I think you should meet," he said. "His name is Robert Kiyosaki. He's a businessman and investor, and he is here applying for a patent on an educational product. I think it's what you have been looking for."

Just What I Was Looking For

My husband, Mike, was so impressed with *CASHFLOW*, the new educational product that Robert Kiyosaki was developing, that he arranged for both of us to participate in a test of the prototype. Because it was an educational game, I also asked my 19-year-old daughter, who was a freshman at a local university, if she would like to take part, and she agreed.

About fifteen people, broken into three groups, participated in the test.

Mike was right. It was the educational product I had been looking for. But it had a twist: It looked like a colorful Monopoly board with a giant well-dressed rat in the middle. Unlike Monopoly, however, there were two tracks: one inside and one outside. The object of the game was to get out of the inside track—what Robert called the "Rat Race"—

and reach the outer track, or the "Fast Track." As Robert put it, the Fast Track simulates how rich people play in real life.

Robert then defined the "Rat Race" for us.

"If you look at the life of the average-educated, hard-working person, there is a similar path. The child is born and goes to school. The proud parents are excited because the child excels, gets fair to good grades, and is accepted into a college. The child graduates, maybe goes on to graduate school and then does exactly as programmed: looks for a safe, secure job or career. The child finds that job, maybe as a doctor or a lawyer, or joins the Army or works for the government. Generally, the child begins to make money, credit cards start to arrive in mass, and the shopping begins, if it already hasn't.

"Having money to burn, the child goes to places where other young people just like them hang out, and they meet people, they date, and sometimes they get married. Life is wonderful now, because today, both men and women work. Two incomes are bliss. They feel successful, their future is bright, and they decide to buy a house, a car, a television, take vacations and have children. The happy bundle arrives. The demand for cash is enormous. The happy couple decides that their careers are vitally important and begin to work harder, seeking promotions and raises. The raises come, and so does another child and the need for a bigger house. They work harder, become better employees, even more dedicated. They go back to school to get more specialized skills so they can earn more money. Maybe they take a second job. Their incomes go up, but so does the tax bracket they're in and the real estate taxes on their new large home, and their Social Security taxes, and all the other taxes. They get their large paycheck and wonder where all the money went. They buy some mutual funds and buy groceries with their credit card. The children reach 5 or 6 years of age, and the need to save for college increases as well as the need to save for their retirement.

"That happy couple, born 35 years ago, is now trapped in the Rat Race for the rest of their working days. They work for the owners of their company, for the government paying taxes, and for the bank paying off a mortgage and credit cards.

"Then, they advise their own children to 'study hard, get good grades, and find a safe job or career.' They learn nothing about money, except from those who profit from their naiveté, and work hard all their lives. The process repeats into another hard-working generation. This is the 'Rat Race'."

The only way to get out of the "Rat Race" is to prove your proficiency at both accounting and investing, arguably two of the most difficult subjects to master. As a trained CPA who once worked for a Big 8 accounting firm, I was surprised that Robert had made the learning of these two subjects both fun and exciting. The process was so well disguised that while we were diligently working to get out of the "Rat Race," we quickly forgot we were learning.

Soon a product test turned into a fun afternoon with my daughter, talking about things we had never discussed before. As an accountant, playing a game that required an Income Statement and Balance Sheet was easy. So I had the time to help my daughter and the other players at my table with concepts they did not understand. I was the first person—and the only person in the entire test group—to get out of the "Rat Race" that day. I was out within 50 minutes, although the game went on for nearly three hours.

At my table was a banker, a business owner and a computer programmer. What greatly disturbed me was how little these people knew about either accounting or investing, subjects so important in their lives. I wondered how they managed their own financial affairs in real life. I could understand why my 19-year-old daughter would not understand, but these were grown adults, at least twice her age.

After I was out of the "Rat Race," for the next two hours I watched my daughter and these educated, affluent adults roll the dice and move their markers. Although I was glad they were all learning so much, I was disturbed by how much the adults did not know about the basics of simple accounting and investing. They had difficulty grasping the relationship between their Income Statement and their Balance Sheet. As they bought and sold assets, they had trouble remembering that each transaction could impact their monthly cash flow. I thought, how many millions of people are out there in the real world struggling financially, only because they have never been taught these subjects?

Thank goodness they're having fun and are distracted by the desire to win the game, I said to myself. After Robert ended the contest, he allowed us fifteen minutes to discuss and critique *CASHFLOW* among ourselves.

The business owner at my table was not happy. He did not like the game. "I don't need to know this," he said out loud. "I hire accountants, bankers and attorneys to tell me about this stuff."

To which Robert replied, "Have you ever noticed that there are a lot of accountants who aren't rich? And bankers, and attorneys, and stockbrokers and real estate brokers. They know a lot, and for the most part are smart people, but most of them are not rich. Since our schools do not teach people what the rich know, we take advice from these people. But one day, you're driving down the highway, stuck in traffic, struggling to get to work, and you look over to your right and you see your accountant stuck in the same traffic jam. You look to your left and you see your banker. That should tell you something."

The computer programmer was also unimpressed by the game: "I can buy software to teach me this."

The banker, however, was moved. "I studied this in school—the accounting part, that is—but I never knew how to apply it to real life. Now I know. I need to get myself out of the 'Rat Race.' "

But it was my daughter's comments that most touched me. "I had fun learning," she said. "I learned a lot about how money really works and how to invest."

Then she added: "Now I know I can choose a profession for the work I want to perform and not because of job security, benefits or how much I get paid. If I learn what this game teaches, I'm free to do and study what my heart wants to study. . .rather than study something because businesses are looking for certain job skills. If I learn this, I won't have to worry about job security and Social Security the way most of my classmates already do."

I was not able to stay and talk with Robert after we had played the game, but we agreed to meet later to further discuss his project. I knew he wanted to use the game to help others become more financially savvy, and I was eager to hear more about his plans.

My husband and I set up a dinner meeting with Robert and his wife within the next week. Although it was our first social get-together, we felt as if we had known each other for years.

We found out we had a lot in common. We covered the gamut, from sports and plays to restaurants and socio-economic issues. We talked about the changing world. We spent a lot of time discussing how most Americans have little or nothing saved for retirement, as well as the almost bankrupt state of Social Security and Medicare. Would my children be required to pay for the retirement of 75 million baby boomers? We wondered if people realize how risky it is to depend on a pension plan.

Robert's primary concern was the growing gap between the haves and have nots, in America and around the world. A self-taught, self-made entrepreneur who traveled the world putting investments together, Robert was able to retire at the age of 47. He came out of retirement because he shares the same concern I have for my own children. He knows that the world has changed, but education has not changed with it. According to Robert, children spend years in an antiquated educational system, studying subjects they will never use, preparing for a world that no longer exists.

"Today, the most dangerous advice you can give a child is 'Go to school, get good grades and look for a safe secure job,' " he likes to say. "That is old advice, and it's bad advice. If you could see what is happening in Asia, Europe, South America, you would be as concerned as I am."

It's bad advice, he believes, "because if you want your child to have a financially secure future, they can't play by the old set of rules. It's just too risky."

I asked him what he meant by "old rules?" .

"People like me play by a different set of rules from what you play by," he said. "What happens when a corporation announces a downsizing?"

"People get laid off," I said. "Families are hurt. Unemployment goes up."

"Yes, but what happens to the company, in particular a public company on the stock exchange?"

"The price of the stock usually goes up when the downsizing is announced," I said. "The market likes it when a company reduces its labor costs, either through automation or just consolidating the labor force in general."

"That's right," he said. "And when stock prices go up, people like me, the shareholders, get richer. That is what I mean by a different set of rules. Employees lose; owners and investors win."

Robert was describing not only the difference between an employee and employer, but also the difference between controlling your own destiny and giving up that control to someone else.

"But it's hard for most people to understand why that happens," I said. "They just think it's not fair."

"That's why it is foolish to simply say to a child, 'Get a good education,' " he said. "It is foolish to assume that the education the school system provides will prepare your children for the world they will face upon graduation. Each child needs more education. Different education. And they need to know the rules. The different sets of rules."

"There are rules of money that the rich play by, and there are the rules that the other 95 percent of the population plays by," he said. "And the 95 percent learns those rules at home and in school. That is why it's risky today to simply say to a child, 'Study hard and look for a job.' A child today needs a more sophisticated education, and the current system is not delivering the goods. I don't care how many computers they put in the classroom or how much money schools spend. How can the education system teach a subject that it does not know?"

So how does a parent teach their children, what the school does not? How do you teach accounting to a child? Won't they get bored? And how do you teach investing when as a parent you yourself are risk averse? Instead of teaching my children to simply play it safe, I decided it was best to teach them to play it smart.

"So how would you teach a child about money and all the things we've talked about?" I asked Robert. "How can we make it easy for parents especially when they don't understand it themselves?"

"I wrote a book on the subject, " he said.

"Where is it?"

"In my computer. It's been there for years in random pieces. I add to it occasionally but I've never gotten around to put it all together. I began writing it after my other book became a best seller, but I never finished the new one. It's in pieces."

And in pieces it was. After reading the scattered sections, I decided the book had merit and needed to be shared, especially in these changing times. We agreed to co-author Robert's book.

I asked him how much financial information he thought a child needed. He said it would depend on the child. He knew at a young age that he wanted to be rich and was fortunate enough to have a father figure who was rich and willing to guide him. Education is the foundation of success, Robert said. Just as scholastic skills are vitally important, so are financial skills and communication skills.

What follows is the story of Robert's two dads, a rich one and a poor one, that expounds on the skills he's developed over a lifetime. The contrast between two dads provides an important perspective. The book is supported, edited and assembled by me. For any accountants who read this book, suspend your academic book knowledge and open your mind to the theories Robert presents. Although many of them challenge the very fundamentals of generally accepted accounting principles, they provide a valuable insight into the way true investors analyze their investment decisions.

When we as parents advise our children to "go to school, study hard and get a good job," we often do that out of cultural habit. It has always been the right thing to do. When I met Robert, his ideas initially startled me. Having been raised by two fathers, he had been taught to strive for two different goals. His educated dad advised him to work for a corporation. His rich dad advised him to own the corporation. Both life paths required education, but the subjects of study were completely different. His educated dad encouraged Robert to be a smart person. His rich dad encouraged Robert to know how to hire smart people.

Having two dads caused many problems. Robert's real dad was the superintendent of education for the state of Hawaii. By the time Robert was 16, the threat of "If you don't get good grades, you won't get a good job" had little effect. He already knew his career path was to own corporations, not to work for them. In fact, if it had not been for a wise and persistent high school guidance counselor, Robert might not have gone on to college. He admits that. He was eager to start building his assets, but finally agreed that the college education would also be a benefit to him.

Truthfully, the ideas in this book are probably too far fetched and radical for most parents today. Some parents are having a hard enough time simply keeping their children in school. But in light of our changing times, as parents we need to be open to new and bold ideas. To encourage children to be employees is to advise your children to pay more than their fair share of taxes over a lifetime, with little or no promise of a pension. And it is true that taxes are a person's greatest expense. In fact, most families work from January to mid-May for the government just to cover their taxes. New ideas are needed and this book provides them.

Robert claims that the rich teach their children differently. They teach their children at home, around the dinner table. These ideas may not be

9

the ideas you choose to discuss with your children, but thank you for looking at them. And I advise you to keep searching. In my opinion, as a mom and a CPA, the concept of simply getting good grades and finding a good job is an old idea. We need to advise our children with a greater degree of sophistication. We need new ideas and different education. Maybe telling our children to strive to be good employees while also striving to own their own investment corporation is not such a bad idea.

It is my hope as a mother that this book helps other parents. It is Robert's hope to inform people that anyone can achieve prosperity if they so choose. If today you are a gardener or a janitor or even unemployed, you have the ability to educate yourself and teach those you love to take care of themselves financially. Remember that financial intelligence is the mental process via which we solve our financial problems.

Today we are facing global and technological changes as great or even greater than those ever faced before. No one has a crystal ball, but one thing is for certain: Changes lie ahead that are beyond our reality. Who knows what the future brings? But whatever happens, we have two fundamental choices: play it safe or play it smart by preparing, getting educated and awakening your own and your children's financial genius.

— *Sharon Lechter*

Rich Dad, Poor Dad

CHAPTER ONE

Rich Dad, Poor Dad

As narrated by Robert Kiyosaki

I had two fathers, a rich one and a poor one. One was highly educated and intelligent; he had a Ph.D. and completed four years of undergraduate work in less than two years. He then went on to Stanford University, the University of Chicago, and Northwestern University to do his advanced studies, all on full financial scholarships. The other father never finished the eighth grade.

Both men were successful in their careers, working hard all their lives. Both earned substantial incomes. Yet one struggled financially all his life. The other would become one of the richest men in Hawaii. One died leaving tens of millions of dollars to his family, charities and his church. The other left bills to be paid.

Both men were strong, charismatic and influential. Both men offered me advice, but they did not advise the same things. Both men believed strongly in education but did not recommend the same course of study.

If I had had only one dad, I would have had to accept or reject his advice. Having two dads advising me offered me the choice of contrasting points of view; one of a rich man and one of a poor man.

Instead of simply accepting or rejecting one or the other, I found myself thinking more, comparing and then choosing for myself.

The problem was, the rich man was not rich yet and the poor man not yet poor. Both were just starting out on their careers, and both were struggling with money and families. But they had very different points of view about the subject of money.

For example, one dad would say, "The love of money is the root of all evil." The other, "The lack of money is the root of all evil."

As a young boy, having two strong fathers both influencing me was difficult. I wanted to be a good son and listen, but the two fathers did not say the same things. The contrast in their points of view, particularly where money was concerned, was so extreme that I grew curious and intrigued. I began to start thinking for long periods of time about what each was saying.

Much of my private time was spent reflecting, asking myself questions such as, "Why does he say that?" and then asking the same question of the other dad's statement. It would have been much easier to simply say, "Yeah, he's right. I agree with that." Or to simply reject the point of view by saying, "The old man doesn't know what he's talking about." Instead, having two dads whom I loved forced me to think and ultimately choose a way of thinking for myself. As a process, choosing for myself turned out to be much more valuable in the long run, rather than simply accepting or rejecting a single point of view.

One of the reasons the rich get richer, the poor get poorer, and the middle class struggles in debt is because the subject of money is taught at home, not in school. Most of us learn about money from our parents. So what can a poor parent tell their child about money? They simply say "Stay in school and study hard." The child may graduate with excellent grades but with a poor person's financial programming and mind-set. It was learned while the child was young.

Money is not taught in schools. Schools focus on scholastic and professional skills, but not on financial skills. This explains how smart bankers, doctors and accountants who earned excellent grades in school may still struggle financially all of their lives. Our staggering national debt is due in large part to highly educated politicians and government officials making financial decisions with little or no training on the subject of money.

I often look ahead to the new millennium and wonder what will happen when we have millions of people who will need financial and medical assistance. They will be dependent on their families or the government for financial support. What will happen when Medicare and Social Security run out of money? How will a nation survive if teaching children about money continues to be left to parents—most of whom will be, or already are, poor?

Because I had two influential fathers, I learned from both of them. I had to think about each dad's advice, and in doing so, I gained valuable insight into the power and effect of one's thoughts on one's life. For example, one dad had a habit of saying, "I can't afford it." The other dad forbade those words to be used. He insisted I say, "How can I afford it?" One is a statement, and the other is a question. One lets you off the hook, and the other forces you to think. My soon-to-be-rich dad would explain that by automatically saying the words "I can't afford it," your brain stops working. By asking the question "How can I afford it?" your brain is put to work. He did not mean buy everything you wanted. He was fanatical about exercising your mind, the most powerful computer in the world. "My brain gets stronger every day because I exercise it. The stronger it gets, the more money I can make." He believed that automatically saying "I can't afford it" was a sign of mental laziness.

Although both dads worked hard, I noticed that one dad had a habit of putting his brain to sleep when it came to money matters, and the other had a habit of exercising his brain. The long-term result was that one dad grew stronger financially and the other grew weaker. It is not much different from a person who goes to the gym to exercise on a regular basis versus someone who sits on the couch watching television. Proper physical exercise increases your chances for health, and proper mental exercise increases your chances for wealth. Laziness decreases both health and wealth.

My two dads had opposing attitudes in thought. One dad thought that the rich should pay more in taxes to take care of those less fortunate. The other said, "Taxes punish those who produce and reward those who don't produce."

One dad recommended, "Study hard so you can find a good company to work for." The other recommended, "Study hard so you can find a good company to buy."

One dad said, "The reason I'm not rich is because I have you kids." The other said, "The reason I must be rich is because I have you kids."

One encouraged talking about money and business at the dinner table. The other forbade the subject of money to be discussed over a meal.

One said, "When it comes to money, play it safe, don't take risks." The other said, "Learn to manage risk."

One believed, "Our home is our largest investment and our greatest asset." The other believed, "My house is a liability, and if your house is your largest investment, you're in trouble."

Both dads paid their bills on time, yet one paid his bills first while the other paid his bills last.

One dad believed in a company or the government taking care of you and your needs. He was always concerned about pay raises, retirement plans, medical benefits, sick leave, vacation days and other perks. He was impressed with two of his uncles who joined the military and earned a retirement and entitlement package for life after twenty years of active service. He loved the idea of medical benefits and PX privileges the military provided its retirees. He also loved the tenure system available through the university. The idea of job protection for life and job benefits seemed more important, at times, than the job. He would often say, "I've worked hard for the government, and I'm entitled to these benefits."

The other believed in total financial self-reliance. He spoke out against the "entitlement" mentality and how it was creating weak and financially needy people. He was emphatic about being financially competent.

One dad struggled to save a few dollars. The other simply created investments.

One dad taught me how to write an impressive resume so I could find a good job. The other taught me how to write strong business and financial plans so I could create jobs.

Being a product of two strong dads allowed me the luxury of observing the effects different thoughts have on one's life. I noticed that people really do shape their life through their thoughts.

For example, my poor dad always said, "I'll never be rich." And that prophesy became reality. My rich dad, on the other hand, always referred to himself as rich. He would say things like, "I'm a rich man, and rich people don't do this." Even when he was flat broke after a major financial setback, he continued to refer to himself as a rich man. He would cover himself by saying, "There is a difference between being poor and being broke. Broke is temporary, and poor is eternal."

My poor dad would also say, "I'm not interested in money," or "Money doesn't matter." My rich dad always said, "Money is power."

The power of our thoughts may never be measured or appreciated, but it became obvious to me as a young boy to be aware of my thoughts and how I expressed myself. I noticed that my poor dad was poor not because of the amount of money he earned, which was significant, but because of his thoughts and actions. As a young boy, having two fathers, I became acutely aware of being careful which thoughts I chose to adopt as my own. Whom should I listen to—my rich dad or my poor dad?

Although both men had tremendous respect for education and learning, they disagreed in what they thought was important to learn. One wanted me to study hard, earn a degree and get a good job to work for money. He wanted me to study to become a professional, an attorney or an accountant or to go to business school for my MBA. The other encouraged me to study to be rich, to understand how money works and to learn how to have it work for me. "I don't work for money!" were words he would repeat over and over, "Money works for me!"

At the age of 9, I decided to listen to and learn from my rich dad about money. In doing so, I chose not to listen to my poor dad, even though he was the one with all the college degrees.

A Lesson From Robert Frost

Robert Frost is my favorite poet. Although I love many of his poems, my favorite is The Road Not Taken. I use its lesson almost daily:

The Road Not Taken

Two roads diverged in a yellow wood,
And sorry I could not travel both
And be one traveler, long I stood
And looked down one as far as I could
To where it bent in the undergrowth;

Then took the other, as just as fair,
And having perhaps the better claim,
Because it was grassy and wanted wear
Though as for that the passing there
Had worn them really about the same,

And both that morning equally lay
In leaves no step had trodden black.
Oh, I kept the first for another day!
Yet knowing how way leads onto way,
I doubted if I should ever come back.

I shall be telling this with a sigh
Somewhere ages and ages hence;
Two roads diverged in a wood, and I—
I took the one less traveled by,
And that has made all the difference.

Robert Frost [1916]

And that made all the difference.

Over the years, I have often reflected upon Robert Frost's poem. Choosing not to listen to my highly educated dad's advice and attitude about money was a painful decision, but it was a decision that shaped the rest of my life.

Once I made up my mind whom to listen to, my education about money began. My rich dad taught me over a period of 30 years, until I was age 39. He stopped once he realized that I knew and fully understood what he had been trying to drum into my often thick skull.

Money is one form of power. But what is more powerful is financial education. Money comes and goes, but if you have the education about how money works, you gain power over it and can begin building wealth. The reason positive thinking alone does not work is because most people went to school and never learned how money works, so they spend their lives working for money.

Because I was only 9 years old when I started, the lessons my rich dad taught me were simple. And when it was all said and done, there were only six main lessons, repeated over 30 years. This book is about those six lessons, put as simply as possible as my rich dad put forth those lessons to me. The lessons are not meant to be answers but guideposts. Guideposts that will assist you and your children to grow wealthier no matter what happens in a world of increasing change and uncertainty.

The Rich Don't Work For Money

"*D*ad, Can You Tell Me How to Get Rich?"

My dad put down the evening paper. "Why do you want to get rich, son?"

"Because today Jimmy's mom drove up in their new Cadillac, and they were going to their beach house for the weekend. He took three of his friends, but Mike and I weren't invited. They told us we weren't invited because we were 'poor kids'."

"They did?" my dad asked incredulously.

"Yeah, they did." I replied in a hurt tone.

My dad silently shook his head, pushed his glasses up the bridge of his nose and went back to reading the paper. I stood waiting for an answer.

The year was 1956. I was 9 years old. By some twist of fate, I attended the same public school where the rich people sent their kids. We were primarily a sugar plantation town. The managers of the plantation and the other affluent people of the town, such as doctors, business owners, and bankers, sent their children to this school, grades 1 to 6. After grade 6, their children were generally sent off to private schools. Because my family lived on one side of the street, I went to this school. Had I lived on the other side of the street, I would have gone to a different school, with kids from families more like mine. After grade 6, these kids and I would go on to the public intermediate and high school. There was no private school for them or for me.

My dad finally put down the paper. I could tell he was thinking.

"Well, son," he began slowly. "If you want to be rich, you have to learn to make money."

"How do I make money?" I asked.

"Well, use your head, son," he said, smiling. Which really meant, "That's all I'm going to tell you," or "I don't know the answer, so don't embarrass me."

A Partnership Is Formed

The next morning, I told my best friend, Mike, what my dad had said. As best I could tell, Mike and I were the only poor kids in this school. Mike was like me in that he was in this school by a twist of fate. Someone had drawn a jog in the line for the school district, and we wound up in school with the rich kids. We weren't really poor, but we felt as if we were because all the other boys had new baseball gloves, new bicycles, new everything.

Mom and dad provided us with the basics, like food, shelter, clothes. But that was about it. My dad used to say, "If you want something, work for it." We wanted things, but there was not much work available for 9-year-old boys.

"So what do we do to make money?" Mike asked.

"I don't know," I said. "But do you want to be my partner?"

He agreed and so on that Saturday morning, Mike became my first business partner. We spent all morning coming up with ideas on how to make money. Occasionally we talked about all the "cool guys" at Jimmy's beach house having fun. It hurt a little, but that hurt was good, for it inspired us to keep thinking of a way to make money. Finally, that afternoon, a bolt of lightning came through our heads. It was an idea Mike had gotten from a science book he had read. Excitedly, we shook hands, and the partnership now had a business.

For the next several weeks, Mike and I ran around our neighborhood, knocking on doors and asking our neighbors if they would save their toothpaste tubes for us. With puzzled looks, most adults consented with a smile. Some asked us what we were doing. To which we replied, "We can't tell you. It's a business secret."

My mom grew distressed as the weeks wore on. We had selected a site next to her washing machine as the place we would stockpile our raw materials. In a brown cardboard box that one time held catsup bottles, our little pile of used toothpaste tubes began to grow.

Finally my mom put her foot down. The sight of her neighbors' messy, crumpled used toothpaste tubes had gotten to her. "What are you boys doing?" she asked. "And I don't want to hear again that it's a business secret. Do something with this mess or I'm going to throw it out."

Mike and I pleaded and begged, explaining that we would soon have enough and then we would begin production. We informed her that we were waiting on a couple of neighbors to finish using up their toothpaste so we could have their tubes. Mom granted us a one-week extension.

The date to begin production was moved up. The pressure was on. My first partnership was already being threatened with an eviction notice from our warehouse space by my own mom. It became Mike's job to tell the neighbors to quickly use up their toothpaste, saying their dentist wanted them to brush more often anyway. I began to put together the production line.

One day my dad drove up with a friend to see two 9-year-old boys in the driveway with a production line operating at full speed. There was fine white powder everywhere. On a long table were small milk cartons from school, and our family's hibachi grill was glowing with red hot coals at maximum heat.

Dad walked up cautiously, having to park the car at the base of the driveway, since the production line blocked the carport. As he and his friend got closer, they saw a steel pot sitting on top of the coals, with the toothpaste tubes being melted down. In those days, toothpaste did not come in plastic tubes. The tubes were made of lead. So once the paint was burned off, the tubes were dropped in the small steel pot, melted until they became liquid, and with my mom's pot holders we were pouring the lead through a small hole in the top of the milk cartons.

The milk cartons were filled with plaster-of-paris. The white powder everywhere was the plaster before we mixed it with water. In my haste, I had knocked the bag over, and the entire area look like it had been hit by a snowstorm. The milk cartons were the outer containers for plaster-of-paris molds.

My dad and his friend watched as we carefully poured the molten lead through a small hole in the top of the plaster-of-paris cube.

"Careful," my dad said.

I nodded without looking up.

Finally, once the pouring was through, I put the steel pot down and smiled at my dad.

"What are you boys doing?" he asked with a cautious smile.

"We're doing what you told me to do. We're going to be rich," I said.

"Yup," said Mike, grinning and nodding his head. "We're partners."

"And what is in those plaster molds?" dad asked.

"Watch," I said. "This should be a good batch."

With a small hammer, I tapped at the seal that divided the cube in half. Cautiously, I pulled up the top half of the plaster mold and a lead nickel fell out."

"Oh, my God!" my dad said. "You're casting nickels out of lead."

"That's right," Mike said. "We doing as you told us to do. We're making money."

My dad's friend turned and burst into laughter. My dad smiled and shook his head. Along with a fire and a box of spent toothpaste tubes, in front of him were two little boys covered with white dust and smiling from ear to ear.

He asked us to put everything down and sit with him on the front step of our house. With a smile, he gently explained what the word "counterfeiting" meant.

Our dreams were dashed. "You mean this is illegal?" asked Mike in a quivering voice.

"Let them go," my dad's friend said. "They might be developing a natural talent."

My dad glared at him.

"Yes, it is illegal," my dad said gently. "But you boys have shown great creativity and original thought. Keep going. I'm really proud of you!"

Disappointed, Mike and I sat in silence for about twenty minutes before we began cleaning up our mess. The business was over on opening day. Sweeping the powder up, I looked at Mike and said, "I guess Jimmy and his friends are right. We are poor."

My father was just leaving as I said that. "Boys," he said. "You're only poor if you give up. The most important thing is that you did something. Most people only talk and dream of getting rich. You've done something. I'm very proud of the two of you. I will say it again.

Keep going. Don't quit."

Mike and I stood there in silence. They were nice words, but we still did not know what to do.

"So how come you're not rich, dad?" I asked.

"Because I chose to be a schoolteacher. Schoolteachers really don't think about being rich. We just like to teach. I wish I could help you, but I really don't know how to make money."

Mike and I turned and continued our clean up.

"I know," said my dad. "If you boys want to learn how to be rich, don't ask me. Talk to your dad, Mike."

"My dad?" asked Mike with a scrunched up face.

"Yeah, your dad," repeated my dad with a smile. "Your dad and I have the same banker, and he raves about your father. He's told me several times that your father is brilliant when it comes to making money."

"My dad?" Mike asked again in disbelief. "Then how come we don't have a nice car and a nice house like the rich kids at school?"

"A nice car and a nice house does not necessarily mean you're rich or you know how to make money," my dad replied. "Jimmy's dad works for the sugar plantation. He's not much different from me. He works for a company, and I work for the government. The company buys the car for him. The sugar company is in financial trouble, and Jimmy's dad may soon have nothing. Your dad is different Mike. He seems to be building an empire, and I suspect in a few years he will be a very rich man."

With that, Mike and I got excited again. With new vigor, we began cleaning up the mess caused by our now defunct first business. As we were cleaning, we made plans on how and when to talk to Mike's dad. The problem was that Mike's dad worked long hours and often did not come home until late. His father owned warehouses, a construction company, a chain of stores, and three restaurants. It was the restaurants that kept him out late.

Mike caught the bus home after we had finished cleaning up. He was going to talk to his dad when he got home that night and ask him if he would teach us how to become rich. Mike promised to call as soon as he had talked to his dad, even if it was late.

The phone rang at 8:30 p.m.

"OK," I said. "Next Saturday." And put the phone down. Mike's dad had agreed to meet with Mike and me.

27

At 7:30 Saturday morning, I caught the bus to the poor side of town.

The Lessons Begin:

"I'll pay you 10 cents an hour."

Even by 1956 pay standards, 10 cents an hour was low.

Michael and I met with his dad that morning at 8 o'clock. He was already busy and had been at work for more than an hour. His construction supervisor was just leaving in his pickup truck as I walked up to his simple, small and tidy home. Mike met me at the door.

"Dad's on the phone, and he said to wait on the back porch," Mike said as he opened the door.

The old wooden floor creaked as I stepped across the threshold of this aging house. There was a cheap mat just inside the door. The mat was there to hide the years of wear from countless footsteps that the floor had supported. Although clean, it needed to be replaced.

I felt claustrophobic as I entered the narrow living room, which was filled with old musty overstuffed furniture that today would be collector's items. Sitting on the couch were two women, a little older than my mom. Across from the women sat a man in workman's clothes. He wore khaki slacks and a khaki shirt, neatly pressed but without starch, and polished work books. He was about 10 years older than my dad; I'd say about 45 years old. They smiled as Mike and I walked past them, heading for the kitchen, which lead to the porch that overlooked the back yard. I smiled back shyly.

"Who are those people?" I asked.

"Oh, they work for my dad. The older man runs his warehouses, and the women are the managers of the restaurants. And you saw the construction supervisor, who is working on a road project about 50 miles from here. His other supervisor, who is building a track of houses, had already left before you got here."

"Does this go on all the time?" I asked.

"Not always, but quite often," said Mike, smiling as he pulled up a chair to sit down next to me.

"I asked him if he would teach us to make money," Mike said.

"Oh, and what did he say to that?" I asked with cautious curiosity.

"Well, he had a funny look on his face at first, and then he said he would make us an offer."

"Oh," I said, rocking my chair back against the wall; I sat there perched on two rear legs of the chair.

Mike did the same thing.

"Do you know what the offer is?" I asked.

"No, but we'll soon find out."

Suddenly, Mike's dad burst through the rickety screen door and onto the porch. Mike and I jumped to our feet, not out of respect but because we were startled.

"Ready boys?" Mike's dad asked as he pulled up a chair to sit down with us.

We nodded our heads as we pulled our chairs away from the wall to sit in front of him.

He was a big man, about 6 feet tall and 200 pounds. My dad was taller, about the same weight, and five years older than Mike's dad. They sort of looked alike, though not of the same ethnic makeup. Maybe their energy was similar.

"Mike says you want to learn to make money? Is that correct, Robert?"

I nodded my head quickly, but with a little intimidation. He had a lot of power behind his words and smile.

"OK, here's my offer. I'll teach you, but I won't do it classroom-style. You work for me, I'll teach you. You don't work for me, I won't teach you. I can teach you faster if you work, and I'm wasting my time if you just want to sit and listen, like you do in school. That's my offer. Take it or leave it."

"Ah... may I ask a question first?" I asked.

"No. Take it or leave it. I've got too much work to do to waste my time. If you can't make up you mind decisively, then you'll never learn to make money anyway. Opportunities come and go. Being able to know when to make quick decisions is an important skill. You have an opportunity that you asked for. School is beginning or it's over in ten seconds," Mike's dad said with a teasing smile.

"Take it," I said.

"Take it," said Mike.

"Good," said Mike's dad. "Mrs. Martin will be by in ten minutes. After I'm through with her, you ride with her to my superette and you can begin working. I'll pay you 10 cents an hour and you will work for three hours every Saturday."

"But I have a softball game today," I said.

29

Mike's dad lowered his voice to a stern tone. "Take it or leave it," he said.

"I'll take it," I replied, choosing to work and learn instead of playing softball.

30 Cents Later

By 9 a.m. on a beautiful Saturday morning, Mike and I were working for Mrs. Martin. She was a kind and patient woman. She always said that Mike and I reminded her of her two sons who were grown and gone. Although kind, she believed in hard work and she kept us working. She was a task master. We spent three hours taking canned goods off the shelves and, with a feather duster, brushing each can to get the dust off, and then re-stacking them neatly. It was excruciatingly boring work.

Mike's dad, whom I call my rich dad, owned nine of these little superettes with large parking lots. They were the early version of the 7-11 convenience stores. Little neighborhood grocery stores where people bought items such as milk, bread, butter and cigarettes. The problem was, this was Hawaii before air conditioning, and the stores could not close its doors because of the heat. On two sides of the store, the doors had to be wide open to the road and parking lot. Every time a car drove by or pulled into the parking lot, dust would swirl and settle in the store.

Hence, we had a job for as long as there was no air conditioning.

For three weeks, Mike and I reported to Mrs. Martin and worked our three hours. By noon, our work was over, and she dropped three little dimes in each of our hands. Now, even at the age of 9 in the mid-1950s, 30 cents was not too exciting. Comic books cost 10 cents back then, so I usually spent my money on comic books and went home.

By Wednesday of the fourth week, I was ready to quit. I had agreed to work only because I wanted to learn to make money from Mike's dad, and now I was a slave for 10 cents an hour. On top of that, I had not seen Mike's dad since that first Saturday.

"I'm quitting," I told Mike at lunchtime. The school lunch was miserable. School was boring, and now I did not even have my Saturdays to look forward to. But it was the 30 cents that really got to me.

This time Mike smiled.

"What are you laughing at?" I asked with anger and frustration.

"Dad said this would happen. He said to meet with him when you were ready to quit."

"What?" I said indignantly. "He's been waiting for me to get fed up?"

"Sort of," Mike said. "Dad's kind of different. He teaches differently from your dad. Your mom and dad lecture a lot. My dad is quiet and a man of few words. You just wait till this Saturday. I'll tell him you're ready."

"You mean I've been set up?"

"No, not really, but maybe. Dad will explain on Saturday."

Waiting in Line on Saturday

I was ready to face him and I was prepared. Even my real dad was angry with him. My real dad, the one I call the poor one, thought that my rich dad was violating child labor laws and should be investigated.

My educated poor dad told me to demand what I deserve. At least 25 cents an hour. My poor dad told me that if I did not get a raise, I was to quit immediately.

"You don't need that damned job anyway," said my poor dad with indignity.

At 8 o'clock Saturday morning, I was going through the same rickety door of Mike's house.

"Take a seat and wait in line," Mike's dad said as I entered. He turned and disappeared into his little office next to a bedroom.

I looked around the room and did not see Mike anywhere. Feeling awkward, I cautiously sat down next to the same two women who where there four weeks earlier. They smiled and slid across the couch to make room for me.

Forty-five minutes went by, and I was steaming. The two women had met with him and left thirty minutes earlier. An older gentleman was in there for twenty minutes and was also gone.

The house was empty, and I sat out in his musty dark living room on a beautiful sunny Hawaiian day, waiting to talk to a cheapskate who exploited children. I could hear him rustling around the office, talking on the phone, and ignoring me. I was now ready to walk out, but for some reason I stayed.

Finally, fifteen minutes later, at exactly 9 o'clock, rich dad walked out of his office, said nothing, and signaled with his hand for me to enter his dingy office.

"I understand you want a raise or you're going to quit," rich dad said as he swiveled in his office chair.

"Well, you're not keeping your end of the bargain," I blurted out nearly in tears. It was really frightening for a 9-year-old boy to confront a grownup.

"You said that you would teach me if I worked for you. Well, I've worked for you. I've worked hard. I've given up my baseball games to work for you. And you don't keep your word. You haven't taught me anything. You are a crook like everyone in town thinks you are. You're greedy. You want all the money and don't take care of your employees. You make me wait and don't show me any respect. I'm only a little boy, and I deserve to be treated better."

Rich dad rocked back in his swivel chair, hands up to his chin, somewhat staring at me. It was like he was studying me.

"Not bad," he said. "In less than a month, you sound like most of my employees."

"What?" I asked. Not understanding what he was saying, I continued with my grievance. "I thought you were going to keep your end of the bargain and teach me. Instead you want to torture me? That's cruel. That's really cruel."

"I am teaching you," rich dad said quietly.

"What have you taught me? Nothing!" I said angrily. "You haven't even talked to me once since I agreed to work for peanuts. Ten cents an hour. Hah! I should notify the government about you.

We have child labor laws, you know. My dad works for the government, you know."

"Wow!" said rich dad. "Now you sound just like most of the people who used to work for me. People I've either fired or they've quit."

"So what do you have to say?" I demanded, feeling pretty brave for a little kid. "You lied to me. I've worked for you, and you have not kept your word. You haven't taught me anything."

"How do you know that I've not taught you anything?" asked rich dad calmly.

"Well, you've never talked to me. I've worked for three weeks, and you have not taught me anything," I said with a pout.

"Does teaching mean talking or a lecture?" rich dad asked.

"Well, yes," I replied.

"That's how they teach you in school," he said smiling. "But that is not how life teaches you, and I would say that life is the best teacher of all. Most of the time, life does not talk to you. It just sort of pushes you around. Each push is life saying, 'Wake up. There's something I want you to learn.' "

"What is this man talking about?" I asked myself silently. "Life pushing me around was life talking to me?" Now I knew I had to quit my job. I was talking to someone who needed to be locked up.

"If you learn life's lessons, you will do well. If not, life will just continue to push you around. People do two things. Some just let life push them around. Others get angry and push back. But they push back against their boss, or their job, or their husband or wife. They do not know it's life that's pushing."

I had no idea what he was talking about.

"Life pushes all of us around. Some give up. Others fight. A few learn the lesson and move on. They welcome life pushing them around. To these few people, it means they need and want to learn something. They learn and move on. Most quit, and a few like you fight."

Rich dad stood and shut the creaky old wooden window that needed repair. "If you learn this lesson, you will grow into a wise, wealthy and happy young man. If you don't, you will spend your life blaming a job, low pay or your boss for your problems. You'll live life hoping for that big break that will solve all your money problems."

Rich dad looked over at me to see if I was still listening. His eyes met mine. We stared at each other, streams of communication going between us through our eyes. Finally, I pulled away once I had absorbed his last message. I knew he was right. I was blaming him, and I did ask to learn. I was fighting.

Rich dad continued. "Or if you're the kind of person who has no guts, you just give up every time life pushes you. If you're that kind of person, you'll live all your life playing it safe, doing the right things, saving yourself for some event that never happens. Then, you die a boring old man. You'll have lots of friends who really like you because you were such a nice hard-working guy. You spent a life playing it safe, doing the right things. But the truth is, you let life push you into submission. Deep down you were terrified of taking risks. You really wanted to win, but the fear of losing was greater than the excitement of winning. Deep inside, you and only you will know you didn't go for it.

You chose to play it safe."

Our eyes met again. For ten seconds, we looked at each other, only pulling away once the message was received.

"You've been pushing me around?" I asked.

"Some people might say that," smiled rich dad. "I would say that I just gave you a taste of life."

"What taste of life?" I asked, still angry, but now curious. Even ready to learn.

"You boys are the first people that have ever asked me to teach them how to make money. I have more than 150 employees, and not one of them has asked me what I know about money. They ask me for a job and a paycheck, but never to teach them about money. So most will spend the best years of their lives working for money, not really understanding what it is they are working for."

I sat there listening intently.

"So when Mike told me about you wanting to learn how to make money, I decided to design a course that was close to real life. I could talk until I was blue in the face, but you wouldn't hear a thing. So I decided to let life push you around a bit so you could hear me. That's why I only paid you 10 cents."

"So what is the lesson I learned from working for only 10 cents an hour?" I asked. "That you're cheap and exploit your workers?"

Rich dad rocked back and laughed heartily. Finally, after his laughing stopped, he said, "You'd best change your point of view. Stop blaming me, thinking I'm the problem. If you think I'm the problem, then you have to change me. If you realize that you're the problem, then you can change yourself, learn something and grow wiser. Most people want everyone else in the world to change but themselves. Let me tell you, it's easier to change yourself than everyone else."

"I don't understand," I said.

"Don't blame me for your problems," rich dad said, growing impatient.

"But you only pay me 10 cents."

"So what are you learning?" rich dad asked, smiling.

"That you're cheap," I said with a sly grin.

"See, you think I'm the problem," said rich dad.

"But you are."

"Well, keep that attitude and you learn nothing. Keep the attitude that I'm the problem and what choices do you have?"

"Well, if you don't pay me more or show me more respect and teach me, I'll quit."

"Well put," rich dad said. "And that's exactly what most people do. They quit and go looking for another job, better opportunity, and higher pay, actually thinking that a new job or more pay will solve the problem. In most cases, it won't."

"So what will solve the problem?" I asked. "Just take this measly 10 cents an hour and smile?"

Rich dad smiled. "That's what the other people do. Just accept a paycheck knowing that they and their family will struggle financially. But that's all they do, waiting for a raise thinking that more money will solve the problem. Most just accept it, and some take a second job working harder, but again accepting a small paycheck."

I sat staring at the floor, beginning to understand the lesson rich dad was presenting. I could sense it was a taste of life. Finally, I looked up and repeated the question. "So what will solve the problem?"

"This," he said tapping me gently on the head. "This stuff between your ears."

It was at that moment that rich dad shared the pivotal point of view that separated him from his employees and my poor dad—and led him to eventually become one of the richest men in Hawaii while my highly educated, but poor, dad struggled financially all his life. It was a singular point of view that made all the difference over a lifetime.

Rich dad said over and over, this point of view, which I call Lesson No.1.

"The poor and the middle class work for money." "The rich have money work for them."

On that bright Saturday morning, I was learning a completely different point of view from what I had been taught by my poor dad. At the age of 9, I grew aware that both dads wanted me to learn. Both dads encouraged me to study... but not the same things.

My highly educated dad recommended that I do what he did. "Son, I want you to study hard, get good grades, so you can find a safe, secure job with a big company. And make sure it has excellent benefits." My rich dad wanted me to learn how money works so I could make it work for me. These lessons I would learn through life with his guidance, not because of a classroom.

My rich dad continued my first lesson, "I'm glad you got angry about working for 10 cents an hour. If you had not gotten angry and had gladly accepted it, I would have to tell you that I could not teach you. You see, true learning takes energy, passion, a burning desire. Anger is a big part of that formula, for passion is anger and love combined. When it comes to money, most people want to play it safe and feel secure. So passion does not direct them. Fear does."

"So is that why they'll take a job with low pay?" I asked.

"Yes," said rich dad. "Some people say I exploit people because I don't pay as much as the sugar plantation or the government. I say the people exploit themselves. It's their fear, not mine."

"But don't you feel you should pay them more?" I asked.

"I don't have to. And besides, more money will not solve the problem. Just look at your dad. He makes a lot of money, and he still can't pay his bills. Most people, given more money, only get into more debt."

"So that's why the 10 cents an hour," I said, smiling. "It's a part of the lesson."

"That's right," smiled rich dad. "You see, your dad went to school and got an excellent education, so he could get a high-paying job. Which he did. But he still has money problems because he never learned anything about money at school. On top of that, he believes in working for money."

"And you don't?" I asked.

"No, not really," said rich dad. "If you want to learn to work for money, then stay in school. That is a great place to learn to do that. But if you want to learn how to have money work for you, then I will teach you that. But only if you want to learn."

"Wouldn't everyone want to learn that?" I asked.

"No," said rich dad. "Simply because it's easier to learn to work for money, especially if fear is your primary emotion when the subject of money is discussed."

"I don't understand," I said with a frown.

"Don't worry about that for now. Just know that it's fear that keeps most people working at a job. The fear of not paying their bills. The fear of being fired. The fear of not having enough money. The fear of starting over. That's the price of studying to learn a profession or trade, and then working for money. Most people become a slave to money... and then get angry at their boss."

"Learning to have money work for you is a completely different course of study?" I asked.

"Absolutely," rich dad answered, "absolutely."

We sat in silence on that beautiful Hawaiian Saturday morning. My friends would have just been starting their Little League baseball game. But for some reason, I was now thankful I had decided to work for 10 cents an hour. I sensed that I was about to learn something my friends would not learn in school.

"Ready to learn?" asked rich dad.

"Absolutely," I said with a grin.

"I have kept my promise. I've been teaching you from afar," my rich dad said. "At 9 years old, you've gotten a taste of what it feels like to work for money. Just multiply your last month by fifty years and you will have an idea of what most people spend their life doing."

"I don't understand," I said.

"How did you feel waiting in line to see me? Once to get hired and once to ask for more money?"

"Terrible," I said.

"If you choose to work for money, that is what life is like for many people," said rich dad.

"And how did you feel when Mrs. Martin dropped three dimes in your hand for three hours' work?"

"I felt like it wasn't enough. It seemed like nothing. I was disappointed," I said.

"And that is how most employees feel when they look at their paychecks. Especially after all the tax and other deductions are taken out. At least you got 100 percent."

"You mean most workers don't get paid everything?" I asked with amazement.

"Heavens no!" said rich dad. "The government always takes its share first."

"How do they do that?" I asked.

"Taxes," said rich dad. "You're taxed when you earn. You're taxed when you spend. You're taxed when you save. You're taxed when you die."

"Why do people let the government do that to them?"

"The rich don't," said rich dad with a smile. "The poor and the middle class do. I'll bet you that I earn more than your dad, yet he pays more in taxes."

"How can that be?" I asked. As a 9-year-old boy, that made no sense to me. "Why would someone let the government do that to them?"

Rich dad sat there in silence. I guess he wanted me to listen instead of jabber away at the mouth.

Finally, I calmed down. I did not like what I had heard. I knew my dad complained constantly about paying so much in taxes, but really did nothing about it. Was that life pushing him around?

Rich dad rocked slowly and silently in his chair, just looking at me.

"Ready to learn?" he asked.

I nodded my head slowly.

"As I said, there is a lot to learn. Learning how to have money work for you is a lifetime study. Most people go to college for four years, and their education ends. I already know that my study of money will continue over my lifetime, simply because the more I find out, the more I find out I need to know. Most people never study the subject. They go to work, get their paycheck, balance their checkbooks, and that's it. On top of that, they wonder why they have money problems. Then, they think that more money will solve the problem. Few realize that it's their lack of financial education that is the problem."

"So my dad has tax problems because he doesn't understand money?" I asked, confused.

"Look," said rich dad. "Taxes are just one small section on learning how to have money work for you. Today, I just wanted to find out if you still have the passion to learn about money. Most people don't. They want to go to school, learn a profession, have fun at their work, and earn lots of money. One day they wake up with big money problems, and then they can't stop working. That's the price of only knowing how to work for money instead of studying how to have money work for you. So do you still have the passion to learn?" asked rich dad.

I nodded my head.

"Good," said rich dad. "Now get back to work. This time, I will pay you nothing."

"What?" I asked in amazement.

"You heard me. Nothing. You will work the same three hours every

Saturday, but this time you will not be paid 10 cents per hour. You said you wanted to learn to not work for money, so I'm not going to pay you anything."

I couldn't believe what I was hearing.

"I've already had this conversation with Mike. He's already working, dusting and stacking canned goods for free. You'd better hurry and get back there."

"That's not fair," I shouted. "You've got to pay something."

"You said you wanted to learn. If you don't learn this now, you'll grow up to be like the two women and the older man sitting in my living room, working for money and hoping I don't fire them. Or like your dad, earning lots of money only to be in debt up to his eyeballs, hoping more money will solve the problem. If that's what you want, I'll go back to our original deal of 10 cents an hour. Or you can do what most people grow up to do. Complain that there is not enough pay, quit and go looking for another job."

"But what do I do?" I asked.

Rich dad tapped me on the head. "Use this," he said. "If you use it well, you will soon thank me for giving you an opportunity, and you will grow into a rich man."

I stood there still not believing what a raw deal I had been handed. Here I came to ask for a raise, and now I was being told to keep working for nothing.

Rich dad tapped me on the head again and said, "Use this. Now get out of here and get back to work."

LESSON #1: *The Rich Don't Work For Money*

I didn't tell my poor dad I wasn't being paid. He would not have understood, and I did not want to try to explain something that I did not yet understand myself.

For three more weeks, Mike and I worked for three hours, every Saturday, for nothing. The work didn't bother me, and the routine got easier. It was the missed baseball games and not being able to afford to buy a few comic books that got to me.

Rich dad stopped by at noon on the third week. We heard his truck pull up in the parking lot and sputter when the engine was turned off. He entered the store and greeted Mrs. Martin with a hug. After finding out how things were going in the store, he reached into the ice-cream freezer, pulled out two bars, paid for them, and signaled to Mike and me.

"Let's go for a walk boys."

We crossed the street, dodging a few cars, and walked across a large grassy field, where a few adults were playing softball. Sitting down at a remote picnic table, he handed Mike and me the ice-cream bars.

"How's it going boys?"

"OK," Mike said.

I nodded in agreement.

"Learn anything yet?" rich dad asked.

Mike and I looked at each other, shrugged our shoulders and shook our heads in unison.

Avoiding One of Life's Biggest Traps

"Well, you boys had better start thinking. You're staring at one of life's biggest lessons. If you learn the lesson, you'll enjoy a life of great freedom and security. If you don't learn the lesson, you'll wind up like Mrs. Martin and most of the people playing softball in this park. They work very hard, for little money, clinging to the illusion of job security, looking forward to a three-week vacation each year and a skimpy pension after forty-five years of work. If that excites you, I'll give you a raise to 25 cents an hour."

"But these are good hard-working people. Are you making fun of them?" I demanded.

A smile came over rich dad's face.

"Mrs. Martin is like a mother to me. I would never be that cruel. I may sound cruel because I'm doing my best to point something out to the two of you. I want to expand your point of view so you can see something. Something most people never have the benefit of seeing because their vision is too narrow. Most people never see the trap they are in."

Mike and I sat there uncertain of his message. He sounded cruel, yet we could sense he was desperately wanting us to know something.

With a smile, rich dad said, "Doesn't that 25 cents an hour sound good? Doesn't it make your heart beat a little faster."

I shook my head "no," but it really did. Twenty five cents an hour would be big bucks to me.

"OK, I'll pay you a dollar an hour," rich dad said, with a sly grin.

Now my heart was beginning to race. My brain was screaming,

"Take it. Take it." I could not believe what I was hearing. Still, I said nothing.

"OK, $2 an hour."

My little 9-year-old brain and heart nearly exploded. After all, it was 1956 and being paid $2 an hour would have made me the richest kid in the world. I couldn't imagine earning that kind of money. I wanted to say "yes." I wanted the deal. I could see a new bicycle, new baseball glove, and adoration of my friends when I flashed some cash. On top of that, Jimmy and his rich friends could never call me poor again. But somehow my mouth stayed silent.

Maybe my brain had overheated and blown a fuse. But deep down, I badly wanted that $2 an hour.

The ice cream had melted and was running down my hand. The ice-cream stick was empty, and under it was a sticky mess of vanilla and chocolate that ants were enjoying. Rich dad was looking at two boys staring back at him, eyes wide open and brains empty. He knew he was testing us, and he knew there was a part of our emotions that wanted to take the deal. He knew that each human being has a weak and needy part of their soul that can be bought. And he knew that each human being also had a part of their soul that was strong and filled with a resolve that could never be bought. It was only a question of which one was stronger. He had tested thousands of souls in his life. He tested souls every time he interviewed someone for a job.

"OK, $5 an hour."

Suddenly there was a silence from inside me. Something had changed. The offer was too big and had gotten ridiculous. Not too many grownups in 1956 made more than $5 an hour. The temptation disappeared, and a calm set in. Slowly I turned to my left to look at Mike. He looked back at me. The part of my soul that was weak and needy was silenced. The part of me that had no price took over. There was a calm and a certainty about money that entered my brain and my soul. I knew Mike had gotten to that point also.

"Good," rich dad said softly. "Most people have a price. And they have a price because of human emotions named fear and greed. First, the fear of being without money motivates us to work hard, and then once we get that paycheck, greed or desire starts us thinking about all the wonderful things money can buy. The pattern is then set."

"What pattern?" I asked.

"The pattern of get up, go to work, pay bills, get up, go to work, pay bills... Their lives are then run forever by two emotions, fear and greed. Offer them more money, and they continue the cycle by also increasing their spending. This is what I call the Rat Race."

"There is another way?" Mike asked.

"Yes," said rich dad slowly. "But only a few people find it."

"And what is that way?" Mike asked.

"That's what I hope you boys will find out as you work and study with me. That is why I took away all forms of pay."

"Any hints?" Mike asked. "We're kind of tired of working hard, especially for nothing."

"Well, the first step is telling the truth," said rich dad.

"We haven't been lying." I said.

"I did not say you were lying. I said to tell the truth," rich dad came back.

"The truth about what?" I asked.

"How you're feeling," rich dad said. "You don't have to say it to anyone else. Just yourself."

"You mean the people in this park, the people who work for you, Mrs. Martin, they don't do that?" I asked.

"I doubt it," said rich dad. "Instead, they feel the fear of not having money. Instead of confronting the fear, they react instead of think. They react emotionally instead of using their heads," rich dad said, tapping us on our heads. "Then, they get a few bucks in their hands, and again the emotion of joy and desire and greed take over, and again they react, instead of think."

"So their emotions do their thinking," Mike said.

"That's correct," said rich dad. "Instead of telling the truth about how they feel, they react to their feeling, fail to think. They feel the fear, they go to work, hoping that money will soothe the fear, but it doesn't. That old fear haunts them, and they go back to work, hoping again that money will calm their fears, and again it doesn't. Fear has them in this trap of working, earning money, working, earning money, hoping the fear will go away. But every day they get up, and that old fear wakes up with them. For millions of people, that old fear keeps them awake all night, causing a night of turmoil and worry. So they get up and go to work, hoping that a paycheck will kill that fear gnawing at their soul. Money is running their lives, and they refuse to tell the truth about that.

Money is in control of their emotions and hence their souls."

Rich dad sat quietly, letting his words sink in. Mike and I heard what he said, but really did not understand fully what he was talking about. I just knew that I often wondered why grownups hurried off to work. It did not seem like much fun, and they never looked that happy, but something kept them hurrying off to work.

Realizing we had absorbed as much as possible of what he was talking about, rich dad said, "I want you boys to avoid that trap. That is really what I want to teach you. Not just to be rich, because being rich does not solve the problem."

"It doesn't?" I asked, surprised.

"No, it doesn't. Let me finish the other emotion, which is desire. Some call it greed, but I prefer desire. It is perfectly normal to desire something better, prettier, more fun or exciting. So people also work for money because of desire. They desire money for the joy they think it can buy. But the joy that money brings is often short lived, and they soon need more money for more joy, more pleasure, more comfort, more security. So they keep working, thinking money will soothe their souls that is troubled by fear and desire. But money cannot do that."

"Even rich people?" Mike asked.

"Rich people included," said rich dad. "In fact, the reason many rich people are rich is not because of desire but because of fear. They actually think that money can eliminate that fear of not having money, of being poor, so they amass tons of it only to find out the fear gets worse. They now fear losing it. I have friends who keep working even though they have plenty. I know people who have millions who are more afraid now than when they were poor. They're terrified of losing all their money. The fears that drove them to get rich got worse. That weak and needy part of their soul is actually screaming louder. They don't want to lose the big houses, the cars, the high life that money has bought them. They worry about what their friends would say if they lost all their money. Many are emotionally desperate and neurotic, although they look rich and have more money."

"So is a poor man happier?" I asked.

"No, I don't think so," replied rich dad. "The avoidance of money is just as psychotic as being attached to money."

As if on cue, the town derelict went past our table, stopping by the large rubbish can and rummaging around in it. The three of us watched him with great interest, when before we probably would have just ignored him.

Rich dad pulled a dollar out of his wallet and gestured to the older man. Seeing the money, the derelict came over immediately, took the bill, thanked rich dad profusely and hurried off ecstatic with his good fortune.

"He's not much different from most of my employees," said rich dad. "I've met so many people who say, 'Oh, I'm not interested in money.' Yet they'll work at a job for eight hours a day. That's a denial of truth. If they weren't interested in money, then why are they working? That kind of thinking is probably more psychotic than a person who hoards money."

As I sat there listening to my rich dad, my mind was flashing back to the countless times my own dad said, "I'm not interested in money." He said those words often. He also covered himself by always saying, "I work because I love my job."

"So what do we do?" I asked. "Not work for money until all traces of fear and greed are gone?"

"No, that would be a waste of time," said rich dad. "Emotions are what make us human. Make us real. The word 'emotion' stands for energy in motion. Be truthful about your emotions, and use your mind and emotions in your favor, not against yourself."

"Whoa!" said Mike.

"Don't worry about what I just said. It will make more sense in years to come. Just be an observer, not a reactor, to your emotions. Most people do not know that it's their emotions that are doing the thinking. Your emotions are your emotions, but you have got to learn to do your own thinking."

"Can you give me an example?" I asked.

"Sure," replied rich dad. "When a person says, 'I need to find a job,' it's most likely an emotion doing the thinking. Fear of not having money generates that thought."

"But people do need money if they have bills to pay," I said.

"Sure they do," smiled rich dad. "All I'm saying is that it's fear that is all too often doing the thinking."

"I don't understand," said Mike.

"For example," said rich dad. "If the fear of not having enough money arises, instead of immediately running out to get a job so they can earn a few bucks to kill the fear, they instead might ask themselves this question. 'Will a job be the best solution to this fear over the long run?' In my opinion, the answer is 'no.' Especially when you look over a person's lifetime. A job is really a short-term solution to a long-term problem."

"But my dad is always saying, 'Stay in school, get good grades, so you can find a safe, secure job.' I spoke out, somewhat confused.

"Yes, I understand he says that," said rich dad, smiling. "Most people recommend that, and it's a good idea for most people. But people make that recommendation primarily out of fear."

"You mean my dad says that because he's afraid?"

"Yes," said rich dad. "He's terrified that you won't be able to earn money and won't fit into society. Don't get me wrong. He loves you and wants the best for you. And I think his fear is justified. An education and a job are important. But it won't handle the fear. You see, that same fear that makes him get up in the morning to earn a few bucks is the fear that is causing him to be so fanatical about you going to school."

"So what do you recommend?" I asked.

"I want to teach you to master the power of money. Not be afraid of it. And they don't teach that in school. If you don't learn it, you become a slave to money."

It was finally making sense. He did want us to widen our views. To see what Mrs. Martin could not see, his employees could not see, or my dad for that matter. He used examples that sounded cruel at the time, but I've never forgotten them. My vision widened that day, and I could begin to see the trap that lay ahead for most people.

"You see, we're all employees ultimately. We just work at different levels," said rich dad. "I just want you boys to have a chance to avoid the trap. The trap caused by those two emotions, fear and desire. Use them in your favor, not against you. That's what I want to teach you. I'm not interested in just teaching you to make a pile of money. That won't handle the fear or desire. If you don't first handle fear and desire, and you get rich, you'll only be a high-paid slave."

"So how do we avoid the trap?" I asked.

"The main cause of poverty or financial struggle is fear and ignorance, not the economy or the government or the rich. It's self-inflicted fear and ignorance that keeps people trapped. So you boys go to school and get your college degrees. I'll teach you how to stay out of the trap."

The pieces of the puzzle were appearing. My highly educated dad had a great education and a great career. But school never told him how to handle money or his fears. It became clear that I could learn different and important things from two fathers.

"So you've been talking about the fear of not having money. How does the desire of money affect our thinking?" Mike asked.

"How did you feel when I tempted you with a pay raise? Did you notice your desires rising?"

We nodded our heads.

"By not giving in to your emotions, you were able to delay your reactions and think. That is most important. We will always have emotions of fear and greed. From here on in, it is most important for you to use those emotions to your advantage and for the long term, and not simply let your emotions run you by controlling your thinking. Most people use fear and greed against themselves. That's the start of ignorance. Most people live their lives chasing paychecks, pay raises and job security because of the emotions of desire and fear, not really questioning where those emotion-driven thoughts are leading them. It's just like the picture of a donkey, dragging a cart, with its owner dangling a carrot just in front of the donkey's nose. The donkey's owner may be going where he wants to go, but the donkey is chasing an illusion. Tomorrow there will only be another carrot for the donkey."

"You mean the moment I began to picture a new baseball glove, candy and toys, that's like a carrot to a donkey?" Mike asked.

"Yeah. And as you get older, your toys get more expensive. A new car, a boat and a big house to impress your friends," said rich dad with a smile. "Fear pushes you out the door, and desire calls to you. Enticing you toward the rocks. That's the trap."

"So what's the answer," Mike asked.

"What intensifies fear and desire is ignorance. That is why rich people with lots of money often have more fear the richer they get. Money is the carrot, the illusion. If the donkey could see the whole picture, it might rethink its choice to chase the carrot."

Rich dad went on to explain that a human's life is a struggle between ignorance and illumination.

He explained that once a person stops searching for information and knowledge of one's self, ignorance sets in. That struggle is a moment-to-moment decision—to learn to open or close one's mind.

"Look, school is very, very important. You go to school to learn a skill or profession so as to be a contributing member of society. Every culture needs teachers, doctors, mechanics, artists, cooks, business people, police officers, firefighters, soldiers. Schools train them so our culture can thrive and flourish," said rich dad. "Unfortunately, for many people, school is the end, not the beginning."

There was a long silence. Rich dad was smiling. I did not comprehend everything he said that day. But as with most great teachers, whose words continue to teach for years, often long after they're gone, his words are still with me today.

"I've been a little cruel today," said rich dad. "Cruel for a reason. I want you to always remember this talk. I want you to always think of Mrs. Martin. I want you always to think of the donkey. Never forget, because your two emotions, fear and desire, can lead you into life's biggest trap, if you're not aware of them controlling your thinking. To spend your life living in fear, never exploring your dreams, is cruel. To work hard for money, thinking that money will buy you things that will make you happy is also cruel. To wake up in the middle of the night terrified about paying bills is a horrible way to live. To live a life dictated by the size of a paycheck is not really a life. Thinking that a job will make you feel secure is lying to yourself. That's cruel, and that's the trap I want you to avoid, if possible. I've seen how money runs people's lives. Don't let that happen to you. Please don't let money run your life."

A softball rolled under our table. Rich dad picked it up and threw it back.

"So what does ignorance have to do with greed and fear?" I asked.

"Because it is ignorance about money that causes so much greed and so much fear," said rich dad. "Let me give you some examples. A doctor, wanting more money to better provide for his family, raises his fees. By raising his fees, it makes health care more expensive for everyone. Now, it hurts the poor people the most, so poor people have worse health than those with money.

"Because the doctors raise their rates, the attorneys raise their rates. Because the attorneys' rates have gone up, schoolteachers want a raise, which raises our taxes, and on and on and on. Soon, there will be such a horrifying gap between the rich and the poor that chaos will break out and another great civilization will collapse. Great civilizations collapsed when the gap between the haves and havenots was too great. America is on the same course, proving once again that history repeats itself, because we do not learn from history. We only memorize historical dates and names, not the lesson.

"Aren't prices supposed to go up?" I asked.

"Not in an educated society with a well-run government. Prices should actually come down. Of course, that is often only true in theory. Prices go up because of greed and fear caused by ignorance. If schools taught people about money, there would be more money and lower prices, but schools focus only on teaching people to work for money, not how to harness money's power."

"But don't we have business schools?" Mike asked. "Aren't you encouraging me to go to business school for my master's degree?"

"Yes," said rich dad. "But all too often, business schools train employees who are sophisticated bean counters. Heaven forbid a bean counter takes over a business. All they do is look at the numbers, fire people and kill the business. I know because I hire bean counters. All they think about is cutting costs and raising prices, which cause more problems. Bean counting is important. I wish more people knew it, but it, too, is not the whole picture," added rich dad angrily.

"So is there an answer?" asked Mike.

"Yes," said rich dad. "Learn to use your emotions to think, not think with your emotions. When you boys mastered your emotions, first by agreeing to work for free, I knew there was hope. When you again resisted your emotions when I tempted you with more money, you were again learning to think in spite of being emotionally charged. That's the first step."

"Why is that step so important?" I asked.

"Well, that's up to you to find out. If you want to learn, I'll take you boys into the briar patch. That place where almost everyone else avoids. I'll take you to that place where most people are afraid to go. If you go with me, you'll let go of the idea of working for money and instead learn to have money work for you."

"And what will we get if we go with you. What if we agree to learn from you? What will we get?" I asked.

"The same thing Briar Rabbit got," said rich dad. "Freedom from the

Tar Baby."

"Is there a briar patch?" I asked.

"Yes," said rich dad. "The briar patch is our fear and our greed. Going into our fear and confronting our greed, our weaknesses, our neediness is the way out. And the way out is through the mind, by choosing our thoughts."

"Choosing our thoughts?" Mike asked, puzzled.

"Yes. Choosing what we think rather than reacting to our emotions. Instead of just getting up and going to work to solve your problems, just because the fear of not having the money to pay your bills is scaring you. Thinking would be taking the time to ask yourself a question. A question like, 'Is working harder at this the best solution to this problem?' Most people are so terrified at not telling themselves the truth—that fear is in control—that they cannot think, and instead run out the door. Tar baby is in control. That's what I mean by choosing your thoughts."

"And how do we do that?" Mike asked.

"That's what I will be teaching you. I'll be teaching you to have a choice of thoughts to consider, rather than knee-jerk reacting, like gulping down your morning coffee and running out the door.

"Remember what I said before: A job is only a short-term solution to a long-term problem. Most people have only one problem in mind, and it's short term. It's the bills at the end of the month, the Tar Baby. Money now runs their lives. Or should I say the fear and ignorance about money. So they do as their parents did, get up every day and go work for money. Not having the time to say, 'Is there another way?' Their emotions now control their thinking, not their heads."

"Can you tell the difference between emotions thinking and the head thinking?" Mike asked.

"Oh, yes. I hear it all the time," said rich dad. "I hear things like, 'Well, everyone has to work.' Or 'The rich are crooks.' Or 'I'll get another job. I deserve this raise. You can't push me around.' Or 'I like this job because it's secure.' Instead of, 'Is there something I'm missing here?' which breaks the emotional thought, and gives you time to think clearly."

I must admit, it was a great lesson to be getting. To know when someone was speaking out of emotions or out of clear thought. It was a lesson that served me well for life. Especially when I was the one speaking out of reaction and not from clear thought.

As we headed back to the store, rich dad explained that the rich really did "make money." They did not work for it. He went on to explain that when Mike and I were casting 5-cent pieces out of lead, thinking we were making money, we were very close to thinking the way the rich think. The problem was that it was illegal for us to do it. It was legal for the government and banks to do it, but not us. He explained that there are legal ways to make money and illegal ways.

Rich dad went on to explain that the rich know that money is an illusion, truly like the carrot for the donkey. It's only out of fear and greed that the illusion of money is held together by billions of people thinking that money is real. Money is really made up. It was only because of the illusion of confidence and the ignorance of the masses that the house of cards stood standing. "In fact," he said, "in many ways the donkey's carrot was more valuable than money."

He talked about the gold standard that America was on, and that each dollar bill was actually a silver certificate. What concerned him was the rumor that we would someday go off the gold standard and our dollars would no longer be silver certificates.

"When that happens, boys, all hell is going to break loose. The poor, the middle class and the ignorant will have their lives ruined simply because they will continue to believe that money is real and that the company they work for, or the government, will look after them."

We really did not understand what he was saying that day, but over the years it made more and more sense.

Seeing What Others Miss

As he climbed into his pickup truck, outside of his little convenience store, he said, "Keep working boys, but the sooner you forget about needing a paycheck, the easier your adult life will be. Keep using your brain, work for free, and soon your mind will show you ways of making money far beyond what I could ever pay you. You will see things that other people never see. Opportunities right in front of their noses. Most people never see these opportunities because they're looking for money and security, so that's all they get. The moment you see one opportunity, you will see them for the rest of your life. The moment you do that, I'll teach you something else. Learn this, and you'll avoid one of life's biggest traps. You'll never, ever, touch that Tar Baby."

Mike and I picked up our things from the store and waved goodbye to Mrs. Martin. We went back to the park, to the same picnic bench, and spent several more hours thinking and talking.

We spent the next week at school, thinking and talking. For two more weeks, we kept thinking, talking, and working for free.

At the end of the second Saturday, I was again saying goodbye to Mrs. Martin and looking at the comic-book stand with a longing gaze. The hard thing about not even getting 30 cents every Saturday was that I didn't have any money to buy comic books. Suddenly, as Mrs. Martin was saying goodbye to Mike and me, I saw something she was doing that I had never seen her do before. I mean, I had seen her do it, but I never took notice of it.

Mrs. Martin was cutting the front page of the comic book in half. She was keeping the top half of the comic book cover and throwing the rest of the comic book into a large brown cardboard box. When I asked her what she did with the comic books, she said, "I throw them away. I give the top half of the cover back to the comic-book distributor for credit when he brings in the new comics. He's coming in an hour."

Mike and I waited for an hour. Soon the distributor arrived and I asked him if we could have the comic books. To which he replied, "You can have them if you work for this store and do not resell them."

Our partnership was revived. Mike's mom had a spare room in the basement that no one used. We cleaned it out, and began piling hundreds of comic books in that room. Soon our comic-book library was open to the public. We hired Mike's younger sister, who loved to study, to be head librarian. She charged each child 10 cents admission to the library, which was open from 2:30 to 4:30 p.m. every day after school. The customers, the children of the neighborhood, could read as many comics as they could in two hours. It was a bargain for them since a comic costs 10 cents each, and they could read five or six in two hours.

Mike's sister would check the kids as they left, to make sure they weren't borrowing any comic books. She also kept the books, logging in how many kids showed up each day, who they were, and any comments they might have. Mike and I averaged $9.50 per week over a three-month period. We paid his sister $1 a week and allowed her to read the comics for free, which she rarely did since she was always studying.

Mike and I kept our agreement by working in the store every Saturday and collecting all the comic books from the different stores. We kept our agreement to the distributor by not selling any comic books. We burned them once they got too tattered. We tried opening a branch office, but we could never quite find someone as dedicated as Mike's sister we could trust.

At an early age, we found out how hard it was to find good staff.

Three months after the library first opened, a fight broke out in the room. Some bullies from another neighborhood pushed their way in and started it. Mike's dad suggested we shut down the business. So our comic-book business shut down, and we stopped working on Saturdays at the convenience store. Anyway, rich dad was excited because he had new things he wanted to teach us. He was happy because we had learned our first lesson so well. We had learned to have money work for us. By not getting paid for our work at the store, we were forced to use our imaginations to identify an opportunity to make money. By starting our own business, the comic-book library, we were in control of our own finances, not dependent on an employer. The best part was that our business generated money for us, even when we weren't physically there. Our money worked for us.

Instead of paying us money, rich dad had given us so much more.

WHY TEACH FINANCIAL LITERACY?

Why Teach Financial Literacy?

*I*n 1990, my best friend, Mike, took over his father's empire and is, in fact, doing a better job than his dad did. We see each other once or twice a year on the golf course. He and his wife are wealthier than you could imagine. Rich dad's empire is in great hands, and Mike is now grooming his son to take his place, as his dad had groomed us.

In 1994, I retired at the age of 47, and my wife, Kim, was 37. Retirement does not mean not working. To my wife and me, it means that barring unforeseen cataclysmic changes, we can work or not work, and our wealth grows automatically, staying way ahead of inflation. I guess it means freedom. The assets are large enough to grow by themselves. It's like planting a tree. You water it for years and then one day it doesn't need you anymore. It's roots have gone down deep enough. Then, the tree provides shade for your enjoyment.

Mike chose to run the empire and I chose to retire.

Whenever I speak to groups of people, they often ask what I would recommend or what could they do? "How do they get started?" "Is there a good book I would recommend?" "What should they do to prepare their children?" "What is the secret to success?" "How do I make millions?" I am always reminded of this article I was once given. It goes as follows.

THE RICHEST BUSINESSMEN

In 1923 a group of our greatest leaders and richest businessmen held a meeting at the Edgewater Beach hotel in Chicago. Among them were Charles Schwab, head of the largest independent steel company; Samuel Insull, president of the world's largest utility; Howard Hopson, head of the largest gas company; Ivar Kreuger president of the International Match Co., one of the world's largest companies at that time; Leon Frazier, president of the Bank of International Settlements; Richard Whitney, president of the New York Stock Exchange; Arthur Cotton and Jesse Livermore, two of the biggest stock speculators; and Albert Fall, a member of President Harding's cabinet. Twenty five years later nine of them (those listed above) ended as follows. Schwab died penniless after living for five years on borrowed money. Insull died broke living in a foreign land. Kreuger and Cotton also died broke. Hopson went insane. Whitney and Albert Fall were just released from prison. Fraser and Livermore committed suicide.

I doubt if anyone can say what really happened to these men. If you look at the date, 1923, it was just before the 1929 market crash and the Great Depression, which I suspect had a great impact on these men and their lives. The point is this: Today we live in times of greater and faster change than these men did. I suspect there will be many booms and busts in the next 25 years that will parallel the ups and downs these men faced. I am concerned that too many people are focused too much on money and not their greatest wealth, which is their education. If people are prepared to be flexible, keep an open mind and learn, they will grow richer and richer through the changes. If they think money will solve problems, I am afraid those people will have a rough ride. Intelligence solves problems and produces money. Money without financial intelligence is money soon gone.

Most people fail to realize that in life, it's not how much money you make, it's how much money you keep. We have all heard stories of lottery winners who are poor, then suddenly rich, then poor again. They win millions and are soon back to where they started. Or stories of professional athletes, who, at the age of 24, are earning millions of dollars a year, and are sleeping under a bridge by age 34. In the paper this morning, as I write this, there is a story of a young basketball player who a year ago had millions. Today, he claims his friends, attorney and accountant took his money, and now he works at a car wash for minimum wage.

He is only 29. He was fired from the car wash because he refused to take off his championship ring as he was wiping off the cars, so his story made the newspaper. He is appealing his termination, claiming hardship and discrimination and that the ring is all he has left. He claims that if you take that away, he'll crumble.

In 1997, I know so many people who are becoming instant millionaires. It's the Roaring '20s one more time. And while I am glad people have been getting richer and richer, I only caution that in the long run, it's not how much you make, it's how much you keep, and how many generations you keep it.

So when people ask, "Where do I get started?" or "Tell me how to get rich quick," they often are greatly disappointed with my answer. I simply say to them what my rich dad said back to me when I was a little kid. "If you want to be rich, you need to be financially literate."

That idea was drummed into my head every time we were together. As I said, my educated dad stressed the importance of reading books, while my rich dad stressed the need to master financial literacy.

If you are going to build the Empire State Building, the first thing you need to do is dig a deep hole and pour a strong foundation. If you are going to build a home in the suburbs, all you need to do is pour a 6-inch slab of concrete. Most people, in their drive to get rich, are trying to build an Empire State Building on a 6-inch slab.

Our school system, having been created in the Agrarian Age, still believes in homes with no foundation. Dirt floors are still the rage. So kids graduate from school with virtually no financial foundation. One day, sleepless and deep in debt in suburbia, living the American Dream, they decide that the answer to their financial problems is to find a way to get rich quick.

Construction on the skyscraper begins. It goes up quickly, and soon, instead of the Empire State Building, we have the Leaning Tower of Suburbia. The sleepless nights return.

As for Mike and me in our adult years, both of our choices were possible because we were taught to pour a strong financial foundation when we were just kids.

Now, accounting is possibly the most boring subject in the world. It also could be the most confusing. But if you want to be rich, long term, it could be the most important subject. The question is, how do you take a boring and confusing subject and teach it to kids? The answer is, make it simple. Teach it first in pictures.

My rich dad poured a strong financial foundation for Mike and me. Since we were just kids, he created a simple way to teach us. For years he only drew pictures and used words. Mike and I understood the simple drawings, the jargon, the movement of money, and then in later years, rich dad began adding numbers. Today, Mike has gone on to master much more complex and sophisticated accounting analysis because he has had to. He has a billion-dollar empire to run. I am not as sophisticated because my empire is smaller, yet we come from the same simple foundation. In the following pages, I offer to you the same simple line drawings Mike's dad created for us. Though simple, those drawings helped guide two little boys in building great sums of wealth on a solid and deep foundation.

Rule One. You must know the difference between an asset and a liability, and buy assets. If you want to be rich, this is all you need to know. It is Rule No. 1. It is the only rule. This may sound absurdly simple, but most people have no idea how profound this rule is. Most people struggle financially because they do not know the difference between an asset and a liability.

"Rich people acquire assets. The poor and middle class acquire liabilities, but they think they are assets"

When rich dad explained this to Mike and me, we thought he was kidding. Here we were, nearly teenagers and waiting for the secret to getting rich, and this was his answer. It was so simple that we had to stop for a long time to think about it.

"What is an asset?" asked Mike.

"Don't worry right now," said rich dad. "Just let the idea sink in. If you can comprehend the simplicity, your life will have a plan and be financially easy. It is simple; that is why the idea is missed."

"You mean all we need to know is what an asset is, acquire them and we'll be rich?" I asked.

Rich dad nodded his head. "It's that simple."

"If it's that simple, how come everyone is not rich?" I asked.

Rich dad smiled. "Because people do not know the difference

between an asset and a liability."

I remember asking, "How could adults be so silly. If it is that simple, if it is that important, why would everyone not want to find out?"

It took our rich dad only a few minutes to explain what assets and liabilities were.

As an adult, I have difficulty explaining it to other adults. Why? Because adults are smarter. In most cases, the simplicity of the idea escapes most adults because they have been educated differently. They have been educated by other educated professionals, such as bankers, accountants, real estate agents, financial planners, and so forth. The difficulty comes in asking adults to unlearn, or become children again. An intelligent adult often feels it is demeaning to pay attention to simplistic definitions.

Rich dad believed in the KISS principle—"Keep It Simple Stupid"—so he kept it simple for two young boys, and that made the financial foundation strong.

So what causes the confusion? Or how could something so simple be so screwed up? Why would someone buy an asset that was really a liability. The answer is found in basic education.

We focus on the word "literacy" and not "financial literacy." What defines something to be an asset, or something to be a liability are not words. In fact, if you really want to be confused, look up the words "asset" and "liability" in the dictionary. I know the definition may sound good to a trained accountant, but for the average person it makes no sense. But we adults are often too proud to admit that something does not make sense.

As young boys, rich dad said, "What defines an asset is not words but numbers. And if you cannot read the numbers, you cannot tell an asset from a hole in the ground."

"In accounting," rich dad would say, "it's not the numbers, but what the numbers are telling you. It's just like words. It's not the words, but the story the words are telling you.

Many people read, but do not understand much. It's called reading comprehension. And we all have different abilities when it comes to reading comprehension. For example, I recently bought a new VCR. It came with an instruction book that explained how to program the VCR. All I wanted to do was record my favorite TV show on Friday night. I nearly went crazy trying to read the manual. Nothing in my world is more complex than learning how to program my VCR. I could read the words, but I understood nothing. I get an "A" for recognizing the words. I get an "F" for comprehension. And so it is with financial statements for most people.

"If you want to be rich, you've got to read and understand numbers." If I heard that once, I heard it a thousand times from my rich dad. And I also heard, "The rich acquire assets and the poor and middle class acquire liabilities."

Here is how to tell the difference between an asset and a liability. Most accountants and financial professionals do not agree with the definitions, but these simple drawings were the start of strong financial foundations for two young boys.

To teach pre-teen boys, rich dad kept everything simple, using as many pictures as possible, as few words as possible, and no numbers for years.

"This is the Cash Flow pattern of an asset."

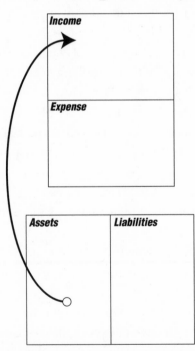

The above box is an Income Statement, often called a Profit and Loss Statement. It measures income and expenses. Money in and money out. The bottom diagram is the Balance Sheet. It is called that because it is supposed to balance assets against liabilities. Many financial novices do not know the relationship between the Income Statement and the Balance Sheet. That relationship is vital to understand.

The primary cause of financial struggle is simply not knowing the difference between an asset and a liability. The cause of the confusion is found in the definition of the two words. If you want a lesson in confusion, simply look up the words "asset" and "liability" in the dictionary.

Now it may make sense to trained accountants, but to the average person, it may as well be written in Mandarin. You read the words in the definition, but true comprehension is difficult.

So as I said earlier, my rich dad simply told two young boys that "assets put money in your pocket." Nice, simple and usable.

"This is Cash Flow pattern of a liability."

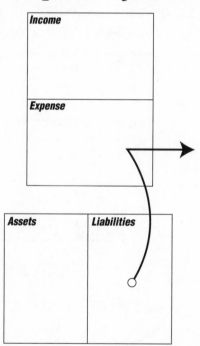

Now that assets and liabilities have been defined through pictures, it may be easier to understand my definitions in words.

An asset is something that puts money in my pocket.

A liability is something that takes money out of my pocket.

This is really all you need to know. If you want to be rich, simply spend your life buying assets. If you want to be poor or middle class, spend your life buying liabilities. It's not knowing the difference that causes most of the financial struggle in the real world.

Illiteracy, both in words and numbers, is the foundation of financial struggle. If people are having difficulties financially, there is something that they cannot read, either in numbers or words. Something is misunderstood. The rich are rich because they are more literate in different areas than people who struggle financially. So if you want to be rich and maintain your wealth, it's important to be financially literate, in words as well as numbers.

The arrows in the diagrams represent the flow of cash, or "cash flow." Numbers alone really mean little. Just as words alone mean little. It's the story that counts. In financial reporting, reading numbers is looking for the plot, the story. The story of where the cash is flowing. In 80 percent of most families, the financial story is a story of working hard in an effort to get ahead. Not because they don't make money. But because they spend their lives buying liabilities instead of assets.

For instance, this is the cash flow pattern of a poor person, or a young person still at home:

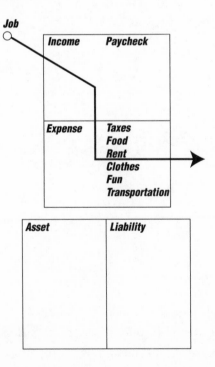

This is the cash flow pattern of a person in the middle class:

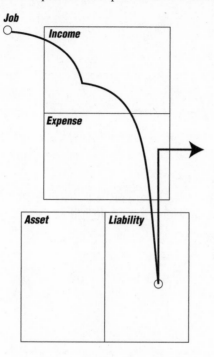

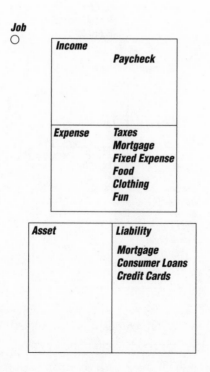

63

This is the cash flow pattern of a wealthy person:

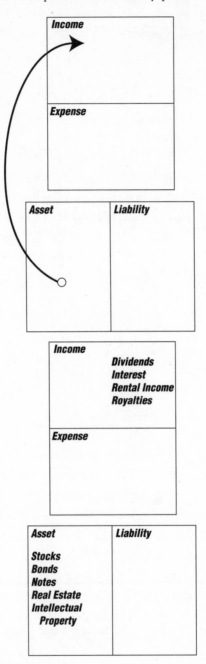

All of these diagrams were obviously oversimplified. Everyone has living expenses, the need for food, shelter and clothing.

The diagrams show the flow of cash through a poor, middle class or wealthy person's life. It is the cash flow that tells the story. It is the story of how a person handles their money, what they do after they get the money in their hand.

The reason I started with the story of the richest men in America is to illustrate the flaw in the thinking of so many people. The flaw is that money will solve all problems. That is why I cringe whenever I hear people ask me how to get rich quicker. Or where do they start? I often hear, "I'm in debt so I need to make more money."

But more money will often not solve the problem; in fact, it may actually accelerate the problem. Money often makes obvious our tragic human flaws. Money often puts a spotlight on what we do not know. That is why, all too often, a person who comes into a sudden windfall of cash—let's say an inheritance, a pay raise or lottery winnings—soon returns to the same financial mess, if not worse than the mess they were in before they received the money. Money only accentuates the cash-flow pattern running in your head. If your pattern is to spend everything you get, most likely an increase in cash will just result in an increase in spending. Thus, the saying, "A fool and his money is one big party."

I have said many times that we go to school to gain scholastic skills and professional skills, both important. We learn to make money with our professional skills. In the 1960s, when I was in high school, if someone did well in school academically, almost immediately people assumed this bright student would go on to be a medical doctor. Often no one asked the child if they wanted to be a doctor. It was assumed. It was the profession with the promise of the greatest financial reward.

Today, doctors are facing financial challenges I would not wish on my worst enemy: insurance companies taking control of the business, managed health care, government intervention, and malpractice suits, to name a few. Today, kids want to be basketball stars, golfers like Tiger Woods, computer nerds, movie stars, rock stars, beauty queens, or traders on Wall Street. Simply because that is where the fame, money and prestige is. That is the reason it is so hard to motivate kids in school today. They know that professional success is no longer solely linked to academic success, as it once was.

Because students leave school without financial skills, millions of educated people pursue their profession successfully, but later find themselves struggling financially. They work harder, but don't get ahead. What is missing from their education is not how to make money, but how to spend money—what to do after you make it. It's called financial aptitude—what you do with the money once you make it, how to keep people from taking it from you, how long you keep it, and how hard that money works for you. Most people cannot tell why they struggle financially because they don't understand cash flow. A person can be highly educated, professionally successful and financially illiterate. These people often work harder than they need to because they learned how to work hard, but not how to have their money work for them.

The story of how the quest for a Financial Dream turns into a financial nightmare

The moving-picture show of hard-working people has a set pattern. Recently married, the happy, highly educated young couple move in together, in one of their cramped rented apartments. Immediately, they realize that they are saving money because two can live as cheaply as one.

The problem is, the apartment is cramped. They decide to save money to buy their dream home so they can have kids. They now have two incomes, and they begin to focus on their careers.

Their incomes begin to increase.

As their incomes go up...

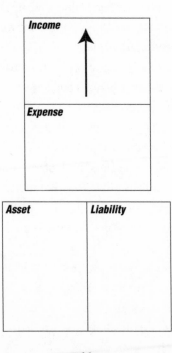

Their expenses go up as well.

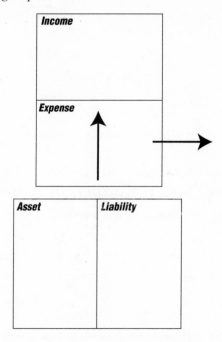

The No. 1 expense for most people is taxes. Many people think it's income tax, but for most Americans their highest tax is Social Security. As an employee, it appears as if the Social Security tax combined with the Medicare tax rate is roughly 7.5 percent, but it's really 15 percent since the employer must match the Social Security amount. In essence, it is money the employer cannot pay you. On top of that, you still have to pay income tax on the amount deducted from your wages for Social Security tax, income you never receive because it went directly to Social Security through withholding.

Then, their liabilities go up.

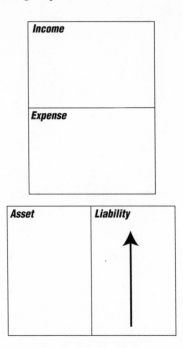

This is best demonstrated by going back to the young couple. As a result of their incomes going up, they decide to go out and buy the house of their dreams. Once in their house, they have a new tax, called property tax. Then, they buy a new car, new furniture and new appliances to match their new house. All of a sudden, they wake up and their liabilities column is full of mortgage debt and credit-card debt.

They're now trapped in the rat race. A child comes along. They work harder. The process repeats itself. More money and higher taxes, also called bracket creep. A credit card comes in the mail. They use it. It maxes out. A loan company calls and says their greatest "asset," their home, has appreciated in value. The company offers a "bill consolidation" loan, because their credit is so good, and tells them the intelligent thing to do is clear off the high-interest consumer debt by paying off their credit card. And besides, interest on their home is a tax deduction. They go for it, and pay off those high-interest credit cards. They breathe a sigh of relief. Their credit cards are paid off. They've now folded their consumer debt into their home mortgage. Their payments go down because they extend their debt over 30 years. It is the smart thing to do.

Their neighbor calls to invite them to go shopping—the Memorial Day sale is on. A chance to save some money. They say to themselves, "I won't buy anything. I'll just go look." But just in case they find something, they tuck that clean credit card inside their wallet.

I run into this young couple all the time. Their names change, but their financial dilemma is the same. They come to one of my talks to hear what I have to say. They ask me, "Can you tell us how to make more money?" Their spending habits have caused them to seek more income.

They don't even know that the trouble is really how they choose to spend the money they do have, and that is the real cause of their financial struggle. It is caused by financial illiteracy and not understanding the difference between an asset and a liability.

More money seldom solves someone's money problems. Intelligence solves problems. There is a saying a friend of mine says over and over to people in debt.

"If you find you have dug yourself into a hole... stop digging."

As a child, my dad often told us that the Japanese were aware of three powers: "The power of the sword, the jewel and the mirror."

The sword symbolizes the power of weapons. America has spent trillions of dollars on weapons and, because of this, is the supreme military presence in the world.

The jewel symbolizes the power of money. There is some degree of truth to the saying, "Remember the golden rule. He who has the gold makes the rules."

The mirror symbolizes the power of self-knowledge. This self-knowledge, according to Japanese legend, was the most treasured of the three.

The poor and middle class all too often allow the power of money to control them. By simply getting up and working harder, failing to ask themselves if what they do makes sense, they shoot themselves in the foot as they leave for work every morning. By not fully understanding money, the vast majority of people allow the awesome power of money to control them. The power of money is used against them.

If they used the power of the mirror, they would have asked themselves, "Does this make sense?" All too often, instead of trusting their inner wisdom, that genius inside of them, most people go along with the crowd. They do things because everybody else does it. They conform rather than question. Often, they mindlessly repeat what they have been told. Ideas such as "diversify" or "your home is an asset." "Your home is your biggest investment." "You get a tax break for going into greater debt." "Get a safe job." "Don't make mistakes." "Don't take risks."

It is said that the fear of public speaking is a fear greater than death for most people. According to psychiatrists, the fear of public speaking is caused by the fear of ostracism, the fear of standing out, the fear of criticism, the fear of ridicule, the fear of being an outcast. The fear of being different prevents most people from seeking new ways to solve their problems.

That is why my educated dad said the Japanese valued the power of the mirror the most, for it is only when we as humans look into the mirror do we find truth. And the main reason that most people say "Play it safe" is out of fear. That goes for anything, be it sports, relationships, career, money.

It is that same fear, the fear of ostracism that causes people to conform and not question commonly accepted opinions or popular trends. "Your home is an asset." "Get a bill consolidation loan and get out of debt." "Work harder." "It's a promotion." "Someday I'll be a vice president." "Save money." "When I get a raise, I'll buy us a bigger house." "Mutual funds are safe." "Tickle Me Elmo dolls are out of stock, but I just happen to have one in back that another customer has not come by for yet."

Many great financial problems are caused by going along with the crowd and trying to keep up with the Joneses. Occasionally, we all need to look in the mirror and be true to our inner wisdom rather than our fears.

By the time Mike and I were 16 years old, we began to have problems in school. We were not bad kids. We just began to separate from the crowd. We worked for Mike's dad after school and on the weekends. Mike and I often spent hours after work just sitting at a table with his dad while he held meetings with his bankers, attorneys, accountants, brokers, investors, managers and employees. Here was a man who had left school at the age of 13, now directing, instructing, ordering and asking questions of educated people. They came at his beck and call, and cringed when he did not approve of them.

Here was a man who had not gone along with the crowd. He was a man who did his own thinking and detested the words, "We have to do it this way because that's the way everyone else does it." He also hated the word "can't." If you wanted him to do something, just say, "I don't think you can do it."

Mike and I learned more sitting at his meetings than we did in all our years of school, college included. Mike's dad was not school educated, but he was financially educated and successful as a result. He use to tell us over and over again. "An intelligent person hires people who are more intelligent than they are." So Mike and I had the benefit of spending hours listening to and, in the process, learning from intelligent people.

But because of this, both Mike and I just could not go along with the standard dogma that our teachers preached. And that caused the problems. Whenever the teacher said, "If you don't get good grades, you won't do well in the real world," Mike and I just raised our eyebrows. When we were told to follow set procedures and not deviate from the rules, we could see how this schooling process actually discouraged creativity. We started to understand why our rich dad told us that schools were designed to produce good employees instead of employers.

Occasionally Mike or I would ask our teachers how what we studied was applicable, or we asked why we never studied money and how it worked. To the later question, we often got the answer that money was not important, that if we excelled in our education, the money would follow.

The more we knew about the power of money, the more distant we grew from the teachers and our classmates.

My highly educated dad never pressured me about my grades. I often wondered why. But we did begin to argue about money. By the time I was 16, I probably had a far better foundation with money than both my mom and dad. I could keep books, I listened to tax accountants, corporate attorneys, bankers, real estate brokers, investors and so forth. My dad talked to teachers.

One day, my dad was telling me why our home was his greatest investment. A not-too-pleasant argument took place when I showed him why I thought a house was not a good investment.

The following diagram illustrates the difference in perception between my rich dad and my poor dad when it came to their homes. One dad thought his house was an asset, and the other dad thought it was a liability.

Rich Dad

Asset	Liability
	Home

Poor Dad

Asset	Liability
Home	

I remember when I drew the following diagram for my dad showing him the direction of cash flow. I also showed him the ancillary expenses that went along with owning the home. A bigger home meant bigger expenses, and the cash flow kept going out through the expense column.

Liability

Income	

Expense	Mortgage
	Real Property
	Taxes
	Insurance
	Maintenance
	Utilities

Asset	Liability
	Mortgage

Today, I am still challenged on the idea of a house not being an asset. And I know that for many people, it is their dream as well as their largest investment. And owning your own home is better than nothing. I simply offer an alternate way of looking at this popular dogma. If my wife and I were to buy a bigger, more flashy house we realize it would not be an asset, it would be a liability, since it would take money out of our pocket.

So here is the argument I put forth. I really do not expect most people to agree with it because a nice home is an emotional thing. And when it comes to money, high emotions tend to lower financial intelligence. I know from personal experience that money has a way of making every decision emotional.

1. When it comes to houses, I point out that most people work all their lives paying for a home they never own. In other words, most people buy a new house every so many years, each time incurring a new 30-year loan to pay off the previous one.

2. Even though people receive a tax deduction for interest on mortgage payments, they pay for all their other expenses with after-tax dollars. Even after they pay off their mortgage.

3. Property taxes. My wife's parents were shocked when the property taxes on their home went to $1,000 a month. This was after they had retired, so the increase put a strain on their retirement budget, and they felt forced to move.

4. Houses do not always go up in value. In 1997, I still have friends who owe a million dollars for a home that will today sell for only $700,000.

5. The greatest losses of all are those from missed opportunities. If all your money is tied up in your house, you may be forced to work harder because your money continues blowing out of the expense column, instead of adding to the asset column, the classic middle class cash flow pattern. If a young couple would put more money into their asset column early on, their later years would get easier, especially as they prepared to send their children to college. Their assets would have grown and would be available to help cover expenses. All too often, a house only serves as a vehicle for incurring a home-equity loan to pay for mounting expenses.

In summary, the end result in making a decision to own a house that is too expensive in lieu of starting an investment portfolio early on impacts an individual in at least the following three ways:

1. Loss of time, during which other assets could have grown in value.
2. Loss of additional capital, which could have been invested instead of paying for high-maintenance expenses related directly to the home.
3. Loss of education. Too often, people count their house, savings and retirement plan as all they have in their asset column. Because they have no money to invest, they simply do not invest. This costs them investment experience. Most never become what the investment world calls a "sophisticated investor." And the best investments are usually first sold to "sophisticated investors," who then turn around and sell them to the people playing it safe.

I am not saying don't buy a house. I am sayig, understand the difference between an asset and a liability. When I want a bigger house, I first buy assets that will generate the cash flow to pay for the house.

My educated dad's personal financial statement best demonstrates the life of someone in the rat race. His expenses seem to always keep up with his income, never allowing him to invest in assets. As a result, his liabilities, such as his mortgage and credit card debts are larger than his assets. The following picture is worth a thousand words:

Educated Dad's Financial Statement

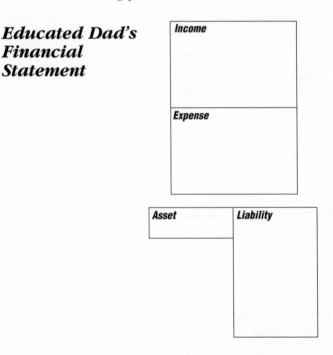

My rich dad's personal financial statement, on the other hand, reflects the results of a life dedicated to investing and minimizing liabilities:

Rich Dad's Financial Statement

Income
Expense

Asset	Liability

A review of my rich dad's financial statement is why the rich get richer. The asset column generates more than enough income to cover expenses, with the balance reinvested into the asset column. The asset column continues to grow and, therefore, the income it produces grows with it.

The result being: The rich get richer!

Why the Rich
Get Richer

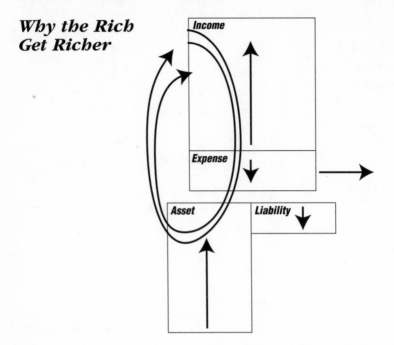

The middle class finds itself in a constant state of financial struggle. Their primary income is through wages, and as their wages increase, so do their taxes. Their expenses tend to increase in equal increments as their wages increase; hence the phrase "the rat race." They treat their home as their primary asset, instead on investing in income-producing assets.

Why the Middle Class Struggle

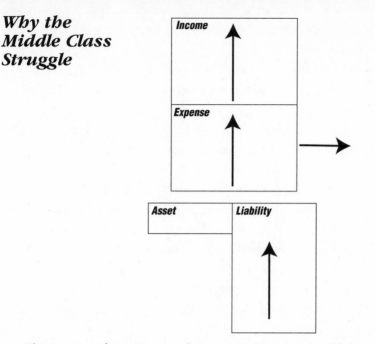

This pattern of treating your home as an investment and the philosophy that a pay raise means you can buy a larger home or spend more is the foundation of today's debt-ridden society. This process of increased spending throws families into greater debt and into more financial uncertainty, even though they may be advancing in their jobs and receiving pay raises on a regular basis. This is high risk living caused by weak financial education.

The massive loss of jobs in the 1990s—the downsizing of businesses—has brought to light how shaky the middle class really is financially. Suddenly, company pension plans are being replaced by 401k plans. Social Security is obviously in trouble and cannot be looked at as a source for retirement. Panic has set in for the middle class. The good thing today is that many of these people have recognized these issues and have begun buying mutual funds. This increase in investing is largely responsible for the huge rally we have seen in the stock market. Today, there are more and more mutual funds being created to answer the demand by the middle class.

Mutual funds are popular because they represent safety. Average mutual fund buyers are too busy working to pay taxes and mortgages, save for their children's college and pay off credit cards. They do not have time to study to learn how to invest, so they rely on the expertise of the manager of a mutual fund. Also, because the mutual fund includes many different types of investments, they feel their money is safer because it is "diversified."

This group of educated middle class subscribes to the "diversify" dogma put out by mutual fund brokers and financial planners. Play it safe. Avoid risk.

The real tragedy is that the lack of early financial education is what creates the risk faced by average middle class people. The reason they have to play it safe is because their financial positions are tenuous at best. Their balance sheets are not balanced. They are loaded with liabilities, with no real assets that generate income. Typically, their only source of income is their paycheck. Their livelihood becomes entirely dependent on their employer.

So when genuine "deals of a lifetime" come along, those same people cannot take advantage of the opportunity. They must play it safe, simply because they are working so hard, are taxed to the max, and are loaded with debt.

As I said at the start of this section, the most important rule is to know the difference between an asset and a liability. Once you understand the difference, concentrate your efforts on only buying income-generating assets. That's the best way to get started on a path to becoming rich. Keep doing that, and your asset column will grow. Focus on keeping liabilities and expenses down. This will make more money available to continue pouring into the asset column. Soon, the asset base will be so deep that you can afford to look at more speculative investments. Investments that may have returns of 100 percent to infinity. Investments that for $5,000 are soon turned into $1 million or more. Investments that the middle class calls "too risky." The investment is not risky. It's the lack of simple financial intelligence, beginning with financial literacy, that causes the individual to be "too risky."

If you do what the masses do, you get the following picture.

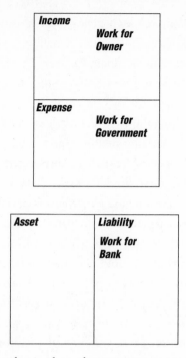

As an employee who is also a homeowner, your working efforts are generally as follows:

1. You work for someone else. Most people, working for a paycheck, are making the owner, or the shareholders richer. Your efforts and success will help provide for the owner's success and retirement.

2. You work for the government. The government takes its share from your paycheck before you even see it. By working harder, you simply increase the amount of taxes taken by the government — most people work from January to May just for the government.

3. You work for the bank. After taxes, your next largest expense is usually your mortgage and credit card debt.

The problem with simply working harder is that each of these three levels takes a greater share of your increased efforts. You need to learn how to have your increased efforts benefit you and your family directly.

Once you have decided to concentrate on minding your own business, how do you set your goals? For most people, they must keep their profession and rely on their wages to fund their acquisition of assets.

As their assets grow, how do they measure the extent of their success? When does someone realize that they are rich, that they have wealth? As well as having my own definitions for assets and liabilities, I also have my own definition for wealth. Actually I borrowed it from a man named Buckminster Fuller. Some call him a quack, and others call him a living genius. Years ago he got all the architects buzzing because he applied for a patent in 1961 for something called a geodesic dome. But in the application, Fuller also said something about wealth. It was pretty confusing at first, but after reading it for awhile, it began to make some sense: Wealth is a person's ability to survive so many number of days forward... or if I stopped working today, how long could I survive?

Unlike net worth—the difference between your assets and liabilities, which is often filled with a person's expensive junk and opinions of what things are worth—this definition creates the possibility for developing a truly accurate measurement. I could now measure and really know where I was in terms of my goal to become financially independent.

Although net worth often includes these non-cash-producing assets, like stuff you bought that now sits in your garage, wealth measures how much money your money is making and, therefore, your financial survivability.

Wealth is the measure of the cash flow from the asset column compared with the expense column.

Let's use an example. Let's say I have cash flow from my asset column of $1,000 a month. And I have monthly expenses of $2,000. What is my wealth?

Let's go back to Buckminster Fuller's definition. Using his definition, how many days forward can I survive? And let's assume a 30-day month. By that definition, I have enough cash flow for half a month.

When I have achieved $2,000 a month cash flow from my assets, then I will be wealthy.

So I am not yet rich, but I am wealthy. I now have income generated from assets each month that fully cover my monthly expenses. If I want to increase my expenses, I first must increase my cash flow from assets to maintain this level of wealth. Take notice that it is at this point that I no longer am dependent on my wages. I have focused on and been successful in building an asset column that has made me financially independent. If I quit my job today, I would be able to cover my monthly expenses with the cash flow from my assets.

My next goal would be to have the excess cash flow from my assets reinvested into the asset column. The more money that goes into my asset column, the more my asset column grows. The more my assets grow, the more my cash flow grows. And as long as I keep my expenses less than the cash flow from these assets, I will grow richer, with more and more income from sources other than my physical labor.

As this reinvestment process continues, I am well on my way to being rich. The actual definition of rich is in the eye of the beholder. You can never be too rich.

Just remember this simple observation:

The rich buy assets.

The poor only have expenses.

The middle class buys liabilities they think are assets.

So how do I start minding my own business? What is the answer? Listen to the founder of McDonald's.

MIND YOUR OWN BUSINESS

Mind Your Own Business

*I*n 1974, Ray Kroc, the founder of McDonald's, was asked to speak to the MBA class at the University of Texas at Austin. A dear friend of mine, Keith Cunningham, was a student in that MBA class. After a powerful and inspiring talk, the class adjourned and the students asked Ray if he would join them at their favorite hangout to have a few beers. Ray graciously accepted.

"What business am I in?" Ray asked, once the group had all their beers in hand.

"Everyone laughed," said Keith. "Most of the MBA students thought Ray was just fooling around."

No one answered, so Ray asked the question again. "What business do you think I'm in?"

The students laughed again, and finally one brave soul yelled out, "Ray, who in the world does not know that you're in the hamburger business."

Ray chuckled. "That is what I thought you would say." He paused and then quickly said, "Ladies and gentlemen, I'm not in the hamburger business. My business is real estate."

Keith said that Ray spent a good amount of time explaining his viewpoint. In their business plan, Ray knew that the primary business focus was to sell hamburger franchises, but what he never lost sight of was the location of each franchise. He knew that the real estate and its location was the most significant factor in the success of each franchise. Basically, the person that bought the franchise was also paying for, buying, the land under the franchise for Ray Kroc's organization.

McDonald's today is the largest single owner of real estate in the world, owning even more than the Catholic Church. Today, McDonald's owns some of the most valuable intersections and street corners in America, as well as in other parts of the world.

Keith said it was one of the most important lessons in his life. Today, Keith owns car washes, but his business is the real estate under those car washes.

The previous chapter ended with the diagrams illustrating that most people work for everyone else but themselves. They work first for the owners of the company, then for the government through taxes, and finally for the bank that owns their mortgage.

As a young boy, we did not have a McDonald's nearby. Yet, my rich dad was responsible for teaching Mike and me the same lesson that Ray Kroc talked about at the University of Texas. It is secret No. 3 of the rich.

The secret is: "Mind your own business." Financial struggle is often directly the result of people working all their life for someone else. Many people will have nothing at the end of their working days.

Again, a picture is worth a thousand words. Here is a diagram of the income statement and balance sheet that best describes Ray Kroc's advice:

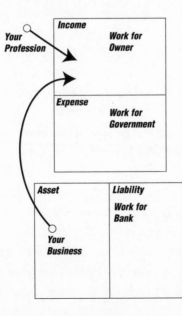

Our current educational system focuses on preparing today's youth to get good jobs by developing scholastic skills. Their lives will revolve around their wages, or as described earlier, their income column. And after developing scholastic skills, they go on to higher levels of schooling to enhance their professional abilities. They study to become engineers, scientists, cooks, police officers, artists, writers and so on. These professional skills allow them to enter the workforce and work for money.

There is a big difference between your profession and your business. Often I ask people, "What is your business?" And they will say, "Oh I'm a banker." Then I ask them if they own the bank? And they usually respond. "No, I work there."

In that instance, they have confused their profession with their business. Their profession may be a banker, but they still need their own business. Ray Kroc was clear on the difference between his profession and his business. His profession was always the same. He was a salesman. At one time he sold mixers for milkshakes, and soon thereafter he was selling hamburger franchises. But while his profession was selling hamburger franchises, his business was the accumulation of income-producing real estate.

A problem with school is that you often become what you study. So if you study, say, cooking, you become a chef. If you study the law, you become an attorney, and a study of auto mechanics makes you a mechanic. The mistake in becoming what you study is that too many people forget to mind their own business. They spend their lives minding someone else's business and making that person rich.

To become financially secure, a person needs to mind their own business. Your business revolves around your asset column, as opposed to your income column. As stated earlier, the No. 1 rule is to know the difference between an asset and a liability, and to buy assets. The rich focus on their asset columns while everyone else focuses on their income statements.

That is why we hear so often: "I need a raise." "If only I had a promotion." "I am going to go back to school to get more training so I can get a better job." "I am going to work overtime." "Maybe I can get a second job." "I'm quitting in two weeks. I found a job that pays more."

In some circles, these are sensible ideas. Yet, if you listen to Ray Kroc, you are still not minding your own business. These ideas all still focus on the income column and will only help a person become more financially secure if the additional money is used to purchase income-generating assets.

The primary reason the majority of the poor and middle class are fiscally conservative—which means, "I can't afford to take risks"—is that they have no financial foundation. They have to cling to their jobs. They have to play it safe.

When downsizing became the "in" thing to do, millions of workers found out their largest so-called asset, their home, was eating them alive. Their asset, called a house, still cost them money every month. Their car, another "asset," was eating them alive. The golf clubs in the garage that cost $1,000 were not worth $1,000 anymore. Without job security, they had nothing to fall back on. What they thought were assets could not help them survive in a time of financial crisis.

I assume most of us have filled out a credit application for a banker to buy a house or to buy a car. It is always interesting to look at the "net worth" section. It is interesting because of what accepted banking and accounting practices allow a person to count as assets.

One day, to get a loan, my financial position did not look too good. So I added my new golf clubs, my art collection, books, stereo, television, Armani suits, wristwatches, shoes and other personal effects to boost the number in the asset column.

But I was turned down for the loan because I had too much investment real estate. The loan committee did not like that I made so much money off of apartment houses. They wanted to know why I did not have a normal job, with a salary. They did not question the Armani suits, golf clubs or art collection. Life is sometimes tough when you do not fit the "standard" profile.

I cringe every time I hear someone say to me that their net worth is a million dollars or $100,000 dollars or whatever. One of the main reasons net worth is not accurate is simply because the moment you begin selling your assets, you are taxed for any gains.

So many people have put themselves in deep financial trouble when they run short of income. To raise cash, they sell their assets. First, their personal assets can generally be sold for only a fraction of the value that is listed in their personal balance sheet. Or if there is a gain on the sale of the assets, they are taxed on the gain. So again, the government takes its share of the gain, thus reducing the amount available to help them out of debt. That is why I say someone's net worth is often "worth less" than they think.

Start minding your own business. Keep your daytime job, but start buying real assets, not liabilities or personal effects that have no real value once you get them home. A new car loses nearly 25 percent of the price you pay for it the moment you drive it off the lot. It is not a true asset even if your banker lets you list it as one. My $400 new titanium driver was worth $150 the moment I teed off.

For adults, keep your expenses low, reduce your liabilities and diligently build a base of solid assets. For young people who have not yet left home, it is important for parents to teach them the difference between an asset and a liability. Get them to start building a solid asset column before they leave home, get married, buy a house, have kids and get stuck in a risky financial position, clinging to a job and buying everything on credit. I see so many young couples who get married and trap themselves into a lifestyle that will not let them get out of debt for most of their working years.

For most people, just as the last child leaves home, the parents realize they have not adequately prepared for retirement and they begin to scramble to put some money away. Then, their own parents become ill and they find themselves with new responsibilities.

So what kind of assets am I suggesting that you or your children acquire? In my world, real assets fall into several different categories:

1. Businesses that do not require my presence. I own them, but they are managed or run by other people. If I have to work there, it's not a business. It becomes my job.
2. Stocks.
3. Bonds.
4. Mutual funds.
5. Income-generating real estate.
6. Notes (IOUs).
7. Royalties from intellectual property such as music, scripts, patents.
8. And anything else that has value, produces income or appreciates and has a ready market.

As a young boy, my educated dad encouraged me to find a safe job. My rich dad, on the other hand, encouraged me to begin acquiring assets that I loved. "If you don't love it, you won't take care of it." I collect real estate simply because I love buildings and land. I love shopping for them. I could look at them all day long. When problems arise, the problems are not so bad that it changes my love for real estate. For people who hate real estate, they shouldn't buy it.

I love stocks of small companies, especially startups. The reason is that I am an entrepreneur, not a corporate person. In my early years, I worked in large organizations, such as Standard Oil of California, the U.S. Marine Corps, and Xerox Corp. I enjoyed my time with those organizations and have fond memories, but I know deep down I am not a company man. I like starting companies, not running them. So my stock buys are usually of small companies, and sometimes I even start the company and take it public. Fortunes are made in new-stock issues, and I love the game. Many people are afraid of small-cap companies and call them risky, and they are. But risk is always diminished if you love what the investment is, understand it and know the game. With small companies, my investment strategy is to be out of the stock in a year. My real estate strategy, on the other hand, is to start small and keep trading the properties up for bigger properties and, therefore, delaying paying taxes on the gain. This allows the value to increase dramatically. I generally hold real estate less than seven years.

For years, even while I was with the Marine Corps and Xerox, I did what my rich dad recommended. I kept my daytime job, but I still minded my own business. I was active in my asset column. I traded real estate and small stocks. Rich dad always stressed the importance of financial literacy. The better I was at understanding the accounting and cash management, the better I would be at analyzing investments and eventually starting and building my own company.

I would not encourage anyone to start a company unless they really want to. Knowing what I know about running a company, I would not wish that task on anyone. There are times when people cannot find employment, where starting a company is a solution for them. The odds are against success: Nine out of 10 companies fail in five years. Of those that survive the first five years, nine out of every 10 of those eventually fail, as well. So only if you really have the desire to own your own company do I recommend it. Otherwise, keep your daytime job and mind your own business.

When I say mind your own business, I mean to build and keep your asset column strong. Once a dollar goes into it, never let it come out. Think of it this way, once a dollar goes into your asset column, it becomes your employee. The best thing about money is that it works 24 hours a day and can work for generations. Keep your daytime job, be a great hard-working employee, but keep building that asset column.

As your cash flow grows, you can buy some luxuries. An important distinction is that rich people buy luxuries last, while the poor and middle class tend to buy luxuries first. The poor and the middle class often buy luxury items such as big houses, diamonds, furs, jewelry or boats because they want to look rich. They look rich, but in reality they just get deeper in debt on credit. The old-money people, the long-term rich, built their asset column first. Then, the income generated from the asset column bought their luxuries. The poor and middle class buy luxuries with their own sweat, blood and children's inheritance.

A true luxury is a reward for investing in and developing a real asset. For example, when my wife and I had extra money coming from our apartment houses, she went out and bought her Mercedes. It did not take any extra work or risk on her part because the apartment house bought the car. She did, however, have to wait for it for four years while the real estate investment portfolio grew and finally began throwing off enough extra cash flow to pay for the car. But the luxury, the Mercedes, was a true reward because she had proved she knew how to grow her asset column. That car now means a lot more to her than simply another pretty car. It means she used her financial intelligence to afford it.

What most people do is they impulsively go out and buy a new car, or some other luxury, on credit. They may feel bored and just want a new toy. Buying a luxury on credit often causes a person to sooner or later actually resent that luxury because the debt on the luxury becomes a financial burden.

After you've taken the time and invested in and built your own business, you are now ready to add the magic touch—the biggest secret of the rich. The secret that puts the rich way ahead of the pack. The reward at the end of the road for diligently taking the time to mind your own business.

THE HISTORY OF TAXES AND THE POWER OF CORPORATIONS

The History of Taxes and The Power of Corporations

I remember in school being told the story of Robin Hood and his Merry Men. My schoolteacher thought it was a wonderful story of a romantic hero, a Kevin Costner type, who robbed from the rich and gave to the poor. My rich dad did not see Robin Hood as a hero. He called Robin Hood a crook.

Robin Hood may be long gone, but his followers live on. How often I still hear people say, "Why don't the rich pay for it?" Or "The rich should pay more in taxes and give it to the poor."

It is this idea of Robin Hood, or taking from the rich to give to the poor that has caused the most pain for the poor and the middle class. The reason the middle class is so heavily taxed is because of the Robin Hood ideal. The real reality is that the rich are not taxed. It's the middle class who pays for the poor, especially the educated upper-income middle class.

Again, to understand fully how things happen, we need to look at the historical perspective. We need to look at the history of taxes. Although my highly educated dad was an expert on the history of education, my rich dad fashioned himself as an expert on the history of taxes.

Rich dad explained to Mike and me that in England and America originally, there were no taxes. Occasionally there were temporary taxes levied in order to pay for wars. The king or the president would put the word out and ask everyone to "chip in." Taxes were levied in Britain for the fight against Napoleon from 1799 to 1816, and in America taxes were levied to pay for the Civil War from 1861 to 1865.

In 1874, England made income tax a permanent levy on its citizens. In 1913, an income tax became permanent in the United States with the adoption of the 16th Amendment to the Constitution. At one time, Americans were anti-tax. It had been the excessive tax on tea that led to the famous Tea Party in Boston Harbor, an incident that helped ignite the Revolutionary War. It took approximately 50 years in both England and the United States to sell the idea of a regular income tax.

What these historical dates fail to reveal is that both of these taxes were initially levied against only the rich. It was this point that rich dad wanted Mike and me to understand. He explained that the idea of taxes was made popular, and accepted by the majority, by telling the poor and the middle class that taxes were created only to punish the rich. This is how the masses voted for the law, and it became constitutionally legal. Although it was intended to punish the rich, in reality it wound up punishing the very people who voted for it, the poor and middle class.

"Once government got a taste of money, the appetite grew," said rich dad. "Your dad and I are exactly opposite. He's a government bureaucrat, and I am a capitalist. We get paid, and our success is measured on opposite behaviors. He gets paid to spend money and hire people. The more he spends and the more people he hires, the larger his organization becomes. In the government, the larger his organization, the more he is respected. On the other hand, within my organization, the fewer people I hire and the less money I spend, the more I am respected by my investors. That's why I don't like government people. They have different objectives from most business people. As the government grows, more and more tax dollars will be needed to support it."

My educated dad sincerely believed that government should help people. He loved John F. Kennedy and especially the idea of the Peace Corps. He loved the idea so much that both he and my mom worked for the Peace Corps training volunteers to go to Malaysia, Thailand and the Philippines. He always strived for additional grants and increases in his budget so he could hire more people, both in his job with the Education Department and in the Peace Corps. That was his job.

From the time I was about 10 years old, I would hear from my rich dad that government workers were a pack of lazy thieves, and from my poor dad I would hear how the rich were greedy crooks who should be made to pay more taxes. Both sides have valid points. It was difficult to go to work for one of the biggest capitalists in town and come home to a father who was a prominent government leader. It was not easy knowing who to believe.

Yet, when you study the history of taxes, an interesting perspective emerges. As I said, the passage of taxes was only possible because the masses believed in the Robin Hood theory of economics, which was to take from the rich and give to everyone else. The problem was that the government's appetite for money was so great that taxes soon needed to be levied on the middle class, and from there it kept "trickling down."

The rich, on the other hand, saw an opportunity. They do not play by the same set of rules. As I've stated, the rich already knew about corporations, which became popular in the days of sailing ships. The rich created the corporation as a vehicle to limit their risk to the assets of each voyage. The rich put their money into a corporation to finance the voyage. The corporation would then hire a crew to sail to the New World to look for treasures. If the ship was lost, the crew lost their lives, but the loss to the rich would be limited only to the money they invested for that particular voyage. The diagram that follows shows how the corporate structure sits outside your personal income statement and balance sheet.

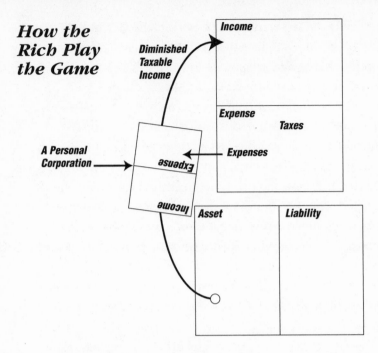

How the Rich Play the Game

Diminished Taxable Income

Income

Expense

Taxes

A Personal Corporation

Expense

Expenses

Income

Asset

Liability

It is the knowledge of the power of the legal structure of the corporation that really gives the rich a vast advantage over the poor and the middle class. Having two fathers teaching me, one a socialist and the other a capitalist, I quickly began to realize that the philosophy of the capitalist made more financial sense to me. It seemed to me that the socialists ultimately penalized themselves, due to their lack of financial education. No matter what the "Take from the rich" crowd came up with, the rich always found a way to outsmart them. That is how taxes were eventually levied on the middle class. The rich outsmarted the intellectuals, solely because they understood the power of money, a subject not taught in schools.

How did the rich outsmart the intellectuals? Once the "Take from the rich" tax was passed, cash started flowing into government coffers. Initially, people were happy. Money was handed out to government workers and the rich. It went to government workers in the form of jobs and pensions. It went to the rich via their factories receiving government contracts. The government became a large pool of money, but the problem was the fiscal management of that money. There really is no recirculation. In other words, the government policy, if you were a government bureaucrat, was to avoid having excess money. If you failed to spend your allotted funding, you risked losing it in the next budget.

You would certainly not be recognized for being efficient. Business people, on the other hand, are rewarded for having excess money and are recognized for their efficiency.

As this cycle of growing government spending continued, the demand for money increased and the "Tax the rich" idea was now being adjusted to include lower-income levels, down to the very people who voted it in, the poor and the middle class.

True capitalists used their financial knowledge to simply find a way to escape. They headed back to the protection of a corporation. A corporation protects the rich. But what many people who have never formed a corporation do not know is that a corporation is not really a thing. A corporation is merely a file folder with some legal documents in it, sitting in some attorney's office registered with a state government agency. It's not a big building with the name of the corporation on it. It's not a factory or a group of people. A corporation is merely a legal document that creates a legal body without a soul. The wealth of the rich was once again protected. Once again, the use of corporations became popular—once the permanent income laws were passed— because the income-tax rate of the corporation was less than the individual income-tax rates. In addition, as described earlier, certain expenses could be paid with pre-tax dollars within the corporation.

This war between the haves and have-nots has been going on for hundreds of years. It is the "Take from the rich" crowd versus the rich. The battle is waged whenever and wherever laws are made. The battle will go on forever. The problem is, the people who lose are the uninformed. The ones who get up every day and diligently go to work and pay taxes. If they only understood the way the rich play the game, they could play it too. Then, they would be on their way to their own financial independence. This is why I cringe every time I hear a parent advise their children to go to school, so they can find a safe, secure job. An employee with a safe, secure job, without financial aptitude, has no escape.

Average Americans today work five to six months for the government before they make enough to cover their taxes. In my opinion, that is a long time. The harder you work, the more you pay the government. That is why I believe that the idea of "Take from the rich" backfired on the very people who voted it in.

Every time people try to punish the rich, the rich don't simply comply, they react. They have the money, power and intent to change things. They do not just sit there and voluntarily pay more taxes. They search for ways to minimize their tax burden. They hire smart attorneys and accountants, and persuade politicians to change laws or create legal loopholes. They have the resources to effect change.

The Tax Code of the United States also allows other ways to save on taxes. Most of these vehicles are available to anyone, but it is the rich who usually look for them because they are minding their own business. For example, "1031" is jargon for Section 1031 of the Internal Revenue Code, which allows a seller to delay paying taxes on a piece of real estate that is sold for a capital gain through an exchange for a more expensive piece of real estate. Real estate is one investment vehicle that allows such a great tax advantage. As long as you keep trading up in value, you will not be taxed on the gains, until you liquidate. People who do not take advantage of these tax savings offered legally are missing a great opportunity to build their asset columns.

The poor and middle class do not have the same resources. They sit there and let the government's needles enter their arm and allow the blood donation to begin. Today, I am constantly shocked at the number of people who pay more taxes, or take fewer deductions, simply because they are afraid of the government. And I do know how frightening and intimidating a government tax agent can be. I have had friends who have had their businesses shut down and destroyed, only to find out it was a mistake on the part of the government. I realize all that. But the price of working from January to mid-May is a high price to pay for that intimidation. My poor dad never fought back. My rich dad didn't either. He just played the game smarter, and he did it through corporations—the biggest secret of the rich.

You may remember the first lesson I learned from my rich dad. I was a little boy of 9 who had to sit and wait for him to choose to talk to me. I often sat in his office waiting for him to "get to me." He was ignoring me on purpose. He wanted me to recognize his power and desire to have that power for myself one day. For all the years I studied and learned from him, he always reminded me that knowledge was power. And with money comes great power that requires the right knowledge to keep it and make it multiply. Without that knowledge, the world pushes you around. Rich dad constantly reminded Mike and me that the biggest bully was not the boss or the supervisor, but the tax man. The tax man will always take more if you let him.

The first lesson of having money work for me, as opposed to working for money, is really all about power. If you work for money, you give the power up to your employer. If your money works for you, you keep and control the power.

Once we had this knowledge of the power of money working for us, he wanted us to be financially smart and not let bullies push us around. You need to know the law and how the system works. If you're ignorant, it is easy to be bullied. If you know what you're talking about, you have a fighting chance. That is why he paid so much for smart tax accountants and attorneys. It was less expensive to pay them than pay the government. His best lesson to me, which I have used most of my life, is "Be smart and you won't be pushed around as much." He knew the law because he was a law-abiding citizen. He knew the law because it was expensive to not know the law. "If you know you're right, you're not afraid of fighting back." Even if you are taking on Robin Hood and his band of Merry Men.

My highly educated dad always encouraged me to seek a good job with a strong corporation. He spoke of the virtues of "working your way up the corporate ladder." He didn't understand that, by relying solely on a paycheck from a corporate employer, I would be a docile cow ready for milking.

When I told my rich dad of my father's advice, he only chuckled. "Why not own the ladder?" was all he said.

As a young boy, I did not understand what rich dad meant by owning my own corporation. It was an idea that seemed impossible, and intimidating. Although I was excited by the idea, my youth would not let me envision the possibility that grownups would someday work for a company I would own.

The point is, if not for my rich dad, I would have probably followed my educated dad's advice. It was merely the occasional reminder of my rich dad that kept the idea of owning my own corporation alive and kept me on a different path. By the time I was 15 or 16, I knew I was not going to continue down the path my educated dad was recommending. I did not know how I was going to do it, but I was determined not to head in the direction most of my classmates were heading. That decision changed my life.

It was not until I was in my mid-20s that my rich dad's advice began to make more sense. I was just out of the Marine Corps and working for Xerox. I was making a lot of money, but every time I looked at my paycheck, I was always disappointed. The deductions were so large, and the more I worked, the greater the deductions. As I became more successful, my bosses talked about promotions and raises. It was flattering, but I could hear my rich dad asking me in my ear: "Who are you working for? Who are you making rich?"

In 1974, while still an employee for Xerox, I formed my first corporation and began "minding my own business." There were already a few assets in my asset column, but now I was determined to focus on making it bigger. Those paychecks with all the deductions made all the years of my rich dad's advice make total sense. I could see the future if I followed my educated dad's advice.

Many employers feel that advising their workers to mind their own business is bad for business. I am sure it can be for certain individuals. But for me, focusing on my own business, developing assets, made me a better employee. I now had a purpose. I came in early and worked diligently, amassing as much money as possible so I could begin investing in real estate. Hawaii was just set to boom, and there were fortunes to be made. The more I realized we were in the beginning stages of a boom, the more Xerox machines I sold. The more I sold, the more money I made, and, of course, the more deductions there were from my paycheck. It was inspiring. I wanted out of the trap of being an employee so badly that I worked harder, not less. By 1978, I was consistently one of the top five salespeople in sales, often No. 1. I badly wanted out of the rat race.

In less than three years, I was making more in my own little corporation, which was a real estate holding company, than I was making at Xerox. And the money I was making in my asset column, in my own corporation, was money working for me. Not me pounding on doors selling copiers. My rich dad's advice made much more sense. Soon the cash flow from my properties was so strong that my company bought me my first Porsche. My fellow Xerox salespeople thought I was spending my commissions. I wasn't. I was investing my commissions in assets.

My money was working hard to make more money. Each dollar in my asset column was a great employee, working hard to make more employees and buy the boss a new Porsche with before-tax dollars. I began to work harder for Xerox. The plan was working, and my Porsche was the proof.

By using the lessons I learned from my rich dad, I was able to get out of the "proverbial rat race" of being an employee at an early age. It was made possible because of the strong financial knowledge I had acquired through these lessons. Without this financial knowledge, which I call financial IQ, my road to financial independence would have been much more difficult. I now teach others through financial seminars in the hope that I may share my knowledge with them. Whenever I do my talks, I remind people that financial IQ is made up of knowledge from four broad areas of expertise.

No. 1 is accounting. What I call financial literacy. A vital skill if you want to build an empire. The more money you are responsible for, the more accuracy is required, or the house comes tumbling down. This is the left brain side, or the details. Financial literacy is the ability to read and understand financial statements. This ability allows you to identify the strengths and weaknesses of any business.

No. 2 is investing. What I call the science of money making money. This involves strategies and formulas. This is the right brain side, or the creative side.

No. 3 is understanding markets. The science of supply and demand. There is a need to know the "technical" aspects of the market, which is emotion driven; the Tickle Me Elmo doll during Christmas 1996 is a case of a technical or emotion-driven market. The other market factor is the "fundamental" or the economic sense of an investment. Does an investment make sense or does it not make sense based on the current market conditions.

Many people think the concepts of investing and understanding the market are too complex for kids. They fail to see that kids know those subjects intuitively. For those not familiar with the Elmo doll, it was a Sesame Street character that was highly touted to the kids just before Christmas. Most all kids wanted one, and put it at the top of their Christmas list. Many parents wondered if the company intentionally held the product off the market, while continuing to advertise it for Christmas. A panic set in due to high demand and lack of supply. Having no dolls to buy in the stores, scalpers saw an opportunity to make a small fortune from desperate parents. The unlucky parents who did not find a doll were forced to buy another toy for Christmas. The incredible popularity of the Tickle Me Elmo doll made no sense to me, but it serves as an excellent example of supply and demand economics. The same thing goes on in the stock, bond, real estate and baseball-card markets.

No. 4 is the law. For instance, utilizing a corporation wrapped around the technical skills of accounting, investing and markets can aid explosive growth. An individual with the knowledge of the tax advantages and protection provided by a corporation can get rich so much faster than someone who is an employee or a small-business sole proprietor. It's like the difference between someone walking and someone flying. The difference is profound when it comes to long-term wealth.

1. Tax advantages: A corporation can do so many things that an individual cannot. Like pay for expenses before it pays taxes. That is a whole area of expertise that is so exciting, but not necessary to get into unless you have sizable assets or a business.

Employees earn and get taxed and they try to live on what is left. A corporation earns, spends everything it can, and is taxed on anything that is left. It's one of the biggest legal tax loopholes that the rich use. They're easy to set up and are not expensive if you own investments that are producing good cash flow. For example; by owning your own corporation — vacations are board meetings in Hawaii. Car payments, insurance, repairs are company expenses. Health club membership is a company expense. Most restaurant meals are partial expenses. And on and on — but do it legally with pre-tax dollars.

2. Protection from lawsuits. We live in a litigious society. Everybody wants a piece of your action. The rich hide much of their wealth using vehicles such as corporations and trusts to protect their assets from creditors. When someone sues a wealthy individual they are often met with layers of legal protection, and often find that the wealthy person actually owns nothing. They control everything, but own nothing. The poor and middle class try to own everything and lose it to the government or to fellow citizens who like to sue the rich. They learned it from the Robin Hood story. Take from the rich, give to the poor.

It is not the purpose of this book to go into the specifics of owning a corporation. But I will say that if you own any kind of legitimate assets, I would consider finding out more about the benefits and protection offered by a corporation as soon as possible. There are many books written on the subject that will detail the benefits and even walk you through the steps necessary to set up a corporation. One book in particular, *Inc. and Grow Rich* provides a wonderful insight into the power of personal corporations.

Financial IQ is actually the synergy of many skills and talents. But I would say it is the combination of the four technical skills listed above that make up basic financial intelligence. If you aspire to great wealth, it is the combination of these skills that will greatly amplify an individual's financial intelligence.

In summary

The Rich with Corporations	People Who Work for Corporations
1. Earn	1. Earn
2. Spend	2. Pay Taxes
3. Pay Taxes	3. Spend

As part of your overall financial strategy, we strongly recommend owning your own corporation wrapped around your assets.

THE RICH
INVENT MONEY

The Rich Invent Money

*L*ast night, I took a break from writing and watched a TV program on the history of a young man named Alexander Graham Bell. Bell had just patented his telephone, and was having growing pains because the demand for his new invention was so strong. Needing a bigger company, he then went to the giant at that time, Western Union, and asked them if they would buy his patent and his tiny company. He wanted $100,000 for the whole package. The president of Western Union scoffed at him and turned him down, saying the price was ridiculous. The rest is history. A multi-billion-dollar industry emerged, and AT&T was born.

The evening news came on right after the story of Alexander Graham Bell ended. On the news was a story of another downsizing at a local company. The workers were angry and complained that the company ownership was unfair. A terminated manager of about 45 years of age had his wife and two babies at the plant and was begging the guards to let him talk to the owners to ask if they would reconsider his termination. He had just bought a house and was afraid of losing it. The camera focused in on his pleading for all the world to see. Needless to say, it held my attention.

I have been teaching professionally since 1984. It has been a great experience and rewarding. It is also a disturbing profession, for I have taught thousands of individuals and I see one thing in common in all of us, myself included. We all have tremendous potential, and we all are blessed with gifts. Yet, the one thing that holds all of us back is some degree of self-doubt. It is not so much the lack of technical information that holds us back, but more the lack of self-confidence. Some are more affected than others.

Once we leave school, most of us know that it is not as much a matter of college degrees or good grades that count. In the real world outside of academics, something more than just grades is required. I have heard it called "guts," "chutzpah," "balls," "audacity," "bravado," "cunning," "daring," "tenacity" and "brilliance." This factor, whatever it is labeled, ultimately decides one's future much more than school grades.

Inside each of us is one of these brave, brilliant and daring characters. There is also the flip side of that character: people who could get down on their knees and beg if necessary. After a year in Vietnam, as a Marine Corps pilot, I intimately got to know both of those characters inside of me. One is not better than the other.

Yet, as a teacher, I recognized that it was excessive fear and self-doubt that were the greatest detractors of personal genius. It broke my heart to see students know the answers, yet lack the courage to act on the answer. Often in the real world, it's not the smart that get ahead but the bold.

In my personal experience, your financial genius requires both technical knowledge as well as courage. If fear is too strong, the genius is suppressed. In my classes I strongly urge students to learn to take risks, to be bold, to let their genius convert that fear into power and brilliance. It works for some and just terrifies others. I have come to realize that for most people, when it comes to the subject of money, they would rather play it safe. I have had to field questions such as: Why take risks? Why should I bother developing my financial IQ? Why should I become financially literate?

And I answer, "Just to have more options."

There are huge changes up head. Just as I started with the story of the young inventor Alexander Graham Bell, in the coming years there will be more people just like him. There will be a hundred people like Bill Gates and hugely successful companies like Microsoft created every year, all over the world. And there also will be many more bankruptcies, layoffs and downsizing.

So why bother developing your financial IQ? No one can answer that but you. Yet, I can tell you why I myself do it. I do it because it is the most exciting time to be alive. I'd rather be welcoming change than dreading change. I'd rather be excited about making millions than worrying about not getting a raise. This period we are in now is a most exciting time, unprecedented in our world's history. Generations from now, people will look back at this period of time and remark at what an exciting era it must have been. It was the death of the old and birth of the new. It was full of turmoil and it was exciting.

So why bother developing your financial IQ? Because if you do, you will prosper greatly. And if you don't, this period of time will be a frightening one. It will be a time of watching people move boldly forward while others cling to decaying life rings.

Land was wealth 300 years ago. So the person who owned the land owned the wealth. Then, it was factories and production, and America rose to dominance. The industrialist owned the wealth. Today, it is information. And the person who has the most timely information owns the wealth. The problem is, information flies all around the world at the speed of light. The new wealth cannot be contained by boundaries and borders as land and factories were. The changes will be faster and more dramatic. There will be a dramatic increase in the number of new multimillionaires. There also will be those who are left behind.

Today, I find so many people struggling, often working harder, simply because they cling to old ideas. They want things to be the way they were; they resist change. I know people who are losing their jobs or their houses, and they blame technology or the economy or their boss. Sadly they fail to realize that they might be the problem. Old ideas are their biggest liability. It is a liability simply because they fail to realize that while that idea or way of doing something was an asset yesterday, yesterday is gone.

One afternoon I was teaching investing using a board game I had invented, *CASHFLOW*, as a teaching tool. A friend had brought someone along to attend the class. This friend of a friend was recently divorced, had been badly burned in the divorce settlement, and was now searching for some answers. Her friend thought the class might help.

The game was designed to help people learn how money works. In playing the game, they learn about the interaction of the income statement with the balance sheet. They learn how "cash flows" between the two and how the road to wealth is through striving to increase your monthly cash flow from the asset column to the point that it exceeds your monthly expenses. Once you accomplish this, you are able to get out of the "Rat Race" and out onto the "Fast Track".

As I have said, some people hate the game, some love it, and others miss the point. This woman missed a valuable opportunity to learn something. In the opening round, she drew a "doodad" card with the boat on it. At first she was happy. "Oh, I've got a boat." Then, as her friend tried to explain how the numbers worked on her income statement and balance sheet, she got frustrated because she had never liked math. The rest of her table waited while her friend continued explaining the relationship between the income statement, balance sheet and monthly cash flow. Suddenly, when she realized how the numbers worked, it dawned on her that her boat was eating her alive. Later on in the game, she was also "downsized" and had a child. It was a horrible game for her.

After the class, her friend came by and told me that she was upset. She had come to the class to learn about investing and did not like the idea that it took so long to play a silly game.

Her friend attempted to tell her to look within herself to see if the game "reflected" on herself in any way. With that suggestion, the woman demanded her money back. She said that the very idea that a game could be a reflection of her was ridiculous. Her money was promptly refunded and she left.

Since 1984, I have made millions simply by doing what the school system does not. In school, most teachers lecture. I hated lectures as a student; I was soon bored and my mind would drift.

In 1984, I began teaching via games and simulations. I always encouraged adult students to look at games as reflecting back to what they know, and what they needed to learn. Most importantly, a game reflects back on one's behavior. It's an instant feedback system. Instead of the teacher lecturing you, the game is feeding back a personalized lecture, custom made just for you.

The friend of the woman who left later called to give me an update. She said her friend was fine and had calmed down. In her cooling-off period, she could see some slight relationship between the game and her life.

Although she and her husband did not own a boat, they did own

112

everything else imaginable. She was angry after their divorce, both because he had run off with a younger woman and because after twenty years of marriage, they had accumulated little in the way of assets. There was virtually nothing for them to split. Their twenty years of married life had been incredible fun, but all they had accumulated was a ton of doodads.

She realized that her anger at doing the numbers—the income statement and balance sheet—came from her embarrassment of not understanding them. She had believed that finances were the man's job. She maintained the house and did the entertaining, and he handled the finances. She was now quite certain that in the last five years of their marriage, he had hidden money from her. She was angry at herself for not being more aware of where the money was going, as well as for not knowing about the other woman.

Just like a board game, the world is always providing us with instant feedback. We could learn a lot if we tuned in more. One day not long ago, I complained to my wife that the cleaners must have shrunk my pants. My wife gently smiled and poked me in the stomach to inform me that the pants had not shrunk, something else had expanded: me!

The game *CASHFLOW* was designed to give every player personal feedback. Its purpose is to give you options. If you draw the boat card and it puts you into debt, the question is, "Now what can you do?" How many different financial options can you come up with? That is the purpose of the game: to teach players to think and create new and various financial options.

I have watched this game played by more than 1,000 people. The people who get out of the "Rat Race" in the game the quickest are the people who understand numbers and have creative financial minds. They recognize different financial options. People who take the longest are people who are not familiar with numbers and often do not understand the power of investing. Rich people are often creative and take calculated risks.

There have been people playing *CASHFLOW* who gain lots of money in the game, but they don't know what to do with it. Most of them have not been financially successful in real life either. Everyone else seems to be getting ahead of them, even though they have money. And that is true in real life. There are a lot of people who have a lot of money and do not get ahead financially.

Limiting your options is the same as hanging on to old ideas. I have a friend from high school who now works at three jobs. Twenty years ago, he was the richest of all my classmates. When the local sugar plantation closed, the company he worked for went down with the plantation. In his mind, he had but one option, and that was the old option: work hard. The problem was, he couldn't find an equivalent job that recognized his seniority in the old company. As a result, he is overqualified for the jobs he currently has, so his salary is lower. He now works three jobs to earn enough to survive.

I have watched people playing *CASHFLOW* complaining that the "right" opportunity cards are not coming their way. So they sit there. I know people who do that in real life. They wait for the "right" opportunity.

I have watched people get the "right" opportunity card and then not have enough money. Then, they complain that they would have gotten out of the Rat Race if they had had more money. So they sit there. I know people in real life who do that also. They see all the great deals, but they have no money.

And I have people pull a great opportunity card, read it out loud and have no idea that it is a great opportunity. They have the money, the time is right, they have the card, but they can't see the opportunity staring at them. They fail to see how it fits into their financial plan for escaping the Rat Race. And I know more people like that than all the others combined. Most people have an opportunity of a lifetime flash right in front of them, and they fail to see it. A year later, they find out about it, after everyone else got rich.

Financial intelligence is simply having more options. If the opportunities aren't coming your way, what else can you do to improve your financial position? If an opportunity lands in your lap, and you have no money, and the bank won't talk to you, what else can you do to get the opportunity to work in your favor? If your hunch is wrong, and what you've been counting on doesn't happen, how can you turn a lemon into millions. That is financial intelligence. It is not so much what happens, but how many different financial solutions you can think of to turn a lemon into millions. It is how creative you are in solving financial problems.

Most people only know one solution: work hard, save and borrow.

So why would you want to increase your financial intelligence?

Because you want to be the kind of person who creates your own luck. You take whatever happens and make it better. Few people realize that luck is created. Just as money is. And if you want to be luckier and create money instead of working hard, then your financial intelligence is important. If you are the kind of person who is waiting for the "right" thing to happen, you might wait for a long time. It's like waiting for all the traffic lights to be green for five miles before starting the trip.

As young boys, Mike and I were constantly told by my rich dad that "Money is not real." Rich dad occasionally reminded us of how close we came to the secret of money on that first day we got together and began "making money" out of plaster of paris. "The poor and middle class work for money," he would say. "The rich make money. The more real you think money is, the harder you will work for it. If you can grasp the idea that money is not real, you will grow richer faster."

"What is it?" was a question Mike and I often came back with. "What is money if it is not real?"

"What we agree it is," was all rich dad would say.

The single most powerful asset we all have is our mind. If it is trained well, it can create enormous wealth in what seems to be an instant. Wealth so far beyond the dreams of kings and queens 300 years ago. An untrained mind can also create extreme poverty that lasts lifetimes by teaching it to their families.

In the Information Age, money is increasing exponentially. A few individuals are getting ridiculously rich from nothing, just ideas and agreements. If you ask many people who trade stocks or other investments for a living, they see it done all the time. Often, millions can be made instantaneously from nothing. And by nothing, I mean no money was exchanged. It is done via agreement: a hand signal in a trading pit; a blip on a trader's screen in Lisbon from a trader's screen in Toronto, and back to Lisbon; a call to my broker to buy and a moment later to sell. Money did not change hands. Agreements did.

So why develop your financial genius? Only you can answer that. I can tell you why I have been developing this area of my intelligence. I do it because I want to make money fast. Not because I need to, but because I want to. It is a fascinating learning process. I develop my financial IQ because I want to participate in the fastest game and biggest game in the world. And in my own small way, I would like to be part of this unprecedented evolution of humanity, the era where humans work purely with their minds and not with their bodies. Besides, it is where the action is. It is what is happening. It's hip. It's scary. And it's fun.

That is why I invest in my financial intelligence, developing the most powerful asset I have. I want to be with people moving boldly forward. I do not want to be with those left behind.

I will give you a simple example of creating money. In the early 1990s the economy of Phoenix was horrible. I was watching the TV show "Good Morning America" when a financial planner came on and began forecasting doom and gloom. His advice was to "save money." Put $100 away every month, he said, and in 40 years you will be a multimillionaire."

Well, putting money away every month is a sound idea. It is one option—the option most people subscribe to. The problem is this: It blinds the person from what is really going on. They miss major opportunities for much more significant growth of their money. The world is passing them by.

As I said, the economy was terrible at that time. For investors, this is the perfect market condition. A chunk of my money was in the stock market and in apartment houses. I was short of cash. Because everyone was giving stuff away, I was buying. I was not saving money; I was investing. My wife and I had more than a million dollars in cash working in a market that was rising fast. It was the best opportunity to invest. The economy was terrible. I just could not pass up these small deals.

Houses that were once $100,000 were now $75,000. But instead of shopping at the local real estate office, I began shopping at the bankruptcy attorney's office, or the courthouse steps. In these shopping places, a $75,000 house could sometimes be bought for $20,000 or less. For $2,000, which was loaned to me from a friend for 90 days for $200, I gave an attorney a cashier's check as a down payment. While the acquisition was being processed, I ran an ad in the paper advertising a $75,000 house for only $60,000 and no money down. The phone rang hard and heavy. Prospective buyers were screened and once the property was legally mine, all the perspective buyers were allowed to look at the house. It was a feeding frenzy. The house sold in a few minutes. I asked for a $2,500 processing fee, which they gladly handed over, and the escrow and title company took over from there. I returned the $2,000 to my friend with an additional $200. He was happy, the home buyer was happy, the attorney was happy, and I was happy. I had sold a house for $60,000 that cost me $20,000. The $40,000 was created from money in my asset column in the form of a promissory note from the buyer. Total working time: five hours.

So now that you are financially literate and read numbers, I will show you why this is an example of money being invented.

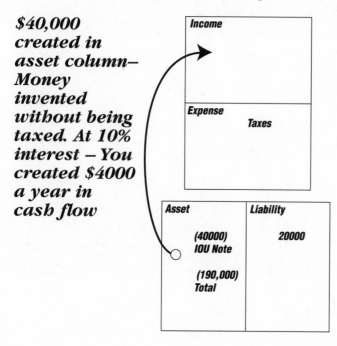

$40,000 created in asset column— Money invented without being taxed. At 10% interest – You created $4000 a year in cash flow

During this depressed market, my wife and I were able to do six of these simple transactions in our spare time. While the bulk of our money was in larger properties and the stock market, we were able to create more than $190,000 in assets (notes at 10 percent interest) in those six buy, create and sell transactions. That comes to approximately $19,000 a year income, much of it sheltered through our private corporation. Much of that $19,000 a year goes to pay for our company cars, gas, trips, insurance, dinners with clients and other things. By the time the government gets a chance to tax that income, it's been spent on legally allowed pre-tax expenses.

Savings–

How long would it take to save $40,000 and how much would it cost at 50% in taxes

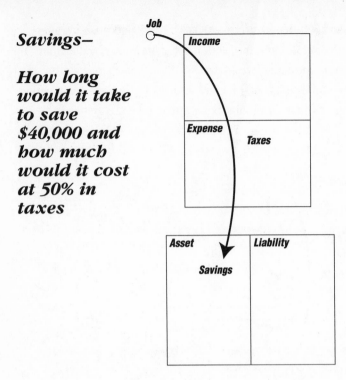

This was a simple example of how money is invented, created and protected using financial intelligence.

Ask yourself how long it would take to save $190,000. Would the bank pay you 10 percent interest on your money? And the note is good for 30 years. I hope they never pay me the $190,000. I have to pay a tax if they pay me the principle, and besides, $19,000 paid over 30 years is a little over $500,000 in income.

I have people ask what happens if the person doesn't pay. That does happen, and it's good news. The Phoenix real estate market, from 1994 to 1997, has been one of the hottest in the nation. That $60,000 home would be taken back and re-sold for $70,000, and another $2,500 is collected as a loan-processing fee. It would still be a zero-down transaction in the mind of the new buyer. And the process would go on.

So if you're quick, the first time I sold the house, I paid back the $2,000. Technically I have no money in the transaction. My return on investment (ROI) is infinity. It's an example of no money making a lot of money.

In the second transaction, when re-sold, I would have put $2,000 in my pocket and re-extended the loan to 30 years. What would my ROI be if I got paid money to make money? I do not know, but it sure beats saving $100 a month, which actually starts out as $150 because it's after-tax income for 40 years at 5 percent, and again you're taxed on the 5 percent. That is not too intelligent. It may be safe, but it's not smart.

Today, in 1997 as I write this book, the market conditions are exactly the opposite of five years ago. The real estate market of Phoenix is the envy of the U.S. Those houses we sold for $60,000 are now worth $110,000. There are foreclosure opportunities still available, but it will cost a valuable asset, my time, to go out looking for them. They are rare. But today, there are thousands of buyers looking for those deals, and only a few available that make financial sense. The market has changed. It is time to move on and look for other opportunities to put in the asset column.

"You can't do that here." "That is against the law." "You're lying."

I hear those comments much more often than "Can you show me how to do that?"

The math is simple. You do not need algebra or calculus. I don't write much because the escrow company handles the legal transaction and the servicing of the payments. I have no roofs to fix or toilets to unplug because the owners do that. It's their house. Occasionally someone does not pay. And that is wonderful because there are late fees, or they move out and the property is sold again. The court system handles that.

And it may not work in your area. The market conditions may be different. But the example illustrates how a simple financial process can create hundreds of thousands of dollars, with little money and low risk. It is an example of money being only an agreement. Anyone with a high school education can do it.

Yet, most people won't. Most people listen to the standard advice of "Work hard and save money."

For about 30 hours of work, approximately $190,000 was created in the asset column, and no taxes were paid.

Which one sounds harder to you?

1. Work hard, pay 50 percent in taxes, save what is left. Your savings then earns 5 percent, which is also taxed.
Or:
2. Take the time to develop your financial intelligence and harness the power of your brain and the asset column.

119

Add to that how much time it takes you, time being one of your greatest assets, to save $190,000 if you used option No. 1?

Now you may understand why I silently shake my head when I hear parents say, "My child is doing well in school and receiving a good education." It may be good, but is it adequate?

I know the above investment strategy is a small one. It is used to illustrate how small can grow into big. Again, my success reflects the importance of a strong financial foundation, which starts with strong financial education. I have said it before, yet it is worth repeating— financial intelligence is made up of these four main technical skills:

1. Financial literacy. The ability to read numbers.
2. Investment strategies. The science of money making money.
3. The market. Supply and demand. Alexander Graham Bell gave the market what it wanted. So did Bill Gates. A $75,000 house offered for $60,000 that cost $20,000 was also the result of seizing an opportunity created by the market. Somebody was buying, and someone was selling.
4. The law. The awareness of accounting, corporate, state and national rules and regulations. I recommend playing within the rules.

It is this basic foundation, or the combination of these skills, that is needed to be successful in the pursuit of wealth, whether it be through the buying of small homes, large apartments, companies, stocks, bonds, mutual funds, precious metals, baseball cards or the like.

By 1996, the real estate market had rebounded and everyone else was getting in. The stock market was booming, and everyone was getting in. The U.S. economy was getting back on its feet. I began selling in 1996 and was now traveling to Peru, Norway, Malaysia and the Philippines. The investments had changed. We were out of the real estate market, as far as buying goes. Now I just watch the values climb inside the asset column and will probably begin selling later this year. It depends on some law changes that may be passed in Congress. I suspect that some of those six little house deals will begin selling and the $40,000 note will be converted to cash. I need to call my accountant to be prepared for cash and seek ways to shelter it.

The point I would like to make is that investments come and go, the market goes up and goes down, economies improve and crash. The world is always handing you opportunities of a lifetime, every day of your life, but all too often we fail to see them. But they are there. And the more the world changes and the more technology changes, the more opportunities there will be to allow you and your family to be financially secure for generations to come.

So why bother developing your financial intelligence? Again, only you can answer that. I know why I continue to learn and develop. I do it because I know there are changes coming. I'd rather welcome change than cling to the past. I know there will be market booms and market crashes. I want to continually develop my financial intelligence because at each market change, some people will be on their knees begging for their jobs. Others, meanwhile, will take the lemons that life hands them—and we are all handed lemons occasionally—and turn them into millions. That's financial intelligence.

I am often asked about the lemons I have turned into millions. As a personal note, I hesitate using many more examples of personal investments. I hesitate because I am afraid it will come across as bragging or tooting my own horn. That is not my intention. I use the examples only as numerical and chronological illustrations of actual and simple cases. I use the examples because I want you to know that it is easy. It is easier, the more familiar you are with the four pillars of financial intelligence.

Personally, I use two main vehicles to achieve financial growth: real estate and small stocks. I use real estate as my foundation. Day in and day out, my properties provide cash flow and occasional spurts of growth in value. The small-cap stocks are used for fast growth.

I do not recommend anything that I do. The examples are just that, examples. If the opportunity is too complex and I do not understand the investment, I don't do it. Simple math and common sense is all that is needed to do well financially.

There are five reasons for using the examples.

1. To inspire people to learn more.
2. To let people know it is easy if the foundation is strong.
3. To show that anyone can achieve great wealth.
4. To show that there are millions of ways to achieve your goals.
5. To show that it's not rocket science.

In 1989, I used to jog through a lovely neighborhood in Portland, Oregon. It was a suburb that had little gingerbread houses. They were small and cute. I almost expected to see Little Red Riding Hood skipping down the sidewalk on her way to Granny's.

There were "for sale" signs everywhere. The timber market was terrible, the stock market had just crashed, and the economy was depressed. On one street, I noticed a for-sale sign that was up longer than most. It looked old. Jogging past it one day, I ran into the owner, who looked troubled.

"What are you asking for your house?" I asked.

The owner turned and smiled weakly. "Make me an offer," he said. "It's been for sale for over a year. Nobody even comes by anymore to look at it."

"I'll look," I said, and I bought the house a half hour later for $20,000 less than his asking price.

It was a cute little two-bedroom home, with gingerbread trim on all the windows. It was light blue with gray accents and had been built in 1930. Inside there was a beautiful rock fireplace, as well as two tiny bedrooms. It was a perfect rental house.

I gave the owner $5,000 down for a $45,000 house that was really worth $65,000, except that no one wanted to buy it. The owner moved out in a week, happy to be free, and my first tenant moved in, a local college professor. After the mortgage, expenses and management fees were paid, I put a little less than $40 in my pocket at the end of each month. Hardly exciting.

A year later, the depressed Oregon real estate market had begun to pick up. California investors, flush with money from their still-booming real estate market, were moving north and buying up Oregon and Washington.

I sold that little house for $95,000 to a young couple from California who thought it was a bargain. My capital gains of approximately $40,000 was placed into a 1031 tax-deferred exchange, and I went shopping for a place to put my money. In about a month, I found a 12-unit apartment house right next to the Intel plant in Beaverton, Oregon. The owners lived in Germany, had no idea what the place was worth, and again, just wanted to get out of it. I offered $275,000 for a $450,000 building. They agreed to $300,000. I bought it and held it for 2 years. Utilizing the same 1031 exchange process, we sold the building for $495,000 and bought a 30-unit apartment building in Phoenix, Arizona. We had moved to Phoenix by then to get out of the rain, and needed to sell anyway. Like the former Oregon market, the real estate market in Phoenix was depressed. The price of the 30-unit apartment building in Phoenix was $875,000, with $225,000 down. The cash flow from the 30 units was a little over $5,000 a month. The Arizona market began moving up and, in 1996, a Colorado investor offered us $1.2 million for the property.

My wife and I considered selling, but we decided to wait to see if the capital-gains law will be changed by Congress. If it does change, we suspect the property will go up another 15 to 20 percent. Besides, the $5,000 a month provides a nice cash flow.

The point of this example is how a small amount can grow into a large amount. Again, it is a matter of understanding financial statements, investment strategies, a sense of the market and the laws. If people are not versed in these subjects, then obviously they must follow standard dogma, which is to play it safe, diversify and only invest in secure investments. The problem with "secure" investments is that they are often sanitized. That is, made so safe that the gains are less.

Most large brokerage houses will not touch speculative transactions to protect themselves and their clients. And that is a wise policy.

The really hot deals are not offered to people who are novices. Often, the best deals that make the rich even richer are reserved for those who understand the game. It is technically illegal to offer someone who is considered not "sophisticated" such speculative deals, but, of course, it happens.

The more so-called "sophisticated" I get, the more opportunities come my way. Another case for developing your financial intelligence, over a lifetime, is simply that more opportunities are presented to you. And the greater your financial intelligence, the easier it is to tell whether a deal is good. It's your intelligence that can spot a bad deal, or make a bad deal good. The more I learn—and there is a lot to learn—the more money I make simply because I gain experience and wisdom as the years go on. I have friends who are playing it safe, working hard at their profession, and failing to gain financial wisdom, which does take time to develop.

My overall philosophy is to plant seeds inside my asset column. That is my formula. I start small and plant seeds. Some grow; some don't.

Inside our real estate corporation, we have several million dollars' worth of property. It is our own REIT, or real estate investment trust.

The point I'm making is that most of those millions started out as little $5,000 to $10,000 investments. All of those down payments were fortunate to catch a fast-rising market, increase tax free, trading in and out several times over a number of years.

We also own a stock portfolio, surrounded by a corporation that my wife and I call our personal mutual fund. We have friends who deal specifically with investors like us that have extra money each month to invest. We buy high-risk, speculative private companies that are just about to go public on a stock exchange in the United States or Canada. An example of how fast gains can be made are 100,000 shares purchased for 25 cents each before the company goes public. Six months later, the company is listed, and the 100,000 shares now are worth $2 each. If the company is well-managed, the price keeps going up, and the stock may go to $20 or more per share. There are years when our $25,000 has gone to a million in less than a year.

It is not gambling if you know what you're doing. It is gambling if you're just throwing money into a deal and praying. The idea in anything is to use your technical knowledge, wisdom and love of the game to cut the odds down, to lower the risk. Of course, there is always risk. It is financial intelligence that improves the odds. Thus, what is risky for one person is less risky to someone else. That is the primary reason I constantly encourage people to invest more in their financial education than in the stock, real estate or other markets. The smarter you are, the better chance you have of beating the odds.

The stock plays I personally invest in are extremely high risk for most people and absolutely not recommended. I have been playing that game since 1979 and have paid more than my share in dues. But if you will reread why investments such as these are high risk for most people, you may be able to set your life up differently, so that the ability to take $25,000 and turn it into $1 million in a year is low risk for you.

As stated earlier, nothing I have written is a recommendation. It is only used as an example of what is simple and possible. What I do is small potatoes in the scheme of things, yet for the average individual, a passive income of more than $100,000 a year is nice and not hard to achieve. Depending on the market and how smart you are, it could be done in five to ten years. If you keep your living expenses modest, $100,000 coming in as additional income is pleasant, regardless of whether you work. You can work if you like or take time off if you choose and use the government tax system in your favor, rather than against you.

My personal basis is real estate. I love real estate because it's stable and slow moving. I keep the base solid. The cash flow is fairly steady and, if properly managed, has a good chance of increasing in value. The beauty of a solid base of real estate is that it allows me to be somewhat riskier with the more speculative stocks I buy.

If I make great profits in the stock market, I pay my capital-gains tax on the gain and then reinvest what's left in real estate, again further securing my asset foundation.

A last word on real estate. I have traveled all over the world and taught investing. In every city, I hear people say you cannot buy real estate cheap. That is not my experience. Even in New York or Tokyo, or just on the outskirts of the city, are prime bargains overlooked by most people. In Singapore, currently undergoing high real estate prices, there are still bargains to be found within a short driving distance. So whenever I hear someone say, "You can't do that here," pointing at me, I remind them that maybe the real statement is, "I don't know how to do that here. . .yet."

Great opportunities are not seen with your eyes. They are seen with your mind. Most people never get wealthy simply because they are not trained financially to recognize opportunities right in front of them.

I am often asked, "How do I start?"

In the last chapter, I offer ten steps that I followed on the road to my financial freedom. But always remember to have fun. This is only a game. Sometimes you win and sometimes you learn. But have fun. Most people never win because they're more afraid of losing. That is why I found school so silly. In school we learn that mistakes are bad, and we are punished for making them. Yet, if you look at the way humans are designed to learn, we learn by making mistakes. We learn to walk by falling down. If we never fell down, we would never walk. The same is true for learning to ride a bike. I still have scars on my knees, but today I can ride a bike without thinking. The same is true for getting rich. Unfortunately the main reason most people are not rich is because they are terrified of losing. Winners are not afraid of losing. But losers are. Failure is part of the process of success. People who avoid failure also avoid success.

I look at money much like my game of tennis. I play hard, make mistakes, correct, make more mistakes, correct and get better. If I lose the game, I reach across the net, shake my opponent's hand, smile and say, "See you next Saturday."

There are two kinds of investors.

1. The first and most common type are people who buy a packaged investment. They call a retail outlet, such as a real estate company or a stockbroker or a financial planner, and they buy something. It could be a mutual fund, a REIT, a stock or a bond. It is a good clean and simple way of investing. An example would be a shopper who goes to a computer store and buys a computer right off the shelf.

2. The second type are investors who create investments. This investor usually assembles a deal, much like there are people who buy components of computers and put it together. It's like customizing. I do not know the first thing about putting components of a computer together. But I do know how to put pieces of opportunities together, or know people who do.

It is this second type of investor that is most probably the professional investor. Sometimes it may take years for all the pieces to come together. And sometimes they never do come together. It was this second type of investor my rich dad encouraged me to be. It is important to learn how to put the pieces together because that is where the huge wins are, and sometimes some huge losses if the tide goes against you.

If you want to be the second type of investor, you need to develop three main skills. These skills are in addition to those required to become financially intelligent:

1. How to find an opportunity that everyone else has missed. You see with your mind what others miss with their eyes. For example, a friend bought this rundown old house. It was spooky to look at. Everyone wondered why he bought it. What he saw that we did not was that the house came with four extra empty lots. He realized that by going to the title company. After buying the house, he tore it down and sold the five lots to a builder for three times what he paid for the entire package. He made $75,000 for two months' work. It's not a lot of money, but it sure beats minimum wage, and it's not technically difficult.

2. How to raise money. The average person only goes to the bank. This second type of investor needs to know how to raise capital, and there

are many ways that don't require a bank. To get started, I learned how to buy houses without a bank. It was not so much the houses, but the learned skill of raising money that is priceless.

All too often I hear people say, "The bank won't lend me money." Or "I don't have the money to buy it." If you want to be a Type 2 investor, you need to learn how to do that which stops most people. In other words, a majority of people let their lack of money stop them from making a deal. If you can avoid that obstacle, you will be millions ahead of those who don't learn those skills. There have been many times I have bought a house, a stock or an apartment building without a penny in the bank. I once bought an apartment house for $1.2 million. I did what is called "Tying it up," with a written contract between seller and buyer. I then raised the $100,000 deposit, which bought me 90 days to raise the rest of the money. Why did I do it? Simply because I knew it was worth $2 million. I never raised the money. Instead, the person who put up the $100,000 gave me $50,000 for finding the deal, he took over my position, and I walked away. Total working time: three days. Again, it's what you know more than what you buy. Investing is not buying. It's more a case of knowing.

3. How to organize smart people. Intelligent people are those who work with or hire a person who is more intelligent than they are. When you need advice, make sure you choose your advisor wisely.

There is a lot to learn, but the rewards can be astronomical. If you do not want to learn those skills, then being a Type 1 investor is highly recommended. It is what you know that is your greatest wealth. It is what you do not know that is your greatest risk.

There is always risk, so learn to manage risk instead of avoid it.

WORK TO LEARN — DON'T WORK FOR MONEY

Work to Learn –
Don't Work
for Money

*I*n 1995, I granted an interview with a newspaper in Singapore. The young female reporter was on time, and the interview got under way immediately. We sat in the lobby of a luxurious hotel, sipping coffee and discussing the purpose of my visit to Singapore. I was to share the platform with Zig Ziglar. He was speaking on motivation, and I was speaking on "The Secrets of the Rich."

"Someday, I would like to be a best-selling author like you," she said. I had seen some of the articles she had written for the paper, and I was impressed. She had a tough, clear style of writing. Her articles held a reader's interest.

"You have a great style," I said in reply. "What holds you back from achieving your dream?"

"My work does not seem to go anywhere," she said quietly. "Everyone says that my novels are excellent, but nothing happens. So I keep my job with the paper. At least it pays the bills. Do you have any suggestions?"

"Yes, I do," I said brightly. "A friend of mine here in Singapore runs a school that trains people to sell. He runs sales-training courses for many of the top corporations here in Singapore, and I think attending one of his courses would greatly enhance your career."

She stiffened. "Are you saying I should go to school to learn to sell?"

I nodded.

"You aren't serious, are you?"

Again, I nodded. "What is wrong with that?" I was now backpeddling. She was offended by something, and now I was wishing I had not said anything. In my attempt to be helpful, I found myself defending my suggestion.

"I have a master's degree in English Literature. Why would I go to school to learn to be a salesperson? I am a professional. I went to school to be trained in a profession so I would not have to be a salesperson. I hate salespeople. All they want is money. So tell me why I should study sales?" She was now packing her briefcase forcibly. The interview was over.

On the coffee table sat a copy of an earlier best-selling book I wrote. I picked it up as well as the notes she had jotted down on her legal pad. "Do you see this?" I said pointing to her notes.

She looked down at her notes. "What," she said, confused.

Again, I pointed deliberately to her notes. On her pad she had written "Robert Kiyosaki, best-selling author."

"It says 'best-selling author,' not best 'writing' author."

Her eyes widened immediately.

"I am a terrible writer. You are a great writer. I went to sales school. You have a master's degree. Put them together and you get a 'best-selling author' and a 'best-writing author.' "

Anger flared from her eyes. "I'll never stoop so low as to learn how to sell. People like you have no business writing. I am a professionally trained writer and you are a salesman. It is not fair."

The rest of her notes were put away, and she hurried out through the large glass doors into the humid Singapore morning.

At least she gave me a fair and favorable write-up the next morning.

The world is filled with smart, talented, educated and gifted people. We meet them every day. They are all around us.

A few days ago, my car was not running well. I pulled into a garage, and the young mechanic had it fixed in just a few minutes. He knew what was wrong by simply listening to the engine. I was amazed.

The sad truth is, great talent is not enough.

I am constantly shocked at how little talented people earn. I heard the other day that less than 5 percent of Americans earn more than $100,000 a year. I have met brilliant, highly educated people who earn less than $20,000 a year. A business consultant who specializes in the medical trade was telling me how many doctors, dentists and chiropractors struggle financially. All this time, I thought that when they graduated, the dollars would pour in. It was this business consultant who gave me the phrase, "They are one skill away from great wealth."

What this phrase means is that most people need only to learn and master one more skill and their income would jump exponentially. I have mentioned before that financial intelligence is a synergy of accounting, investing, marketing and law. Combine those four technical skills and making money with money is easier. When it comes to money, the only skill most people know is to work hard.

The classic example of a synergy of skills was that young writer for the newspaper. If she diligently learned the skills of sales and marketing, her income would jump dramatically. If I were her, I would take some courses in advertising copywriting as well as sales. Then, instead of working at the newspaper, I would seek a job at an advertising agency. Even if it were a cut in pay, she would learn how to communicate in "short cuts" that are used in successful advertising. She also would spend time learning public relations, an important skill. She would learn how to get millions in free publicity. Then, at night and on weekends, she could be writing her great novel. When it was finished, she would be better able to sell her book. Then, in a short while, she could be a "best-selling author."

When I first came out with my first book *If You Want To Be Rich and Happy, Don't Go to School?* a publisher suggested I change the title to The Economics of Education. I told the publisher that with a title like that, I would sell two books: one to my family and one to my best friend. The problem is, they would expect it for free. The obnoxious title *If You Want To Be Rich and Happy, Don't Go to School?* was chosen because we knew it would get tons of publicity. I am pro-education and believe in education reform. Otherwise, why would I continue to press for changing our antiquated educational system? So I chose a title that would get me on more TV and radio shows, simply because I was willing to be controversial. Many people thought I was a fruitcake, but the book sold and sold.

When I graduated from the U.S. Merchant Marine Academy in 1969, my educated dad was happy. Standard Oil of California had hired me for its oil-tanker fleet. I was a third mate, and the pay was low compared with my classmates, but it was OK for a first real job after college. My starting pay was about $42,000 a year, including overtime, and I only had to work for seven months. I had five months of vacation. If I had wanted to, I could have taken the run to Vietnam with a subsidiary shipping company, and easily doubled my pay instead of taking the five months' vacation.

I had a great career ahead of me, yet I resigned after six months with the company and joined the Marine Corps to learn how to fly. My educated dad was devastated. Rich dad congratulated me.

In school and in the workplace, the popular opinion is the idea of "specialization." That is, in order to make more money or get promoted, you need to "specialize." That is why medical doctors immediately begin to seek a specialty such as orthopedics or pediatrics. The same is true for accountants, architects, lawyers, pilots and others.

My educated dad believed in the same dogma. That is why he was thrilled when he eventually achieved his doctorate. He often admitted that schools reward people who study more and more about less and less.

Rich dad encouraged me to do exactly the opposite. "You want to know a little about a lot" was his suggestion. That is why for years I worked in different areas of his companies. For awhile, I worked in his accounting department. Although I would probably never have been an accountant, he wanted me to learn via "osmosis." Rich dad knew I would pick up "jargon" and a sense of what is important and what is not. I also worked as a bus boy and construction worker, as well as in sales, reservations and marketing. He was "grooming" Mike and me. That is why he insisted we sit in on the meetings with his bankers, lawyers, accountants and brokers. He wanted us to know a little about every aspect of his empire.

When I quit my high-paying job with Standard Oil, my educated dad had a heart-to-heart with me. He was bewildered. He could not understand my decision to resign from a career that offered high pay, great benefits, lots of time off, and opportunity for promotion. When he asked me one evening, "Why did you quit?" I could not explain it to him, as much as I tried. My logic did not fit his logic. The big problem was that my logic was my rich dad's logic.

Job security meant everything to my educated dad. Learning meant everything to my rich dad.

Educated dad thought I went to school to learn to be a ship's officer. Rich dad knew that I went to school to study international trade. So as a student, I made cargo runs, navigating large freighters, oil tankers and passenger ships to the Far East and the South Pacific. Rich dad emphasized that I stay in the Pacific instead of taking ships to Europe because he knew that the "emerging nations" were in Asia, not Europe. While most of my classmates, including Mike, were partying at their fraternity houses, I was studying trade, people, business styles and cultures in Japan, Taiwan, Thailand, Singapore, Hong Kong, Vietnam, Korea, Tahiti, Samoa and the Philippines. I also was partying, but it was not in any frat house. I grew up rapidly.

Educated dad just could not understand why I decided to quit and join the Marine Corps. I told him I wanted to learn to fly, but really I wanted to learn to lead troops. Rich dad explained to me that the hardest part of running a company is managing people. He had spent three years in the Army; my educated dad was draft-exempt. Rich dad told me of the value of learning to lead men into dangerous situations. "Leadership is what you need to learn next," he said. "If you're not a good leader, you'll get shot in the back, just like they do in business."

Returning from Vietnam in 1973, I resigned my commission, even though I loved flying. I found a job with Xerox Corp. I joined it for one reason, and it was not for the benefits. I was a shy person, and the thought of selling was the most frightening subject in the world. Xerox has one of the best sales-training programs in America.

Rich dad was proud of me. My educated dad was ashamed. Being an intellectual, he thought that salespeople were below him. I worked with Xerox for four years until I overcame my fear of knocking on doors and being rejected. Once I could consistently be in the top five in sales, I again resigned and moved on, leaving behind another great career with an excellent company.

In 1977, I formed my first company. Rich dad had groomed Mike and me to take over companies. So I now had to learn to form them and put them together. My first product, the nylon and velcro wallet, was manufactured in the Far East and shipped to a warehouse in New York, near where I had gone to school. My formal education was complete, and it was time to test my wings. If I failed, I went broke. Rich dad thought it best to go broke before 30. "You still have time to recover" was his advice. On the eve of my 30th birthday, my first shipment left Korea for New York.

Today, I still do business internationally. And as my rich dad encouraged me to do, I keep seeking the emerging nations. Today my investment company invests in South America, Asia, Norway and Russia.

There is an old cliche that goes, "Job is an acronym for 'Just Over Broke.' " And unfortunately, I would say that the saying applies to millions of people. Because school does not think financial intelligence is an intelligence, most workers "live within their means." They work and they pay the bills.

There is another horrible management theory that goes, "Workers work hard enough to not be fired, and owners pay just enough so that workers won't quit." And if you look at the pay scales of most companies, again I would say there is a degree of truth in that statement.

The net result is that most workers never get ahead. They do what they've been taught to do: "Get a secure job." Most workers focus on working for pay and benefits that reward them in the short term, but is often disastrous in the long run.

Instead I recommend to young people to seek work for what they will learn, more than what they will earn. Look down the road at what skills they want to acquire before choosing a specific profession and before getting trapped in the "Rat Race."

Once people are trapped in the lifelong process of bill paying, they become like those little hamsters running around in those little metal wheels. Their little furry legs are spinning furiously, the wheel is turning furiously, but come tomorrow morning, they'll still be in the same cage: great job.

In the movie *Jerry Maguire*, starring Tom Cruise, there are many great one liners. Probably the most memorable is "Show me the money." But there is one line I thought most truthful. It comes from the scene where Tom Cruise is leaving the firm. He has just been fired, and he is asking the entire company "Who wants to come with me?" And the whole place is silent and frozen. Only one woman speaks up and says, "I'd like to but I'm due for a promotion in three months."

That statement is probably the most truthful statement in the whole movie. It is the type of statement that people use to keep themselves busy working away to pay bills. I know my educated dad looked forward to his pay raise every year, and every year he was disappointed. So he would go back to school to earn more qualifications so he could get another raise, but again, it would be another disappointment.

The question I often ask people is, "Where is this daily activity taking you?" Just like the little hamster, I wonder if people look at where their hard work is taking them. What does the future hold?

Cyril Brickfield, the former executive director of The American Association of Retired People, reports that "private pensions are in a state of chaos. First of all, 50 percent of the workforce today has no pension. That alone should be of great concern. And 75 to 80 percent of the other 50 percent have ineffective pensions that pay $55 or $150 or $300 a month."

In his book *The Retirement Myth*, Craig S. Karpel writes: "I visited the headquarters of a major national pension consulting firm and met with a managing director who specializes in designing lush retirement plans for top management. When I asked her what people who don't have corner offices will be able to expect in the way of pension income, she said with a confident smile: 'The Silver Bullet.'

" 'What,' I asked, 'is The Silver Bullet?'

"She shrugged, 'If baby boomers discover they don't have enough money to live on when they're older, they can always blow their brains out.' " Karpel goes on to explain the difference between the old Defined Benefit retirement plans and the new 401K plans which are riskier. It is not a pretty picture for most people working today. And that is just for retirement. When medical fees and long-term nursing home care are added to the picture, the picture is frightening. In his 1995 book, he indicates that nursing-home fees run from $30,000 to $125,000 per year. He went to a clean no-frills nursing home in his area and found the price to be $88,000 a year in 1995.

Already, many hospitals in countries with socialized medicine need to make tough decisions such as "Who will live and who will die?" They make those decisions purely on how much money they have and how old the patients are. If the patient is old, they often will give the medical care to someone younger. The older poor patient gets put to the back of the line. So just as the rich can afford better education, the rich will be able to keep themselves alive, while those who have little wealth will die.

So I wonder, are workers looking into the future or just until their next paycheck, never questioning where they are headed?

When I speak to adults who want to earn more money, I always recommend the same thing. I suggest taking a long view of their life. Instead of simply working for the money and security, which I admit are important, I suggest they take a second job that will teach them a second skill. Often I recommend joining a network marketing company, also called multilevel marketing, if they want to learn sales skills. Some of these companies have excellent training programs that help people get over their fear of failure and rejection, which are the main reasons people are unsuccessful. Education is more valuable than money, in the long run.

When I offer this suggestion, I often hear in response, "Oh that is too much hassle," or "I only want to do what I am interested in."

To the statement of "It's too much of a hassle," I ask, "So you would rather work all your life giving 50 percent of what you earn to the government?" To the other statement—"I only do what I am interested in"—I say, "I'm not interested in going to the gym, but I go because I want to feel better and live longer."

Unfortunately, there is some truth to the old statement "You can't teach an old dog new tricks." Unless a person is used to changing, it's hard to change.

But for those of you who might be on the fence when it comes to the idea of working to learn something new, I offer this word of encouragement: Life is much like going to the gym. The most painful part is deciding to go. Once you get past that, it's easy. There have been many days I have dreaded going to the gym, but once I am there and in motion, it is a pleasure. After the workout is over, I am always glad I talked myself into going.

If you are unwilling to work to learn something new and insist on, instead, becoming highly specialized within your field, make sure the company you work for is unionized. Labor unions are designed to protect specialists.

My educated dad, after falling from grace with the governor, became the head of the teachers union in Hawaii. He told me that it was the hardest job he ever held. My rich dad, on the other hand, spent his life doing his best to keep his companies from becoming unionized. He was successful. Although the unions came close, rich dad was always able to fight them off.

Personally, I take no sides because I can see the need for and the benefits of both sides. If you do as school recommends, become highly specialized, then seek union protection. For example, had I continued on with my flying career, I would have sought a company that had a strong pilots union. Why? Because my life would be dedicated to learn a skill that was valuable in only one industry. If I were pushed out of that industry, my life's skills would not be as valuable to another industry. A displaced senior pilot—with 100,000 hours of heavy airline transport time, earning $150,000 a year—would have a hard time finding an equivalent high-paying job in school teaching. The skills do not necessarily transfer from industry to industry, because the skills the pilots are paid for in the airline industry are not as important in, say, the school system.

The same is true even for doctors today. With all the changes in medicine, many medical specialists are needing to conform to medical organizations such as HMO's. Schoolteachers definitely need to be union members. Today in America, the teachers union is the largest and the richest labor union of all. The NEA, National Education Association, has tremendous political clout. Teachers need the protection of their union because their skills are also of limited value to an industry outside of education. So the rule of thumb is, "Highly specialized, then unionize." It's the smart thing to do.

When I ask the classes I teach, "How many of you can cook a better hamburger than McDonald's?" almost all the students raise their hands. I then ask, "So if most of you can cook a better hamburger, how come McDonald's makes more money than you?"

The answer is obvious: McDonald's is excellent at business systems. The reason so many talented people are poor is because they focus on building a better hamburger and know little to nothing about business systems.

A friend of mine in Hawaii is a great artist. He makes a sizable amount of money. One day his mother's attorney called to tell him that she had left him $35,000. That is what was left of her estate after the attorney and the government took their shares. Immediately, he saw an opportunity to increase his business by using some of this money to advertise. Two months later, his first four-color, full-page ad appeared in an expensive magazine that targeted the very rich. The ad ran for three months. He received no replies from the ad, and all of his inheritance is now gone. He now wants to sue the magazine for misrepresentation.

This is a common case of someone who can build a beautiful hamburger, but knows little about business. When I asked him what he learned, his only reply was that "advertising salespeople are crooks." I then asked him if he would be willing to take a course in sales and a course in direct marketing. His reply, "I don't have the time, and I don't want to waste my money."

The world is filled with talented poor people. All too often, they're poor or struggle financially or earn less than they are capable of, not because of what they know but because of what they do not know. They focus on perfecting their skills at building a better hamburger rather than the skills of selling and delivering the hamburger. Maybe McDonald's does not make the best hamburger, but they are the best at selling and delivering a basic average burger.

Poor dad wanted me to specialize. That was his view on how to be paid more. Even after being told by the governor of Hawaii that he could no longer work in state government, my educated dad continued to encourage me to get specialized. Educated dad then took up the cause of the teachers union, campaigning for further protection and benefits for these highly skilled and educated professionals. We argued often, but I know he never agreed that overspecialization is what caused the need for union protection. He never understood that the more specialized you become, the more you are trapped and dependent on that specialty.

Rich dad advised that Mike and I "groom" ourselves. Many corporations do the same thing. They find a young bright student out of business school and begin "grooming" that person to someday take over the company. So these bright young employees do not specialize in one department; they are moved from department to department to learn all the aspects of business systems. The rich often "groom" their children or the children of others. By doing so, their children gain an overall knowledge of the operations of the business and how the various departments interrelate.

For the World War II generation, it was considered "bad" to skip from company to company. Today, it is considered smart. Since people will skip from company to company, rather than seek greater specialization, why not seek to "learn" more than "earn." In the short term, it may earn you less. In the long term, it will pay off in large dividends.

The main management skills needed for success are:

1. The management of cash flow.
2. The management of systems (including yourself and time with family).
3. The management of people.

The most important specialized skills are sales and understanding marketing. It is the ability to sell—therefore, to communicate to another human being, be it a customer, employee, boss, spouse or child—that is the base skill of personal success. It is communication skills such as writing, speaking and negotiating that are crucial to a life of success. It is a skill that I work on constantly, attending courses or buying educational tapes to expand my knowledge.

As I have mentioned, my educated dad worked harder and harder the more competent he became. He also became more trapped the more specialized he got. Although his salary went up, his choices diminished. Soon after he was locked out of government work, he found out how vulnerable he really was professionally. It is like professional athletes who suddenly are injured or are too old to play. Their once high-paying position is gone, and they have limited skills to fall back on. I think that is why my educated dad sided so much with unions after that. He realized how much a union would have benefited him.

Rich dad encouraged Mike and me to know a little about a lot. He encouraged us to work with people smarter than we were and to bring smart people together to work as a team. Today it would be called a synergy of professional specialities.

Today, I meet ex-schoolteachers earning hundreds of thousands of dollars a year. They earn that much because they have specialized skills in their field as well as other skills. They can teach as well as sell and market. I know of no other skills to be more important than selling as well as marketing. The skills of selling and marketing are difficult for most people primarily due to their fear of rejection. The better you are at communicating, negotiating and handling your fear of rejection, the easier life is. Just as I advised that newspaper writer who wanted to become a "best-selling author," I advise anyone else today. Being technically specialized has its strengths as well as its weaknesses. I have friends who are geniuses, but they cannot communicate effectively with other human beings and, as a result, their earnings are pitiful. I advise them to just spend a year learning to sell. Even if they earn nothing, their communication skills will improve. And that is priceless.

In addition to being good learners, sellers and marketers, we need to be good teachers as well as good students. To be truly rich, we need to be able to give as well as to receive. In cases of financial or professional struggle, there is often a lack of giving and receiving. I know many people who are poor because they are neither good students nor good teachers.

Both of my dads were generous men. Both made it a practice to give first. Teaching was one of their ways of giving. The more they gave, the more they received. One glaring difference was in the giving of money. My rich dad gave lots of money away. He gave to his church, to charities, to his foundation. He knew that to receive money, you had to give money. Giving money is the secret to most great wealthy families. That is why there are organizations like the Rockefeller Foundation and the Ford Foundation. These are organizations designed to take their wealth and increase it, as well as give it away in perpetuity.

My educated dad always said, "When I have some extra money, I'll give it." The problem was, there was never any extra. So he worked harder to draw more money in rather than focus on the most important law of money: "Give and you shall receive." Instead, he believed in "Receive and then you give."

In conclusion, I became both dads. One part of me is a hard-core capitalist who loves the game of money making money. The other side is a socially responsible teacher who is deeply concerned with this ever-widening gap between the haves and have nots. I personally hold the archaic educational system primarily responsible for this growing gap.

BEGINNINGS

CHAPTER EIGHT

Overcoming Obstacles

Once people have studied and become financially literate, they may still face roadblocks to becoming financially independent. There are five main reasons why financially literate people may still not develop abundant asset columns. Asset columns that could produce large sums of cash flow. Asset columns that could free them to live the life they dream of, instead of working full time just to pay bills. The five reasons are:

1. Fear.
2. Cynicism.
3. Laziness.
4. Bad habits.
5. Arrogance.

Reason No. 1. Overcoming the fear of losing money. I have never met anyone who really likes losing money. And in all my years, I have never met a rich person who has never lost money. But I have met a lot of poor people who have never lost a dime. . .investing, that is.

The fear of losing money is real. Everyone has it. Even the rich. But it's not fear that is the problem. It's how you handle fear. It's how you handle losing. It's how you handle failure that makes the difference in one's life. That goes for anything in life, not just money. The primary difference between a rich person and a poor person is how they handle that fear.

It's OK to be fearful. It's OK to be a coward when it comes to money. You can still be rich. We're all heroes at something and cowards at something else. My friend's wife is an emergency room nurse. When she sees blood, she flies into action. When I mention investing, she runs away. When I see blood, I don't run. I pass out.

My rich dad understood phobias about money. "Some people are terrified of snakes. Some people are terrified about losing money. Both are phobias," he would say. So his solution to the phobia of losing money was this little rhyme:

"If you hate risk and worry. . .start early."

That's why banks recommend savings as a habit when you're young. If you start young, it's easy to be rich. I won't go into it here, but there is a large difference between a person who starts saving at age 20 versus age 30. A staggering difference.

It is said that one of the wonders of the world is the power of compound interest. The purchase of Manhattan Island is said to be one of the greatest bargains of all time. New York was purchased for $24 in trinkets and beads. Yet, if that $24 had been invested, at 8 percent annually, that $24 would have been worth more than $28 trillion by 1995. Manhattan could be repurchased with money left over to buy much of L.A., especially at 1995's real estate prices.

My neighbor works for a major computer company. He has been there 25 years. In five more years he will leave the company with $4 million in his 401k retirement plan. It is invested mostly in high-growth mutual funds, which he will convert to bonds and government securities. He'll only be 55 when he gets out, and he will have a passive cash flow of over $300,000 a year, more than he makes from his salary. So it can be done, even if you hate losing or hate risk. But you must start early and definitely set up a retirement plan, and you should hire a financial planner you trust to guide you before investing in anything.

But what if you don't have much time left or would like to retire early? How do you handle the fear of losing money?

My poor dad did nothing. He simply avoided the issue, refusing to discuss the subject.

My rich dad, on the other hand, recommended that I think like a Texan. "I like Texas and Texans," he used to say. "In Texas, everything is bigger. When Texans win, they win big. And when they lose, it's spectacular."

"They like losing?" I asked.

"That's not what I'm saying. Nobody likes losing. Show me a happy loser, and I'll show you a loser," said rich dad. "It's a Texan's attitude toward risk, reward and failure I'm talking about. It's how they handle life. They live it big. Not like most of the people around here, living like roaches when it comes to money. Roaches terrified that someone will shine a light on them. Whimpering when the grocery clerk shortchanges them a quarter."

Rich dad went on to explain.

"What I like best is the Texas attitude. They're proud when they win, and they brag when they lose. Texans have a saying, "If you're going to go broke, go big. You don't want to admit you went broke over a duplex. Most people around here are so afraid of losing, they don't have a duplex to go broke with."

He constantly told Mike and me that the greatest reason for lack of financial success was because most people played it too safe. "People are so afraid of losing that they lose" were his words.

Fran Tarkenton, a one-time great NFL quarterback, says it still another way: "Winning means being unafraid to lose."

In my own life, I've noticed that winning usually follows losing. Before I finally learned to ride a bike, I first fell down many times. I've never met a golfer who has never lost a golf ball. I've never met people who have fallen in love who have never had their heart broken. And I've never met someone rich who has never lost money.

So for most people, the reason they don't win financially is because the pain of losing money is far greater than the joy of being rich. Another saying in Texas is, "Everyone wants to go to Heaven, but no one wants to die." Most people dream of being rich, but are terrified of losing money. So they never get to Heaven.

Rich dad used to tell Mike and me stories about his trips to Texas. "If you really want to learn the attitude of how to handle risk, losing and failure, go to San Antonio and visit the Alamo. The Alamo is a great story of brave people who chose to fight, knowing there was no hope of success against overwhelming odds. They chose to die instead of surrendering. It's an inspiring story worthy of study; nonetheless, it's still a tragic military defeat. They got their butts kicked. A failure if you will. They lost. So how do Texans handle failure? They still shout, 'Remember the Alamo!' "

Mike and I heard this story a lot. He always told us this story when he was about to go into a big deal and he was nervous. After he had done all his due diligence and now it was put up or shut up, he told us this story. Every time he was afraid of making a mistake, or losing money, he told us this story. It gave him strength, for it reminded him that he could always turn a financial loss into a financial win. Rich dad knew that failure would only make him stronger and smarter. It's not that he wanted to lose; he just knew who he was and how he would take a loss. He would take a loss and make it a win. That's what made him a winner and others losers. It gave him the courage to cross the line when others backed out. "That's why I like Texans so much. They took a great failure and turned it into a tourist destination that makes them millions."

But probably his words that mean the most to me today are these: "Texans don't bury their failures. They get inspired by them. They take their failures and turn them into rallying cries. Failure inspires Texans to become winners. But that formula is not just the formula for Texans. It is the formula for all winners."

Just as I also said that falling off my bike was part of learning to ride. I remember falling off only made me more determined to learn to ride. Not less. I also said that I have never met a golfer who has never lost a ball. To be a top professional golfer, losing a ball or a tournament only inspires golfers to be better, to practice harder, to study more. That's what makes them better. For winners, losing inspires them. For losers, losing defeats them.

Quoting John D. Rockefeller, "I always tried to turn every disaster into an opportunity."

And being Japanese-American, I can say this. Many people say that Pearl Harbor was an American mistake. I say it was a Japanese mistake. From the movie *Tora, Tora, Tora*, a somber Japanese admiral says to his cheering subordinates, "I am afraid we have awakened a sleeping giant." "Remember Pearl Harbor" became a rallying cry. It turned one of America's greatest losses into the reason to win. This great defeat gave America strength, and America soon emerged as a world power.

Failure inspires winners. And failure defeats losers. It is the biggest secret of winners. It's the secret that losers do not know. The greatest secret of winners is that failure inspires winning; thus, they're not afraid of losing. Repeating Fran Tarkenton's quote, "Winning means being unafraid to lose." People like Fran Tarkenton are not afraid of losing because they know who they are. They hate losing, so they know that losing will only inspire them to become better. There is a big difference between hating losing and being afraid to lose. Most people are so afraid of losing money that they lose. They go broke over a duplex. Financially they play life too safe and too small. They buy big houses and big cars, but not big investments. The main reason that over 90 percent of the American public struggles financially is because they play not to lose. They don't play to win.

They go to their financial planners or accountants or stockbrokers and buy a balanced portfolio. Most have lots of cash in CDs, low-yield bonds, mutual funds that can be traded within a mutual-fund family, and a few individual stocks. It is a safe and sensible portfolio. But it is not a winning portfolio. It is a portfolio of someone playing not to lose.

Don't get me wrong. It's probably a better portfolio than more than 70 percent of the population, and that's frightening. Because a safe portfolio is a lot better than no portfolio. It's a great portfolio for someone who loves safety. But playing it safe and going "balanced" on your investment portfolio is not the way successful investors play the game. If you have little money and you want to be rich, you must first be "focused," not "balanced." If you look at anyone successful, at the start they were not balanced. Balanced people go nowhere. They stay in one spot. To make progress, you must first go unbalanced. Just look at how you make progress walking.

Thomas Edison was not balanced. He was focused. Bill Gates was not balanced. He was focused. Donald Trump is focused. George Soros is focused. George Patton did not take his tanks wide. He focused them and blew through the weak spots in the German line. The French went wide with the Maginot Line, and you know what happened to them.

If you have any desire of being rich, you must focus. Put a lot of your eggs in a few baskets. Do not do what poor and middle class people do: put their few eggs in many baskets.

If you hate losing, play it safe. If losing makes you weak, play it safe. Go with balanced investments. If you're over 25 years old and are terrified of taking risks, don't change. Play it safe, but start early. Start accumulating your nest egg early because it will take time.

But if you have dreams of freedom—of getting out of the rat race— the first question to ask yourself is, "How do I respond to failure?" If failure inspires you to win, maybe you should go for it—but only maybe. If failure makes you weak or causes you to throw temper tantrums—like spoiled brats who call an attorney to file a lawsuit every time something does not go their way—then play it safe. Keep your daytime job. Or buy bonds or mutual funds. But remember, there is risk in those financial instruments also, even though they are safer.

I say all this, mentioning Texas and Fran Tarkenton, because stacking the asset column is easy. It's really a low-aptitude game. It doesn't take much education. Fifth-grade math will do. But staking the asset column is a high-attitude game. It takes guts, patience and a great attitude toward failure. Losers avoid failing. And failure turns losers into winners. Just remember the Alamo.

Reason No. 2. Overcoming cynicism. "The sky is falling. The sky is falling." Most of us know the story of "Chicken Little," who ran around warning the barnyard of impending doom. We all know people who are that way. But we all have a "Chicken Little" inside each of us.

And as I stated earlier, the cynic is really a little chicken. We all get a little chicken when fear and doubt cloud our thoughts.

All of us have doubts. "I'm not smart." "I'm not good enough." "So and so is better than me." Or our doubts often paralyze us. We play the "What if?" game. "What if the economy crashes right after I invest?" Or "What if I lose control and I can't pay the money back?" "What if things don't go as I planned?" Or we have friends or loved ones who will remind us of our shortcomings regardless of whether we ask. They often say, "What makes you think you can do that?" Or "If it's such a good idea, how come someone else hasn't done it?" Or "That will never work. You don't know what you're talking about." These words of doubt often get so loud that we fail to act. A horrible feeling builds in our stomach. Sometimes we can't sleep. We fail to move forward. So we stay with what is safe and opportunities pass us by. We watch life passing by as we sit immobilized with a cold knot in our body. We have all felt this at one time in our lives, some more than others.

Peter Lynch of Fidelity Magellan mutual fund fame refers to warnings about the sky falling as "noise," and we all hear it.

"Noise" is either created inside our heads or comes from outside. Often from friends, family, co-workers and the media. Lynch recalls the time during the 1950s when the threat of nuclear war was so prevalent in the news that people began building fallout shelters and storing food and water. If they had invested that money wisely in the market, instead of building a fallout shelter, they'd probably be financially independent today.

When the riots broke out in Los Angeles a few years ago, gun sales went up all over the country. A person dies from rare hamburger meat in Washington State and the Arizona Health Department orders restaurants to have all beef cooked well-done. A drug company runs a national TV commercial showing people catching the flu. The ad runs in February. Colds go up as well as sales of their cold medicine.

Most people are poor because when it comes to investing, the world is filled with Chicken Littles running around yelling, "The sky is falling. The sky is falling." And Chicken Littles are effective because everyone of us is a little chicken. It often takes great courage to not let rumors and talk of doom and gloom affect your doubts and fears.

In 1992, a friend named Richard came from Boston to visit my wife and me in Phoenix. He was impressed with what we had done through stocks and real estate. The prices of real estate in Phoenix were depressed. We spent two days with him showing him what we thought were excellent opportunities for cash flow and capital appreciation.

My wife and I are not real estate agents. We are strictly investors. After identifying a unit in a resort community, we called an agent who sold it to him that afternoon. The price was a mere $42,000 for a two-bedroom townhome. Similar units were going for $65,000. He had found a bargain. Excited, he bought it and returned to Boston.

Two weeks later, the agent called to say that our friend had backed out. I called immediately to find out why. All he said was that he talked to his neighbor, and his neighbor told him it was a bad deal. He was paying too much.

I asked Richard if his neighbor was an investor. Richard said "no." When I asked why he listened to him, Richard got defensive and simply said he wanted to keep looking.

The real estate market in Phoenix turned, and by 1994, that little unit was renting for $1,000 a month—$2,500 in the peak winter months. The unit was worth $95,000 in 1995. All Richard had to put down was $5,000 and he would have had a start at getting out of the rat race. Today, he still has done nothing. And the bargains in Phoenix are still here; you just have to look a lot harder.

Richard's backing out did not surprise me. It's called "buyer's remorse," and it affects all of us. It's those doubts that get us. The little chicken won, and a chance at freedom was lost.

In another example, I hold a small portion of my assets in tax lien certificates instead of CDs. I earn 16 percent per year on my money, which certainly beats the 5 percent the bank offers. The certificates are secured by real estate and enforced by state law, which is also better than most banks. The formula they're bought on makes them safe. They just lack liquidity. So I look at them as 2 to 7-year CDs. Almost every time I tell someone, especially if they have money in CDs, that I hold my money this way, they will tell me it's risky. They tell me why I should not do it. When I ask them where they get their information, they say from a friend or an investment magazine. They've never done it, and they're telling someone who's doing it why they shouldn't. The lowest yield I look for is 16 percent, but people who are filled with doubt are willing to accept 5 percent. Doubt is expensive.

My point is that it's those doubts and cynicism that keep most people poor and playing it safe. The real world is simply waiting for you to get rich. Only a person's doubts keep them poor. As I said, getting out of the rat race is technically easy. It doesn't take much education, but those doubts are cripplers for most people.

"Cynics never win," said rich dad. "Unchecked doubt and fear creates a cynic. Cynics criticize, and winners analyze" was another of his favorite sayings. Rich dad explained that criticism blinded while analysis opened eyes. Analysis allowed winners to see that critics were blind, and to see opportunities that everyone else missed. And finding what people miss is key to any success.

Real estate is a powerful investment tool for anyone seeking financial independence or freedom. It is a unique investment tool. Yet, every time I mention real estate as a vehicle, I often hear, "I don't want to fix toilets." That's what Peter Lynch calls "noise." That's what my rich dad would say is the cynic talking. Someone who criticizes and does not analyze. Someone who lets their doubts and fears close their mind instead of open their eyes.

So when someone says, "I don't want to fix toilets," I want to fire back, "What makes you think I want to?" They're saying a toilet is more important than what they want. I talk about freedom from the rat race, and they focus on toilets. That is the thought pattern that keeps most people poor. They criticize instead of analyze.

" 'I don't wants' hold the key to your success," rich dad would say.

Because I, too, do not want to fix toilets, I shop hard for a property manager who does fix toilets. And by finding a great property manager who runs houses or apartments, well, my cash flow goes up. But more importantly a great property manager allows me to buy a lot more real estate since I don't have to fix toilets. A great property manager is key to success in real estate. Finding a good manager is more important to me than the real estate. A great property manager often hears of great deals before real estate agents do, which makes them even more valuable.

That is what rich dad meant by " 'I don't wants' hold the key to your success." Because I do not want to fix toilets either, I figured out how to buy more real estate and expedite my getting out of the rat race. The people who continue to say "I don't want to fix toilets" often deny themselves the use of this powerful investment vehicle. Toilets are more important than their freedom.

In the stock market, I often hear people say, "I don't want to lose money." Well, what makes them think I or anyone else likes losing money? They don't make money because they chose to not lose money. Instead of analyzing, they close their minds to another powerful investment vehicle, the stock market.

In December 1996, I was riding with a friend past our neighborhood gas station. He looked up and saw that the price of oil was going up. My friend is a worry wart or a "Chicken Little." To him, the sky is always going to fall, and it usually does, on him.

When we got home, he showed me all the stats as to why the price of oil was going to go up over the next few years. Statistics I had never seen before, even though I already owned a substantial share block of an existing oil company. With that information, I immediately began looking for and found a new undervalued oil company that was about to find some oil deposits. My broker was excited about this new company, and I bought 15,000 shares for 65 cents per share.

In February 1997, this same friend and I drove by the same gas station, and sure enough, the price per gallon had gone up nearly 15 percent. Again, the "Chicken Little" worried and complained. I smiled because in January 1997, that little oil company hit oil and those 15,000 shares went up to more than $3 per share since he had first given me the tip. And the price of gas will continue to go up if what my friend says is true.

Instead of analyzing, their little chicken closes their mind. If most people understood how a "stop" worked in stock-market investing, there would be more people investing to win instead of investing not to lose. A "stop" is simply a computer command that sells your stock automatically if the price begins to drop, helping to minimize your losses and maximize some gains. It's a great tool for those who are terrified of losing.

So whenever I hear people focusing on their "I don't wants," rather than what they do want, I know the "noise" in their head must be loud. Chicken Little has taken over their brain and is yelling, "The sky is falling and toilets are breaking." So they avoid their "don't wants," but they pay a huge price. They may never get what they want in life.

Rich dad gave me a way of looking at Chicken Little. "Just do what Colonel Sanders did." At the age of 66, he lost his business and began to live on his Social Security check. It wasn't enough. He went around the country selling his recipe for fried chicken. He was turned down 1,009 times before someone said "yes." And he went on to become a multimillionaire at an age when most people are quitting. "He was a brave and tenacious man," rich dad said of Harlan Sanders.

So when you're in doubt and feeling a little afraid, just do what Col. Sanders did to his little chicken. He fried it.

Reason No. 3. Laziness. Busy people are often the most lazy. We have all heard stories of a businessman who works hard to earn money. He works hard to be a good provider for his wife and children. He spends long hours at the office and brings work home on weekends. One day he comes home to an empty house. His wife has left with the kids. He knew he and his wife had problems, but rather than work to make the relationship strong, he stayed busy at work. Dismayed, his performance at work slips and he loses his job.

Today, I often meet people who are too busy to take care of their wealth. And there are people too busy to take care of their health. The cause is the same. They're busy, and they stay busy as a way of avoiding something they do not want to face. Nobody has to tell them. Deep down they know. In fact, if you remind them, they often respond with anger or irritation.

If they aren't busy at work or with the kids, they're often busy watching TV, fishing, playing golf or shopping. Yet, deep down they know they are avoiding something important. That's the most common form of laziness. Laziness by staying busy.

So what is the cure for laziness? The answer is a little greed.

For many of us, we were raised thinking of greed or desire as bad. "Greedy people are bad people," my mom use to say. Yet, we all have inside of us this yearning to have nice things, new things or exciting things. So to keep that emotion of desire under control, often parents found ways of suppressing that desire with guilt.

"You only think about yourself. Don't you know you have brothers and sisters?" was one of my mom's favorites. Or "You want me to buy you what?" was a favorite of my dad. "Do you think we're made of money? Do you think money grows on trees? We're not rich people, you know."

It wasn't so much the words but the angry guilt-trip that went with the words that got to me.

Or the reverse guilt-trip was the "I'm sacrificing my life to buy this for you. I'm buying this for you because I never had this advantage when I was a kid." I have a neighbor who is stone broke, but can't park his car in his garage. The garage is filled with toys for his kids. Those spoiled brats get everything they ask for. "I don't want them to know the feeling of want" are his everyday words. He has nothing set aside for their college or his retirement, but his kids have every toy ever made. He recently got a new credit card in the mail and took his kids to visit Las Vegas. "I'm doing it for the kids," he said with great sacrifice.

Rich dad forbade the words "I can't afford it."

In my real home, that's all I heard. Instead, rich dad required his children to say, "How can I afford it?" His reasoning, the words "I can't afford it" shut down your brain. It didn't have to think anymore. "How can I afford it?" opened up the brain. Forced it to think and search for answers.

But most importantly, he felt the words "I can't afford it" were a lie. And the human spirit knew it. "The human spirit is very, very, powerful," he would say. "It knows it can do anything." By having a lazy mind that says, "I can't afford it," a war breaks out inside you. Your spirit is angry, and your lazy mind must defend its lie. The spirit is screaming, "Come on. Let's go to the gym and work out." And the lazy mind says, "But I'm tired. I worked really hard today." Or the human spirit says, "I'm sick and tired of being poor. Let's get out there and get rich." To which the lazy mind says, "Rich people are greedy. Besides it's too much bother.

It's not safe. I might lose money. I'm working hard enough as it is. I've got too much to do at work anyway. Look at what I have to do tonight. My boss wants it finished by the morning."

"I can't afford it" also brings up sadness. A helplessness that leads to despondency and often depression. "Apathy" is another word. "How can I afford it?" opens up possibilities, excitement and dreams. So rich dad was not so concerned about what you wanted to buy, but that "How can I afford it?" created a stronger mind and a dynamic spirit.

Thus, he rarely gave Mike or me anything. Instead he would ask, "How can you afford it?" and that included college, which we paid for ourselves. It was not the goal but the process of attaining the goal we desired that he wanted us to learn.

The problem I sense today is that there are millions of people who feel guilty about their greed. It's an old conditioning from their childhood. Their desire to have the finer things that life offers. Most have been conditioned subconsciously to say, "You can't have that," or "You'll never afford that."

When I decided to exit the rat race, it was simply a question. "How can I afford to never work again?" And my mind began to kick out answers and solutions. The hardest part was fighting my real parents' dogma of "We can't afford that." Or "Stop thinking only about yourself." Or "Why don't you think about others?" and other such words designed to instill guilt to suppress my greed.

So how do you beat laziness? The answer is a little greed. It's that radio station WII-FM, which stands for "What's In It-For Me?" A person needs to sit down and ask, "What's in it for me if I'm healthy, sexy and good looking?" Or "What would my life be like if I never had to work again?" Or "What would I do if I had all the money I needed?" Without that little greed, the desire to have something better, progress is not made. Our world progresses because we all desire a better life. New inventions are made because we desire something better. We go to school and study hard because we want something better. So whenever you find yourself avoiding something you know you should be doing, then the only thing to ask yourself is "What's in it for me?" Be a little greedy. It's the best cure for laziness.

Too much greed, however, as anything in excess can be, is not good. But just remember what Michael Douglas said in the movie *Wall Street*. "Greed is good." Rich dad said it differently: "Guilt is worse than greed.

158

For guilt robs the body of its soul." And to me, Eleanor Roosevelt said it best: "Do what you feel in your heart to be right—for you'll be criticized anyway. You'll be damned if you do, and damned if you don't."

Reason No. 4. Habits. Our lives are a reflection of our habits more than our education. After seeing the movie *Conan*, starring Arnold Schwarzenegger, a friend said, "I'd love to have a body like Schwarzenegger." Most of the guys nodded in agreement.

"I even heard he was really puny and skinny at one time," another friend added.

"Yeah, I heard that too," another one added. "I heard he has a habit of working out almost every day in the gym."

"Yeah, I'll bet he has to."

"Nah," said the group cynic. "I'll bet he was born that way. Besides, let's stop talking about Arnold and get some beers."

This is an example of habits controlling behavior. I remember asking my rich dad about the habits of the rich. Instead of answering me outright, he wanted me to learn through example, as usual.

"When does your dad pay his bills?" rich dad asked.

"The first of the month," I said.

"Does he have anything left over?" he asked.

"Very little," I said.

"That's the main reason he struggles," said rich dad. "He has bad habits."

"Your dad pays everyone else first. He pays himself last, but only if he has anything left over."

"Which he usually doesn't," I said. "But he has to pay his bills, doesn't he? You're saying he shouldn't pay his bills?"

"Of course not," said rich dad. "I firmly believe in paying my bills on time. I just pay myself first. Before I pay even the government."

"But what happens if you don't have enough money?" I asked. "What do you do then?"

"The same," said rich dad. "I still pay myself first. Even if I'm short of money. My asset column is far more important to me than the government."

"But," I said. "Don't they come after you?"

"Yes, if you don't pay," said rich dad. "Look, I did not say not to pay. I just said I pay myself first, even if I'm short of money."

"But," I replied. "How do you do that?"

"It's not how. The question is 'Why,' " rich dad said.

"OK, why?"

"Motivation," said rich dad "Who do you think will complain louder if I don't pay them—me or my creditors?"

"Your creditors will definitely scream louder than you," I said, responding to the obvious. "You wouldn't say anything if you didn't pay yourself."

"So you see, after paying myself, the pressure to pay my taxes and the other creditors is so great that it forces me to seek other forms of income. The pressure to pay becomes my motivation. I've worked extra jobs, started other companies, traded in the stock market, anything just to make sure those guys don't start yelling at me. That pressure made me work harder, forced me to think, and all in all made me smarter and more active when it comes to money. If I had paid myself last, I would have felt no pressure, but I'd be broke."

"So it is the fear of the government or other people you owe money to that motivates you?"

"That's right," said rich dad. "You see, government bill collectors are big bullies. So are bill collectors in general. Most people give into these bullies. They pay them and never pay themselves. You know the story of the 96-pound weakling who gets sand kicked in his face?"

I nodded. "I see that ad for weightlifting and bodybuilding lessons in the comic books all the time."

"Well, most people let the bullies kick sand in their faces. I decided to use the fear of the bully to make me stronger. Others get weaker. Forcing myself to think about how to make extra money is like going to the gym and working out with weights. The more I work my mental money muscles out, the stronger I get. Now, I'm not afraid of those bullies.

I liked what rich dad was saying. "So if I pay myself first, I get financially stronger, mentally and fiscally."

Rich dad nodded.

"And if I pay myself last, or not at all, I get weaker. So people like bosses, managers, tax collectors, bill collectors and landlords push me around all my life. Just because I don't have good money habits."

Rich dad nodded. "Just like the 96-pound weakling."

Reason No. 5. Arrogance. Arrogance is ego plus ignorance.

"What I know makes me money. What I don't know loses me

160

money. Every time I have been arrogant, I have lost money. Because when I'm arrogant, I truly believe that what I don't know is not important," rich dad would often tell me.

I have found that many people use arrogance to try to hide their own ignorance. It often happens when I am discussing financial statements with accountants or even other investors.

They try to bluster their way through the discussion. It is clear to me that they don't know what they're talking about. They're not lying, but they are not telling the truth.

There are many people in the world of money, finances and investments who have absolutely no idea what they're talking about. Most people in the money industry are just spouting off sales pitches like used-car salesmen.

When you know you are ignorant in a subject, start educating yourself by finding an expert in the field or find a book on the subject.

GETTING STARTED

CHAPTER NINE

Getting Started

I wish I could say acquiring wealth was easy for me, but it wasn't.

So in response to the question "How do I start?" I offer the thought process I go through on a day-by-day basis. It really is easy to find great deals. I promise you that. It's just like riding a bike. After a little wobbling, it's a piece of cake. But when it comes to money, it's the determination to get through the wobbling that's a personal thing.

To find million-dollar "deals of a lifetime" requires us to call on our financial genius. I believe that each of us has a financial genius within us. The problem is, our financial genius lies asleep, waiting to be called upon. It lies asleep because our culture has educated us into believing that the love of money is the root of all evil. It has encouraged us to learn a profession so we can work for money, but failed to teach us how to have money work for us. It taught us not to worry about our financial future, our company or the government would take care of us when our working days are over. However, it is our children, educated in the same school system, who will end up paying for it. The message is still to work hard, earn money and spend it, and when we run short, we can always borrow more.

Unfortunately, 90 percent of the Western world subscribes to the above dogma, simply because it's easier to find a job and work for money. If you are not one of the masses, I offer you the following ten steps to awaken your financial genius. I simply offer you the steps I have personally followed. If you want to follow some of them, great. If you don't, make up your own. Your financial genius is smart enough to develop its own list.

While in Peru, with a gold miner of 45 years, I asked him how he was so confident about finding a gold mine. He replied, "There is gold everywhere. Most people are not trained to see it."

And I would say that is true. In real estate, I can go out and in a day come up with four or five great potential deals, while the average person will go out and find nothing. Even looking in the same neighborhood. The reason is they have not taken the time to develop their financial genius.

I offer you the following ten steps as a process to develop your God-given powers. Powers only you have control over.

1. **I NEED A REASON GREATER THAN REALITY:** The power of spirit. If you ask most people if they would like to be rich or financially free, they would say "yes." But then reality sets in. The road seems too long with too many hills to climb. It's easier to just work for money and hand the excess over to your broker.

I once met a young woman who had dreams of swimming for the U.S Olympic team. The reality was, she had to get up every morning at 4 a.m. to swim for three hours before going to school. She did not party with her friends on Saturday night. She had to study and keep her grades up, just like everyone else.

When I asked her what compelled her with such super-human ambition and sacrifice, she simply said, "I do it for myself and the people I love. It's love that gets me over the hurdles and sacrifices."

A reason or a purpose is a combination of "wants" and "don't wants." When people ask me what my reason for wanting to be rich is, it is a combination of deep emotional "wants" and "don't wants."

I will list a few. First the "don't wants," for they create the "wants." I don't want to work all my life. I don't want what my parents aspired for, which was job security and a house in the suburbs. I don't like being an employee. I hated that my dad always missed my football games because he was so busy working on his career. I hated it when my dad worked hard all his life and the government took most of what he worked for at his death. He could not even pass on what he worked so hard for when he died. The rich don't do that. They work hard and pass it on to their children.

Now the wants. I want to be free to travel the world and live in the

166

lifestyle I love. I want to be young when I do this. I want to simply be free. I want control over my time and my life. I want money to work for me.

Those are my deep-seated, emotional reasons. What are yours? If they are not strong enough, then the reality of the road ahead may be greater than your reasons. I have lost money and been set back many times, but it was the deep emotional reasons that kept me standing up and going forward. I wanted to be free by age 40, but it took me until I was 47 with many learning experiences along the way.

As I said, I wish I could say it was easy. It wasn't, but it wasn't hard either. But without a strong reason or purpose, anything in life is hard.

IF YOU DO NOT HAVE A STRONG REASON, THERE IS NO SENSE READING FURTHER. IT WILL SOUND LIKE TOO MUCH WORK.

2. I CHOOSE DAILY: The power of choice. That is the main reason people want to live in a free country. We want the power to choose.

Financially, with every dollar we get in our hands, we hold the power to choose our future to be rich, poor or middle class. Our spending habits reflect who we are. Poor people simply have poor spending habits.

The benefit I had as a boy was that I loved playing Monopoly constantly. Nobody told me Monopoly was only for kids, so I just kept playing the game as an adult. I also had a rich dad who pointed out to me the difference between an asset and a liability. So a long time ago, as a little boy, I chose to be rich, and I knew that all I had to do was learn to acquire assets, real assets. My best friend, Mike, had an asset column handed to him, but he still had to choose to learn to keep it. Many rich families lose their assets in the next generation simply because there was no one trained to be a good steward over their assets.

Most people choose not to be rich. For 90 percent of the population, being rich is "too much of a hassle." So they invent sayings that go, "I'm not interested in money." Or "I'll never be rich." Or "I don't have to worry, I'm still young." Or "When I make some money, then I'll think about my future." Or "My husband/wife handles the finances." The problem with those statements is they rob the person who chooses to think such thoughts of two things: one is time, which is your most precious asset, and two is learning. Just because you have no money, it should not be an excuse to not learn. But that is a choice we all make daily, the choice of what we do with our time, our money and what we put in our heads. That is the power of choice. All of us have choice. I just choose to be rich, and I make that choice every day.

INVEST FIRST IN EDUCATION: In reality, the only real asset you have is your mind, the most powerful tool we have dominion over. Just as I said about the power of choice, each of us has the choice of what we put in our brain once we're old enough. You can watch MTV all day, or read golf magazines, or go to ceramics class or a class on financial planning. You choose. Most people simply buy investments rather than first invest in learning about investing.

A friend of mine, who is a rich woman, recently had her apartment burglarized. The thieves took her TV and VCR and left all the books she reads. And we all have that choice. Again, 90 percent of the population buys TV sets and only about 10 percent buy books on business or tapes on investments.

So what do I do? I go to seminars. I like it when they are at least two days long because I like to immerse myself in a subject. In 1973, I was watching TV and this guy came on advertising a three-day seminar on how to buy real estate for nothing down. I spent $385 and that course has made me at least $2 million, if not more. But more importantly, it bought me life. I don't have to work for the rest of my life because of that one course. I go to at least two such courses every year.

I love audio tapes. The reason: I can rewind quickly. I was listening to a tape by Peter Lynch, and he said something I completely disagreed with. Instead of becoming arrogant and critical, I simply pushed "rewind" and I listened to that five-minute stretch of tape at least twenty times. Possibly more. But suddenly, by keeping my mind open, I understood why he said what he said. It was like magic. I felt like I had a window into the mind of one of the greatest investors of our time. I gained tremendous depth and insight into the vast resources of his education and experience.

The net result: I still have the old way I used to think, and I have Peter's way of looking at the same problem or situation. I have two thoughts instead of one. One more way to analyze a problem or trend, and that is priceless. Today, I often say, "How would Peter Lynch do this, or Donald Trump or Warren Buffett or George Soros?" The only way I can access their vast mental power is to be humble enough to read or listen to what they have to say. Arrogant or critical people are often people with low self-esteem who are afraid of taking risks. You see, if you learn something new, you are then required to make mistakes in order to fully understand what you have learned.

If you have read this far, arrogance is not one of your problems. Arrogant people rarely read or buy tapes. Why should they? They are the center of the universe.

There are so many "intelligent" people who argue or defend when a new idea clashes with the way they think. In this case, their so-called "intelligence" combined with "arrogance" equals "ignorance". Each of us knows people who are highly educated, or believe they are smart, but their balance sheet paints a different picture. A truly intelligent person welcomes new ideas, for new ideas can add to the synergy of other accumulated ideas. Listening is more important than talking. If that was not true, God would not have given us two ears and only one mouth. Too many people think with their mouth instead of listening to absorb new ideas and possibilities. They argue instead of asking questions.

I take a long view on my wealth. I do not subscribe to the "Get rich quick" mentality most lottery players or casino gamblers have. I may go in and out of stocks, but I am long on education. If you want to fly an airplane, I advise taking lessons first. I am always shocked at people who buy stocks or real estate, but never invest in their greatest asset, their mind. Just because you bought a house or two does not make you an expert at real estate.

3. **CHOOSE FRIENDS CAREFULLY:** The power of association. First of all, I do not choose my friends by their financial statements. I have friends who have actually taken the vow of poverty as well as friends who earn millions every year. The point is I learn from all of them, and I consciously make the effort to learn from them.

Now I will admit that there are people I have actually sought out because they had money. But I was not after their money; I was seeking their knowledge. In some cases, these people who had money have become dear friends, but not all.

But there is one distinction that I would like to point out. I've

169

noticed that my friends with money talk about money. And I do not mean brag. They're interested in the subject. So I learn from them, and they learn from me. My friends, whom I know are in dire straits financially, do not like talking about money, business or investing. They often think it rude or unintellectual. So I also learn from my friends who struggle financially. I find out what not to do.

I have several friends who have generated over a billion dollars in their short lifetimes. The three of them report the same phenomenon: Their friends who have no money have never come to them to ask them how they did it. But they do come asking for one of two things, or both: 1. a loan, or 2. a job.

A WARNING: Don't listen to poor or frightened people. I have such friends, and I love them dearly, but they are the "Chicken Littles" of life. When it comes to money, especially investments, "The sky is always falling." They can always tell you why something won't work. The problem is, people listen to them, but people who blindly accept doom-and-gloom information are also "Chicken Littles." As that old saying goes, "Chickens of a feather agree together."

If you watch CNBC, which is a goldmine of investment information, they often have a panel of so-called "experts." One expert will say the market is going to crash, and the other will say it's going to boom. If you're smart, you listen to both. Keep your mind open because both have valid points. Unfortunately, most poor people listen to "Chicken Little."

I have had more close friends try to talk me out of a deal or an investment. A few years ago, a friend told me he was excited because he found a 6 percent certificate of deposit. I told him I earn 16 percent from the state government. The next day he sent me an article about why my investment was dangerous. I have received 16 percent for years now, and he still receives 6 percent.

I would say that one of the hardest things about wealth building is to be true to yourself and be willing to not go along with the crowd. For in the market, it is usually the crowd that shows up late and is slaughtered. If a great deal is on the front page, it's too late in most instances. Look for a new deal. As we used to say as surfers: "There is always another wave." People who hurry and catch a wave late usually are the ones who wipe out.

Smart investors don't time markets. If they miss a wave, they search for the next one and get themselves in position. Why this is hard for most investors is because buying what is not popular is frightening to them. Timid investors are like sheep going along with the crowd. Or their greed gets them in when wise investors have already taken their profits and moved on. Wise investors buy an investment when it's not popular. They know their profits are made when they buy, not when they sell. They wait patiently. As I said, they do not time the market. Just like a surfer, they get in position for the next big swell.

It's all "insider trading." There are forms of insider trading that are illegal, and there are forms of insider trading that are legal. But either way, it's insider trading. The only distinction is how far away from the inside are you? The reason you want to have rich friends who are close to the inside is because that is where the money is made. It's made on information. You want to hear about the next boom, get in and get out before the next bust. I'm not saying do it illegally, but the sooner you know, the better your chances are for profits with minimal risk. That is what friends are for. And that is financial intelligence.

4. **MASTER A FORMULA AND THEN LEARN A NEW ONE:** The power of learning quickly. In order to make bread, every baker follows a recipe, even if it's only held in their head. The same is true for making money. That's why money is often called "dough."

Most of us have heard the saying "You are what you eat." I have a different slant on the same saying. I say, "You become what you study." In other words, be careful what you study and learn, because your mind is so powerful that you become what you put in your head. For example, if you study cooking, you then tend to cook. You become a cook. If you don't want to be a cook anymore, then you need to study something else. Let's say, a schoolteacher. After studying teaching, you often become a teacher. And so on. Choose what you study carefully.

When it comes to money, the masses generally have one basic formula they learned in school. And that is, work for money. The formula I see that is predominant in the world is that every day millions of people get up and go to work, earn money, pay bills, balance checkbooks, buy some mutual funds and go back to work. That is the basic formula, or recipe.

If you're tired of what you're doing, or you're not making enough, it's simply a case of changing the formula via which you make money.

Years ago, when I was 26, I took a weekend class called "How to Buy Real Estate Foreclosures." I learned a formula. The next trick was to have the discipline to actually put into action what I had learned. That is where most people stop. For three years, while working for Xerox, I spent my spare time learning to master the art of buying foreclosures. I've made several million dollars using that formula, but today, it's too slow and too many other people are doing it.

So after I mastered that formula, I went in search of other formulas. For many of the classes, I did not use the information I learned directly, but I always learned something new.

I have attended classes designed for only derivative traders, also a class for commodity option traders and a class for Chaologists. I was way out of my league, being in a room full of people with doctorates in nuclear physics and space science. Yet, I learned a lot that made my stock and real estate investing more meaningful and lucrative.

Most junior colleges and community colleges have classes on financial planning and buying of traditional investments. They are great places to start.

So I always search for a faster formula. That is why, on a fairly regular basis, I make more in a day than many people will make in their lifetime.

Another side note. In today's fast-changing world, it's not so much what you know anymore that counts, because often what you know is old. It is how fast you learn. That skill is priceless. It's priceless in finding faster formulas—recipes, if you will, for making dough. Working hard for money is an old formula born in the day of cave men.

5. **PAY YOURSELF FIRST:** The power of self-discipline. If you cannot get control of yourself, do not try to get rich. You might first want to join the Marine Corps or some religious order so you can get control of yourself. It makes no sense to invest, make money and blow it. It is the lack of self-discipline that causes most lottery winners to go broke soon after winning millions. It is the lack of self-discipline that causes people who get a raise to immediately go out and buy a new car or take a cruise.

It is difficult to say which of the ten steps is the most important. But of all the steps, this step is probably the most difficult to master if it is not already a part of your makeup. I would venture to say that it is the lack of personal self-discipline that is the No. 1 delineating factor between the rich, the poor and the middle class.

Simply put, people who have low self-esteem and low tolerance for financial pressure can never, and I mean never, be rich. As I have said, a lesson learned from my rich dad was that "the world will push you around." The world pushes people around not because other people are bullies, but because the individual lacks internal control and discipline. People who lack internal fortitude often become victims of those who have self-discipline.

In the entrepreneur classes I teach, I constantly remind people to not focus on their product, service or widget, but to focus on developing management skills. The three most important management skills necessary to start your own business are:

1. Management of cash flow.
2. Management of people.
3. Management of personal time.

I would say, the skills to manage these three apply to anything, not just entrepreneurs. The three matter in the way you live your life as an individual, or as part of a family, a business, a charitable organization, a city or a nation.

Each of these skills is enhanced by the mastery of self discipline. I do not take the saying "pay yourself first" lightly.

The Richest Man in Babylon, by George Classen, is where the statement "pay yourself first" comes from. Millions of copies have been sold. But while millions of people freely repeat that powerful statement, few follow the advice. As I said, financial literacy allows one to read numbers, and numbers tell the story. By looking at a person's income statement and balance sheet, I can readily see if people who spout the words "pay yourself first" actually practice what they preach.

A picture is worth a thousand words. So let's again compare the financial statements of people who pay themselves first against someone who doesn't.

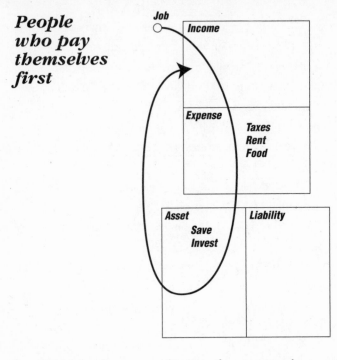

People who pay themselves first

Job

Income

Expense

Taxes
Rent
Food

Asset

Save
Invest

Liability

Study the diagrams and notice if you can pick up some distinctions. Again, it has to do with understanding cash flow, which tells the story. Most people look at the numbers and miss the story. If you can truly begin to understand the power of cash flow, you will soon realize what is wrong with the picture on the next page, or why 90 percent of most people work hard all their lives and need government support like Social Security when they are no longer able to work.

Do you see it? The diagram above reflects the actions of an individual who chooses to pay himself first. Each month, they allocate money to their asset column before they pay their monthly expenses. Although millions of people have read Classen's book and understand the words "pay yourself first," in reality they pay themselves last.

Now I can hear the howls from those of you who sincerely believe in paying your bills first. And I can hear all the "responsible" people who pay their bills on time. I am not saying be irresponsible and not pay your bills. All I am saying is do what the book says, which is "pay yourself first." And the diagram above is the correct accounting picture of that action. Not the one that follows.

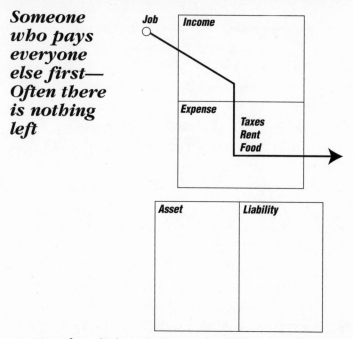

Someone who pays everyone else first— Often there is nothing left

My wife and I have had many bookkeepers and accountants and bankers who have had a major problem with this way of looking at "pay yourself first." The reason is that these financial professionals actually do what the masses do, which is pay themselves last. They pay everyone else first.

There have been months in my life, when for whatever reason, cash flow was far less than my bills. I still paid myself first. My accountant and bookkeeper screamed in panic. "They're going to come after you. The IRS is going to put you in jail." "You're going to ruin your credit rating." "They'll cut off the electricity." I still paid myself first.

"Why?" you ask. Because that's what the story *The Richest Man In Babylon* was all about. The power of self-discipline and the power of internal fortitude. "Guts," in less elegant terms. As my rich dad taught me the first month I worked for him, most people allow the world to push them around. A bill collector calls and you "pay or else." So you pay and not pay yourself. A sales clerk says, "Oh, just put it on your charge card." Your real estate agent tells you to "go ahead—the government allows you a tax deduction on your home." That is what the book is really about. Having the guts to go against the tide and get rich. You may not be weak, but when it comes to money, many people get wimpy.

I am not saying be irresponsible. The reason I don't have high credit card debt, and doodad debt, is because I want to pay myself first. The reason I minimize my income is because I don't want to pay it to the government. That is why, for those of you who have watched the video *The Secrets of the Rich*, my income comes from my asset column, through a Nevada corporation. If I work for money, the government takes it.

Although I pay my bills last, I am financially astute enough to not get into a tough financial situation. I don't like consumer debt. I actually have liabilities that are higher than 99 percent of the population, but I don't pay for them; other people pay for my liabilities. They're called tenants. So rule No. 1 in paying yourself first is don't get into debt in the first place. Although I pay my bills last, I set it up to have only small unimportant bills, that I will have to pay.

Secondly, when I occasionally come up short, I still pay myself first. I let the creditors and even the government scream. I like it when they get tough. Why? Because those guys do me a favor. They inspire me to go out and create more money. So I pay myself first, invest the money, and let the creditors yell. I generally pay them right away anyway. My wife and I have excellent credit. We just don't cave into the pressure and spend our savings or liquidate stocks to pay for consumer debt. That is not too financially intelligent.

So the answer is:

1. Don't get into large debt positions that you have to pay for. Keep your expenses low. Build up assets first. Then, buy the big house or nice car. Being stuck in the rat race is not intelligent.

2. When you come up short, let the pressure build and don't dip into your savings or investments. Use the pressure to inspire your financial genius to come up with new ways of making more money and then pay your bills. You will have increased your ability to make more money as well as your financial intelligence.

So many times I have gotten into financial hot water, and used my brain to create more income, while staunchly defending the assets in my asset column. My bookkeeper has screamed and dived for cover, but I was like a good trooper defending the fort, Fort Assets.

Poor people have poor habits. A common bad habit is innocently called "Dipping into savings." The rich know that savings are only used to create more money, not to pay bills.

I know that sounds tough, but as I said, if you're not tough inside, the world will always push you around anyway.

If you do not like financial pressure, then find a formula that works for you. A good one is to cut expenses, put your money in the bank, pay more than your fair share of income tax, buy safe mutual funds and take the vow of the average. But this violates the "pay yourself first" rule.

The rule does not encourage self-sacrifice or financial abstinence. It doesn't mean pay yourself first and starve. Life was meant to be enjoyed. If you call on your financial genius, you can have all the goodies of life, get rich and pay bills, without sacrificing the good life. And that is financial intelligence.

6. **PAY YOUR BROKERS WELL:** The power of good advice. I often see people posting a sign in front of their house that says, "For Sale by Owner." Or I see on TV today many people claiming to be "Discount Brokers."

My rich dad taught me to take the opposite tack. He believed in paying professionals well, and I have adopted that policy also. Today, I have expensive attorneys, accountants, real estate brokers and stockbrokers. Why? Because if, and I do mean if, the people are professionals, their services should make you money. And the more money they make, the more money I make.

We live in the Information Age. Information is priceless. A good broker should provide you with information as well as take the time to educate you. I have several brokers who are willing to do that for me. Some taught me when I had little or no money, and I am still with them today.

What I pay a broker is tiny in comparison with what kind of money I can make because of the information they provide. I love it when my real estate broker or stockbroker makes a lot of money. Because it usually means I made a lot of money.

A good broker saves me time in addition to making me money—as when I bought the piece of vacant land for $9,000 and sold it immediately for over $25,000, so I could buy my Porsche quicker.

A broker is your eyes and ears to the market. They're there every day so I do not have to be. I'd rather play golf.

Also, people who sell their house on their own must not value their time much. Why would I want to save a few bucks when I could use that time to make more money or spend it with those I love? What I find

177

funny is that so many poor and middle class people insist on tipping restaurant help 15 to 20 percent even for bad service and complain about paying a broker 3 to 7 percent. They enjoy tipping people in the expense column and stiffing people in the asset column. That is not financially intelligent.

All brokers are not created equal. Unfortunately, most brokers are only salespeople. I would say the real estate salespeople are the worst. They sell, but they themselves own little or no real estate. There is a tremendous difference between a broker who sells houses and a broker who sells investments. And that is true for stock, bond, mutual fund and insurance brokers who call themselves financial planners. As in the fairy tale, you kiss a lot of frogs to find one prince. Just remember the old saying, "Never ask an encyclopedia salesperson if you need an encyclopedia."

When I interview any paid professional, I first find out how much property or stocks they personally own and what percentage they pay in taxes. And that applies to my tax attorney as well as my accountant. I have an accountant who minds her own business. Her profession is accounting, but her business is real estate. I used to have an accountant that was a small business accountant, but he had no real estate. I switched because we did not love the same business.

Find a broker who has your best interests at heart. Many brokers will spend the time educating you, and they could be the best asset you find. Just be fair, and most of them will be fair to you. If all you can think about is cutting their commissions, then why should they want to be around you? It's just simple logic.

As I said earlier, one of the management skills is the management of people. Many people only manage people they feel smarter than and they have power over, such as subordinates in a work situation. Many middle managers remain middle managers, failing to get promoted because they know how to work with people below them, but not with people above them. The real skill is to manage and pay well the people who are smarter than you in some technical area. That is why companies have a board of directors. You should have one, too. And that is financial intelligence.

7. **BE AN "INDIAN GIVER":** This is the power of getting something for nothing. When the first white settlers came to America, they

were taken aback by a cultural practice some American Indians had. For example, if a settler was cold, the Indian would give the person a blanket. Mistaking it for a gift, the settler was often offended when the Indian asked for it back.

The Indians also got upset when they realized the settlers did not want to give it back. That is where the term "Indian giver" came from. A simple cultural misunderstanding.

In the world of the "asset column," being an Indian giver is vital to wealth. The sophisticated investor's first question is, "How fast do I get my money back?" They also want to know what they get for free, also called a piece of the action. That is why the ROI, or return of and on investment, is so important.

For example, I found a small condominium, a few blocks from where I live, that was in foreclosure. The bank wanted $60,000, and I submitted a bid for $50,000, which they took, simply because, along with my bid, was a cashier's check for $50,000. They realized I was serious. Most investors would say, aren't you tying up a lot of cash? Would it not be better to get a loan on it? The answer is, not in this case. My investment company uses this as a vacation rental in the winter months, when the "snowbirds" come to Arizona, and rent it for $2,500 a month for four months out of the year. For rental during the off-season, it rents for only $1,000 a month. I had my money back in about three years. Now I own this asset, which pumps money out for me, month in and month out.

The same is done with stocks. Frequently, my broker will call me and recommend I move a sizable amount of money into the stock of a company that he feels is just about to make a move that will add value to the stock, like announcing a new product. I will move my money in for a week to a month while the stock moves up. Then, I pull my initial dollar amount out, and stop worrying about the fluctuations of the market, because my initial money is back and ready to work on another asset. So my money goes in, and then it comes out, and I own an asset that was technically free.

True, I have lost money on many occasions. But I only play with money I can afford to lose. I would say, on an average ten investments, I hit home runs on two or three, while five or six do nothing, and I lose on two or three. But I limit my losses to only the money I have in at that time.

179

For people who hate risk, they put their money in the bank. And in the long run, savings are better than no savings. But it takes a long time to get your money back and, in most instances, you don't get anything for free with it. They used to hand out toasters, but they rarely do that these days.

On every one of my investments, there must be an upside, something for free. A condominium, a mini-storage, a piece of free land, a house, stock shares, office building. And there must be limited risk, or a low-risk idea. There are books devoted entirely to this subject that I will not get into here. Ray Kroc, of McDonald's fame, sold hamburger franchises, not because he loved hamburgers, but because he wanted the real estate under the franchise for free.

So wise investors must look at more than ROI; it's the assets you get for free once you get your money back. That is financial intelligence.

8. **ASSETS BUY LUXURIES:** The power of focus. A friend's child has been developing a nasty habit of burning a hole in his pocket. Just 16, he naturally wanted his own car. The excuse, "All his friends' parents gave their kids cars." The child wanted to go into his savings and use it for a down payment. That was when his father called me.

"Do you think I should let him do it, or should I just do as other parents do and just buy him a car?"

To which I answered. "It might relieve the pressure in the short term, but what have you taught him in the long term? Can you use this desire to own a car and inspire your son to learn something?" Suddenly the lights went on, and he hurried home.

Two months later I ran into my friend again. "Does your son have his new car?" I asked.

"No, he doesn't. But I went and handed him $3,000 for the car. I told him to use my money instead of his college money."

"Well, that's generous of you," I said.

"Not really. The money came with a hitch. I took your advice of using his strong desire to buy a car and use that energy so he could learn something."

"So what was the hitch?" I asked.

"Well, first we broke out your game again, *CASHFLOW*. We played it

180

and had a long discussion about the wise use of money. I then gave him a subscription to the Wall Street Journal, and a few books on the stock market."

"Then what?" I asked. "What was the catch?"

"I told him the $3,000 was his, but he could not directly buy a car with it. He could use it to buy and sell stocks, find his own stockbroker, and once he had made $6,000 with the $3,000, the money would be his for the car, and the $3,000 would go into his college fund."

"And what are the results?" I asked.

"Well, he got lucky early in his trading, but lost all he gained a few days later. Then, he really got interested. Today, I would say he is down $2,000, but his interest is up. He has read all the books I bought him and he's gone to the library to get more. He reads the Wall Street Journal voraciously, watching for indicators, and he watches CNBC instead of MTV. He's got only $1,000 left, but his interest and learning are sky high. He knows that if he loses that money, he walks for two more years. But he does not seem to care. He even seems uninterested in getting a car because he's found a game that is more fun."

"What happens if he loses all the money?" I asked.

"We'll cross that bridge when we get to it. I'd rather have him lose everything now rather than wait till he's our age to risk losing everything. And besides, that is the best $3,000 I've ever spent on his education. What he is learning will serve him for life, and he seems to have gained a new respect for the power of money. I think he's stopped the burning of holes in his pockets."

As I said in the section "Pay Yourself First," if a person cannot master the power of self-discipline, it is best not to try to get rich. For while the process of developing cash flow from an asset column in theory is easy, it is the mental fortitude of directing money that is hard. Due to external temptations, it is much easier in today's consumer world to simply blow it out the expense column. Because of weak mental fortitude, that money flows into the paths of least resistance. That is the cause of poverty and financial struggle.

I gave this numerical example of financial intelligence, in this case the ability to direct money to make more money.

If we gave 100 people $10,000 at the start of the year, I gave my opinion that at the end of the year:

- 80 would have nothing left. In fact, many would have created greater debt by making a down payment on a new car, refrigerator, TV, VCR or a holiday.
- 16 would have increased that $10,000 by 5 percent to 10 percent.
- 4 would have increased it to $20,000 or into the millions.

We go to school to learn a profession so we can work for money. It is my opinion that it is also important to learn how to have money work for you.

I love my luxuries as much as anyone else. The difference is, some people buy their luxuries on credit. It's the keep-up-with-the-Joneses trap. When I wanted to buy a Porsche, the easy road would have been to call my banker and get a loan. Instead of choosing to focus in the liability column, I chose to focus in the asset column.

As a habit, I used my desire to consume to inspire and motivate my financial genius to invest.

Too often today, we focus to borrowing money to get the things we want instead of focusing on creating money. One is easier in the short term, but harder in the long term. It's a bad habit that we as individuals and as a nation have gotten into. Remember, the easy road often becomes hard, and the hard road often becomes easy.

The earlier you can train yourself and those you love to be masters of money, the better. Money is a powerful force. Unfortunately, people use the power of money against them. If your financial intelligence is low, money will run all over you. It will be smarter than you. If money is smarter than you, you will work for it all your life.

To be the master of money, you need to be smarter than it. Then money will do as it is told. It will obey you. Instead of being a slave to it, you will be the master of it. That is financial intelligence.

9. **THE NEED FOR HEROES:** The power of myth. When I was a kid, I greatly admired Willie Mays, Hank Aaron, Yogi Berra. They were my heroes. As a kid playing Little League, I wanted to be just like them. I treasured their baseball cards. I wanted to know everything about them. I knew the stats, the RBI, the ERAs, their batting averages, how much they got paid, and how they came up from the minors. I wanted to know everything because I wanted to be just like them.

Every time, as a 9 or 10 year-old kid, when I stepped up to bat or played first base or catcher, I wasn't me. I was Yogi or Hank. It's one of the most powerful ways we learn that we often lose as adults. We lose our heroes. We lose our naiveté.

Today, I watch young kids playing basketball near my home. On the court they're not little Johnny; they're Michael Jordan, Sir Charles or Clyde. Copying or emulating heroes is true power learning. And that is why when someone like O.J. Simpson falls from grace, there is such a huge outcry.

There is more than just a courtroom trial. It is the loss of a hero. Someone people grew up with, looked up to, and wanted to be like. Suddenly we need to rid ourselves of that person.

I have new heroes as I grow older. I have golf heroes such as Peter Jacobsen, Fred Couples and Tiger Woods. I copy their swings and do my best to read everything I can about them. I also have heroes such as Donald Trump, Warren Buffett, Peter Lynch, George Soros and Jim Rogers. In my older years, I know their stats just like I knew the ERAs and RBI of my baseball heroes. I follow what Warren Buffett invests in, and read anything I can about his point of view on the market. I read Peter Lynch's book to understand how he chooses stocks. And I read about Donald Trump, trying to find out how he negotiates and puts deals together.

Just as I was not me when I was up to bat, when I'm in the market or I'm negotiating a deal, I am subconsciously acting with the bravado of Trump. Or when analyzing a trend, I look at it as though Peter Lynch were doing it. By having heroes, we tap into a tremendous source of raw genius.

But heroes do more than simply inspire us. Heroes make things look easy. It's the making it look easy that convinces us to want to be just like them. "If they can do it, so can I."

When it comes to investing, too many people make it sound hard. Instead find heroes who make it look easy.

10. **TEACH AND YOU SHALL RECEIVE:** The power of giving. Both of my dads were teachers. My rich dad taught me a lesson I have carried all my life, and that was the necessity of being charitable or giving. My educated dad gave a lot by the way of time and knowledge, but almost never gave away money. As I

said, he usually said that he would give when he had some extra money. Of course, there was rarely any extra.

My rich dad gave money as well as education. He believed firmly in tithing. "If you want something, you first need to give," he would always say. When he was short of money, he simply gave money to his church or to his favorite charity.

If I could leave one single idea with you, it is that idea. Whenever you feel "short" or in "need" of something, give what you want first and it will come back in buckets. That is true for money, a smile, love, friendship. I know it is often the last thing a person may want to do, but it has always worked for me. I just trust that the principle of reciprocity is true, and I give what I want. I want money, so I give money, and it comes back in multiples. I want sales, so I help someone else sell something, and sales come to me. I want contacts and I help someone else get contacts, and like magic, contacts come to me. I heard a saying years ago that went, "God does not need to receive, but humans need to give."

My rich dad would often say, "Poor people are more greedy than rich people." He would explain that if a person was rich, that person was providing something that other people wanted. In my life, over all these years, whenever I have felt needy or short of money or short of help, I simply went out or found in my heart what I wanted, and decided to give it first. And when I gave, it always came back.

It reminds me of the story of the guy sitting with firewood in his arms on a cold freezing night, and he is yelling at the pot-bellied stove, "When you give me some heat, then I'll put some wood in." And when it comes to money, love, happiness, sales and contacts, all one needs to remember is first to give what you want and it will come back in droves. Often just the process of thinking of what I want, and how could I give what I want to someone else, breaks free a torrent of bounty. Whenever I feel that people aren't smiling at me, I simply begin smiling and saying hello, and like magic, there are suddenly more smiling people around me. It is true that your world is only a mirror of you.

So that's why I say, "Teach and you shall receive." I have found that the more I sincerely teach those who want to learn, the more I learn. If you want to learn about money, teach it to someone else. A torrent of new ideas and finer distinctions will come in.

There are times when I have given and nothing has come back or what I have received is not what I wanted. But upon closer inspection and soul searching, I was often giving to receive in those instances, instead of giving to give.

My dad taught teachers, and he became a master teacher. My rich dad always taught young people his way of doing business. In retrospect, it was their generosity with what they knew that made them smarter. There are powers in this world that are much smarter than we are. You can get there on your own, but it's easier with the help of the powers that be. All you need to be is generous with what you have, and the powers will be generous with you.

CHAPTER TEN

Still Want More? Here are Some To Do's

*M*any people may not be satisfied with my ten steps. They see them more as philosophies than actions. I think understanding the philosophy is just as important as the action. There are many people who want to do, instead of think, and then there are people who think but do not do. I would say that I am both. I love new ideas and I love action.

So for those who want "to dos" on how to get started, I will share with you some of the things I do, in abbreviated form.

- Stop doing what you're doing. In other words, take a break and assess what is working and what is not working. The definition of insanity is doing the same thing and expecting a different result. Stop doing what is not working and look for something new to do.
- Look for new ideas. For new investing ideas, I go to bookstores and look for books on different and unique subjects. I call them formulas. I buy how-to books on a formula I know nothing about. For example, it was in the bookstore that I found the book *The 16 Percent Solution*, by Joel Moskowitz. I bought the book and read it.

TAKE ACTION! The next Thursday, I did exactly as the book said. Step by step. I have also done that with finding real estate bargains in attorneys' offices and in banks. Most people do not take action, or they let someone talk them out of whatever new formula they are studying. My neighbor told me why 16 percent would not work. I did not listen to him because he's never done it.

- Find someone who has done what you want to do. Take them to lunch. Ask them for tips, for little tricks of the trade. As for 16 percent tax lien certificates, I went to the county tax office and found the government employee who worked in the office. I found out that she, too, invested in the tax liens. Immediately, she was invited to lunch. She was thrilled to tell me everything she knew and how to do it. After lunch, she spent all afternoon showing me everything. By the next day, I found two great properties with her help and have been accruing interest at 16 percent ever since. It took a day to read the book, a day to take action, an hour for lunch, and a day to acquire two great deals.
- Take classes and buy tapes. I search the newspapers for new and interesting classes. Many are for free or a small fee. I also attend and pay for expensive seminars on what I want to learn. I am wealthy and free from needing a job simply because of the courses I took. I have friends who did not take those classes who told me I was wasting my money, and yet they're still at the same job.
- Make lots of offers. When I want a piece of real estate, I look at many properties and generally write an offer. If you don't know what the "right offer" is, neither do I. That is the job of the real estate agent. They make the offers. I do as little work as possible.

A friend wanted me to show her how to buy apartment houses. So one Saturday she, her agent and I went and looked at six apartment houses. Four were dogs, but two were good. I said to write offers on all six, offering half of what the owners asked for. She and the agent nearly had heart attacks. They thought it would be rude, that I might offend the sellers, but I really don't think the agent wanted to work that hard. So they did nothing and went on looking for a better deal.

No offers were ever made, and that person is still looking for the "right" deal at the right price. Well, you don't know what the right price is until you have a second party who wants to deal. Most sellers ask too much. It is rare that a seller will actually ask a price that is less than something is worth.

Moral of the story: Make offers. People who are not investors have no idea what it feels like to be trying to sell something. I have had a piece of real estate that I wanted to sell for months. I would have welcomed anything. I would not care how low the price. They could have offered me ten pigs and I would have been happy. Not at the offer, but just because someone was interested. I would have countered, maybe for a pig farm in exchange. But that's how the game works. The game of buying and selling is fun. Keep that in mind. It's fun and only a game. Make offers. Someone might say "yes."

And I always make offers with escape clauses. In real estate, I make an offer with the words "subject to approval of business partner." I never specify who the business partner is. Most people do not know my partner is my cat. If they accept the offer, and I don't want the deal, I call my home and speak to my cat. I make this absurd statement to illustrate how absurdly easy and simple the game is. So many people make things too difficult and take them too seriously.

Finding a good deal, the right business, the right people, the right investors, or whatever is just like dating. You must go to the market and talk to a lot of people, make a lot of offers, counteroffers, negotiate, reject and accept. I know single people who sit at home and wait for the phone to ring, but unless you're Cindy Crawford or Tom Cruise, I think you'd best go to the market, even if it's only the supermarket. Search, offer, reject, negotiate and accept are all parts of the process of almost everything in life.

- Jog, walk or drive a certain area once a month for ten minutes. I have found some of my best real estate investments while jogging. I will jog a certain neighborhood for a year. What I look for is change. For there to be profit in a deal, there must be two elements: a bargain and change. There are lots of bargains, but it's change that turns a bargain into a profitable opportunity. So when I jog, I jog a neighborhood I might like to invest in. It is the repetition that causes me to notice slight differences. I notice real estate signs that are up for a long time. That means the seller might be more agreeable to deal. I watch for moving trucks, going

189

in or out. I stop and talk to the drivers. I talk to the postal carriers. It's amazing how much information they acquire about an area.

I find a bad area, especially an area that the news has scared everyone away from. I drive it for sometimes a year waiting for signs of something changing for the better. I talk to retailers, especially new ones, and find out why they're moving in. It takes only a few minutes a month, and I do it while doing something else, like exercising, or going to and from the store.

- As for stocks, I like Peter Lynch's book *Beating the Street* for his formula for selecting stocks that grow in value. I have found that the principles of finding value are the same regardless if it's real estate, stocks, mutual funds, new companies, a new pet, a new home, a new spouse, or a bargain on laundry detergent.

The process is always the same. You need to know what you're looking for and then go look for it!

- Why consumers will always be poor. When the supermarket has a sale on, say, toilet paper, the consumer runs in and stocks up. When the stock market has a sale, most often called a crash or correction, the consumer runs away from it. When the supermarket raises its prices, the consumer shops elsewhere. When the stock market raises its prices, the consumer starts buying.

- Look in the right places. A neighbor bought a condominium for $100,000. I bought the identical condo next door to his for $50,000. He told me he's waiting for the price to go up. I told him that his profit is made when you buy, not when you sell. He shopped with a real estate broker who owns no property of her own. I shopped at the foreclosure department of a bank. I paid $500 for a class on how to do this. My neighbor thought that the $500 for a real estate investment class was too expensive. He said he could not afford it, and he couldn't afford the time. So he waits for the price to go up.

- I look for people who want to buy first, then I look for someone who wants to sell. A friend was looking for a certain piece of land. He had the money and did not have the time. I found a large piece of land larger than what my friend wanted to buy, tied it up with an option, called my friend and he wanted a piece of it. So I sold the piece to him and then bought the land. I kept the remaining land as mine for free. Moral of the story: Buy the pie and cut it in pieces. Most people look for what they can afford, so they look too small. They buy only a piece of the pie, so they end up paying more for less. Small thinkers don't get the big breaks. If you want to get richer, think bigger first.

Retailers love giving volume discounts, simply because most business people love big spenders. So even if you're small, you can always think big. When my company was in the market for computers, I called several friends and asked them if they were ready to buy also. We then went to different dealers and negotiated a great deal because we wanted to buy so many. I have done the same with stocks. Small people remain small because they think small; act alone, or don't act all.

- Learn from history. All the big companies on the stock exchange started out as small companies. Colonel Sanders did not get rich until after he lost everything in his 60s. Bill Gates was one of the richest men in the world before he was 30.
- Action always beats inaction.

These are just a few of the things I have done and continue to do to recognize opportunities. The important words being "done" and "do". As repeated many times throughout the book, you must take action before you can receive the financial rewards. Act now!

How To Pay for a Child's College Education for Only $7,000

As the book draws to a close and approaches publication, I would like to share a final thought with you.

The main reason I wrote this book was to share insights into how increased financial intelligence can be used to solve many of life's common problems. Without financial training, we all too often use the standard formulas to get through life, such as to work hard, save, borrow and pay excessive taxes. Today we need better information.

I use the following story as a final example of a financial problem that confronts many young families today. How do you afford a good education for your children and provide for your own retirement? It is an example of using financial intelligence instead of hard work to achieve the same goal.

A friend of mine was griping one day about how hard it was to save money for his four children's college education. He was putting $300 away in a mutual fund each month and had so far accumulated about

$12,000. He estimated he needed $400,000 to get four children through college. He had 12 years to save for it, since his oldest child was then 6 years of age.

The year was 1991, and the real estate market in Phoenix was terrible. People were giving houses away. I suggested to my classmate that he buy a house with some of the money in his mutual fund. The idea intrigued him and we began to discuss the possibility. His primary concern was that he did not have the credit with the bank to buy another house, since he was so over-extended. I assured him that there were other ways to finance a property other than through the bank.

We looked for a house for two weeks, a house that would fit all the criteria we were looking for. There were a lot to choose from, so the shopping was kind of fun. Finally, we found a 3 bedroom 2 bath home in a prime neighborhood. The owner had been downsized and needed to sell that day because he and his family were moving to California where another job waited.

He wanted $102,000, but we offered only $79,000. He took it immediately. The home had on it what is called a non-qualifying loan, which means even a bum without a job could buy it without a banker's approval. The owner owed $72,000 so all my friend had to come up with was $7,000, the difference in price between what was owed and what it sold for. As soon as the owner moved, my friend put the house up for rent. After all expenses were paid, including the mortgage, he put about $125 in his pocket each month.

His plan was to keep the house for 12 years and let the mortgage get paid down faster, by applying the extra $125 to the principle each month. We figured that in 12 years, a large portion of the mortgage would be paid off and he could possibly be clearing $800 a month by the time his first child went to college. He could also sell the house if it had appreciated in value.

In 1994, the real estate market suddenly changed in Phoenix and he was offered $156,000 for the same house by the tenant who lived in it and loved it. Again, he asked me what I thought, and I naturally said sell, on a 1031 tax-deferred exchange.

Suddenly, he had nearly $80,000 to operate with. I called another friend in Austin, Texas who then moved this tax deferred money into a mini-storage facility. Within three months, he began receiving checks for a little less than a $1,000 a month in income which he then poured back into the college mutual fund that was now building much faster. In 1996, the mini-warehouse sold and he received a check for nearly $330,000 as proceeds from the sale which was again rolled into a new project that would now throw off over $3,000 a month in income, again, going into the college mutual fund. He is now very confident that his goal of $400,000 will be met easily, and it only took $7,000 to start and a little financial intelligence. His children will be able to afford the education that they want and he will then use the underlying asset, wrapped in his C Corporation, to pay for his retirement. As a result of this successful investment strategy he will be able to retire early.

Thank you for reading this book. I hope it has provided some insights into utilizing the power of money to work for you. Today, we need greater financial intelligence to simply survive. The idea that it takes money to make money is the thinking of financially unsophisticated people. It does not mean that they're not intelligent. They have simply not learned the science of making money.

Money is only an idea. If you want more money simply change your thinking. Every self-made person started small with an idea, then turned it into something big. The same applies with investing. It takes only a few dollars to start and grow it into something big. I meet so many people who spend their lives chasing the big deal, or trying to mass a lot of money to get into a big deal, but to me that is foolish. Too often I have seen unsophisticated investors put their large nest egg into one deal and lose most of it rapidly. They may have been good workers but they were not good investors.

Education and wisdom about money are important. Start early. Buy a book. Go to a seminar. Practice. Start small. I turned $5,000 cash into a $1 million dollar asset producing $5,000 a month cash flow in less than six years. But I started learning as a kid. I encourage you to learn because it's not that hard. In fact, it's kind of easy once you get the hang of it.

I think I have made my message clear. It's what is in your head that determines what is in your hands. Money is only an idea. There is a great book called *Think and Grow Rich*. The title is not Work Hard and Grow Rich. Learn to have money work hard for you and your life will be easier and happier. Today, don't play it safe, play it smart.

Rich Dad's Guide to Financial Freedom

By Robert T. Kiyosaki
with Sharon L. Lechter C.P.A.

BUSINESS PLUS

NEW YORK   BOSTON

"Man is born free;
and everywhere he is in chains.
One thinks himself the master of others,
and still remains a greater slave than they."

Jean Jacques Rousseau

My rich dad used to say, "You can never
have true freedom without financial freedom."
He would go on to say, "Freedom may be free,
but it has a price." This book is dedicated to
those people willing to pay the price.

To Our Friends,

The phenomenal success of *Rich Dad Poor Dad* has brought us thousands of new friends all over the world. Their kind words and friendship inspired us to write *The CASHFLOW Quadrant* which, in reality, is a continuation of *Rich Dad Poor Dad.*

So to our friends, old and new, for their enthusiastic support beyond our wildest dreams, we say thank you.

Table of Contents

Which Quadrant Are You In? Is It The Right One For You?

Are you financially free? *The CASHFLOW Quadrant* was written for you if your life has come to a financial fork in the road. If you want to take control of what you do today in order to change your financial destiny it will help you chart your course. This is the *CASHFLOW Quadrant*:

The letters in each quadrant represent:

    E   for employee
    S   for self-employed
    B   for business owner
    I   for investor

Each of us resides in at least one of the four quadrants of the *CASHFLOW Quadrant*. Where we are is determined by where our cash comes from. Many of us rely on paychecks and are therefore employees, while others are self-employed. Employees and self-employed individuals reside on the left side of the *CASHFLOW Quadrant*. The right side of the *CASHFLOW Quadrant* is for individuals who receive their cash from businesses they own or investments they own.

The CASHFLOW Quadrant is about the four different types of people who make up the world of business, who they are and what makes individuals in each quadrant unique. It will help you define where you are in the *Quadrant* today and help you chart a course for where you want to be in the future as you choose your own path to financial freedom. While financial freedom can be found in all four of the quadrants, the skills of a "B" or "I" will help you reach your financial goals more quickly. A successful "E" should also become a successful "I".

WHAT DO YOU WANT TO BE WHEN YOU GROW UP?

This book is in many ways Part II of my book, *Rich Dad Poor Dad*. For those of you who may not have read *Rich Dad Poor Dad*, it was about the different lessons my two dads taught me about the subject of money and life choices. One was my real dad and the other my best friend's dad. One was highly educated and the other a high school drop out. One was poor and the other rich.

Whenever I was asked the question, "What do you want to be when you grow up?"

My highly educated but poor dad always recommended,

"Go to school, get good grades, and then find a safe secure job."

He was recommending a life's path that looked like this.

SCHOOL

Poor Dad's Advice

Poor dad was recommending that I choose to become either a high paid "E", employee, or a high paid "S", self employed professional, such as a medical doctor, lawyer, or accountant. My poor dad was very concerned about a steady paycheck, benefits, and job security. That is why he was a high paid government official; the head of education for the State of Hawaii.

My rich, but uneducated dad, on the other hand, offered very different advice. He recommended,

"Go to school, graduate, build businesses and become a successful investor."

He was recommending a life's path that looked like this.

Rich Dad's Advice

SCHOOL

This book is about the mental, emotional, and educational process I went through in following my rich dad's advice.

WHO THIS BOOK IS FOR

This book is written for people who are ready to change quadrants. This book is especially for individuals who are currently in the "E" and "S" categories and are contemplating becoming "B's" or "I's". It is for people who are ready to move beyond job security and begin to achieve financial security. It is not an easy life's path but the prize at the end of the journey is worth the journey. It is the journey to financial freedom.

Rich dad told me a simple story when I was 12 years old that has guided me to great wealth and financial freedom. It was rich dad's way of explaining the difference between the left side of the *CASHFLOW Quadrant*, the "E" and "S" quadrants, from the right side or the "B" and "I" quadrants. It goes:

"Once upon a time there was this quaint little village. It was a great place to live except for one problem. The village had no water unless it rained. To solve this problem once and for all, the village elders decided to put out to bid the contract to have water delivered to the village on a daily basis. Two people volunteered to take on the task and the elders awarded the contract to both of them. They felt that a little competition would keep prices low and insure a back up supply of water.

The first of the two people who won the contract, Ed, immediately ran out, bought two galvanized steel buckets and began running back and forth along the trail to the lake which was a mile away. He immediately began making money as he labored morning to dusk hauling water from the lake with his two buckets. He would empty them into the large concrete holding tank the village had built. Each morning he had to get up before the rest of the village awoke to make sure there was enough water for the village when it wanted it. It was hard work, but he was very happy to be making money and for having one of the two exclusive contracts for this business.

The second winning contractor, Bill, disappeared for a while. He was not seen for months, which made Ed very happy since he had no competition. Ed was making all the money.

Instead of buying two buckets to compete with Ed, Bill had written a business plan, created a corporation, found four investors, employed a president to do the work, and returned six months later with a construction crew. Within a year his team had built a large volume stainless steel pipeline which connected the village to the lake.

At the grand opening celebration, Bill announced that his water was cleaner than Ed's water. Bill knew that there had been complaints about dirt in Ed's water. Bill also announced that he could supply the village with water 24 hours a day, 7 days a week. Ed could only deliver water on the weekdays...he did not work on weekends. Then Bill announced that he would charge 75% less than Ed did for this higher quality and more reliable source of water. The village cheered and ran immediately for the faucet at the end of Bill's pipeline.

In order to compete, Ed immediately lowered his rates by 75%, bought two more buckets, added covers to his buckets and began hauling four buckets each trip. In order to provide better service, he hired his two sons to give him a hand for the night shift and on weekends. When his boys went off to college, he said to them,

'Hurry back because someday this business will belong to you.'

For some reason, after college, his two sons never returned. Eventually Ed had employees and union problems. The union was demanding higher wages, better benefits, and wanted its members to only haul one bucket at a time.

Bill, on the other hand, realized that if this village needed water then other villages must need water too. He rewrote his business plan and went off to sell his high speed, high volume, low cost, and clean water delivery system to villages throughout the world. He only makes a penny per bucket of water delivered, but he delivers billions of buckets of water everyday. Regardless if he works or not, billions of people consume billions of buckets of water, and all that money pours into his bank account. Bill had developed a pipeline to deliver money to himself as well as water to the villages.

Bill lived happily ever after and Ed worked hard for the rest of his life and had financial problems forever after. The end."

That story about Bill and Ed has guided me for years. It has assisted me in my life's decision making process. I often ask myself,

"Am I building a pipeline or hauling buckets?"

"Am I working hard or am I working smart?"

And the answers to those questions have made me financially free.

And that is what this book is about. It is about what it takes to become a "B" and an "I". It is for people who are tired of hauling buckets and are ready to build pipelines for cash to flow into their pockets... not out of their pockets.

This book is divided into three parts.

Part One: The first part of this book is about the core differences between people in the four quadrants. It is about why certain people gravitate to certain quadrants and often get stuck there without realizing it. It will help you identify where you are today in the *Quadrant* and where you want to be in five years.

Part Two: The second part of this book is about personal change. It is more about "who" you have to be instead of what you have to do.

Part Three: The third part of this book defines seven steps you can take on your path to the right side of the *Quadrant*. I will share more of my rich dad's secrets on the skills required to be a successful "B" and "I". It will help you choose your own path to financial freedom.

Throughout *The CASHFLOW Quadrant* I continue to stress the importance of financial intelligence. If you want to operate on the right side of the quadrant, the "B" and "I" side, a person needs to be smarter than if you choose to stay on the left side as an "E" or "S".

To be a "B" or "I", you must be able to control the direction your cash flow is flowing. This book is written for people who are ready to make changes in their lives. It is written for people who are ready to move beyond job security and begin to build their own pipelines to achieve financial freedom.

We are in the dawning of the Information Age and this age will offer more opportunities than ever before for financial reward. It will be individuals with the skills of the "B's" and "I's" who will be able to identify and seize those opportunities. To be successful in the Information Age, a person will need information from all four quadrants. Unfortunately, our schools are still in the Industrial Age and still prepare students for only the left side of the *Quadrant.*

If you are looking for new answers to move forward into the Information Age, then this book is written for you. It is written to assist you in your journey into the Information Age. It does not have all the answers...but it will share the deep personal and guiding insights I gained as I traveled from the "E" and "S" side of the *CASHFLOW Quadrant*, to the "B" and "I" side.

If you are ready to begin your journey or are already on your journey to financial freedom this book is written for you.

As my way of saying "Thank You" for reading this book and increasing your knowledge about money and business, I make available to you a special audio report entitled,

"What My Rich Dad Taught Me About Investing."

It is an educational tape that offers further insights into what my rich dad taught me about investing. It is offered to further enhance your education and explain why we create our educational products for people like you. With a retail value of $19.95 we offer this tape as a gift to you.

This tape does not discuss what I call "Middle Class" investment strategies... especially those heavily dependent upon mutual funds. In fact you will find out why many rich people don't buy mutual funds. As with all our products, we do our best to provide distinctions between how the rich, the poor, and the middle class think... and then leave the choice up to you as to which way you want to think. After all, one of the benefits of living in a free society is that we all have the choice to be rich, poor, or middle class. That decision is up to you, regardless of which class you are in today.

All you have to do to get this audio report is visit our special website at www.richdadbook2.com and the report is yours free.

Thank you

CHAPTER ONE

"Why Don't You Get A Job?"

In 1985, my wife, Kim, and I were homeless. We were unemployed and had little money left from our savings; our credit cards were exhausted; and we lived in an old brown Toyota with reclining seats that served as beds. At the end of one week, the harsh reality of who we were, what we were doing, and where we were headed began to sink in.

Our homelessness lasted for another two weeks. A friend, when she realized our desperate financial situation, offered us a room in her basement. We lived there for nine months.

We kept our situation quiet. For the most part, my wife and I looked quite normal on the surface. When friends and family were informed of our plight, the first question was always, "Why don't you get a job?"

At first we attempted to explain, but in most instances, we failed to clarify our reasons. To someone who values a job, it is difficult to explain why you might not want a job.

Occasionally, we did a few odd jobs and earned a few dollars here and there. But we did that only to keep food in our stomachs and gas in the car. Those few extra dollars were only fuel to keep us going toward our singular goal. I must admit that during moments of deep personal doubt, the idea of a safe, secure job with a paycheck was appealing. But because job security was not what we were looking for, we kept pushing on, living day to day, on the brink of the financial abyss.

That year, 1985, was the worst of our lives, as well as one of the longest. Anyone who says that money isn't important obviously has not been without it for long. Kim and I fought and argued often. Fear, uncertainty and hunger shortens the human emotional fuse, and often we fight with the person who loves us the most. Yet, love held the two of us together and our bond as a couple grew stronger because of the adversity. We knew where we were going; we just did not know if we would ever get there.

We knew we could always find a safe, secure, high-paying job. Both of us were college graduates with good job skills and solid work ethics. But we were not going for job security. We were going for financial freedom.

By 1989, we were millionaires. Although financially successful in some people's eyes, we still had not reached our dreams. We had not yet achieved true financial freedom. That took until 1994. By then, we never had to work again for the rest of our lives. Barring any unforeseen financial disaster, we were both financially free. Kim was 37, and I was 47.

IT DOESN'T TAKE MONEY TO MAKE MONEY

I started this book about being homeless and having nothing because I often hear people say, "It takes money to make money."

I disagree. To get from homeless in 1985 to rich in 1989 and then to become financially free by 1994 did not take money. We had no money when we started, and we were in debt.

It also does not take a good formal education. I have a college degree, and I can honestly say that achieving financial freedom had nothing to do with what I learned in college. I did not find much call for my years of studying calculus, spherical trigonometry, chemistry, physics, French, and English literature.

Many successful people have left school without receiving a college degree. People such as Thomas Edison, founder of General Electric; Henry Ford, founder of Ford Motor Co.; Bill Gates, founder of Microsoft; Ted Turner, founder of CNN; Michael Dell, founder of Dell Computers; Steve Jobs, founder of Apple Computer; and Ralph Lauren, founder of Polo. A college education is important for traditional professions, but not for how these people found great wealth. They developed their own successful businesses and that was what Kim and I were striving for.

SO WHAT DOES IT TAKE?

I am often asked, "If it doesn't take money to make money, and schools do not teach you how to become financially free, then what does it take?

My answer: It takes a dream, a lot of determination, a willingness to learn quickly, and the ability to use your God-given assets properly and to know which sector of the *CASHFLOW Quadrant* to generate your income from.

WHAT IS THE CASHFLOW QUADRANT?

The diagram below is the *CASHFLOW Quadrant*.

The letters in each quadrant represent:

E   for employee
S   for self-employed
B   for business owner
I   for investor

WHICH QUADRANT DO YOU GENERATE YOUR INCOME FROM?

The *CASHFLOW Quadrant* represents the different methods by which income or money is generated. For example, an employee earns money by holding a job and working for someone else or a company. Self-employed people earn money working for themselves. A business owner owns a business that generates money, and investors earn money from their various investments-in other words, money generating more money.

Different methods of income generation require different frames of mind, different technical skills, different educational paths, and different types of people. Different people are attracted to different quadrants.

While money is all the same, the way it is earned can be vastly different. If you begin to look at the four different labels for each quadrant, you might want to ask yourself, "Which quadrant do you generate the majority of your income from?"

Each quadrant is different. To generate income from different quadrants requires different skills and a different personality, even if the person found in each quadrant is the same. Changing from quadrant to quadrant is like playing golf in the morning and then attending the ballet at night.

YOU CAN EARN INCOME IN ALL FOUR QUADRANTS

Most of us have the potential to generate income from all four quadrants. Which quadrant you or I choose to earn our primary income from is not so much what we learned in school; it is more about who we are at the core-our core values, strengths, weaknesses and interests. It is these core differences that attract us to or repel us from the four quadrants.

Yet, regardless of what we "do" professionally, we can still work in all four quadrants. For example, a medical doctor could choose to earn income as an "E," an employee, and join the staff of a large hospital, or work for the government in the public-health service, or become a military doctor, or join the staff of an insurance company needing a doctor on its staff.

This same doctor could also decide to earn income as an "S," a self-employed person, and start a private practice, setting up an office, hiring staff and building a private list of clients.

Or the doctor could decide to become a "B" and own a clinic or laboratory and have other doctors on staff. This doctor probably would hire a business manager to run the organization. In this case, the doctor would own the business, but not have to work in it. The doctor also could decide to own a business that has nothing to do with the medical field, while still practicing medicine somewhere else. In this case, the doctor would be earning income as both an "E" and as a "B."

As an "I," the doctor also could generate income from being an investor in someone else's business or in vehicles like the stock market, bond market and real estate.

The important words are "generate income from." It is not so much what we do, but more how we generate income.

DIFFERENT METHODS OF INCOME GENERATION

More than anything, it is the internal differences of our core values, strengths, weaknesses and interests that affect which quadrant we decide to generate our income from. Some people love being employees, while others hate it. Some people love owning companies, but do not want to run them. Others love owning companies and also love running them. Certain people love investing, while others only see the risk of losing money. Most of us are a little of each of these characters. Being successful in the four quadrants often means redirecting some internal core values.

YOU CAN BE RICH OR POOR IN ALL FOUR QUADRANTS

It also is important to note that you can be rich or poor in all four quadrants. There are people who earn millions and people who go bankrupt in each of the quadrants. Being in one quadrant or the other does not necessarily guarantee financial success.

NOT ALL QUADRANTS ARE EQUAL

By knowing the different features of each quadrant, you'll have a better idea as to which quadrant, or quadrants, might be best for you.

For example, one of the many reasons I chose to work predominantly in the "B" and "I" quadrants is because of tax advantages. For most people working on the left side of the *Quadrant*, there are few legal tax breaks available. Yet, legal tax breaks abound on the right side of the *Quadrant*. By working to generate income in the "B" and "I" quadrants, I could acquire money faster and keep that money working for me longer, without losing large chunks to pay taxes.

DIFFERENT WAYS OF EARNING MONEY

When people ask why Kim and I were homeless, I tell them it was because of what my rich dad taught me about money. For me, money is important, yet I did not want to spend my life working for it. That is why I did not want a job. If we were going to be responsible citizens, Kim and I wanted to have our money work for us rather than spend our lives physically working for money.

That is why the *CASHFLOW Quadrant* is important. It distinguishes between the different ways in which money is generated. There are ways of being responsible and creating money, other than physically working for it.

DIFFERENT FATHERS-DIFFERENT IDEAS ABOUT MONEY

My highly educated dad had a strong belief that the love of money was evil. That to profit excessively meant you were greedy. He felt embarrassed when the newspapers published how much he made, because he felt he was too highly paid when compared with the schoolteachers who worked for him. He was a good, honest, hard working man who did his best to defend his point of view that money was not important to his life.

My highly educated, yet poor, dad constantly said,
"I'm not that interested in money."

"I'll never be rich."

"I can't afford it."

"Investing is risky."

"Money isn't everything."

MONEY SUPPORTS LIFE

My rich dad had a different point of view. He thought it foolish to spend your life working for money and to pretend that money was not important. Rich dad believed that life was more important than money, but money was important for supporting life. He often said, "You only have so many hours in a day and you can only work so hard. So why work hard for money? Learn to have money and people work hard for you, and you can be free to do the things that are important."

To my rich dad, what was important was:

1. Having lots of time to raise his kids.
2. Having money to donate to charities and projects he supported.
3. Bringing jobs and financial stability to the community.
4. Having time and money to take care of his health.
5. Being able to travel the world with his family.

"Those things take money," said rich dad. "That is why money is important to me. Money is important, but I don't want to spend my life working for it."

CHOOSING THE QUADRANTS

One reason my wife and I focused on the "B" and "I" quadrants while we were homeless was because I had more training and education in those quadrants. It was because of my rich dad's guidance that I knew the different financial and professional advantages of each quadrant. For me, the quadrants of the right side, the "B" and "I" quadrants, offered the best opportunity for financial success and financial freedom.

Also, at 37 years old, I had experienced successes and failures in all four quadrants, which allowed me some degree of understanding about my own personal temperament, likes, dislikes, strengths and weaknesses. I knew which quadrants I did best in.

PARENTS ARE TEACHERS

It was my rich dad who often referred to the *CASHFLOW Quadrant* when I was a young boy. He would explain to me the difference between someone who was successful on the left side vs. the right side. Yet being young, I really did not pay much attention to what he said. I did not understand the difference between an employee's mind-set and a business owner's mind-set. I was just trying to survive in school.

Yet, I did hear his words, and soon his words began to make sense. Having two dynamic and successful father figures around me gave meaning to what each was saying. But it was what they were doing that allowed me to begin to notice the differences between the "E-S" side of the *Quadrant* and the "B-I" side. At first the differences were subtle, and then they became glaring.

For example, one painful lesson I experienced as a young boy was simply how much time one dad had available to spend with me vs. the other. As the success and prominence of both dads grew, it was obvious that one dad had less and less time to spend with his wife and four children. My real dad was always on the road, at meetings, or dashing off to the airport for more meetings. The more successful he got, the fewer dinners we had together as a family. Weekends, he spent at home in his crowded little office, buried under paperwork.

My rich dad, on the other hand, had more and more free time as his success grew. One of the reasons I learned so much about money, finance, business and life was simply because my rich dad had more and more free time for his children and me.

Another example is that both dads made more and more money as they became successful, but my real dad, the educated one, also got further into debt. So he'd work harder and suddenly find himself in a higher income-tax bracket. His banker and accountant would then tell him to buy a bigger house for the so-called "tax break." My dad would follow the advice and buy a bigger house, and soon he was working harder than ever so he could make more money to pay for the new house... taking him even further away from his family.

My rich dad was different. He made more and more money, but paid less in taxes. He, too, had bankers and accountants, but he was not getting the same advice my highly educated dad was getting.

THE MAIN REASON

Yet, the driving force that would not allow me to stay on the left side of the *Quadrant* was what happened to my highly educated but poor dad at the peak of his career.

In the early 1970s, I was already out of college and in Pensacola, Florida, going through pilot training for the Marine Corps, on my way to Vietnam. My educated dad was now the Superintendent of Education for the State of Hawaii and a member of the governor's staff. One evening, my dad phoned me in my room on base.

"Son," he said. "I'm going to resign from my job and run for lieutenant governor of the state of Hawaii for the Republican Party."

I gulped and then said, "You're going to run for office against your boss?"

"That's right," he replied.

"Why?" I asked. "Republicans do not have a chance in Hawaii. The Democratic Party and the labor unions are too strong."

"I know, son. I also know that we do not have a prayer of winning. Judge Samuel King will be the candidate for governor, and I will be his running mate."

"Why?" I asked again. "Why run against your boss if you know you're going to lose?"

"Because my conscience won't let me do anything else. The games these politicians are playing disturb me."

"Are you saying they're corrupt?" I asked.

"I don't want to say that," said my real dad. He was an honest and moral man who rarely spoke badly about anyone. He was always a diplomat. Yet, I could tell from his voice that he was angry and upset when he said, "I'll just say that my conscience bothers me when I see what goes on behind the scenes. I could not live with myself if I turned a blind eye and did nothing. My job and paycheck are not as important as my conscience."

After a long silence, I realized that my dad's mind was made up. "Good luck," I said quietly. "I'm proud of you for your courage, and I'm proud to be your son."

My dad and the Republican ticket were crushed, as expected. The re-elected governor sent the word out that my dad was never to get a job again with the government for the state of Hawaii... and he never did. At the age of 54, my dad went looking for a job, and I was on my way to Vietnam.

At middle age my dad was looking for a new job. He went from jobs with big titles and low pay to more jobs with big titles and low pay. Jobs where he was the executive director of XYZ Services, a nonprofit organization, or managing director of ABC Services, another nonprofit.

He was a tall, brilliant and dynamic man who was no longer welcome in the only world he knew, the world of government employees. He tried starting several small businesses. He was a consultant for a while, and even bought a famous franchise, but they all failed. As he grew older, and his strength slipped away, so did his drive to start over again; his lack of will became even more pronounced after each business failure. He was a successful "E" trying to survive as an "S," a quadrant in which he had no training or experience and for which he had no heart. He loved the world of public education, but he could not find a way to get back in. The ban on his employment in the state government was silently in place. In some circles, the word is called "blacklisted."

If not for Social Security and Medicare, the last years of his life would have been a complete disaster. He died frustrated and a little angry, yet he died with a clear conscience.

So what kept me going in the darkest of hours? It was the haunting memory of my educated dad sitting at home, waiting for the phone to ring, trying to succeed in the world of business, a world he knew nothing about.

That, and the joyous memory of seeing my rich dad grow happier and more successful as his years went on inspired me. Instead of declining at age 54, rich dad blossomed. He had become rich years before that, but now he was becoming mega-rich. He was constantly in the newspapers as the man who was buying up Waikiki and Maui. His years of methodically building businesses and investing was paying off, and he was on his way to becoming one of the richest men in the Islands.

SMALL DIFFERENCES BECOME
LARGE DIFFERENCES

Because my rich dad had explained the *Quadrant* to me, I was better able to see the small differences that grew into large differences when measured over the years a person spends working. Because of the *Quadrant*, I knew it was better to decide not so much what I wanted to do, but more who I wanted to become as my working years progressed. In the darkest hours, it was this deep knowledge, and lessons from two powerful dads, that kept me going.

IT IS MORE THAN THE QUADRANT

The *CASHFLOW Quadrant* is more than two lines and some letters.

If you look below the surface of this simple diagram, you will find completely different worlds as well as different ways of looking at the world. As a person who has looked at the world from both the left side of the *Quadrant* and the right side, I can honestly say the world looks much different depending on which side you are on... and those differences are what this book is about.

One quadrant is not better than another... each has strengths, and each has weaknesses. This book is written to allow you to glimpse into the different quadrants, and into the personal development required to be financially successful in each of them. It is my hope that you will gain further insights into choosing the financial life path that is best suited for you.

Many of the skills essential to be successful on the right side of the *Quadrant* are not taught in school, which might explain why people like Bill Gates of Microsoft, and Ted Turner of CNN, and Thomas Edison left school early. This book will identify the skills, as well as the personal core temperament, that are necessary to find success on the "B" and "I" side of the *Quadrant.*

First, I offer a broad overview of the four quadrants and then a closer focus on the "B" and "I" side. There are already plenty of books written about what it takes to be successful on the "E" and "S" side.

After reading this book, some of you might want to make a change in how you earn your income, and some of you will be happy to stay just where you are. You might choose to operate in more than one quadrant, and maybe in all four quadrants. We are all different, and one quadrant is not more important or better than another. In every village, town, city and nation in the world, there is a need for people operating in all four quadrants to ensure the financial stability of the community.

Also, as we grow older and gain different experiences, our interests change. For example, I notice that many young people right out of school are often happy to get a job. Yet, after a couple of years, a few of them decide they are not interested in climbing the corporate ladder, or they lose interest in the field of business they are in. These changes of age and experience often cause a person to search for new avenues of growth, challenge, financial reward and personal happiness. I hope this book offers some fresh ideas for attaining those goals.

In short, this book is not about homelessness but about finding a home... a home in a quadrant or quadrants.

CHAPTER 2

Different Quadrants... Different People

"Y ou can't teach an old dog new tricks," my highly educated dad always said.

I had sat with him on several occasions, doing my best to explain the *CASHFLOW Quadrant* in an effort to show him some new financial directions. Nearing 60 years of age, he was realizing that many of his dreams were not going to be fulfilled. His "blacklisting" seemed to go beyond the walls of the state government. He was now "blacklisting" himself.

"I tried it, but it didn't work," he said.

My dad was referring to his attempts to be successful in the "S" quadrant with his own business as a self-employed consultant, and as a "B" when he poured much of his life savings into a famous ice-cream franchise that failed.

Being bright, he conceptually understood the different technical skills required in each of the four quadrants. He knew he could learn them if he wanted to. But there was something else holding him back.

One day over lunch, I talked to my rich dad about my educated dad.

"Your father and I are not the same people at the core," said rich dad. "While we are both human beings, and we both have fears, doubts, beliefs, strengths and weaknesses, we respond or handle those core similarities... differently."

"Can you tell me the differences?" I asked.

"Not over one lunch," said rich dad. "But how we respond to those differences is what causes us to remain in one quadrant or another. When your dad tried to cross over from the 'E' quadrant to the 'B' quadrant, intellectually he could understand the process, but he couldn't handle it emotionally. When things did not go smoothly, and he began to lose money, he did not know what to do to solve the problems... so he went back to the quadrant he felt most comfortable in."

"The 'E' and sometimes 'S' quadrant," I said.

Rich dad nodded his head. "When the fear of losing money and failing becomes too painful inside, a fear we both have, he chooses to seek security, and I choose to seek freedom."

"And that is the core difference," I said, signaling the waiter for our check.

"Even though we're all human beings," restated rich dad, "when it comes to money and the emotions attached to money, we all respond differently. And it's how we respond to those emotions that often determines which quadrant we choose to generate our income from."

"Different quadrants... different people," I said.

"That's right," said rich dad as we stood and headed for the door. "And if you're going to be successful in any quadrant, you need to know more than just technical skills. You also need to know the core differences that cause people to seek different quadrants. Know that, and life will be much easier."

We were shaking hands and saying goodbye as the valet brought my rich dad's car around.

"Oh, one last thing," I said hurriedly. "Can my dad change?"

"Oh sure," said rich dad. "Anyone can change. But changing quadrants is not like changing jobs or changing professions. Changing quadrants is often a change at the core of who you are, how you think, and how you look at the world. The change is easier for some people than for others simply because some people welcome change and others fight it. And changing quadrants is most often a life-changing experience. It is a change as profound as the age-old story of the caterpillar becoming a butterfly. Not only will you change but so will your friends. While you'll still be friends with your old friends, it's just harder for caterpillars to do the same things butterflies do. So the changes are big changes, and not too many people choose to make them."

The valet closed the door, and as my rich dad drove off, I was left thinking about the differences.

WHAT ARE THE DIFFERENCES?

How do I tell if people are an "E, S, B or I" without knowing much about them? One of the ways is by listening to their words.

One of my rich dad's greatest skills was being able to "read" people, but he also believed you could not "judge a book by its cover." Rich dad, like Henry Ford, did not have an excellent education, but both men knew how to hire and work with people who did. Rich dad always explained to me that the ability to bring smart people together and work as a team was one of his primary skills.

From the age of 9, my rich dad began to teach me the skills necessary to be successful in the "B" and "I" quadrants. One of those skills was to get beyond the surface of a person and begin to gaze into their core. Rich dad used to say, "If I listen to a person's words, I begin to see and feel their souls."

So at the age of 9, I began to sit in with my rich dad when he hired people. From these interviews I learned to listen not so much for words but for core values. Values that my rich dad said came from their souls.

"E" QUADRANT WORDS

A person who comes from the "E," or employee, quadrant might say:
"I am looking for a safe, secure job with good pay and excellent benefits."

"S" QUADRANT WORDS

A person who comes from the "S," or self-employed, quadrant might say:
"My rate is $35 per hour."
Or "My normal commission rate is 6 percent of the total price."
Or "I can't seem to find people who want to work and do the job right."
Or "I've got more than 20 hours into this project."

"B" QUADRANT WORDS

A person operating out of the "B," or business-owner, quadrant might say:
"I'm looking for a new president to run my company."

"I" QUADRANT WORDS

Someone operating out of the "I," or investor, quadrant might say:
"Is my cash flow based on an internal rate of return or net rate of return?"

WORDS ARE TOOLS

Once my rich dad knew who the person he was interviewing was at the core, at least for that moment, he would know what they were really looking for, what he had to offer, and what words to use when speaking to them. Rich dad always said, "Words are powerful tools."

Rich dad constantly reminded his son and me of this. "If you want to be a leader of people, then you need to be a master of words."

So one of the skills necessary to be a great "B" is to be a master of words, knowing which words work on which kinds of people. He trained us to first listen carefully to the words a person used, and then we would know which words we should use, and when to use them in order to respond to them in the most effective way.

Rich dad explained, "One word may excite one type of person while that same word would completely turn off another person."

For example, the word "risk" might be exciting to a person in the "I" quadrant, while evoking total fear to someone in the "E" quadrant.

To be great leaders, rich dad stressed that we first had to be great listeners. If you did not listen to the words a person used, you would not be able to feel their soul. If you did not listen to their soul, you would never know to whom you were talking.

CORE DIFFERENCES

The reason he would say, "Hear their words, feel their souls," is because behind the words a person chooses are the core values and core differences of that individual. The following are some of the generalities that separate people in one quadrant from those in another.

1. **The "E" (employee).** When I hear the word "secure" or "benefits," I get a sense of who they might be at the core. The word "secure" is a word often used in response to the emotion of fear. If a person feels fear, then the need for security is often a commonly used phrase for someone who comes predominantly from the "E" quadrant. When it comes to money and jobs, there are many people who simply hate the feeling of fear that comes with economic uncertainty... hence the desire for security.

   The word "benefit" means people would also like some kind of additional reward that is spelled out– a defined and assured extra compensation, such as a health-care or retirement plan. The key is that they want to feel secure and see it in writing. Uncertainty does not make them happy; certainty does. Their internal workings say, "I'll give you this… and you promise to give me that in return."

They want their fear satisfied with some degree of certainty, so they seek security and strong agreements when it comes to employment. They are accurate when they say, "I'm not that interested in money."

For them, the idea of security is often more important than money.

Employees can be presidents of companies or janitors of companies. It is not so much what they do, but the contractual agreement they have with the person or organization that hires them.

2. The "S" (self-employed). These are people who want to: "Be their own boss." Or they like to: "Do their own thing."

I call this group the "do-it-yourselfers."

Often, when it comes to the subject of money, a hard core "S" does not like to have his or her income be dependent on other people. In other words, if "S's" work hard, they expect to get paid for their work. Those who are "S's" do not like having the amount of money they earn dictated by someone else or by a group of people who might not work as hard as they do. If they work hard, pay them well. They also understand that if they do not work hard, then they don't deserve to be paid much. When it comes to money, they have fiercely independent souls.

THE EMOTION OF FEAR

So while the "E," or employee, often will respond to the fear of not having money by seeking "security," the "S" often will respond differently. The people in this quadrant respond to fear not by seeking security, but by taking control of the situation and doing it on their own. That is why I call the "S" group the "do-it-yourself" group. When it comes to fear and financial risk, they want to "take the bull by the horns."

In this group you find well-educated "professionals" who spend years in school, such as doctors, lawyers and dentists.

Also in the "S" group are people who took educational paths other than, or in addition to, traditional school. In this group are direct-commission salespeople– real estate agents, for instance– as well as small business owners such as retail shopkeepers, cleaners, restaurateurs, consultants, therapists, travel agents, car mechanics, plumbers, carpenters, preachers, electricians, hair stylists, and artists.

This group's favorite song would be either "Nobody Does It Better," or "I Did It My Way."

Self-employed people are often hard-core "perfectionists." They often want to do something exceptionally well. In their mind, they do not think anyone else does it better than they can do it, so they really do not trust anyone else to do it the way they like it... the way they think is the "right way." In many respects, they are true artists with their own style and methods of doing things.

And that is why we hire them. If you hire a brain surgeon, you want that brain surgeon to have had years of training and experience, but most importantly, you want this brain surgeon to be a perfectionist. The same goes for a dentist, hairstylist, marketing consultant, plumber, electrician, tarot-card reader, lawyer or a corporate trainer. You, as the client hiring this person, want someone who is the best.

For this group, money is not the most important thing about their work. Their independence, the freedom to do things their way, and to be respected as experts in their field, are much more important than mere money. When hiring them, it is best to tell them what you want done and then leave them alone to do it. They do not need or want supervision. If you meddle too much, they'll simply walk off the job and tell you to hire someone else. The money really does not come first; their independence does.

This group often has a hard time hiring other people to do what they do simply because in their mind, nobody is up to the task. Which causes this group to often say: "It's hard to find good help these days."

Also, if this group trains someone to do what they do, that newly trained person often ends up leaving to "do their own thing," and "be their own boss," and "do things their way," and "to have a chance to express their individuality."

Many "S" types are hesitant to hire and train other people because once trained they often end up as their competition. This, in turn, keeps them working harder and doing things on their own.

3. The "B" (business owner). This group of people could almost be the opposite of the "S." Those who are true "B's" like to surround themselves with smart people from all four categories, "E, S, B and I." Unlike the "S," who does not like to delegate work (because no one could do it better), the true "B" likes to delegate. The true motto of a "B" is, "Why do it yourself when you can hire someone to do it for you, and they can do it better?"

Henry Ford fit this mold. As one popular story goes, a group of so-called intellectuals came by to condemn Ford for being "ignorant." They claimed he really did not know much. So Ford invited them into his office and challenged them to ask him any question and he would answer it. So this panel assembled around America's most powerful industrialist, and began to ask him questions. Ford listened to their questions, and when they were through, he simply reached for several phones on his desk and called in some of his bright assistants, and asked them to give the panel the answers they sought. He ended by informing the panel that he would rather hire smart people who went to school to come up with answers so he could leave his mind clear to do more important tasks. Tasks like "thinking."

One of the quotes credited to Ford goes: "Thinking is the hardest work there is. That is why so few people engage in it."

LEADERSHIP IS BRINGING OUT THE BEST IN PEOPLE

My rich dad's idol was Henry Ford. He had me read books about people like Ford and John D. Rockefeller, the founder of Standard Oil. Rich dad constantly encouraged his son and me to learn the essence of leadership and the technical skills of business. In retrospect, I understand now that many people may have one or the other, but to be a successful "B," you really do need to have both. I also now realize that both skills can be learned. There is a science to business and leadership as well as an art to business and leadership. For me, both are lifelong studies.

When I was a boy my rich dad gave me a children's book entitled *Stone Soup*, written in 1947 by Marcia Brown and still available today from leading bookstores. He had me read this book to begin my training as a leader in business.

Leadership, rich dad said, is "the ability to bring out the best in people." So he trained his son and me in the technical skills necessary to become successful in business, technical skills such as reading financial statements, marketing, sales, accounting, management, production and negotiations, and he really stressed that we learn to work with and lead people. Rich dad always said, "The technical skills of business are easy. . .the hard part is working with people."

As a reminder, I still read *Stone Soup* today, for I personally have a tendency to be a tyrant, instead of a leader, when things do not go my way.

ENTREPRENEURIAL DEVELOPMENT

I have often heard the words, "I'm going to start my own business."

Many people tend to believe that the way to financial security and happiness is to "do your own thing," or to "develop a new product no one else has."

So they rush out and start their own business. In many cases, this is the path they take.

Many wind up starting an "S" type of business and not a "B" type of business. Again, not that one is necessarily better than the other. Both have different strengths and weakness, risks and rewards. But many people who want to start a "B" type of business wind up with an "S" type of business and become stalled in their quest to move to the right side of the *Quadrant*.

Many new entrepreneurs want to do this:

But wind up instead doing this and getting stuck there.

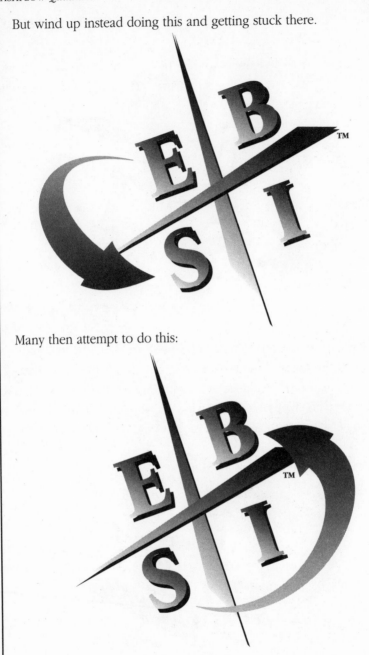

Many then attempt to do this:

But only a few who attempt actually make it. Why? Because the technical skills and human skills to be successful in each quadrant are often different. You must learn the skills and mind-set required by a quadrant in order to find true success there.

THE DIFFERENCE BETWEEN AN "S" TYPE OF BUSINESS AND A "B" TYPE OF BUSINESS

Those who are true "B's" can leave their business for a year or more and return to find their business more profitable and running better than when they left it. In a true "S" type of business, if the "S" left for a year or more, the chances are there would be no business left to return to.

So what causes the difference? Saying it simply, an "S" owns a job. A "B" owns a system and then hires competent people to operate the system. Or put another way: In many cases, the "S" is the system. That is why they cannot leave.

Let's take a dentist. A dentist spends years in school learning to become a self-contained system. You, as the client, get a toothache. You go see your dentist. He fixes your tooth. You pay and go home. You're happy and then tell all of your friends about your great dentist. In most cases, the dentist can do the entire job by himself. The problem is that if the dentist goes on vacation, so does his income.

"B" business owners can go on vacation forever because they own a system, not a job. If the "B" is on vacation, the money still comes in.

To be successful as a "B" requires:
A. Ownership or control of systems, and
B. The ability to lead people.

For "S's" to evolve into "B's," they need to convert who they are and what they know into a system... and many are not able to do that... or they are often too attached to the system.

CAN YOU MAKE A BETTER HAMBURGER THAN McDONALD'S?

Many people come to me for advice on how to start a company or to ask me how to raise money for a new product or idea.

I listen, usually for about 10 minutes, and within that time I can tell where their focus is. Is it the product or the system of business? In those 10 minutes, I most often hear words such as these (remember the importance of being a good listener and allowing words to direct you to the core values of a person's soul):

"This is a far better product than company XYZ makes."
"I've looked everywhere, and nobody has this product."
"I'll give you the idea for this product; all I want is 25 percent of the profits."
"I've been working on this (product, book, music score, invention) for years."

These are the words of a person generally operating from the left side of the *Quadrant*, the "E" or "S" side.

It is important to be gentle at this time, because we are dealing with core values and ideas that have been entrenched often for years… maybe handed down for generations. If I am not gentle or patient, I could damage a fragile and sensitive launch of an idea and, more importantly, a human being ready to evolve into another quadrant.

THE HAMBURGER AND THE BUSINESS

Since I need to be gentle, at this point in the conversation I often use the "McDonald's hamburger" example for clarification. After listening to their pitch, I slowly ask, "Can you personally make a better hamburger than McDonald's?"

So far, 100 percent of the people I have talked with about their new idea or product have said "yes." They can all prepare, cook and serve a better quality hamburger than McDonald's.

At this point, I ask them the next question: "Can you personally build a better business system than McDonald's?"

Some people see the difference immediately, and some do not. And I would say the difference is whether the person is fixated on the left side of the *Quadrant*, which is focused on the idea of the better burger, or on the right side of the *Quadrant*, which is focused on the system of business.

I do my best to explain that there are a lot of entrepreneurs out there offering far superior products or services than are offered by the mega-rich multinational corporations, just as there are billions of people who can make a better burger than McDonald's. But only McDonald's has the system that has served billions of burgers.

SEE THE OTHER SIDE

If people can begin to see the other side, I then suggest they go to McDonald's, buy a burger, and sit and look at the system that delivered that burger. Take note of the trucks that delivered the raw burger, the rancher that raised the beef, the buyer who bought the beef, and the TV ads with Ronald McDonald. Notice the training of young inexperienced people to say the same words, "Hello, welcome to McDonald's," as well as the decor of the franchise, the regional offices, the bakeries that bake the buns, and the millions of pounds of French fries that taste exactly the same all over the world. Then include the stockbrokers raising money for McDonald's on Wall Street. If they can begin to understand the "whole picture," then they have a chance at moving to the "B" or "I" side of the *Quadrant.*

The reality is, there are unlimited new ideas, billions of people with services or products to offer, millions of products, and only a few people who know how to build excellent business systems.

Bill Gates of Microsoft did not build a great product. He bought somebody else's product and built a powerful global system around it.

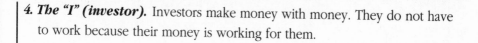

4. The "I" (investor). Investors make money with money. They do not have to work because their money is working for them.

The "I" quadrant is the playground of the rich. Regardless of which quadrant people make their money in, if they hope someday to be rich, they ultimately must come to the "I" quadrant. It is in the "I" quadrant that money becomes converted to wealth.

THE CASHFLOW QUADRANT

That is the *CASHFLOW Quadrant*. The *Quadrant* simply makes distinctions on how income is generated, whether as an "E" (employee), "S" (self-employed), "B" (business owner) or "I" (investor). The differences are summarized below.

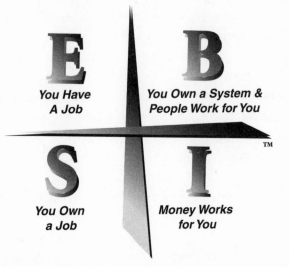

OPT AND OPM

Most of us have heard that the secrets to great riches and wealth are:

1. OPT-Other People's Time.
2. OPM-Other People's Money.

OPT and OPM are found on the right side of the *Quadrant*. For the most part, people who work on the left side of the *Quadrant* are the OP (Other People) whose time and money are being used.

A primary reason Kim and I took time to build a "B" type of business, rather than an "S" type, was because we recognized the long-term benefit of using "other people's time". One of the drawbacks to being a successful "S" is that success simply means more hard work. In other words, good work results in more hard work and longer hours.

In designing a "B" type of business, success simply means increasing the system and hiring more people. In other words, you work less, earn more and enjoy more free time.

The remainder of this book goes through the skills and mind-set required for the right side of the *Quadrant*. It is my experience that being successful on the right side requires a different mind-set and different technical skills. If people are flexible enough to make a mind-set change, I think they will find the process of achieving greater financial security or freedom easy. For other people, the process might be too difficult... because many people are frozen in one quadrant, one mind-set.

At a minimum, you will find out why some people work less, earn more, pay less in taxes, and feel more financially secure than others. It is simply a matter of knowing which quadrant to work out of and when.

A GUIDE TO FREEDOM

The CASHFLOW Quadrant is not a set of rules. It is only a guide for those who wish to use it. It guided Kim and me from financial struggle to financial security, and then to financial freedom. We did not want to spend every day of our lives having to get up and work for money.

THE DIFFERENCE BETWEEN THE RICH AND EVERYONE ELSE

A few years ago, I read this article that said most rich people received 70 percent of their income from investments, or the "I" quadrant, and less than 30 percent from wages, or the "E" quadrant. And if they were an "E," the chances were that they were employees of their own corporation.

Their income looked like this:

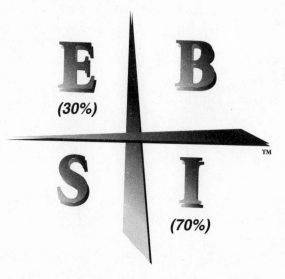

For most everyone else, the poor and the middle class, at least 80 percent of their income comes from wages from the "E" or "S" quadrants and less than 20 percent from investments, or the "I" quadrant.

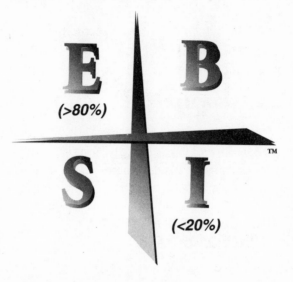

THE DIFFERENCE BETWEEN BEING RICH AND BEING WEALTHY

In Chapter 1, I wrote that my wife and I were millionaires by 1989, but we were not financially free until 1994. There is a difference between being rich and being wealthy. By 1989, our business was making us a lot of money. We were earning more and working less because the business system was growing without any more physical effort on our part. We had achieved what most people would consider financial success.

We still needed to convert the cash flow coming from the business into even more tangible assets that would throw off additional cash flow. We had grown our business into a success, and it was now time to focus on growing our assets to the point where the cash flow from all of our assets would be greater than our living expenses.

Our diagram looked like this:

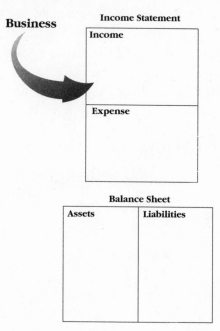

By 1994, the passive income from all of our assets was greater than our expenses. Then, we were wealthy.

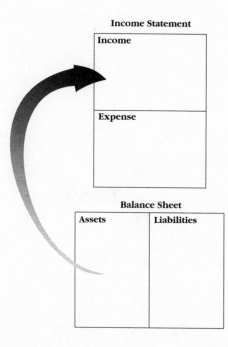

In actuality, our business would also be considered an asset because it generated income and operated without much physical input. For our own personal sense of wealth, we wanted to make sure we had tangible assets such as real estate and stocks that were throwing off more passive income than our expenses, so we could really say we were wealthy. Once the income from our asset column was greater than the money coming in from the business, we sold the business to our partner. We were now wealthy.

THE DEFINITION OF WEALTH

The definition of wealth is: "The number of days you can survive, without physically working (or anyone else in your household physically working) and still maintain your standard of living."

For example: If your monthly expenses are $1,000 a month, and if you have $3,000 in savings, your wealth is approximately 3 months or 90 days. Wealth is measured in time, not dollars.

By 1994, my wife and I were wealthy indefinitely (barring great economic changes) because the income from our investments was greater than our monthly expenses.

Ultimately, it is not how much money you make that matters, but how much money you keep and how long that money works for you. Every day I meet many people who make a lot of money, but all of their money goes out the expense column. Their cash flow pattern looks like this:

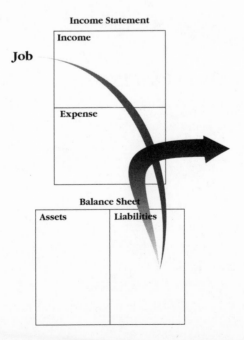

Every time they make a little more money, they go shopping. They often buy a bigger house or new car, which results in long-term debt and more hard work, and nothing is left to go into the asset column. The money goes out so fast, you'd think they took some kind of financial laxative.

RED LINE FINANCES

In the world of cars, there is a saying about "keeping the engine at red line." "Red line" means the throttle is keeping the RPMs of the engine as close to the "red line," or the maximum speed the car's engine can maintain, without blowing up.

When it comes to personal finances, there are many people, rich and poor, who operate constantly at the financial "red line." No matter how much money they make, they spend it as fast as it comes in. The trouble with operating your car's engine at "red line" is that the life expectancy of the engine is shortened. The same is true with operating your finances at the "red line."

Several of my medical doctor friends say the main problem they see today is stress caused by working hard and never having enough money. One says that the biggest cause of health disorders is something she calls, "cancer of the wallet."

MONEY MAKING MONEY

Regardless of how much money people make, ultimately they should put some in the "I" quadrant. The "I" quadrant deals specifically with the idea of money making money. Or the idea that your money works so that you do not have to work. Yet it is important to acknowledge that there are other forms of investing.

OTHER FORMS OF INVESTING

People invest in their education. Traditional education is important because the better your education, the better your chances of earning money. You can spend four years in college and have your income earning potential go from $24,000 a year to $50,000 a year or more. Given that the average person spends 40 years or more actively working, four years' worth of college or some type of higher education is an excellent investment.

Loyalty and hard work is another form of investing, like being a lifelong employee of a company or the government. In return, via contract, that individual is rewarded with a pension for life. That is a form of investment popular in the Industrial Age but obsolete in the Information Age.

Other people invest in having large families and, in turn, have their children care for them in their old age. That form of investing was the norm in the past, yet due to economic constraints in the present, it is becoming more difficult for families to handle the living and medical expenses of parents.

Government retirement programs such as Social Security and Medicare in America, which are often paid for through payroll deduction, is another form of investment mandated by law. But due to massive changes in demographics and costs, this form of investment may not be able to keep some of the promises it has made.

And there are independent investment vehicles for retirement that are called individual retirement plans. Often, the federal government will offer tax incentives to both the employer and employee to participate in such plans. In America, one popular plan is the 401(k) retirement plan, and in countries such as Australia, they are called "Superannuation" plans.

INCOME RECEIVED FROM INVESTMENTS

Although the above are all forms of investing, the "I" quadrant focuses on investments that generate income on an ongoing basis during your working years. So to qualify as a person who operates as an "I," use the same criteria used in all the other quadrants. Do you receive current income from the "I" quadrant? In other words, is your money working for you and generating current income for you?

Let's look at a person who buys a house as an investment and rents it out. If the rent collected is greater than the expenses to operate the property, that income is coming from the "I" quadrant. The same is true for people who receive income as interest from savings, or dividends from stocks and bonds. So the qualifier for the "I" quadrant is how much income you generate from the quadrant without working in it.

IS MY RETIREMENT ACCOUNT A FORM OF INVESTMENT?

Regularly putting money into a retirement account is a form of investing and is a wise thing to do. Most of us hope to be considered investors when our working years are over... but for the sake of this book, the "I" quadrant represents a person whose income comes from investments during their working years. In reality, most people are not investing in a retirement account. Most are saving money in their retirement account, hoping that, when they retire, there will be more money coming out than they put in.

There is a difference between people who save money in their retirement accounts and people who, through investing, actively use their money to make more money as income.

ARE STOCKBROKERS INVESTORS?

Many people who are advisers in the investment world are, by definition, not really people who generate their income from the "I" quadrant.

For example, most stockbrokers, real estate agents, financial advisers, bankers and accountants are predominantly "E's" or "S's." In other words, their income comes from their professional work, not necessarily from assets they own.

I also have friends who are stock traders. They buy stocks low and hope to sell high. In reality, their profession is "trading," much like a person who owns a retail shop and buys items at wholesale and sells them at retail. There is still something they physically must do to generate the money. So they would fit more into the "S" quadrant than the "I" quadrant.

Can all of these people be investors? The answer is "yes," but it is important to know the difference between someone who earns money from commissions, or sells advice by the hour, or gives advice for a salary, or tries to buy low and sell high, and someone who earns money from spotting or creating good investments.

There's one way to find out how good your advisers are: Ask them what percentage of their income comes from commissions or fees for their advice vs. income that comes from passive income, income from their investments or other businesses they own.

I have several CPA friends who tell me, without violating client confidentiality, that many professional investment advisers have little in the way of income from investments. In other words, "They do not practice what they preach."

ADVANTAGES OF INCOME FROM THE "I" QUADRANT

So the primary distinction of people who earn their money from the "I" quadrant is that they focus on having their money make money. If they are good at it, they can have that money work for them and for their family for hundreds of years.

Besides the obvious advantages of knowing how to make money with money and not having to get up and go to work, there also are many tax advantages that are not available to people who have to work for their money.

One of the reasons the rich get richer is because they sometimes can make millions and legally not pay taxes on that money. That's because they make money in the "asset column," not in the "income column." Or they make money as investors, not workers.

For people who work for money, not only are they often taxed at higher rates, their taxes are withheld from their wages and they never even see that portion of their income.

WHY AREN'T MORE PEOPLE INVESTORS?

The "I" quadrant is the quadrant for working less, earning more, and paying less in taxes. So why aren't more people investors? The same reason many people do not start their own businesses. It can be summed up in one word: "risk."

Many people do not like the idea of handing over their hard earned money and not having it come back. Many people are so afraid of losing, they choose not to invest or risk their money at all... no matter how much money they could make in return.

A Hollywood celebrity once said: "It's not return on the investment that I worry about. It's the return of the investment."

This fear of losing money seems to divide investors into four broad categories:

1. People who are risk-adverse and do nothing but play it safe, keeping their money in the bank.
2. People who turn the job of investing over to someone else, such as a financial adviser or mutual fund manager.
3. Gamblers.
4. Investors.

The difference between a gambler and an investor is this. For a gambler, investing is a game of chance. For an investor, investing is a game of skill. And for the people who turn their money over to someone else to invest, investing is often a game they do not want to learn. The important thing for these individuals is to choose a financial adviser carefully.

In an upcoming chapter, this book will go into the seven levels of investors, which should shed more light on this subject.

RISK CAN BE VIRTUALLY ELIMINATED

The good news about investing is that risk can be greatly minimized or even eliminated, and you can still receive high yields on your money, if you know the game.

A true investor will be heard speaking these words: "How soon do I get my money back and how much income will I receive for the rest of my life after I get that initial investment money back?"

A true investor wants to know how soon they get their money back. People who have a retirement account have to wait years to find out if they will ever get their money back. This is the most extreme difference between a professional investor and someone who sets money aside for retirement.

It is the fear of losing money that causes most people to seek security. Yet the "I" quadrant is not as treacherous as many people think. The "I" quadrant is like any other quadrant. It has its own skills and mind-set. The skills to be successful in the "I" quadrant can be learned if you're willing to take the time to learn them.

A NEW AGE BEGINS

In 1989, the Berlin Wall came down. In the history of the world, that was one of the most important events. More than signifying the failure of communism, in my opinion, that event marked the official end of the Industrial Age and the beginning of the Information Age.

THE DIFFERENCE BETWEEN INDUSTRIAL-AGE PENSION PLANS AND INFORMATION-AGE PENSION PLANS

The voyage of Columbus in 1492 roughly coincides with the start of the Industrial Age. The fall of the Berlin Wall in 1989 is the event that marked the end of that age. For some reason, it seems that every 500 years in modern history, great cataclysmic changes have occurred. We are in one such period right now.

That change has already threatened the financial security of hundreds of millions of people, most of whom are not yet aware of the financial impact of that change and many of whom cannot afford it. The change is found in the difference between an Industrial Age pension plan and an Information Age pension plan.

When I was a boy, my rich dad encouraged me to take risks with my money and learn to invest. He would always say: "If you want to get rich, you need to learn how to take risks. Learn to be an investor."

At home, I told my educated dad about my rich dad's suggestion that we learn how to invest and learn to manage risk. My educated dad replied, "I don't need to learn how to invest. I have a government pension plan, a pension from the Teachers Union, and Social Security benefits guaranteed. Why take risks with my money?"

My educated dad believed in Industrial Age pension plans, such as government-employee pensions and Social Security. He was happy when I signed up for the U.S. Marine Corps. Instead of being worried that I might lose my life in Vietnam, he simply said, "Stay in for 20 years and you will get a pension and medical benefits for life."

Although still in use, such pension plans officially have become obsolete. The idea of a company being financially responsible for your retirement and the government picking up the balance of your retirement needs through pension schemes is an old idea that is no longer valid.

PEOPLE NEED TO BECOME INVESTORS

As we move from Defined Benefit pension plans, or what I call Industrial Age retirement plans, to Defined Contribution pension plans, or Information Age pension plans, the result is that you as an individual must now be financially responsible for yourself. Few people have noticed the change.

INDUSTRIAL AGE PENSION PLAN

In the Industrial Age, a Defined Benefit pension plan meant that the company guaranteed you, the worker, a defined amount of money (usually paid monthly) for as long as you lived. People felt secure because these plans assured a steady income.

INFORMATION AGE PENSION PLAN

Somebody changed the deal, and companies suddenly were no longer guaranteeing financial security at the end of your working days. Instead, companies began offering Defined Contribution retirement plans. "Defined Contribution" means that you are only going to get back what you and the company have contributed while you were working. In other words, your pension is defined solely by what has been contributed. If you and your company put no money in, you get no money out.

The good news is that in the Information Age, life expectancy will go up. The bad news is that you might outlive your pension.

RISKY PENSION PLANS

And worse than that, what you and your employer put into the plan is no longer guaranteed to exist when you decide to pull it out. This is because plans like 401(k)s and Superannuations, are subject to market forces. In other words, one day you could have a million dollars in the account, and if there were a stock-market crash, which every market occasionally has, your million dollars could be cut in half or even wiped out. The guarantee of lifelong income is gone... and I wonder how many people who have these plans realize what this means.

It could mean that people who retire at 65, and begin to live on their Defined Contribution plan, could run out of money by, let's say, age 75. Then, what do they do? Dust off the resume.

And what about the government's Defined Benefit pension plan? Well, in the

United States, Social Security is expected to be bankrupt by the year 2032 and Medicare bankrupt by 2005, just when baby boomers begin needing it. Even today, Social Security does not provide much in the way of income. What will happen when 77 million baby boomers begin to want the money they paid in... but it's not there?

In 1998, President Clinton's popular cry of "Save Social Security" was well received. Yet as Democratic Senator Ernest Hollings pointed out, "Obviously the first way to save Social Security is to stop looting it." For decades, the federal government has been responsible for "borrowing" the retirement money for expenditures.

Many politicians seem to think that Social Security is income that can be spent rather than an asset that should be held in trust.

TOO MANY PEOPLE COUNTING ON THE GOVERNMENT

I write my books and build my products, such as the educational board game *CASHFLOW*, because we are at the end of the Industrial Age and just getting started in the Information Age.

My concern as a private citizen is that from my generation forward, we are not properly prepared to handle the differences between the Industrial Age and the Information Age... and one of those differences is how we prepare financially for our retirement years. The idea of "go to school and get a safe, secure job" was a good idea for people born before 1930. Today, everyone needs to go to school to learn to get a good job, but we also need to know how to invest, and investing is not a subject taught in school.

One of the hangovers of the Industrial Age is that too many people have become dependent on the government to solve their individual problems. Today we are facing even bigger problems because of the delegation to the government of our personal financial responsibility.

It is estimated that by the year 2020, there will be 275 million Americans, with 100 million of them expecting some kind of government support. This will include federal employees, military retirees, postal workers, schoolteachers and other government employees, as well as retirees expecting Social Security and Medicare payments. And they are contractually correct in expecting it because, in one way or another, most have been investing in that promise. Unfortunately, there have been too many promises made for years, and now the bill is coming due.

And I do not think those financial promises can be kept. If our government begins to raise taxes even higher to pay for those promises, those who can escape will escape to countries that have lower taxes. In the Information Age, the term "offshore" will not mean another country as a tax haven... "offshore" could mean "cyberspace."

A GREAT CHANGE IS AT HAND

I recall President John F. Kennedy warning, "A great change is at hand." Well, that change is here.

INVESTING WITHOUT BEING INVESTORS

The change from Defined Benefit to Defined Contribution pension plans is forcing millions of people throughout the world to become investors, with little investor education. Many people who have spent their lives avoiding financial risks are now being forced to take them... financial risks with their future, their old age, the end of their working years. Most will find out if they were wise investors or careless gamblers only when it comes time to retire.

Today, the stock market is the talk of the world. It is fueled by many things, one of which is non-investors trying to become investors. Their financial path looks like this:

A large majority of these people, the "E's" and "S's," are people who by nature are security oriented. That is why they seek secure jobs or secure careers, or start small businesses they can control. They are migrating today, because of the

Defined Contribution retirement plans, to the "I" quadrant, where they hope they will find "security" for when their working years are over. Unfortunately, the "I" quadrant is not known for its security. The "I" quadrant is the quadrant of risk.

Because so many people on the left side of the *CASHFLOW Quadrant* come looking for security, the stock market responds in kind. That is why you hear so often the following words:

1. "Diversification." People who seek security use the word "diversification" a lot. Why? Because the strategy of diversification is an investment strategy for "not losing." It is not an investment strategy for winning. Successful or rich investors do not diversify. They focus their efforts.

   Warren Buffett, possibly the world's greatest investor, says this about " diversification": "The strategy we've adopted precludes our following standard diversification dogma. Many pundits would therefore say the strategy must be riskier than that employed by more conventional investors. We disagree. We believe that a policy of portfolio concentration may well decrease risk if it raises, as it should, both the intensity with which an investor thinks about a business and the comfort level he must feel with its economic characteristics before buying into it."

   In other words, Warren Buffett is saying that portfolio concentration or focusing on a few investments, rather than diversifying, is a better strategy. In his mind, concentration rather than diversification requires you to become smarter, more intense in your thoughts and actions. His article goes on to say that average investors avoid volatility because they think volatility is risky. Warren Buffet says instead, "In fact, the true investor welcomes volatility."

   For my wife and me to get out of financial struggle and find financial freedom, we did not diversify. We concentrated our investments.

2. "Blue Chip Stocks." Security-minded investors usually buy "Blue Chip" companies. Why? Because in their mind, they are safer. While the company might be safer, the stock market is not.

3. "Mutual Funds." People who know little about investing feel more secure about turning their money over to a fund manager they hope will do a

better job than they can. And this is a smart strategy for people who have no intention of becoming professional investors. The problem is, as smart as this strategy is, it does not mean that mutual funds are less risky. In fact, if there is a stock-market crash, we might see what I call the "Mutual Fund Meltdown," a financial catastrophe as devastating as the "Tulipomania" crash in 1610, the "South Seas Bubble" meltdown of 1620, and the "Junk Bond" bombshell of 1990.

Today, the market is filled with millions of people who, by nature, are security minded, but due to the changing economy are being forced to cross from the left side of the *CASHFLOW Quadrant* into the right side, where their brand of security does not really exist. That causes me concern. Many people think their pension plans are safe, when they really are not. If there is a crash or a major depression, their plans could be wiped out. Their retirement plans are not as safe as the retirement plans our parents had.

GREAT ECONOMIC UPHEAVALS COMING

The stage is set for a great economic upheaval. Such upheavals have always marked the end of an old era and the birth of a new era. At the end of every age there are people who move forward and other people who cling to ideas of the past. I am afraid that for people who still expect that their financial security is the responsibility of a big company or big government, they will be disappointed in the coming years. Those are ideas of the Industrial Age, not the Information Age.

No one has a crystal ball. I subscribe to many investment news services. Each one says something different. Some say the near future is bright. Some say a market crash and major depression are right around the corner. To remain objective, I listen to both sides, because both sides have points worth listening to. The tack I take is not one of playing fortuneteller and trying to predict the future; instead I work at staying educated in both the "B" and "I" quadrants and being prepared for whatever happens. A person who is prepared will prosper no matter which direction the economy goes, whenever it goes.

If history is any indicator, a person who lives to the age of 75 should anticipate going through one depression and two major recessions. Well, my parents went through their depression, but the baby boomers have not... yet. And it has been approximately 60 years since the last depression hit.

Today we all need to be concerned with more than just job security. I think we also need to be concerned about our own long-term financial security... and not leave that responsibility to a company or the government. The times officially changed when companies said that they were no longer responsible for your retirement years. Once they switched to the Defined Contribution retirement plan, the message was that you were now responsible for investing in your own retirement. Today, we all need to become wiser investors, ever vigilant of the changes in the ups and downs of the financial markets. I recommend learning to be an investor rather than giving your money to somebody else to invest for you. If you simply turn your money over to a mutual fund or to an adviser, you may have to wait until you're 65 to find out if that person did a good job. If they did a lousy job, you may have to work for the rest of your life. Millions of people will have to do just that because it will be too late for them to invest or learn about investing.

LEARN TO MANAGE RISK

It is possible to invest for high returns with low risk. All you have to do is learn how it's done. It is not hard. In fact, it's much like learning how to ride a bike. In the early stages, you may fall down, but after a while, the falling stops and investing becomes second nature, just as riding a bicycle is for most of us.

The problem with the left side of the *CASHFLOW Quadrant* is that most people go there to avoid financial risk. Instead of avoiding risk, I recommend learning how to manage financial risk.

TAKE A RISK

People who take risks change the world. Few people ever get rich without taking risks. Too many people have come to depend on government to eliminate the risks of life. The beginning of the Information Age is the end of big government as we know it. Big government has just become too expensive. Unfortunately, the millions of people around the world that have come to depend upon the idea of "entitlements" and pensions for life will be left behind financially. The Information Age means we all need to become more self-sufficient and begin to grow up.

The idea of "study hard and find a safe, secure job" is an idea born in the Industrial Age. We're not in that age anymore. The times are changing. The problem is many people's ideas have not. They still think they're entitled to something. Many still think that the "I" quadrant is not their responsibility. They continue to think that the government or a big business or the labor union or their mutual fund or their family will take care of them when their working days are over. For their sake, I hope they're right. These individuals have no need to read farther.

It is my concern for those people who recognize the need to become investors that prompted me to write *The CASHFLOW Quadrant*. It was written to help individuals who want to make the move from the left side of the *Quadrant* to the right side, but don't know where to start. Anyone can make the move with the right skills and determination.

If you have already found your own financial freedom, I say, "Congratulations." Please tell others about your path, and guide them if they want to be guided. Guide them, but let them find their own path, for there are many paths to financial freedom.

Regardless of what you decide, please remember this. Financial freedom might be free, but it does not come cheap. Freedom has a price... and to me it is worth the price. The big secret is this: It takes neither money to be financially free nor a good formal education. It also doesn't have to be risky. Instead, freedom's price is measured in dreams, desire and the ability to overcome disappointments that occur to all of us along the way. Are you willing to pay the price?

One of my fathers paid the price; the other didn't. He paid a different kind of price.

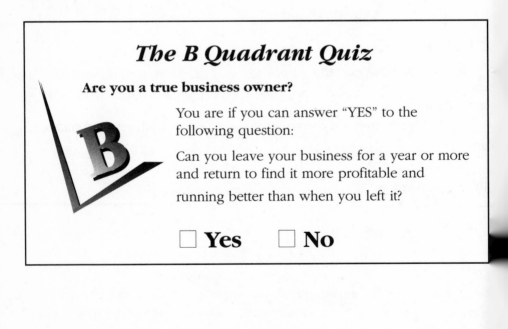

The B Quadrant Quiz

Are you a true business owner?

You are if you can answer "YES" to the following question:

Can you leave your business for a year or more and return to find it more profitable and running better than when you left it?

☐ **Yes**   ☐ **No**

CHAPTER 3

Why People Choose Security Over Freedom

Both of my dads recommended that I go to college and get a college degree. But it was after receiving the degree that their advice to me changed.

My highly educated dad constantly advised: "Go to school, get good grades, and then get a good safe, secure job."

He was recommending a life path focused on the left side of the *Quadrant* that looked like this.

SCHOOL

47

My uneducated but rich dad advised focusing on the right side of the *Quadrant*: "Go to school, get good grades, and then start your own company."

SCHOOL

Their advice was different because one dad was concerned with job security, and the other was more concerned about financial freedom.

WHY PEOPLE SEEK JOB SECURITY

The primary reason many people seek job security is because that is what they are taught to seek, at home and at school.

Millions of people continue to follow that advice. Many of us have been conditioned from our earliest days to think about job security, rather than financial security or financial freedom. And because most of us learn little to nothing about money at home or at school, it is only natural that many of us cling even more tightly to the idea of job security. . .instead of reaching for freedom.

If you look at the *CASHFLOW Quadrant*, you will notice that the left side is motivated by security, and the right side is motivated by freedom.

TRAPPED BY DEBT

The main reason that 90 percent of the population is working on the left side is simply because that is the side they learn about at school. They then leave school and are soon deeply in debt. So deeply in debt that they must cling even tighter to a job, or professional security, just to pay the bills.

Often I meet young people who receive their college diploma along with the bill for their college loans. Several of them have reported being depressed when they see that they are $50,000 to $150,000 in debt for their college education. If the parents paid for their education, then the parents are strapped financially for years.

I recently read that most Americans today will receive a credit card while still in school and will be in debt for the rest of their lives. That is because they are often following a script that became popular in the Industrial Age.

FOLLOWING THE SCRIPT

If we track the life of average educated people, the financial script often goes like this:

The child goes to school, graduates, finds a job and soon has some money to spend. The young adult now can afford to rent an apartment, buy a TV set, new clothes, some furniture and, of course, a car. And now the bills begin to come in. One day, the adult meets someone special, sparks fly, they fall in love and get married. For a while, life is blissful because two can live as cheaply one. They now have two incomes, only one rent to pay, and they can afford to set a few dollars aside to buy the dream of all young couples, their own home. They find their dream home, pull the money from savings and use it for a down payment on the house, and they now have a mortgage. Because they have a new house, they need new furnishings, so they find a furniture store that advertises those magic words, "No money down, easy monthly payments."

Life is wonderful, and they throw a party to have all their friends over to see their new house, new car, new furniture, and new toys. They are now deeply in debt for the rest of their lives. Then, the first child arrives.

The average well-educated, hard-working couple, after dropping the child off at nursery school, must now put their nose to the grindstone and go to work. They become trapped by the need for job security simply because, on average, they are less than three months away from financial bankruptcy. From these people you often hear, "I can't afford to quit. I have bills to pay," or a modification from a song from Snow White and the Seven Dwarfs, "I owe, I owe, so it's off to work I go."

THE SUCCESS TRAP

One of the reasons I learned so much from my rich dad was because he had the free time to teach me. As he grew more successful, he had more free time and money. If business got better, he did not have to work harder. He simply had his president expand the system and hire more people to do the work. If his investments did well, he reinvested the money and made more money. Because of his success, he had more free time. He spent hours with both his son and me explaining to us everything he was doing in business and investing. I was learning more from him than I was learning at school. That is what happens when you work hard on the right side of the *Quadrant*, the "B" and "I" side.

My highly educated dad worked hard also, but he worked hard on the left side of the *Quadrant*. By working hard, getting promoted and gaining more responsibility, he had less and less free time to spend with his kids. He would leave for work at 7 a.m., and many times we would not see him because we had to go to bed before he got home. That is what happens when you work hard and become successful on the left side of the *Quadrant*. Success brings you less and less time... even if it does bring more money.

THE MONEY TRAP

Success on the right side of the *Quadrant* requires a knowledge about money called "financial intelligence." Rich dad defined it this way: "Financial intelligence is not so much how much money you make, but how much money you keep, how hard that money works for you, and how many generations you keep it for."

Success on the right side of the *Quadrant* requires financial intelligence. If people lack basic financial intelligence, they will, in most cases, not survive on the right-side of the *Quadrant*.

My rich dad was good with money and with people at work. He had to be. He was responsible for creating money, managing as few people as possible, keeping costs low, and keeping profits high. Those are the skills necessary for success on the right side of the *Quadrant*.

It was my rich dad who stressed to me that your home is not an asset but a liability. He could prove it because he taught us to be financially literate so we were able to read numbers. He had the free time to teach his son and me because he was good at managing people. His skills from work carried over into his home life.

My educated dad did not manage money and people at work, although he thought he did. As the state Superintendent of Education, he was a government official with a multimillion dollar budget and thousands of employees. But it was not money he created. It was taxpayers' money, and his job was to spend all of it. If he did not spend it, the government would give him less money the next year. So at the end of each fiscal year, he was looking for ways to spend it all, which meant he often hired more people to justify next year's budget. The funny thing was, the more people he hired, the more problems he had.

As a young boy, observing both fathers, I began to take mental notes of what kind of life I wanted to lead.

My educated dad was a voracious reader of books, so he was word literate, but he was not financially literate. Because he could not read numbers, he had to take the advice of his banker and accountant, and both told him that his house was an asset, and that it should be his largest investment.

Because of this financial advice, not only did my highly educated dad work harder, but he also got further into debt. Every time he received a promotion for his hard work, he also got a pay raise, and with each pay raise he went into a higher tax bracket. Because he was in a higher tax bracket, and taxes for high-income workers in the 1960s and 1970s were extremely high, his accountant and banker would tell him to buy a bigger house so he could write off the interest payments. He made more money, but all that happened was his taxes increased and his debt increased. The more successful he got, the harder he had to work, and the less time he had with the people he loved. Soon, all the children were gone from home, and he was still working hard just to keep up with the bills.

He always thought that the next promotion and pay raise would solve his problem. But the more money he made, the more the same things happened. He got deeper into debt and paid more in taxes.

The more frazzled he got, both at home and at work, the more he seemed to depend on job security. The more emotionally attached he got to his job, and a paycheck to pay the bills, the more he encouraged his kids to "get a safe, secure job."

The more insecure he felt, the more he sought security.

YOUR TWO BIGGEST EXPENSES

Because my dad could not read financial statements, he could not see the money trap he was getting into as he grew more successful. It's the same money trap I see millions of other successful hard-working people fall into.

The reason so many people struggle financially is because every time they make more money, they also increase their two biggest expenses:

1. Taxes.
2. Interest on debt.

To top it off, the government often offers you tax breaks to get deeper into debt. Doesn't that make you a little suspicious?

As my rich dad defined financial intelligence: "It's not so much how much you make, but how much you keep, how hard it works for you, and how many generations you keep it for."

At the end of my hard-working educated dad's life, the little money he did have to pass on... was taken by the government in probate taxes.

THE SEARCH FOR FREEDOM

I know many people search for freedom and happiness. The problem is most people have not been trained to work from the "B" and "I" quadrants. Because of this lack of training, the programming into job security, and their increasing amount of debt, most people limit their search for financial freedom to the left side of the *CASHFLOW Quadrant.* Unfortunately, financial security or financial freedom are seldom found in the "E" or "S" quadrant. True security and freedom are found on the right side.

GOING FROM JOB TO JOB IN SEARCH OF FREEDOM

One thing the *CASHFLOW Quadrant* is useful for is to track or observe a person's life pattern. Many people spend their life in search of security or freedom, but wind up instead going from job to job. For example:

I have a friend from high school. I hear from him about every five years, and he is always excited because he has found the perfect job. He is ecstatic because he has found the company of his dreams. He loves the company. It's doing exciting things. He loves his work, he has an important title, the pay is great, the people are great, the benefits are great, and his chances for promotion are great. About four and a half years later, I hear from him again, and by this time, he is dissatisfied. The company he works for is now corrupt and dishonest, in his opinion; it doesn't treat its workers with respect; he hates his boss; he was passed over for a promotion, and they don't pay him enough. Six months go by and he's happy again. He's ecstatic because he's found the perfect job... again.

His life's path looks something like a dog chasing its tail. It looks like this.

His life pattern is going from job to job. So far, he lives well because he is smart, attractive and personable. But the years are catching up with him, and younger people are now getting the jobs he used to get. He has a few thousand dollars in savings, nothing set aside for retirement, a house he will never own, child support payments, and college yet to pay for. His youngest child, 8, lives with his ex-wife, and his oldest child, 14, lives with him.

He used to always say to me, "I don't have to worry. I'm still young. I have time."

I wonder if he's saying that now.

In my opinion, he needs to make a serious effort to begin moving to either the "B" or the "I" quadrant quickly. A new attitude and a new educational process need to begin. Unless he gets lucky and wins the lottery, or finds a rich woman to marry, he is on a course of working hard for the rest of his life.

DOING YOUR OWN THING

"E's" BECOME "S's"

Another common pattern is someone going from "E" to "S." During this current period of massive downsizing, many people are getting the message and are leaving their jobs with big companies to start their own businesses. There is a boom in so-called "home-based businesses." So many people made the decision to "Start their own business," "Do their own thing" and "Be their own boss."

Their career path looks like this.

Of all the life paths, this is the one I feel for the most. In my opinion, being an "S" can be the most rewarding and also the most risky. I think the "S" quadrant is the hardest quadrant there is. The failure rates are high. And if you make it, being successful can be worse than failing. That is because if you are successful as an "S," you will work harder than if you were in any of the other quadrants… and you will work harder for a long time. For as long as you are successful.

The reason "S's" work the hardest is because they typically are the proverbial "chief cook and bottle washer." They have to do or be responsible for all the jobs that in a bigger company are done by many managers and employees. An "S" just starting out often answers the phone, pays the bills, makes sales calls, tries to advertise on a small budget, handles customers, hires employees, fires employees, fills in when employees do not show up, talks to the tax man, fights off the government inspectors, and on and on.

Personally I cringe whenever I hear someone say they're going to start their own business. I wish them well, yet I feel great concern for them. I have seen so many "E's" take their life savings or borrow money from friends and family to start their own business. After three or so years of struggle and hard work, the business folds, and instead of life savings, they have debt to pay off.

Nationally, nine out of 10 of these types of businesses fail in five years. Of the one that is remaining, nine out of 10 of them fail in the next five years. In other words, 99 out of 100 small businesses ultimately disappear in 10 years.

I think the reason most fail in the first five years is due to the lack of experience and lack of capital. The reason the one survivor often fails in the second five years is not due to lack of capital, but lack of energy. The hours of long, hard work finally get to the person. Many "S's" just burn out. That is why so many highly educated professionals change firms or try to start something new, or die. Maybe that is why the average life expectancy for doctors and lawyers is lower than it is for most others. Their average life expectancy is 58. For everyone else, it is in the 70s.

For those who do survive, they seem to have become used to the idea of getting up, going to work and working hard forever. That seems to be all they know.

A friend's parents remind me of this. For 45 years they have spent long hours in their liquor store on a street corner. As crime increased in their neighborhood, they had to put steel bars up on the doors and all the windows. Today, money is passed through a slot, much like in a bank. I go by occasionally to see them. They are wonderful, sweet people, but it saddens me to see them as virtual prisoners in their own business, from 10 in the morning until 2 the next morning, staring out from behind the bars.

Many wise "S's" sell their businesses at their peak, before they run out of steam, to someone with energy and money. They take some time off, and then start something new. They keep doing their own thing and love it. But they have to know when to get out.

THE WORST ADVICE TO GIVE YOUR CHILDREN

If you were born prior to 1930, the advice "Go to school, get good grades, and find a safe, secure job" was good advice. But if you were born after 1930, it is bad advice.

Why?

The answer is found in: 1. Taxes. 2. Debt.

For people who earn their income out of the "E" quadrant, there are virtually no tax breaks left. Today in America, being an employee means you are a 50/50 partner with the government. That means the government ultimately will take 50 percent or more of an employee's earnings, and much of that even before the employee sees the paycheck.

When you consider that the government offers you tax breaks for going further into debt, the path to financial freedom is virtually impossible for most people in the "E" quadrant and for most in the "S" Quadrant. I often hear accountants tell clients who begin earning more income from the "E" quadrant to buy a bigger house so they can receive a bigger tax break. While that might make sense to someone on the left side of the *CASHFLOW Quadrant*, that makes no sense to someone on the right side of the *Quadrant*.

WHO PAYS THE MOST TAXES?

The rich pay few income taxes. Why? Simply because they do not earn their money as employees. The ultra rich know that the best way to avoid taxes legally is by generating that income out of the "B" and "I" quadrants.

If people earn money in the "E" quadrant, the only tax break they are offered is to buy a bigger house and go into greater debt. From the right side of the *CASHFLOW Quadrant,* that is not too financially intelligent. To people on the right side, that is the same as saying, "Give me $1, and I will give you $.50 back."

TAXES ARE UNFAIR

I often hear people say, "It's un-American not to pay taxes."

Americans who say this seem to have forgotten their history. America was founded out of tax protest. Have they forgotten the infamous Boston Tea Party of 1773? The rebellion that led to the Revolutionary War which separated the American colonies from the oppressive taxes of England.

This rebellion was followed by the Shay's Rebellion, The Whiskey Rebellion, Fries Rebellion, The Tariff Wars and many others throughout the history of the United States.

There are two other famous tax revolts that were not American, but also demonstrate the passion with which people object to taxation:

The story of William Tell is a story of tax protest. That is why the arrow was shot off his son's head. He was angry about taxes and risked his son's life in protest.

And then there was Lady Godiva. She asked that taxes in her town be lowered. The heads of the government said they would lower the taxes if she would ride naked through the town. She took them up on their dare.

TAX ADVANTAGES

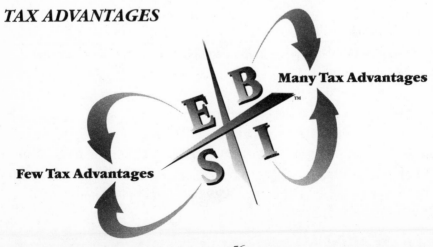

Many Tax Advantages

Few Tax Advantages

Taxes are a necessity of modern civilization. Problems arise when taxes become abusive and mismanaged. In the next few years, millions of baby boomers will begin to retire. They will shift from the role of taxpayers to retirement and Social Security recipients. There will be a need to collect more taxes to support this shift. America and other great nations will decline financially. Individuals with money will leave in search of countries that welcome their money, instead of penalize them for having it.

A BIG MISTAKE

Earlier this year, I was interviewed by a newspaper reporter. During the interview, he asked me how much money I made during the prior year. I replied, "Approximately a million dollars."

"And how much did you pay in taxes?" he asked.

"Nothing," I said. "That money was made in capital gains, and I was able to indefinitely defer paying those taxes. I sold three pieces of real estate and put them through a Tax Code Section 1031 exchange. I never touched the money. I just reinvested it into a much larger property." A few days later, the newspaper ran this story.

"Rich man makes $1 million and admits to paying nothing in taxes."

I did say something like that, but a few choice words are missing, thus distorting the message. I do not know if the reporter was being malicious or if he simply did not understand what a 1031 exchange was. Whatever the reason, it is a perfect example of different points of view coming from different quadrants. As I said, not all income is equal. Some income is much less taxed than others.

MOST PEOPLE FOCUS ON INCOME NOT INVESTMENTS

The reporter earns his income in this column:

I earn my money in this column:

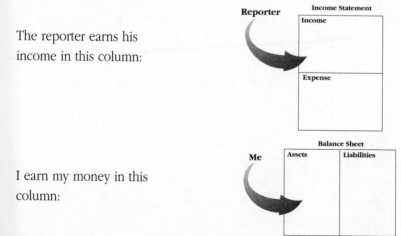

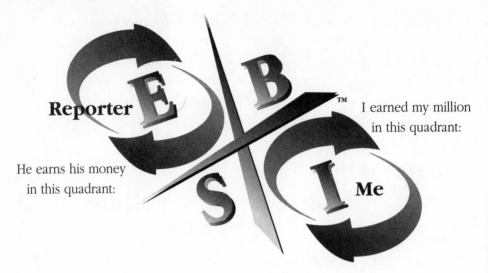

Reporter

He earns his money
in this quadrant:

I earned my million
in this quadrant:

Me

And today, I still hear people saying, "I'm going back to school so I can get a raise," or "I'm working hard so I can get a promotion."

Those are words or ideas of a person who is focusing on the income column of the financial statement or the "E" quadrant of the *CASHFLOW Quadrant*. Those are the words of a person who will give half of that raise to the government and work harder and longer to do it.

In an upcoming chapter, I will explain how people on the right-hand side of the *Quadrant* utilize taxes as an asset, instead of the liability it is for most people on the left side of the *Quadrant*. It is not a matter of being unpatriotic; it's a matter of being a person who protests, and fights back legally, to defend the right to keep as much money as possible. People and countries that do not protest their taxes are often people or countries with depressed economies.

GET RICH QUICKLY

For my wife and me to go from homeless to financially free quickly meant earning our money in the "B" and "I" quadrants. In the right-hand quadrants, you can get rich quickly because you can avoid paying taxes legally. And by being able to keep more money and have that money work for us, we found freedom quickly.

HOW TO GET FREE

Taxes and debt are two of the main reasons most people never feel financially secure or achieve financial freedom. The path to security or freedom is found on the right-hand side of the *CASHFLOW Quadrant*. You need to go beyond job security. It is time to know the difference between financial security and financial freedom.

WHAT IS THE DIFFERENCE BETWEEN

1. JOB SECURITY,
2. FINANCIAL SECURITY, and
3. FINANCIAL FREEDOM?

As you know, my highly educated dad was fixated on job security, as are most people of his generation. He assumed that job security meant financial security... that was, until he lost his job and could not get another job. My rich dad never talked about job security. He talked instead about financial freedom.

The answer to finding the kind of security or freedom you desire can be found in observing the patterns found in the *CASHFLOW Quadrant.*

1. THIS IS THE PATTERN FOR JOB SECURITY

SCHOOL

People with this pattern are often good at performing their job. Many spent years in school, and years on the job gaining experience. The problem is they know little about the "B" quadrant or the "I" quadrant, even if they have a retirement plan. They feel financially insecure because they have been trained only for job or professional security.

TWO LEGS ARE BETTER THAN ONE

To become more financially secure, I suggest, in addition to performing their jobs in the "E" or "S" quadrants, individuals become educated in the "B" or "I" quadrants. By having confidence in their abilities on both sides of the *Quadrant,* they will naturally feel more secure, even if they have only a little money. Knowledge is power... all they have to do is wait for the opportunity to use their knowledge and then they'll have the money.

That is why our maker gave us two legs. If we had only one leg, we would always feel wobbly and insecure. By having knowledge in two quadrants, one on the left and one on the right, we tend to feel more secure. People who know about their job or their profession only have one leg. Every time the economic winds blow, they tend to wobble more than people with two legs.

2. THIS IS THE PATTERN FOR FINANCIAL SECURITY

This is what financial security looks like for an "E":

Instead of just putting money into a retirement account and hoping for the best, this loop signifies that people feel confident in their education as both an investor and an employee. Just as we study at school to learn a job, I suggest you study to learn to be a professional investor.

The reporter who was upset about me making a million dollars in my asset column and not paying taxes never asked me the question, "How did you make the million dollars?"

To me, that is the real question. Legally avoiding the taxes is easy. Making the million was not so easy.

A second path to financial security could be:

And this is what financial security looks like for an "S":

This is the pattern described by the book *The Millionaire Next Door*, written by Thomas Stanley. It is an excellent book. The average American millionaire is self-employed, lives frugally, and invests for the long term. The pattern above reflects that financial life path.

This path, the "S to the B," is often the path that many great entrepreneurs, like Bill Gates, take. It is not the easiest, but in my mind, it is one of the best.

TWO IS BETTER THAN ONE

So being educated in more than one quadrant, especially one on the left and one on the right, is much better than being good in just one. In Chapter 2, I refer to the fact that the average rich person earns 70 percent from the right side and 30 percent from the left side of the *Quadrant.* I have found that no matter how much money people make, they will feel more secure if they operate in more than one quadrant. Financial security is having a secure footing on both sides of the *CASHFLOW Quadrant.*

MILLIONAIRE FIREFIGHTERS

I have two friends who are examples of success on both sides of the *CASHFLOW Quadrant.* They have tremendous job security with benefits, and they have also achieved great financial wealth on the right side of the *Quadrant.* Both are firefighters working for the city government. They have good, steady pay, excellent benefits and retirement plans, and work only two days a week. Three days a week they work as professional investors. The remaining two days, they relax and spend with their families.

One buys old houses, fixes them up and collects rent. At the time of this writing, he owns 45 houses that pay him $10,000 a month net, after debt, taxes, maintenance, management and insurance. He earns $3,500 as a firefighter, making his total monthly income more than $13,000 and annual income about $150,000 and growing. He has five more years before retirement, and his goal is to have

$200,000 a year in income at age 56. Not bad for a government employee with four kids.

The other friend spends his time analyzing companies and taking major long-term positions in stocks and options. His portfolio is now more than $3 million. If he cashed it out and earned 10 percent interest a year, he would have an income of $300,000 per year, barring any major market changes, for life. Again, not bad for a government employee with two kids.

Both friends have enough passive income from their 20 years of investing to have retired by age 40... but they both enjoy their work and want to retire with full benefits from local government. They then will be free because they will enjoy the benefits of success from both sides of the *Quadrant.*

MONEY ALONE DOES NOT BRING SECURITY

I have met many people who have millions in their retirement accounts and still feel insecure. Why? Because it's money generated from their job or business. They often have the money invested in a retirement account, but know little to nothing about the subject of investments. If that money disappears, and their working days are over, what do they do then?

In times of great economic change, there are always great transfers of wealth. Even if you do not have much money, it is important to invest in your education... for when the changes come, you will be better prepared for them. Don't be caught unaware and afraid. As I said, no one can predict what will happen, yet it is best to be prepared for whatever happens. And that means getting educated now.

3. THIS IS THE PATTERN FOR FINANCIAL FREEDOM

This is the pattern of study my rich dad recommended. It is the path to financial freedom. This is true financial freedom because in the "B" quadrant, people are working for you, and in the "I" quadrant, your money is working for you. You are free to work or not to work. Your knowledge in these two quadrants has brought you complete physical freedom from work.

If you look at the ultra rich, this is their pattern in the *Quadrant*. The loop around the "B" and the "I" signifies the income pattern of Bill Gates of Microsoft, Rupert Murdoch of News Corp., Warren Buffet of Berkshire Hathaway, and Ross Perot.

A quick word of caution. The "B" quadrant is much different from the "I" quadrant. I have seen many successful "B's" sell their businesses for millions, and their new-found wealth goes to their head. They tend to think that their dollars are a measure of their IQ, so they swagger on down to the "I" quadrant and lose it all. The game and rules are different in all of the quadrants... which is why I recommend education over ego.

Just as in the case of financial security, having two quadrants gives you greater stability in the world of financial freedom.

A CHOICE OF PATHS

These are the different financial paths people can choose. Unfortunately, most people choose the path of job security. When the economy starts wobbling, they often cling more desperately to job security. They wind up spending their lives there.

At a minimum, I recommend becoming educated in financial security, which is feeling confident about your job and feeling confident about your ability to invest in good times and in bad times. A big secret is that true investors make more money in bad markets. They make their money because the non-investors are panicking and selling when they should be buying. That is why I am not afraid of the possible coming economic changes... because change means wealth is being transferred.

YOUR BOSS CANNOT MAKE YOU RICH

The economic changes currently happening are partly from the sales and mergers of companies. Recently, a friend of mine sold his company. He put more than $15 million into his bank account the day of the sale. His employees had to look for new jobs.

At the farewell party, which was filled with tears, there were also undercurrents of extreme anger and resentment. Although he had paid them well for years, most workers were no financially better off on their last day of work than they were on their first day of work. Many people realized that the owner of the company had gotten rich while they spent all those years collecting their paychecks and paying bills.

The reality is, your boss's job is not to make you rich. Your boss's job is to make sure you get your paycheck. It is your job to become rich, if you want to. And that job begins the moment you receive your paycheck. If you have poor money-management skills, then all the money in the world cannot save you. If you budget your money wisely, and learn about either the "B" or "I" quadrant, then you are on your own path to great personal fortune and, most importantly, freedom.

My rich dad used to say to his son and me, "The only difference between a rich person and a poor person is what they do in their spare time."

I agree with that statement. I realize that people are busier than ever before, and free time is more and more precious. Yet, I would like to suggest that if you are going to be busy anyway, be busy on both sides of the *Quadrant*. If you do that, you will have a better chance of eventually finding more free time and more financial freedom. When at work, work hard. Please do not read the "Wall Street Journal" on company time. Your boss will appreciate and respect you more. What you do after work with your paycheck and your spare time will determine your future. If you work hard on the left side of the *Quadrant*, you will work hard forever. If you work hard on the right side of the *Quadrant*, you have a chance of finding freedom.

THE PATH I RECOMMEND

I am often asked by people on the left side of the *Quadrant,* "What would you recommend?" I recommend the same path my rich dad recommended to me. The same path that people like Ross Perot, Bill Gates and others took. The path looks like this:

I occasionally receive this complaint, "But I'd rather be an investor."

To which I reply, "Then go to the "I" quadrant. If you have plenty of money and lots of free time, go straight to the "I" quadrant. But if you don't have an abundance of time and money, the path I recommend is safer."

In most cases, people do not have an abundance of time or money, so they then ask another question, "Why? Why do you recommend the "B" quadrant first?"

This discussion usually takes an hour or so, which I will not go into here. But I will summarize my reasons in the next few lines.

1. **Experience and education.** If you are first successful as a "B," you will have a better chance of developing into a powerful "I."

"I's" invest in "B's"

If you first develop a solid business sense, you can become a better investor. You will be better able to identify other good "B's." True investors invest in successful "B's" with stable business systems. It is risky to invest in an "E" or an "S" who does not know the difference between a system and a product... or who lacks excellent leadership skills.

2. Cash Flow. If you have a business that is up and running, you then should have the free time and the cash flow to support the ups and downs of the "I" quadrant.

Many times I meet people from the "E-S" quadrants who are so tight on cash, they could not afford to take any kind of financial loss. One market swing and they are wiped out financially because they operate financially at "red line."

The reality is, investing is capital and knowledge intensive. Sometimes it takes lots of capital and time to gain that knowledge. Many successful investors have lost many times before winning. Successful people know that success is a poor teacher. Learning comes from making mistakes, and in the "I" quadrant, mistakes cost money. If you lack both knowledge and capital, it's financial suicide to try to become an investor.

By developing the skill of becoming a good "B" first, you will also be providing the cash flow necessary to move on to becoming a good investor. The business you develop as a "B" will provide the cash to support you as you gain the education to become a good investor. Once you have gained the education to become a successful investor you will understand how I can say "It does not always take money to make money."

GOOD NEWS

The good news is that it is now easier than ever before to be successful in the "B" quadrant. Just as there have been technological advances that have made many things easier, technology also has made it easier to be successful in the "B" quadrant. Although it's not as easy as just getting a minimum-wage job, the systems are in place now for more and more people to find financial success as "B's."

CHAPTER 4

The 3 Kinds Of Business Systems

In moving to the "B" quadrant, remember that your goal is to own a system and have people work that system for you. You can develop the business system yourself or you can look for a system to purchase. Think of the system as the bridge that will allow you to cross safely from the left side of the *CASHFLOW Quadrant* to the right side… your bridge to financial freedom.

There are three main types of business systems commonly in use today. They are:

1. Traditional C-type corporations – where you develop your own system.
2. Franchises – where you buy an existing system.
3. Network Marketing – where you buy into and become part of an existing system.

Each has its strengths and weaknesses, yet each ultimately does the same thing. If operated properly, each system will provide a steady stream of income without much physical effort on the part of the owner… once it is up and running. The problem is getting it up and running.

In 1985, when people asked, "Why were you homeless?" Kim and I simply said, "We were building a business system."

It was a business system that was a hybrid of the traditional C-type corporation and a franchise. As stated before, the "B" quadrant requires a knowledge of both systems and people.

Our decision to develop our own system meant a lot of hard work. I had taken this route before, and my company had failed. Although it was successful for years, it suddenly went broke in its fifth year. When success came to us, we were not ready with an adequate system. The system began to break down even though we had hard-working people. We felt like we were on a good-size yacht that had sprung a leak, but we could not find the leak. All of us were trying to figure out where the leak was, but we could not bail water fast enough to find the leak and fix it. Even if we found it, we were not certain we could plug it.

"YOU MAY LOSE 2 OR 3 COMPANIES"

When I was in high school, my rich dad told his son and me that he had lost a company when he was in his 20s. "That was the best and worst experience of my life," he said. "As much as I hated it, I learned more by repairing it and eventually turning it into a huge success."

Knowing that I was contemplating starting my own company, rich dad said to me, "You may lose two or three companies, before you build a successful one that lasts."

He was training Mike, his son, to take over his empire. Because my dad was a government employee, I was not going to inherit an empire. I had to build my own.

SUCCESS IS A POOR TEACHER

"Success is a poor teacher," Rich dad always said. "We learn the most about ourselves when we fail... so don't be afraid of failing. Failing is part of the process of success. You cannot have success without failure. So unsuccessful people are people who never fail."

Maybe it was a self-fulfilling prophecy, but in 1984, the company that went down was company No. 3. I had made millions and had lost millions and was starting all over again when I met Kim. The reason I know she did not marry me for my money is because I did not have any money. When I told her what I was going to do, build company No. 4, she did not back away.

"I'll build it with you," was her reply, and she was true to her word. Along with another partner, we built a business system with 11 offices worldwide that generated income regardless of whether we worked. Building it from nothing to 11 offices took five years of blood, sweat and tears... but it worked. Both dads were happy for me and sincerely congratulated me (they had both lost money in my previous experiments at starting companies).

THE HARD PART

Mike, my rich dad's son, has often said to me, "I will never know if I can do what you did or my dad did. The system was handed to me, and all I had to do was learn how to run it."

I am certain he could have developed his own successful system because he learned well from his dad. Yet, I understand what he meant. The hard thing about building a company from scratch is that you have two big variables: the system and the people building the system. If both the people and the system are leaky, the chances for failure are great. Sometimes it is hard to know whether the problem is the person or the system that is failing.

BEFORE FRANCHISES

When my rich dad began teaching me about becoming a "B," there was only one kind of business. That was big business... a major corporation that usually dominated the town. In our town in Hawaii, it was the sugar plantation that controlled virtually every thing... including the other big businesses. So there were big businesses and mom-and-pop "S"-type businesses with little in between.

To be able to work at the top levels of those big sugar companies was not a likely goal for people like rich dad and me. Minorities, such as the Japanese, Chinese and Hawaiians worked in the fields, but were never allowed in the boardroom. So rich dad learned everything he knew simply by trial and error.

As I started high school, we began to hear about a thing called "franchises," but none had come to our little town. We had not heard about McDonald's or Kentucky Fried Chicken or Taco Bell. They were not a part of our vocabulary while I was studying with rich dad. When we did hear rumors about them, we heard they were "illegal, fraudulent scams and dangerous." Naturally, upon hearing those rumors, rich dad flew to California to begin checking franchises out, rather than believing the gossip. When he returned, all he said was, "Franchises are the wave of the future," and he bought the rights to two of them. His wealth skyrocketed as the idea of franchises caught on, and he began selling his rights to other people so they could have a chance at building their own businesses.

When I asked him if I should buy one from him, he simply said, "No. You've come this far in learning how to build your own business system; don't stop now. Franchises are for people who do not want to build or do not know how to build their own systems. Besides, you don't have the $250,000 it takes to buy a franchise from me."

It is hard to imagine today a city without a McDonald's or Burger King or Pizza Hut on every corner. Yet, there was a time, not too long ago, when they did not exist. And I'm old enough to remember those days.

HOW TO LEARN TO BECOME A "B"

The way I learned to become a "B" was by being an apprentice to my rich dad. His son and I were both "E's" learning to be "B's." And that is the way many people learn. It's called "on-the-job training." This is the way many closely held family empires are passed on from one generation to the next.

The problem is, not too many people are privileged or lucky enough to learn the "behind-the-scene" aspects of becoming a "B." Most corporate "management-training programs" are just that – the company only trains you to be a manager. Few teach what it takes to be a "B."

Often people get stuck in the "S" quadrant in their journey to the "B" quadrant. This happens primarily because they do not develop a strong enough system, and so they end up becoming an integral part of the system. Successful "B's" develop a system that will run without their involvement.

There are three ways you can make it to the "B" side quickly.

1. **Find a mentor.** My rich dad was my mentor. A mentor is someone who has already done what you want to do… and is successful at doing it. Do not find an adviser. An adviser is someone who tells you how to do it, but has not personally done it. Most advisers are in the "S" quadrant. The world

is filled with "S's" trying to tell you how to be a "B" or an "I." My rich dad was a mentor, not an adviser. One of the biggest tips my rich dad gave me was this:

"Be careful of the advice you take. While you must keep your mind open, always be first aware of which quadrant the advice is coming from."

My rich dad taught me about systems and how to be a leader of people, not a manager of people. Managers often see their subordinates as inferiors. Leaders must direct people who are often smarter.

If you would like to read an excellent book about the basics of starting your own business system, check out *E-Myth*, by Michael Gerber. For people who want to learn to develop their own system, this book is priceless.

A traditional way of learning about systems is to get your MBA from a prestigious school and get a fast-track job up the corporate ladder. An MBA is important because you learn the basics of accounting and how the financial numbers relate to the systems of a business. Yet, just because you have an MBA does not automatically mean you are competent to run all the systems that ultimately make up a complete business system.

To learn about all the systems necessary in a big company, you'll need to spend 10 to 15 years there, learning all the different aspect of the business. You should then be prepared to leave and start your own company. Working for a successful major corporation is like being paid by your mentor.

Even with a mentor and/or years of experience, this first method is labor intensive. To create your own system requires a lot of trial and error, up-front legal costs, and paperwork. All of this occurs at the same time you are trying to develop your people.

2. Franchises. Another way to learn about systems is to buy a franchise. When you buy a franchise, you are buying a "tried and proven" operating system. There are many excellent franchises.

By buying the franchise system, instead of trying to create your own, you can focus on developing your people. Buying the system removes one big variable when you are learning how to be a "B." The reason many banks will loan money on a franchise and not to a small start-up business is because the banks recognize the importance of systems and how starting with a good system will lower their risk.

A word of caution if you buy a franchise. Please do not be an "S" who wants to "do their own thing." If you buy a franchise system, be an "E." Just do it exactly the way they tell you to do it. Nothing is more tragic than the courtroom fights between franchisees and franchisors. The fights occur usually because the people who buy the system really want to do it their way, not the way the person who created the system wants it run. If you want to do your own thing, then do it after you've mastered both systems and people.

My highly educated dad failed even though he bought a famous and expensive ice-cream franchise. Although the system was excellent, the business still failed. In my opinion, the franchise failed because the people he was in partnership with were all "E's" and "S's" who did not know what to do when things started to get bad, and did not ask for support from the parent company. In the end, the partners fought among themselves, and the business went down. They forgot that a true "B" is more than a system. It is also dependent on good people to operate the system.

BANKS DON'T LEND MONEY TO PEOPLE WITHOUT SYSTEMS

If a bank will not lend money to a small business without a system, why should you? Almost daily, people come to me with business plans with the hope of raising money for their idea or their project.

Most of the time I turn them down for one main reason. The people raising the money do not know the difference between a product and a system. I have had friends (singers in a band) ask me to invest money in developing a new music CD, and others who want me to help form a new nonprofit to change the world. As much as I might like the project, the product or the person, I will turn them down if they have little or no experience in creating and running business systems.

Just because you can sing does not mean you understand the system of marketing, or the system of finance and accounting, and the system of sales, and the system of hiring and firing people, and the legal system, and the many other systems that are required to keep a business afloat and make it successful.

For a business to survive and thrive, 100 percent of all the systems must be functioning and accountable. For example:

An airplane is a system of systems. If an airplane takes off and, let's say, the fuel system fails, there often is a crash. The same things happen in business. It's not the systems that you know about that are the problem – it's the systems you are not aware of that cause you to crash.

The human body is a system of systems. Most of us have had a loved one die because one of the body systems has failed – like the blood system, which causes disease to spread to all of the other systems.

That is why building a tried-and-true business system is not easy. It is the systems you forget about or do not pay attention to that cause you to crash and burn. That is why I rarely invest with an "E" or "S" who has a new product or idea. Professional investors tend to invest in proven systems with people who know how to run those systems.

So if banks lend based only on tried-and-true systems, and look to the person who is going to run them, then you should do the same – if you want to be a smart investor.

3. **Network marketing.** Also called multilevel marketing or direct distribution systems. Just as with franchises, the legal system initially attempted to outlaw network marketing, and I know of some countries that have succeeded in outlawing or severely restricting it. Any new system or idea often goes through this period of being classified as "strange and suspicious." At first, I also thought that network marketing was a scam. But over the years, I have studied the various systems available through network marketing, and I have watched several friends become successful at this form of "B." I have changed my mind.

After I dropped my prejudices and began researching network marketing, I found that there were many people who were sincerely and diligently building successful network marketing businesses. When I met these people, I saw the impact their business had on other people's lives and financial futures. I began to truly appreciate the value of the network marketing system. For a reasonable entry fee (often around $200), people can buy into an existing system and immediately start building their business. Due to the technological advances in the computer industry, these organizations are totally automated, and the headaches of paperwork, order processing, distribution, accounting and follow-up are almost entirely managed by the network marketing software systems. New distributors can focus all of their efforts in building their business through sharing this automated business opportunity instead of worrying about the normal start-up headaches of a small business.

One of my old friends who did more than a billion dollars in real estate in 1997 recently signed on as a network marketing distributor and began building his business. I was surprised to find him so diligently building a network marketing business because he definitely did not need the money. When I asked him why, he explained it this way:

"I went to school to become a CPA, and I have an MBA in finance. When people ask me how I became so rich, I tell them about the multimillion-dollar real estate transactions I do and the hundreds of thousands of dollars in passive income I receive each year from my real estate. I then notice that some of them withdraw or shy away. We both know that their chances of doing multimillion-dollar real estate investments like I do are slim to none. Besides not having the educational background, they do not have the extra capital to invest. So I began to look for a way I could help them achieve the same level of passive income I developed from real estate... without going back to school for six years and spending 12 years investing in real estate. I believe network marketing gives people the opportunity to build up the passive income they need for support while they learn to become professional investors. That is why I recommend network marketing to them. Even if they have little money, they can still invest 'sweat equity' for five years and begin to generate more than enough passive income to begin investing. By developing their own business, they have the free time to learn and the capital to invest with me in my bigger deals."

My friend joined a network marketing company as a distributor, after researching several, and started a network marketing business with people who someday want to invest with him. He is now doing well in his network marketing business as well as in his investment business. He told me, "I did it initially because I wanted to help people find the money to invest, and now I'm getting rich from a whole new business."

Twice a month, he holds classes on Saturdays. At the first meeting, he teaches people about business systems and people, or how to develop into a successful "B." On the second meeting of the month, he teaches them about financial literacy and financial intelligence. He is teaching them to be savvy "I's." His class sizes are growing rapidly.

The pattern he recommends is the same one I recommend.

A PERSONAL FRANCHISE

And that's why today I recommend people consider network marketing. Many famous franchises cost a million dollars or more to buy. Network marketing is like buying a personal franchise, often for less than $200.

I know much of network marketing is hard work. But success in any quadrant is hard work. I personally generate no income as a network marketing distributor. I have researched several network marketing companies and their compensation plans. While doing my research, I did join several companies, just because their products were so good and I use them as a consumer.

Yet, if I could give you a recommendation as to finding a good organization to help you get over to the right side of the *Quadrant*, the key is not so much the product but the education the organization offers. There are network marketing organizations that are only interested in having you sell their system to your friends. And there are organizations primarily interested in educating you and helping you succeed.

From my research into network marketing, I have found two important things you can learn through their programs that are essential in becoming a successful "B":

1. To be successful, you need to learn to overcome your fear of being rejected, and to stop worrying about what other people will say about you. So many times I have met people who hold themselves back simply because of what their friends might say if they did something different. I know because I was the same way. Coming from a small town, everyone knew what everyone else was up to. If someone did not like what you were doing, the whole town heard about it and made your business their business.

One of the best phrases I said over and over to myself was, "What you think of me is none of my business. What is most important is what I think about myself."

One of the reasons my rich dad encouraged me to work in sales for Xerox Corporation for four years was not because he liked copiers, but because he wanted me to overcome my shyness and fear of rejection.

2. To learn to lead people. Working with different kinds of people is the hardest thing about business. The people I have met who are successful in any business are those who are natural leaders. The ability to get along with and inspire people is a priceless skill. A skill that can be learned.

As I said, the transition from the left quadrant to the right quadrant is not so much what you do, but who you have to become. Learn how to handle rejection, how not to be affected by what other people think of you, and learn to lead people and you will find prosperity. So I endorse any network marketing organization that is first committed to developing you as a human being, more than developing you into a salesperson. I would seek organizations that:

1. Are proven organizations that have successful track records and a distribution system and a compensation plan that has been successful for years.
2. Have a business opportunity you can succeed with, believe in and share confidently with others.
3. Have ongoing, long-term educational programs to develop you as a human being. Self-confidence is vital on the right side of the *Quadrant.*
4. Have a strong mentor program. You want to learn from leaders, not advisers. People who are already leaders on the right side of the *Quadrant* and want you to succeed.
5. Have people you respect and enjoy being with.

If the organization meets these five criteria, then and only then look at the product. Too many people look at the product and not the business system and organization behind the product. In some of the organizations I have looked into, one of their pitches was, "The product sells itself. It's easy." If you're looking to be a salesperson, an "S," then the product is the most important thing. But if you're developing into a long term "B," then the system, lifelong education, and the people are more important.

A friend and colleague of mine knowledgeable in this industry reminded me about the value of time, one of our most precious assets. A true success story in a network marketing company is when your commitment of time and hard work in the short term results in significant long-term passive income. Once you have built a strong organization below you, you can stop working and your revenue stream will continue from the efforts of the organization you have built. The most important key to success with a network marketing company is still, however, a long-term commitment on your part, as well as the organization's part, to mold you into the business leader you want to become.

A SYSTEM IS A BRIDGE TO FREEDOM

Being homeless was not an experience I want to repeat. Yet, for Kim and me, the experience was priceless. Today, freedom and security are found not so much in what we have, but what we know we can create with confidence.

Since that time we have created or helped develop a real estate company, an oil company, a mining company, and two education companies. So the process of learning how to create a successful system was beneficial for us. Yet, I would not recommend the process to anyone, unless they truly want to go through it.

Until only a few years ago, the possibility of a person becoming successful in the "B" quadrant was only available to those who were brave or rich. Kim and I must have been brave because we certainly weren't rich. The reason so many people stay stuck in the left side of the *Quadrant* is because they feel the risks involved in developing their own system are too great. For them, it is smarter to remain safe and secure in a job.

Today, primarily due to changes in technology, the risk in becoming a successful business owner has been greatly reduced... and the opportunity to own your own business system has been made available to virtually everyone.

Franchises and network marketing took away the hard part of developing your own system. You acquire the rights to a proven system, and then your only job is to develop your people.

Think of these business systems as bridges. Bridges that will provide a path for you to cross safely from the left side to the right side of the *CASHFLOW Quadrant*... your bridge to financial freedom.

In the next chapter, I will cover the second half of the right side of the *Quadrant*, the "I," or investor.

CHAPTER 5

The 7 Levels Of Investors

My rich dad once asked me, "What is the difference between a person who bets on horses and a person who picks stocks?"

"I don't know," was my response.

"Not much," was his answer, "Never be the person who buys the stock. What you want to be when you grow up is the person who creates the stock that brokers sell and others buy."

For a long time, I did not understand what my rich dad really meant. It was not until I started teaching investing to others that I really understood the different types of investors.

A special thanks goes to John Burley for this chapter. John is considered one of the brightest minds in the world of real estate investing. In his late 20s and early 30s, he purchased more than 130 homes using none of his own money. By the time he was 32, he was financially free and never had to work again. So, like me, he chooses to teach. But his knowledge goes far beyond just real estate. He began his career as a financial planner, so he has a deep understanding of the world of finance and taxes. But he also has the unique ability to explain it clearly. He has the gift of taking the complex or abstract and making it simple to understand. Through his teaching, he developed a way to identify investors into six categories by their level of sophistication in their investing as well as their differences in personality traits. I have revised and expanded his categories to include a seventh.

Using this identification method in concert with the *CASHFLOW Quadrant* has helped me teach others about the world of investors. As you read about the different levels, you will probably recognize people you know at each level.

OPTIONAL LEARNING EXERCISE

At the end of each level, I have left a blank space where you can fill in the person or persons who, in your judgment, fit this level. When you find the level you are at, you may want to put your own name there.

As I said, this is only an optional exercise for the purpose of increasing your understanding of the different levels. It is in no way meant to degrade or put down your friends. The subject of money is as volatile as politics, religion and sex. That is why I recommend keeping your personal thoughts private. The blank space at the end of every level is merely there to enhance your learning, if you choose to use it.

I use this list often at the beginning of my investment classes. It has made the learning more powerful and has helped many students become clear on which level they are on and which level they want to go to.

Over the years, I have, with John's permission, modified the content to match my own experiences. Please read the seven levels carefully.

THE SEVEN LEVELS OF INVESTORS

LEVEL 0: THOSE WITH NOTHING TO INVEST

These people have no money to invest. They either spend everything they make or spend more than they make. There are many "rich" people who would fall into this category because they spend as much, or more, than they make. Unfortunately this zero level is where about 50 percent of the adult population would be categorized.

Do you know any Level 0 investors? (optional)

_____

_____

LEVEL 1: BORROWERS

These people solve financial problems by borrowing money. Often they even invest with borrowed money. Their idea of financial planning is robbing Peter to pay Paul. They live their financial lives with their head in the sand like an ostrich, hoping and praying that everything will work out. While they may have a few assets, the reality is that their level of debt is simply too high. For the most part, they are not conscious about money and their spending habits.

Anything they own of value has debt attached to it. They use credit cards impulsively and then roll that debt into a long-term home-equity loan so they can clean up their credit cards and then start charging again. If the value of their home goes up, they borrow on the equity again, or buy a larger and more expensive home. They believe the value of real estate only goes up.

The words "low down, easy monthly payments" always draw their attention. They often purchase depreciating toys (or doodads) such as boats, swimming pools, vacations and cars with those words in mind. They list these depreciating toys as assets and go back to the bank for another loan and wonder why they get turned down.

Shopping is their favorite form of exercise. They buy things they don't need, saying these words to themselves: "Oh, go ahead. You deserve it." Or "You're worth it." Or "If I don't buy it now, I may never find it again at such a great price." Or "It's on sale." Or "I want the kids to have what I never had."

They think spreading debt over a long period of time is smart, always kidding themselves that they'll work harder and pay off their bills someday. They spend everything they make and then some. They are known as consumers. Shop owners and car dealers love these people. If they have money, it gets spent. If they don't have the money, they borrow it.

When asked what their problem is, they will say that they just don't make enough money. They think more money will solve the problem. No matter how much they make, they only get deeper into debt. Little do most of them realize that the money they earn today seemed like a fortune or dream to them just yesterday. But today, even though they have achieved their dream income, it still is not enough.

They fail to see that the problem is not necessarily their income (or lack of it), but rather their money habits. Some eventually believe deep down that their situation is hopeless and have given up. So they bury their head deeper and keep on doing the same things. Their habits of borrowing, shopping and spending are out of control. Just as a binge eater eats when depressed, these people spend when depressed. They spend, get depressed and spend more.

They often argue with loved ones about money, emphatically defending their need to buy this or that. They live in complete financial denial, pretending that miraculously their money problems will someday disappear, or they pretend they will always have enough money to spend on whatever they desire.

This level of investor can often look rich. They may have big houses and flashy cars... but if you check, they buy on borrowed money. They may also make a lot of money, but they are one professional accident away from financial ruin.

I had an ex-business owner in one of my classes. He was well known in the "make big bucks, spend big bucks" category. He had a thriving chain of jewelry stores for years. But one downturn in the economy and his business disappeared. His debts, however, did not go away. It took less than six months for those debts to eat him alive. He was in my class looking for new answers and refused to even entertain the idea that he and his wife were Level 1 investors.

He came from the "B" quadrant, hoping to get rich in the "I" quadrant. He clung to the idea that he was once a successful businessman and could use the same formulas to invest his way to financial freedom. It was a classic case of a businessman thinking he could automatically become a successful investor. The rules of business are not always the same as the rules of investing.

Unless these investors are willing to change, their financial future is bleak... unless they marry someone rich who will put up with such habits.

Do you know any Level 1 investors? (optional)

_____

_____

Level 2: SAVERS

These people put aside a "small" amount of money (usually) on a regular basis. The money is in a low-risk, low-return vehicle such as a money-market checking account, savings account or certificate of deposit (CD).

If they have an Individual Retirement Account (IRA), they have it with a bank or in a mutual-fund cash account.

They often save to consume rather than to invest (e.g. they save for a new TV, car, vacation, etc.). They believe in paying in cash. They are afraid of credit and debt. Instead, they like the "security" of money in the bank.

Even when shown that in today's economic environment savings give a negative return (after inflation and taxes), they are still unwilling to take on much risk. Little do they know that the U.S. dollar has lost 90 percent of its value since 1950, and continues to lose value annually at a rate greater than the interest a bank pays them. They often have whole-life insurance policies because they love the feeling of security.

People in this group often waste their most precious asset, which is time, trying to save pennies. They spend hours clipping coupons from the newspaper, and then at the supermarket, they hold up everyone else in line, fumbling to find those big savings.

Instead of trying to save pennies, they could have put that time into learning how to invest. If they had put $10,000 into John Templeton's fund in 1954 and forgotten about it, it would have been worth $2.4 million in 1994. Or if they had put $10,000 into George Soros' Quantum Fund in 1969, it would have been worth $22.1 million in 1994. Instead, their deep need for security, which is fear-based, keeps them saving in low-yield investments, such as bank CD's.

You often hear these people saying, "A penny saved is a penny earned." Or "I'm saving for the kids." The real truth is there is often some deep insecurity running them and their lives. In truth, they often "shortchange" themselves and the people they are saving for. They are almost the exact opposite of the Level 1 investor.

Saving money was a good idea during the Agrarian Age. But once we entered the Industrial Age, savings was not the smart choice. Simply saving money became an even worse choice once the U.S. went off the gold standard and we hit the era of inflation with government rampantly printing money. People who save money during times of inflation end up as losers. Of course, if we go into a period of deflation, they may be winners... but only if the printed money is still worth something.

It is good to have some savings. It is recommended that you have six months' to a year's worth of living expenses held in cash. But after that, there are far better and safer investment vehicles than money in the bank. To hold your money in the bank earning 5 percent while others are getting 15 percent and more is not a wise investment strategy.

Yet, if you are unwilling to study investing and you live in constant fear of financial risk, then saving is a better choice than investing. You don't have to think as much if you just keep the money in the bank... and your bankers will love you. Why shouldn't they? The bank lends $10 to $20 for every $1 you have in savings and charges up to 19 percent interest, then turns around and pays you less than 5 percent. We should all be bankers.

Do you know any Level 2 investors? (optional)

_____

_____

LEVEL 3: "SMART" INVESTORS

There are three different types of investors in this group. This level of investor is aware of the need to invest. They may even participate in the company retirement plan 401(k), SEP, Superannuation, pension, etc. Sometimes they even have outside investments in mutual funds, stocks, bonds or limited partnerships.

Generally they are intelligent people who have a solid education. They make up the two-thirds of the country we call the "middle class." However, when it comes to investing, they are often not educated... or lack what the investment industry calls "sophistication." Rarely will they read a company annual report or company prospectus. How could they? They were not trained to read financial reports. They lack financial literacy. They may have advanced college degrees, and may be doctors or even accountants, but few have ever been formally trained and educated in the win/lose world of investing.

These are the three main categories in this level. They are often smart people who are well educated and often make substantial incomes, and they do invest. Yet, there are differences.

Level 3-A. People in this level make up the "I Can't Be Bothered" group. They have convinced themselves they don't understand money and never will. They say things like,

"I'm just not very good with numbers."

"I'll never understand how investing works."

"I'm just too busy."

"There's too much paperwork."

"It's just too complicated."

"Investing is too risky."

"I prefer to leave the money decisions to the professionals."

"It's too much of a hassle."

"My husband/wife handles the investments for our family."

These people just let the money sit and do little in their retirement plan or turn it over to a financial planner who recommends "diversification." They block their financial future out of their minds, work hard day to day, and say to themselves, "At least I have a retirement plan."

When they retire, then they'll look at how their investments did.

Do you know any Level 3-A investors? (optional)

_____

_____

Level 3-B. The second category is the "Cynic." These people know all the reasons why an investment will not work. They are dangerous to have around. They often sound intelligent, speak with authority, are successful in their chosen field, but are really cowards under their intellectual exterior. They can tell you exactly how and why you will get "swindled" with every investment known to man. When you ask for their opinion on a stock or other investment, you walk away feeling terrible, often afraid or doubtful. Their most commonly repeated words are, "Well, I've been taken before. They're not going to do that to me again."

They often drop names and say things like, "My broker at Merrill Lynch, or Dean Witter… " Name dropping helps cover their deep insecurity.

Yet strangely, these same cynics often follow the market like sheep. At work, they're always reading the financial pages or the "Wall Street Journal". They read the paper and then tell everyone else what they know at the coffee break. Their language is filled with the latest investment jargon and technical terms. They talk about the big deals, but are never in them. They look for stocks that make the front page and, if the report is favorable, they often buy. The problem is they buy late because if you get your news from the newspaper… it is too late. The truly smart investors have bought way before it makes the news. The cynic does not know that.

When bad news comes, they criticize and say things like, "I knew it." They think they're in the game, but they are really only a spectator standing on the sidelines. They often want to get into the game, but deep down they are terribly afraid of getting hurt. Security is more important than fun.

Psychiatrists report that cynicism is the combination of fear and ignorance, which in turn causes arrogance. These people often enter major market swings late, waiting for the crowd or social proof that their investment decision is the right decision. Because they wait for social proof, they buy late at market tops and sell at market bottoms, just as the market crashes. They label buying high and selling low as getting "swindled" again. Everything they were so afraid of happening… happens, again and again.

Cynics are often what professional traders call "pigs." They squeal a lot and then run to their own slaughter. They buy high and sell low. Why? Because they're so "smart", they have become overly cautious. They are smart, but are terrified of taking risks and making mistakes, so they study harder, get smarter. The more they know, the more risk they see, so they study even harder. Their cynical caution causes them to wait until it's too late. They come to market when greed finally overpowers their fear. They come to the trough with the other pigs and get slaughtered.

But the worst part of the cynic is that they infect the people around them with their deep fear, disguised as intelligence. When it comes to investing, they can tell you why things won't work, but they can't tell you how it could work. The worlds of academia, government, religion and the media are filled with these people. They love hearing about financial disaster or wrong doings so they can "spread the word." They are truly "Monday-morning quarterbacks" when it comes to investing. Yet, rarely do they have anything good to say about financial success. A cynic finds it easy to discover what is wrong. It is their way of protecting themselves from revealing their lack of knowledge – or lack of courage.

The original Cynics were an ancient Greek sect despised because of their arrogance and sarcastic contempt for merit and success. They were nicknamed the dog-men (cynic comes from the Greek word for dog). When it comes to money, there are many dog-people... many who are smart, and well-educated. Be careful about allowing dog-people to squelch your financial dreams. While it is true that the world of money is filled with crooks, con-men and charlatans, what industry isn't?

It is possible to get rich quickly, with little money, and with little risk. It is possible, but only if you are willing to do your part to make it possible. One of the things you need to do is keep an open mind and be aware of cynics as well as con-men. They are both financially dangerous.

Do you know any Level 3-B investors? (optional)

_____

_____

Level 3-C: The third category of this level is the "Gambler." This group is also called "pigs" by professional traders. But while the "cynic" is overly cautious, this group is not cautious enough. They look at the stock market, or any investment market, about the same way they look at a Las Vegas craps table. It's just luck. Throw the dice and pray.

This group has no set trading rules or principles. They want to act like the "Big Boys," so they fake it until they make it or lose it all. The latter is most probable. They are searching for the "secret" to investing, or the "Holy Grail." They are always looking for new and exciting ways to invest. Instead of long-term diligence and study and understanding, they seek "tips" or "shortcuts."

They jump into commodities, initial public offerings (IPOs), penny stocks, gas and oil, cattle and every other investment known to mankind. They like to use "sophisticated" investment techniques such as margins, puts, calls and options. They jump into the "game" without knowing who the players are and who makes up the rules.

These people are the worst investors the planet has ever known. They always try to hit a "home run." They usually "strike out." When asked how they are doing, they always are "about even," or "a little bit up." In actuality, they have lost money. Lots of money. Often huge amounts of money. This type of investor loses money over 90 percent of the time. They never discuss their losses. They only remember the "killing" they made six years ago. They think they were smart and fail to recognize they were merely lucky. They think that all they need is "the one big deal" and then they'll be on easy street. Society calls this person an "incurable gambler." Deep down, they are simply lazy when it comes to investing money.

Do you know any Level 3-C investors? (optional)

_____

_____

LEVEL 4: LONG-TERM INVESTORS

These investors are clearly aware of the need to invest. They are actively involved in their own investment decisions. They have a clearly laid out long-term plan that will allow them to reach their financial objectives. They invest in their education before actually buying an investment. They take advantage of periodic investing and, whenever possible, invest in a tax-advantaged way. Most importantly they seek out advice from competent financial planners.

Please understand this type of investor is not what you would think of as some big-time investor. Far from it. It is doubtful that they are investing in real estate, businesses, commodities, or any other exciting investment vehicles. Rather, they take the conservative long-term approach recommended by investors such as Peter Lynch of Fidelity's Magellan Fund fame, or Warren Buffett.

If you are not yet a long-term investor, get yourself there as fast as you can. What does this mean? This means that you sit down and map out a plan. Get control of your spending habits. Minimize your debt and liabilities. Live within your means and then increase your means. Find out how much invested per month for how many months at a realistic rate of return it will take to reach your goals. Goals such as: At what age do you plan to stop working? How much money will you need per month?

Simply having a long-term plan that reduces your consumer debt while putting away a small amount of money (on a periodic basis) into a top mutual fund will give you a head start on retiring wealthy, if you start early enough and keep an eye on what you're doing.

At this level, keep it simple. Don't get fancy. Forget the sophisticated investments. Just do solid stock and mutual fund investments. Learn how to buy closed-end mutual funds soon, if you haven't already. Don't try to outsmart the market. Use insurance vehicles wisely as protection but not as wealth accumulation. A mutual fund like the Vanguard Index 500 fund, which in the past has outperformed two-thirds of all mutual funds year-in and year-out is worth using as a benchmark. Over 10 years, this type of fund may give you a return that exceeds 90 percent of the "professional" mutual-fund money managers. But always remember, there is no "100 percent safe investment." Index funds have their own inherent tragic flaws.

Stop waiting for the "big deal." Get into the "game" with small deals (like my first small condo that allowed me to start investing for just a few dollars). Don't worry about being right or wrong at first, just start. You'll learn a lot more once you put some money down... just a little to start. Money has a way of increasing intelligence quickly. Fear and hesitation retards you. You can always move up to a bigger game, but you can never get back the time and education you lost by waiting to do the right thing or make the big deal. Remember, small deals often lead to bigger deals... but you must start.

Start today, don't wait. Cut up your credit cards, get rid of "doodads" and call a good no-load mutual fund (although there is no such thing as a true "no-load" fund). Sit down with your loved ones and work out a plan, call a financial planner or go to the library and read about financial planning, and start putting money away (even if it's only $50 a month) for yourself. The longer you wait, the more you waste one of your most precious assets... the intangible and priceless asset of time.

An interesting note. Level 4 is where most of the millionaires in America come from. The book *The Millionaire Next Door* describes average millionaires as driving a Ford Taurus, owning a company and living within their means. They study or are informed about investing, have a plan, and invest for the long term. They do nothing fancy, risky or sexy when it comes to investing. They are truly conservative and their well-balanced financial habits are what make them rich and successful over the long haul.

For people who don't like risk, and would rather focus on their profession, job or career, instead of spending a lot of time studying the subject of investing, Level 4 is a must if you want to live a prosperous and financially abundant life. For these individuals, it is even more important to seek the advice of financial planners. They can help you develop your investment strategy and get you started on the right track with a long-term investing pattern.

This level of investor is patient and uses the advantage of time. If you start early and invest regularly, you can make it to phenomenal wealth. If you start late in life, past age 45, this level may not work, especially between now and the year 2010.

Do you know any Level 4 investors? (optional)

_____

_____

Level 5: SOPHISTICATED INVESTORS

These investors can "afford" to seek more aggressive or risky investment strategies. Why? Because they have good money habits, a solid foundation of money and also investment savvy. They are not new to the game. They are focused, not usually diversified. They have a long track record of winning on a consistent basis, and they have had enough losses that give them the wisdom that only comes from making mistakes and learning from them.

These are the investors that often buy investments "wholesale" rather than "retail." They put their own deals together for their own use. Or they are "sophisticated" enough to get into deals that their Level 6 friends have put together that need investment capital.

What determines whether people are "sophisticated?" They have a financial base that is sound, from their profession, business or retirement income, or have a base of solid, conservative investments. These people have their personal debt/equity ratios in control, which means they have much more income than expenses. They are well educated in the world of investing and actively seek new information. They are cautious, yet not cynical, always keeping an open mind.

They risk less than 20 percent of all their capital in speculative ventures. They often start small, putting a little money down, so they can learn the business of investing, be it stocks, a business acquisition, a real estate syndication, buying foreclosures, etc. If they lost this 20 percent, it would not damage them or take food off their table. They will look at the loss as a lesson, learn from it, and get back into the game to learn more, knowing that failure is part of the process of success. While hating to lose, they are not afraid of losing. Losing inspires them to move forward, to learn, rather than to dive into their emotional cave and call their attorney.

If people are sophisticated, they can create their own deals with returns of 25 percent to infinity. They are classified as sophisticated because they have the extra money, a team of hand-picked professional advisers, and a track record to prove it.

As mentioned earlier, investors at this level put their own deals together. Just as there are some who buy computers right off the retailer's shelf, there are some people who buy components and create their own customized computer system. Level 5 investors can assemble their investments by bringing different components together.

These investors know that bad economic times or markets offer them the best opportunities for success. They get into markets when others are getting out. They usually know when to get out. At this level, an exit strategy is more important than entry into the market.

They are clear on their own "principles" and their "rules" of investing. Their vehicle of choice might be real estate, discounted paper, businesses, bankruptcies or new issues of stocks. While they take risks greater than the average person, they abhor gambling. They have a plan and specific goals. They study on a daily basis. They read the paper, read magazines, subscribe to investment newsletters, and attend investment seminars. They actively participate in the management of their investments. They understand money and know how to have money work for them. Their main focus is on increasing their assets, rather than investing so they can make a few extra bucks to spend. They reinvest their gains to build a bigger asset base. They know that building a strong asset base that throws off high cash yields or high returns with minimal tax exposure is the path to great long-term wealth.

They often teach this information to their children and pass on the family fortune to the generations that follow in the form of corporations, trusts and partnerships. They personally own little. Nothing is found in their names for tax purposes as well as protection from Robin Hoods who believe in taking from the rich to give to the poor. But although they own nothing, they control everything through corporations. They control the legal entities that own their assets.

They have a personal board of directors to help them manage their assets. They take advice and learn. This informal board is comprised of a team of bankers, accountants, attorneys and brokers. They spend a small fortune on solid professional advice not only to increase their wealth but also to protect their wealth from family, friends, lawsuits and the government. Even after they have departed this life, they are still controlling their wealth. These people are often called "stewards of money." Even after death, they continue to direct the fate of the money they created.

Do you know any Level 5 investors? (optional)

_____

_____

LEVEL 6: CAPITALISTS

Few people in the world reach this level of investment excellence. In America, less than one person in a hundred is a true capitalist. This person is usually an excellent "B" as well as an "I" because he or she can create a business and an investment opportunity simultaneously.

A capitalist's purpose is to make more money by synergistically orchestrating other people's money, other people's talents, and other people's time. Often they are the "movers and shakers" that allow America and other great countries to become great financial powers. These are the Kennedys, Rockefellers, Fords, J. Paul Gettys, and Ross Perots. It is the capitalists that provide the money that create the jobs, the businesses, and the goods that make a country prosper.

Level 5 investors generally create investments only for their own portfolio using their own money. True capitalists, on the other hand, create investments for themselves and others by using the talents and finances of other people. True capitalists create investments and sell them to the market. True capitalists do not need money to make money simply because they know how to use other people's money and other people's time. Level 6 investors create the investments that other people buy.

They often make other people rich, create jobs, and make things happen. In good economic times, true capitalists do well. In bad economic times, true capitalists get even richer. Capitalists know that economic chaos means new opportunities. They are most often involved early in a project, product, company or country years before the masses find it popular. When you read in the paper about a country in trouble or in a war or a disaster, you can be assured that a true capitalist is going in soon, or may already be there. A true capitalist is going in while most people are saying, "Stay away. That country, or that business, is in turmoil. It's too risky."

Returns of 100 percent to infinity are expected. That's because they know how to manage risk and how to make money without money. They can do this because they know that money is not a thing, but merely an idea created in their head. While these people have the same fears everyone has, they use that fear and turn it into excitement. They convert fear into new knowledge and new wealth. Their game in life is the game of money making money. They love the game of money more than any other game... more than golf, gardening or goofing off. This is the game that gives them life. Whether they're winning or losing money, you can always hear them say, "I love this game." That's what makes them capitalists.

Like those at Level 5, investors at this level are also excellent "stewards of money." When studying most of the people at this level, you often find they are generous to their friends, family, churches and to education. Look at some of the famous people who founded our well known institutions of learning. Rockefeller helped create the University of Chicago, and J.P. Morgan influenced Harvard with more than money. Other capitalists who gave their names to the institutions they helped found include Vanderbilt, Duke and Stanford. They represent the great captains not only of industry but also of education.

Today, Sir John Templeton gives generously to religion and spirituality, and George Soros donates hundreds of millions to causes he believes in. Also don't forget the Ford Foundation and the Getty Foundation, and Ted Turner pledging a billion dollars to the United Nations.

So contrary to what many of the intellectual cynics and critics in our schools, government, churches and our media may say, true capitalists have contributed in more ways than just being captains of industry, providing jobs and making a lot of money. To create a better world, we need more capitalists, not fewer, as many cynics would have you believe.

In reality, there are many more cynics than capitalists. Cynics, who make more noise and keep millions of people in fear, seeking security instead of freedom. As my friend Keith Cunningham always says, "I've never seen a statue erected to a cynic, or a university funded by a cynic."

Do you know any Level 6 investors? (optional)

_____

_____

BEFORE READING FURTHER

This completes the explanation part of the *CASHFLOW Quadrant*. This last chapter dealt with the "I" section of the *Quadrant*. Before we go on, here is another question:

1. What level of investor are you? _____.

If you are truly sincere about getting wealthy quickly, read and re-read the seven levels. Each time I read the levels, I see a little of myself in all the levels. I recognize not only strengths but also, as Zig Ziglar says, "character flaws" that hold me back. The way to great financial wealth is to strengthen your strengths and address your character flaws. And the way to do that is by first recognizing them rather than pretending you are flawless.

We all want to think the best of ourselves. I have dreamed of being a Level 6 capitalist for most of my life. I knew this is what I wanted to become from the moment my rich dad explained the similarities between a stock picker and a person who bets on horses. But after studying the different levels of this list, I could see the character flaws that hold me back. Although I do operate today as a Level 6 investor, I continue to read and re-read the seven levels and work on improving myself.

I found character flaws in myself from Level 3-C that would often raise their ugly heads in times of pressure. The gambler in me was good, but it was also not good. So with the guidance of my wife and friends, and additional schooling, I immediately began addressing my own character flaws and turning them into strengths. My effectiveness as a Level 6 investor improved immediately.

Here's another question for you:

2. What level of investor do you want or need to be in the near future?

_____

If your answer to question No. 2 is the same as that in question No. 1, then you are where you want to be. If you are happy where you are, relative to being an investor, then there is not much need to read any further in this book. For example, if today you are a solid Level 4 investor and you have no desire to become a Level 5 or Level 6, then read no further. One of life's greatest joys is to be happy where you are. Congratulations!

WARNING

Anyone with the goal of becoming a Level 5 or 6 investor must develop their skills FIRST as a Level 4 investor. Level 4 cannot be skipped on your path to Level 5 or 6. Anyone who tries to become a Level 5 or 6 investor without the skills of a Level 4 investor is really a Level 3 investor... a Gambler!

If you still want and need to know more financially and continue to be interested in pursuing your financial freedom, read on. The remaining chapters will focus primarily on the characteristics of someone in the "B" and "I" quadrants. In these chapters, you will learn how to move from the left side of the *Quadrant* to the right side easily and with low risk. The shift from the left side to the right will continue to focus on intangible assets that make possible the tangible assets on the right side of the *Quadrant.*

Before going on, I have one last question: To go from homeless to millionaires in less than 10 years, what level of investor do you think Kim and I had to be? The answer is found in the next chapter, where I will share some learning experiences from my personal journey to financial freedom.

CHAPTER 6

You Cannot See Money With Your Eyes

In late 1974, I purchased a small condominium on the fringes of Waikiki as one of my first investment properties. The price was $56,000 for a cute two-bedroom, one-bath unit in an average building. It was a perfect rental unit... and I knew it would rent quickly.

I drove over to my rich dad's office, all excited about showing him the deal. He glanced at the documents and in less than a minute he looked up and asked: "How much money are you losing a month?"

"About $100 a month," I said.

"Don't be foolish," rich dad said. "I haven't gone over the numbers, but I can already tell from the written documents that you're losing much more than that. And besides, why in the world would you knowingly invest in something that loses money?"

"Well, the unit looked nice, and I thought it was a good deal. A little paint and the place would be as good as new," I said.

"That doesn't justify knowingly losing money," smirked rich dad.

"Well, my real estate agent said not to worry about losing money every month. He said that in a few years the price of this unit will double, and in addition, the government gives me a tax break on the money I lose. Besides, it was such a good deal that I was afraid someone else would buy it if I didn't."

Rich dad stood and closed his office door. When he did that, I knew I was about to be chewed out as well as be taught an important lesson. I had been through these types of educational sessions before.

"So how much money are you losing a month?" rich dad asked again.

"About $100 a month," I repeated nervously.

Rich dad shook his head as he scanned the documents. The lesson was about to begin. On that day, I learned more about money and investing than I had in all my previous 27 years of life. Rich dad was happy that I had taken the initiative and invested in a property... but I had made some grave mistakes that could have been a financial disaster. However, the lessons I learned from that one investment have made me millions over the years.

MONEY IS SEEN WITH YOUR MIND

"It's not what your eyes see," said rich dad. "A piece of real estate is a piece of real estate. A company's stock certificate is a company's stock certificate. You can see those things. But it's what you cannot see that is important. It's the deal, the financial agreement, the market, the management, the risk factors, the cash flow, the corporate structuring, the tax laws, and a thousand other things that make something a good investment or not."

He then proceeded to tear the deal apart with questions. "Why would you pay such a high interest rate? What do you figure your return on investment to be? How does this investment fit into your long-term financial strategy? What vacancy factor are you using? What is your cap rate? Have you checked the association's history of assessments? Have you figured in management costs? What percentage rate did you use to compute repairs? Did you know that the city has just announced it will be tearing up the roads in that area and changing the traffic pattern? A major thoroughfare will run right in front of your building. Residents are moving to avoid the year-long project. Did you know that? I know the market trend is up today, but do you know what is driving that trend? Business economics or greed? How long do you think the trend will be up? What happens if this place is not rented? And if it isn't, how long can you keep it afloat and yourself afloat? And again, what goes on in your head to make you think that losing money is a good deal? This really has me worried."

"It looked like a good deal," I said, deflated.

Rich dad smiled, stood up and shook my hand. "I'm glad you took action," he said. "Most people think, but never do. If you do something, you make mistakes, and it's from our mistakes that we learn the most. Remember that anything important cannot really be learned in the classroom. It must be learned by taking action, making mistakes, and then correcting them. That is when wisdom sets in."

I felt a little better, and now I was ready to learn.

"Most people," said rich dad, "invest 95 percent with their eyes and only 5 percent with their minds."

Rich dad went on to explain that people look at a piece of real estate, or the name of a stock, and often make their decision based on what their eyes see or what a broker tells them, or on a hot tip from a fellow worker. They often buy emotionally instead of rationally.

"That is why 9 out of 10 investors do not make money," said rich dad. "While they do not necessarily lose money, they just do not make money. They just sort of break even, making some and losing some. That's because they invest with their eyes and emotions, rather than with their minds. Many people invest because they want to get rich quickly. So instead of becoming investors, they wind up being dreamers, hustlers, gamblers and crooks. The world is filled with them. So let's sit down, go back over this losing deal you just bought, and I will teach you how to turn it into a winning deal. I'll begin to teach your mind to see what your eyes cannot."

FROM BAD TO GOOD

The next morning, I went back to the real estate agent, rejected the agreement and reopened negotiation. It was not a pleasant process, but I learned a lot.

Three days later, I returned to see my rich dad. The price had stayed the same, the agent got his full commission because he deserved it. He had worked hard for it. But while the price remained the same, the terms of the investment were vastly different. By re-negotiating the interest rate, payment terms and the amortization period, instead of losing money, I was now certain of making a net profit of $80 per month, even after the management fee and an allowance for vacancy was factored in. I could even lower my rent, and still make money, if the market went bad. I would definitely raise the rent if the market got better.

"I estimated that you were going to lose at least $150 per month," said rich dad. "Probably more. If you had continued to lose $150 per month, based on your salary and expenses, how many of these deals could you afford?"

"Barely one," I replied. "Most months, I do not have an extra $150. If I had done the original deal, I would have struggled financially every month. Even after the tax breaks. I might even have had to take an extra job to pay for this investment."

"And now, how many of these deals at $80 positive cash flow can you afford?"

asked rich dad.

I smiled and said, "As many as I can get my hands on."

Rich dad nodded in approval. "Now go out there and get your hands on more of them."

A few years later, the real estate prices in Hawaii did skyrocket. But instead of having only one property go up in value, I had seven double in value. That is the power of a little financial intelligence.

"YOU CAN'T DO THAT"

An important side note to my first real estate investment: When I took my new offer back to the real estate agent, all he said to me was, "You can't do that."

What took the longest time was convincing the agent to start thinking about how we could do what I wanted done. In any event, there were many lessons I learned from this one investment, and one of those lessons was to realize that when someone says to you, "You can't do that," they may have one finger pointing forward at you... but three fingers are pointing backward at them.

Rich dad taught me "You can't do that" doesn't necessarily mean "you can't." It more often means "they can't."

A classic example took place many years ago when people said to the Wright Brothers, "You can't do that." Thank goodness, the Wright Brothers did not listen.

$1.4 TRILLION LOOKING FOR A HOME

Every day, $1.4 trillion orbits the planet electronically, and it is increasing. There is more money being created and available today than ever before. The problem is, money is invisible. Today, the bulk of it is electronic. So when people look for money with their eyes, they fail to see anything. Most people struggle to live from paycheck to paycheck, and yet, $1.4 trillion flies around the world every day looking for someone who wants it. Looking for someone who knows how to take care of it, nurture it and grow it. If you know how to take care of money, money will flock to you, and be thrown at you. People will beg you to take it.

But if you do not know how to care for money, money will stay away from you. Remember rich dad's definition of financial intelligence: "It's not how much money you make, but how much money you keep, how hard it works for you, and how many generations you keep it for."

THE BLIND LEADING THE BLIND

"The average person is 95 percent eyes and only 5 percent mind when they invest," said rich dad. "If you want to become a professional on the "B" and "I" side of the *Quadrant,* you need to train your eyes to be only 5 percent and train your mind to see the other 95 percent. Rich dad went on to explain that people who trained their minds to see money had tremendous power over people who did not.

He was adamant about whom I took financial advice from. "The reason most people struggle financially is because they take advice from people who are also mentally blind to money. It's the classic tale of the blind leading the blind. If you want money to come to you, you must know how to take care of it. If money is not first in your head, it will not stick to your hands. If it does not stick to your hands, then money, and people with money, will stay away from you."

TRAIN YOUR BRAIN TO SEE MONEY

So what is the first step in training your brain to see money? The answer is easy. The answer is financial literacy. It begins with the ability to understand the words and the number systems of capitalism. If you do not understand the words or the numbers, you might as well be speaking a foreign language... and in many cases, each quadrant represents a foreign language.

If you look at the *CASHFLOW Quadrant,*

each quadrant is like a different country. They do not all use the same words, and if you do not understand the words, you will not understand the numbers.

For example, if a medial doctor says, "Your systolic is 120 and your diastolic is 80," is that good or bad? Is that all you need to know for your health? The answer is obviously "no." Yet, it is a start.

It would be like asking, "My stock's p/e is 12, and my apartment house cap rate is 12. Is this all I need to know for my wealth? Again, the answer is "no," but it is a start. At least we're beginning to speak the same words and use the same numbers. And that is where financial literacy, which is the basis of financial intelligence, begins. It begins with knowing the words and numbers.

The doctor is speaking from the "S" quadrant, and the other is speaking with the words and numbers of the "I" quadrant. They might as well be different foreign languages.

I disagree when someone says to me, "It takes money to make money."

In my opinion, the ability to make money with money begins with understanding the words and numbers. As my rich dad always said, "If money is not first in your head, it will not stick to your hands."

KNOW WHAT REAL RISK IS

The second step in training your brain to see money is to learn to recognize what real risk is. When people say to me that investing is risky, I simply say, "Investing is not risky. Being uneducated is risky."

Investing is much like flying. If you've been to flight school and spent a number of years gaining experience, then flying is fun and exciting. But if you've never been to flight school, I would recommend leaving the flying to someone else.

BAD ADVICE IS RISKY

Rich dad firmly believed that any financial advice was better than no financial advice. He was a man with an open mind. He was courteous and listened to many people. But ultimately, he relied on his own financial intelligence to make his decisions: "If you do not know anything, then any advice is better than no advice. But if you cannot tell the difference between bad advice and good advice, then that is risky."

Rich dad firmly believed that most people struggled financially because they operated on financial information handed down from parent to child… and most people do not come from financially sound families. "Bad financial advice is risky, and most of the bad advice is handed out at home," he often said. "Not because of what is said, but because of what is done. Children learn by example more than words."

YOUR ADVISERS ARE ONLY AS SMART AS YOU

Rich dad said, "Your advisers can only be as smart as you are. If you are not smart, they cannot tell you that much. If you are financially well educated, competent advisers can give you more sophisticated financial advice. If you are financially naive, they must by law offer you only safe and secure financial strategies. If you are an unsophisticated investor, they can only offer low risk, low yield investments. They'll often recommend "diversification" for unsophisticated investors. Few advisers choose to take the time to teach you. Their time is also money. So if you will take it upon yourself to become financially educated and manage your money well, then a competent adviser can inform you about investments and strategies that only a few will ever see. But first, you must do your part to get educated. Always remember, your adviser can only be as smart as you."

IS YOUR BANKER LYING TO YOU?

Rich dad had several bankers he dealt with. They were an important part of his financial team. While he was close friends with and respected his bankers, he always felt that he had to watch out for his own best interests... as he expected the bankers to look out for their own best interests.

After my 1974 investment experience, he asked me this: "When a banker says that your house is an asset, are they telling you the truth?"

Since most people are not financially literate and do not know the game of money, they often must take the opinion and advice of people they tend to trust. If you are not financially literate, then you need to trust someone you hope is financially literate. Many people invest or manage their money based on someone else's recommendations more than their own. And that is risky.

THEY ARE NOT LYING...
THEY'RE JUST NOT TELLING YOU THE TRUTH

The fact is, when a banker tells you your house is an asset, they are not really lying to you. They're just not telling you the whole truth. While your house is an asset, they simply do not say whose asset it is. For if you read financial statements, it is easy to see that your house is not your asset. It's the bank's asset. Remember my rich dad's definitions of an asset and a liability from Rich Dad Poor Dad:

"An asset puts money into my pocket.

A liability takes money out of my pocket."

People on the left side of the *Quadrant* do not really need to know the difference. Most of them are happy to feel secure in their jobs, have a nice house they think they own, they feel proud of, and think they are in control of. Nobody will take it away from them as long as they make those payments. And make those payments they do.

But people on the right side of the *Quadrant* need to know the difference. To be financially literate and financially intelligent means being able to understand the big picture of money. Financially astute people know that a mortgage does not show up as an asset but as a liability on your balance sheet. Your mortgage actually shows up as an asset on a balance sheet across town. It shows up as an asset on the bank's balance sheet... not yours.

Your Balance Sheet

Assets	Liabilities
	Mortgage

Anyone who has taken accounting knows that a balance sheet must balance. But where does it balance? It does not really balance on your balance sheet. If you look at the bank's balance sheet, this is the story the numbers really tell.

Bank's Balance Sheet

Assets	Liabilities
Your Mortgage	

Now it balances. Now it makes sense. That is "B and I" accounting. But this is not the way it is taught in basic accounting. In accounting, you would show the "value" of your home as an asset and the mortgage as a liability. Also an important point to note is that the "value" of your home is an opinion which fluctuates with the market while your mortgage is a definite liability not affected by the market.

For a "B and I," however, the "value" of your home is not considered an asset because it does not generate cash flow.

WHAT HAPPENS IF YOU PAY OFF YOUR MORTGAGE?

Many people ask me, "What happens if I pay off my mortgage? Is my house an asset then?"

And my reply is, "In most cases, the answer is still 'no.' It's still a liability."

There are several reasons for my answer. One is maintenance and general upkeep. Property is like a car. Even if you own it free and clear, it still costs you money to operate… and once things start to break, everything begins to break. And in most cases, people pay for repairs on their house and their car with after-tax dollars. A person in the "B and I" quadrants only includes property as an asset if it generates income through positive cash flow.

But the main reason a house, even without a mortgage, is still a liability is because you still do not own it… really. The government still taxes you even if you own it. Just stop paying your property taxes, and again you will find out who really owns your property.

That is where tax-lien certificates come from… which I wrote about in *Rich Dad, Poor Dad.* Tax-lien certificates are an excellent way to receive at least 16 percent interest on your money. If homeowners do not pay their property taxes, the government charges them interest on the taxes owed, at rates from 10 percent to 50 percent. Talk about usury. If you don't pay the property taxes, and someone like me pays them for you… then in many states, you owe me the taxes plus the interest. If you do not pay the taxes and the interest within a certain amount of time, I get to take your house just for the money I put up. In most states, property taxes take priority in repayment, even before the bank's mortgage. I have had the opportunity to buy houses I paid the taxes on for less than $3,500.

THE DEFINITION OF REAL ESTATE

Again, to be able to see money, you must see it with your mind, not your eyes. In order to train your mind, you must know the real definitions of words, and the system of numbers.

By now, you should know the difference between an asset and a liability, and you should know the definition of the word "mortgage," which is an "agreement until death," and the word "finance," which means penalty. You will now learn the origin of the words "real estate" and a popular financial vehicle called "derivatives." Many people think "derivatives" are new, but in reality, they are literally ages old.

A simple definition of "derivative" is "something that comes from something else." An example of a derivative is orange juice. Orange juice is a derivative of an orange.

I used to think that real estate meant "real" or something that was tangible. My rich dad explained to me that it really comes from the Spanish word real, which means "royal." El Camino Real means the royal's road. Real estate means the royal's estate.

Once the Agrarian Age came to an end and the Industrial Age began around 1500, the power was no longer based on the land and agriculture. The monarchs realized they had to change in response to the land-reform acts that allowed peasants to own the land. Then, the royalty created derivatives. Derivatives such as "taxes" on land ownership and "mortgages" as a way of allowing the commoners to finance their land. Taxes and mortgages are derivatives because they are derived from the land. Your banker would not call the mortgage a derivative; they would say it is "secured" by the land... different words, similar meanings. So once the royalty realized that money was no longer in the land but in the "derivatives" that came from the land, the monarchs set up banks to handle the increased business. Today, land is still called "real estate" because no matter how much you pay for it, it never really belongs to you. It still belongs to the "royals."

WHAT IS YOUR INTEREST RATE... REALLY?

Rich dad fought and negotiated tough for every single point of interest he paid. He asked me this question: "When a banker tells you your interest rate is 8 percent per annum... is it really?" I found out it's not if you learn to read numbers.

Let's say you buy a $100,000 home, make a down payment of $20,000 and borrow the remaining $80,000 at 8 percent interest with a 30-year term from your bank.

In five years you will pay a total of $35,220 to the bank: $31,276 for interest, and only $3,944 for debt reduction.

If you take the loan to term, or 30 years, you will have paid $211,323 total principal and interest, less what you originally borrowed – $80,000. The total interest you will have paid: $131,323.

By the way, that $211,323 does not include property taxes and insurance on the loan.

Funny, $131,323 seems to be a little bit more than 8 percent of $80,000. It's more like 160 percent in interest over 30 years. As I said, they are not lying... they are just not telling the whole truth. And if you cannot read numbers, you'd really never know. And if you're happy with your house, you'll never really care. But, of course, the industry knows that in a few years... you're going to want a new house, a bigger house, a smaller house, a vacation house, or to refinance your mortgage. They know it and, in fact, they count on it.

INDUSTRY AVERAGE

In the banking industry, a seven-year average is used as the life expectancy for a mortgage. That means, banks expect the average person to buy a new house, or refinance every seven years. And that means in this example, they expect to get their original $80,000 back every seven years, plus $43,291 in interest.

And that's why it is called a "mortgage," which comes from the French word "mortir" or "agreement until death." The reality is that most people will continue to work hard, get pay raises and buy new houses... with new mortgages. On top of that, the government gives a tax break to encourage taxpayers to buy more expensive houses, which will mean higher property taxes for the government. And let's not forget the insurance that every mortgage company requires you to pay on your mortgage.

Every time I watch television, I see commercials where handsome professional baseball and football players smile and tell you to take all your credit card debt and roll it into a "bill consolidation loan." That way, you can pay off all those credit cards and carry a new loan at a lower interest rate. And then they tell you why it's financially intelligent to do this: "A bill consolidation loan is a smart move on your part because the government will give you a tax deduction for the interest payments you make on your home mortgage."

Viewers, thinking they see the light, run down to their finance company, refinance their houses, pay off their credit cards and feel intelligent.

A few weeks later, they're shopping and see a new dress, a new lawn mower, or realize their kid needs a new bicycle, or they need to take a vacation because they're exhausted. They just happen to now have a clean credit card... or they suddenly receive a new credit card in the mail because they paid off the other one. They have excellent credit, they pay their bills, their little heart goes pitter-patter, and they say to themselves, "Oh, go on. You deserve it. You can pay it off a little every month."

Emotions overpower logic, and the clean new credit card comes out of hiding.

As I said, when bankers say your house is an asset... they aren't lying. When the government gives you a tax break for being in debt, it isn't because it's concerned about your financial future. The government is concerned about its financial future. So when your banker, your accountant, your attorney and your schoolteachers tell you your house is an asset, they just failed to say whose asset it is.

WHAT ABOUT SAVINGS? ARE THEY ASSETS?

Now, your savings really are assets. That's the good news. But again, if you read financial statements, you will see the total picture. While it is true that your savings are assets, when you look across town at the bank's balance sheet, your savings show up as a liability. This is what your savings and checkbook balance look like in your asset column.

Your Balance Sheet

Assets	Liabilities
Savings	
Checkbook Balance	

And this is how your savings and your checkbook balance are carried on your bank's balance sheet.

Bank's Balance Sheet

Assets	Liabilities
	Your Savings
	Your Checkbook Balance

Why is your savings and checkbook balance a liability to banks? They have to pay you interest for your money, and it costs them money to safeguard it.

If you can get the significance of these few drawings and words, you might begin to better understand what the eyes cannot see about the game of money.

WHY YOU DON'T GET A TAX BREAK FOR SAVING MONEY?

If you notice, you get a tax break for buying a house and going into debt... but you do not get a tax break for saving money. Have you ever wondered why?

I do not have the exact answer, but I can speculate. One big reason is because your savings are a liability to banks. Why would they ask the government to pass a law that would encourage you to put money in their bank... money that would be a liability to them?

THEY DON'T NEED YOUR SAVINGS

Besides, banks really do not need your savings. They don't need much in deposits because they can magnify money at least 10 times. If you put a single $1 note in the bank, by law, the bank can lend out $10 and, depending upon the reserve limits imposed by the central bank, possibly as much as $20. That means your single $1 suddenly becomes $10 or more. It's magic! When my rich dad showed me that, I fell in love with the idea. At that point I knew that I wanted to own a bank, and not go to school to become a banker.

On top of that, the bank might pay you only 5 percent interest on that $1. You as a consumer feel secure because the bank is paying you some money on your money. Banks see this as good customer relations, because if you have savings with them, you may come in and borrow from them. They want you to borrow because they can then charge 9 percent or more to you on what you borrow. While you may make 5 percent on your $1, the bank can make 9 percent or more on the $10 of debt your single dollar has generated. Recently, I received a new credit card that advertised 8.9 percent interest... but if you understood the legal jargon in the fine print, it was really 23 percent. Needless to say, that credit card was cut in half and mailed back.

THEY GET YOUR SAVINGS ANYWAY

The other reason they don't offer a tax break for savings is more obvious. If you can read the numbers and see which way the cash is flowing, you'll notice that they'll get your savings anyway. The money you could be saving in your asset column is flowing instead out of your liability column, in the form of interest payments on your mortgage in their asset column. The cash flow pattern looks like this:

Your Financial Statement

Income Statement

Income	
Expense	
Interest	

Balance Sheet

Assets	Liabilities
	Mortgage

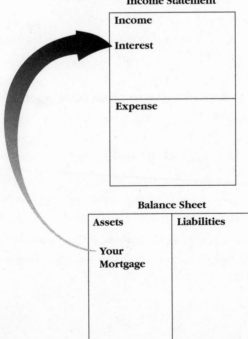

Your Bank's Financial Statement

Income Statement

Income	
Interest	
Expense	

Balance Sheet

Assets	Liabilities
Your	
Mortgage	

That is why they don't need the government to give you a tax incentive to save. They'll get your savings anyway... in the form of interest payments on debt.

Politicians are not about to mess with the system because the banks, insurance companies, building industry, brokerage houses and others contribute a lot of money to political campaigns... and the politicians know the name of the game.

THE NAME OF THE GAME

In 1974, my rich dad was upset because the game was played against me, and I did not know it. I had bought this investment real estate and had taken a losing position... yet, I had been led to believe it was a winning position.

"I'm glad you entered the game," said rich dad. "But because no one has ever told you what the game is, you've just been suckered over to the losing team."

Rich dad then explained the basics of the game. "The name of the game of capitalism is "Who is indebted to whom?"

Once I knew the game, he said, then I could be a better player... instead of someone who just had the game run all over them.

THE MORE PEOPLE YOU ARE INDEBTED TO, THE POORER YOU ARE

"The more people you are indebted to, the poorer you are," said rich dad. "And the more people you have indebted to you, the wealthier you are. That is the game."

As I said, I struggled to keep my mind open. So I stayed silent and let him explain. He was not saying it maliciously; he was just explaining the game as he saw it.

"We are all in debt to someone else. The problems occur when the debt gets out of balance. Unfortunately, the poor people of this world have been run over so hard by the game, they often can't get any deeper into debt. The same is true for poor countries. The world simply takes from the poor, the weak, the financially uninformed. If you have too much debt, the world takes everything you have... your time, your work, your home, your life, your confidence, and then they take your dignity, if you let them. I did not make up this game, I do not make the rules, but I do know the game... and I play the game well. I will explain the game to you. I want you to learn to play the game. Then, after you've mastered the game, you can decide what to do with what you know."

MONEY IS DEBT

Rich dad went on to explain that even our currency is not an instrument of equity, but an instrument of debt. Every dollar bill used to be backed by gold or silver, but is now an IOU guaranteed to be paid by the taxpayers of the issuing country. As long as the rest of the world has confidence in the American taxpayer to work and pay for this IOU called money, the world will have confidence in our dollar. If that key element of money, which is "confidence," suddenly disappears, the economy comes down like a house of cards... and the house of cards has come down many times throughout history.

Take the example of the German Weimar-government marks that became utterly worthless just before World War II. As one story goes, this elderly woman was pushing a wheelbarrow full of marks to buy a loaf of bread. When she turned her back, someone stole the wheelbarrow and left the pile of worthless money all over the street.

That is why most money today is known as "fiat" money, which is money that cannot be converted to something tangible... like gold or silver. The money is only as good as long as people have confidence in the government backing it. The other definition for "fiat" is a "dictatorial order or decree given by a person or group having complete authority."

Today, much of the global economy is based on debt and confidence. As long as we all keep holding hands, and no one breaks ranks, everything will be fine...and the word "fine" is my acronym for, Feeling Insecure Neurotic and Emotional.

"WHO OWES YOU?"

Going back to 1974, when I was learning how to buy that $56,000 condo, my rich dad taught me an important lesson on how to structure deals.

" 'Who is indebted to whom?' is the name of the game," said rich dad. "And somebody just stuck you with the debt. It's like going to dinner with 10 friends. You go to the restroom and when you come back, the bill is there, but all 10 friends are gone. If you're going to play the game, then you had best learn the game, know the rules, speak the same language, and know with whom you're playing. If not, instead of playing the game, the game will be played on you."

IT'S ONLY A GAME

At first I got angry at what my rich dad told me... but I listened and did my best to understand. Finally he put it into a context that I could understand. "You love playing football, don't you?" he asked.

I nodded my head. "I love the game," I said.

"Well, money is my game," said rich dad. "I love the money game."

"But for many people, money is not a game," I said.

"That is correct," said rich dad. "For most people, it's survival. For most people, money is a game they are forced to play, and they hate it. Unfortunately, the more civilized we get, the more money becomes a part of our lives."

Rich dad drew the *CASHFLOW Quadrant.*

"Just look at this as a tennis court, or football field, or soccer field. If you're going to play the money game, which team do you want to be on? The "E's, S's, B's or I's"? Or which side of the court do you want to be on – the right side or the left?"

I pointed to the right side of the *Quadrant.*

IF YOU TAKE ON DEBT AND RISK, YOU SHOULD BE PAID

"Good," said rich dad. "That is why you cannot go out there to play the game and believe some sales agent when he tells you that to lose $150 a month for 30 years is a good deal... because the government will give you a tax break for losing money and he expects the price of real estate to go up. You simply cannot play the game with that mind-set. While those opinions might come true, that is just not the way the game is played on the right side of the *Quadrant.* Somebody is telling you to get into debt, take all the risks, and pay for it. People on the left side think that is a good idea... but not the people on the right."

I was shaking a little.

"Look at it my way," said rich dad. "You're willing to pay $56,000 for this condo in the sky. You're signing for the debt. You take the risk. The tenant pays less in rent than what it costs to live there. So you are subsidizing that person's housing. Does that make sense to you?"

I shook my head. "No."

"This is the way I play the game," said rich dad. "From now on, if you take on debt and risk, then you should get paid. Got that?"

I nodded my head.

"Making money is common sense," said rich dad. "It's not rocket science. But unfortunately, when it comes to money, common sense is uncommon. A banker tells you to take on debt, tells you that the government will give you a tax break for something that really does not make fundamental economic sense, and then a real estate sales person tells you to sign the papers because he can find a tenant who will pay you less than you are paying, just because in his opinion the price will go up. If that makes sense to you, then you and I do not share the same common sense."

I just stood there. I heard everything he said, and I had to admit that I had gotten so excited by what I thought looked like a good deal that my logic went out of the window. I could not analyze the deal. Because the deal "looked" good, I had gotten emotional with greed and excitement, and I was no longer able to hear what the numbers and the words were trying to tell me.

It was then that rich dad gave me an important rule that he has always used, "Your profit is made when you buy... not when you sell."

Rich dad had to be certain that whatever debt or risk he took on, it had to make sense from the day he bought it... it had to make sense if the economy got worse, and it had to make sense if the economy got better. He never bought on tax tricks or crystal ball forecasts of the future. A deal had to make sound economic sense in good times and in bad.

I was beginning to understand the game of money as he saw it. And the game of money was to see others become indebted to you and to be careful whom you became indebted to. Today, I still hear his words: "If you take on risk and debt, make sure you get paid for it."

Rich dad had debt, but he was careful when he took it on. "Be careful when you take on debt," was his advice. "If you take on debt personally, make sure it's small. If you take on large debt, make sure someone else is paying for it."

He saw the game of money and debt as a game that is played on you, played on me, played on everyone. It's played from business to business, and it's played from country to country. He saw it only as a game. The problem is, for most people, money is not a game. For many people, money is survival... often life itself. And because no one explained the game to them, they still believe bankers who say a house is an asset.

THE IMPORTANCE OF FACTS VERSUS OPINIONS

Rich dad continued his lesson: "If you want to be successful on the right side, when it comes to money, you have got to know the difference between facts and opinions. You cannot blindly accept financial advice the way people on the left side do. You must know the numbers. You must know the facts. And numbers tell you the facts. Your financial survival depends upon facts, not some friend or adviser's wordy opinions.

"I don't understand. What is the big deal about something being a fact or opinion?" I asked. "Is one better than the other?"

"No." replied rich dad. "Just know when something is a fact and when something is an opinion."

Still puzzled I stood there with a confused look on my face.

"What is your family's home worth?" asked rich dad. He was using an example to help me out of my confusion.

"Oh I know." I replied quickly. "My parents are thinking about selling so they had a real estate agent come in and give us an appraisal. They said the house was worth $36,000. That means my dad's net worth increased by $16,000 because he only paid $20,000 for it 5 years ago."

"So is the appraisal and your dad's net worth a fact or an opinion?" asked rich dad.

I thought about it for a while and understood what he was getting at. "Both are opinions. Aren't they?"

Rich dad nodded his head. "Very good. Most people struggle financially because they spend their lives using opinions rather than facts when making financial decisions. Opinions such as "Your house is an asset." "The price of real estate always goes up." "Blue chip stocks are your best investment." "It takes money to make money." "Stocks have always out performed real estate." "You should diversify your portfolio." "You have to be dishonest to be rich." "Investing is risky." "Play it safe."

I sat there deep in thought, realizing that most of what I heard about money at home was really people's opinions, not facts.

"Is gold an asset?" asked rich dad, snapping me out of my daydream.

"Yes. Of course." I replied. "It has been the only real money that has withstood the test of time."

"See there you go again." smiled rich dad. "All you are doing is repeating someone else's opinion about what is an asset rather than checking out the facts."

"Gold is only an asset, by my definition, if you buy it for less than you sell it for." rich dad said slowly. "In other words, if you bought it for $100 and sold it for $200, then it was an asset. But if you bought one ounce for $200 and you sold it for $100 then gold in this transaction was a liability. It's the actual financial numbers of the transaction that ultimately tell you the facts. In reality, the only thing that is an asset or liability is you... for ultimately it is you that can make gold an asset and only you can make it a liability. That is why financial education is so important. I have seen so many people take a perfectly good business, or piece of real estate and turn it into a financial nightmare. Many people do the same with their personal life. They take hard earned money and create a lifetime of financial liabilities."

I was even more confused, a little hurt inside, and wanted to argue. Rich dad was toying with my brain.

"Many a man has been suckered because he did not know the facts. Everyday I hear horror stories of someone who lost all their money because they thought an opinion was a fact. It's OK to use an opinion when making a financial decision... but you'd best know the difference. Millions upon millions of people have made life decisions based upon opinions handed down from generation to generation... and then they wonder why they struggle financially."

"What kind of opinions?" I asked.

Rich dad chuckled to himself before he answered. "Well, let me give you a few common ones we have all heard."

Rich dad began listing a few as he chuckled quietly, apparently laughing at the humor of being human beings. Some of the examples he gave that day were:

1. "You should marry him. He'll make a good husband."
2. "Find a secure job and stay there all your life."
3. "Doctors make a lot of money."
4. "They have a big house. They must be rich."
5. "He has big muscles. He must be healthy."
6. "This is a nice car, only driven by a little old lady."
7. "There is not enough money for everyone to be rich."
8. "The earth is flat."
9. "Humans will never fly."
10. "He's smarter than his sister."
11. "Bonds are safer than stocks."

12. "People who make mistakes are stupid."

13. "He'll never sell for such a low price."

14. "She'll never go out with me."

15. "Investing is risky."

16. "I'll never be rich."

17. "I didn't go to college so I'll never get ahead."

18. "You should diversify your investments."

19. "You shouldn't diversify your investments."

Rich dad went on and on until finally he could tell I was tired of hearing his examples of opinions.

"OK!" I finally said. "I've heard enough. What is your point?"

"Thought you'd never stop me." smiled rich dad. "The point is most people's lives are determined by their opinions, rather than the facts. For a person's life to change, they first need to change their opinions... then start looking at the facts. If you can read financial statements, you will be able to see the facts not only of a company's financial success... if you can read financial statements you can tell immediately how an individual is doing... rather than going by yours or somebody else's opinions. As I said, one is not better than the other. To be successful in life, especially financially, you must know the difference. If you cannot verify something is a fact, then it is an opinion. Financial blindness is when a person cannot read numbers... so they must take someone else's opinion. Financial insanity is caused when opinions are used as facts. If you want to be on the right side of the *Quadrant*, you must know the difference between facts and opinions. Few lessons are more important than this one."

I sat there listening quietly doing my best to understand what he was saying. It was obviously a simple concept yet it was larger than my brain could accept at that moment.

"Do you know what 'due diligence' means?" rich dad asked.

I shook my head.

"Due diligence simply means finding out what are opinions and what are facts. When it comes to money, most people are either lazy or searching for shortcuts, so they do not do enough due diligence. And there are still others who are so afraid of making mistakes that all they do is due diligence and then do nothing. Too much due diligence is also called 'analysis paralysis'. The point is you must know how to sift through the facts and opinions, and then make your decision. As I said, most people are in financial trouble today simply because they've taken too many shortcuts and are making their life's financial decisions based upon opinions, often the opinions of an "E" or an "S", and not the facts. If you want to be a "B" or an "I", you must be keenly aware of this difference."

I did not fully appreciate rich dad's lesson that day, yet few lessons have served me better than to know the difference between facts and opinions, especially when it comes to handling my money.

Years later, in the early 1990's, my rich dad watched the stock market climb out of sight. His only comment was,

"That is what happens when highly paid employees or self-employed people, with big pay checks, paying excessive amounts in taxes, greatly in debt, and with only paper assets in their portfolio begin handing out investment advice. Millions are about to get hurt following the opinions of people who think they know the facts."

Warren Buffet, America's greatest investor, once said,

"If you are in a poker game and after 20 minutes you do not know who the patsy is, then you're the patsy."

WHY PEOPLE STRUGGLE FINANCIALLY

I heard recently that most people will be in debt from the day they leave school until the day they die.

This is the average middle class American's financial picture:

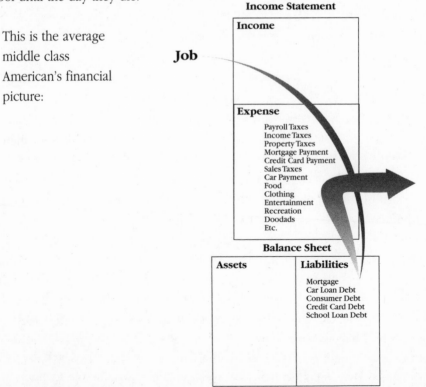

SOMEONE ELSE'S BALANCE SHEET

If you now understand the game, then you may realize that those liabilities listed must show up on someone else's balance sheet like this.

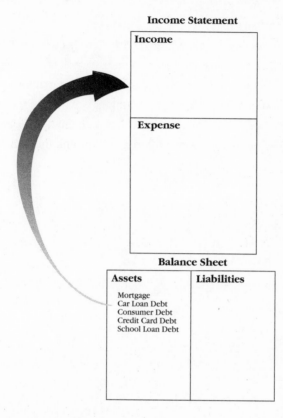

Anytime you hear these words, "Low down, easy monthly payments," or "Don't worry, the government will give you a tax break for those losses," then you know someone is luring you into the game. If you want to be financially free, you've got to be a little smarter than that.

For most people, no one is indebted to them. They have no real assets (things that put money in their pocket)... and they are often indebted to everyone else. That is why they cling to job security and struggle financially. If it were not for their job, they'd be broke in a flash. It has been said that the average American is less than three paychecks away from bankruptcy, just because they sought a better life and got run over by the game. The deck is stacked against them. They still think their house, car, golf clubs, clothes, vacation home, and other doodads are assets. They believed what someone else told them. They have to believe it because they cannot read financial numbers. They cannot tell facts from opinions. Most people go to school and learn to be players in the game, but no one explained the game to them. No one told them that the name of the game is "Who is indebted to whom?" And because no one told them that, they're the ones who become indebted to everyone else.

MONEY IS AN IDEA

I hope you now understand the basics of the *CASHFLOW Quadrant* and know that money really is an idea that is more clearly seen with your mind than your eyes. Learning the game of money and how it is played is an important part of your journey to financial freedom. More important, though, is who you need to become to move to the right side of the *CASHFLOW Quadrant*. Part II of this book will focus on "Bringing Out The Best In You" and in analyzing the formula:

BE-DO-HAVE

Bringing Out The Best In You

CHAPTER 7

Becoming Who You Are

"It's not being homeless that matters," my rich dad said. "It's about who you are. Keep striving and you become somebody. Quit and you also become somebody... but not the same person."

THE CHANGES YOU GO THROUGH

For those of you contemplating going from job security to financial security, all I can offer you are words of encouragement. For Kim and me, it took being homeless and desperate before I found the courage to move forward. That was our path, but it definitely does not have to be your path. As I described earlier, there are ready-made systems that can help you cross the bridge to the right side of the *Quadrant.*

The real issue is the changes you go through internally and who you become in the process. For some people, the process is easy. For others, the journey is impossible.

MONEY IS A DRUG

Rich dad would always say to Mike and me, "Money is a drug."

The main reason he refused to pay us while we worked for him was because he never wanted us to become addicted to working for money. "If you become addicted to money," he said, "it's hard to break that addiction."

When I was calling him from California as a grown man to ask him for money, he was not about to break a pattern he had started with Mike and me when we were 9. He did not give us money as kids, and he was not about to start now. Instead he continued to be tough and guide me away from the addiction of working for money.

He called money a drug because he had observed people who were happy when they had money, and upset or moody when they did not. Just as heroine addicts get high when they inject the drug, they also get moody and violent when they don't have it.

"Be careful of money's addictive power," he often said. "Once you get used to receiving it, that addiction keeps you attached to the way you got it."

Put another way, if you receive money as an employee, then you tend to get accustomed to that way of acquiring it. If you get used to generating money by being self-employed, it is often difficult to break the attachment to earning money in that way. And if you get used to government handouts, that, too, is a hard pattern to break.

"The hardest part about moving from the left side to the right side is the attachment you have to the way you have been earning money," said rich dad. "It's more than breaking a habit; it's breaking an addiction."

That is why he stressed to Mike and me to never work for money. He insisted we learn to create our own systems as a way of acquiring money.

THE PATTERNS

For Kim and me, the hardest part in trying to become people who generated income in the "B" quadrant was that all of our past conditioning was still holding us back. It was tough when friends said, "Why are you doing this? Why don't you just get a job?"

It was even more difficult because there was a part of us that also wanted to go back to the security of a paycheck.

Rich dad explained to Mike and me that the world of money was one large system. And we as individuals learn how to operate in certain patterns within that system. For example:

An "E" works for the system.

An "S" is the system.

A "B" creates, owns or controls the system.

An "I" invests money into the system.

The pattern rich dad was talking about was the pattern in our body, mind and soul of how we naturally gravitate to the subject of money.

"When a person feels the need for money," rich dad explained, "an 'E' will automatically look for a job, an 'S' often will do something alone, a 'B' will create or buy a system that produces money, and an 'I' will look for an opportunity to invest in an asset that produces more money."

WHY IT'S HARD TO CHANGE A PATTERN

"The reason it's hard to change a pattern," said rich dad, "is because money today is essential for life. In the Agrarian Age, money was not that important because the land could provide food, shelter, warmth and water without money. Once we moved into the cities during the Industrial Age, money signified life itself. Today, even water costs money."

Rich dad went on to explain that when you begin to move from, let's say, the "E" quadrant to the "B" quadrant, the part of you that is addicted to being an "E," or afraid that life will end, begins to kick and fight back. It's like a drowning person beginning to fight for air, or a starving man who will eat anything to survive.

"It's this battle that goes on inside of you that makes it so hard. It's the battle between who you no longer are and who you want to become that is the problem," rich dad explained to me over the phone. "The part of you that still seeks security is in a war with that part of you that wants freedom. Only you can decide which one will win. You'll either build that business or you'll go back to finding a job-forever."

FIND YOUR PASSION

"Do you really want to move forward?" asked rich dad.

"Yes!" I said hurriedly.

"Have you forgotten what you set out to do? Have you forgotten about your passion and what caused you to get into this predicament in the first place?" asked rich dad.

"Oh," I replied, a little startled. I had forgotten. So I stood there at the pay phone, clearing my head so I could remember what got me into this mess in the first place.

"I knew it," said rich dad, his voice booming over the phone. "You're more worried about your own personal survival than keeping your dream alive. Your fear has pushed aside your passion. The best way to keep going is to keep the flame in your heart going. Always remember what you set out to do, and the trip will be easy. Start worrying more about yourself, and your fear begins to eat away at your soul. Passion builds businesses. Not fear. You've gone this far. You're close, so don't turn back now. Remember what you set out to do, keep that memory in your heart and keep the flame going. You can always quit... so why quit now?"

With that, rich dad wished me luck and hung up the phone.

He was correct. I had forgotten why I set out on this journey. I had forgotten about my dream and allowed my fears to fill my head as well as my heart.

Just a few years earlier, there had been a movie entitled "Flash Dance." The theme song said something about, "Take your passion and make it happen."

Well, I had forgotten my passion. It was now time to make it happen or go back home and forget about it. I stood there for a while, and again I heard rich dad's last words: "You can always quit. So why quit now?"

I decided to delay quitting until I had made things happen.

BECOMING A TEACHER WHO OWNED THE SYSTEM

I stood at the phone booth after rich dad and I had hung up. My fears and lack of success were beating me, and my dream had been pushed aside. My dream of creating a different kind of school system. An educational program for people who wanted to be entrepreneurs and investors. As I stood there, my mind drifted back to my days in high school.

When I was 15 years old, my high school guidance counselor asked me, "What are you going to do when you grow up? Are you going to become a teacher like your dad?"

Looking straight at my counselor, my answer was straightforward, strong and filled with conviction. "I'll never be a teacher. Becoming a teacher is the last thing I would ever do."

I did not dislike school. I hated it. I absolutely hated being forced to sit and listen to someone I did not particularly like or respect speak for months on a subject I had no interest in. I fidgeted, squirmed, caused problems in the back of the room, unless I just left instead of going to class.

So when my guidance counselor asked me if I was planning to seek a career, following in my father's footsteps as a teacher, I nearly jumped out of my skin.

Little did I know at the time that passion is a combination of love and hate. I loved learning, but I hated school. I absolutely detested sitting there and being programmed into becoming something I did not want to be. I was not alone.

NOTABLE QUOTES ON EDUCATION

Winston Churchill once said: "I am always ready to learn, but I do not always like being taught."

John Updike said: "The founding fathers in their wisdom decided that children were an unnatural strain on their parents. So they provided jails called school, equipped with tortures called education."

Norman Douglas said: "Education is the state-controlled manufactory of echoes."

H.L. Mencken said: "School days, I believe, are the unhappiest in the whole span of human existence. They are full of dull, unintelligible tasks, new and unpleasant ordinances, and brutal violations of common sense and common decency."

Galileo said: "You cannot teach a person anything; you can only help him find it within himself."

Mark Twain said: "I never let schooling interfere with my education."

Albert Einstein said: "There is too much education altogether, especially in American schools."

A GIFT FROM MY EDUCATED DAD

The person who shared these quotes with me was my highly educated but poor dad. He also despised the school system... although he did well in it. He became a teacher because he had dreams of changing the 300 year old system, but instead, the system crushed him. He took his passion, tried to change the system, and ran into a brick wall. It was a system that too many people were making money in, and no one wanted it changed... although there was a lot of talk about the need for change.

Maybe my guidance counselor was psychic because years later I did indeed follow in my father's footsteps. I just didn't follow him into the same system. I was taking that same passion and creating my own system. That is why I was homeless. My passion was to create an educational system that taught people differently.

When my educated dad learned that Kim and I were struggling financially, doing our best to set up our own educational system, he sent us those quotes. Scribbled across the top of the page of the quotes were these words:

"Keep going." Love, Dad,

Up until that moment, I never knew how much my educated dad had hated the system and what it did to young people. But after this gesture of encouragement, things began to make sense. The passion that was driving me then was the same passion that had driven him years earlier. I was just like my real dad, and I had unwittingly picked up the torch from him. I was a teacher at the core... maybe that is why I hated the system so much.

In hindsight, I had become both dads. From my rich dad, I had learned the secrets of being a capitalist. From my highly educated dad, I inherited the passion for teaching. And given the combination of the two dads, I could now do something about the educational system. I did not have the desire or ability to change the current system. But I did have the knowledge to create my own system.

THE YEARS OF TRAINING BEGIN TO PAY OFF

For years, my rich dad groomed me to be a person who created businesses and business systems. The business I set up, in 1977, was a manufacturing company. We were one of the first companies to produce the nylon and velcro "surfer wallets" that came in bright colors. We followed that product with the "shoe pocket"– a miniature wallet, also made of nylon and velcro, that attached to the shoe laces of running shoes. In 1978, jogging was the new craze, and joggers always wanted a place to put their keys, and to carry money or ID cards in case they got hurt. That is why I designed the "shoe pocket" and marketed it to the world.

Our meteoric success was phenomenal, but soon the passion for the product line and the business drifted away. It began to weaken once my little company began to be pounded by foreign competition. Countries like Taiwan, Korea and Hong Kong were shipping products identical to mine and were wiping out the markets we had developed. Their prices were so low that there was no way we could compete. They were retailing products for less than it cost us to manufacture them.

Our little company was faced with a dilemma: fight them or join them. The partners realized we could not fight the competition. The companies flooding the market with cheap products were too strong. A vote was taken, and we decided to join them.

The tragedy was, in order to stay afloat, we had to let go of most of our faithful and hard-working staff. That broke my heart. When I went over to inspect the new factories we contracted with for our manufacturing in Korea and Taiwan, again my soul died a little. The conditions these young workers were forced to work in were cruel and inhumane. I saw five workers stacked one on top of the other, in a space where we would only allow one worker. My conscience began to bother me deeply. Not only for the workers we let go in America, but for the workers overseas who were now working for us.

Although we had solved the financial problem of foreign competition and began to make a lot of money, my heart was no longer in the business... and the business began to sag. Its spirit was gone because my spirit was gone. I no longer wanted to become rich if it meant exploiting so many low-paid workers. I began to think about educating people to be owners of businesses, not employees of business. At the age of 32, I was beginning to become a teacher, but didn't realize it at the time. The business began to decline not due to a lack of systems but because of a lack of heart, or passion. By the time Kim and I started out on our new business venture, the wallet company was gone.

DOWNSIZING COMING

In 1983, I was invited to give a talk to the MBA class at the University of Hawaii. I gave them my views on job security. They did not like what I said: "In a few years, many of you will lose your jobs, or be forced to work for less and less money, with less and less security."

Because my work caused me to travel the world, I witnessed firsthand the combined power of cheap labor and innovations from technology. I began to realize that a worker in Asia or Europe or Russia or South America was really competing with workers in America. I knew the idea of high pay and a safe, secure job for workers and middle managers was an idea whose time had past. Big companies would soon have to make cuts, both in the numbers of people and in the dollars they paid to workers, just to be able to compete globally.

I was never asked back to the University of Hawaii. A few years later, the word "downsizing" became standard practice. Every time a big company merged, and workers became redundant, downsizing occurred. Every time the owners wanted to make their shareholders happy, a downsizing occurred. With each downsizing, I saw the people at the top get richer and richer, and the people at the bottom pay the price.

Every time I heard someone say, "I'm sending my child to a good school so he or she can get a good safe, secure job," I cringed. Being prepared for a job is a good idea for the short term, but it is not enough for the long term. Slowly but surely, I was becoming a teacher.

BUILD A SYSTEM AROUND YOUR PASSION

Although my manufacturing company had turned around and was doing well again, my passion was gone. My rich dad summed up my frustration when he said: "School days are over. It's time to build a system around your heart. Build a system around your passion. Let the manufacturing company go and build what you know you must build. You have learned well from me, but you are still your father's son.

You and your dad are teachers deep in your souls."

Kim and I packed up everything and moved to California to learn new teaching methods, so we could create a business around those methods. Before we could get the business off the ground, we ran out of money and were out on the street. It was that phone call to my rich dad, my wife standing by me, anger at myself, and a rekindling of the passion, that got us out of the mess we were in.

Soon we were back at building a company. The company was an educational company using teaching methods almost exactly opposite of what traditional schools use. Instead of asking students to sit still, we encouraged them to be active. Instead of teaching via lecture, we taught by playing games. Instead of being boring, we insisted our teachers be fun. Instead of teachers, we sought out business people who had actually started their own companies, and taught our style of teaching. Instead of grading the students, the students graded the teacher. If the teacher got a lousy grade, the teacher was either put through another intensive training program, or asked to leave.

Age, educational background, sex and religious beliefs were not criteria. All we asked for was a sincere desire to learn and to learn quickly. We were eventually able to teach a year's worth of accounting in one day.

Although we mainly taught adults, we had many young people, some 16 years old, learning right alongside highly paid, well-educated 60 year old business executives. Instead of competing on tests, we asked them to cooperate on teams. Then, we had the team taking a test competing against other teams taking the same test. Instead of striving for grades, we bet money. Winner take all. The competition and desire to do well as a team was fierce. The teacher did not have to motivate the class. The teacher just had to get out of the way once the learning competition was on. Instead of quiet at test time, there was yelling, screaming, laughter and tears. People were excited about learning. They were "turned on" by learning... and they wanted to learn more.

We focused on teaching just two subjects: entrepreneurship and investing. The "B" and "I" side of the *Quadrant*. The people who wanted to learn these subjects in our style of education showed up in droves. We did no advertising. Everything spread by word of mouth. The people who showed up were people who wanted to create jobs, not people looking for jobs.

Once I made up my mind not to quit that night at the phone booth, things began to move forward. In less than five years, we had a multimillion-dollar business with 11 offices throughout the world. We had built a new system of education, and the market loved it. Our passion had made it happen, because passion and a good system overcame fear and past programming.

A TEACHER CAN BE RICH

Whenever I hear teachers say they are not paid enough, I feel for them. The irony is that they are a product of their own system's programming. They look at being a teacher from the point of view of the "E" quadrant rather than the "B" or "I" quadrant. Remember you can be anything you want to be in any of the quadrants... even a teacher.

WE CAN BE ANYTHING WE WANT

Most of us have the potential to be successful in all of the quadrants. It all depends on how determined we are to be successful. As my rich dad said, "Passion builds businesses. Not fear."

The problem of changing quadrants is often found in our past conditioning. Many of us came from families where the emotion of fear was used as a prime motivator to get us to think and act in a certain way. For example:

"Did you do your homework? If you don't do your homework, you'll flunk out of school and all your friends will laugh at you."

"If you keep making faces, your face will get stuck in that position."

And the classic, "If you don't get good grades, you won't get a safe, secure job with benefits."

Well, today many people have gotten good grades, but there are fewer safe, secure jobs and even fewer with benefits, like retirement plans. So many people, even those with good grades, need to "mind their own business" and not just look for a job where they will mind someone else's business.

IT'S RISKY ON THE LEFT SIDE

I know many friends who still seek security in a job or a position. Ironically, the march of technology continues moving at an even faster pace. To keep up in the job market, each person will need to constantly be trained in the latest technology. If you're going to be re-educated anyway, why not spend some time educating yourself on the skills needed for the right side of the *Quadrant*? If people could see what I see when I travel the world, they would not be looking for more security. Security is a myth. Learn something new and take on this brave new world. Don't hide from it.

It is also risky for self-employed people, in my opinion. If they get sick, injured or die, their income is directly impacted. As I get older, I meet more self-employed people my age who are physically, mentally and emotionally burned out from hard work. The more fatigue a person endures, the less secure they become, and the risk of them having an accident also goes up.

IT IS MORE SECURE ON THE RIGHT SIDE

The irony is, life is actually more secure on the right side of the *Quadrant*. For example, if you have a secure system that produces more and more money with less and less work, then you really do not need a job, or need to worry about losing your job or need to live life below your means. Instead of living below your means, expand your means. To make more money, simply expand the system and hire more people.

People who are high-level investors are not concerned about the market going up or going down because their knowledge will allow them to make money either way. If there is a market crash and/or a depression in the next 30 years, many baby boomers will panic, and lose much of the money they had set aside for retirement. If that happens in their old age, instead of retiring, they will have to work for as long as they can.

As for fear of losing money, professional investors are people who risk little of their own money and yet still make the highest returns. It is the people who know little about investing who take the risks and earn the least in return. From my point of view, all the risk is on the left side of the *Quadrant.*

WHY THE LEFT SIDE IS RISKIER

"If you cannot read numbers, then you must take someone else's opinion," said rich dad. "In the case of buying a house, your dad just blindly accepts your banker's opinion that his house is an asset."

Both Mike and I noticed his emphasis on the word "blindly."

"Most people on the left side really do not need to be that good with financial numbers. But if you want to be successful on the right side of the *Quadrant,* then numbers become your eyes. Numbers allow you to see what most people cannot see," rich dad went on.

"You mean like Superman's X-ray vision," said Mike.

Rich dad chuckled and nodded. "Exactly," he said. "The ability to read numbers, financial systems and business systems gives you vision that mere mortals do not have." Even he laughed at that silliness. "Having financial vision lowers your risk. Being financially blind increases risk. But you only need that vision if you want to operate on the right side of the *Quadrant.* In fact, people on the left side think in words, and to be successful on the right, especially the "I" quadrant, you must think in numbers... not words. It's really risky trying to be an investor while still thinking predominantly in words."

"Are you saying that people on the left side of the *Quadrant* do not need to know about financial numbers?" I asked.

"For most of them, that is correct," said rich dad. "As long as they are content to operate strictly within the confines of being an "E" or "S," then the numbers they learn in school are adequate. But if they want to survive on the right side, understanding financial numbers and systems becomes crucial. If you want to build a small business, you don't need to master numbers. But if you want build a large worldwide business, numbers become everything. Not words. That is why so many large companies are often run by bean counters."

Rich dad continued his lesson: "If you want to be successful on the right side, when it comes to money, you have got to know the difference between facts and opinions. You cannot blindly accept financial advice the way people on the left side do. You must know your numbers. You must know the facts. And numbers tell you the facts."

WHO PAYS TO TAKE THE RISK?

"Besides the left side being risky, people on that side pay to take that risk," said rich dad.

"What did you mean by that last remark?" I asked. "Doesn't everyone pay to take risks?

"No," said rich dad. "Not on the right side."

"Are you trying to say that people on the left pay to take risks and the people on the right side get paid to take risks?"

"Exactly what I mean," said rich dad, smiling. "That is the biggest difference between the left side and the right side. That is why the left side is riskier than the right.

"Can you give me an example?" I asked.

"Sure," said rich dad. "If you buy shares of stock in a company, who takes the financial risk? You or the company?"

"I guess I do," I said, still puzzled.

"And if I am a medical insurance company and I insure your health and take on your health risk, do I pay you?"

"No," I said. "If they insure my health, and they take that risk, I pay for it."

"That's right," said rich dad. "I have yet to find an insurance company that will insure your health or accident risk and pay you for that privilege. But that is what people on the left side do."

"It's kind of confusing," said Mike. "It still does not make sense."

Rich dad smiled, "Once you better understand the right side, you will begin to see the differences more clearly. Most people do not know there is a difference. They just assume everything is risky... and they pay for it. But as the years go on, and you become more comfortable with your experience and education on the right side of the *Quadrant*, your vision will improve and you will begin to see what people on the left side cannot see. And you will understand why seeking security to avoid risk is the riskiest thing you can do. You'll develop your own financial vision and not have to accept other people's opinions simply because they have a job title of banker, or stockbroker, or accountant, or whatever. You'll be able to see for yourself, and know the difference between financial facts and financial opinions."

It was a good day. In fact, it was one of the better lessons I could remember. It was great because it began to open my mind to things my eyes could not see.

NUMBERS REDUCE RISK

Without those simple lessons from my rich dad, I doubt if I could have taken my passion and built the educational system of my dreams. Without his insistence on financial literacy and accuracy, I know I could not have invested as wisely, with so little of my own money and earned such high returns. I always remembered the bigger the project and the faster you want to succeed, the more you need to be accurate. If you want to get rich slowly, or just work all your life and let someone else manage your money, then you do not need to be as accurate. The faster you want to get rich, the more accurate with numbers you must be.

The good news is that due to advances in technology and new products, it is much easier today to learn the necessary skills for building your own system and quickly developing your financial literacy.

YOU CAN GO FAST... BUT DON'T TAKE SHORTCUTS

"To reduce your taxes, buy a bigger house and get deeper into debt so you can get a tax write-off."

"Your home should be your largest investment."

"You'd better buy now because the prices always go up."

"Get rich slowly."

"Live below your means."

If you put in the time to study and learn about the subjects required on the right side of the *Quadrant*, such statements won't make much sense. It might make sense to someone on the left side of the *Quadrant*, but not to someone on the right side. You can do anything you like, go as fast as you like, make as much money as you like, but you have to pay the price. You can go quickly, but remember, there are no shortcuts.

This book is not about answers. This book is about looking at financial challenges and objectives from a different point of view. It's not that one point of view is better than another; it's simply smarter to have more than one point of view.

In reading the following chapters, you may begin looking at finances, business and life from a different point of view.

CHAPTER 8

How Do I Get Rich?

When I am asked, "Where did I learn my formula for getting rich?" I reply, "Playing the game of *Monopoly* as a kid."

Some people think I am kidding, and others wait for the punch line, expecting a joke. Yet, it is not meant as a joke, and I am not kidding. The formula for getting rich in *Monopoly* is simple, and it works in real life as well as in the game.

FOUR GREEN HOUSES... ONE RED HOTEL

You may recall that the secret to wealth when playing *Monopoly* is simply to buy four green houses and then trade them in to buy a large red hotel. That is all it takes, and that is the same investment formula for wealth my wife and I used.

When the real estate market was really bad, we bought as many small houses as we could, with the limited money we had. When the market improved, we traded in the four green houses and bought a large red hotel. We never have to work because the cash flow from our large red hotel, apartment houses and mini storages pays for our lifestyle.

IT WORKS FOR HAMBURGERS ALSO

Or if you do not like real estate, all you have to do is make hamburgers, build a business around that hamburger, and franchise it. Within a few years, the increasing cash flow will provide you with more money than you can spend.

In reality, that is how simple the path to extraordinary wealth can be. In other words, in this high-tech world, the principles of great wealth remain simple and low tech. I would say that it's merely common sense. But unfortunately, when it comes to the subject of money, common sense is uncommon.

For example, it makes no sense to me to give people a tax break to lose money and spend their lives in debt. Or to call your home an asset when it really is a liability that drains cash from you every day. Or to have a national government that spends more money than it collects in taxes. Or to send a child to school to study in the hope of getting a job, but not teach that child anything about money.

IT IS EASY TO DO WHAT RICH PEOPLE DO

Doing what rich people do is easy. One of the reasons there are so many wealthy people who did not do well in school is because the "to do" part of becoming wealthy is simple. You do not have to go to school to become rich. The "to do" part of becoming rich is definitely not rocket science.

There is a classic book I recommend you read: *Think and Grow Rich* by Napolean Hill. I read this book as a youngster, and it greatly influenced the direction of my life. In fact, it was my rich dad who first recommended I read this book and others like it.

There is a good reason why it's titled *Think and Grow Rich* and not Work Hard and Grow Rich or Get a Job and Grow Rich. The fact is, people who work the hardest do not wind up rich. If you want to be rich, you need to "think." Think independently rather than go along with the crowd. In my opinion, one great asset of the rich is they think differently from everyone else. If you do what everyone else does, you'll wind up having what everyone else has. And for most people, what they have is years of hard work, unfair taxes and a lifetime of debt.

When someone asks me, "What do I have to do to move from the left side of the *Quadrant* to the right side?" my response is, "It's not what you have to 'do' that needs to change. It's first how you 'think' that needs to change. In other words, it's who you have to 'be' in order to 'do' what needs to be done."

Do you want to be the kind of person who thinks buying four green houses and turning them in for one red hotel is easy? Or do you want to be the kind of person who thinks buying four green houses and turning them in for one red hotel is hard?

Years ago I was in this class on goal setting. It was the mid-1970s, and I really could not believe I was spending $150 and a beautiful Saturday and Sunday to learn how to set goals. I would rather have been surfing. Instead, here I was paying someone to teach me how to set goals. I nearly backed out several times, but what I learned from that class has helped me achieve what I want in life.

The instructor put up on the board these three words.

BE — DO — HAVE

She then said, "Goals are the 'have' part of these three words. Goals such as to have a nice body, or to have the perfect relationship, or to have millions of dollars, or to have great health, or to have fame. Once most people figure out what they want to have, their goal, they begin listing what they have 'to do.' That is why most people have 'To Do' lists. They set their goal and then begin 'doing.' "

She first used the goal of the perfect body. "What most people do when they want a perfect body is go on a diet, and then go to the gym. This lasts for a few weeks and then most are back to the old diet of French fries and pizza, and instead of going to the gym, they watch baseball on TV. This is an example of 'doing' instead of 'being.' "

"It's not the diet that counts; it's who you have to be to follow the diet that counts. Yet, every year millions of people look for the perfect diet to follow in order to become thin. They focus on what they have to do, rather than who they have to be. A diet will not help if your thoughts do not change."

She used golf as another example: "Many people buy a new set of golf clubs in hopes that they can improve their game, instead of starting with the attitude, mind-set and beliefs of a professional golfer. A lousy golfer with a new set of golf clubs is still a lousy golfer."

Then, she discussed investments: "Many people think that buying stocks or mutual funds will make them rich. Well, simply buying stocks, mutual funds, real estate and bonds will not make you rich. Just doing what professional investors do does not guarantee financial success. A person who has a loser mentality will always lose no matter what stock, bond, real estate or mutual fund they buy."

Next, she used an example of finding the perfect romantic partner: "So many people go to bars or to work or to their church looking for the perfect person, the person of their dreams. That is what they 'do'. What they 'do' is go and look for the 'right person' instead of work on 'being the right person.' "

Here's one of her examples about relationships: "In marriage, many people try to change the other person so they can have a better marriage. Instead of trying to change the other person, which often leads to fights, it is better to change yourself first," she said. "Don't work on the other person; work on your thoughts about that other person."

As she was talking about relationships, my mind drifted to the many people I had met over the years who were out to "change the world" but were not getting anywhere. They wanted to change everyone else, but not change themselves.

For her example of money, she said, "And when it comes to money, many people try 'to do' what the rich do and 'to have' what the rich have. So they go out and buy a house that looks rich, a car that looks rich, and send their kids to the schools where the rich send their kids. All this does is cause these people 'to do' by working harder and 'to have' more debt, which causes them to work even harder... which is not what the truly rich do."

I was nodding my head in the back of the room in agreement. My rich dad did not use these same words to explain things, but he did often say to me, "People think that working hard for money, and then buying things that make them look rich, will make them rich. In most cases it doesn't. It only makes them more tired. They call it 'Keeping up with the Joneses,' and if you notice, the Joneses are exhausted."

During that weekend class, much of what my rich dad had been telling me began to make more sense. For years he lived modestly. Instead of working hard to pay bills, he worked hard to acquire assets. If you saw him on the street, he looked like everyone else. He drove a pickup truck, not an expensive car. Then one day, when he was in his late 30s, he emerged as a financial powerhouse. People took notice when he suddenly bought one of the prime pieces of real estate in Hawaii. After his name hit the paper, it was then people realized that this quiet unpretentious man owned many other businesses, lots of prime real estate, and when he spoke, his bankers listened. Few people ever saw the modest house he lived in. After he was flush with cash and cash flow from his assets, he then bought a new large house for his family. He did not take out a loan. He paid cash.

After that weekend class on goal setting, I realized that many people tried "doing" what they thought the rich did and tried "having" what the rich had. They often would buy big houses and invest in the stock market because that is what they thought the rich did. Yet, what my rich dad was trying to tell me was if they still thought and had the beliefs and ideas of a poor person or middle-class person, and then did what the rich did, they would still wind up having what the poor and middle class have. "Be-Do-Have" began to make sense.

THE CASHFLOW QUADRANT IS ABOUT BEING...
NOT DOING

Moving from the left side of the *Quadrant* to the right side of the *Quadrant* is not so much about "doing" but more about "being."

It is not so much what the "B" or "I" does that makes the difference; it is more how they "think." Who they are at their core "being."

The good news is that it does not cost much money to change your thinking. In fact, it can be done for free. The bad news is that sometimes it's hard to change some deep core thoughts about money that are handed down from generation to generation, or thoughts that you learned from friends, from work and from school. Yet, it can be done. And this is what this book is primarily about. It's not so much a "How-to book" on "What to do" to become financially free. This book is not about what stocks to buy, or what mutual fund is safest. This book is primarily about strengthening your thoughts (being), so that you can take the action (doing) that will enable you to become financially free (having).

SECURITY IS THE ISSUE FOR "E's"

As a generalization, people who seek out the "E" quadrant, when it comes to money, often greatly value security. For them, it is often true that money is not as important as security. They may take great risks in other areas of their lives, such as sport parachuting, but not when it comes to money.

PERFECTIONISM IS THE ISSUE FOR "S's"

Again, this is a generalization... yet what I have observed among people who are currently in the "S" quadrant, but are trying to switch from the left quadrant to right quadrant, is the "Do it yourself" mentality. They like to "Do it themselves" because they often have a great need to make sure things are done "right." And since they have a hard time finding someone else to do it "right," they do it on their own.

For many "S's," the real issue is "control." They need to be in control. They hate making mistakes. What they hate even more is someone else making mistakes and making them look bad. That is what makes them excellent "S's" and the reason you hire them to do certain tasks for you. You want your dentist to be a perfectionist. You want your attorney to be a perfectionist. You want your brain surgeon to be a perfectionist. You want your architect to be a perfectionist. That is what you pay them for. That is their strength. It is also their weakness.

EMOTIONAL INTELLIGENCE

A big part of being a human being is being human. And being human means having emotions. All of us have the same emotions. We all feel fear, sadness, anger, love, hate, disappointment, joy, happiness and other emotions. What makes us individuals is how we each handle those emotions.

When it comes to risking money, we all experience fear... even the rich. The difference is how we handle that fear. For many people, that emotion of fear generates the thought, "Play it safe. Don't take risks."

For others, especially those on the right side, fear of losing money may have them think this thought: "Play it smart. Learn to manage risk."

Same emotion, different thought... different being... different doing...different having.

THE FEAR OF LOSING MONEY

In my opinion, the greatest cause of human financial struggle is the fear of losing money. And because of this fear, people often operate too safely, or with too much personal control, or they just give their money to someone they think is an expert and hope and pray that money will be there when they need it.

If fear keeps you prisoner in one of the financial quadrants, I recommend you read *Emotional Intelligence*, by Daniel Goleman. In his book, Goleman explains the age-old puzzle of why people who do well academically in school do not always do well financially in the real world. His answer is that Emotional IQ is more powerful than Academic IQ. That is why people who take risks, make mistakes and recover often do better than people who learned not to make mistakes because they were afraid of risk. Too many people leave school with passing grades, yet are not emotionally prepared to take risks... especially financial risks. The reason so many teachers are not rich is because they operate in a "punish people who make mistakes environment," and they themselves are often people who are emotionally afraid of making mistakes. Instead, to be financially free, we need to learn how to make mistakes and manage risk.

If people spend their life terrified of losing money, afraid of doing things differently from what the crowd does, then getting rich is almost impossible, even if it's as simple as buying four green houses and trading them in for one large red hotel.

EMOTIONAL IQ IS STRONGER

After reading Goleman's book, I came to realize that Financial IQ is 90 percent Emotional IQ and only 10 percent technical information about finance or money. Goleman quotes 16th century humanist Erasmus of Rotterdam, who wrote a satirical vein of the perennial tension between reason and emotion. In his writing, he uses the ratio of 24:1 in comparing the power of the emotional brain to the rational brain. In other words, when emotions are in high gear, emotions are 24 times stronger than the rational mind. Now I do not know if the ratio is valid, but it does have some usefulness as a reference to the power of emotional thinking vs. rational thinking.

24 : 1

Emotional Brain : Rational Brain

All of us, if we are human, have experienced events in our lives when our emotions overtook our rational thoughts. I am certain most of us have:

1. Said something out of anger that we later wish we had not said.
2. Been attracted to someone we knew was not good for us... but still went out with them or, worse, married them.
3. Have cried, or seen someone cry uncontrollably, because of the loss of a loved one.
4. Did something intentionally to hurt someone we love because we were hurt.
5. Had our heart broken and not gotten over it for a long time.

Those are just a few examples of emotions being stronger than rational thought.

There are times when emotions are more than 24:1, and these are often called:

1. Addictions, such as compulsive eating, smoking, sex, shopping, drugs.
2. Phobias, such as fear of snakes, heights, tight spaces, the dark, strangers.

These and other behaviors are often 100 percent emotionally driven. There is little power that rational thought has over the emotional thought when something as strong as addictions and phobias are involved.

SNAKES PHOBIA

When I was in flight school, I had a friend who had a phobia about snakes. During a class on how to survive in the wild after being shot down, the teacher brought out a harmless garden snake to show us how to eat it. My friend, a grown man, jumped up, screamed and ran out of the room. He could not control himself. Not only was his phobia of snakes strong, but the idea of eating a snake was just too much for his emotions to bear.

MONEY PHOBIA

When it comes to risking money, I have seen people do the same thing. Instead of finding out about the investment, they also jump up, scream and run out of the room.

When it comes to the subject of money, there are many deep emotional phobias... too many to list. I have them. You have them. We all have them. Why? Because like it or not, money is an emotional subject. And because it's an emotional subject, most people cannot think logically about money. If you don't think money is emotional, just watch the stock market. In most markets, there is no logic... only the emotions of greed and fear. Or just watch people climb into a new car and have them smell the leather interior. All the salesperson has to do is whisper these magic words in their ear, "Low down, easy monthly payments," and all logic goes out the window.

EMOTIONAL THOUGHTS SOUND LOGICAL

The problem with core emotional thoughts is that they sound logical. To someone in the "E" quadrant, when the emotion of fear is present, the logical thought is: "Play it safe, don't take risks." To someone in the "I" quadrant, however, this thought does not sound logical.

For people in the "S" quadrant, when the issue of trusting other people to do a good job comes up, their logical thought may go like this: "I'll just do it myself."

That is a reason why so many "S" type businesses are often family businesses. There is a greater sense of trust. For them, "Blood is definitely thicker than water."

So different quadrants... different logic... different thoughts... different actions... different haves... same emotions. Therefore, emotions make us human beings, and recognizing that we have emotions is a large part of being human.

What determines what we do is how we individually respond to those emotions.

I DON'T FEEL LIKE IT

One way to know if you're thinking emotionally and not rationally is when you use the word "feel" in conversation. For example, many people who are run by their emotions or their feelings will say things like: "I don't feel like exercising today." Logically they know they should exercise.

Many people who struggle financially are not able to control how they feel, or they let their feelings dictate their thoughts. I hear them say:

"I don't feel like learning about investing. It's too much trouble."

"Investing doesn't feel right for me."

"I don't feel like telling my friends about my business."

"I hate the feeling of being rejected."

PARENT-CHILD-ADULT

Those are thoughts generated from emotions, more than rationality. In pop psychology, it's the battle between the parent and child. The parent usually speaks in "should's." For example, a parent might say, "You should be doing your homework," while the child speaks in "feeling." In response to homework, a child would say, "But I don't feel like doing it."

Financially, the parent in you would say silently, "You should save more money." But the child in you would reply, "But I really feel like taking a vacation. I'll just put the vacation on my credit card."

WHEN ARE YOU AN ADULT?

In going from left quadrant to right quadrant, we need to be adults. We all need to grow up financially. Instead of being parent or child, we need to look at money, work, and investing as adults. And what being an adult means is knowing what you have to do and doing it, even though you may not feel like doing it.

CONVERSATIONS WITHIN YOU

For people contemplating making the crossing from one quadrant to another, an important part of the process is to be aware of your internal dialogue... or conversations within you. Always remember the importance of the book *Think and Grow Rich*. A significant part of the process is to be constantly vigilant regarding your silent thoughts, your internal dialogue, and always remember that what sounds logical in one quadrant does not make sense in another quadrant. The process of going from job or financial security to financial freedom is primarily a process of changing your thinking. It is a process of doing your best to know which thoughts are emotion-based and which thoughts are logic-based. If you can keep your emotions in check and go for what you know to be logical, you have a good chance of making the journey. No matter what anyone is saying to you from the outside, the most important conversation is the one you are having with yourself on the inside.

When Kim and I were temporarily homeless and financially unstable, our emotions were out of control. Many times, what sounded logical was pure emotions talking. Our emotions were saying the same thing our friends were saying: "Play it safe. Just get a safe, secure job and enjoy life."

Yet, logically, we both agreed that freedom made more sense to us than security. In going for financial freedom, we knew we could find a sense of security that job security could never give us. That made sense to us. The only things in our way were our emotionally driven thoughts. Thoughts that sounded logical but in the long term made no sense. The good news is that once we made it across, the old thoughts stopped screaming and the new thoughts we desired became our reality... the thoughts of the "B" and "I" quadrants.

Today, I understand the emotions when a person says:

"I can't take risks. I have a family to think about. I must have a secure job."

Or "It takes money to make money. That is why I can't invest."

Or "I'll do it on my own."

I feel their thoughts, for I have had those thoughts myself. But looking across the *Quadrant* and having achieved financial freedom from the "B" and "I" quadrants, I can faithfully say that having financial freedom is a much more peaceful and secure way of thinking.

DIFFERENCES BETWEEN "E" AND "B"

Core emotional values cause different points of view. The struggle in communication between owners of a business and the employees of a business is often caused by differences in emotional values. There has always been a struggle between the "E" and the "B" because one wants more pay and the other wants more work. That is why we often hear, "I'm overworked and underpaid."

And from the other side we often hear, "What can we do to motivate them to work harder and be more loyal without paying them any more?"

DIFFERENCES BETWEEN "B" AND "I"

Another is the constant tension between business operators and the investors in that business, often called the shareholders, the "B" and the "I." One wants more money to operate with and the other wants greater dividends.

A conversation at a shareholders meeting may sound like this:

Company managers: "We need a private jet so our executives can get to their meetings faster."

Investors: "We need fewer executives. Then, we won't need a private jet."

DIFFERENCES BETWEEN "S" AND "B"

In business transactions, I have often seen a bright "S," such as an attorney, put a multimillion-dollar deal together for a "B", business owner, and when the transaction is completed, the attorney becomes silently disturbed because the "B" makes millions and the "S" earns an hourly wage.

Their words may sound like this:

Attorney: "We did all the work, and he made all the money."

The "B": "How many hours did those guys bill us for? We could have bought the whole law firm for what they charged us."

DIFFERENCES BETWEEN "E" AND "I"

Another example is a bank manager who gives an investor a loan to buy some real estate. The investor makes hundreds of thousands of dollars, tax free, and the banker gets a paycheck that is taxed heavily. That would be an example of an "E" dealing with an "I" that often causes a mild emotional reaction.

The "E" might say: "I give that guy a loan, and he doesn't even say 'Thank you.' I don't think he knows how hard we worked for him."

The "I" might say: "Boy, those guys are picky. Look at all this useless paperwork we have to do just to get a lousy loan."

EMOTIONALLY DISTURBED MARRIAGE

The most emotionally disturbed marriage I ever witnessed was a couple where the wife was a hard core "E" who believed in job and financial security. The husband, on the other hand, fancied himself as a high-flying "I." He thought he was a future Warren Buffet, but in reality he was an "S," a commission-only salesman by profession, but he was a chronic gambler at heart. He was always looking for the investment that would help him "Get rich quick." He was all ears for any new stock offering, or off-shore investment scheme that promised ultra-high returns, or a real estate deal he could take an option on. This couple is still together, yet I really do not know why. Each drives the other nuts. One person thrives on risk; the other hates risk. Different quadrants, different core values.

IF YOU ARE MARRIED OR IN A PRIMARY RELATIONSHIP

If you are married or in a primary relationship, circle the quadrant you generate the majority of your income from and then circle the quadrant your spouse or partner generates income from.

The reason I ask you to do this is because the discussion between partners is often difficult if one partner does not understand where the other is coming from.

THE BATTLE BETWEEN THE RICH AND THE EDUCATED

There is another unspoken battlefield I have noticed, and that is the differences in points of view between the educated and the rich.

In my years of researching the differences between the different quadrants, I have often heard bankers, attorneys, accountants and others like them grumble silently that they are the educated ones, and it's often the so-called less-educated person who makes the "big bucks." This is what I label the battle between the educated and the rich, which is more often the difference between people on the left side of the *Quadrant* and people on the right side of the *Quadrant*... or the "E-S's" vs. the "B-I's." It's not that people in the "B" and "I" quadrant are uneducated... because many are highly educated; it's just that many "B's" and "I's" were not academic whiz kids in school... and were not trained in graduate schools like attorneys, accountants and MBAs were.

For those of you who read my book *Rich Dad Poor Dad,* you know it is about the struggle between the educated and the rich. My highly educated but poor dad took great pride in the fact that he had done years of advanced studies in prestigious schools such as Stanford University and The University of Chicago. My rich dad was a man who dropped out of school to run his family's business when his father died... so he never finished high school, yet he acquired tremendous wealth.

As I grew older and seemed to be more influenced by my rich but uneducated dad, my educated dad was occasionally defensive of his station in life. One day, when I was about 16 years of age, my educated dad blurted out,

"I have advanced degrees from prestigious schools. What does your friend's dad have?"

I paused and replied quietly, "Money and free time."

MORE THAN A MENTAL CHANGE

As stated earlier, to find success in the "B" or "I" quadrant requires more than simply academic or technical knowledge. It often requires a change in core emotional thinking, feelings, beliefs and attitude. Remember the

BE — DO — HAVE.

What the rich do is relatively simple. It's the "Be" that is different. The difference is found in their thoughts and, more specifically, their internal dialogue with themselves. That is why my rich dad forbade me from saying:

"I can't afford it."

"I can't do that."

"Play it safe."

'Don't lose money."

"What if you fail and never recover?"

He forbade me from saying those words because he truly believed that words are the most powerful tools available to humans. What a person says and thinks becomes real.

He often quoted from the Bible, although he was not that religious: "And the word became flesh and dwelt amongst us."

Rich dad firmly believed that what we said to ourselves, at our core, became our reality. That is why I suspect that for people who struggle financially, their emotions often do the talking and run their lives. Until a person learns to overcome those emotionally driven thoughts, their words do become flesh. Words such as:

"I'll never be rich."

"That idea will never work."

"It's too expensive for me."

If they are emotionally based thoughts, they are powerful. The good news is that they can be changed with support of new friends, new ideas and a little time.

People who are not able to control their fear of losing should never invest on their own. They are best served by turning that job over to a professional and not interfering with them.

As an interesting note, I have met many professional people who are fearless when investing other people's money and able to make lots of money. But when it comes to investing or risking their own money, their fear of losing becomes too strong and they ultimately lose. Their emotions do the thinking rather than their logic.

I have also met people who can invest their money and win constantly, but lose their calm when someone asks them to invest money for them.

The making and losing of money is an emotional subject. So my rich dad gave me the secret to handling these emotions. Rich dad always said, "To be successful as an investor or a business owner, you have to be emotionally neutral to winning and losing. Winning and losing are just part of the game."

QUITTING MY SECURE JOB

My friend Mike had a system that belonged to him. His father had built it. I did not have that good fortune. I knew that someday I was going to have to leave the comfort and security of the nest, and begin to build my own.

In 1978, I resigned from my full-time secure job with Xerox, and took the hard step forward with no safety net. The noise in my head was loud from my fear and doubt. I was nearly paralyzed with fear as I signed my letter of resignation, collected my last paycheck, and walked out the door. I had an orchestra of self-damaging thoughts and feelings playing inside me. I was "bad-mouthing" myself so loudly and with such conviction that I could not hear anything else. It's a good thing, because so many of the people I worked with were saying, "He'll be back. He'll never make it."

The problem was, I was saying the same thing to myself. Those emotional words of self-doubt haunted me for years until my wife and I were successful in both the "B" and "I" quadrants. Today, I still hear those words; they just have less authority. In the process of putting up with my own self-doubt, I learned to create other words, words of personal encouragement, statements such as:

"Keep calm, think clearly, keep an open mind, keep going, ask someone who has gone before you for some guidance, trust, and keep the faith in a higher power wanting the best for you."

I learned to create these words of encouragement internally, even though there was a part of me that was frightened and afraid."

I knew that I had little chance of success my first time out. Yet, the positive human emotions, emotions such as trust, faith, courage and good friends moved me forward. I knew that I had to take risks. I knew that risk led to mistakes, and mistakes led to wisdom and knowledge, both of which I lacked. For me, failure would have been to let fear win, so I was willing to move forward with little in guarantees. My rich dad had instilled in me the idea that "failure is part of the process of success."

INTERNAL JOURNEY

The journey from one quadrant to the next is an internal journey. It is a journey from one set of core beliefs and technical skills to a new set of core beliefs and a new set of technical skills. The process is much like learning to ride a bicycle. At first you fall down many times. Often times it's frustrating and embarrassing, especially if your friends are watching. But after a while, the falling stops and riding becomes automatic. If you fall down again, it's not that big of a deal because, internally, you now know that you can get up and ride again. The process is the same when going from an emotional mind-set of job security to the emotional mind-set of financial freedom. Once my wife and I made the crossing, we were less afraid of failing because we were confident in our ability to stand back up.

There are two statements that kept me going personally. One was my rich dad's words of advice, when I was on the brink of quitting and turning back: "You can always quit... so why quit now?"

That statement kept my spirits higher and emotions calm. That statement reminded me that I was halfway across... so why turn back because the distance going home was just as far as going for the quadrant on the other side. It would be like Columbus quitting and turning back halfway across the Atlantic. Either way, the distance was the same.

And a word of caution: Intelligence is also knowing when to quit. Too often I meet people who are so stubborn, they keep going forward on a project that has no chance of success. The problem of knowing when to quit or when to keep going is an age-old problem with anyone who takes risks. One way to manage this problem of "to keep going or quit" is to find mentors who have already successfully made the crossing before, and seek their advice. Such a person, who is already on the other side, can best guide you. But be careful of advice from someone who has only read books about the crossing and gets paid to lecture on the subject.

The other statement that often kept me going was:

"Giants often trip and fall.

But worms don't, because

All they do is dig and crawl."

The main reason so many people struggle financially is not because they lack a good education, or are not hard working. It's because they're afraid of losing. If the fear of losing stops them, they've already lost.

LOSERS CUT THEIR WINNERS AND RIDE THEIR LOSERS

Fear of "being" a loser affects what people "do" in strange ways. I have seen people who bought a stock at $20, sell their shares when they reached $30 because they're so afraid of losing what they've gained, only to have the stock go to $100, split and go up to $100 again.

That same person, having bought a stock at $20, will watch it go down to, say, $3 and still hang on, hoping the price will come back up... and they may hang on to that $3 stock for 20 years. This is an example of a person "being" so afraid of losing, or admitting they lost, that they wind up losing.

WINNERS CUT THEIR LOSERS AND RIDE THEIR WINNERS

Winners "do" things almost exactly the opposite. Often, the moment they know they took a losing position, i.e. their stock price starts to go down instead of up, they will sell immediately and take their losses. Most are not ashamed to say they took a loss, for a winner knows that losing is part of the process of winning.

When they find a winner, they will ride it up as far as it can go. The moment they know the free ride is over and the price has peaked, they cut and sell.

The key to being a great investor is to be neutral to winning and losing. Then, you don't have emotionally driven thoughts such as fear and greed doing your thinking for you.

LOSERS DO THE SAME THINGS IN LIFE

People who are afraid of losing do the same things in real life. We all know of:
1. People who stay in marriages where there is no longer any love.
2. People who stay at dead-end jobs.
3. People who hang on to old clothes and "stuff" they will never use.
4. People who stay in towns where they have no future.
5. People who stay friends with people who hold them back.

EMOTIONAL INTELLIGENCE CAN BE CONTROLLED

Financial intelligence is closely linked to emotional intelligence. In my opinion, most people suffer financially because their emotions are in control of their thoughts. We as human BE-ings, all have the same emotions. What determines the differences in what we "DO" and what we "HAVE" in life is primarily how we handle those emotions.

For example, the emotion of fear can cause some of us to be cowards. The same emotion of fear can cause others to become courageous. Unfortunately, when it comes to the subject of money, most people in our society are conditioned to be financial cowards. When the fear of losing money comes up, most people's minds automatically start chanting these words:
1. "Security," rather than "freedom."
2. "Avoid risk," rather than "learn to manage risk."
3. "Play it safe," rather than "play it smart."
4. "I can't afford it," rather than "how can I afford it?"
5. "It's too expensive," rather than "what is it worth, long term?"
6. "Diversify," rather than "focus."
7. "What will my friends think?" rather than "what do I think?"

THE WISDOM OF RISK

There is a science to taking risks, especially financial risks. One of the best books I have read on the subject of money and risk management is *Trading for a Living*, by Dr. Alexander Elder.

Although it was written for people who trade stocks and options professionally, the wisdom of risk and risk management applies to all areas of money, money management, personal psychology and investing. One of the reasons many successful "B's" are not always as successful as "I's" is because they do not fully understand the psychology behind purely risking money. While "B's" understand risk when it involves business systems and people, that knowledge does not always translate into the systems of money making money.

IT'S EMOTIONAL MORE THAN TECHNICAL

In summary, moving from quadrants on the left to quadrants on the right is more emotional than technical. If people are not able to control their emotional thoughts, I would not recommend the journey.

The reason things look so risky on the right side of the *Quadrant* to people on the left side is because the emotion of fear is often affecting their thinking. People on the left side think "play it safe" is a logical thought. It isn't. It's an emotional thought. And it's the emotional thoughts that keep people stuck to one quadrant or the other.

What people "DO" on the right side of the equation is not that hard. I am sincere when I say that it is as easy as buying four green houses for low prices, waiting until the market improves, selling them and then buying a big red hotel.

Life really is a game of *Monopoly* for people on the right side of the quadrant. Sure, there is winning and losing, but that is part of the game. Winning and losing is a part of life. To be successful on the right side of the *Quadrant* is to "BE" a person who loves the game. Tiger Woods loses more than he wins, yet he still loves the game. Donald Trump went broke and battled back. He didn't quit because he lost. Losing only made him smarter and more determined. Many wealthy people went broke before they became rich. It's a part of the game.

If a person's emotions are thinking for them, those emotional thoughts often blind that person from seeing anything else. It is because of those knee-jerk emotional thoughts that people react, rather than think. It is those emotions that cause people from different quadrants to argue. The arguments are caused by people not having the same emotional points of view. It is that emotional reaction that blinds a person from seeing how easy, and often risk free, things are on the right side of the *Quadrant.* If a person cannot control their emotional thoughts, and many cannot, then they should not attempt to make the crossing.

I encourage all of you wanting to make the crossing to make sure you have a long-term positive support group with you and a mentor on the other side guiding you. To me, the struggle my wife and I went through was worth it. For us, the most important thing about crossing from the left side to the right side of the *Quadrant* is not what we had to "do," but who we became in the process. To me, that is priceless.

CHAPTER 9

Be The Bank...
Not The Banker

I have focused on the "BE" portion of the formula "BE-DO-HAVE" because without the proper mind-set and attitude, you cannot be prepared for the great economic changes that are facing us today. By "being" someone with the skills and mind-set of the right side of the *Quadrant,* you will be prepared to recognize opportunities that arise from these changes and be prepared to "DO" what will result in your "HAVING" financial success.

I remember a phone call I received from my rich dad in late 1986:

"Are you in the real estate market or the stock market?" he asked.

"Neither," I replied. "Everything I have is invested in building my business."

"Good," he said. "Stay out of all markets. Keep building your business. Something big is about to happen."

That year, the U.S. Congress passed the Tax Reform Act of 1986. In a swift 43 days, Congress took away many of the tax loopholes that people counted on to shelter their income. For people who were using those "passive losses" from their income property as tax deductions, they suddenly still had their losses, but the government had taken away the tax deduction. All across America, real estate prices began to plunge. Property prices began to slide, in some cases as much as a 70 percent. Suddenly, properties were worth far less than the amount of their mortgages. Panic swept the entire property market. Banks and savings and loans began to shake, many began to fail. People could not get their money out of the banks and then Wall Street crashed in October 1987. The world went into financial crisis.

Fundamentally, the Tax Reform Act of 1986 took away many of the tax loopholes that, on the left side of the *Quadrant*, high-income "E's" and "S's" depended on. Many of them had invested in real estate properties or limited partnerships in order to utilize these losses to offset their earnings from the "E" and/or "S" quadrants. And while the crash and recession did affect the people on the right side of the *Quadrant*, the "B" and "I" quadrants, many of their tax-avoidance mechanisms were left in tack.

During this period, "E's" learned a new word. That word was "downsizing." They soon realized that when a major layoff was announced, the share price of the stock of the company announcing the lay off went up. Sadly, most did not understand why. There were many "S's" who were also struggling to cope with the recession, due to a decrease in business, higher insurance rates, as well as losses from the real estate and share markets. As a result, I feel that individuals primarily focused in the left side of the *Quadrant* were hurt and suffered the most financially as a direct result of the Tax Reform Act of 1986.

TRANSFER OF WEALTH

While people on the left side were suffering, many people who operated on the "B" and "I" side of the *Quadrant* were getting rich, thanks to the government taking away from some people to give to others.

By changing the tax code, all the "tax trick" reasons for investing were taken away from people who were simply buying real estate to lose money. Many were high-income employees, or professional people such as doctors, attorneys, accountants and small-business owners. Prior to this period, they had so much taxable income that their advisers told them to buy real estate to lose money, and then with any extra money, invest in the stock market. When the government took that loophole away with the Tax Reform Act... one of the most massive transfers of wealth began. In my opinion, much of the wealth was taken away from the "E" and "S" side of the *Quadrant* and handed to the "B" and "I" side for pennies on the dollar.

When the savings and loans, the organizations that issued the bad loans, failed, billions of dollars in deposits were at risk. The money had to be paid back. So who was left to pay back the billions of dollars lost in savings and real estate foreclosures? Well, the taxpayers of course. The very people who were already hurting enough as it was. And the taxpayers were stuck with a multibillion dollar bill for this tax law change.

Some of you may also remember a governmental agency called the Resolution Trust Corporation, or the RTC as it was commonly known. The RTC was the agency responsible for taking the foreclosures from the real estate crash, and transferring them to people who knew how to handle them. For me and many of my friends, it was like a blessing from financial heaven.

Money, you'll recall, is seen with the mind... not the eyes. During this period of time, emotions ran high and visions were blurred. People saw what they were trained to see. Three things happened to the people on the left side of the *Quadrant.*

1. Panic was everywhere. When emotions are high, financial intelligence often disappears. Because people were so concerned about their jobs, the falling value of their property, the crash of the stock market, and the general slowdown of business, they failed to see the massive opportunities right in front of them. Their emotional thoughts had blinded them. Instead of moving forward and beating the bushes, most people went into their caves and hid.

2. They lacked the technical skills required on the right side of the *Quadrant.* Just as a doctor must have technical skills developed from years of schooling and then from on-the-job training, someone in the "B" quadrant and the "I" quadrant must also possess highly specialized technical skills. Technical skills that include financial literacy, which is knowing the vocabulary, how to restructure debt, how to structure an offering, who your market is, how to raise capital, and other learnable skills.

   When the RTC said, "We have a banker's box for sale, and in it is property that used to be worth $20 million... but you can have it today for $4 million," most people on the left side of the *Quadrant* did not have a clue how to raise the $4 million to buy the gift from financial heaven or know how to recognize the good deals from the bad deals.

3. They lacked a cash machine. Most people during this period had to work harder just to survive. By operating as a "B," my business could expand with little physical effort on my part. By 1990, my business was up and running and growing. During this period, the business grew from a start-up to 11

offices worldwide. The more it expanded, the less physical work I had to do, and the more money came in. The system and the people in the system were working hard. With the extra money and free time, my wife and I were able to spend a lot of time looking at "deals"... and there were many of them.

IT WAS THE BEST OF TIMES...
IT WAS THE WORST OF TIMES

There is a saying that goes: "It is not what happens in one's life that matters... but it is the meaning one puts on what happens that matters."

The period from 1986 to 1996 was, for some people, the worst time of their lives. For others, it was the best of times. When I received that phone call from my rich dad in 1986, I recognized the fantastic opportunity that this economic change presented me. Even though I did not have a lot of extra cash at the time, I was able to create assets by utilizing my skills as a "B" and an "I." Later in this chapter, I will describe in greater detail how I created assets that helped me become financially free.

One of the keys to a successful and happy life is to be flexible enough to respond appropriately to whatever change comes your way – to be able to respond and make a good thing out of anything. Unfortunately, most people have not been equipped to handle the fast-breaking economic changes that have happened and continue to happen. There is one thing that is a blessing with human beings: They are generally optimistic, and have the ability to forget. After about 10 to 12 years, they forget... and then things change again.

HISTORY REPEATS ITSELF

Today, people have more or less forgotten about the Tax Reform Act of 1986. The "E's" and "S's" are working harder than ever. Why? Because their tax loopholes were taken away. As they have worked harder to get back what they lost, the economy has improved, their incomes have gone up, and their tax accountant has again started whispering the same old words of wisdom:

"Go buy a bigger house. Interest on your debt is your best tax deduction. And besides, your home is an asset, and it should be your largest investment."

So they look at "the easy monthly payments," and they get sucked into a higher debt position.

The housing market is booming, people have more disposable income, and interest rates are low. People are buying bigger houses, their mood is euphoric, and they are pouring money into the stock market because they want to get rich quickly and they have realized they need to invest for retirement.

Again, in my opinion, a great transfer of wealth is about to happen. It may not happen this year, but it will happen. It will just not happen in exactly the same way. Something different will happen. This is why my rich dad had me read books on economic history. Economics change, but history repeats. It just does not read on the same set of circumstances.

Money continues to flow from the left side to the right side of the *Quadrant*. It always has. Many people are deeply in debt, yet they pour money into the biggest stock market boom in the history of the world. The people on the right side of the *Quadrant* will sell at the top of the market, just when the last cautious people on the left side overcome their fear and enter the market. Something newsworthy will happen, the market will crash, and when the dust settles, the investors will move back in. They will buy back what they just sold. Again, we will have another great transfer of wealth from the left side to the right side of the *Quadrant*.

It will take at least another 12 years for the emotional scars to heal of those who lose money… but the wounds will heal, just as another market is nearing its peak.

At about that time, people will begin quoting Yogi Berra, the great New York Yankees baseball player: "It's deja vu all over again."

IS IT A CONSPIRACY?

Often I hear people, especially people on the left side of the *Quadrant*, say that there is some kind of global conspiracy, held together by a few ultra-rich families that control the banks. These banking conspiracy theories have been around for years.

Is there a conspiracy? I do not know. Could there be a conspiracy? Anything is possible. I know there are powerful families who control massive sums of money. But does one group control the world? I don't think so.

I see it differently. I see it more or less as one group of people on one side of the *Quadrant* with one mind-set and another group of people on the other side of the *Quadrant* with a different mind-set. They're all playing this one big game of money, but each quadrant is playing from a different point of view and with a different set of rules.

The big problem is, the people on the left side are unable to see what the people on the right side are doing, but the people on the right side know what the people on the left are doing.

WITCH HUNTS

Many people on the left side of the *Quadrant*, instead of finding out what the people on the right side know that they do not, go on witch hunts. Only a few centuries ago, when there was a plague, or something bad happened to a community, townspeople would go on a "witch hunt." They needed someone to blame for their plight. Until science invented the microscope and people could see what their naked eyes could not, which were germs, people blamed other people for their diseases. They burned witches at the stake to solve their problems. Little did they know that most of the disease was caused by people living in cities with poor garbage and sewage disposal. People had caused their own problems by using unsanitary conditions... not the "witches".

Well, witch hunts still go on today. Many people look for someone to blame for their financial plight. These people often want to blame the rich for their personal financial problems, rather than realize it is often their own lack of information about money that is a fundamental reason for their plight.

HEROES BECOME VILLAINS

Every few years a new financial guru appears and seems to have the new magic formula for wealth. In the late 1970s, it was the Hunt brothers who tried to corner the silver market. The world applauded their genius. Almost overnight, they were hunted down as criminals because so many people lost money after they followed the brothers' advice. In the late 1980s, it was Michael Milken, the junk-bond king. One day he was a financial genius, and right after the crash he was tracked down and sent to jail. The individuals change, but history repeats.

Today, we have new investment geniuses. They come across on television, their names are in the paper, they are the new celebrities. One of them is Alan Greenspan, the chairman of the Federal Reserve Board. Today, he is nearly a god. People think he is responsible for our wonderful economy. Warren Buffet is also touted as a near god. When he buys something, everybody rushes in and buys what he buys. And when Warren Buffet sells, prices crash. Bill Gates is also watched carefully. Money will follow him freely. If there is a major market correction in the near future, will today's financial heroes be tomorrow's hated? Only time will tell.

In every "up" cycle of the economy, there are heroes, and in every "down" cycle, there are villains. In reviewing history, they have often been the same people. People will always need witches to burn or conspiracies to blame for their own financial blindness. History will repeat itself... and again a great transfer of wealth will take place. And when it does, which side of the transfer will you be on? The left side or the right side?

In my opinion, people simply fail to realize that they are in this large global game… a virtual casino in the sky, but no one told them that they were an important player in the game. The game is "Who Is Indebted To Whom?"

BEING THE BANK… NOT THE BANKER

In my mid-20s, it dawned on me that the name of the game was to be the bank, but that didn't mean to get a job as a banker. My advanced education was about to begin. It was during this period that my rich dad had me look up words like "mortgage," "real estate" and "finance." I was beginning to train my mind to see what my eyes could not.

He encouraged me to learn and understand the game, and then after I learned the game, I could do what I wanted with what I found. I decided to share my knowledge with anyone who was interested.

He also had me read books on the great leaders of capitalism. People such as John D. Rockefeller, J.P. Morgan, Henry Ford. One of the most important books I read was *The Worldly Philosophers*, by Robert Heilbroner. For people who want to operate on the "B" and "I" side, his book is a must read, for it traces the greatest economists of all time, starting with Adam Smith, who wrote *The Wealth of Nations*. It is fascinating to look into the minds of some of our most important philosophers, the economists. These people interpreted the evolution of modern capitalism over its brief history. In my opinion, if you want to be a leader on the right side of the *Quadrant*, a historical view of economic history is important to understanding both our history and future.

After *The Worldly Philosophers*, I recommend reading Paul Zane Pilzer's *Unlimited Wealth*, James Dale Davidson's *The Sovereign Individual*, Robert Prechter's *The Crest of the Wave*, and Harry Dent's *The Great Boom Ahead*. Heilbroner's book gives you insight into where we have come from economically, and the other authors give their views on where we are headed. Their contrasting viewpoints are important in allowing me to see what my eyes cannot… something called the future. By reading books like these, I have been able to gain insights into the ups and downs of cycles and trends of the economy. A common theme in all of these books is that one of the biggest changes of all is right around the corner.

HOW TO PLAY THE BANK

After the 1986 Tax Reform Act, there were opportunities everywhere. Real estate, stocks and businesses were available for low prices. While it was devastating for many people on the left side of the *Quadrant*, it was wonderful for me because I could utilize my skills as a "B" and "I" to take advantage of the opportunities around me. Instead of being greedy and chasing everything that looked like a good deal, I decided to focus on real estate.

Why real estate? For these five simple reasons:

1. **Pricing.** The prices of real estate were so low that mortgage payments were far lower than the fair market rent for most properties. These properties made great economic sense... which meant there was little risk. It was like going to a sale at a department store when everything was priced 50 percent off.

2. **Financing.** The banks would give me a loan on real estate, but not on stocks. Since I wanted to buy as much as I could while the market was depressed, I bought real estate so that what cash I had could be combined with financing through banks.

   For example: Let's say I had $10,000 in savings to invest. If I bought stocks, I could buy $10,000 worth of stocks. I could have gone on margin (when you buy on margin you put up only part of the total cost and the broker company lends you the remainder), but I was not financially strong enough to risk a downturn in the market.

   With $10,000 in real estate, and a 90 percent loan, I could buy a $100,000 property.

   If both markets went up 10 percent, I would make $1,000 in stocks, but $10,000 in real estate.

3. **Taxes.** If I made $1 million in profit from stocks, I would have to pay nearly 30 percent in capital gains tax on my profit. In real estate, however, the $1 million could be rolled tax free into the next real estate transaction. On top of that, I could depreciate the property for even greater tax advantages.

   Important note: An investment must make economic sense before the tax benefit for me to invest in it. Any tax benefit only makes the investment more attractive.

4. Cash flow. Rents had not declined even though the real estate prices had declined. This put a lot of money into my pocket, paid for the mortgages, and most importantly allowed me to "time" the market. Rents bought me time to wait until real estate prices went up again. When they did, I was able to sell. Although I carried large debt, it never hurt me because the rents were far greater than the cost of carrying the loan.

5. An opportunity to become a bank. Real estate allowed me to become a bank, something I had always wanted to do since 1974.

BE THE BANK, NOT A BANKER

In *Rich Dad Poor Dad*, I wrote about how the rich create money and often play the role of banker. The following is a simple example that almost anyone can follow.

Let's say I find a house that is worth $100,000 and I get a heck of a deal and only pay $80,000 for it (a $10,000 down payment plus a $70,000 mortgage I am responsible for.)

I then advertise that the house is available for sale for $100,000, which is its appraised price, and use these magic words in the ad: "House for sale. Owner desperate. No bank qualifying. Low down payment, easy monthly payments."

The phone rings like crazy. The house is sold on what is called a "wrap" or a "lease purchase contract," depending on which country you're in. In simple terms, I sell the house for a $100,000 IOU. This is what the transaction looks like:

My Balance Sheet

on my
balance sheet:

Assets	Liabilities
$100,000 IOU	$70,000 Mortgage

Buyer's Balance Sheet

on the buyers
balance sheet:

Assets	Liabilities
	$100,000 IOU

This transaction is then registered with a title and escrow office, which often handles the payments. If the person defaults on the $100,000, I simply foreclose and sell the property to the next person who wants a "low down, easy monthly payment" home to live in. People line up for the opportunity to buy a home on these terms.

The net effect is that I have created $30,000 in my asset column for which I am paid interest, just like a bank gets paid interest for loans it makes.

I was beginning to be a bank, and I loved it. If you recall from the last chapter, rich dad said: "Be careful when you take on debt. If you take on debt personally, make sure it's small. If you take on large debt, make sure someone else is paying for it."

In the language of the right side of the *Quadrant*, I "laid off" my risk, or "hedged" my risk on to another buyer. That is the game in the world of finance.

This type of transaction is done all over the world. Yet, wherever I go, people come up to me and say those magic words, "You can't do that here."

What most small investors fail to realize is that many large commercial buildings are bought and sold exactly in the manner described above. Sometimes they go through a bank, but many times they do not.

IT'S LIKE SAVING $30,000 WITHOUT SAVING

If you remember from a previous chapter, I wrote about why the government did not give people a tax advantage for saving money. Well, I doubt if the banks ever will ask the government to do so because your savings are their liability. The U.S. has a low savings rate simply because banks do not want your money or need your savings to do well. So this example is a way of playing bank and increasing your savings without a great deal of effort. The cash flow from this $30,000 is reflected as follows:

Income Statement

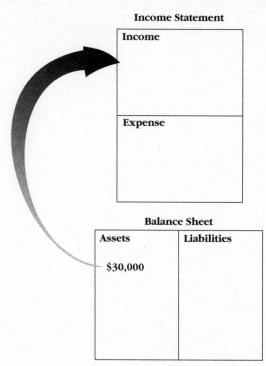

Income

Expense

Balance Sheet

Assets	Liabilities
$30,000	

There are several interesting things about this diagram:

1. I determine the interest rate from my $30,000. Often it's 10 percent interest. Most banks don't pay you more than 5 percent on your savings today. So even if I did use my own $10,000 as a down payment, which I try not to do, the interest on it is often better than the bank would pay me.

2. It's like creating $20,000 ($30,000-$10,000 down payment) that did not exist before. Just like the bank does... it creates, an asset and then charges interest on it.

3. This $20,000 was created tax free. For the average person in the "E" quadrant, it would have taken nearly $40,000 of wages to be able to set aside $20,000. Income earned as an employee is a 50-50 proposition, with the government taking its 50 percent before you ever see it through withholding.

4. All property taxes, maintenance and management fees are now the responsibility of the buyer, because I sold the property to the buyer.

5. And there is more. Many creative things can be done on the right side of the

Quadrant to create money from nothing, just by playing the role of the bank.

A transaction like this may take a week to a month to put together. The question is how long would it take for most people to earn an additional $40,000 so they can save $20,000 after running the gauntlet of taxes and other expenses incurred to earn that money.

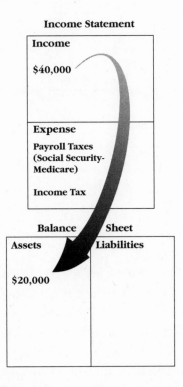

Income Statement

Income
$40,000

Expense
Payroll Taxes (Social Security-Medicare)
Income Tax

Balance Sheet

Assets	Liabilities
$20,000	

THE INCOME STREAM IS THEN SHELTERED

In *Rich Dad Poor Dad*, I briefly covered why the rich use corporations:

1. Asset protection. If you're rich, people tend to want to take what you have through litigation. It is called, "Look for someone with deep pockets." The rich often don't own anything in their own names. Their assets are held in trusts and corporations to protect them.

2. Income protection. By passing the income stream from assets through your own corporation, much of what is normally taken from you by the government can be sheltered.

The harsh reality: If you are an employee, the sequence goes like this.

EARN — TAXED — SPEND

As an employee, your earnings are taxed and taken through withholding even before you get your paycheck. So if an employee is paid $30,000 per year, by the time the government gets through with it, it's down to $15,000. With this $15,000 you must then pay your mortgage. (But at least you get a tax deduction for the interest paid on your mortgage... which is how the bank convinces you to buy a bigger house.)

If you pass your income stream through a corporate entity first, this is what the pattern would look like.

EARN — SPEND — TAXED

By passing the income stream from the $30,000 you invented first through a corporation, you can "expense" much of the earnings before the government gets it. If you own the corporation, you make the rules... as long as it conforms with the tax code.

For example, if you make the rules, you can write into the bylaws of your company that child care is part of your employment package. The company may pay $400 per month for child care out of pre-tax dollars. If you pay for it with after-tax dollars, you have to effectively earn close to $800 to pay for that same child care with after-tax dollars. The list is long and the requirements are specific as to what an owner of a corporation can write off that an employee cannot. Even certain travel expenses can be written off with pre-tax dollars as long as you can document that you conducted business on the trip (eg. You hold a board meeting). Just make sure you follow the rules. Even retirement plans are different for owners and employees in many instances. Having said all of this, I want to stress that you must follow the regulations required to make these expenses deductible. I believe in taking advantage of the legal deductions allowed by the tax code but I do not recommend breaking the law.

Again, the key to being able to take advantage of some of these provisions is which quadrant you earn your income from. If all of your income is generated as an employee from a company that you do not own or control, there is little income or asset protection available to you.

That's why I recommend that if you are an employee, keep your job, but begin to spend time in the "B" or "I" quadrants. Your road to faster freedom is through those two quadrants. To feel more financially secure, the secret is to operate in more than one quadrant.

FREE LAND

A few years ago, my wife and I wanted some property away from the maddening crowds. We got the urge to own some acreage with tall oak trees with a stream running through it. We also wanted privacy.

We found a parcel with a price of $75,000 for 20 acres. The seller was willing to take 10 percent down and carry the balance at 10 percent interest. It was a fair transaction. The problem was it violated the rule on debt that my rich dad had taught me, which was: "Be careful when you take on debt. If you take on debt personally, make sure it's small. If you take on large debt, make sure someone else pays for it."

My wife and I passed on the $75,000 piece of land and went looking for a piece of land that made more sense. To me, $75,000 is a lot of debt because our cash flow would have looked like this:

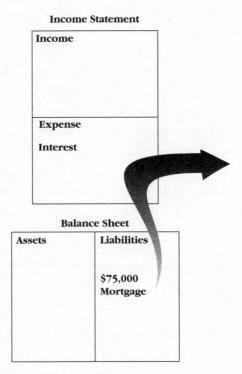

Income Statement

Income

| Expense |
| Interest |

Balance Sheet

Assets	Liabilities
	$75,000 Mortgage

And remember my rich dad's rule:

"If you take on debt and risk, then you should be paid."

Well, in this transaction, I would have taken on both the debt and the risk, and I was paying for it.

About a month later, we found a piece of land that was even more beautiful. It was 87 acres of tall oak trees with a stream, and it had a house on it, for $115,000. I offered the seller full price, if he would give me my terms... and he did. To make a long story short, we spent a few dollars fixing the house and sold the house and 30 acres for $215,000, using the same idea of "low down, easy monthly payments," all while keeping 57 acres for ourselves.

This is what the transaction looks like on my balance sheet.

Balance Sheet

Assets	Liabilities
$215,000	$115,000

The new owner was thrilled because it was a beautiful home and he was able to buy it for almost nothing down. As an aside, he also bought it through his company for use as a corporate retreat for his employees, which allowed him to depreciate the purchase price as a company asset as well as deduct the maintenance costs. This, all in addition to being able to deduct the interest payments. His interest payments more than paid for my interest payments. A few years later, he sold some of his company stock and paid off the loan to me, and I, in turn, paid off my loan. The debt was gone.

With the extra $100,000 profit I made, I was able to pay the taxes from the gain of the land and the house.

The net result was zero debt, a few dollars profit ($15,000 after taxes), and the 57 acres of gorgeous land. It was like getting paid for getting what you want.

Today, my balance sheet from that one transaction looks like this:

Balance Sheet

Assets	Liabilities
57 Acres Land **$15,000 Cash**	

THE IPO

An initial public offering (IPO), or taking a private company public through a stock offering, is based on the same principles. While the words, the market and the players are different, there are basic underlying principles that remain the same. When my organization forms a company to take public, we often create a value out of thin air, even though we try to base it on an accurate opinion of the fair market value. We take the offering to the public market, and instead of this equity being sold to one person, it is sold to thousands of people as shares of a company.

THE VALUE OF EXPERIENCE

This is another reason I recommend people start in the "B" quadrant before proceeding to the "I" quadrant. Regardless of whether the investment is in real estate, a business, stocks or bonds, there is an underlying "comprehensive business sense" that is essential to being a sound investor. Some people have this comprehensive sense, but many do not. Primarily because school trains us to be highly specialized... not comprehensively trained.

One more point, for those thinking about starting to move over to the "B" or "I" quadrants, I recommend starting small... and taking your time. Do bigger deals as your confidence grows and experience grows. Remember, the only difference between an $80,000 deal and an $800,000 deal is a zero. The process of going through a small deal is much the same as going through a much larger multimil-lion-dollar public offering. It's only a matter of more people, more zeros and more fun.

Once a person gains experience and a good reputation, it takes less and less money to create bigger and bigger investments. Many times it takes no money to make a lot of money. Why? Experience is valuable. As stated earlier, if you know how to make money with money, people and money will flock to you. Start small and take your time. Experience is more important than money.

IT IS SIMPLE AND EASY

In theory, the numbers and transactions on the right side of the *Quadrant* are that simple, regardless of whether we're talking about stocks, bonds, real estate or businesses. To be financially well off simply means being able to think differently... to think from different quadrants and to have the courage to do things differently. To me, one of the hardest things a person who is new to this way of thinking has to go through is the countless number of people who will say to you: "You can't do that."

If you can overcome that kind of limited thinking, and seek out people who say to you, "Yes, I know how to do that. I'd be happy to teach you," your life will be easy.

THE LAWS

I started this chapter with the Tax Reform Act of 1986. While that was a significant rule change, it is not and will not be the last rule change. I only use the '86 Act as an example of how powerful some rules and laws can be. If a person is to be successful on the "B" or "I" side of the *Quadrant*, he or she needs to be aware of market forces and any changes in the law that affect those market forces.

Today in America, there are more than 100,000 pages of tax code. That's for the IRS alone. The federal laws come to more than 1.2 million pages of laws. It would take the average reader 23,000 years to read the entire U.S. Code. Every year more laws are created, deleted and changed. It would be more than a full-time job just to keep up with those changes.

Every time someone tells me, "That's against the law," I reply by asking them if they've read every line of code in America. If they say "yes," I leave slowly, backing up toward the door. Never turn your back on someone who thinks they know every law.

To be successful on the right side of the *Quadrant* requires seeing 5 percent with your eyes and 95 percent with your mind. Understanding the laws and market forces is vital for financial success. Great transfers of wealth often occur when laws and markets change. So it is important to pay attention if you want to have those changes work in your favor and not against you.

THE GOVERNMENT NEEDS YOUR MONEY

I believe in paying taxes. I know the government provides many important and vital services essential for a well run civilization. Unfortunately, in my opinion, government is mismanaged, is too big, and has made too many promises it cannot keep. But it is not the fault of the politicians and lawmakers in office today, because most of the financial problems we face today were created more than 60 years ago by their predecessors. Today's lawmakers are trying to handle the problem and to find solutions. Unfortunately, if lawmakers want to stay in office, they cannot tell the masses the truth. If they did, they would be thrown out of office... because the masses still rely on the government to solve their financial and medical problems for them. Government cannot. Government is getting smaller, and the problems are getting bigger.

In the meantime, government will have to continue to come after more taxes... even if the politicians promise not to. That is why Congress passed the Tax Reform Act of 1986. It needed to plug a tax loophole in order to collect more in taxes. In the next few years, many of our Western governments must begin to collect even more in taxes to prevent a default on some of those promises made long ago. Promises made such as Medicare and Social Security, as well as federal pensions due to millions of federal workers. A mass public realization will probably not occur now, but the magnitude of the problem will be apparent by 2010. The world will realize that the U.S. will not be able to borrow its way out of these problems.

Forbes magazine ran this projection about the escalating U.S. debt:

"If you notice, it goes down until 2010, and then it zooms up. It zooms up just as the biggest group of people in the history of America begins to retire. In the year 2010, the first baby boomers turn 65. In the year 2010, instead of adding money to the stock market, baby boomers will begin withdrawing money from the stock market... if not earlier. By the year 2010, 75 million baby boomers will decide that their biggest "asset," their home, is too big since the kids are gone, and will begin selling their big houses so they can move to a more crime-free part of the country, small-town America."

Suddenly, the current retirement vehicles, called the 401(k)s in America, or The Superannuation Funds in many Commonwealth countries, will begin to shrink. They will shrink because they are subject to market fluctuations... which means they go up with the market and they come down with the market. Mutual funds will begin to liquidate their stocks in order to pay for the sell orders from baby boomers needing to use the money for retirement. Baby boomers will suddenly be stuck with huge capital-gains taxes from the gains accrued by these mutual funds and taxable to them on withdrawal. The capital gains will come from selling these overvalued stocks at higher prices, which the funds pass on to its members. Instead of cash, many baby boomers will be stuck with a tax bill for capital gains they never received. Remember, the tax man always gets the money first.

Simultaneously, the health of millions of poorer baby boomers will begin to fail because poor people historically have worse health than affluent people. Medicare will be bankrupt and the cry for more government support will go up in cities all across America.

Add to this the eclipsing of America by China as the nation with the largest GNP and the advent of the European Monetary Union. I suspect that both wages and the prices of goods will have to come down... and/or productivity must skyrocket in order to meet the challenges of these two large economic blocks.

All this will happen by 2010, which is not too far away. The next great transfer of wealth will take place, not by conspiracy but by ignorance. We are in the final gasp of the entitlement mentality of big government and big business of the Industrial Age, and we are officially entering the Information Age. In 1989, the Berlin Wall came down. In my opinion, that event was as significant as the year 1492, when Columbus bumped into the Americas in his search for Asia. In some circles, 1492 was the official beginning of the Industrial Age. The end was marked in 1989. The rules have changed.

HISTORY IS A GUIDE

My rich dad encouraged me to learn the game well. After I learned it well, then I could do what I wanted with what I knew. I write and teach out of concern and a sense that more people need to know how to take care of themselves financially... and not become dependent upon the government or a company for life support.

I hope I am wrong about what I see coming down the road economically. Maybe governments can keep making promises to take care of people: keep on raising taxes, and keep on going into greater debt. Maybe the stock market will always go up and never come down again... and maybe real estate prices will always go up and your home will become your best investment. And maybe millions of people will find happiness earning a minimum wage and be able to provide a good life for their family. Maybe this can all happen. But I don't think so. Not if history is any guide.

Historically, if people lived to be 75 years of age, they lived through two recessions and one depression. As baby boomers we have gone through two recessions, but we have not yet seen that depression. Maybe there will never be a depression again. But history does not say that. The reason my rich dad had me read books on the great capitalists and the economists was so that I could gain a longer view and a better perspective on where we have come from and where we are going.

Just as there are waves on the ocean, there are great waves in markets. Instead of the wind and sun driving the waves of the ocean, the waves of the financial markets are driven by two human emotions: greed and fear. I do not think that depressions are things of the past because we are all human beings and we will always have those emotions of greed and fear. And when greed and fear collide, and a person loses badly, the next human emotion is depression. Depression is made up of the two human emotions, anger and sadness. Anger with one's self and sadness over the loss. Economic depressions are emotional depressions. People lose and they get depressed.

Even though the economy overall may appear to be in great shape, there are millions of people who are in various stages of depression. They may have a job, but deep down they know they aren't getting ahead financially. They are angry at themselves and sad over their loss of time. Little do most know that they have been trapped by the Industrial Age idea of "find a safe, secure job, and don't worry about the future."

A GREAT CHANGE... AND OPPORTUNITY

We are entering into the era of tremendous change and opportunity. For some people, it will be the best of times and for others it will be the worst of times.

President John Kennedy said: "A great change is at hand."

Kennedy was a man who came from the "B-I" side of the *Quadrant*, and he tried desperately to elevate the lives of those stuck in time warps. Unfortunately, millions of people are still in those time warps, following ideas in their heads that were handed down from ages past. Ideas such as "go to school so you can find a secure job." Education is more important than ever before, but we need to teach people to think a little further than just looking for a secure job and expecting the company or the government to look after them once their working days are through. That is an Industrial Age idea... and we aren't there anymore.

Nobody said it was fair... for this is not a fair country. We are a free country. There are people who work harder, are smarter, are more driven for success, are more talented, or are more desirous of the good life than others. We are free to pursue those ambitions if we have the determination. Yet every time somebody does better, some people say it is unfair. The same people think that it would be fair if the rich shared with the poor. Well, nobody said it was fair. And the more we try to make things fair, the less free we become.

When someone says to me that there is racial discrimination or a "glass ceiling," I agree with them. I know such things exist. I personally detest any kind of discrimination and, being of Japanese ancestry, I have experienced discrimination firsthand. On the left side of the *Quadrant*, discrimination does exist, especially in companies. Your looks, your school, whether you're white or black or brown or yellow, or are male or female... all of those things count on the left side of the *Quadrant*. But they do not count on the right side of the *Quadrant*. The right side is concerned not with fairness or security, but with freedom and the love of the game. If you want to play the game on the right side, the players will welcome you. If you play and win, fine. They will welcome you even more and ask you for your secrets. If you play and lose, they will gladly take all your money, but don't complain or blame someone else for your failures. That is not the way the game is played on the right side of the *Quadrant*. It is not meant to be fair. Being fair is not the name of the game.

SO WHY DOES GOVERNMENT LEAVE THE "B-I" SIDE ALONE?

In reality, governments do not leave the "B-I" side alone. It is more that the "B-I" side has more ways of escaping and hiding wealth. In *Rich Dad Poor Dad*, I talked about the power of corporations. One big reason the rich keep more of their wealth is simply because they operate as corporate bodies and not human bodies. A human body needs a passport to go from country to country. A corporate body does not. A corporate body travels the world freely and can often work freely. A human body needs to register with the government, and in America they need a "green card" to work. A corporate body does not.

While governments would like to take more money from corporate bodies they realize that if they pass abusive tax laws, the corporate bodies will take both their money and their jobs to some other country. In the Industrial Age, people talked about "off-shore" as a country. The rich have always sought tax havens where their money would be treated kindly. Today, "off-shore" is not a country; it is cyberspace. Money, being an idea and invisible, can now hide in the invisible, or at least out of sight from the human eye. Soon, if it is not already being done, people will do their banking on a geo-synchronous satellite orbiting in space... free from any laws, or they may choose to operate in a country whose laws are more favorable to rich people.

In *Rich Dad Poor Dad*, I wrote that corporations became popular at the start of the Industrial Age... just after Columbus discovered a new world filled with riches. Each time the rich sent a vessel out to sea they were at risk because if the ship did not come back the rich did not want to be indebted to the families of the sailors who died. So corporations were formed for legal protection and to limit the risk of loss to the amount of money ventured, and not beyond that. So the rich risked only their money, and the crews risked their lives. Not much has changed since then.

Wherever I travel in the world, the people I deal with primarily deal in this manner... as employees of their own corporations. In theory, they own nothing and really do not exist as private citizens. They exist as officers of their rich corporations, but as private citizens they own nothing. And wherever I go in the world, I meet people who tell me, "You can't do that in this country. That is against the law."

Little do most people realize that most countries' laws in the Western world are similar. They may use different words to describe the same things, but in principle, their laws are pretty much the same.

I recommend that, if possible, you at least consider being an employee of your own corporation. It is especially advisable for high income "S's" and for "B's," even if they own franchises or earn their income from network marketing. Seek advice from competent financial advisers. They can help you choose and implement the best structure for your particular situation.

THERE ARE TWO KINDS OF LAWS

On the surface, it seems as if there are laws for the rich and there are laws for everyone else. But in reality, the laws are the same. The only difference is the rich use the laws to their advantage while the poor and middle class do not. That is the fundamental difference. The laws are the same... they are written for everyone... and I strongly suggest you hire smart advisers and obey the laws. It's too easy to make money legally rather than break the laws and wind up in jail. Besides, your legal advisers will serve as your early warning system for upcoming law changes... and when laws change, wealth changes hands.

TWO CHOICES

One advantage of living in a free society is the freedom to make choices. In my opinion, there are two big choices... the choice of security and the choice of freedom. If you choose security, there is a huge price to pay for that security in the form of excessive taxes and punishing interest payments. If you choose freedom, then you need to learn the whole game and then play the game. It is your choice which quadrant you want to play the game from.

Part I of this book defined the specifics of the *CASHFLOW Quadrant*, while Part II has focused on developing the mind-set and attitude of someone who chooses the right side of the *Quadrant*. So now you should understand where you are currently in the *Quadrant*, as well as have an idea of where you want to be. You also should have a better understanding of the mental process and mind-set of operating from the right side of the *Quadrant*.

While I have shown you ways to cross from the left side to the right side of the *Quadrant*, I now would like to provide you with more specifics. In the final section of the book, Part III, I will identify 7 steps to finding your financial fast track that I consider to be essential in moving to the right side of the *Quadrant*.

AUTHOR'S NOTE

In 1943, the U.S. began taxing all working American's via pay roll deduction. In other words, the government got paid before people in the "E" quadrant got paid. Anyone who was purely an "E" had little escape from the government. It also meant that instead of only the rich being taxed, which was the hope of the 16th Amendment, it now meant everyone on the left side of the *Quadrant* got taxed, rich or poor. As stated earlier, the lowest paid in America today pay more in taxes as a percentage of total income than the rich and the middle class.

In 1986, the Tax Reform Act went after the highly paid professionals in the "S" quadrant. The act specifically listed doctors, lawyers, architects, dentists, engineers, and other such professions, and made it difficult, if not impossible, for them to shelter their income the way that the rich can do in the "B" and "I" quadrants.

These professionals were forced to operate their businesses through S corporations instead of through C corporations, or pay a tax penalty. The rich do not pay this penalty. Income for these highly compensated professionals is then passed through the S corporation and taxed at the highest individual tax rate possible. They don't have the opportunity to shelter their income through deductions allowed to a C corporation. And, at the same time, the law was changed to force all S corporations to have a calendar year end. This again forced all income to be taxed at the highest rate.

When I was discussing these changes recently with my personal CPA, she reminded me that the biggest shock to newly self-employed people generally comes at the end of their first business year when they realize that the biggest tax they are paying is a "self-employment" tax. This tax is double for "S's", or self-employed, over what they paid as "E's", or employees. And it is calculated based on income before the individual can deduct any itemized deductions or personal exemptions. It is possible for a self-employed person to have no taxable income, yet still owe self-employment tax. Corporations, on the other hand, do not pay self-employment tax.

The 1986 Tax Reform Act also effectively pushed the "E's" and "S's" of America out of real estate as an investment and into paper assets such as stocks and mutual funds. Once the downsizing began, millions not only felt less secure about their jobs, they also felt less secure about their retirement, simply because they were basing their future financial well-being upon paper assets subject to the ups and downs of the market.

The 1986 Tax Reform Act also appears to have had the intention of shutting down the smaller community banks in America and shifting all banking to large national banks. I suspect that the reason this was done was so that America could compete with the large banks of Germany and Japan. If that was the intent, it was successful. Today in America, banking is less personal and purely by the numbers, the net result being that it is harder for certain classes of people to qualify for home loans. Instead of a small town banker knowing you by your character, today a central computer spits your name out if you don't meet it's impersonal qualification requirements.

After the 1986 Tax Reform Act, the rich continue to earn more, work less, pay less in taxes, and enjoy greater asset protection by using the formula my rich dad gave me 40 years ago, which was, "Build a business and buy real estate." Make a lot of money via C corporations, and shelter your income through real estate. While millions upon millions of Americans work; pay more and more in taxes; and then pour billions each month into mutual funds, the rich are quietly selling the shares of their C corporations, making them even richer, and then buying billions in investment real estate. A share of a C corporation allows the buyer to share in the risk of owning the company. A share of stock does not allow the shareholder the advantages that owning a C corporation and investing in real estate offers.

Why did my rich dad recommend building businesses in C corporations and then buying real estate? Because the tax laws reward people who operate that way... but this is a subject that is beyond the scope of this book. Just remember the words of such immensely wealthy people such as Ray Kroc, founder of McDonald's.

"My business is not hamburgers. My business is real estate."

My rich dad, who drummed into my head,

"Build businesses and buy real estate."

In other words, seek my fortune on the right side of the *CASHFLOW Quadrant* to take full advantage of the tax laws.

In 1990, President George Bush raised taxes after promising, "Watch my lips. No new taxes." In 1992, President Clinton signed into law the largest tax increase in recent history. Again, those increases affected the "E's" and "S's" but the "B's" and "I's" were for the most part, not affected.

As we progress further and further away from the Industrial Age and into the

Information Age, we all need to continue to gather information from different quadrants. In the Information Age, quality information is our most important asset. As Erik Hoffer once said,

"In times of change…
　　Learners inherit the earth,
While the learned
　　Find themselves beautifully equipped
to deal with a world
　　that no longer exists."

REMEMBER

Everyone's financial situation is different. That is why I always recommend:

1. Seek out the best professional and financial advice you can find. For example while a C corporation may work well in some instances, it does not work well in all instances. Even on the right side of the *Quadrant*, occasionally an S corporation is appropriate.

2. Remember that there are different advisors for the rich, the poor, and the middle class, just as there are different advisors for people who earn their money on the right side and on the left. Also consider seeking advice from people who are already where you want to go.

3. Never do business or investing for tax reasons. A tax break is an extra bonus for doing things the way the government wants. It should be a bonus, not the reason.

4. If you are a reader who is not a U.S. citizen, this advice remains the same. Our laws may be different, yet the principles of seeking competent advice remain the same. People on the right side operate very similarly throughout the world.

PART III

How To Become A Successful "B" and "I"

CHAPTER 10

Take Baby Steps

Most of us have heard the saying, "A journey of a thousand miles begins with a single step." I would like to modify that statement a little. Instead I would say, "A journey of a thousand miles begins with a baby step."

I emphasize this because I have seen too many people attempt to take the "Great Leap Forward" instead of taking baby steps. We have all seen people, who are completely out of shape, suddenly decide to lose 20 pounds and get into shape. They begin a crash diet, go to the gym for two hours, and then jog 10 miles. This lasts maybe a week. They lose a few pounds, and then the pain, boredom, and hunger begin to wear away at their will power and determination. By the third week, their old habits of overeating, lack of exercise, and television are back in control.

Instead of taking a "Great Leap Forward." I would strongly recommend taking a baby step forward. Long term financial success is not measured in how big your stride is. Long term financial success is measured in the number of steps, in which direction you're moving and in numbers of years. In reality, that is the formula for success or failure in any endeavor. When it comes to money, I have seen too many people, myself included, attempt to do too much with too little... and then crash and burn. It's hard to take a baby step forward when you first need a ladder to get yourself out of the financial hole you have dug for yourself.

HOW DO YOU EAT AN ELEPHANT?

This section of the book describes 7 steps to guide you on your path to the right side of the *Quadrant*. With the guidance of my rich dad, I began working and acting on these 7 steps from the age of 9. I will continue to follow them for as long as I live. I warn you before you read the 7 steps because, for some people, the task may seem overwhelming and it will be if you try to do it all in one week. So please begin with baby steps.

We have all heard the saying, "Rome was not built in a day." The saying I use whenever I find myself feeling overwhelmed by how much I have to learn is "How do you eat an elephant?" The answer is "One bite at a time." And that is how I would recommend you proceed if you find yourself feeling even a little bit overwhelmed by how much you may have to learn, in order to make the journey from the "E" and "S" side to the "B" and "I" side. Please be kind to yourself and realize that the transition is more than just mental learning, the process also involves emotional learning. After you can take baby steps for six months to a year, you are ready for the next saying which is, "You've got to walk before you can run." In other words you go from baby steps, to walking, and then to running. This is the path I recommend. If you don't like this path, then you can do what millions of people do who want to get rich quickly the fast and easy way, which is to buy a lottery ticket. Who knows? It might be your lucky day.

ACTION BEATS INACTION

To me, one of the primary reasons "E's" and "S's" have difficulty moving to the "B" and "I" side is because they are too afraid of making mistakes. They often say, "I have a fear of failing." Or they say, " I need more information, or can you recommend another book?" Their fear or self doubt is primarily what keeps them trapped in their quadrant. Please take the time to read the 7 steps and complete the action steps at the end of each step. That for most people is enough of a baby step to get you moving in the direction towards the "B" and "I" side. Just doing those 7 action steps will open whole new worlds of possibility and change. Then just keep taking small baby steps.

Nike's slogan "Just do it" says it best. Unfortunately our schools also say, "Don't make mistakes." Millions of highly educated people who want to take action are paralyzed by the emotional fear of making mistakes. One of the most important lessons I have learned as a teacher is that true learning requires mental, emotional, and physical learning. That is why action always beats inaction. If you take action and make a mistake, at least you've learned something be it mentally, emotionally, and/or physically. A person who continually searches for the "right" answer is often afflicted with the disease known as "analysis paralysis" which seems to affect many well-educated people. Ultimately, the way we learn is by making mistakes. We learned to walk and ride a bicycle by making mistakes. People who are afraid of taking action, out of fear of making mistakes, may be mentally smart but emotionally and physically handicapped.

There was a study done a number of years ago of rich and poor all around the world. The study wanted to find out how people born into poverty eventually become wealthy. The study found that these people, regardless of in which country they lived, possessed three qualities. These qualities were:

1. They maintained a long term vision and plan.
2. They believed in delayed gratification.
3. They used the power of compounding in their favor.

The study found that these people thought and planned for the long term and knew that they could ultimately achieve financial success by holding to a dream or a vision. They were willing to make short term sacrifices to gain long-term success, the basis of delayed gratification. Albert Einstein was amazed at how money could multiply just by the power of compounding. He considered the compounding of money as one of the most amazing inventions of human. This study took compounding to another level beyond money. The study reinforced the idea of baby steps... because each baby step in learning compounded over the years. People who had taken no steps at all did not have the leverage of magnified accumulation of knowledge and experience that comes from compounding.

The study also found what caused people to go from wealthy to poor. There are many rich families who lose most of their wealth after only three generations. Not surprisingly the study found that these people possessed the following three qualities:

1. They have short term vision.
2. They have a desire for instantaneous gratification.
3. They abuse the power of compounding.

Today I meet people who get frustrated with me because they want me to tell them how they can make more money today. They do not like the idea of thinking long term. Many are desperately seeking short term answers because they have money problems to be solved today... money problems such as consumer debt and lack of investments caused by their uncontrolled desire for instantaneous gratification. They have the idea of "Eat, drink, and be merry while we're young." This abuses the power of compounding, which leads to long-term debt, instead of long-term wealth.

They want the quick answer and want me to tell them "What to do." Instead of hearing "Who they need 'to be' in order 'to do' what they need to do to acquire great wealth," they want short-term answers to a long-term problem. In other words, too many people are fixated upon the "Get rich quick" philosophy of life. To these people I wish them luck because luck is what they will need.

A HOT TIP

Most of us have heard that people who write down their goals are more successful than those who do not. There is a teacher named Raymond Aaron, from Ontario, Canada who has seminars and tapes on subjects such as sales, goal setting, doubling your income, and how to be a better networker. While these are subjects taught by many people, I recommend his work simply because he has some fascinating insights into these important subjects. Insights that can help you achieve more of what you want in the world of business and investing.

On the subject of goal setting, he recommends something that follows in line with the idea of taking baby steps instead of great leaps forward. He recommends having great big long-term dreams and wishes. Yet, when it comes to setting goals, instead of trying to be an overachiever, he recommends being an underachiever. In other words, take baby steps. For example, if I wanted to have a beautiful body, instead of trying to take a great leap forward, he recommends underachieving by doing less than you would want to. Instead of going to the gym for one hour, commit to going for only 20 minutes. In other words, set an underachieving goal and force yourself to stick with it. The result will be instead of being overwhelmed, you will feel underwhelmed. By feeling underwhelmed, I have found myself looking forward to going to the gym, or anything else I need to do or change in my life. The strange thing is that I find I achieve today by being an underachiever instead of trying to kill myself and be an overachiever. In summary, dream big daring dreams, and then underachieve a little bit each day. In other words, baby steps instead of great leaps over the cliff. Set attainable daily goals that, when achieved, provide positive reinforcement to help you stay on the path to the big goal.

An example of the way I underachieve is that I set a written goal to listen to two audio cassette tapes a week. I may listen to the same tape two or more times if it's good… but it still counts towards my 2 cassettes a week. My wife and I also have a written goal to attend at least two seminars a year on subjects about the "B" and "I" quadrants. We go on vacations with people who are experts on subjects found in the "B" and "I" quadrants. Again we learn a lot while playing, resting, and dining out. Those are ways of underachieving and yet still moving towards big and bold dreams. I thank Raymond Aaron and his tape on goal setting for assisting me in achieving more with a lot less stress.

Now read on, and remember to dream big, think long-term, underachieve on a daily basis, and take baby steps. That is the key to long-term success and the key to crossing from the left side of the *CASHFLOW Quadrant* to the right side.

IF YOU WANT TO BE RICH, YOU'VE GOT TO CHANGE YOUR RULES

I have often been quoted as saying "The rules have changed." When people hear these words, they nod their head in agreement and say, "Yes. The rules have changed. Nothing is the same anymore." But then they go on and do the same old thing.

INDUSTRIAL AGE FINANCIAL STATEMENTS

When I teach classes on the topic of "Getting Your Financial Life In Order," I start by asking the students to fill out a personal financial statement. It often becomes a life-changing experience. Financial statements are much like X-rays. Both financial statements and X-rays let you see what your unassisted eye cannot. After the class members have filled out their statements, it is easy to see who has "financial cancer" and who is financially healthy. Generally, the ones with financial cancer are those with Industrial Age ideas.

Why do I say that? Because in the Industrial Age, people did not have to "think about tomorrow." The rules were, "Work hard and your employer or the government will take care of your tomorrows." Which is why so many of the my friends and family often said, "Get a job with the government. It has great benefits." Or: "Make sure the company you work for has an excellent retirement plan." Or: "Make sure the company you work for has a strong union." Those are words of advice based on Industrial Age rules, which I refer to as the "entitlement" mentality. Although the rules have changed, many people have not changed their personal rules... especially their financial rules. They're still spending like there is no need to plan for tomorrow. That is what I look for when I read a person's financial statement – whether or not they have a tomorrow.

DO YOU HAVE A TOMORROW?

Keeping things simple – this is what I look for on a personal financial statement.

Income Statement

Income
Expense (Today)

Balance Sheet

Assets	Liabilities
(Tomorrow)	(Yesterday)

People with no assets, which throw off cash flow, have no tomorrows. When I find people who have no assets, they generally are working hard for a paycheck to pay bills. If you look at most people's "Expense column," the two biggest monthly expenses are taxes and debt service for long-term liabilities. Their expense statements look like this:

Income Statement

Income

Expense
Taxes (Approximately 50%) **Debt (Approximately 35%)** **Living Expenses**

Balance Sheet

Assets	Liabilities

In other words, the government and the bank get paid before they do. People who cannot get control of their cash flow generally have no financial future and will find themselves in serious trouble in the next few years.

Why? A person who is only in the "E" quadrant has little protection from taxes and debt. Even an "S" can do something about these two financial cancers.

If this does not make sense to you, I would suggest reading or re-reading *Rich Dad Poor Dad*, which should make this and the next few chapters easier to understand.

THREE CASH FLOW PATTERNS

As stated in *Rich Dad Poor Dad*, there are three basic cash flow patterns: one for the rich, one for the poor, and one for the middle class. This is the cash flow pattern of the poor:

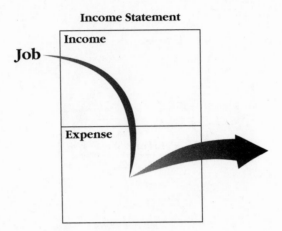

Income Statement

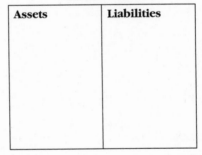

This is the cash flow pattern of the middle class.

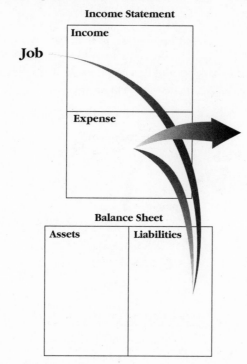

This cash flow pattern is considered "normal" and "intelligent" by our society. After all, the people who have this pattern probably have good high-paying jobs, nice homes, cars and credit cards. This is what my rich dad called the "working-class dream."

When I play my educational board game, *CASHFLOW*, with adults they usually struggle mentally. Why? Because they are being introduced to financial literacy, which means understanding the numbers and words of money. The game takes several hours to play, not because the game is long, but because the players are learning a completely new subject. It is almost like learning a foreign language. But the good news is that this new literacy can be learned quickly, and then the game picks up speed. It picks up speed because the players are smarter... and the more they play the game, the smarter and faster they become, all the while having fun.

Something else also happens. Because they are now becoming financially literate, many begin to realize that they are personally in financial trouble, even though the rest of society thinks they are "financially normal." You see, to have a middle class cash flow pattern was normal in the Industrial Age, but it could be disastrous in the Information Age.

Many people, once they successfully learn and understand the game, begin to seek new answers. It becomes a financial wake-up call about their personal financial health, just as a mild heart attack is an alert about a person's medical health.

At that moment of understanding, many people begin thinking like a rich person instead of a hard-working middle class person. After playing *CASHFLOW* several times, some people begin to change their thinking pattern to that of the rich, and they begin to seek a cash flow pattern that looks like this.

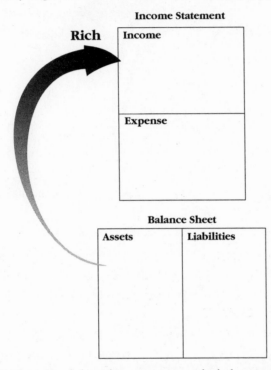

This is the mental thought pattern my rich dad wanted his son and me to have as young children, which is why he took away our paychecks and refused to give us raises. He never wanted us to become addicted to the idea of a high-paying job. He wanted us to develop the thought pattern of thinking only in assets and income in the form of capital gains, dividends, rental income, residual income from businesses, and royalties.

For people who want to be successful in the Information Age, the faster they begin to develop their financial intelligence and emotional intelligence to think in this pattern, the faster they will feel more financially secure and find financial freedom. In a world of less and less job security, this cash flow pattern makes much more sense to me. And to achieve this pattern a person needs to see the world from the "B" and "I" quadrants, not just the "E" and "S" quadrants.

I also call this an Information Age financial statement because the income is generated strictly from information, not hard work. In the Information Age, the idea of hard work does not mean the same thing as it did in the Agrarian Age and the Industrial Age. In the Information Age, the people who work physically the hardest will be paid the least. It is already true today and has been true through history.

However, today when people say, "Don't work hard, work smart," they do not mean work smart in the "E" or "S" quadrants. They actually mean work smart in the "B" or "I" quadrants. That is Information Age thinking which is why financial intelligence and emotional intelligence are vital today and will be vital in the future.

SO WHAT IS THE ANSWER?

Obviously my answer is to re-educate yourself to think like a rich person, not a poor or middle class person. In other words, to think and look at the world from the "B" or "I" quadrant. However, the solution is not as simple as going back to school and taking a few courses. To be successful in the "B" or "I" quadrant requires financial intelligence, systems intelligence and emotional intelligence. These things cannot be learned in school.

The reason these intelligences are hard to learn is because most adults are "wired" to the "hard work and spend" mode of life. They feel financial anxiety, so they hurry off to work and work hard. They come home and hear about the stock market going up and down. The anxiety grows, so they go shopping for a new house or car, or they go and play golf to avoid the anxiety.

The problem is that the anxiety returns on Monday morning.

HOW DO YOU START THINKING
LIKE A RICH PERSON?

People often ask me how to get started thinking like a rich person. I always recommend starting small and seeking education, rather than running out and simply buying a mutual fund or a rental property. If people are serious about learning and retraining themselves to think like a rich person, I recommend my board game, *CASHFLOW*.

I created the game to help people improve their financial intelligence. It gives people the mental, physical and emotional training required to allow them to make the gradual change from thinking like a poor or middle class person to thinking like a rich person. It teaches people to think about what my rich dad said was important... which was not a large paycheck or big house.

CASH FLOW, NOT MONEY, RELIEVES ANXIETY

Financial struggle and poverty are really financial anxiety problems. They are mental and emotional loops that keep people stuck in what I call the "rat race." Unless the mental and emotional hooks are broken, the pattern remains intact.

I worked with a banker a few months ago on breaking his pattern of financial struggle. I am not a therapist, but I have had experience in breaking my own financial habits instilled by my family.

This banker makes more than $120,000 a year, but is always in some sort of financial trouble. He has a beautiful family, three cars, a big house, a vacation home, and he looks the part of a prosperous banker. When I looked at his financial statement however, I found he had a financial cancer that would be terminal in a few years if he did not change his ways.

The first time he and his wife played *CASHFLOW*, he struggled and fidgeted almost uncontrollably. His mind was wandering, and he could not seem to grasp the game. After four hours of play, he was still stuck. Everyone else had completed the game, but he was still in the "Rat Race".

So I asked him, as we put the game away, what was going on. His only answer was that the game was too hard, too slow and too boring. I then reminded him of what I had told him before the game started: that all games are reflections of the people playing. In other words, a game is like a mirror that allows you to look at yourself.

That statement angered him, so I backed off, and asked if he was still committed to getting his financial life in order. He said he was still committed, so I invited him and his wife, who loved the game, to come play again with an investment group I was coaching.

A week later, he showed up reluctantly. This time, a few lights began to go on inside his head. For him, the accounting part was easy, so he was naturally neat and tidy with his numbers, which is important for the game to be valuable. But now he was beginning to understand the world of business and investing. He could finally "see" with his mind his own life's patterns and what he was doing to cause his own financial struggle. He still did not finish the game after four hours, but he was beginning to learn. As he left this time, he invited himself back.

By the third meeting, he was a new man. He was now in control of the game, his accounting and his investments. His confidence soared, and this time he successfully exited the "Rat Race" and was on the "Fast Track." This time as he left, he purchased a game and said, "I'm going to teach my kids."

By the fourth meeting, he told me his own personal expenses were down, he had changed his spending habits and cut up several credit cards, and he was now taking an active interest in learning to invest and build his asset column. His thinking was now on track to make him an Information Age thinker.

At the fifth meeting, he beta tested *CASHFLOW 202*, which is the advanced game for people who have mastered the original *CASHFLOW (101)*. He was now ready and eager to play the fast and risky game that true "B's" and "I's" play. The best news was that he had taken control of his financial future. This man was completely different from the one who had asked me to make *CASHFLOW* easier the first time he played it. I told him that if he wanted an easier game, he should play *Monopoly*, which is also an excellent teaching game. A few weeks later, instead of wanting things to be easier, he was actively seeking bigger challenges and he was optimistic about his financial future.

He had re-educated himself not only mentally but also – more importantly – emotionally, via the power of the repetitive learning process that comes from a game. In my opinion, games are a superior teaching tool because they require the player to become fully involved in the learning process, while having fun. Playing a game involves a person mentally, emotionally and physically.

The 7 Steps To Finding Your Financial Fast Track

Chapter 11

STEP 1:
It's Time To
Mind Your
Own Business

Have you been working hard and making everyone else rich? Early in life, most people are programmed to mind other people's businesses and make other people rich. It begins innocently enough with words of advice such as these:

1. "Go to school and get good grades, so you can find a safe, secure job with good pay and excellent benefits."
2. "Work hard so you can buy the home of your dreams. After all, your home is an asset and it is your most important investment."
3. "Having a large mortgage is good because the government gives you a tax deduction for your interest payments."
4. "Buy now, pay later," or "Low down, easy monthly payments." Or, "Come in and save money."

People who blindly follow these words of advice often become:
1. Employees, making their bosses and owners rich.
2. Debtors, making banks and money lenders rich.

3. Taxpayers, making the government rich.

4. Consumers, making many other businesses rich.

Instead of finding their own financial fast track, they help everyone else find theirs. Instead of minding their own business, they work all their lives minding everyone else's.

By looking at the Income Statement and Balance Sheet, you can easily begin to see how we have been programmed from an early age to mind everyone else's business, and ignore our own business.

Income Statement

Income
1. You mind your boss's business.
Expense
2. You mind the government's business via taxes. With every other line item expense, you mind a lot of other people's businesses.

Balance Sheet

Assets	Liabilities
4. This is your business.	**3. You mind your banker's business.**

TAKE ACTION

In my classes, I often ask people to fill out their financial statements. For many people, their financial statements are not a pretty picture simply because they've been misled into minding everyone else's business instead of minding their own business.

1) YOUR FIRST STEP:

Fill out your own personal financial statement. I have included a sample income statement and balance sheet as shown in the game, *CASHFLOW.*

In order to get where you want to go you need to know where you are. This is your first step to take control of your life and spend more time minding your own business.

2) SET FINANCIAL GOALS:

Set a long-term financial goal for where you want to be in 5 years and a smaller, short-term financial goal for where you want to be in 12 months. (The smaller financial goal is a stepping stone along the way to your 5-year goal.) Set goals that are realistic and attainable.

A) Within the next twelve months:
   1. I want to decrease my debt by $_____.
   2. I want to increase my cash flow from my assets, or passive income, (passive income is income you earn without you working for it) to $_____ per month.

B) My 5-year financial goals are:
   1) Increase my cash flow from my assets to $_____ per month.
   2) Have these investment vehicles in my asset column (i.e. real estate, stocks, businesses, etc.) _____

   _____

   _____

C) Use your 5-year goals to develop your income statement and balance sheet for 5 years from today.

Now that you know where you are financially today and have set your goals, you need to get control of your cash flow so that you can achieve your goals.

Profession

Player

Goal: To get out of the Rat Race and onto the Fast Track by building up your
Passive Income to be greater than your Total Expenses

Income Statement

Income

Auditor

Person on your right

Salary:

Interest:

Dividends:

Real Estate: Cash Flow

Passive Income= _____

(Interest + Dividends +
Real Estate + Business Cash Flows)

Businesses: Cash Flow

**Total
Income:** _____

Expenses

Taxes:

Home Mortgage:

School Loan Payment:

Car Payment:

Credit Card Payment:

Retail Payment:

Other Expenses:

Child Expenses:

Bank Loan Payment:

**Number of
Children:** _____
(Begin game with 0 Children)

**Per Child
Expense:** _____

**Total
Expenses:** _____

**Monthly
Cash Flow:** _____
(Pay Check)

Balance Sheet

Assets

Liabilities

Savings:

Stocks/Mutual's/CD's   No. of Shares: Cost/Share:

Home Mortgage:

School Loans:

Car Loans:

Credit Cards:

Real Estate: Down Pay: Cost:

Retail Debt:

RE Mortgage:

Business: Down Pay: Cost:

Liability: (Business)

Bank Loan:

©1998, CASHFLOW Technologies, Inc.

CHAPTER 12

STEP 2:
Take Control Of Your Cash Flow

Many people believe that simply making more money will solve their money problems but, in most cases, it only causes bigger money problems.

The primary reason most people have money problems is they were never schooled in the science of cash flow management. They were taught how to read, write, drive cars and swim, but they were not taught how to manage their cash flow. Without this training they wind up having money problems, then work harder believing that more money will solve the problem.

As my rich dad often said, "More money will not solve the problem, if cash flow management is the problem."

THE MOST IMPORTANT SKILL

After deciding to mind your own business, the next step as the CEO of the business of your life, is to take control of your cash flow. If you do not, making more money will not make you richer... in fact, more money makes most people poorer because they often go out and get deeper into debt every time they get a pay raise.

WHO IS SMARTER – YOU OR YOUR BANKER?

The majority of people do not prepare personal financial statements. At most, they try to balance their checkbooks each month. So congratulate yourself, you are now ahead of most of your colleagues simply by completing your financial statement and setting goals for yourself.

As CEO of your own life, you can learn to be smarter than most people, even your banker.

Most people will say that "two sets of books" is illegal. And that is true in some instances. Yet, in reality, if you truly understand the world of finances, there must always be two sets of books. Once you realize this, you will be as smart, and maybe smarter, than your banker. The following is an example of a legal "two sets of books" – yours and your banker's.

As CEO of your life, always remember these simple words and diagrams from my rich dad, who often said, "For every liability you have, you are somebody else's asset."

And he would draw this simple diagram.

Your Balance Sheet

Assets	Liabilities
	Mortgage

Your Bank's Balance Sheet

Bank's Balance Sheet

Assets	Liabilities
Your Mortgage	

As CEO of your life, you must always remember that for each of your liabilities, or debts, you are someone else's asset. That is the real "two sets of books accounting." For every liability, such as a mortgage, car loan, school loan and credit card, you're an employee of the people lending the money. You're working hard to make someone else rich.

GOOD DEBT AND BAD DEBT

Rich dad often cautioned me about "good debt and bad debt." He would often say, "Every time you owe someone money, you become an employee of their money. If you take out a 30 year loan, you've become a 30 year employee, and they do not give you a gold watch when the debt is retired."

Rich dad did borrow money, but he did his best to not become the person who paid for his loans. He would explain to his son and me that good debt was debt that someone else paid for you, and bad debt was debt that you paid for with your own sweat and blood. That is why he loved rental properties. He would encourage me to buy rental property because "the bank gives you the loan, but your tenant pays for it."

INCOME AND EXPENSE

Not only do the two sets of books apply to assets and liabilities, but they also apply to income and expenses. The more complete verbal lesson from my rich dad was this: "For most every asset, there must be a liability, but they do not appear on the same set of financial statements. For every expense, there must also be income, and again they do not appear on the same set of financial statements."

This simple drawing will make that lesson clearer:

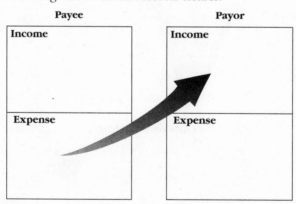

Most people cannot get ahead financially because every month, they have bills to pay. They have phone bills, tax bills, electric bills, gas bills, credit card bills, food bills, and so forth. Every month, most people pay everyone else first and pay themselves last, if they have anything left over. Hence, most people violate the golden rule of personal finance, which is, "Pay yourself first."

That is why rich dad stressed the importance of cash flow management and basic financial literacy. Rich dad would often say, "People who cannot control their cash flow work for those who can."

THE FINANCIAL FAST TRACK AND THE RAT RACE

The concept of "two sets of books" can be used to show you the "Financial Fast Track" and the "Rat Race". There are many different types of financial fast tracks. The diagram below is one of the most common. It is the track between a creditor and a debtor.

It is overly simplified, yet if you take time to study it, your mind will begin to see what most people's eyes cannot. Study it and you will see the relationship between the rich and the poor, the haves and have nots, the borrowers and the lenders, and those who create jobs and those who look for jobs.

THIS IS THE FINANCIAL FAST TRACK AND YOU'RE ALREADY ON IT

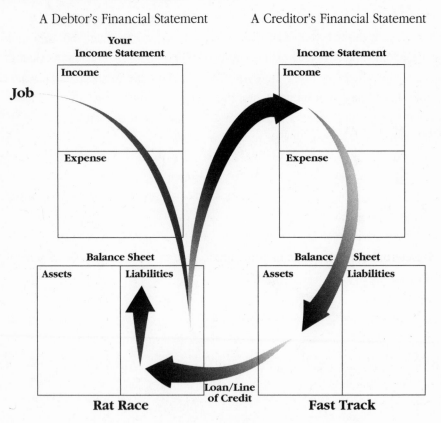

A Debtor's Financial Statement   A Creditor's Financial Statement

At this point, the creditor will say, "Because of your good credit, we'd like to offer you a bill consolidation loan." Or: "Would you like to open line of credit just in case you need some extra money in the future?"

DO YOU KNOW THE DIFFERENCE?

The path of money flowing between the two sets of books is what my rich dad called the "Financial Fast Track." It is also the "Financial Rat Race." For one to exist, so must the other. Hence, there must be at minimum two financial statements. The question is, which one is yours? And which one do you want to have?

This is why my rich dad constantly told me, "Making more money will not solve your problems, if cash flow management is the problem," and "the people who understand the power of financial numbers have power over those who do not."

This is why Step No. 2 to finding your own financial fast track is, "Take control of your cash flow."

You need to sit down and map out a plan to get control of your spending habits. Minimize your debt and liabilities. Live within your means before you try to increase your means. If you need assistance seek the help of a qualified financial planner. He or she can help you lay out a plan where you can improve your cash flow and start to pay yourself first.

TAKE ACTION

1) Review your financial statements from the previous chapter.

2) Determine which quadrant of the *CASHFLOW Quadrant* you receive your income from today. _____

3) Determine which quadrant you want to receive the bulk of your income from in five years. _____

4) Begin Your Cashflow Management Plan:

A) Pay yourself first. Put aside a set percentage from each paycheck or each payment you receive from other sources. Deposit that money into an investment savings account. Once your money goes into the account, NEVER take it out, until you are ready to invest it.

Congratulations! You have just started managing your cash flow.

B) Focus on reducing your personal debt.

The following are some simple and ready-to-apply tips for reducing and eliminating your personal debt.

Tip #1: If you have credit cards with outstanding balances...
1. Cut up all your credit cards, except for 1 or 2.
2. Any new charges you add to the 1 or 2 cards you now have must be paid off every month. Do not incur any further long-term debt.

Tip #2: Come up with $150-$200 extra per month. Now that you are becoming more and more financially literate this should be relatively easy to do. If you cannot generate an additional $150-$200 per month then your chances for financial freedom may only be a pipe dream.

Tip #3: Apply the additional $150-$200 to your monthly payment of ONLY ONE of your credit cards. You will now pay the minimum PLUS the $150-$200 on that one credit card.

Pay only the minimum amount due on all other credit cards. Often people try to pay a little extra each month on all their cards, but those cards surprisingly never get paid off.

Tip #4: Once the first card is paid off, then apply the total amount you were paying each month on that card to your next credit card. You are now paying the minimum amount due on the second card PLUS the total monthly payment you were paying on your first credit card.

Continue this process with all your credit cards and other consumer credit such as store charges, etc. With each debt you pay off, apply the full amount you were paying on that debt to the minimum payment of your next debt. As you pay off each debt, the monthly amount you are paying on the next debt will escalate.

Tip #5: Once all your credit cards and other consumer debt is paid off, now continue the procedure with your car and house payments.

If you follow this procedure you will be amazed at the shortened amount of time it takes for you to be completely debt-free. Most people can be debt-free within 5 to 7 years.

Tip #6: Now that you are completely debt-free, take the monthly amount you were paying on your last debt, and put that money towards investments. Build your asset column.

That's how simple it is.

Chapter 13

STEP 3: Know The Difference Between Risk And Risky

I often hear people saying, "Investing is risky."
I disagree. Instead I say, "Being uneducated is risky."

WHAT IS PROPER CASH FLOW MANAGEMENT?

Proper cash flow management begins with knowing the difference between an asset and a liability... and not the definition your banker gives you.

The following diagram is a picture of an individual who is 45 years old and who has properly managed his or her cash flow.

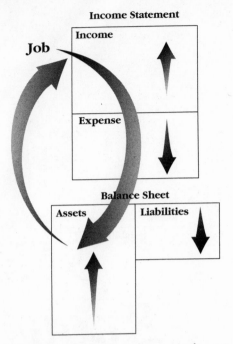

I use the age 45 because it is halfway between the age 25, when most people begin to work and 65, the age when most people plan on retiring. By age 45, if they have properly managed their cash flow, their asset column should be longer than their liability column.

This is a financial picture of people who take risks, but are not risky.

They are also in the upper 10 percent of the population. But if they do what the other 90 percent of the population does, which is mismanage their cash flow and not know the difference between an asset and a liability, their financial picture looks like this at age 45:

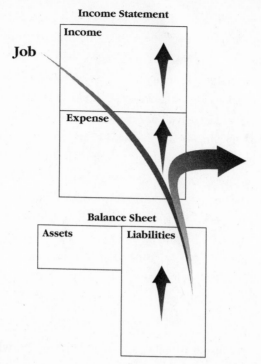

These are the people who most often say, "Investing is risky." For them, that statement is true – but not because investing is risky. It is their lack of formal financial training and knowledge that is risky.

FINANCIAL LITERACY

In *Rich Dad Poor Dad*, I told the story of how my rich dad demanded that I become financially literate.

Financial literacy is simply looking at the numbers with your eyes, but it is also your trained mind that tells you which way the cash is flowing. Rich dad often said, "The direction of cash flow is everything."

So a house could be an asset or a liability depending on the direction of the cash flow. If the cash flows into your pocket, it is an asset, and if it flows out of your pocket, it is a liability.

FINANCIAL INTELLIGENCE

Rich dad had many definitions for "financial intelligence," such as "the ability to convert cash or labor into assets that provide cash flow."

But one of his favorite definitions was, "Who is smarter? You or your money?"

To my rich dad, to spend your life working hard for money only to have it go out as fast as it comes in is not a sign of high intelligence. You may want to review the cash flow patterns of a poor person, a middle-class person and a rich person as presented in Chapter 10 and remember that a rich person focuses his or her efforts on acquiring assets, not working harder.

Due to the lack of financial intelligence, many educated people will put themselves into positions of high financial risk. My rich dad called it "financial red line," meaning income and expenses are nearly the same every month. These are the people who cling desperately to job security, are unable to change when the economy changes, and often destroy their health with stress and worry. And these are often the same people who say: "Business and investing is risky."

In my opinion, business and investing is not risky. Being under-educated is. Similarly, being misinformed is risky and relying on a "safe secure job" is the highest risk anyone can take. Buying an asset is not risky. Buying liabilities you have been told are assets is risky. Minding your own business is not risky. Minding everyone else's business and paying them first is risky.

So Step 3 is to know the difference between risk and risky.

TAKE ACTION

1) Define risk in your own words.
   a) Is relying on a paycheck risky to you?
   b) Is having debt to pay each month risky to you?
   c) Is owning an asset that generates cash flow into your pocket each month risky to you?
   d) Is spending time to learn about financial education risky to you?
   e) Is spending time learning about different types of investments risky to you?

2) Commit 5 hours of your time each week to do one or more of the following:
   a) Read the business page of your newspaper and the *Wall Street Journal.*
   b) Listen to the financial news on television or radio.
   c) Listen to educational cassettes on investing and financial education.
   d) Read financial magazines and newsletters.
   e) Play *CASHFLOW.*

CHAPTER 14

STEP 4:
Decide What Kind Of Investor You Want To Be

Have you ever wondered why some investors make more money with a lot less risk than others?

Most people struggle financially because they avoid financial problems. One of the biggest secrets my rich dad taught me was this: "If you want to acquire great wealth quickly, take on great financial problems."

In Section I of this book, I went into the 7 levels of investors. I would like to add one more distinction that defines the three different types of investors:

Type A: Investors who seek problems.

Type B: Investors who seek answers.

Type C: Sgt. Schultz investors: "I know nothing."

TYPE C INVESTORS

The name Sgt. Schultz comes from the lovable character in the TV series

Hogan's Heroes. In the program, Sgt. Schultz is a guard in a German POW camp who knows the POWs are trying to escape or sabotage the German war effort.

When he knows something is wrong, all Schultz says is, "I know nothing." Most people, when it comes to investing, take the same attitude.

Can Sgt. Schultz investors still achieve great wealth? The answer is yes. They can get a job with the federal government, marry someone rich, or win the lottery.

TYPE B INVESTORS

Type B investors often ask such questions as:

"What do you recommend I invest in?"

"Do you think I should buy real estate?"

"What mutual funds are good for me?

"I talked to my broker and he recommended I diversify."

"My parents gave me a few shares of stock. Should I sell them?"

Type B investors should immediately interview several financial planners, choose one and start taking their advice. Financial planners, if they're good, provide excellent technical knowledge and can often help you establish a financial game plan for your life.

The reason I do not offer specific financial advice in my books is because everyone's financial position is different. A financial planner can best evaluate where you are today, and then give you an idea on how to become a Level 4 investor.

An interesting side note – I often find that many high income "E's" and "S's" fall into the Type B investor category because they have little time to spend looking for investment opportunities. Because they are so busy, they often have little time to learn about the right side of the *Quadrant.* Hence, they seek answers rather than knowledge. So this group often buys what the Type A investor calls "retail investments," which are investments that have been packaged for sale to the masses.

TYPE A INVESTORS

Type A investors look for problems. In particular they look for problems caused by those who get into financial trouble. Investors who are good at solving problems expect to make returns of 25 percent to infinity on their money. They are typically Level 5 and Level 6 investors who have strong financial foundations. They possess the skills necessary to succeed as business owners and investors, and they use those skills to solve problems caused by people who lack such skills.

For example, when I first started investing, all I looked for were small condominiums and houses that were in foreclosure. I started with $18,000 problems that had been created by investors who did not manage their cash flow well and ran out of money.

After a few years, I was still looking for problems, but this time, the numbers were bigger. Three years ago, I was working on acquiring a $30 million mining company in Peru. While the problem and numbers were bigger, the process was the same.

HOW TO GET ON THE FAST TRACK FASTER

The lesson is to start small and learn to solve problems, and you will eventually gain immense wealth as you become better at solving problems.

For those who wish to acquire assets faster, I again emphasize the need to first learn the skills of the "B" and "I" side of the *Quadrant.* I recommend learning how to build a business first, because a business provides vital educational experience, improves personal skills, provides cash flow to soften the ups and downs of the marketplace, and provides free time. It is the cash flow from my business that bought me the free time to begin looking for financial problems to solve.

CAN YOU BE ALL THREE TYPES OF INVESTORS?

In reality, I operate as all three types of investors. I am a Sgt. Schultz, or a Type C investor, when it comes to mutual funds or picking stocks. When I am asked, "What mutual funds do you recommend?" or "What stocks are you buying?" I turn into Sgt. Schultz and respond "I know nothing."

I do have a few mutual funds, but I really do not spend much time studying them. I can achieve better results with my apartment houses than with mutual funds. As a type B investor, I seek professional answers to my financial problems. I seek answers from financial planners, stockbrokers, bankers and real estate brokers. If they are good, these professionals provide a wealth of information I do not personally have the time to acquire. They are also closer to the market and are, I trust, more up to date with changes in the laws and the markets.

The advice from my financial planner is priceless simply because she knows trusts, wills and insurance far better than I ever will. Everyone should have a plan, and that is why there is a financial planning profession. There is much more to investing than simply buying and selling.

I also give my money to other investors to invest for me. In other words, I know other level 5 and level 6 investors who seek partners in their investments. These are individuals I personally know and trust. If they choose to invest in an area I know nothing about, such as low-income housing or large office buildings, I may choose to give my money to them because I know they are good at what they do and I trust their knowledge.

WHY YOU SHOULD GET STARTED QUICKLY

One of the main reasons I recommend people find their own financial fast track quickly and take getting rich seriously is because in America, and most of the world, there are two sets of rules, one for the rich and one for everyone else. Many laws are written against people stuck in the financial rat race. In the world of business and investing, which is the world I am most familiar with, I find it shocking how little the middle class knows when it comes to where its tax dollars are going. Although tax dollars are going to many worthwhile causes, many of the larger tax breaks, incentives and payments are going to the rich, while the middle class is paying for them.

For example, low-income housing in America is a huge problem and a political hot potato. To help solve this problem, city, state and federal governments offer substantial tax credits, tax breaks and subsidized rents to people who finance and build low-income housing. Just by knowing the laws, financiers and builders become wealthier by having taxpayers subsidize their investments in low-income housing.

WHY IT'S UNFAIR

Thus, not only do most people on the left side of the *CASHFLOW Quadrant* pay more in personal income tax, but they are often not able to participate in tax-advantaged investments. This may be one source for the saying "the rich get richer."

I know it's unfair, and I understand both sides of the story. I have met people who protest and write letters to the editor of their newspaper. Some people try to change the system by running for political office. I say it's much easier to simply mind your own business, take control of your cash flow, find your own financial fast track and get rich. I contend that it is easier to change yourself than to change the political system.

PROBLEMS LEAD TO OPPORTUNITIES

Years ago, my rich dad encouraged me to develop my skills as a business owner and investor. He also said, "Then practice solving problems."

For years, that is all I have done. I solve business and investment problems. Some people prefer to call them challenges, yet I like to call them problems, because that is what they are, for the most part.

I think people like the word "challenges" more than "problems" because they think one word sounds more positive than the other. Yet, to me, the word "problem" has a positive meaning, because I know that inside of every problem lies an "opportunity," and opportunities are what real investors are after. And with every financial or business problem I address, regardless of whether I solve the problem, I wind up learning something. I may learn something new about finance, marketing, people or legal affairs. I often meet new people who become invaluable assets on other projects. Many become lifelong friends which is a priceless bonus.

FIND YOUR FAST TRACK

So for those of you who want to find your financial fast track, start by:

1. Minding your own business.
2. Taking control of your cash flow.
3. Knowing the difference between risk and risky.
4. Knowing the difference between a Type A, B and C investor, and choosing to be all three.

To get on the financial fast track, become an expert at solving a certain type of problem. Do not "diversify," as people who are only Type B investors are advised to do. Become an expert at solving that one type of problem, and people will come to you with money to invest. Then, if you are good and trustworthy, you will reach your financial fast track more quickly. Here are a few examples:

Bill Gates is an expert at solving software marketing problems. He is so good at it the federal government is after him. Donald Trump is an expert at solving problems in real estate. Warren Buffet is an expert at solving problems in business and the stock market, which in turn allows him to buy valuable stocks and manage a successful portfolio. George Soros is an expert at solving problems resulting from market volatility. That is what makes him an excellent hedge-fund manager. Rupert Murdock is an expert at solving the business problems of global television networks.

My wife and I are pretty good at solving problems in apartment housing that will eventually pay off with passive income. We know little outside the realm of the small to medium-size apartment house market we primarily invest in, and we do not diversify. If I choose to invest in areas outside those arenas I become a Type B investor, which means I give my money to people who have an excellent track record in their fields of expertise.

I have one focused objective, and that is to "mind my own business." Although my wife and I do work for charities and help other people in their efforts, we never lose sight of the importance of minding our own business and continually adding to our asset column.

So to become rich quicker, become a student of the skills needed by a business owner and investor, and seek to solve bigger problems... because inside of big problems lie huge financial opportunities. That is why I recommend becoming a "B" first, before becoming an "I." If you are a master of solving business problems, you will have excess cash flow and your knowledge of business will make you a much smarter investor. I've said it many times before, yet it is worth saying again: Many people come to the "I" quadrant in hopes that investing will solve their financial problems. In most cases, it doesn't. Investing only makes their financial problems worse if they are not already sound business owners.

There is no scarcity of financial problems. In fact, there is one right around the corner from you, waiting to be solved.

TAKE ACTION

GET EDUCATED IN INVESTING:

Once again, I recommend you become proficient as a level 4 investor before trying to become a level 5 or 6 investor. Start small and continue your education.

Each week do at least two of the following:

1. Attend financial seminars and classes. (I attribute much of my success to a real estate course I took as a young man that cost me $385. It has earned me millions over the years because I took action.)

2. Look for real estate "for sale" signs in your area. Call on three or four per week and ask the sales person to tell you about the property. Ask questions like: Is it an investment property?
   If it is:
   Is it rented? What is the current rent? What is the vacancy rate? What are the average rents in that area? What are the maintenance costs? Is there deferred maintenance? Will the owner finance? What type of financing terms are available?

   Practice calculating the monthly cash flow statement for each property and then go over it with the agent for the property to see what you forgot. Each property is a unique business system and should be viewed as an individual business system.

3. Meet with several stockbrokers and listen to the companies they recommend for stock buys. Then research these companies at the library or over the internet. Call the companies and ask for their annual reports.
4. Subscribe to investment newsletters and study them.
5. Continue to read, listen to tapes & videos, watch financial TV programs, and play *CASHFLOW.*

GET EDUCATED IN BUSINESS:

1. Meet with several business brokers to see what existing businesses are for sale in your area. It is amazing the terminology you can learn by just asking questions and listening.
2. Attend a network marketing seminar to learn about its business system. (I recommend researching at least three different network marketing companies)
3. Attend business opportunity conventions or trade expos in your area to see what franchises or business systems are available.
4. Subscribe to business newspapers and magazines.

CHAPTER 15

STEP 5:
Seek Mentors

Who guides you to places you're never been to before?

A mentor is someone who tells you what is important and what is not important.

MENTORS TELL US WHAT IS IMPORTANT

The following is the score sheet from my educational board game, *CASHFLOW*. It was created to be a mentor, because it trains people to think like my rich dad thought and point out what he thought was financially important.

Salary

Poor Dad thought this area of a financial statement was important.

Passive Income

Rich dad taught me that these areas are important if you want to be rich.

Profession		Player

Goal: To get out of the Rat Race and onto the Fast Track by building up your
Passive Income to be greater than your Total Expenses

Income Statement

Income		Auditor

Person on your right

Salary:
Interest:
Dividends:
Real Estate: _____ Cash Flow

Passive Income= _____
(Interest + Dividends +
Real Estate + Business Cash Flows)

Businesses: _____ Cash Flow

Total Income: _____

Expenses

Taxes:
Home Mortgage:
School Loan Payment:
Car Payment:
Credit Card Payment:
Retail Payment:
Other Expenses:
Child Expenses:
Bank Loan Payment:

Number of Children: _____
(Begin game with 0 Children)
Per Child Expense: _____

Total Expenses: _____

Monthly Cash Flow: _____
(Pay Check)

Balance Sheet

Assets			Liabilities

Savings:
Stocks/Mutual's/CD's No. of Shares: Cost/Share:

Home Mortgage:
School Loans:
Car Loans:
Credit Cards:
Retail Debt:
RE Mortgage:

Real Estate: Down Pay: Cost:

Business: Down Pay: Cost:

Liability: (Business)

Bank Loan:

My highly educated but poor dad thought that a job with a high salary was important, and that buying the house of your dreams was important. He also believed in paying bills first and living below your means.

My rich dad taught me to focus on passive income and spend my time acquiring the assets that provided passive or long-term residual income. He did not believe in living below your means. To his son and me, he often said, "Instead of living below your means, focus on increasing your means."

To do that, he recommended we focus on building the asset column and increasing passive income from capital gains, dividends, residual income from businesses, rental income from real estate, and royalties.

Both dads served as strong mentors for me as I grew up. The fact that I chose to follow the financial advice of my rich dad did not lessen the impact that my educated by poor dad had on me as well. I would not be who I am today without the strong influence of both these men.

REVERSE ROLE MODELS

Just as there are mentors who are excellent role models, there are people who are also reverse role models. In most instances, we all have both.

For example, I have a friend who has personally made more than $800 million in his lifetime. Today as I write, he is personally bankrupt. I have had other friends ask me why I continue to spend time with him. The answer to that question is because he is both an excellent role model and an excellent reverse role model. I can learn from both role models.

SPIRITUAL ROLE MODELS

Both of my dads were spiritual men, yet when it came to money and spirituality, they had different points of view. For instance, they interpreted the saying "the love of money is the root of all evil" differently.

My highly educated but poor dad felt any desire to have more money or to improve your financial position was wrong.

On the other hand, my rich dad interpreted this quote quite differently. He felt that temptation, greed and financial ignorance were wrong.

In other words, rich dad did not think money by itself was evil. He did believe that working all your life as a slave to money was evil and to be in financial slavery to personal debt was evil.

My rich dad often had a way of converting religious teachings into financial lessons, and I would like to share one of those lessons with you now.

THE POWER OF TEMPTATION

Rich dad believed individuals who worked hard, were chronically in debt and lived beyond their means were poor role models for their children. Not only were they poor role models in his eyes, but he also felt that people in debt had given into temptation and greed.

He would often draw a diagram like the following and say:

Asset	Liability

"And lead us not into temptation," as he pointed to the liability column.

Rich dad believed that many financial problems came from the desire to possess items that had little value. When credit cards arrived, he foresaw that millions of people would go into debt and that the debt would eventually control their lives. We see people going into tremendous personal debt for homes, furnishings, clothes, vacations and cars, because they lacked control over that human emotion called "temptation." Today people work harder and harder, buying things they think are assets, but their spending habits will never allow them to acquire real assets.

He then would point to the asset column that follows and say,

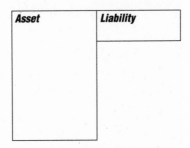

"But deliver us from evil."

Which was rich dad's way of saying that delaying gratification (a sign of emotional intelligence), minding your own business, and building your asset column first would help you avoid the degradation of the human spirit caused by temptation, lack of financial education, and the influence of financially poor role models.

For those of you seeking your own personal fast track, I can only caution you to be careful about the people you are around every day. Ask yourself: Are they good role models? If not, I suggest consciously seeking to spend more time with people who are heading in the same direction you are.

If you cannot find them during working hours, you can find them in investment clubs, network marketing groups, and other business associations.

FIND SOMEONE WHO'S BEEN THERE

Choose your mentors wisely. Be careful from whom you take advice. If you want to go somewhere, it is best to find someone who has already been there.

For example, if you decide you are going to climb Mount Everest next year, obviously you'd seek advice from someone who had climbed the mountain before. However, when it comes to climbing financial mountains, most people ask advice from people who are also personally stuck in financial swamps.

The hard part of finding mentors who are "B's" and "I's" is that most people giving advice about those quadrants, and about money, are people who actually come from the "E" and "S" side of the *Quadrant*.

Rich dad encouraged me to always have a coach or mentor. He constantly said, "Professionals have coaches. Amateurs do not."

For example, I play golf and I take lessons, but I do not have a full-time coach. This is probably why I pay money to play golf instead of getting paid to play. Yet, when it comes to the game of business and investing, I do have coaches, several of them. Why do I have coaches? I have coaches because I get paid to play those games.

So choose your mentors wisely. It is one of the most important things you can do.

TAKE ACTION

1) Seek Mentors - Seek out individuals in both the investment and business arenas who might act as mentors to you.
   a) Seek out role models. Learn from them.
   b) Seek out reverse role models. Learn from them.

2) WHO YOU SPEND YOUR TIME WITH IS YOUR FUTURE
   a) Write down the six people you spend the most time with. All of your children count as one person. Remember that the qualifier is who you spend the most time with, not the type of your relationship. (DO NOT READ ANY FURTHER UNTIL YOU HAVE WRITTEN DOWN YOUR 6 NAMES.)

   I was at a seminar about fifteen years ago when the instructor asked us to do the same. I wrote down my 6 names.

   He then asked us to look at the names we had written and announced, "You are looking at your future. The six people you spend the most time with are your future."

   The six people you spend the most time with may not necessarily always be personal friends. For some of you it may be your co-workers, spouse and children, or members of your church or charity. My list was made up of co-workers, business associates, and rugby players. The list was pretty revealing once I began to look below the surface. I gained insights about myself that I liked and even more that I did not like.

The instructor had us go around the room and meet with other people to discuss our lists. After a while the relevance of the exercise began to sink in even deeper. The more I discussed my list with other people, and the more I listened to them, I realized that I needed to make some changes. This exercise had little to do with the people I was spending my time with. It had everything to do with where I was going and what I was doing with my life.

Fifteen years later, the people I spend the most time with are all different except one. The five others on my earlier list are still dear friends, but we rarely see each other. They are great people and they are happy with their lives. My change had only to do with me. I wanted to change my future. To successfully change my future, I had to change my thoughts, and as a result, the people I spent time with.

b) Now that you have your list of 6 people, the next step is:

1) After each person's name list the quadrant they operate from.

Are they an "E, S, B, or I"? A reminder: the quadrant reflects the way in which a person generates the majority of their income. If they are unemployed or retired, list the quadrant they earned their income in. Leave a blank for young children and students.

Note: A person can have more than one designation. For example, my wife, Kim, would have a "B" and an "I" next to her name since she generates 50% of her income from each.

So my list would have Kim at the top since she and I spend almost all of our time together.

NAME	Quadrant
1. Kim Kiyosaki	B-I
2.	
3.	
4.	
5.	
6.	

c) The next step is to list each person's level as an investor. Please refer to chapter 5 and the 7 Levels of Investors. Kim is a level 6 investor.

If you do not know a person's investor level, just do your best and take an educated guess.

So a name would be complete with the quadrant and investor level listed.

NAME	QUADRANT	INVESTOR LEVEL
1. Kim Kiyosaki	B-I	6
2.		
3.		
4.		
5.		
6.		

SOME PEOPLE GET ANGRY

I've had mixed reviews from people in doing this exercise. Some people get very angry. I have heard, "How dare you ask me to classify the people around me?" So if this exercise has caused any emotional upset, please accept my apologies. This exercise is not intended to upset anyone. It is simply an exercise that is designed to shine some light on an individual's life. It does for some, but not for everyone.

When I did this exercise over 15 years ago, I realized that I was playing it safe and hiding. I was not happy with where I was and I used the people I worked with as the excuse as to why I was not making progress in my life. There were two people in particular that I argued with constantly, blaming them for holding our company back. My daily routine at work was to find their faults, point the faults out to them and then blame them for the problems we were having as an organization.

After completing this exercise, I realized that the two people I was always bumping heads with were very happy with where they were. I was the one who wanted to change. So instead of changing myself, I was pressuring them to change. After doing this exercise, I realized that I was projecting my personal expectations onto others. I wanted them to do what I did not want to do. I also thought that they should want and have the same things I did. It was not a healthy relationship. Once I realized what was happening, I was able to take the steps to change myself.

d) Take a look at the *CASHFLOW Quadrant* and place the initials of the people you spend time with in the appropriate quadrant.

Then put your initials in the quadrant you are in at present. Next put your initials in the quadrant you want to operate from in the future. If they are all primarily in the same quadrant, the chances are, you are a happy person. You are surrounded by like minded people. If they are not, you may want to consider some changes in your life.

CHAPTER 16

STEP 6: Make Disappointment Your Strength

Who do you become when things do not go the way you want?

When I left the Marine Corps my rich dad recommended I get a job that taught me to sell. He knew I was shy. Learning to sell was the last thing in the world I wanted to do.

For two years I was the worst salesman in my company. I could not sell a life preserver to a drowning man. My shyness was painful not only to me but also to the customers I was trying to sell to. For those two years I was on and off probation which meant I was always on the verge of being fired.

Often I would blame the economy or the product I was selling, or even the customers, as the reasons for my lack of success. Rich dad had another way of looking at it. He would say, "When people are lame, they love to blame."

This meant that the emotional pain from the disappointment was so strong that the individual with the pain wants to push the pain onto someone else through blame. In order to learn to sell, I had to come face to face with the pain of disappointment. In the process of learning to sell, I found a priceless lesson: how to turn disappointment into an asset rather than a liability.

Whenever I meet people who are afraid to "try" something new, in most cases the reason lies in their fear of being disappointed. They are afraid they might make a mistake, or get rejected. If you are prepared to embark on your journey to find your own financial fast track, I would like to offer you the same words of advice and encouragement my rich dad offered me when I was learning something new:

"Be prepared to be disappointed."

He meant this in a positive sense, not a negative sense. His reasoning was that if you're prepared for disappointment, you have a chance of turning that disappointment into an asset. Most people turn disappointment into a liability – a long-term one. And you know it's long-term when you hear a person say, "I'll never do that again." Or: "I should have known I would fail."

Just as inside every problem lies an opportunity... inside every disappointment lies a priceless gem of wisdom.

Whenever I hear someone say, "I'll never do that again," I know I am listening to someone who has stopped learning. They have let disappointment stop them. Disappointment has turned into a wall erected around them, instead of a foundation from which to grow taller.

My rich dad helped me learn how to deal with deep emotional disappointments. Rich dad would often say, "The reason there are few self-made rich people is because few people can tolerate disappointment. Instead of learning to face disappointment, they spend their lives avoiding it."

He also said, "Instead of avoiding it, be prepared for it. Disappointment is an important part of learning. Just as we learn from our mistakes, we gain character from our disappointments." Following are some of the words of advice he gave me over the years:

1. **Expect to be disappointed.** Rich dad often said, "Only fools expect everything to go the way they want. To expect to be disappointed does not mean being passive or a defeated loser. Expecting to be disappointed is a way of mentally and emotionally preparing yourself to be ready for surprises that you may not want. By being emotionally prepared, you can act with calm and dignity when things do not go your way. If you're calm, you can think better."

Many times I have seen people with great new business ideas. Their excitement lasts for about a month, then the disappointments begin to wear

them down. Soon, their excitement is di~~~ished, and all you hear them say
is, "That was a good idea, but it didn't wor~~~

It's not the idea that didn't work. It was disappoi~~~
They allowed their impatience to turn into disappo~~~ that worked harder.
allowed the disappointment to defeat them. Many time~~~ and then they
the result of them not receiving immediate financial rewa~~~ patience is
owners and investors may wait for years to see cash flow fr~~~ss
investment, but they go into it with the knowledge that success~~~
time. They also know that when success is achieved the financial~~~ss or
will be well worth the wait.

2. **Have a mentor standing by.** In the front of your phone book are listings
   for the hospital, fire department and police department. I have the same list
   of numbers for financial emergencies, except they are the phone numbers
   of my mentors.

Often, before I go into a deal or venture, I call one of my friends and
explain what I'm doing and what I intend to accomplish. I also ask them to
stand by in case I find myself in over my head, which is often.

Recently, I was negotiating for a large piece of real estate. The seller was
playing hardball and changing the terms at the closing. He knew I wanted
the property, and he was doing his best to get more money from me at the
last minute. Having a hot temper, my emotions went out of control. Instead
of blowing the deal by yelling and shouting, which is my normal inclination,
I simply asked if I could use the phone to call my partner.

After talking to three of my friends, who were standing by, and getting their
advice on how to handle the situation, I calmed down and learned three
new ways to negotiate I had not known before. The deal never went
through, but I still use those three negotiation techniques today – techniques
I would never have learned if I had not gone into the deal at all. That
knowledge is priceless.

The point is, we can never know everything beforehand, and we often only
learn things when we need to learn them. That is why I recommend you try
new things and expect disappointment, but always have a mentor standing

...perience. Many people never start projects by to coach you through the ...ave all the answers. You will never have all the simply because they do p... As my friend Keith Cunningham always says, answers, but begin a... ...ad down the street until all the lights are green. "Many people will go anywhere."

That is why the...

3. Be kind ...self. One of the most painful aspects about making a ...ing disappointed or failing at something is not what other ...bout us. It is how hard we are on ourselves. Most people who mist... ...akes often beat themselves up far harder than anyone else would. ...ould turn themselves into the police for personal emotional abuse.

...ave found that people who are hard on themselves mentally and emotionally are often too cautious when taking risks, or adopting new ideas, or attempting something new. It is hard to learn anything new if you punish yourself or blame someone else for your personal disappointments.

4. **Tell the truth.** One of the worst punishments I ever received as a child was the day I accidentally broke my sister's front tooth. She ran home to tell my dad, and I ran to hide. After my father found me, he was very angry.

He scolded me, "The reason I am punishing you is not because you broke your sister's tooth… but because you ran away."

Financially, there have been many times I could have run away from my mistakes. Running away is an easy thing to do but my dad's words have served me well for most of my life.

In short, we all make mistakes. We all feel upset and disappointed when things do not go our way. Yet, the difference lies in how we internally process that disappointment. Rich dad summarized it this way. He said, "The size of your success is measured by the strength of your desire; the size of your dream; and how you handle disappointment along the way."

In the next few years, we are going to have financial changes that will test our courage. It is the people who are most in control of their emotions, who do not let their emotions hold them back, and who have the emotional maturity to learn new financial skills who will flourish in the years ahead.

As Bob Dylan sang, "The times they are a-c ... ng."

And the future belongs to those who can change personal disappointments as building blocks for the

TAKE ACTION

1) Make mistakes. That is why I recommend you start with ba. Remember that losing is part of winning. "E's" and "S's" were t. making mistakes was not acceptable. "B's" and "I's" know that ma. mistakes is how they learn.

2) Put a little money down. Start small. If you find an investment you want to invest in, put a little money down. It's amazing how quickly your intelligence grows when you have some money on the line. Don't bet the ranch, your mortgage payment, or your child's college education. Simply put a little money down... and then pay attention and learn.

3) The key to this take action step is to TAKE ACTION!

Reading, watching and listening are all crucial to your education. But you must also start "DOING". Make offers on small real estate deals that will generate positive cash flow, join a network marketing company and learn about it from the inside, invest in some stock after researching the company. Seek advice from your mentor, financial or tax advisor if you need it. But as Nike says, "Just Do It!"

CHAPTER 17

STEP 7: *The Power Of Faith*

hat is your deepest fear?

In my senior year of high school, rich dad's son and I were lined up in front of a small group of students made up primarily of the leaders of the senior class. Our guidance counselor said to us, "The two of you will never amount to anything."

There was some snickering from some of the seniors as the guidance counselor continued. "From now on, I am not going to waste any more time on either of you. I am only going to spend my time with these students who are the class leaders. You two are the class clowns with bad grades, and you will never amount to anything. Now get out of here."

BIGGEST FAVOR OF ALL

That counselor did Mike and me the biggest favor of all. While what she said was true in many ways and her words hurt us deeply, her words also inspired both of us to strive even harder. Her words carried us through college and into our own businesses.

HIGH SCHOOL REUNION

A few years ago, Mike and I went back to our high school reunion, always an interesting experience. It was nice to visit with people with whom we had spent three years during a period of time when none of us really knew who we were. It was also interesting to see that most of the so-called senior leaders had not become successful in the years after high school.

I tell this story because Mike and I were not academic whiz kids. We were neither financial geniuses nor athletic stars. For the most part, we were slow-to-average learners and students. We were not leaders in our class. In my opinion, we were not as naturally gifted as our fathers. Yet it was our guidance counselor's stinging words and the snickering from our classmates that gave us the fire to plod along, to learn from our mistakes, and to keep going in both good times and bad times.

Just because you did not do well in school, were not popular, are not good in math, are rich or poor, or have other reasons to sell yourself short – none of it counts in the long run. Those so-called shortcomings only count if you think they count.

For those of you who are considering embarking on your own financial fast track, you may have some doubts about your abilities. All I can say is trust that you have everything you need right now to be successful financially. All it takes to bring out your natural God-given gifts is your desire, determination and a deep faith that you have a genius and a gift that is unique.

LOOK IN THE MIRROR AND LISTEN TO THE WORDS

A mirror reflects back more than just a visual image. A mirror often reflects back our thoughts. How often have we seen people, look in the mirror and say such things as:

"Oh, I look horrible."

"Have I put on that much weight?"

"I'm really getting old."

or

"My, my, my! I am damned good looking. I am God's gift to women."

THOUGHTS ARE REFLECTIONS

As I said, mirrors reflect back much more than just what the eyes see. Mirrors also reflect back our thoughts, often our opinions of ourselves. These thoughts or opinions are much more important than our outwardly appearance.

Many of us have met people who are beautiful on the outside, but inside they think they're ugly. Or people who are greatly loved by others, but they cannot love themselves. Our deepest thoughts are often reflections of our souls. Thoughts are a reflection of our love for ourselves, our egos, our dislike of ourselves, how we treat ourselves, and our overall opinion of ourselves.

MONEY DOES NOT STAY WITH PEOPLE WHO DO NOT TRUST THEMSELVES

Personal truths are often spoken in moments of peak emotions.

After explaining the *CASHFLOW Quadrant* to a class or an individual I give them a moment to decide their next step. First they decide which quadrant they are in, which is easy because it's simply the quadrant that generates the most money for them. Second, I ask them, which quadrant they would like to move to, if they need to move.

They then look at the *Quadrant* and make their choices.

Some people look and say, "I'm happy exactly where I am."

Others say, "I'm not happy with where I am, but I am not willing to change or move at this time."

And then there are people who are unhappy where they are, and know they need to do something immediately. People in this condition often speak most clearly about their personal truths. They use words that reflect their opinions of themselves, words that reflect their soul. And that is why I say, "Personal truths are spoken at moments of peak emotions."

At these moments of truth I often hear:

"I can't do that. I can't move from "S" to "B". Are you crazy? I have a wife and three kids to feed."

"I can't do that. I can't wait five years before I get another paycheck."

"Invest? You want me to lose all my money don't you?"

"I don't have any money to invest."

"I need more information before I do anything."

"I tried that before. It will never work."

"I don't need to know how to read financial statements. I can get by."

"I don't have to worry. I'm still young."

"I'm not smart enough."

"I would do it if I could find the right people to do it with me."

"My husband would never go for it."

"My wife would never understand."

"What would my friends say?"

"I would if I was younger."

"It's too late for me."

"It's not worth it."

"I'm not worth it."

ALL WORDS ARE MIRRORS

Personal truths are spoken at moments of peak emotion. All words are mirrors for they reflect back some insight as to what people think about themselves, even though they may be speaking about someone else.

MY BEST ADVICE

For those of you who are ready to move from one quadrant to another, the most important advice I know to give you is to be very aware of your words. Especially be aware of the words that come from your heart, your stomach, and your soul. If you are going to make a change, you must be aware of the thoughts and words generated by your emotions. If you cannot be aware of when your emotions are doing your thinking, you will never survive the journey. You will hold yourself back. For even if you are talking about somebody else, for example by saying, "My spouse will never understand." You are really saying something more about yourself. You may be using your spouse as an excuse for your own inaction, or you might actually be saying "I don't have the courage or communication skills to convey these new ideas to her." All words are mirrors that provide opportunities for you to look into your soul.

Or you might say,

"I can't stop working and start my own business. I have a mortgage and a family to think about."

You might be saying:

"I'm tired. I don't want to do anything more."

or,

"I really don't want to learn anything more."

These are personal truths.

PERSONAL TRUTHS ARE ALSO PERSONAL LIES

These are truths and they are also lies. If you lie to yourself, I would say the journey will never be completed. So my best advice is to listen to your doubts, fears, and limiting thoughts, and then dig deeper for the deeper truth.

For example saying "I'm tired, I don't want to learn something new" may be a truth but it is also a lie. The real truth may be "If I don't learn something new, I'll be even more tired. And even deeper than that, "The truth is I love learning new things. I would love to learn new things and be excited about life again. Maybe whole new worlds would open to me." Once you can get to that point of the deeper truth, you may find a part of you that is powerful enough to help you change.

OUR JOURNEY

For Kim and me to move forward we first had to be willing to live with the opinions and criticisms we individually had about ourselves. We had to be willing to live with the personal thoughts that kept us small, but not let them stop us. Occasionally the pressure would go to the boiling point and our self-criticisms would flare up and I would blame her for my self doubts and she would blame me for hers. Yet, we both knew before starting out on this journey that the only thing we had to face was ultimately our own personal doubts, criticisms and inadequacies. Our real job as husband and wife, business partners, and soul mates along this journey was to keep reminding each other that each of us was much more powerful than our individual doubts, pettiness, and inadequacies. In that process, we learned to trust ourselves more. The ultimate goal for us was more than to simply get rich it was to learn to be trustworthy with ourselves as well as with money.

Remember the only person that determines the thoughts you choose to believe about yourself is you. So the reward from the journey is not only the freedom that money buys but the trust you gain in yourself... for they really are the same thing. My best advice to you is to prepare daily to be bigger than your smallness. In my opinion, the reason most people stop and turn back from their dreams is because the tiny person found inside each of us beats the person that is bigger.

Even though you may not be good at everything, take time developing what you need to learn and your world will change rapidly. Never run from what you know you need to learn. Face your fears and doubts, and new worlds will open to you.

TAKE ACTION

Believe in yourself and start today!

CHAPTER 18

In Summary

These are the seven steps my wife and I used to move from being homeless to being financially free in a few short years. These seven steps helped us find our own financial fast track and we continue to use them today. I trust they can assist you in charting your own course to financial freedom.

To do that, I recommend being true to yourself. If you are not yet a long-term investor, get yourself there as fast as you can. What does this mean? Sit down and map out a plan to get control of your spending habits. Minimize your debt and liabilities. Live within your means and then increase your means. Find out how much invested per month, for how many months, at a realistic rate of return it will take to reach your goals. Goals such as: At what age do you plan to stop working? How much money per month will you need to live at the standard you desire?

Simply having a long-term plan that reduces your consumer debt while putting away a small amount of money regularly will give you a head start if you start early enough and keep an eye on what you're doing.

At this level, keep it simple. Don't get fancy.

The reason I introduce you to the *CASHFLOW Quadrant*,

the 7 Levels of Investors and my three types of investors is to offer you many glimpses into who you are, what your interests may be, and who you want to ultimately become. I like to believe that anyone can find their own unique path to the financial fast track, regardless of which quadrant they operate from. Yet, it is ultimately up to you to find your own path.

Remember what I said in a previous chapter: "Your boss's job is to give you a job. It's your job to make yourself rich."

Are you ready to stop hauling water buckets and begin building pipelines of cash flow to support you, your family and your lifestyle?

Minding your own business might be difficult and sometimes confusing, especially at first. There is a lot to learn, regardless of how much you know. It is a lifelong process. But the good news is that the hardest part of the process is at the start. Once you make the commitment, life really does get easier and easier. Minding your business is not hard to do. It's just common sense.

The Quick Reference Guide to Wealth

by Alan Jacques*, Inspired by Robert Kiyosaki

	Broke Masses
1. Who	Employees
2. Education	High school or college graduate
3. Major financial goal	To survive until next payday
4. Focus	Salary or hourly wage
5. Cash Flow Management (CFM)	"How much do I have in my wallet?"
6. Definition of an asset	A 6-pack in the fridge
7. Home	Would like to own one
8. Investment vehicles	• Government pension • Lotteries
9. Investment sources	The government
10. Investment systems	• Hope
11. Expected rate of return	Get rich quick
12. Risk	Has no idea how to evaluate
13. What Works	If it doesn't work, keep doing it.
14. Time horizon	Next payday
15. Real Estate	Would like some
16. Most valuable resource	Paycheck
17. Why work?	Work for the weekend
18. Advisors	Broke friends & family
19. Resources	• TV
20. Key indicator event	Savings account with $100 in it
21. Questions & Answers	Don't really understand the distinction
22. Delegation	"If you want it done right, you have to do it yourself."

Alan Jacques is president of a successful consulting company in Canada. He is a great teacher of money, wealth and entrepreneurial business.

Successful Middle Class Investor	Rich
Employees & self-employed	Business owners & investors
• Values education, often college graduate • Attends course & seminars on investing	Values only "street smart" education, often acquired from peers and/or self-learned
To build up a significant net worth by age 55 – 65	Freedom
Net worth	Cash flow
Understands the value of CFM	Understands that CFM is the foundation to all wealth
Anything that has market value	Anything that produces positive cash flow
One of their most important assets	A home is a liability, not an asset
mutual funds blue chip stocks real estate: condos, houses & duplexes	• stocks: IPOs as investors and/or key shareholders • real estate: larger projects • businesses
Invests in financial products created by others	Create products and services to sell to the Middle Class and the masses
dollar cost averaging (DCA) low down real estate systems	• Create their own and/or modify others • Often learn from other rich investors who are their peers
% to 30%	50% to 500%+++
accepts moderate risk	Most investments are low or very low risk
learn what works and keep doing it no matter what	Keep learning and innovate, innovate, innovate
long term	Tailored to each goal and/or investment
buy & hold, waits for it to go up in value	"You make money when you buy, not when you sell."
investments	Time
work for money of which 10 – % goes to investments	Money works so they don't have to
financial planners, accountants	Themselves, each other, coaches, selected professionals
The Millionaire Next Door The Wealthy Barber	• Rich Dad/Poor Dad • The CASHFLOW Quadrant • The CASHFLOW Game • Robert Kiyosaki tape sets
million in net worth	Passive income exceeds expenses
asks questions and seeks the right answer	Knows there are many answers
you can delegate what you don't know."	"If you don't know the fundamentals, you can get slaughtered!"

*Recommended Reading

For Improving Your Financial Intelligence

At the Crest of the Tidal Wave, (Economics) *by Robert Prechter*
Awaken The Giant Within, (Personal Development) *by Anthony Robbins*
Creating Wealth, (Real Estate) *by Robert Allen*
Deals on Wheels, (Real Estate) *by Lonnie Scruggs*
E-Myth, (Business) *by Michael Gerber*
Emotional Intelligence, (Personal Development) *by Daniel Goleman*
God Wants You To Be Rich, (Wealth) *by Paul Zane Pilzer*
The Great Boom Ahead, (Economics) *by Harry S. Dent, Jr.*
How To Make Money in Stocks, (Stocks) *by William J. O'Neil.*
Influence, (Personal Development) *by Robert Cialdini*
Over The Top, (Sales) *by Zig Ziglar*
Rich Dad Poor Dad, (Personal Finance) *by Robert Kiyosaki with Sharon Lechter*
The Sovereign Individual, (Economics)
      by James Dale Davidson and Lord William Rees-Mogg
Stone Soup, (Leadership) *by Marcia Brown*
Trade Your Way To Financial Freedom, (Trading) *by Dr. Van Tharp*
Trading For a Living, (Trading) *by Dr. Alexander Elder*
The Wealth of Nations, (Economics) *by Adam Smith*
Think and Grow Rich, (Wealth) *by Napolean Hill*
Unlimited Wealth, (Wealth) *by Paul Zane Pilzer*
What Works On Wall Street, (Stocks) *by James O'Shaughnessy*
Who Stole the American Dream?,(Network Marketing) *by Burke Hedges*
The Worldly Philosophers, (Economics) *by Robert Heilbronner*

*Audio Tape Sets Recommended

Closing the Sale, (Sales) *by Raymond Aaron*
Goals, Crossing the Goal Line, (Goal Setting) *by Raymond Aaron*
Secrets of the Great Investors, (Investing) *by Knowledge Products*
Power-Talk (Personal Development) *by Anthony Robbins*

*These books and tapes are suggested resources and may be time sensitive. We always recommend
 seeking your own professional, legal, financial and investment advice.

Rich Dad's
GUIDE TO
INVESTING

What the Rich Invest In That the Poor and Middle Class Do Not!

By Robert T. Kiyosaki
with Sharon L. Lechter, C.P.A.

**BUSINESS
PLUS**

NEW YORK   BOSTON

ACKNOWLEDGMENTS

On April 8, 1997, *Rich Dad Poor Dad* was formally launched. We printed a thousand copies, thinking that quantity would last us for at least a year. Over a million copies later, and not a dollar spent on formal advertising, the success of *Rich Dad Poor Dad* and the *CASHFLOW Quadrant* continues to amaze us. Sales have been driven primarily by word of mouth, the best kind of marketing.

Rich Dad's Guide to Investing is a thank you to you for helping make *Rich Dad Poor Dad* and the *CASHFLOW Quadrant* so successful.

We have made many new friends through this success and some of them have contributed to the development of this book. The following are friends, new and old, whom we would like to personally thank for their contribution to this book. If you are not on this list, and you have helped in any way, please pardon our oversight and know that we also thank you.

For both technical and moral support we thank: Diane Kennedy, CPA; Rolf Parta, CPA; Dr. Ann Nevin, Educational Psychologist; Kim Butler, CFP, Frank Crerie, Investment Banker; Rudy Miller, Venture Capitalist; Michael Lechter, Intellectual Property Attorney; Chris Johnson, Securities Attorney; Dr. Van Tharp, Investor Psychologist; Craig Coppola, Commercial Real Estate; Dr. Dolf DeRoos, Investment Real Estate; Bill and Cindy Shopoff, Investment Real Estate; Keith Cunningham, Corporate Restructuring; Wayne and Lynn Morgan, Real Estate Education; Hayden Holland, Trusts; Larry Clark, Real Estate Entrepreneur; Marty Weber, Social Entrepreneur; Tom Weisenborn, Stockbroker; Mike Wolf, Entrepreneur; John Burley, Real Estate Investor; Dr. Paul Johnson, Professor of Business at Thunderbird University; The American School of International Management; Carolita Oliveros, Professor-University of Arizona and Thunderbird; Larry Gutsch, Investor Advisor; Liz Berkenkamp, Investment Advisor; John Milton Fogg, Publishing; Dexter Yager and the Internet Services family; John Addison, Trish Adams, Mortgage Banker; Bruce Whiting, CPA, Australia; Michael Talarico, Real Estate Investor, Australia; Harry Rosenberg CPA, Australia; Dr. Ed Koken, Financial Advisor, Australia; John Hallas, Business Owner, Australia, Dan Osborn, Foreign Exchange Advisor, Australia, Nigel Brunel, Securities Trader, Australia, David Reid, Securities Attorney, Canada, Thomas Allen, Securities Attorney, Canada; Kelvin Dushnisky, General Counsel, Canada; Alan Jacques Business, Canada; Raymond Aaron Business, Canada; Dan Sullivan, Business Canada, Brian Cameron, Securities, Canada; Jannie Tay, Business Investments-Singapore, Patrick Lim, Real Estate Investments-Singapore, Dennis Wee, Real Estate Investments, Singapore; Richard and Veronica Tan, Business, Singapore;

Bellum and Doreen Tan, Business, Singapore; C.K. Teo, Business, Singapore; Nazim Kahn, Attorney, Singapore, K.C. See, Business, Malaysia; Siew Ka Wei, Business, Malaysia; Kevin Stock, Sara Woolard, Joe Sposi, Ron Barry, Loral Langemeier, Mary Painter and Kim Arries.

With great appreciation and in loving memory we acknowledge Cynthia Oti. Cynthia was a Financial Commentator for radio station KSFO-San Francisco, California, a stockbroker, a fellow teacher, and most importantly, a friend. She is truly missed.

Our list would not be complete without thanking the incredible team members we have at CASHFLOW Technologies.

Thank you,

Robert and Kim Kiyosaki   *Sharon Lechter*

Rich Dad's
Guide to Investing

A Father's Advice on Investing

Years ago, I asked my rich dad,
*"What advice would you give
to the average investor?"*

His reply was,
"Don't be average."

The 90/10 Rule of Money

Most of us have heard of the 80/20 rule. In other words, 80% of our success comes from 20% of our efforts. Originated by the Italian economist Vilfredo Pareto in 1897 it is also known as the Principle of Least Effort.

Rich dad agreed with the 80/20 rule for overall success in all areas but money. When it came to money, he believed in the 90/10 rule. Rich dad noticed that 10% of the people had 90% of the money. He pointed out that in the world of movies, 10% of the actors made 90% of the money. He also noticed that 10% of the athletes made 90% of the money as did 10% of the musicians. The same 90/10 rule applies to the world of investing, which is why his advice to investors was "Don't be average." An article in *The Wall Street Journal* recently validated his opinion. It stated that 90% of all corporate shares of stock in America are owned by just 10% of the people.

This book explains how some of the investors in the 10% have gained 90% of the wealth and how you might be able to do the same.

Rich Dad's Guide to Investing

The Introduction

What You Will Learn from Reading this Book

The Securities and Exchange Commission (SEC) of the United States defines an individual as an Accredited Investor if the individual has:

1. $200,000 or more in annual income or
2. $300,000 or more in annual income as a couple, or
3. $1 million or more in net worth.

The SEC established these requirements to protect the average investor from some of the worst and most risky investments in the world. The problem is, these investor requirements also shield the average investor from some of the best investments in the world, which is one reason why rich dad's advice to the average investor was, "Don't be average."

Starting with Nothing

This book begins with me returning from Vietnam in 1973. I had less than a year to go before I was going to be discharged from the Marine Corps. That meant that in less than a year, I was going to have no job, no money, and no assets. So this book begins at a point that many of you may recognize and that is a point of starting with nothing.

Writing this book has been a challenge. I have written and rewritten it four times. The first draft began at the SEC's Accredited Investor Level, the level that begins with a $200,000 minimum annual income. After the book was completed the first time, it was Sharon Lechter, my co-author, who reminded me of rich dad's 90/10 rule of money. She said, "While this book is about the investments that the rich invest in, the reality is less than 10%

of the population in America earn more than $200,000 a year. In fact, I believe it is less than 3% that earns enough to qualify as an Accredited Investor." So the challenge of this book was to write about the investments the rich invest in, investments that begin at the minimum requirement of $200,000 in earnings and still include all readers regardless if they have money to invest or not. That was quite a challenge and why it required writing and rewriting the book four times.

It now begins at the most basic of investor levels and goes to the most sophisticated investor level. Instead of beginning at the Accredited Investor level, the book now begins in 1973 because that is when I had no job, no money, and no assets. A point in life many of us have shared. All I had in 1973 was the dream of someday being very rich and becoming an investor who qualified to invest in the investments of the rich. Investments that few people ever hear about, or that are written about in the financial newspapers, or sold over the counter by investments brokers. This book begins when I had nothing but a dream and my rich dad's guidance to become an investor who could invest in the investments of the rich.

So regardless if you have very little money to invest or have a lot to invest today, and regardless if you know very little about investing or you know a lot about investing, this book should be of interest to you. It is written as simply as possible about a very complex subject. It is written to include anyone interested in becoming a better informed investor regardless of how much money they have.

If this is your first book on investing, and you are concerned that it might be too complicated, please do not be concerned. All Sharon and I ask is that you have a willingness to learn and read this book from the beginning to the end with an open mind. If there are parts of the book that you do not understand, then just read the words but continue on to the end. Even if you do not understand everything, just by reading all the way through to the conclusion of this book, you will know more about the subject of investing than many people who are currently investing in the market. In fact, by reading the entire book, you will know a lot more about investing than many people who are giving investment advice and being paid to give their investment advice. This book begins with the simple and goes into the sophisticated without getting too bogged down in detail and complexity. In many ways, this book starts simple and remains simple although covering some very sophisticated investor strategies. This is a story of a rich man guiding a young man, with pictures and diagrams to help explain the often confusing subject of investing.

The 90/10 Rule of Money

My rich dad appreciated Italian economist, Vilfredo Pareto's discovery of the 80/20 rule, also known as the Principle of Least Effort. Yet when it came to money, rich dad was more aware of the 90/10 rule which meant that 10% of the people always made 90% of the money.

The September 13, 1999, issue of *The Wall Street Journal* ran an article supporting my rich dad's point of view on the 90/10 rule of money. A section of the article read:

> "For all the talk of mutual funds for the masses, of barbers and shoe shine boys giving investment tips, the stock market has remained the privilege of a relatively elite group. Only 43.3% of all households owned any stock in 1997, the most recent year for which data is available, according to New York University economist Edward Wolf. Of those, many portfolios were relatively small. Nearly 90% of all shares were held by the wealthiest 10% of households. The bottom line: That top 10% held 73% of the country's net worth in 1997, up from 68% in 1983."

In other words, even though more people are investing today, the rich continue to get richer. When it comes to stocks, the 90/10 rule of money holds true.

Personally I am concerned because more and more families are counting on their investments to support them in the future. The problem is that while more people are investing very few of them are well educated investors. If or when the market crashes, what will happen to all these new investors? The federal government of the United States insures our savings from catastrophic loss but it does not insure our investments. That is why when I ask my rich dad, "What advice would you give the average investor?" His reply was, "Don't be average."

How Not to Be Average

I became very aware of the subject of investing when I was just 12 years old. Up until that age, the concept of investing was not really in my head. Baseball and football were on my mind but not investing. I had heard the word, but I had not really paid much attention to the word until I saw what the power of investing could do. I remember walking along a small beach with the man I call my rich dad and his son Mike, my best friend. Rich dad was showing his son and me this piece of real estate he had just purchased. Although only 12 years old, I did realize that my rich dad had just purchased one of the most valuable pieces of property in our town. Even though I was young I knew that oceanfront property with a sandy beach in front of it was more valuable than property without a beach on it. My first thought was, "How can Mike's dad afford such an expensive piece of property?" I stood there with the waves washing over my bare feet looking at a man the same age as my real dad, who was making one of the biggest financial investments in his life. I was in awe of how he could afford such a piece of land. I knew that my dad made much more money because he was a highly paid government official with a bigger salary. But I also knew that my real dad could never afford to buy land right on the ocean. So how could Mike's dad afford this land when my dad couldn't? Little did I know that my career as a professional investor had begun the moment I realized the power built into the word "investing."

Some 40 years after that walk on the beach with my rich dad and his son Mike, I now have people asking me many of the same questions I began asking that day. In the investment classes I teach, people are now asking me similar questions I began asking my rich dad questions such as:

1. "How can I invest when I don't have any money?"
2. "I have $10,000 to invest. What would you recommend I invest in?"
3. "Do you recommend investing in real estate, mutual funds, or stocks?"
4. "Can I buy real estate or stocks without any money?"
5. "Doesn't it take money to make money?"
6. "Isn't investing risky?"
7. "How do you get such high returns with low risk?"
8. "Can I invest with you?"

Today more and more people are beginning to realize the power hidden in the word investing. Many want to find out how to acquire that power for themselves. After reading this book, it is my intention that many of these questions will be answered for you and if not answered, it should inspire you to dig further to find the answers that work for you. Over 40 years ago, the most important thing my rich dad did for me was spark my curiosity on this subject of investing. My curiosity was aroused when I realized that my best friend's dad, a man who made less money than my real dad, at least when comparing paycheck to paycheck, could afford to acquire investments that only rich people could afford. I realized that my rich dad had a power my real dad did not have and I wanted to have that power also.

Many people are afraid of this power, stay away from it and many even fall victim to it. Instead of running from the power or condemning it by saying such things as, "The rich exploit the poor," or "Investing is risky," or "I'm not interested in becoming rich," I became curious. It is my curiosity and my desire to acquire this power, also known as knowledge and abilities, that set me off on a life long path of inquiry and learning.

Investing Like a Rich Person

While this book may not give you all the technical answers you may want, the intention is to offer you an insight into how many of the richest self-made individuals made their money and went on to acquire great wealth. Standing on the beach at the age of 12, looking at my rich dad's newly acquired piece of real estate, my mind was opened to a world of possibilities that did not exist in my home. I realized that it was not money that made my rich dad a rich investor. I realized that my rich dad had a thinking pattern that was almost exactly opposite and often contradicted the thinking of my real dad. I realized that I needed to understand the thinking pattern of my rich dad if I wanted to have the same financial power he had. I knew that if I thought like him I would be rich forever. I knew that if I did not think like him, I would never really be rich, regardless of how much money I had. Rich dad had just invested in one of the most expensive pieces of land in our town, and he had no money. I realized that wealth was a way of thinking and not a dollar amount in the bank. It is this thinking pattern of rich investors that Sharon and I want to deliver to you in this book, and why we rewrote the book four times.

Rich Dad's Answer

Standing on the beach 40 years ago, I finally worked up the courage to ask my rich dad, "How can you afford to buy these 10 acres of very expensive oceanfront land, when my dad can't afford it?" Rich dad then put his hand on my shoulder and gave me an answer I have never forgotten. With his arm draped over my shoulder, we turned and began walking down the beach at the water line and he began to warmly explain to me the fundamentals of the way he thought about money and investing. His answer began with, "I can't afford this land either. But my business can." We walked on the beach for an hour that day, rich dad with his son on one side and me on his other side. My investor lessons had begun.

A few years ago, I was teaching a three-day investment course in Sydney, Australia. The first day and a half I spent discussing the ins and outs of building a business. Finally in frustration, a participant raised his hand and said, "I came to learn about investing. Why are you spending so much time on business?"

My reply was, "There are two reasons. Reason number one is because what we ultimately invest in is a business. If you invest in stocks, you are investing in a business. If you buy a piece of real estate, such as an apartment building, that building is also a business. If you buy a bond, you are also investing in a business. In order to be a good investor, you first need to be good at business. Reason number two is the best way to invest is to have your business buy your investments for you. The worst way to invest is to invest as an individual. The average investor knows very little about business and often invests as an individual. That is why I spend so much time on the subject of business in an investment course." And that is why this book will spend some time on how to build a business as well as how to analyze a business. I will also spend time on investing through a business because that is how rich dad taught me to invest. As he said to me 40 years ago, "I can't afford to buy this land either. But my business can." In other words my rich dad's rule was "My business buys my investments. Most people are not rich because they invest as individuals and not as owners of businesses." In this book, you will see why most of the 10% who own 90% of the stocks are owners of businesses and invest through their businesses and how you can do the same."

Later in the course the individual understood why I spent so much time on business. As the course progressed, that individual and the class began to realize that the richest investors in the world do not buy investments, most of the 90/10 investors created their own investments. The reason we have billionaires who are still in their twenties is not because they bought investments. They created investments, called businesses, that millions of people want to buy.

Nearly every day I hear people say, "I have an idea for a new product that will make millions." Unfortunately most of those creative ideas will never be turned into fortunes. The second half of this book will focus on how the 10% turn their ideas into multi-million even multi-billion dollar businesses that other investors invest in. That is why rich dad spent so much time teaching me to build businesses as well as to analyze businesses to invest in. So if you have an idea that you think could make you rich, maybe even help you join the 90/10 club, the second half of this book is for you.

Buy, Hold, and Pray

Over the years rich dad pointed out that investing means different things to different people. Today I often hear people saying such things as:

1. "I just bought 500 shares of XYZ company for $5.00 a share, the price went up to $15.00 and I sold it. I made $5,000 in less than a week."
2. "My husband and I buy old houses, we fix them up and sell them for a profit."
3. "I trade commodity futures."
4. "I have over a million dollars in my retirement account."

5. "Safe as money in the bank."
6. "I have a diversified portfolio."
7. "I'm investing for the long term."

As rich dad said, "Investing means different things to different people." While the above statements reflect different types of investment products and procedures, rich dad did not invest in the same way. He said instead, "Most people are not investors. Most people are speculators or gamblers. Most people have the 'buy, hold, and pray the price goes up mentality.' Most investors live in hopes that the market stays up and live in fear of the market crashing. A true investor makes money regardless if the market is going up or crashing down; they make money regardless if they are winning or losing, and they go both long and short. The average investor does not know how to do that and that is why most investors are average investors who fall into the 90% that make only 10% of the money."

More than Buying, Holding and Praying

Investing meant more to rich dad than buying, holding, and praying. This book will cover such subjects as:

1. The 10 Investor Controls: Many people say that investing is risky. Rich dad said, "Investing is not risky. Being out of control is risky." This book will go into rich dad's 10 investor controls that can reduce risk and increase profits.

2. The 5 phases of rich dad's plan to guide me from having no money to investing with a lot of money. Phase one of rich dad's plan was preparing my mind to become a rich investor. This is a simple yet very important phase for anyone who wants to invest with confidence.

3. The different tax laws for different investors. In book number two, *CASHFLOW Quadrant*, I cover the four different people found in the world of business.

They are:

The E stands for employee. The S stands for Self-employed or small business. The B stands for business owner. The I stands for investor.

The reason rich dad encouraged me to invest from the B quadrant is because the tax laws are better for investing from the B quadrant. Rich dad always said, "The tax laws are not fair; they are written for the rich and by the rich. If you want to be rich, you need to use the same tax laws the rich use." One of the reasons why 10% of the people control most of the wealth is because only 10% know which tax laws to use.

In 1943, the federal government plugged most tax loopholes for all employees. In 1986, the federal government took away the tax loopholes enjoyed by the B quadrant from individuals in the S quadrant, individuals such as doctors, lawyers, accountants, engineers, and architects.

In other words, another reason 10% of the investors make 90% of the money is because only 10% of all investors know how to invest from the four different quadrants in order to gain different tax advantages. The average investor often only invests from one quadrant.

4. Why and how a true investor will make money regardless if the market goes up or crashes down.

5. The difference between Fundamental Investors and Technical Investors.

6. In *CASHFLOW Quadrant*, I went into the six levels of investors. This book starts at the last two levels of investors and further classifies them into the following types of investors:

> The Accredited Investor
> The Qualified Investor
> The Sophisticated Investor
> The Inside Investor
> The Ultimate Investor

By the end of this book, you will know the different skill and education requirements between each different investor.

7. Many people say, "When I make a lot of money, my money problems will be over." What they fail to realize is that having too much money is as big a problem as having not enough money. In this book you will learn the difference between the two kinds of money problems. One problem is the problem of not enough

money. The other problem is the problem of too much money. Few people realize how big a problem having too much money can be.

One of the reasons so many people go broke after making a lot of money, is because they do not know how to handle the problem of too much money.

In this book you will learn how to start with the problem of having not enough money, how to make a lot of money and then how to handle the problem of too much money. In other words, this book will not only teach you how to make a lot of money but more importantly it will teach you how to keep it. As rich dad said, "What good is making a lot of money if you wind up losing it all?"

A stockbroker friend of mine once said to me, "The average investor does not make money in the market. They do not necessarily lose money, they just fail to make money. I have seen so many investors make money one year and give it all back the next year."

8. How to make much more than just $200,000, the minimum income level to begin investing in the investments of the rich. Rich dad said to me, "Money is just a point of view. How can you be rich if you think $200,000 is a lot of money? If you want to be a rich investor, you need to see that $200,000, the minimum dollar amount to qualify as an accredited investor, is just a drop in the bucket." And that is why Phase One of this book is so important.

9. Phase One of this book, which is preparing yourself mentally to be a rich investor, has a short mental quiz for you at the end of each chapter.

Although the quiz questions are simple, they are designed to have you think and maybe discuss your answers with the people you love. It was the soul searching questions my rich dad asked me that helped me find the answers I was looking for. In other words, many of the answers I was looking for, regarding the subject of investing, were really inside of me all along.

What Makes the 90/10 Investor Different?

One of the most important aspects of this book is the mental differences between the average investor and the 90/10 investor. Rich dad often said, "If you want to be rich, just find out what everyone else is doing and do exactly the opposite." As you read this book you will find out that most of the differences between the 10% of investors who make 90% of the money and the 90% that make only 10% of the money is not what they invest in, but that their thinking is different. For example:

1. Most investors say "Don't take risks." The rich investor takes risks.
2. Most investors say "diversify." The rich investor focuses.
3. The average investor tries to minimize debt. The rich investor increases debt in their favor.
4. The average investor tries to decrease expenses. The rich investor knows how to increase expenses to make themselves richer.
5. The average investor has a job. The rich investor creates jobs.
6. The average investor works hard. The rich investor works less and less to make more and more.

The Other Side of the Coin

So an important aspect of reading this book is to notice when your thoughts are often 180 degrees out from the guiding thoughts of my rich dad. Rich dad said, "One of the reasons so few people become rich is because they become set in one way of thinking. They think there is only one way to think or do something. While the average investor thinks 'Play it safe and don't take risks,' the rich investor must also think about how to improve skills so he or she can take more risks." Rich dad called this kind of thinking, "Thinking on both sides of the coin." He went on to say "The rich investor must have more flexible thinking than the average investor. For example, while both the average investor and rich investor must think about safety, the rich investor must also think about how to take more risks. While the average investor thinks about cutting down debt, the rich investor is thinking about how to increase debt. While the average investor lives in fear of market crashes, the rich investor looks forward to market crashes. While this may sound like a contradiction to the average investor, it is this contradiction that makes the rich investor rich."

As you read through this book, be aware of the contradictions in thinking between average investors and rich investors. As rich dad said, "The rich investor is very aware that there are two sides to every coin. The average investor sees only one side. And it is the side the average investor does not see that keeps the average investor average and the rich investor rich." The second part of this book is about the other side of the coin.

Do You Want to Be More than an Average Investor?

This book is much more than just a book about investing, hot tips, and magic formulas. One of the main purposes for writing it is to offer you the opportunity to gain a different point of view on the subject of investing. It begins with me returning from Vietnam in 1973 and preparing myself to begin investing as a rich investor. In 1973, rich dad began teaching me how to acquire the same financial power he possessed, a power I first became aware of at the age of 12. While standing on the sandy beach in front of my rich dad's latest investment 40 years ago, I realized that when it came to the subject of investing, the difference between my rich dad and my poor dad went far deeper than merely how much money each man had to invest. The difference is first found in a person's deep desire to be much more than just an average investor. If you have such a desire, then read on.

FREE!

A Special Audio Report from Robert Kiyosaki
For Readers of *Rich Dad's Guide to Investing* Only

As our way of saying thank you for taking an active role in your financial education, Robert has prepared a special audio report. "My rich dad said that one of the most important investor skills an investor can learn is how to get rich when a market is crashing. When everyone else is panicking and selling, how do you stay calm, stay in the market and make a lot of money?"

Please listen to
"My Rich Dad Said, 'Profit Don't Panic'"

All you have to do to get this audio report is visit our special website at www.richdadbook3.com, and the report is yours free.

Thank you and good luck.

Are You Mentally Prepared to Be an Investor?

Investor Control #1
Control Over Yourself

Chapter 1

What Should I Invest In?

In 1973, I returned home from my tour of Vietnam. I felt fortunate to have been assigned to a base in Hawaii near home rather than to a base on the East Coast. After settling in at the Marine Corps Air Station, I called my friend Mike and we set up a time to have lunch together with his dad, the man I call my rich dad. Mike was anxious to show me his new baby and his new home so we agreed to have lunch at his house the following Saturday. When Mike's limousine came to pick me up at the drab gray base BOQ, the Bachelor Officers' Quarters, I began to realize how much had changed since we had graduated together from high school in 1965.

"Welcome home," Mike said as I walked into the foyer of his beautiful home with marble floors. Mike was beaming from ear to ear as he held his seven-month-old son. "Glad you made it back in one piece."

"So am I," I replied as I looked past Mike at the shimmering blue Pacific Ocean, which touched the white sand in front of his home. The home was spectacular. It was a tropical one-level mansion with all the grace and charm of old and new Hawaiian living. There were beautiful Persian carpets, tall dark green potted plants, and a large pool that was surrounded on three sides by his home, with the ocean on the fourth side. It was very open, breezy, and the model of gracious island living with the finest of detail. The home fit my fantasies of living the luxurious life in Hawaii.

"Meet my son James," said Mike.

"Oh," I said in a startled voice. My jaw must have been hanging open as I had slipped into a trance taking in the stunning beauty of this home. "What a cute kid." I replied as any person should reply when looking at a new baby. But as I stood there waving and making faces at a baby blankly staring back at me, my mind was still in shock at how much had changed in eight years. I was living on a military base in old barracks, sharing a room with three other messy beer-drinking young pilots, while Mike was living in a multi-million-dollar estate with his gorgeous wife and newborn baby.

"Come on in," Mike continued. "Dad and Connie are waiting for us on the patio."

The lunch was spectacular and served by their full-time maid. I sat there enjoying the meal, the scenery, and the company when I thought about my three roommates who were probably dining at the officer's mess hall at that very moment. Since it was Saturday, lunch on the base was probably a sub sandwich and a bowl of soup.

After the pleasantries and catching up on old times was over, rich dad said, "As you can see, Mike has done an excellent job investing the profits from the business. We have made more money in the last two years than I made in the first twenty. There is a lot of truth to the statement that the first million is the hardest."

"So business has been good?" I asked, encouraging further disclosure on how their fortunes had jumped so radically.

"Business is excellent," said rich dad. "These new 747s bring so many tourists from all over the world to Hawaii that business cannot help but keep growing. But our real success is from our investments more than our business. And Mike is in charge of the investments."

"Congratulations," I said to Mike. "Well done."

"Thank you," said Mike. "But I can't take all the credit. It's dad's investment formula that is really working. I'm just doing exactly what he has been teaching us about business and investing for all these years."

"It must be paying off," I said. "I can't believe you live here in the richest neighborhood in the city. Do you remember when we were poor kids, running with our surfboards between houses trying to get to the beach?"

Mike laughed. "Yes I do. And I remember being chased by all those mean old rich guys. Now I'm the mean old rich guy who is chasing those kids away. Who would have ever thought that you and I would be living...?"

Mike suddenly stopped talking once he realized what he was saying. He realized that while he was living here, I was living on the other side of the island in drab military barracks.

"I'm sorry," he said. "I...didn't mean to..."

"No apologies necessary," I said with a grin. "I'm happy for you. I'm glad you're so wealthy and successful. You deserve it because you took the time to learn to run the business. I'll be out of the barracks in a couple of years as soon as my contract with the Marine Corps is done."

Rich dad, sensing the tension between Mike and me, broke in and said, "And he's done a better job than I have. I'm very proud of him. I'm proud of both my son and his wife. They are a great team and have earned everything they have. Now that you're back from the war, it's your turn Robert."

May I Invest With You?

"I'd love to invest with you," I eagerly replied. "I saved nearly $3,000 while I was in Vietnam and I'd like to invest it before I spend it. Can I invest with you?"

"Well, I'll give you the name of a good stockbroker," rich dad said. "I'm sure he'll give you some good advice, maybe even a hot tip or two."

"No, no, no," I said. "I want to invest in what you are investing in. Come on. You know how long I've known you two. I know you've always got something that you're working on or investing in. I don't want to go to a stockbroker. I want to be in a deal with you guys."

The room went silent as I waited for rich dad or Mike to respond. The silence grew into tension.

"Did I say something wrong?" I asked finally.

"No," said Mike. "Dad and I are investing in a couple of new projects that are exciting but I think it is best you call one of our stockbrokers first and begin investing with him."

Again there was silence, punctuated only by the clinking of the dishes and glasses as the maid cleared the table. Mike's wife Connie excused herself and took the baby to another room.

"I don't understand," I said. Turning to rich dad more than Mike, I continued, "All these years I've worked right along side the two of you building your business. I've worked for close to nothing. I went to college as you advised and I fought for my country as you said a young man should. Now that I'm old enough and I finally have a few dollars to invest, you seem to hesitate when I say I want to invest in what you invest in. I don't understand. Why the cold shoulder—are you trying to snub me or push me away? Don't you want me to get rich like you?"

"It's not a cold shoulder," Mike replied. "And we would never snub you or not wish you to attain great wealth. It's that things are different now."

Rich dad nodded his head in slow and silent agreement.

"We'd love to have you invest in what we invest in," rich dad finally said. "But it would be against the law."

"Against the law?" I echoed in loud disbelief. "Are you two doing something illegal?"

"No, no," said rich dad with a chuckle. "We would never do anything illegal. It's too easy to get rich legally to ever risk going to jail for something illegal."

"And it is because we want to always remain on the right side of the law that we say it would be illegal for you to invest with us," said Mike.

"It's not illegal for Mike and me to invest in what we invest in. But it would be illegal for you," rich dad tried to summarize.

"Why?" I asked.

"Because you're not rich," said Mike softly and gently. "What we invest in is for rich people only."

Mike's words went straight through me. Since he was my best friend, I knew they were difficult words for him to say to me. And although he said them as gently as possible, they still hurt and cut like a knife through my heart. I was beginning to sense how wide the financial gap between us was. While his dad and my dad both started out with nothing, he and his dad had achieved great wealth. My dad and I were still from the other side of the tracks, as they say. I could sense that this big house with the lovely white-sand beach was still far away for me, and the distance was measured in more than miles. Leaning back in my chair and crossing my arms in introspective thought, I sat there nodding quietly as I summarized that moment in our lives. We were both 25 years old but in many ways, Mike was 25 years ahead of me financially. My own dad had just been more or less fired from his government job and he was starting over with nothing at age 52. I had not even begun.

"Are you OK?" asked rich dad gently.

"Yeah, I'm OK," I replied, doing my best to hide the hurt that came from feeling sorry for myself and for my family. "I'm just doing some deep thinking and some soul searching," I said, mustering a brave grin.

The room was silent as we listened to the waves and as the cool breeze blew through the beautiful home. Mike, rich dad, and I sat there while I came to terms with the message and its reality.

"So I can't invest with you because I'm not rich," I finally said as I came out of my trance. "And if I did invest in what you invest in, it would be against the law?"

Rich dad and Mike nodded. "In some instances," Mike added.

"And who made this law?" I asked.

"The federal government," Mike replied.

"The SEC," rich dad added.

"The SEC?" I asked. "What is the SEC?"

"The Securities and Exchange Commission," rich dad responded. "It was created in the 1930s under the direction of Joseph Kennedy, father of our late President John Kennedy."

"Why was it created?" I asked.

Rich dad laughed. "It was created to protect the public from wild unscrupulous dealmakers, businessmen, brokers, and investors."

"Why do you laugh?" I asked. "It seems like that would be a good thing to do."

"Yes, it is a very good thing," rich dad replied, still chuckling a little. "Prior to the stock market crash of 1929, many shady, slippery, and shoddy investments were being sold to the public. A lot of lying and misinformation was being put forth. So the SEC was formed to be the watchdog. It is the agency that helps make—as well as enforce—the rules. It serves a very important role. Without the SEC, there would be chaos."

"So why do you laugh?" I persisted.

"Because while it protects the public from the bad investments, it also keeps the public out of the best investments," replied rich dad in a more serious tone.

"So if the SEC protects the public from the worst investments and from the best investments, what does the public invest in?" I asked.

"The sanitized investments," rich dad replied. "The investments that follow the guidelines of the SEC."

"Well, what is wrong with that?" I asked.

"Nothing," said rich dad. "I think it's a good idea. We must have rules and enforce the rules. The SEC does that."

"But why the chuckle?" I asked. "I've known you too many years and I know you are holding back something that is causing you to laugh."

"I've already told you," said rich dad. "I chuckle because in protecting the public from the bad investments, the SEC also protects the public from the best investments."

"Which is one of the reasons the rich get richer?" I asked tenuously.

"You got it," said rich dad. "I chuckle because I see the irony in the big picture. People invest because they want to get rich. But because they're not rich, they're not allowed to invest in the investments that could make them rich. Only if you're rich can you invest in a rich person's investments. And so the rich get richer. To me, that is ironic."

"But why is it done this way?" I asked. "Is it to protect the poor and middle class from the rich?"

"No, not necessarily," Mike responded. "I think it is really to protect the poor and the middle class from themselves."

"Why do you say that?" I asked.

"Because there are many more bad deals than good deals. If a person is not aware, all deals—good and bad—look the same. It takes a great deal of education and experience to sort the more sophisticated investments into good and bad investments. To be sophisticated means you have the ability to know what makes one investment good and the others dangerous. And most people simply do not have that education and experience," said rich dad. "Mike, why don't you bring out the latest deal we are considering?"

Mike left the table for his office and returned with a three-ring binder that was about two inches thick filled with pages, pictures, figures, and maps.

"This is an example of something we would consider investing in," said Mike as he sat down. "It is known as a non-registered security. This particular investment is sometimes called a private placement memorandum."

My mind went numb as Mike flipped though the pages and showed me the graphs, charts, maps, and pages of written text that described the risks and rewards of the investment. I felt drowsy as Mike explained what he was looking at and why he thought it was such a great investment opportunity.

Rich dad, seeing me begin to fade away with the overload of unfamiliar information, stopped Mike and said, "This is what I wanted Robert to see."

Rich dad then pointed to a small paragraph at the front of the book that read "Exemptions from the Securities Act of 1933."

"This is what I want you to understand," he said.

I leaned forward to be better able to read the fine print his finger was pointing to. The fine print said,

"This investment is for accredited investors only. An accredited investor is generally accepted to be someone who:

- has a net worth of $1 million or more; or

- has had an annual income of $200,000 or more in each of the most recent years (or $300,000 jointly with a spouse) and who has a reasonable expectation of reaching the same income level in the current year."

Leaning back in my chair, I said, "This is why you say I cannot invest in what you invest in. This investment is for rich people only."

"Or people with high incomes," said Mike.

"Not only are these guidelines tough, but the minimum amount you can invest in this investment is $35,000. That is how much each investment 'unit,' as it is called, costs."

"$35,000!" I said with a gasp. "That is a lot of money and a lot of risk. You mean that is the least someone can invest in this deal?"

Rich dad nodded. "How much does the government pay you as a Marine Corps pilot?"

"I was earning about $12,000 a year with flight pay and combat pay in Vietnam. I really don't know what my pay will be here now that I am stationed in Hawaii. I might get some COLA, cost of living allowance, but it sure isn't going to be much, and it certainly will not cover the cost of living in Hawaii."

"So for you to have saved $3,000 was quite an accomplishment," said rich dad, doing his best to cheer me up. "You saved nearly 25% of your gross income."

I nodded yet silently I realized how very, very far behind I was from becoming a so-called accredited investor. I realized that even if I became a General in the Marine Corps, I would probably not earn enough money to be considered an accredited investor. Not even the president of the United States, unless he or she were already rich, could qualify on salary alone.

"So what should I do?" I finally asked. "Why can't I just give you my $3,000 and you combine it with your money and we split the profits when the deal pays off?"

"We could do that," said rich dad. "But I wouldn't recommend it. Not for you anyway."

"Why?" I asked. "Why not for me?"

"You already have a pretty good financial education foundation. So you can go way beyond just being an accredited investor. If you want, you could become a sophisticated investor. Then you will find wealth far beyond your wildest dreams."

"Accredited investor? Sophisticated investor? What's the difference?" I asked, actually feeling a spark of renewed hope.

"Good question," Mike said with a smile, sensing that his friend was coming out of a slump.

"An accredited investor is by definition someone who qualifies because he or she has money. That is why an accredited investor is often called a qualified investor," rich dad explained. "But money alone does not qualify you to be a sophisticated investor."

"What is the difference?" I asked.

"Well, did you see the headlines in yesterday's newspaper about the Hollywood movie star who lost millions in an investment scam?" asked rich dad.

I nodded my head saying, "Yes I did. Not only did he lose millions, he had to pay the tax department for untaxed income that went into that deal."

"Well, that is an example of an accredited or qualified investor," rich dad continued. "But just because you have money does not mean you're a sophisticated investor. This is why we often hear of so many high-income people such as doctors, lawyers, rock stars, and professional athletes losing money in less-than-sound investments. They have the money but they lack the sophistication. They have money but don't know how to invest it safely and for high returns. All the deals look the same to them. They can't tell a good investment from a bad one. People like them should stay only in sanitized investments or hire a professional money manager they trust to invest for them."

"So what is your definition of a sophisticated investor?" I asked.

"A sophisticated investor knows the 3-Es," said rich dad.

"The 3-Es," I repeated. "What are the 3-Es?"

Rich dad then turned over the private placement memorandum we were looking at and wrote the following on the back of one of the pages.

1. Education
2. Experience
3. Excessive cash

"Those are the 3-Es," he said, looking up from the page. "Achieve those three items and you will be a sophisticated investor."

Looking at the three items, I said, "So the movie star had excessive cash, but he lacked the first two items."

Rich dad nodded. "And there are many people with the right education but they lack the experience, and without real life experience, they often lack the excessive cash."

"People like that often say, 'I know' when you explain things to them, but they do not do what they know," added Mike. "Our banker always says, 'I know' to what dad and I do, but for some reason, he does not do what he claims he knows."

"And that is why your banker lacks the excessive cash," I said.

Rich dad and Mike nodded.

Again, the room went silent as the conversation ended. All three of us were deep in our own private thoughts. Rich dad signaled the maid for more coffee and Mike began putting the three-ring binder away. I sat with my arms crossed, gazing out upon the deep blue Pacific Ocean at Mike's beautiful home and contemplating my next direction in life. I had finished college as my parents had wished, my military obligation would soon be over, and then I would be free to choose the path that was best for me.

"What are you thinking about?" asked rich dad, sipping from his fresh cup of coffee.

"I'm thinking about what I want to become now that I have grown up," I replied.

"And what is that?" asked Mike.

"I'm thinking that maybe I should become a sophisticated investor," I replied quietly. "Whatever that is."

"That would be a wise choice," said rich dad. You've got a pretty good start, a financial education foundation. Now it's time to get some experience."

"And how will I know when I have enough of both?" I asked.

"When you have excessive cash," smiled rich dad.

With that, the three of us laughed and raised our water glasses, toasting, "To excessive cash."

Rich dad then toasted, "And to being a sophisticated investor."

"To being a sophisticated investor and to excessive cash," I repeated again silently to myself. I liked the ring of those words in my head.

Mike's limousine driver was summoned and I returned to my dingy bachelor officers quarters to think about what I was going to do with the rest of my life. I was an adult and I had fulfilled my parents' expectations... expectations such as getting a college education and serving my country during a time of war. It was now time for me to decide what I wanted to do for myself. The thought of studying to become a sophisticated investor appealed to me. I could continue my education with rich dad as I gained the experience I needed. This time, my rich dad would be guiding me as an adult.

20 Years Later

By 1993, rich dad's wealth was split between his children, grandchildren, and their future children. For the next hundred years or so, his heirs would not have to worry about money. Mike received the primary assets of the business and has done a magnificent job of growing the balance of rich dad's financial empire, a financial empire that rich dad had built from nothing. I had seen it start and grow during my lifetime.

It took me 20 years to achieve what I thought I should have been able to do in 10 years. There is some truth to that saying, "It's the first million that is the hardest."

In retrospect, making $1 million was not that difficult. It's keeping the million and having it work hard for you that I found to be difficult. Nevertheless, I was able to retire in 1994 at the age of 47, financially free with ample money with which to enjoy life.

Yet, it was not retirement that I found exciting. It was finally being able to invest as a sophisticated investor that was exciting. To be able to invest alongside Mike and rich dad was a goal worth achieving. That day back in 1973, when Mike and rich dad said I was not rich enough to invest with them, was a turning point in my life and the day I set the goal to become a sophisticated investor.

The following is a list of some of the investments in which so-called "Accredited Investors and Sophisticated Investors" invest:

1. Private placements
2. Real estate syndication and limited partnerships
3. Pre-initial public offerings (IPOs)
4. IPOs (while available to all investors,
   IPOs are not usually easily accessible)
5. Sub-prime financing
6. Mergers and acquisitions
7. Loans for startups
8. Hedge funds

For the average investor, these investments are too risky, not because the investment itself is necessarily risky, but because all too often, the average investor lacks the education, experience, and excessive capital to know what he or she is getting into. I now tend to side with the SEC that it is better to protect unqualified investors by restricting their access to these types of investments because I made some errors and false steps along the way.

As a sophisticated investor today, I now invest in such ventures. If you know what you're doing, the risk is very low while the potential reward can be huge. Investments such as these are where the rich routinely invest their money.

Although I have taken some losses, the returns on the investments that do well have been spectacular, far exceeding the few losses. A 35% return on capital is normal, but returns of 1,000% and more are occasionally achieved. I would rather invest in these investments because I find them more exciting and more challenging. It's not simply a matter of "Buy me 100 shares of this or sell 100 shares of that." Nor is it "Is the p/e high or is the p/e low?" That is not what being a sophisticated investor is about.

Investing in these investments is about getting very close to the engine of Capitalism. In fact, some of the investments listed are venture capital investments, which for the average investor are far too risky. In reality, the investments are not risky, it's the lack of education, experience, and excessive cash that makes the average investor risky.

This Book is not about investments.
This Book is about the investor.

The Path

This book is not necessarily about investments. This book is about the investor specifically, and the path to becoming a sophisticated investor. It is about you finding your path to acquiring the 3-Es: education, experience, and excessive cash.

Rich Dad Poor Dad is a book about my educational path as a child. *CASHFLOW Quadrant* is *Rich Dad Poor Dad* part II and is my educational path as a young adult between the years 1973 and 1994. This book, *Rich Dad's Guide to Investing*, builds on the lessons from all previous years with my real life experiences and converts the lessons into the 3-E's in order to qualify as a sophisticated investor.

In 1973, I barely had $3,000 to invest and I did not have much education and real-life experience. By 1994, I had become a sophisticated investor.

Over 20 years ago, rich dad said, "Just as there are houses for the rich, the poor, and the middle class, there are investments for each of them. If you want to invest in investments that the rich invest in, you have to be more than rich. You need to become a sophisticated investor, not just a rich person who invests."

The Five Phases of Becoming a Sophisticated Investor

Rich dad broke my development program into five distinct phases, which I have organized into phases, lessons, and chapters. The phases are:

1. Are You Mentally Prepared to Be an Investor?
2. What Type of Investor Do You Want to Become?
3. How Do You Build a Strong Business?
4. Who Is the Sophisticated Investor?
5. Giving It Back.

This book is written as a guide. It will not give you specific answers. The purpose of this book is to help you understand what questions to ask. And if this book does that, it has done its job. Rich dad said, "You cannot teach someone to be a sophisticated investor. But a person can learn to become a sophisticated investor. It's like learning to ride a bicycle. I cannot teach you to ride a bicycle, but you can learn to ride a bicycle. Learning to ride a bicycle requires risk, trial and error, and proper guidance. The same is true with investing. If you do not want to take risks, then you're saying you do not want to learn. And if you do not want to learn, then I cannot teach you."

If you're looking for a book on hot investment tips, or how to get rich quick, or the secret investment formula of the rich, this book is not for you. This book is really about learning more than investing. It is written for people who are students of investing, students who seek their own path to wealth rather than look for the easy road to wealth.

This book is about rich dad's five phases of development, the five phases that he went through and that I am currently going through. If you are a student of great wealth, you may notice while reading this book that rich dad's five phases are the same five phases that the richest business people and investors in the world went through in order to become very, very rich. Bill Gates, founder of Microsoft; Warren Buffet, America's richest investor; and Thomas Edison, founder of General Electric, all went through these five phases. They are the same five phases that the young new millionaires and billionaires of the Internet or the "dot com" generation are currently going through while still in their twenties and thirties. The only difference is that because of the Information Age, these young people went through the same phases faster...and maybe so can you.

Are You Part of the Revolution?

Great wealth, vast fortunes, and mega-rich families were created during the Industrial Revolution. The same is going on today during the Information Revolution.

I find it interesting that today we have self-made multi-millionaires and billionaires who are twenty, thirty, and forty years of age; yet we still have people forty and over having a tough time hanging on to $50,000-a-year jobs. One reason causing this great disparity is the shift from the Industrial Age to the Information Age. When we shifted into the Industrial Age, people like Henry Ford and Thomas Edison became billionaires. Today, shifting into the Information Age, we have Bill Gates, Michael Dell, and the founders of the Internet companies becoming young millionaires and billionaires. These twenty-somethings will soon be passing Bill Gates— who is old at 39—in wealth. That is the power of a shift in ages, the shift from the Industrial Age to the Information Age. It has been said that there is nothing so powerful as an idea whose time has come...and there is nothing so detrimental than someone who is still thinking old ideas.

For you, this book may be about looking at old ideas and possibly finding new ideas for wealth. It may also be about a paradigm shift in your life. It may be about a transition as radical as the shift from the Industrial Age to the Information Age. It may be about you defining a new financial path for your life. It may be about thinking more like a businessperson and investor rather than an employee or a self-employed person.

It took me years to go through the phases, and in fact, I am still going through them. After reading this book, you may consider going through the same five phases or you may decide that this developmental path is not for you. If you decide to embark upon the same path, how fast you choose to go through these five phases of development is up to you. Remember that this book is not about getting rich quickly. The choice to undergo such a personal development and education program begins in phase one...the phase of mental preparation.

Are You Mentally Prepared to Be an Investor?

Rich dad often said, "Money will be anything you want it to be."

What he meant was that money comes from our minds, our thoughts. If a person says, "Money is hard to get," it will probably be hard to get. If a person says, "Oh I'll never be rich," or "It's really hard to get rich," it will probably be true for that person. If a person says, "The only way to get rich is to work hard," then that person will probably work hard. If the person says, "If I had a lot of money, I would put it in the bank because I wouldn't know what to do with it," then it will probably happen just that way. You'd be surprised how many people think and do just that. And if a person says, "Investing is risky," then it is. As rich dad said, "Money will be anything you want it to be."

Rich dad warned me that the mental preparation needed to become a sophisticated investor was probably similar to the mental preparation it would take to climb Mt. Everest, or to prepare for the priesthood. He was kidding, yet he was putting me on notice that such an undertaking was not to be taken lightly. He said to me, "You start as I did. You start without any money. All you have is hope and a dream of attaining great wealth. While many people dream of it, only a few achieve it. Think hard and prepare mentally because you are about to learn to invest in a way that very few people are allowed to invest. You will see the investment world from the inside rather than from the outside. There are far easier paths in life and easier ways to invest. So think it over and be prepared if you decide this is the path for your life."

Chapter 2

Pouring a Foundation of Wealth

Returning to the dingy gray officers' quarters on base that night was very difficult. They had been fine when I left earlier that day, but after spending the afternoon in Mike's new home, the officers' quarters seemed cheap, old, and tired.

As expected, my three roommates were drinking beer and watching a baseball game on television. There were pizza boxes and beer cans everywhere. They did not say much as I passed through the shared living area. They just stared at the TV set. As I retired to my room and closed the door, I felt grateful that we all had private rooms. I had much to think about.

At 25 years of age, I finally realized things that I could not understand as a kid of 9, the age at which I first began working with rich dad. I realized that my rich dad had been working hard for years pouring a solid foundation of wealth. They had started on the poor side of town, living frugally, building businesses, buying real estate, and working on their plan. I now understood that rich dad's plan was to become very wealthy. While Mike and I were in high school, rich dad had made his move by expanding to different islands of the Hawaiian chain, buying businesses and real estate. While Mike and I were in college, he made his big move and became one of the major private investors in businesses in Honolulu and parts of Waikiki. While I was flying for the Marine Corps in Vietnam, his foundation of wealth was set in place. It was a strong and firm foundation.

Now he and his family were enjoying the fruits of their labor. Instead of living in the poorest of neighborhoods on an outer island, they lived in one of the wealthiest neighborhoods in Honolulu. They did not just look rich on the surface as many of the people in that neighborhood did. I knew that Mike and his dad were rich because they allowed me to review their audited financial statements. Not many people were given that privilege.

My real dad, on the other hand, had just lost his job. He had been climbing the ladder in the state government when he fell from grace from the political machine that ran the State of Hawaii. My dad lost everything he had worked to achieve when he ran against his boss for governor and lost. He had been blacklisted from state government and was trying to start over. He had no foundation of wealth. Although he was 52 and I was 25, we were in exactly the same financial position. We had no money. We both had a college education and we could both get another job, but when it came to real assets, we had nothing. That night, lying quietly on my bunk, I knew I had a rare opportunity to choose a direction for my life. I say rare because very few people have the luxury of comparing the life paths of two fathers and then choosing the path that was right for them. It was a choice I did not take lightly.

Investments of the Rich

Although many things ran through my mind that night, I was most intrigued by the idea that there were investments only for the rich, and then there were investments for everyone else. I remembered that when I was a kid working for rich dad, all he talked about was building his businesses. But now that he was rich, all he talked about was his investments...investments for the rich. That day over lunch, he had explained, "The only reason I built businesses was so I could invest in the investments of the rich. The only reason you build a business is so that your business can buy your assets. Without my businesses, I could not afford to invest in the investments of the rich."

Rich dad went on to stress the difference between an employee buying an investment and a business buying an investment. He said, "Most investments are too expensive when you purchase them as an employee. But they are much more affordable if my business buys them for me." I did not know what he meant by that statement, but I knew this distinction was important. I was now curious and anxious to find out what the difference was. Rich dad had studied corporate and tax law and had found ways to make a lot of money using the laws to his advantage. I drifted off that night excited about calling rich dad in the morning and saying softly to myself, "investments of the rich."

The Lessons Resume

I had spent many hours as a child sitting at a table in one of rich dad's restaurants as rich dad discussed the affairs of his business. At these discussions, I would sit and sip my soda, while rich dad talked with his bankers, accountants, attorneys, stockbrokers, real estate brokers, financial planners, and insurance agents. It was the beginning of my business education. Between the ages of 9 and 18, I spent hours listening to these men and women solve intricate business problems. But those lessons around the table ended when I left for four years of college in New York, followed by five years of service with the Marine Corps. Now that my college education was complete and my military duty nearly over, I was ready to continue the lessons with rich dad.

When I called him the next day, he was ready to begin my lessons again. He had turned the businesses over to Mike and was now semi-retired. He was looking for something to do rather than play golf all day.

When I was young, I did not know which dad to listen to when it came to the subject of money. Both were good, hard-working men. Both were strong and charismatic. Both said I should go to college and serve my country in the military. But they did not say the same things about money or give the same advice about what to become when I grew up. Now I could compare the results of the career paths chosen by my rich dad and my poor dad.

In *CASHFLOW Quadrant*, the book that follows *Rich Dad Poor Dad*, my poor dad advised me to "Go to school, get good grades, and then find a safe secure job with benefits." He was recommending a career path in this direction:

On the other hand, my rich dad said, "Learn to build businesses and invest through your businesses." He was recommending a career path that looked like this:

SCHOOL

The *CASHFLOW Quadrant* is about the core emotional differences and the technical differences among the people found in each of the quadrants. These core emotional and technical differences are important because they ultimately determine which quadrant a person tends to favor and operate from. For example, a person who needs job security will most likely seek the E quadrant. In the E quadrant are people from janitors to presidents of companies. A person who needs to do things on his or her own is often found in the S quadrant, the quadrant of the self-employed or small business. I also say that "S" stands for solo and smart, because this is where many of the professionals such as doctors, attorneys, accountants, and other technical consultants are found.

The *CASHFLOW Quadrant* explains a lot about the difference between the S quadrant—which is where most small-business owners operate—and the B quadrant—which is the quadrant where big businesses are found. In this book, we will go into much more detail about the technical differences, because it is here that the differences between the rich and everyone else are found.

The Tax Laws Are Different

The differences between the quadrants play a very important role in this book. The tax laws are different for the different quadrants. What may be legal in one quadrant is illegal in another. These subtle differences make big differences when it comes to the subject of investing. When discussing the subject of investing, my rich dad was very careful to ask me from which quadrant I was planning to earn my money.

The Lessons Begin

While Mike was busy running their empire, rich dad and I were having lunch at a hotel on Waikiki Beach. The sun was warm, the ocean beautiful, the breeze light, and the setting as close to paradise as you can get. Rich dad was shocked to see me walk in wearing my uniform. He had never seen me in uniform before. He had only seen me as a kid, dressed in casual clothes such as shorts, jeans, and T-shirts. I guess he finally realized that I had grown up since leaving high school, and by now had seen a lot of the world and fought in a war. I had worn my uniform to the meeting because I was between flights and had to get back to the base to fly that evening.

"So that is what you have been doing since leaving high school," said rich dad.

I nodded my head and said, "Four years at the military academy in New York, and four years in the Marine Corps. One more year to go."

"I am very proud of you," said rich dad.

"Thanks," I replied. "But it will be nice to get out of a military uniform. It's really tough being spit on or stared at, or called 'baby-killers' by all these hippies and people who are against the war. I just hope it ends soon for all of us."

"I'm just glad Mike did not have to go," said rich dad. "He wanted to enlist but his poor health kept him out."

"He was fortunate," I replied. "I lost enough friends to that war. I would have hated to have lost Mike too."

Rich dad nodded his head and asked, "So what are your plans once your military contract is up next year?"

"Well, three of my friends have been offered jobs with the airlines as pilots. It's tough getting hired right now but they say they can get me in through some contacts they have."

"So you're thinking of flying with the airlines?" asked rich dad.

I nodded slowly. "Well, that's all I've been doing...thinking about it. The pay is OK, and benefits are good. And besides, my flight training has been pretty intense," I said. "I've become a pretty good pilot after flying in combat. If I fly for a year with a small airline and get some multi-engine time, I will be ready for the major carriers."

"So is that what you think you are going to do?" asked rich dad.

"No," I replied. "Not after what has happened to my dad and after having lunch at Mike's new home. I lay awake for hours that night and thought about what you said about investing. I realized that if I took a job with the airlines I might someday become an accredited investor. But I realized that I might never go beyond that level."

Rich dad sat in silence, nodding ever so slightly. "So what I said hit home," rich dad said in a low voice.

"Very much so," I replied. "I reflected on all the lessons you gave me as a kid. Now I am an adult and the lessons have a new meaning to me."

"And what did you remember?" asked rich dad.

"I remember you taking away my 10 cents per hour and making me work for free," I replied. "I remembered that lesson of not becoming addicted to a paycheck."

Rich dad laughed at himself and said, "That was a pretty tough lesson."

"Yes it was," I replied. "But a great lesson. My dad was really angry with you. But now he is the one trying to live without a paycheck. The difference is he's 52 and I was 9 when I got that lesson. After lunch at Mike's, I vowed that I would not spend my life clinging to job security just because I needed a paycheck. That is why I doubt that I will seek a job with the airlines. And that is why I'm here having lunch with you. I want to review your lessons on how to have money work for me, so I don't have to spend my life working for money. But this time, I want your lessons as an adult. Make the lessons harder and give me more detail."

"And what was my first lesson?" asked rich dad.

"The rich don't work for money," I said promptly. "They know how to have money work for them."

A broad smile came over rich dad's face. He knew that I had been listening to him all those years as a kid. "Very good," he said. "And that is the basis of becoming an investor. All investors do is learn how to have their money work hard for them."

"And that is what I want to learn," I said quietly. "I want to learn and maybe teach my dad what you know. He is in a very bad way right now, trying to start over again at the age of 52."

"I know," said rich dad. "I know."

So on a sunny day, with surfers riding the beautiful waves of the deep blue ocean, my lessons on investing began. The lessons came in five phases, each phase taking me to a higher level of understanding... understanding the thought process of rich dad and his investment plan. The lessons began with preparing mentally and taking control of myself...because that is the only place that investing really takes place anyway. Investing ultimately begins and ends with taking control of yourself.

The lessons on investment in Phase One of rich dad's investment plan are all about the mental preparation it takes before actually beginning to invest. Lying in my bunk that night in 1973, in a dingy room on base, my mental preparation had begun. Mike was fortunate enough to have a father who had accumulated great wealth. I was not that fortunate. In many ways, he had a 50-year head start on me. I had yet to start. That night, I began my mental preparation by making a decision between job security as chosen by my poor dad, or pouring a foundation of real wealth as chosen by my rich dad. That is where the process of investing truly begins and where rich dad's lessons on investing start. It starts with a very personal decision...a mental choice to be rich, poor, or middle class. It is an important decision, because whichever financial position in life you choose—be it rich, poor, or middle class—everything in your life then changes.

Chapter 3

Investor Lesson #1:

The Choice

Rich dad's lessons on investing began. "When it comes to money and investing, people have three fundamental reasons or choices for investing. They are:

1. To be secure,
2. To be comfortable, or
3. To be rich."

Rich dad went on to say, "All three choices are important. The difference in one's life occurs when the choices are prioritized." He continued by saying that most people make their money and investment choices in that exact order. In other words, their first choice when it comes to money decisions is security, second is comfort, and third is to be rich. That is why most people make job security their highest priority. After they have a secure job or profession, then they focus on comfort. The last choice for most people is to be rich.

That day in 1973, rich dad said, "Most people dream of becoming rich, but it is not their first choice." He went on to say, "Only three out of a hundred people in America are rich because of this priority of choices. For most people, if becoming rich disturbs their comfort or makes them feel insecure, they will forsake becoming rich. That is why so many people want that one hot investment tip. People who make security and comfort their first and second choices look for ways to get rich quick that are easy, risk free, and comfortable. A few people do get rich on one lucky investment, but all too often they lose it all again."

Rich or Happy

I often hear people say, "I'd rather be happy than be rich." That comment has always sounded very strange to me since I have been both rich and poor. And in both financial positions, I have been both happy and unhappy. I wonder why people think they have to choose between happiness and being rich.

When I reflect upon this lesson, it occurs to me that what people are really saying is that "I'd rather feel secure and comfortable than be rich." That is because if they felt insecure or uncomfortable, they were not happy. For me, I was willing to feel insecure and uncomfortable in order to be rich. I have been rich and poor as well as happy and unhappy. But I assure you that when I was poor and unhappy, I was much unhappier than when I was rich and unhappy.

I have also never understood the statement "Money does not make you happy." While there is some truth in it, I have always noticed that when I have money, I feel pretty good. The other day, I found a $10 bill in my jeans pocket. Even though it was only $10, it felt great finding it. Receiving money has always felt better than receiving a bill for money I owe. At least that is my experience with money. I feel happy when it comes in and sad when it leaves me.

Back in 1973, I put my priorities in this order:
1. To be rich
2. To be comfortable
3. To be secure

As stated earlier, when it comes to money and investing, all three priorities are important. Which order you put them in is a very personal decision that should be made before beginning to invest. My poor dad put "to be secure" as priority one, and rich dad put "to be rich" as priority one. Before beginning to invest, it is important to decide what your priorities are.

Mental Attitude Quiz

To be rich, comfortable, and secure are really personal core values. One is not better than the other. I do know, however, that making the choice of which core values are most important to you often has a significant long-term impact upon the kind of life you choose. That is why it is important to know which core values are most important to you, especially when it comes to the subject of money and financial planning.

So the mental attitude quiz is:

List in order of importance which core values are most important to you:

1. _____

2. _____

3. _____

Some of you may need to work through your true feelings. Talk seriously with your spouse or mentor. Make "pro" and "con" lists. Knowing what your personal priorities are will save you many agonizing decisions and sleepless nights later.

One of the reasons the 90/10 rule of money applies may be because 90% of the people choose comfort and security over being rich.

Chapter 4

Investor Lesson #2:

What Kind of World Do You See?

One of the most startling differences between my rich dad and poor dad was what kind of world they saw. My poor dad always saw a world of financial scarcity. That view was reflected when he said, "Do you think money grows on trees?" or "Do you think I'm made of money?" or "I can't afford it."

When I spent time with my rich dad, I began to realize that he saw a completely different world. He could see a world of too much money. That view was reflected when he said, "Don't worry about money. If we do the right things, there will always be plenty of money," or "Don't let not having money be an excuse for not getting what you want."

In 1973, during one of rich dad's lessons, he said, "There are only two kinds of money problems. One problem is not enough money. The other problem is too much money. Which type of money problem do you want?"

In my classes on investing, I spend a lot of time on this subject. Most people come from families where the money problem was not enough money. Since money is only an idea, if your idea is that there is not enough money, then that is what your reality will be. One of the advantages I had, coming from two families, was that I could see both types of problems...and rest assured, both are problems. My poor dad always had problems of not enough money and my rich dad always had problems of too much money.

Rich dad had a comment on that strange phenomenon. He said, "People who suddenly become rich—by things such as inheritance, a big jackpot from Las Vegas, or the lottery—suddenly become poor again because psychologically, all they know is a world of not enough money. So they lose all their suddenly found wealth and go back to repeating the only world of money they know: a world of not enough money."

One of my personal struggles was shaking the idea that the world was a world of not enough money. From 1973 on, rich dad had me become very aware of my thoughts when it came to the subjects of money, working, and becoming rich. Rich dad truly believed that poor people remained poor simply because that was the only world they knew. Rich dad would say, "Whatever your reality is about money inside of you is the reality of money outside of you. You cannot change your outside reality until you first change your inside reality about money."

Rich dad once outlined what he saw as some of the causes of scarcity as differences in peoples' attitudes:

1. The more security your need, the more scarcity there is in your life.

2. The more competitive you are, the more scarcity in your life. Which is why people compete for jobs and promotions at work and compete for grades in school.

3. To gain more abundance a person needs more skills and needs to be more creative and cooperative. People who are creative, have good financial and business skills, and are cooperative often have lives of increasing financial abundance.

I could see these differences in attitudes between my two dads. My real dad always encouraged me to play it safe and seek security. My rich dad encouraged me to develop skills and be creative. The second half of this book is about how to take your creative ideas and create a world of abundance rather than a world of scarcity.

During our discussions about scarcity rich dad would break out a coin and say, "When a person says 'I can't afford it,' that person sees only one side of the coin. The moment you say 'How can I afford it?,' you begin to see the other side. The problem is, even when people see the other side, they see it with only their eyes. That is why poor people see rich people doing what rich people do on the surface but they fail to see what rich people are doing inside their minds. If you want to see the other side of the coin, you have to see what is going on inside a very rich person's mind." The second half of this book is about what goes on in a rich person's mind.

Years later, when lottery winners began going broke I asked rich dad why this was happening. His reply was, "A person who suddenly comes into a lot of money and goes broke, goes broke because they still see only one side of the coin. In other words they handle the money in the same way they always did, which was the reason they were poor or struggled in the first place. They see only a world of not enough money. The safest thing that person can do is just put the money in the bank and live off the interest only. People who can see the other side of the coin would take that money and multiply it rapidly and safely. They can do that because they see the other side of the coin, the side of the coin where there is a world of too much money and they use their money to get to the other side faster while everyone else uses money to become poorer faster."

In the late 1980's after rich dad retired and turned his empire over to Mike, he called me in for a brief meeting. Before the meeting began he showed me a bank statement with $39 million dollars in cash in it. I gasped as he said, "And this is only in one bank. I am retired now because it is a full time job to keep taking this cash out of my banks and moving it into more productive investments. I repeat it is a full time job that becomes more challenging every year."

As the meeting ended rich dad said, "I spent years training Mike to build the engine that produces this much money. Now that I am retired he is running the engine that I built. The reason I can retire with confidence is because Mike knows not only how to run the engine, he can fix it if it breaks. Most rich kids lose their parents' money because although they grew up in extreme wealth, they never really learned how to build an engine or fix it after it is broken. In fact, too many rich kids are the very people who break the engine. They grew up on the rich side of the coin, but they never learned what it takes to get to that side. You have a chance, with my guidance, to make the transition and stay on the other side."

A big part of taking control of myself was taking control of my internal reality about money. I have had to constantly remind myself that there is a world of too much money, because in my heart and soul, I have often felt like a poor person.

One of the exercises rich dad had me do whenever I felt the surge of panic in my heart and stomach, the panic that comes from the fear of not having enough money, was to simply say, "There are two kinds of money problems. One problem is not enough money and the other is too much money. Which one do I want?" I would ask this question mentally even though my core being was in a state of financial panic.

I am not one of these wishful-thinking people or a person who believes solely in the power of affirmation. I asked myself that question to combat my inherited point of view on money. Once my gut was calmed down, I would then ask my mind to begin finding solutions to whatever was financially challenging me at the time. Solutions could mean seeking new answers, finding new advisors, or attending a class on a subject I was weak on. The main purpose for combating my core panic was to allow me to calm down so I could move forward again.

I have noticed that most people let their panic about money defeat them and dictate the terms and conditions of their lives. Hence, they remain terrified about risk and money. As I wrote in *CASHFLOW Quadrant*, people's emotions often run their lives. Emotions such as fear and doubt lead to low self-esteem and a lack of self-confidence.

In the early 1990s, Donald Trump was nearly $1 billion in debt personally and $9 billion in debt corporately. An interviewer asked Trump if he was worried. Trump replied, "Worrying is a waste of time. Worrying gets in my way of working to solve these problems." I have noticed that one of the main reasons people are not rich is that they worry too much about things that might never happen.

Rich dad's investment lesson #2 was to mentally choose to see both worlds... a world of not enough money and a world of too much money. Later, rich dad went into the importance of a financial plan. Rich dad strongly believed in having a financial plan for when you did not have enough money as well as a financial plan for when you will have too much money. He said, "If you do not have a plan for having too much money, then you will lose all your money and go back to the only plan you know, which is what 90% of the population knows: a world of not enough money."

Security and Scarcity

Rich dad said, "The more a person seeks security the more scarcity they will have in their life. Security and scarcity go hand in hand. That is why people who seek job security or guarantees are often the people with less abundance in their life. One of the reasons the 90/10 rule of money holds true is because most people spend their lives seeking more security instead of seeking more financial skills. The more financial skills you have the more abundance you will have in your life."

It was these financial skills that gave rich dad the power to begin acquiring some of the most valuable real estate in Hawaii even though he had very little money. These same financial skills give people the power to take an opportunity and turn it into millions of dollars. Most people can see opportunities, they just cannot turn that opportunity into money and that is why they often seek even more security. Rich dad also said, "The more a person seeks security, the less they can see of the opportunities that abound. They see only one side of the coin and never see the other side.

That is why the more they seek security the less opportunity they see on the flip side of the coin. As the great baseball player Yogi Bera once said, 'Strike out just 7 out of 10 times and you're in the Hall of Fame.'" In other words, if he came to bat one thousand times in his baseball career, and if he could strike out only 700 times, he would be in the Hall of Fame. After reading Yogi Bera's quote, rich dad said, "Most people are so security conscious that they live their entire lives avoiding striking out just once."

Mental Attitude Quiz

I came from a family that saw the world as a world of not enough money. My personal challenge was to repeatedly remind myself that another kind of world existed and that I needed to keep an open mind to see a world of both possibilities for me.

So the mental attitude questions are:

1. Can you see that two different worlds of money can exist? A world of not enough money and a world of too much money.

    Yes___   No ____

2. If you currently live in a world of not enough money, are you willing to see the possibility of you living in a world of too much money?

    Yes___   No _____

Chapter 5
Investor Lesson #3:

Why Investing Is Confusing

One day, I was waiting in rich dad's office and he was speaking on the phone. He was saying things such as, "So you're long today?" and "If the prime drops, what will that do to the spread?" and "OK, OK, OK, now I understand why you're buying an option straddle to cover that position" and "You're going to short that stock? Why not use a put option instead of a short?"

After rich dad put his phone down, I said, "I have no idea what you were talking about. Investing seems so confusing."

Rich dad smiled and said, "What I was talking about was not really investing."

"It wasn't investing? Then what was it? It sounded like what investors on TV and in the movies sound like."

Rich dad smiled and laughed, saying, "First of all, investing means different things to different people. That is why it seems so confusing. What most people call investing is not really investing. People are all talking about different things yet they often think they are talking about the same thing."

"What?" I said, screwing up my face. "People are talking about different things yet thinking they are talking about the same thing?"

Again rich dad laughed. The lesson had begun.

Investing Means Different Things to Different People

As rich dad began the lesson that day, he repeatedly stressed that main point. Investing means different things to different people. The following are some of the highlights of this important lesson:

Different People Invest in Different Things

1. Rich dad explained some of the differences in value.

    a. Some people invest in large families. A large extended family is a way to ensure care for the parents in their old age.

    b. People invest in a good education, job security, and benefits. The individual and his or her marketable skills become the assets.

    c. Some people invest in external assets. In America, about 45% of the population owns shares in companies. This number is growing as people realize that job security and lifetime employment are less and less guaranteed.

There Are Many Different Investment Products

2. Here is a sample of some of the different types of investments:

    a. Stocks, bonds, mutual funds, real estate, insurance, commodities, savings, collectibles, precious metals, hedge funds, etc.

    b. Each one of these groups can then be broken down into different subgroups. Let's take stocks, for example.

Stocks can be subdivided into:

    1. Common stock
    2. Preferred stock
    3. Stocks with warrants
    4. Small cap stock
    5. Blue chip stock
    6. Convertible stock
    7. Technical stock
    8. Industrial stock
    9. And on and on and on

Real estate can be subdivided into:

    1. Single family
    2. Commercial office
    3. Commercial retail

4. Multi-family

5. Warehouse

6. Industrial

7. Raw land

8. Raw land to the curb

9. And on and on and on

Mutual funds can be subdivided into:

1. Index fund

2. Aggressive growth fund

3. Sector fund

4. Income fund

5. Closed end fund

6. Balanced fund

7. Municipal bond fund

8. Country fund

9. And on and on and on

Insurance can be subdivided into:

1. Whole, Term, Variable Life

2. Universal, Variable Universal

3. Blended (whole and term in one policy)

4. First, second, or last to die

5. Used for Funding Buy-Sell Agreement

6. Used for Executive Bonus and Defferred Compensation

7. Used for Funding Estate taxes

8. Used for Non Qualified retirement benefits

9. And on and on and on

c. There are many different investment products, each designed to do something different. That is another reason why the subject of investing is so confusing.

There Are Different Investment Procedures

3. Rich dad used the word "procedure" to describe the technique, method, or formula for buying, selling, trading, or holding these investment products. The following are some of the different types of investment procedures:

1. Buy, hold, and pray (long)

2. Buy and sell (trade)

3. Sell then buy (short)

4. Option buying and selling (trade)

5. Dollar cost averaging (long)

     6. Brokering (trade no position)

     7. Saving (collecting)

  4. Many investors are classified by their procedures and their products. For example:

     1. I am a stock trader

     2. I speculate in real estate.

     3. I collect rare coins.

     4. I trade commodity future options.

     5. I am a day trader.

     6. I believe in money in the bank.

These are all examples of different types of investors, their product specialties, and their investing procedure. All of this adds to the confusion on the subject of investing because under the banner of investing there are people who are really:

     a. Gamblers

     b. Speculators

     c. Traders

     d. Savers

     e. Dreamers

     f. Losers

Many of these individuals call themselves investors and, technically they are, which is why the subject of investing is even more confusing.

No One Is an Expert at Everything

"Investing means different things to different people." Rich dad also said, "There is no one person who can possibly be an expert at the entire subject. There are many different investment products and many different investment procedures."

Everyone Has a Bias

A person who is good at stocks will say, "Stocks are your best investment." A person who loves real estate will say, "Real estate is the basis of all wealth." Someone who hates gold will say, "Gold is an obsolete commodity."

Then you add procedure bias and you really become confused. Some people say "Diversify. Don't put all your eggs in one basket," and still others such as Warren Buffet, America's greatest investor, says, "Don't diversify. Put all your eggs in one basket and watch that basket closely."

All of this personal bias from so-called experts adds to the confusion that shrouds the subject of investing.

Same Market, Different Directions

Adding to the confusion is that everyone has a different opinion on the direction of the market and the future of the world. If you watch the financial news stations, they will have one so-called expert who says, "The market is over-heated. It will crash in the next six weeks." Ten minutes later, another expert will come on and say, "The market is set to go up even further. There will be no crash."

Late to the Party

A friend of mine recently asked, "Every time I hear of a hot stock, by the time I buy it, the stock is heading down. So I buy at the top because it's the hot popular stock and then a day later it starts heading down. Why am I always late to the party?"

Another complaint I often hear is: "The stock drops in price so I sell it, and the next day it goes up. Why does that happen?"

I call this the "late to the party" phenomenon or the "you sold too early" phenomenon. The problem with investing in something because it's popular or rated as the #1 fund for the past two years is that real investors have already made their money in that investment. They were in it early and got out at the top. For me, nothing is more frustrating than to hear someone say, "I bought it at $2 a share and it's now at $35 a share." Such stories or hot tips do me no good and only frustrate me. That is why today, when I hear such tales of instant wealth and fast money in the market, I just walk away and choose not to listen...because such stories are not really stories about investing.

This Is Why Investing Is Confusing

Rich dad often said, "Investing is confusing because it is a very large subject. If you look around you, you'll see that people have invested in many different things. Look at your appliances. Those are all products from companies that people invested in. You receive your electricity from a utility company that people invest in. Once you understand that, then look at your car, the gas, the tires, seat belts, windshield wipers, spark plugs, the roads, the stripes on the road, your soft drinks, the furniture in your house, the shopping center your favorite store is in, the office buildings, the bank, the hotels, the airplane overhead, the carpet in the airport, etc. All of these things are there because someone invested in the business or building that delivers you the things that make life civilized. That is what investing really is all about."

Rich dad often ended his lessons on investing with this statement: "Investing is such a confusing subject for most people because what most people call investing is not really investing."

In the next chapter, rich dad guides me into reducing the confusion and into what investing really is.

Mental Attittude Quiz

Investing is a vast subject with many different people having as many different opinions:

1. Do you realize that investing means different things to different people?

    Yes_____ No_____

2. Do you realize that no one person can know all there is to know about the subject of investing?

    Yes_____ No_____

3. Do you realize that one person may say an investment is good and another person may say the same investment is bad, and realize both could have valid points?

    Yes_____ No_____

4. Are you willing to keep an open mind to the subject of investing and listen to different points of view on the subject?

    Yes_____ No_____

5. Are you now aware that focusing on specific products and procedures may not necessarily be investing?

    Yes_____ No_____

6. Do you realize that an investment product that is good for one person may not be good for you?

    Yes_____ No_____

Chapter 6
Investor Lesson #4:

Investing Is a Plan, Not a Product or Procedure

I am often asked questions like, "I have $10,000 to invest. What do you recommend I invest in?"

And my standard reply is, "Do you have a plan?"

A few months ago, I was on a radio station in San Francisco. The program was on investing and was hosted by a very popular local stockbroker. A call came in from a listener wanting some investment advice. "I am 42 years old, I have a good job, but I have no money. My mother has a house with a lot of equity in it. Her home is worth about $800,000 and she owes only $100,000 on it. She said she would let me borrow some of the equity out so I could begin investing. What do you think I should invest in? Should it be stocks or real estate?"

Again my reply was, "Do you have a plan?"

"I don't need a plan," was the reply. "I just want you to tell me what to invest in. I want to know if you think the real estate market is better or the stock market."

"I know that is what you want to know...but do you have a plan?" I again asked as politely as possible.

"I told you I don't need a plan," said the caller. "I told you my mother will give me the money. So I have money. That's why I don't need a plan. I'm ready to invest. I just want to know which market you think is better, the stock market or the real estate market. I also want to know how much of my mom's money I should spend on my own home. Prices are going up so fast here in the Bay Area that I don't want to wait any longer."

Deciding to take another tack, I asked, "If you're 42 years old and have a good job, why is that you have no money? And if you lose your mother's equity money from her home, can she continue to afford the home with the added debt? And if you lose your job or the market crashes, can you continue to afford a new house if you can't sell it for what you paid for it?"

To an estimated 400,000 listeners came his answer. "That is none of your business. I thought you were an investor. You don't need to dig into my private life to give me tips on investing. And leave my mother out of this. All I want is investment advice, not personal advice."

Investment Advice Is Personal Advice

One of the most important lessons I learned from my rich dad was that "Investing is a plan, not a product or procedure." He went on to say, "Investing is a very personal plan."

During one of my lessons on investing, he asked, "Do you know why there are so many different types of cars and trucks?"

I thought about the question for a while, finally replying, "I guess because there are so many different types of people and people have different needs. A single person may not need a large nine-passenger station wagon but a family with five kids would need one. And a farmer would rather have a pickup truck than a two-seater sports car."

"That's correct," said rich dad. "And that is why investment products are often called 'investment vehicles.'"

"They're called 'vehicles'?" I repeated. "Why investment vehicles?"

"Because that is all they are," said rich dad. "There are many different investment products, or vehicles, because there are many different people with many different needs, just as a family with five children has different needs than a single person or a farmer."

"But why the word 'vehicles'?" I again asked.

"Because all a vehicle does is get you from point A to point B," said rich dad. "An investment product or vehicle simply takes you from where you are financially to where you want to be, sometime in the future, financially."

"And that is why investing is a plan," I said nodding my head quietly. I was beginning to understand.

"Investing is like planning a trip, let's say from Hawaii to New York. Obviously, you know that for the first leg of your trip, a bicycle or car will not do. That means you will need a boat or a plane to get across the ocean," said rich dad.

"And once I reach land, I can walk, ride a bike, travel by car, train, bus, or fly to New York," I added. "All are different vehicles."

Rich dad nodded his head. "And one is not necessarily better than the other. If you have a lot of time and really want to see the country, then walking or riding a bike would be the best. Not only that, you will be much healthier at the end of the trip. But if you need to be in New York tomorrow, then obviously flying from Hawaii to New York is your best and only choice if you want to make it on time."

"So many people focus on a product, let's say stocks, and then a procedure, let's say trading, but they don't really have a plan. Is that what you are saying?" I asked.

Rich dad nodded. "Most people are trying to make money by what they think is investing. But trading is not investing."

"What is it, if it is not investing?" I asked.

"It's trading," said rich dad. "And trading is a procedure or technique. A person trading stocks is not much different than a person who buys a house, fixes it up, and sells it for a higher profit. One trades stocks; the other trades real estate. It's still trading. In reality, trading is centuries old. Camels carried exotic wares across the desert to consumers in Europe. So a retailer is also a trader in a sense. And trading is a profession. But it is not what I call investing."

"And to you, investing is a plan, a plan to get you from where you are to where you want to be," I said, doing my best to understand rich dad's distinctions.

Rich dad nodded and said, "I know it's picky and seems a minor detail. Yet, I want to do my best to reduce the confusion around this subject of investing. Every day, I meet people who think they're investing, but financially they're going nowhere. They might as well be pushing a wheelbarrow in a circle."

It Takes More Than One Vehicle

In the previous chapter, I listed a few of the different types of investment products and procedures available. More are being created every day because so many people have so many different needs. When people are not clear on their own personal financial plans, all these different products and procedures become over-whelming and confusing.

Rich dad used the wheelbarrow as his vehicle of choice when describing many investors. "Too many so-called investors get attached to one investment product and one investment procedure. For example, a person may invest only in stocks or a person may invest only in real estate. The person becomes attached to the vehicle and then fails to see all the other investment vehicles and procedures available. The person becomes an expert at that one wheelbarrow and pushes it in a circle forever."

One day when he was laughing about investors and their wheelbarrows, I had to ask for further clarification. His response was, "Some people become experts at one type of product and one procedure. That is what I mean by becoming attached to the wheelbarrow. The wheelbarrow works; it hauls a lot of cash around, but it is still a wheelbarrow. A true investor does not become attached to the vehicles or the procedures. A true investor has a plan and has multiple options as to investment vehicles and procedures. All a true investor wants to do is get from point A to point B safely and within a desired time frame. That person doesn't want to own or push the wheelbarrow."

Still confused, I asked for greater clarification. "Look," he said, becoming a little frustrated, "if I want to go from Hawaii to New York, I have a choice of many vehicles. I don't really want to own them. I just want to use them. When I climb on a 747, I don't want to fly it. I don't want to fall in love with it. I just want to get from where I am to where I am going. When I land at Kennedy Airport, I want to use the taxi to get from the airport to my hotel. Once I arrive at the hotel, the porter uses a handcart to move my bags from the curb to the room. I don't want to own or push that handcart."

"So what is the difference?" I asked.

"Many people who think they are investors get attached to the investment vehicle. They think they have to like stocks or like real estate to use them as investment vehicles. So they look for investments they like and fail to put together a plan. These are the investors who wind up traveling in circles, never getting from financial point A to financial point B."

"So you don't necessarily fall in love with the 747 you fly on, just as you don't necessarily fall in love with your stocks, bonds, mutual funds, or office buildings. They are all simply vehicles," I stated, "vehicles to take you to where you want to go."

Rich dad nodded. "I appreciate those vehicles, I trust that people take care of those vehicles, I just don't get attached to the vehicles...nor do I necessarily want to own or spend my time driving them."

"What happens when people get attached to their investment vehicles?" I asked.

"They think that their investment vehicle is the only vehicle, or it is the best vehicle. I know people who invest only in stocks as well as people who invest only in mutual funds or real estate. That is what I mean by getting attached to the wheelbarrow. There is not anything necessarily wrong with that type of thinking. It's just that they often focus on the vehicle rather than their plan. So even though they may make a lot of money buying, holding, and selling investment products, that money may not take them to where they want to go."

"So I need a plan," I said. "And my plan will then determine the different types of investment vehicles I will need."

Rich dad nodded, saying, "In fact, don't invest until you have a plan. Always remember that investing is a plan...not a product or procedure. That is a very important lesson."

Mental Attitude Quiz

Before a person builds a house, he or she usually calls in an architect to draw up the plans. Could you imagine what could happen if someone just called in some people and began to build a house without a plan? Well, that is what happens to many people's financial houses.

Rich dad guided me in writing out financial plans. It was not necessarily an easy process, nor did it make sense at first. But after a while, I became very clear on where I was financially, and where I wanted to go. Once I knew that, the planning process became easier. In other words, for me, the hardest part was figuring out what I wanted. So the mental attitude questions are:

1. Are you willing to invest the time to find out where you are financially today and where you want to be financially, and are you willing to spell out how you plan to get there? In addition, always remember that a plan is not really a plan until it is in writing and you can show it to someone else.

   Yes _____ No _____

2. Are you willing to meet with at least one professional financial advisor and find out how his or her services may help you with your long term investment plans?

   Yes _____ No _____

You may want to meet with two ot three financial advisors just to find out the differences in their approach to financial planning.

Chapter 7
Investor Lesson #5:

Are You Planning to Be Rich or Are You Planning to Be Poor?

"Most people are planning to be poor," said rich dad.

"What?" I replied in disbelief. "Why do you say that and how can you say that?"

"I just listen to what people say," said rich dad. "If you want to see a person's past, present, and future, just listen to his or her words."

The Power of Words

Rich dad's lesson on the power of words was very powerful. He asked, "Have you ever heard someone say, 'It takes money to make money'?"

Standing to get two soft drinks from the refrigerator, I replied, "Yes. I hear it all the time. Why do you ask?"

"Because the idea that it takes money to make money is one of the worst ideas there is. Especially if a person wants more money," said rich dad.

Handing rich dad his soft drink, I said, "I don't understand. You mean it doesn't take money to make money?"

"No," said rich dad, shaking his head. "It does not take money to make money. It takes something available to all of us and is a lot less expensive to obtain than money. In fact, in many cases, what it takes is free."

That statement made me very curious but he would not tell me what it was. Instead, as the lesson on investing ended, he gave me an assignment. "Before we meet again, I want you to invite your dad out to dinner...a long, slow dinner. All through the dinner, I want you to pay careful attention to the specific words he uses. After you hear his words, begin to pay attention to the message his words are sending."

By this time, I was accustomed to rich dad giving me strange assignments, assignments that seemed unrelated to the subject we were discussing or studying. Yet he was a firm believer in experience first and lesson second. So I called my dad and set up a date for dinner at his favorite restaurant.

About a week later, rich dad and I met again. "How was dinner?" he asked.

"Interesting," I replied. "I listened very carefully to his choice of words and the meaning of, or thoughts behind, the words."

"And what did you hear?"

"I heard, 'I'll never be rich,'" I said. "But I've heard that most of my life. In fact, he often said to the family, 'The moment I decided to become a schoolteacher, I knew I'd never be rich.'"

"So you've heard some of the same lines before?" inquired rich dad.

I nodded, saying, "Many times. Over and over again."

"What else have you heard repeatedly?" asked rich dad.

"'Do you think money grows on trees?' 'Do you think I'm made of money?' 'The rich don't care about people like I do.' 'Money is hard to get.' 'I'd rather be happy than be rich,'" I replied.

"Now do you know what I mean when I say you can see people's past, present, and future by listening to their words?" asked rich dad.

Nodding, I said, "And I noticed something else."

"And what was that?" asked rich dad.

"You have the vocabulary of a businessman and an investor. My dad has the vocabulary of a schoolteacher. You use words such as 'capitalization rates,' 'financial leverage,' 'EBIT,' 'producer price index,' 'profits,' and 'cash flow.' He uses words such as 'test scores,' 'grants,' 'grammar,' 'literature,' 'government appropriations,' and 'tenure.'"

Rich dad smiled as he said, "It does not take money to make money. It takes words. The difference between a rich person and a poor person is that person's vocabulary. All a person needs to do to become richer is increase his or her financial vocabulary. And the best news is, most words are free."

During the 1980s, I spent much time teaching entrepreneurship and investing. During that time, I became acutely aware of people's vocabulary and how their words related to their financial well-being. Upon further research, I found out that there are approximately 2 million words in the English language. The average person has command of approximately 5,000 words. If people want to begin increasing their financial success, it begins with increasing their vocabulary in a certain subject. For example, when I was investing in small real estate deals such as single-family rental properties, my vocabulary increased in that subject area. When I shifted to investing in private companies, my vocabulary had to increase before I felt comfortable investing in such companies.

In school, lawyers learn the vocabulary of law, medical doctors learn the vocabulary of medicine, and teachers learn the vocabulary of teachers. If a person leaves school without learning the vocabulary of investing, finance, money, accounting, corporate law, taxation, it is difficult to feel comfortable as an investor.

One reason I created the educational board game *CASHFLOW* was to familiarize non-investors with the vocabulary of investing. In all our games, the players quickly learn the relationships behind the words of accounting, business, and investing. By repeatedly playing the games, the players learn the true definition of such misused words as "asset" and "liability."

Rich dad often said, "More than not knowing the definitions of words, using the wrong definition to a word is what really causes long-term financial problems. Nothing is more destructive to a person's financial stability than to call a 'liability' an 'asset.'" That is why he was a stickler for the definition of financial words. He would say, the word "mortgage" comes from "mortir," French for "death." So a mortgage is "an engagement until death." "Real estate" does not mean "real" in English. Real estate really comes from the Spanish words meaning royal estate. That is why to this day, we do not own our property. We only technically control our real estate. We do not really own it. The government owns our property and taxes us to use it.

And that is why rich dad would often say, "It does not take money to make money. It takes a rich person's vocabulary to make money and more importantly, keep money."

So as you read this book, please be aware of the different words that may be used. And always remember that one of the fundamental differences between a rich person and a poor person is his or her words...and words are free.

Planning to Be Poor

After this lesson with rich dad, by simply listening to others' words, I began to notice why most people are unconsciously planning to be poor. Today, I often hear people say, "When I retire, my income will go down." And it does.

They also often say, "My needs will go down after I retire, so that is why I will need less income." But what they often fail to realize is that while some expenses do go down, other expenses go up. And often these expenses—such as full-time nursing home care when they are very old, if they are lucky enough to become very old—are large. An average nursing home for the elderly can cost $5,000 a month. That is more than many people's monthly incomes today.

Other people say, "I don't need to plan. I have a retirement and medical plan from my work." The problem with such thinking is that there is more to an investment plan than simply investments and money. A financial plan is important before someone begins to invest because it needs to take into consideration many different financial needs. These needs include college education, retirement, medical costs, and long-term health care. Many of these often-large and pressing needs can be provided for by investing in products other than stocks and bonds or real estate, such as insurance products and different investment vehicles.

The Future

I write about money to help educate people to provide for their long-term financial well-being. Ever since the advent of Information Age retirement plans, which are 401Ks in America and Superannuation plans in Australia and Registered Retirement Savings Plans (RRSP) in Canada, I have grown concerned about the people who are not prepared for the Information Age. At least in the Industrial Age a company and the government did provide some financial aid for a person after his or her working days were over. Today, when a person's 401K or "cash balance retirement plan" (which isn't a traditional pension) is drained dry, it will be the individual's problem, not the company's.

It is imperative that our schools begin to teach young people to invest for their long-term health and financial well-being. If we do not, we will have a massive socioeconomic time bomb on our hands.

I often say to my classes, "Be sure you have a plan. First, ask yourself if you are planning to be rich or if you are planning to be poor. If you are planning to be poor, the older you get, the more difficult you will find the financial world." Rich dad said to me many years ago, "The trouble with being young is that you don't know what it feels like to be old. If you knew what being old felt like, you would plan your financial life differently."

Planning for Being Old

It is important to plan as early in life as possible. When I say this to my classes, most of my students nod in agreement. No one disagrees on the importance of planning. The problem is, very few people actually do it.

Realizing that most people agreed that they needed to write a financial plan, but few were going to take the time to do it, I decided to do something about it. About an hour before lunch in one of these classes, I found some cotton clothesline and cut it into different lengths. I asked the students to take one piece of line and tie each end around one of their ankles, much like one would hobble a horse. With their ankles tied about a foot apart, I gave them another piece of the line and had them loop it around their neck and tie it back down at their ankles. The overall result was that they were hobbled at the ankles and instead of standing erect, they stooped over at about a 45-degree angle.

One of the students asked if this was a new form of Chinese water torture. "No," I replied. "I'm just taking each of you into the future, if you're lucky to live so long. The ropes now represent what old age could feel like."

A slow moan came from the class. A few were getting the picture. The hotel staff then brought in lunch on long tables. The lunch consisted of sandwiches, salad, and beverages. The problem was, the cold cuts were simply stacked, the bread was not sliced, the salad was not made, and the beverages were the dry mix type that had to be combined with water. The students, now stooped and aged, had to prepare their own lunch. For the next two hours, they struggled to slice their bread, stack their sandwiches, make their salads, mix their drinks, sit, eat, and clean up. Naturally, many also needed to go to the rest room during these two hours.

At the end of the two hours, I asked them if they wanted to take a few moments to write out a financial plan for their life. The answer was an enthusiastic "Yes." It was interesting to observe them actively taking an interest in what they planned to do once the ropes came off. Their interest in planning had increased dramatically once their point of view on life had been changed.

As rich dad said, "The problem with being young is that you don't know what it feels like to be old. If you knew what being old felt like, you would plan your financial life differently." He also said, "The problem with many people is that they plan only up to retirement. Planning to retirement is not enough. You need to plan far beyond retirement. In fact, if you're rich, you should plan for at least three generations beyond you. If you don't, the money could be gone soon after you're gone. Besides, if you don't have a plan for your money before you depart this earth, the government does."

Mental Attitude Quiz

Many times, we do not pay close attention to our silent and seemingly unimportant thoughts. Rich dad said, "It's not what we say out loud that determines our lives. It's what we whisper to ourselves that has the most power."

So the mental attitude questions are:

1. Are you planning to be rich or are you planning to be poor?

Rich_____ Poor_____

2. Are you willing to pay more attention to your deep, often silent, thoughts?

Yes_____ No_____

3. Are you willing to invest time to increase your financial vocabulary? A first goal of learning one new financial word a week is doable. Simply find a word, look it up in the dictionary, find more than one definition for the word, and make a mental note to use the word in a sentence that week.

Yes_____ No_____

Rich dad was a stickler for words. He often said, "Words form thoughts, thoughts form realities, and realities become life. The primary difference between a rich person and a poor person is the words he or she uses. If you want to change a person's external reality, you need to first change that person's internal reality. That is done through first changing, improving, or updating the words he or she uses. If you want to change people's lives, first change their words. And the good news is, words are free."

Getting Rich Is Automatic...If You Have a Good Plan and Stick to It

My friend Tom is an excellent stockbroker. He often says, "The sad thing is that nine out of ten investors do not make money." Tom goes on to explain that while these nine out of ten investors do not lose money, they just fail to make money.

Rich dad said a similar thing to me: "Most people who consider themselves investors make money one day and then give it back a week later. So they do not lose money, they simply fail to make money. Yet they consider themselves investors."

Years ago, rich dad explained to me that much of what people think is investing is really the Hollywood version of investing. The average person often has mental images of floor traders shouting buy/sell orders at the start of the trading day, or images of tycoons making millions of dollars in a single trade, or images of stock prices plummeting and investors diving out of tall office buildings. To rich dad, that was not investing.

I remember watching a program where Warren Buffet was being interviewed. During the course of the interview, I heard him say, "The only reason I go to the market is to see if someone is about to do something silly." Buffet went on to explain that he did not watch the pundits on TV or watch the ups and downs of share prices to gain his investing advice. In fact, his investing was actually done far away from all the noise and promotion of stock promoters and people who make money from so-called investment news.

Investing Is Not What Most People Think

Years ago, rich dad explained to me that investing was not what most people thought it was. He said, "Many people think investing is this exciting process where there is a lot of drama. Many people think investing involves a lot of risk, luck, timing, and hot tips. Some realize they know little about this mysterious subject of investing, so they entrust their faith and money to someone they hope knows more than they do. Many other so-called investors want to prove they know more than other people...so they invest, hoping to prove that they can outsmart the market. But while many people think this is investing, it is not what investing is to me. To me, investing is a plan, often a dull, boring, and almost mechanical process of getting rich."

When I heard rich dad make that statement, I repeated it back to him several times. "Investing is a plan, often a dull, boring, and almost mechanical process of getting rich?" I asked. "What do you mean by a dull, boring, and almost mechanical process of getting rich?"

"That is exactly what I said and what I mean," said rich dad. "Investing is simply a plan, made up of formulas and strategies, a system for getting rich...almost guaranteed."

"A plan that guarantees that you get rich?" I asked.

"I said almost guarantees," repeated rich dad. "There is always some risk."

"You mean investing doesn't have to be risky, dangerous, and exciting?" I asked hesitantly.

"That's correct," rich dad answered. "Unless, of course, you want it to be that way or you think that is the way investing has to be. But for me, investing is as simple and boring as following a recipe to bake bread. Personally, I hate risk. I just want to be rich. So I'll simply follow the plan, the recipe, or the formula. That is all investing is to me."

"So if investing is simply a matter of following a recipe, then how come so many people don't follow the same formula?" I asked.

"I don't know," said rich dad. "I've often asked myself the same question.   I've also wondered why only three out of every hundred Americans is rich. How can so few people become rich in a country that was founded on the idea that each of us has the opportunity to become rich? I wanted to be rich. I had no money. So to me, it was just common sense to find a plan or recipe to be rich and follow it. Why try and make up your own plan when someone else has already shown you the way?"

"I don't know," I said. "I guess I did not know that it was a recipe."

Rich dad continued. "I now realize why it is so hard for most people to follow a simple plan."

"And why is that?" I asked.

"Because following a simple plan to become rich is boring," said rich dad. "Human beings are quickly bored and want to find something more exciting and amusing. That is why only three out of a hundred people become rich. They start following a plan, and soon they are bored. So they stop following the plan and then they look for a magic way to get rich quick. They repeat the process of boredom, amusement, and boredom again for the rest of their lives. That is why they do not get rich. They cannot stand the boredom of following a simple, uncomplicated plan to get rich. Most people think there is some magic to getting rich through investing. Or they think that if it is not complicated, it cannot be a good plan. Trust me; when it comes to investing, simple is better than complex."

"And where did you find your formula?" I asked.

"Playing *Monopoly*," said rich dad. "Most of us have played *Monopoly* as children. The difference is, I did not stop playing the game once I grew up. Do you remember that years ago, I would play *Monopoly* by the hours with you and Mike?"

I nodded.

"And do you remember the formula for tremendous wealth that this simple game teaches?"

Again I nodded.

"And what is that simple formula and strategy?" asked rich dad.

"Buy four green houses. Then exchange the four green houses for a red hotel," I said quietly as my childhood memories came rushing back. "You told us over and over again while you were poor and just starting out that playing *Monopoly* in real life was what you were doing."

"And I did," said rich dad. "Do you remember me taking you to see my green houses and red hotels in real life?"

"I do," I replied. "I remember how impressed I was that you actually played the game in real life. I was only 12 years old, but I knew that for you, *Monopoly* was more than a game. I just didn't realize that this simple game was teaching you a strategy, a recipe, or a formula to become rich. I did not see it that way."

"Once I learned the formula, the process of buying four green houses and then exchanging them for one red hotel, the formula became automatic. I could do it in my sleep, and many times, it seemed like I did. I did it automatically without much thinking. I just followed the plan for ten years, and one day I woke up and realized I was rich."

"Was that the only part of your plan?" I asked.

"No, it wasn't. But that strategy was one of the simple formulas I followed. To me, if the formula is complex, it is not worth following. If you can't do it automatically after you learn it, you shouldn't follow it. That is how automatic investing and getting rich is, if you have a simple strategy and follow it."

A Great Book for People Who Think Investing Is Difficult

In my investment classes, there is always the cynic or doubter to the idea that investing is a simple and boring process of following a plan. This type of person always wants more facts, more data, more proof from smart people. Since I am not a technical specialist, I did not have the scholarly proof that these types of individuals demanded—that is, until I read a great book on investing.

James P. O'Shaughnessy wrote the perfect book for people who think that investing has to be risky, complex, and dangerous. It is also the perfect book for those who want to think that they can outsmart the market. This book has the academic and numerical proof that a passive or mechanical system of investing will in most cases beat a human system of investing...even professional investors such as fund managers. This book also explains why nine out of ten investors do not make money.

O'Shaughnessy's best-selling book is titled *What Works On Wall Street: A Guide to the Best Performing Investment Strategies of All Time.* O'Shaughnessy distinguishes between two basic types of decision-making:

1. The clinical or intuitive method. This method relies on knowledge, experience, and common sense.
2. The quantitative or actuarial method. This method relies solely on proven relationships based on large samples of data.

O'Shaughnessy found that most investors prefer the intuitive method of investment decision-making. In most instances, the investor who used the intuitive method was wrong or beaten by the nearly mechanical method. He quotes David Faust, author of *The Limits of Scientific Reasoning*, who writes, "Human judgment is far more limited than we think."

O'Shaughnessy also writes, "All (speaking of money managers) of them think they have superior insights, intelligence, and ability to pick winning stocks, yet 80 percent are routinely out performed by the S&P 500 index." In other words, a purely mechanical method of picking stocks out performs 80 percent of the professional stock pickers. That means, even if you knew nothing about stock picking, you could beat most of the so-called well-trained and educated professionals if you followed a purely mechanical, non-intuitive method of investing. It is exactly as rich dad said: "It's automatic." Or, the less you think, the more money you make with less risk and with a lot less worry.

Other interesting ideas that O'Shaughnessy's book points out are:

1. Most investors prefer personal experience to simple basic facts or base rates. Again, they prefer intuition to reality.

2. Most investors prefer complex rather than simple formulas. There seems to be this idea that if the formula is not complex and difficult, it can't be a good formula.

3. Keeping it simple is the best rule for investing. He states that instead of keeping things simple, "We make things complex, follow the crowd, fall in love with the story of a stock, let our emotions dictate decisions, buy and sell on tips and hunches, and approach each investment on a case-by-case basis, with no underlying consistency or strategy."

4. He also states that professional institutional investors tend to make the same mistakes that average investors make. O'Shaughnessy writes, "Institutional investors say they make decisions objectively and unemotionally, but they don't." Here's a quotation from the book *Fortune and Folly*: "While institutional investors' desks are cluttered with in-depth analytical reports, the majority of pension executives select outside managers based on gut feelings and keep managers with consistently poor performance simply because they have good personal relationships with them."

5. "The path to achieving investment success is to study long-term results and find a strategy or group of strategies that make sense. Then stay on the path." He also states, "We must look at how well strategies, not stocks, perform."

6. History does repeat itself. Yet people want to believe that this time, things will be different. He writes, "People want to believe that the present is different from the past. Markets are now computerized, block traders dominate, individual investors are gone, and in their

place sit money managers controlling huge mutual funds to which they have given their money. Some people think these masters of money make decisions differently, and believe that a strategy perfected in the 1950s and 1960s offers little insight into how it will perform in the future."

But not much has changed since Sir Isaac Newton, a brilliant man indeed, lost a fortune in the South Sea Trading Company bubble of 1720. Newton lamented that he could "calculate the motions of heavenly bodies but not the madness of men."

7. O'Shaughnessy was not necessarily saying to invest in the S&P 500. He simply used that example as a comparison between intuitive human investors and a mechanical formula. He went on to say that investing in the S&P 500 was not necessarily the best performing formula, although it was a good one. He explained that in the last five to ten years, large cap stocks have done the best. Yet over the past 46 years of data, it was actually small cap stocks, companies of less than $25 million in capitalization, that have made the investor the most money.

The lesson was, the longer period of time for which you had data, the better your judgment. He looked for the formula that performed the best over the longest amount of time.

Rich dad had a similar view. That is why his formula was to build businesses and have his businesses buy his real estate as well as his paper assets. That formula has been a winning formula for wealth for at least 200 years. Rich dad said, "The formula I use, and the formula I am teaching you, is the formula that has created the richest individuals over a long period of time."

Many people think the Indians who sold Manhattan Island, a.k.a. New York City, to Peter Minuit of the Dutch West India Company for $24 in beads and trinkets got a bad deal. Yet if the Indians had invested that money for an 8 percent annual return, that $24 would be worth over $27 trillion today. They could buy Manhattan back and have plenty of money left over. The problem was not the amount of money but the lack of a plan for their money.

8. "There is a chasm of difference between what we think might work and what really works."

Find a Formula That Works and Follow It

So rich dad's simple message to me years ago was: "Find a formula that will make you rich and follow it." I am often disturbed when people come up to me and start telling me about the stock they bought for $5 and how it went up to $30 and they sold it. I find myself disturbed because those kinds of stories distract from their plan, their success.

Such stories of hot tips and quick cash often remind me of a story rich dad told me. He said, "Many investors are like a family taking a drive in the country. Suddenly, on the road ahead of them appear several large deer with massive horns. The driver, usually the male of the household, shouts, 'Look at the big bucks.' The bucks instinctively bolt from the road and onto the farmland alongside the road. The driver veers the car off the road and begins chasing the big bucks across the farm and into the trees. The ride is rough and bumpy. The family is screaming for the driver to stop. Suddenly, the car goes over a stream embankment and crashes into the water below. The moral of the story is that this is what happens when you stop following your simple plan and begin chasing the big bucks."

Mental Attitude Quiz

Whenever I hear someone say to me, "It takes money to make money," I cringe. I cringe because my rich dad said, "You don't have to be a rocket scientist to be rich. You don't need a college education, a high-paying job, or any money at all to start. All you have to do is know what you want, have a plan, and stick to it." In other words, all it takes is a little discipline. The problem when it comes to money, however, is a little discipline is often a rare commodity.

O'Shaughnessy highlights one of my favorite quotations. It comes from the famous cartoon character Pogo, who said, "We've met the enemy, and he is us." That statement is very true for me. I'd be a lot better off financially if I had simply listened to rich dad and just followed my formula.

So the mental attitude question is:

1. Are you ready to find a simple formula as part of your plan and stick to it until you reach your financial goal?

Yes_____ No _____

How Can You Find The Plan That Is Right for You?

"How do I find the plan that is right for me?" is a question I am asked often.

My standard answer is that it comes in steps:

1. Take your time. Think quietly about your life up to this point. Take days to think quietly. Take weeks if you need to.

2. Ask yourself in these moments of quiet, "What do I want from this gift called my life?"

3. Don't talk to anyone else for a while, at least until you are certain you know what you think you want. All too often, people either innocently or aggressively want to impose what they want for you instead of what you want for yourself. The biggest killers of deep inner dreams are your friends and family members who say, "Oh don't be silly," or "You can't do that," or "What about me?

Remember Bill Gates was in his 20s when he started with $50,000 and became the richest man in the world with $90 billion. It's a good thing he did not ask too many people for their ideas on what they thought was possible for his life.

4. Call a financial advisor. All investment plans begin with a financial plan. If you do not like what the financial advisor says, find another one. You would ask for a second opinion for a medical problem, so why not ask for many opinions for financial challenges? Financial advisors come in many forms; a reference list is provided later in this chapter. Choose an advisor equipped to assist you in developing a written financial plan.

Many financial advisors sell different types of products. One such product is insurance. Insurance is a very important product and needs to be considered as part of your financial plan, especially when you are first starting out. For example, if you have no money but have three children, insurance is important in case you die, are injured, or for whatever reason are unable to complete your investment plan. Insurance is a safety net, or a hedge against financial liabilities and weak spots. Also, as you become rich, the role of insurance and type of insurance in your financial plan may change as your financial position and needs change. So keep that part of your plan up to date.

Two years ago, a tenant in one of my apartment buildings left his Christmas tree lights on and went out for the day. A fire broke out. Immediately, the fire crews were there to put out the fire. I was never so grateful to a bunch of men and women. The next people on the scene were my insurance agent and his assistant. They were the second most important group of people I was grateful to see that day.

Rich dad always said, "Insurance is a very important product in anyone's life plan. The trouble with insurance is that you can never buy it when you need it. So you have to anticipate what you need and buy it hoping you'll never need it. Insurance is simply peace of mind."

IMPORTANT NOTE: Some financial advisors specialize in helping people at different financial levels. In other words, some advisors work only with rich people. Regardless of whether or not you have money, find an advisor you like and who is willing to work with you. If your advisor has done a good job, you may find yourself outgrowing your advisor. My wife Kim and I have often changed our professional advisors, which include doctors, attorneys, accountants, etc. If the person is professional, he or she will understand. But even if you change advisors, be sure you stick to your plan.

So How Do You Find Your Plan?

I had a goal of being a multi-millionaire before I was 30 years old. That was the end result of my plan. The problem was, I made it and then immediately lost all my money. So while I found out that there were flaws in my plan, my overall plan did not change. After losing my money after reaching my goal, I simply needed to refine my plan by what I had learned from that experience. I then had to reset my goal, which was to be financially free and a millionaire by age 45. It took me to age 47 to reach the new goal.

The point is, my plan remains the same. It just gets improved upon as I learn more and more.

So how do you find your own plan? The answer is to begin with a financial advisor. Ask the advisors to provide their qualifications to you and interview several. If you have never had a financial plan done for you, it is an eye-opening experience for most people.

Set realistic goals. I set a goal of becoming a multi-millionaire in five years because it was realistic for me. It was realistic because I had my rich dad guiding me. Yet, even though he guided me, it did not mean I was free from making mistakes...and I made many of them, which is why I lost my money so quickly. As I said, life would have been easier if I had just followed rich dad's plan. Being young, however, I had to do things my way.

So start with realistic goals, and then improve upon or add to the goals as your education and experience increase. Always remember that it is best to start by walking before you begin to run in a marathon.

You find your own plan first by taking action. Begin by calling an advisor, set realistic goals, knowing the goals will change as you change...but stick to the plan. For most people, the ultimate plan is to find a sense of financial freedom, freedom from the day-to-day drudgery of working for money.

The second step is to realize that investing is a team sport. In this book, I will go into the importance of my financial team. I have noticed that too many people think they need to do things on their own. Well, there are definitely things you need to do on your own, but sometimes you need a team. Financial intelligence helps you know when to do things on your own and when to ask for help.

When it comes to money, many people often suffer alone and in silence. Chances are, their parents did the same thing. As your plan evolves, you will begin to meet the new members of your team, which will assist you in helping make your financial dreams come true. Members of your financial team may include:

1. Financial planner
2. Banker
3. Accountant
4. Lawyer
5. Broker
6. Bookkeeper
7. Insurance agent
8. Successful mentor

You may want to hold meetings over lunch with all these people on a regular basis. That is what rich dad did, and it was at these meetings that I learned the most about business, investing, and the process of becoming very rich.

Remember, that finding a team member is much like finding a business partner, because that is what team members are in many ways. They are partners in minding the most important business of all—the business of your life. Always remember what rich dad said: "Regardless of if you work for someone else or for yourself, if you want to be rich, you've got to mind your own business." And in minding your own business, the plan that works best for you will slowly appear. So take your time, yet keep taking one step a day and you will have a good chance of getting everything you want in your life.

Mental Attitude Quiz

My plan has not really changed, yet in many ways, it has changed dramatically. What has not changed about my plan is where I started and what I ultimately want for my life. Through many of the mistakes, the learning experiences, the wins, the losses, the highs, and the lows, I have grown up and gained knowledge and wisdom along the way. Therefore, my plan is constantly under revision because I am under revision.

As someone once said, "Life is a cruel teacher. It punishes you first, and then gives you the lesson." Yet like it or not, that is the process of true learning. Most of us have said, "If I knew back then what I knew today, life would be different." Well, for me, that is exactly what has happened as I traveled along my plan. So my plan is basically the same, yet it is very different since I am different. I would not do today what I did 20 years ago. However, if I had not done what I did 20 years ago, I would not be where I am and know what I know today. For example, I would not run my business today the way I ran my business 20 years ago. Yet, it was losing my first major business and digging myself out from under the rubble and wreckage that helped me become a better businessperson. So although I did reach my goal of becoming a millionaire by age 30, it was losing the money that made me a millionaire today...all according to plan. It just took a little longer than I wanted.

And when it comes to investing, I learned more from my bad investments, investments where I lost money, than I learned from the investments that went smoothly. My rich dad said, if I have ten investments, three of them will go smoothly and be financial home runs. Five will probably be dogs and do nothing, and two would be disasters. Yet, I would learn more from the two financial disasters than I would from the three home runs...In fact, those two disasters are what make it easier to hit the home runs the next time I am up to bat. And that is all part of the plan.

So the mental attitude question is:

1. Are you willing to start with a simple plan, keep the plan simple, but keep learning and improving as the plan reveals to you what you need to learn along the way? In other words, the plan doesn't really change, but are you willing to allow the plan to change you?

       Yes____ No ____

Decide Now What You Want to Be When You Grow Up

In Investor Lesson #1, which was the importance of choice, there were three financial core value choices offered. They were:

1. To be secure
2. To be comfortable
3. To be rich

These are very important personal choices and should not be taken lightly.

In 1973, when I returned from the Vietnam War, I was faced with these choices. When rich dad discussed my option of taking a job with the airlines as a pilot, he said, "A job with the airlines may not be that secure. I suspect that they will be having a rough time in the next few years. Yet, if you keep your record clean, you might find job security in that profession...if that is what you really want."

He then asked me if I wanted to get my job back with Standard Oil of California, a job I held for only five months...the five months before I went to flight school for the Marine Corps. "Didn't you receive a letter saying that Standard Oil would take you back as an employee once your military duty was over?"

"They said they would be happy to have me reapply," I replied. "But they guaranteed nothing."

"But wouldn't that be a good company to work for? Wasn't the pay pretty good?" asked rich dad.

"Very good," I said. "It was an excellent company to work for, but I don't want to go back. I want to move on."

"And what do you want most?" asked rich dad as he pointed to the three choices. "Do you want security, comfort, or to be rich the most?"

From deep inside me, the answer was a loud "To be rich." It had not changed in years, although that desire and core value was pushed down quite a bit in my family, a family where job and financial security was the highest priority and rich people were considered evil, uneducated, and greedy. I grew up in a family where money was not discussed at the table because it was an unclean subject, a subject not worthy of intellectual discussion. But now that I was 25 years old, I could let my personal truth out. I knew the priority of core values of security and comfort were not first on my list. To be rich was core value number one for me.

My rich dad then had me list my core financial priorities. My list went in this order:

1. To be rich
2. To be comfortable
3. To be secure

Rich dad looked at my list and said, "OK. Step one is to write out a financial plan to be financially secure."

"What?" I asked. "I just told you I wanted to be rich. Why should I bother with a plan to be secure?"

Rich dad laughed. "Just as I thought," he said. "The world is filled with guys like you who only want to be rich. The problem is, most guys like you don't make it because you don't understand being secure, or being comfortable financially. While a few people like you do make it, the reality is, the road to wealth is littered with wrecked lives...wrecked lives of reckless people...people just like you."

I sat there ready to scream. All my life, I had lived with my poor dad, a man who valued security above all. Now, I'm finally old enough to be outside of my poor dad's values and now my rich dad is saying the same thing. I was ready to scream. I was ready to get rich, not be secure.

It was three weeks before I could talk to rich dad again. I was very upset. Everything I had done my best to get away from he put back in my face. Finally I calmed down and called him for another lesson.

"Are you ready to listen?" rich dad asked when we met again.

I nodded, saying, "I'm ready but not really willing."

"Step one," rich dad started. "Call my financial advisor. Say, 'I want a written financial plan for lifetime financial security.'"

"OK," I said.

"Step two," said rich dad. "After you have a written plan for basic financial security, call me and we'll go over it. Lesson is over. Goodbye."

It was a month before I called him. I had my plan and I showed it to him. "Good" was all he said. "Are you going to follow it?"

"I don't think so," I said. "It's just too boring and automatic."

"That is what it is supposed to be," said rich dad. "It's supposed to be mechanical, automatic, and boring. But I can't make you follow it, although I do recommend you do."

I was calming down as I said, "Now what?"

"Now you find your own advisor and you write a plan on how to be financially comfortable," said rich dad.

"You mean a long-term financial plan that is little bit more aggressive?" I asked.

"That is correct," said rich dad.

"That is more exciting," I said. "That one I can get into."

"Good," said rich dad. "Call me when you have that one ready."

It was four months before I could meet with rich dad again. This plan was not that easy...or as easy as I thought it would be. I checked in by phone with rich dad every so often, but the plan was still taking longer than I wanted. Yet the process was extremely valuable because I learned a tremendous amount talking to different financial advisors. I was gaining a better understanding of the concepts rich dad was trying to teach me. The lesson I learned was that unless I am clear, it is hard for the advisor to be clear and able to help me.

Finally, I was able to meet with rich dad and show him my plan. "Good" was all he said for a while. He sat there looking at the plan and then asked, "So what did you learn about yourself?"

"I learned that it is not that easy to really define what it is I want from my life because today we have so many choices...and so many of them look exciting."

"Very good," he said. "And that is why so many people today go from job to job or from business to business...but never really get to where they want to go financially. So they often spend their most precious asset, their time, and wander through life without much of a plan. They might be happy doing what they are doing, but they really do not know what they are missing out on."

"Exactly," I agreed. "This time, instead of just being secure, I really had to think what I wanted to do with my life...and surprisingly, I had to explore ideas that would never have occurred to me before."

"Like what?" asked rich dad.

"Well, if I really wanted to be comfortable with my life, then I had to think about what I wanted to have in my life. Things like travel to far away lands, fancy cars, expensive vacations, nice clothes, big houses, etc. I really had to expand my thoughts into the future and find out what I wanted for my life."

"And what did you find out?" asked rich dad.

"I found out that security was so easy because I was planning on being secure only. I did not know what true comfort meant. So security was easy, defining comfort was more difficult, and I now cannot wait to define what rich means and how I plan to achieve great wealth."

"That's good," said rich dad. "Very good." He then continued on by saying, "So many people have been conditioned to 'live below their means' or 'save for a rainy day' that they never know what could be possible for their lives. So people splurge, get into debt by taking the annual vacation or buying a nice car, then feel guilty. They never take the time to figure out what could be financially possible if only they had a good financial plan...and that is a waste."

"That is exactly what happened," I said. "By meeting with advisors and discussing what was possible, I learned a lot. I learned that I was really selling myself short. In fact, I felt like I have been walking in a house with a low ceiling for years, trying to scrimp, save, be secure, and live below my means. Now that I have a plan of what is possible relative to being comfortable, I am now excited about defining what the word 'rich' means."

"Good," said rich dad with a smile. "The key to staying young is to decide what you want to be when you grow up, and then keep growing up. Nothing is more tragic than to see people who have sold themselves short on what is possible for their lives. They try to live frugally, scrimping and saving, and they think that is being financially smart. In reality, it is financially limiting...and it shows up in their faces and in their attitude in life the older they get. Most people spend their lives mentally caged in financial ignorance. They begin to look like wild lions trapped in small cages at the zoo. They just pace back and forth wondering what happened to the life they once knew. One of the most important discoveries people can make by taking the time to learn how to plan is to find out what is financially possible for their lives...and that is priceless.

"The continual planning process also keeps me young. I am often asked why I spend my time building more businesses, investing, and making more money. The reason is I feel good doing it. While I make a lot of money doing what I do, I do it because making money keeps me young and alive. You wouldn't ask a great painter to stop painting once he or she was successful, so why should I stop building businesses, investing, and making more money? That is what I do, just as painting is what artists do to keep their spirits young and alive, even though the body ages."

"So the reason you asked me to take the time to plan at different levels is for me to find out what is financially possible for my life?" I asked.

"That's it," said rich dad. "That is why you want to plan. The more you find out what might be possible for this tremendous gift called life, the younger at heart you remain. People who plan only for security or who say, 'My income will go down when I retire' are planning for a life of less, not a life of more. If our maker has created a life of unlimited abundance, why should you plan on limiting yourself to having less?"

"Maybe that is what they were taught to think," I said.

"And that is tragic," rich dad replied. "Very tragic."

As rich dad and I sat there, my mind and heart drifted to my poor dad. I knew he was hurting and struggling to start his life over again. Many times I had sat down with him and attempted to show him a few of the things I knew about money. However, we usually got into an argument. I think there is often that kind of breakdown in communication when two parties communicate from two different core values, one of security and the other of being rich. As much as I loved my dad, the subject of money, wealth, and abundance was not a subject we could communicate about. Finally, I decided to let him live his life and I would focus on living mine. If he ever wanted to know about money, I would let him ask, rather than trying to help when my help had not been requested. He never asked. Instead of trying to help him financially, I decided to just love him for his strengths and not get into what I thought were his weaknesses. After all, love and respect are far more important than money.

Mental Attitude Quiz

In retrospect, my real dad had a plan only for financial security via job security. The problem was that his plan failed when he ran for public office against his boss. He failed to update his plan and continued to plan only for security. Luckily, he did have his financial security needs covered by a teacher's pension, Social Security, and Medicare. If not for those safety nets, he would have been in very bad financial shape. The reality was that he planned for a world of scarcity, a world of bare minimum survival, and that is what he got. My rich dad, on the other hand, planned for a world of financial abundance, and that is what he achieved.

Both lifestyles require planning. Sadly, most people plan for a world of not enough, although a parallel world of financial plenty is also possible. All it requires is a plan.

So the mental attitude question is:

Do you have a written financial plan to be:

1. Secure?   Yes_____ No_____

2. Comfortable?   Yes_____ No_____

3. Rich?   Yes_____ No_____

Please remember rich dad's lesson that all three plans are important. But security and comfort still come before being rich, even though being rich may be your first choice. The point is that if you want to be rich, you will need all three plans. To be comfortable, you need only two plans. And to be secure, you need only one plan. Remember that only three out of every hundred Americans are rich. Most fail to have more than one plan. Many don't have any kind of written financial plan at all.

Chapter 11
Investor Lesson #9:

Each Plan
Has a Price

"What is the difference between the plan to be rich and the other two core values?" I asked.

Rich dad turned to his yellow legal tablet and wrote down the following words:

1. To be secure
2. To be comfortable
3. To be rich

"You mean the difference between rich and secure and comfortable?"

"That's what I am asking," I responded.

"The difference is the price," said rich dad. "There is a tremendous price difference between a financial plan to be rich and the other two positions."

"You mean the investments in the rich financial plan cost more money?" I asked.

"Well, to most people, it looks like the price is measured in terms of money. But if you look closer, you'll see that the price is not measured in money; it is really measured in time. And of the assets of time and money, time is really the more precious asset."

A scowl came over my face as I tried to comprehend what rich dad was saying. "What do you mean the price is measured in time? Give me an example."

"Sure," said rich dad. "If I wanted to go from LA to New York, how much would a bus ticket cost?"

"I don't know. I'd guess under $100," I replied. "I've never purchased a bus ticket from LA to New York."

"Neither have I," said rich dad. "Now tell me how much a ticket by a 747 jetliner from LA to New York would cost."

"Again, I don't really know. But I guess it would be around $500," I replied.

"That's close enough," said rich dad. "Now let me ask you. Why the difference in price? You're traveling from LA to New York in both instances. Why would you pay so much more for a ticket on a jet airliner?"

"Oh, I got it," I said as I began to understand what rich dad was getting at. "I pay more for the jet airliner ticket because I am saving time."

"Think of it more like buying time than saving time. The moment you begin to think of time as precious and that it has a price, the richer you will become."

I sat thinking silently. I really was not getting what rich dad was talking about...yet I knew that it was important to him. I wanted to say something but I did not know what to say. I did understand the idea that time was precious but I never really thought of it as having a price. And the idea of buying time rather than saving time was important to rich dad, but it was not important to me yet.

Finally, sensing my mental struggle, rich dad broke the silence by saying, "I'll bet in your family you use the words 'save' or 'saving' a lot. I'll bet your mom often says she goes shopping and tries to save money. And your dad thinks that how much money he has in savings is important."

"Yes they do," I replied. "So what does that mean to you?"

"Well they may work hard at trying to save but they waste a lot of time. I've seen shoppers in grocery stores spend hours trying to save a few dollars," said rich dad. "They may save money but they waste a lot of time."

"But isn't saving important?" I asked. "Can't you get rich by saving?"

"I'm not saying that saving is not important," rich dad continued. "And yes you can become rich by saving. All I am saying is that the price is really measured in time."

Again I scrunched up my face, struggling with what he was saying.

"Look," said rich dad. "You can get rich by saving and you can become rich by being cheap, but it takes a heck of a long time, just as you can go from LA to New York by bus so you can save some money. However, your real price will be measured in time. In other words, it takes five hours by jet for $500 or it can take up to five days by bus for $100. Poor people measure in money and rich people measure in time. That may be why there are more poor people who ride buses."

"Because they have more time than money?" I asked. "That is why they ride the bus?"

"That is part of it," said rich dad, shaking his head, indicating that he was not happy with the way our conversation was going.

"Because they value money more than time?" I asked, guessing in the dark.

"Closer," said rich dad. "I have noticed that the less money a person has the harder that person clings to it. I have met a lot of poor people with a lot of money."

"Poor people with a lot of money?" I asked.

"Yes," said rich dad. "They have a lot of money because they cling to money like it has some magical value. So they have a lot of money but are just as poor as if they had no money."

"So poor people often cling to money more than rich people?" I asked.

"I think of money as only a medium of exchange. In reality, money by itself has very little value. So as soon as I have money, I want to exchange it for something of value. The irony is that for many people who cling desperately to money, the money they spend for things of very little value...is why they are poor. They say things like 'safe as money in the bank,' and when they do spend their hard-earned money, they turn their cash into trash."

"So they value money more than you do," I said.

"Yes," said rich dad. "In many cases, the poor and middle class struggle because they place far too much importance on money itself. So they cling to it, work hard for it, work hard at living frugally, shop at sales, and do their best to save as much of it as they can. Many of these people try to get rich by being cheap. But at the end of the day, you may have a lot of money, but you're still cheap."

"I don't understand," I replied. "You're talking about the values my mom and dad tried to instill in us. You're talking about the way I currently think. I'm in the Marine Corps, and they don't pay much money so I find myself naturally thinking that way."

"I understand," rich dad replied. "Thrift and frugality have their place. But today we are talking about the difference between the plan to be rich and the other two plans."

"And the difference is the price," I restated.

"Yes," said rich dad. "And most people think the price is measured in money."

"And what you're saying is that the price is measured in time," I added, beginning to understand what rich dad was getting at. "Because time is more important than money."

Nodding, rich dad said, "Many people want to get rich, or invest in the investments the rich invest in, but most are not willing to invest the time. That is why only three out of a hundred Americans are rich—and one of those three inherited that money."

Rich dad again wrote on his yellow legal tablet the three core values we had been discussing:

1. To be secure
2. To be comfortable
3. To be rich

"You can invest to be secure and comfortable using an automatic system or plan. In fact, I recommend that for most people. Simply work and turn your money over to professional managers or institutions and invest for the long term. People who invest in this manner will probably do better than the individual who thinks he or she is the Tarzan of Wall Street. A steady program of putting money away following a plan is the best way to invest for most people."

"But if I want to be rich, I have to invest in something more valuable than money, and that is time. Is this what you've been getting at with this lesson?"

"I wanted to make sure you understood the lesson," said rich dad. "You see, most people want to be rich but they are not willing to first invest the time. They operate on hot tips or wild get-rich-quick schemes. Or they want to start a business so they rush out and start a business without the basic skills of business. And then we wonder why 95% of all small businesses fail in the first five to ten years."

"They are in such a hurry to make money, they eventually lose both time and money," I added. "They want to do things on their own rather than invest in a little study."

"Or follow a simple long-term plan," rich dad repeated. "You see, almost anyone in the Western world can easily become a millionaire if he or she simply follows a long-term plan. But again, most people aren't willing to invest the time; they want to get rich now."

"Instead they say things like 'investing is risky' or 'it takes money to make money' or 'I don't have the time to learn to invest. I'm too busy working and I have bills to pay,'" I added as I began to understand rich dad's point.

Rich dad nodded. "And those very common ideas or excuses are why so few people achieve great wealth in a world that is filled with money.

Those ideas or words are why 90% of the population has the problem of having not enough money rather than the problem of too much money. Their ideas about money and investing cause their money problems. All they have to do is change a few words, a few ideas, and their financial world will change like magic. But most people are too busy working and they do not have the time. Many often say, "I'm not interested in learning to invest. It is a subject that does not interest me." Yet they fail to see that by saying that, they become slaves to money, working for money, having money dictate the financial boundaries of their lives, living frugally and within their means, instead of investing a little time, following a plan, and having money work for them."

"So time is more important than money," I said.

"That is true for me," said rich dad. "So if you want to move on to the rich level of investing, you are going to have to invest much more time than you do at the other two levels. Most people do not go beyond secure and comfortable because they are not willing to invest the time. That is a personal decision we all need to make. At least the person has a financial plan to be secure and/or comfortable. There is nothing more high risk than a person who does not have those two basic plans, who is focused only on becoming rich. While a few make it, most don't. You see them in the later years of their lives, broke, spent, and talking about the deal they almost made or the money they once had. At the end of their lives, they have neither time nor money. "

"So I think it is time I begin to invest more time, especially since I want to invest at the rich level," I said, shuddering at the thought of being a broke and broken old man, muttering in my beer about the deals that almost happened. I had already seen and met such investors. It is not pretty to see a person who is out of both time and money.

Mental Attitude Quiz

Investing at the secure level and the comfortable level should be as mechanical or as formulated as possible. They should be "no-brainers." All you do is turn your money over to professional—and hopefully reputable—managers, and all they do is follow your plan. If you start early and if the stars shine on you, at the end of the rainbow should be the pot of gold. Investing can—and should be—that simple, at these two fundamental levels.

There is a word of caution, however. There is no such thing in life as risk free. There are lower-risk things, and that is so for investing. So, if you feel uncertain about the fate of the financial world and don't trust the people or the industry, then you have much more research to do.

It is important to be true to your emotions and instinct but don't let them run your entire life. So if you cannot shake this nervousness, then invest with greater caution...but always remember the price: the more secure an investment, the more time it takes to make money...if it makes money. So there is always a tradeoff, or as they say, "There is no such thing as a free lunch." Everything has a price, and in the investment world, that price is measured in both time and money.

Once your investment plans of being financially secure and/or comfortable are in place and on track, then you are better able to speculate on that hot stock tip you heard from a friend. Speculating in the world of financial products is fun, yet it should be done responsibly. There are many so-called investors in the markets who are really addicts with a gambling problem.

When people ask me questions such as "What stocks are you investing in?" I have to say, "I don't pick stocks. Professional money managers do that for me. "

They then often say, "I thought you were a professional investor."

And I reply, "I am. But I do not invest in the ways that most people invest. I invest how my rich dad taught me to invest."

I personally and actively invest in the rich level of investing. Very few people invest or play the game of investing at this level. The remainder of this book is dedicated to that level of investing, which my rich dad taught me. It is not a method for everyone...especially if you do not already have the secure and comfort levels already in place.

So the mental attitude questions are:

1. Are you willing to set in place an investment plan to cover your financial needs to be secure and/or comfortable?

    Yes _____ No _____

2. Are you willing to invest the time to learn to invest at the rich level, the level of my rich dad?

    Yes _____ No _____

If you are not sure of your answer and want to find out what level of commitment rich dad's investment in study requires, the rest of the book will give you some insights as to what it takes to invest at the rich level.

Why Investing Isn't Risky

People say, "investing is risky" for three main reasons:

1. They have not been trained to be investors. If you read
   CASHFLOW Quadrant, the sequel to *Rich Dad Poor Dad,*
   you will recall that most people go to school to be trained
   for the left side of the Quadrant rather than the right side
   of the Quadrant.

2. Secondly, most investors lack control or are out of control. My rich dad used this example: He would say, "There is risk driving a car. But driving the car with your hands off the steering wheel is really risky." He then said, "When it comes to investing, most people are driving with their hands off the steering wheel." Phase One of this book is taking control of yourself before investing. If you didn't have a plan, a little discipline, and some determination, the other investor controls would not mean much. The rest of this book will go into the remainder of rich dad's ten investor controls.

3. Thirdly, people say investing is risky because most people invest from the outside rather than from the inside. Most of us know intuitively that if you want a real deal, you have to be on the inside. You often hear someone say, "I have a friend in the business." It does not matter what the business is. It could be to buy a car, tickets to a play, or a new dress. We all know that on the inside is where the deals are made. The investment world is no different. As Gordon Gekko, the villainous character played by Michael Douglas in the movie *Wall Street*, said, "If you're not on the inside, you're outside."

We will review this relationship between being on the outside or inside later. What is interesting to note at this time is that people on the left side of the Quadrant usually invest from the outside. In contrast, Bs and Is are able to invest from the inside as well as the outside.

An Important Note

As this book progresses, many sacred money cows may be slaughtered. Inside investing is one of them. In the real world, there is legal inside investing and there is illegal inside investing. That is an important distinction. What makes the news is the illegal insider investing. Yet, there is more legal insider investing in the real world that does not make the news, and that is the type of inside investing I am talking about.

A hot tip from a taxi driver is in many ways an insider tip. The real question in insider investing is really: "How close to the inside are you?"

Rich Dad's Plan

When rich dad listed the three core financial values, which are:

    1. To be secure,
    2. To be comfortable and
    3. To be rich,

he said, "It makes perfect sense to invest from the outside when you invest at the secure and the comfortable level of investing. That is why you turn your money over to a professional you hope is closer to the inside than you. But if you want to be rich, you have to be closer to the inside than the professional to whom most people entrust their money."

And that was the focus of rich dad's plan to be rich. That is what he did and that was why he was so rich. To follow his plan, I needed the education and experiences found on the right side of the quadrant, not the left. To do that, I needed to invest a lot more time than the average investor...and that is what the rest of this book is really about. This book is about what it takes to move from the outside to the inside.

Before You Decide

I realize that many people do not want to invest that much time into the subject of investing just to get to the inside. But before you decide, and before getting into a little more detail about rich dad's plan, I thought I would give you a very simplified overview of the subject of investing. Hopefully, after reading the next few chapters, you may learn a few new ways to reduce your investment risk to become more successful as an investor, even if you do not want to be an inside investor. As I said earlier, investing is a very personal subject, and I completely respect that reality. I know that many people do not want to commit the time to the subject of investing the way rich dad and I did.

Before going into rich dad's educational plan to teach me to be an investor at the rich level, the next few chapters are dedicated to offering the reader a simple overview of rich dad's investment plan.

Mental Attitude Quiz

The business of investing has many parallels to the business of professional sports. For example, let's use the game of professional football. At Super Bowl time, the entire world watches. On the field are the players, the fans, the blimp overhead, the cheerleaders, the vendors, the sports commentators, and the fans at home watching the event on television.

Today, for many investors, the world of investing looks like a professional football game. You have the same cast of characters. You have the TV commentators describing the play-by-play battle of the blue chip giants on the field. There are the adoring fans purchasing shares instead of tickets, cheering for their favorite team. You also have the cheerleaders, telling you why the stock price is going up; or, if the market goes down, they want to keep cheering you up with new hope that the price will soon rise. There are the bookmakers, called stockbrokers, who give you stock quotes over the phone and record your bets. Instead of reading the sports page, you read the financial pages. There are even the equivalent of ticket scalpers, but in the financial world they don't sell over-priced tickets to latecomers; they sell over-priced financial tip sheets to people who want to get closer to the inside game. Then there are the hot dog vendors, who also dispense antacid pills, as well as the people who sweep up the mess after the trading day is over. And of course we have the viewers at home.

What most people do not see in both arenas of the sports world and the investment world is what is going on behind the scenes. And that is the business behind both games. Oh, you may see the owner of the team occasionally, just as you may see a CEO or the president of the company, but the figurehead is not really the business. So as rich dad said, "The business behind the business is the real game. It's the business behind the business that makes money regardless of who wins the game or which way the market goes—up or down. It's the business that sells the tickets to the game; it does not buy the tickets." That is the investment game rich dad taught me, and what the rest of this book is about. It is the investment game that creates the richest people in the world.

So the mental attitude questions are:

1. Are you willing to start taking control over yourself?

        Yes_____   No_____

2. Based on what you know so far, are you willing to invest the time to gain the education and experience to become a successful investor as an insider?

        Yes_____   No_____

Chapter 13
Investor Lesson #11:

On Which Side of the Table Do You Want to Sit?

Why Investing Isn't Risky

My poor dad always said "Work hard and save money."

My rich dad said, "Working hard and saving money are important if you want to be secure and comfortable. But if you want to be rich, working hard and saving money will probably not get you there. On top of that, people who work hard and save money are often the same people that say, 'Investing is risky.'"

There were many reasons rich dad reminded Mike and me that working hard and saving money was not the way he got rich. He knew that working hard and saving money was good for the masses but not for anyone wanting to become rich.

There were three reasons why he recommended finding a different plan to becoming rich. These are the reasons.

1. He would say, "People who work hard and save money have a hard time getting rich because they pay more than their fair share of taxes. The government taxes people like this when they earn, when they save, when they spend, and when they die. If you want to be rich

you will need greater financial sophistication than merely working hard and saving money."

Rich dad explained further by saying, "To put $1,000 in savings, the government has already taken its fair share out in taxes. So it might take $1,300 or more in earnings just to save $1,000. Then that $1,000 is immediately being eaten away by inflation, so each year your $1,000 is worth less. The meager sum of interest you are paid is also eaten by inflation as well as taxes. So let's say your bank pays you 5% interest, and inflation runs at 4% and taxes run at 30% of the interest, your net result is a loss of money. That is why rich dad thought that working hard and saving money was a hard way to try and get rich.

2. The second reason was, "People who work hard and save often think investing is risky. People who think things are risky often also avoid learning something new."

3. The third reason was, "People who believe in hard work, saving, and that investing is risky, rarely ever see the other side of the coin."

This chapter covers some of the reasons why or how investing does not have to be risky.

Rich dad had a way of taking very complex subjects and simplifying them so almost everyone could understand at least the basics of what he was talking about. In *Rich Dad Poor Dad*, I shared the diagrams of the income statement and the balance sheet that he used to teach me the basics of accounting and financial literacy. In *CASHFLOW Quadrant*, I shared his diagram that explains the core emotional and educational differences between the people found in the four quadrants. In order for me to understand investing, I first needed to fully understand the lessons taught in those two books.

When I was between the ages of 12 and 15, rich dad would occasionally have me sit at his side while he interviewed people who were looking for a job. At 4:30 p.m., which was the time he did all his interviews, I would sit behind a large brown wooden table in a chair next to rich dad. Across the table was a single wooden chair for the person being interviewed. One by one, his secretary would let the prospective employees into the large room and instruct each person to sit in the lone open chair.

I saw grown adults asking for jobs that paid $1.00 an hour, with minimal benefits. Even though I was a young teenager, I knew that it was difficult to raise a family, much less get rich, on $8.00 a day. I also saw people with college degrees, even several with Ph.D.s asking rich dad for managerial or technical jobs that paid less than $500 a month.

After a while, the novelty of sitting behind the table on rich dad's side wore off. Rich dad never said anything to me before, during, or after these interviewing days. Finally, when I was 15 and bored of sitting behind the table, I asked him, "Why do you want me to sit here and watch people ask for jobs? I'm not learning anything and it's getting boring. Besides, it is painful to see grownups so needy for a job and money. Some of those people are really desperate. They can't afford to quit their present job unless you give them another job. I doubt some of them could last three months without a paycheck. And some of them are older than you and obviously have no money. What's happened to them? Why do you want me to see this? It hurts me every time I do this with you. I have no problem with them asking for a job, but it's the desperation for money I can see in their eyes that really bothers me."

Rich dad sat still at the table for a moment, collecting his thoughts. "I've been waiting for you to ask this question," he said. "It hurts me too and that is why I wanted you to see this before you got much older." Rich dad took his legal pad and drew the *CASHFLOW Quadrant.*

"You are just starting high school. You are soon going to be making some very important decisions about what you will be when you grow up, if you haven't already made them. I know your dad is encouraging you to go to college so you can get a high-paying job. If you listen to his advice, you will be going in this direction." Rich dad then drew an arrow to the E and S side of the Quadrant.

"If you listen to me, you will be studying to become a person on this side of the Quadrant." He then drew an arrow to the B and I side of the Quadrant.

SCHOOL

Rich dad

"You've shown me this and told me this many times," I replied quietly. "Why do you continue to go over it?"

"Because if you listen to your dad, you will soon find yourself sitting in that solitary wooden chair on the other side of the table. If you listen to me, you will be sitting in the wooden chair on my side of the table. That is the decision you are making, consciously or unconsciously, as you enter high school. I've had you sit on my side of the table because I wanted you to know that there is a difference in points of view. I'm not saying one side of the table is better than the other side. Each side has its pluses and minuses. I just want you to start choosing now which side you want to sit on because what you study from this day forward will determine which side of the table you wind up on. Will you wind up on the E and S side or the B and I side of the table?"

A Gentle Reminder 10 Years Later

In 1973, rich dad reminded me of that discussion we had when I was 15 years old. "Do you remember me asking you which side of the table you want to sit on?" he asked.

I nodded and said, "Who could have predicted back then that my dad, the proponent for job security and lifelong employment, would be sitting on the other side of the table again, at the age of 50? He had everything going for him at 40, and it was all over just 10 years later."

"Well, your dad is a very courageous man. Unfortunately, he did not plan for this happening to him and now he's getting into professional as well as financial trouble. It could get worse if he does not make some rapid changes. If he keeps going with his old beliefs about jobs and job security, I am afraid he will waste the last years of his life. I cannot help him right now but I can help guide you," said rich dad.

"So you're saying choose which side of the table to sit on?" I replied. "You mean choose a job as a pilot with the airlines or make my own path?"

"Not necessarily," said rich dad. "All I want to do in this lesson is point something out to you."

"And what is that?" I asked.

Rich dad again drew the *CASHFLOW Quadrant*:

He then said, "Too many young people focus on only one side of the Quadrant. Most people are asked as children, "What do you want to be when you grow up?" If you notice, most children will reply such things as 'a fireman,' or 'a ballerina,' or 'a doctor,' or 'a teacher.'"

"So most kids choose the E and S side of the Quadrant," I added.

"Yes," said rich dad. "And the I quadrant, the investor quadrant, is an afterthought, if any thought is given to it at all. In many families, the only thought given to the 'I' quadrant is when parents say, 'Make sure the job you have has excellent benefits and a strong retirement plan.' In other words, the idea is to let the company be responsible for your long-term investment needs. That is changing rapidly as we speak."

"Why do you say that?" I asked. "Why do you say it's changing?"

"We are entering a period of a global economy," said rich dad. "For companies to compete in the world, they need to get their costs down. And one of their major costs is employee compensation and employee retirement plan funding. You mark my words, in the next few years businesses will begin shifting the responsibility of investing for retirement to the employee."

"You mean people will have to provide for their own pension instead of relying on their employer or the government?" I asked.

"Yes. The problem will be the worst for poor people, and they are who I worry about," said rich dad. "That is why I reminded you about sitting across the table from people whose only financial support was a job. By the time you are my age, what to do with people without financial and medical support when they are older will be a massive problem. And your generation, the Baby Boomer generation, will probably be tasked with solving that problem. The severity of this problem will be very prominent sometime around 2010."

"So what should I do?" I asked.

"Make the 'I' quadrant the most important quadrant, not the others. Choose to be an investor when you're grown up. You'll want to have your money working for you so you don't have to work if you don't want to, or cannot, work. You don't want to be like your dad at 50—starting all over again, trying to figure out which quadrant he can earn the most money from, and realizing he is trapped in the E quadrant," said rich dad.

"You want to learn how to operate from all quadrants. Being able to sit on both sides of the table allows you to see both sides of the coin," rich dad said in summary, referring to his two-sided coin story.

The Most Important Quadrant

Rich dad explained to me that one of the differences between rich people and poor people comes from what the parents teach their kids at home. He said, "Mike already had a personal investment portfolio of over $200,000 by the time he was 15. You had nothing. All you had was the idea of going to school so you could get a job with benefits. That is what your dad thought was important."

Rich dad reminded me that his son Mike knew how to be an investor before he left high school. "I never tried to influence him in his choice of careers," said rich dad. "I wanted him to follow his interests, even if it meant he did not take over my business. But whether he chose to be a policeman, politician, or a poet, I wanted him to first be an investor. You'll become far richer if you learn to be an investor, regardless of what you do to earn the money along the way."

Years later, as I met more and more people who came from well-to-do families, many of them said the same thing. Many of my wealthy friends said that their families started an investment portfolio for them when they were very young and then guided them in learning to be investors—before deciding what type of profession they wanted to enter.

Mental Attitude Quiz

In the Industrial Age, the rules of employment were that your company would employ you for life and take care of your investing needs once your working days were over. In 1980, the average length of retirement before death was only one year for men and two years for women. In other words, all you had to do was focus on the E quadrant and your employer would take care of the I quadrant. That message was very comforting, especially to my parents' generation, since they lived through a horrible world war, and the Great Depression. Those events had a tremendous impact upon their mental attitude and financial priorities. Many still live with that financial attitude and they often taught that same attitude to their children. Many people also continue to believe that their home is an asset and their most important investment. That idea is an Industrial Age way of thinking. In the Industrial Age, that was all a person needed to know about money management because the company or labor union and the government took care of the rest.

The rules have changed. In the Information Age of today, most of us need greater financial sophistication. We need to know the difference between an asset and a liability. We are living much longer and therefore need more financial stability for our retirement years. If your home is your biggest investment, then you're probably in financial trouble. Your financial portfolio needs to be a much bigger investment than your home.

The good news is that the I quadrant is a great quadrant to place first—to learn to be responsible for—because freedom comes from this quadrant.

So the mental attitude questions are:

1. Which quadrant will you place first (is the most important to you)?

> E___ S___ B___ I___

2. What side of the table do you eventually plan to sit on?

I have asked question two and left it without an answer because of this phenomenon: You may have noticed that when a major company announces a lay-off of thousands of employees, the company's share price often goes up. That is an example of the two sides of the table. When a person shifts to the other side, his or her point of view of the world also changes. And when a person shifts quadrants, if only mentally and emotionally, then loyalties often change. And I believe that this shift is brought on by the change of ages, the change from Industrial Age thinking to Information Age thinking, and it will cause businesses and business leaders some of the biggest challenges in the future. As they say, "The rules have just begun to change."

Chapter 14
Investor Lesson #12:

The Basic Rules of Investing

One day, I was feeling frustrated about my financial progress in life. I had about four months before I was to leave the military and enter the civilian world. I had stopped all efforts to get a job with the airlines. I had decided that I was going to enter the business world in June of 1974 and see if I could make it in the B quadrant. It was not a hard decision since rich dad was willing to guide me, but the pressure to become financially successful was building. I felt that I was so far behind financially, especially when I compared myself to Mike.

During one of our meetings, I shared my thoughts and frustrations with rich dad. I said, "I've got my two plans in place. One plan is to ensure that I have basic financial security, and the other, more aggressive, investment plan is so I will be comfortable financially. But at the rates those plans will be successful, if they are successful, I'll never be rich like you and Mike."

Rich dad grinned when he heard that. Smiling and laughing quietly to himself, he said, "Investing is not a race. You are not in competition with anyone else. People who compete usually have huge ups and downs in their financial life. You are not here to try to finish first. All you need to do to make more money is simply focus on becoming a better investor. If you focus on improving your experience and education as an investor, you will gain tremendous wealth. If all you want to do is to get rich quickly, or have more money than Mike, then the chances are you will be the big loser. It's OK to compare and compete a little, but the real objective of this process is for you to become a better and more educated investor. Anything other than that is foolish and risky."

I sat there nodding and feeling a little bit better. I knew then that rather than try to make more money and take bigger risks, I would focus on studying harder. That made more sense to me, it seemed less risky, and it certainly took less money...and money was not something I had much of then.

Rich dad went on to explain his reasons for starting Mike out in the I quadrant, rather than the B or E quadrant. He said, "Since the objective of the rich is to have your money work for you so you don't have to work, why not start where you want to wind up." He went on to explain why he encouraged Mike and me to play golf when we were 10 years old. He said, "Golf is a game you can play all your life. Football is a game you can play for only a few years. So why not start with the game you will end with?"

Of course I had not listened to him. Mike continued playing golf and I went on to baseball, football, and rugby. I was not very good at any of them, but I loved the games and I am glad I played them.

Fifteen years after starting to play golf and beginning to invest, Mike was now a great golfer, had a substantial investment portfolio, and had years more investment experience than I did. At 25, I was just beginning to learn the basics of the game of golf and the game of investing.

I make this point because regardless of how young or old you are, learning the basics of anything, especially a game, is important. Most people take some kind of golf lessons to learn the basics before playing golf, but unfortunately, most people never learn the simple basics of investing before investing their hard-earned money.

The Basics of Investing

"Now that your two plans are in place—the plan for security and the plan for comfort—I will explain the basics of investing," said rich dad. He went on to explain that too many people begin investing without having the first two plans in place, and that was risky in his mind. He said, "After you have those two plans firmly in place, then you can experiment and learn more exotic techniques utilizing different investment vehicles. That is why I waited for you to take the time to put those two automatic or mechanical investment plans in place before I continued on with your lessons."

Basic Rule Number One

"Investment basic rule number one," said rich dad, "is to always know what kind of income you are working for."

For years, rich dad had always said to Mike and me that there were three different kinds of income:

1. **Earned Income:** income generally derived from a job or some form of labor. In its most common form, it is income from a paycheck. It is also the highest-taxed income, so it is the hardest income with which to build wealth. When you say to a child, "Get a good job," you are advising the child to work for earned income.

2. **Portfolio Income:** income generally derived from paper assets such as stocks, bonds, mutual funds, etc. Portfolio income is by far the most popular form of investment income, simply because paper assets are so much easier to manage and maintain than any others.

3. **Passive Income:** income generally derived from real estate. It can also be income derived from royalties from patents or license agreements. Yet approximately 80% of the time, passive income is from real estate. There are many tax advantages available for real estate.

One of the running battles between my two dads was what a parent should say to a child. My poor dad always said to me, "Work hard at school so you can get good grades. When you get good grades, you will be able to get a good job. Then you become a good hardworking man." While Mike and I were in high school, rich dad would snicker at that idea. He used to say, "Your dad is a good hardworking man but he will never get rich if he continues to think that way. If you boys listen to me, you will work hard for portfolio income and passive income if you want to become rich."

Back then, I did not fully understand what either man was saying or what the difference in philosophies was all about. At age 25, I was beginning to understand a little better. My dad at age 52 was starting all over again, focused only on earned income, something he had thought was the right thing to do all his life. My rich dad was rich and enjoying life simply because he had lots of all three types of income. I knew now which type of income I was going to work hard for and it was not earned income.

Basic Rule Number Two

"Investment basic rule number two," said rich dad, "is to convert earned income into portfolio income or passive income as efficiently as possible." Rich dad then drew this diagram on his yellow legal tablet:

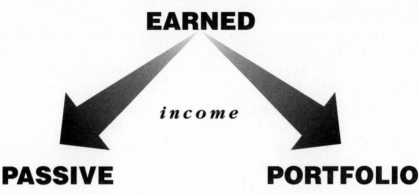

"And that, in a nutshell, is all an investor is supposed to do," rich dad summarized with a smile. "That is about as basic as it can get."

"But how do I do it?" I asked. "How do I get the money if I don't already have the money? What happens if I lose the money?" I kept asking.

"How, how, how?" said rich dad. "You sound like an Indian Chief from an old movie."

"But those are real questions," I whined.

"I know they are real questions. But for now, I just want you to understand the basics. Later, I'll go into the how. OK? And watch out for the negative thoughts. Look, risk is always part of investing, as it is with life. People who are too negative and avoid risk back themselves out of most opportunities because of their negativity and fear of risk. Got it?"

I nodded. "I got it. Start with the basics."

Basic Rule Number Three

"Investment basic rule number three," said rich dad, nodding to my last statement, "is to keep your earned income secure by purchasing a security you hope converts your earned income into passive income or portfolio income."

"Secure in a security?" I asked. "I'm confused. What happened to assets and liabilities?"

"Good question," said rich dad. "I'm now expanding your vocabulary. It is time for you to go beyond the simple understanding of assets and liabilities—an understanding that most people never achieve, I might add. But the point I am making here is that all securities are not necessarily assets, as many people think they are."

"You mean a stock or piece of real estate is a security, but it may not be an asset?" I asked.

"That is correct. However, many average investors cannot distinguish between a security and an asset. Many people, including many professionals, do not know the difference. Many people call any security an asset."

"So what is the difference?" I asked.

"A security is something you hope will keep your money secure. And generally, these securities are bound up tight by government regulations. And that is why the organization that watches over much of the world of investing is called the Securities and Exchange Commission, a.k.a. the SEC. You may notice that its title is not the Assets and Exchange Commission."

"So the government knows that securities are not necessarily assets," I stated.

Rich dad nodded and said, "And neither is it called the Securities and Guarantees Commission. The government knows that all it can do is maintain a tight set of rules and do its best to maintain order by enforcing those rules. It does not guarantee that everyone who acquires a security will make money. That is why securities are not called assets. If you remember the basic definition, an asset puts money in your pocket, or the income column; a liability takes money from your pocket, and that shows up in your expense column. It's simply a matter of basic financial literacy."

I nodded. "So it is up to the investor to know which securities are assets and which securities are liabilities," I stated, beginning to understand where rich dad was going with this.

"That is correct," said rich dad, again reaching for his legal tablet. He drew this diagram on it:

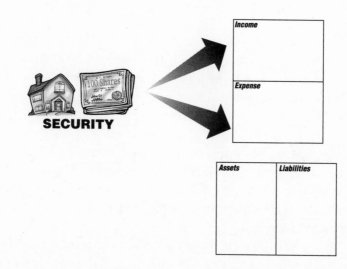

"The confusion begins for most investors when someone tells them that securities are assets. Average investors are nervous about investing because they know that just because they buy a security, it does not mean they will make money. The problem with buying a security is that the investor can also lose money," said rich dad.

"So if the security makes money, as your diagram shows, it puts money into the income column of the financial statement, and it is an asset. But if it loses money, and that event is recorded in the expense column of the financial statement, then that security is a liability. In fact, the same security can change from being an asset into a liability. For example, I bought a hundred shares of stock in ABC Company in December for which I paid $20 per share. In January, I sold ten shares for $30 per share. Those ten shares of stock were assets because they generated income for me. But in March, I sold ten more shares for only $10, so that same stock had become a liability because it generated a loss (expense)."

Rich dad cleared his throat before speaking. "So the way I look at this is that there are instruments called securities in which I invest. It is up to me as the investor to determine if each security is an asset or liability."

"And that is where the risk comes in," I said. "It is the investor not knowing the difference between an asset or liability that makes investing risky."

Basic Rule Number Four

"And why I say investor basic rule number four is, it is the investor that is really the asset or the liability," said rich dad.

"What?" I asked. "The investor is the asset or liability, not the investment or security?"

Rich dad nodded. "You often hear people say, 'Investing is risky.' It's the investor who is risky. It is ultimately the investor who is the asset or the liability. I have seen many so-called investors lose money when everyone else is making money. I have sold businesses to many so-called business people and watch the businesses soon go bust. I have seen people take a perfectly good piece of real estate, real estate that is making a lot of money, and in a few years, that same piece of real estate is running at a loss and falling apart. And then I hear people say, investing is risky. It's the investor who is risky, not the investment. In fact, a good investor loves to follow behind a risky investor because that is where the real investment bargains are found."

"And that is why you love to listen to investors who are crying the blues about their investment losses," I said. "You want to find out what they did wrong and see if you can find a bargain."

"You've got it," said rich dad. "I'm always looking for the skipper of the *Titanic*."

"And that is why you don't like to hear stories about people making a lot of money in the stock market or the real estate market. You hate it when someone tells you that he or she bought a stock at $5 and it went to $25."

"You have observed me well," said rich dad. "Listening to tales of quick money and instant wealth is a fool's game. Such stories draw in only the losers. If a stock is well known or has made a lot of money, the party is often already over or soon to be over. I'd rather hear tales of woe and misery because that is where the bargains are. As a person who operates on the B and I side of the quadrant, I want to find securities that are liabilities and turn them into assets, or wait for someone else to begin turning them into assets."

"So that would make you a contrarian investor," I ventured, "a contrarian being someone who goes against the popular sentiment of the market."

"That is the lay person's idea of what a contrarian investor is. Most people just think a contrarian investor is anti-social and does not like going along with the crowd. But that is not true. As someone who operates on the B and I side of the Quadrant, I like to think of myself as a repairman. I want to look at the wreck and see if it can be fixed. If it can be fixed, then it would still be a good investment only if other investors also want it fixed. If it cannot be fixed or if no one would want it even after it is fixed, I don't want it either. So a true investor must also like what the crowd likes, and that is why I would not say I am a pure contrarian. I will not buy something just because no one else wants it."

"So is there an investor basic rule number five?" I asked.

Basic Rule Number Five

"Yes, there is," said rich dad. "Investor basic rule number five is that a true investor is prepared for whatever happens. A non-investor tries to predict what and when things will happen."

"What does that mean?" I asked.

"Have you ever heard someone say, 'I could have bought that land for $500 an acre twenty years ago. And look at it now. Someone built a shopping center right next to it, and now that same land is $500,000 an acre'?"

"Yes, I have heard those stories many times."

"We all have," said rich dad. "Well, that is a case of someone who was not prepared. Most investments that will make you rich are available for only a narrow window of time—a few moments in the world of trading or a window of opportunity that is open for years, as it is in real estate. But regardless of how long the window of opportunity is open, if you are not prepared with education and experience, or extra cash, the opportunity, if it is good, will pass.

"So how does one prepare?"

"You need to focus and keep in mind what others are already looking for. If you want to buy a stock, then attend classes on how to spot bargains in stocks. The same is true for real estate. It all begins with training your brain to know what to look for and being prepared for the moment the investment is presented to you. It is much like the sport of soccer. You play and play, and then all of a sudden the winning kick at the goal appears. You're either prepared or you're not. You're either in position or you're not. But even if you miss the shot in soccer or in investing, there is always another shot at the goal, or an investment 'opportunity of a lifetime' right around the corner. The good news is that there are more and more opportunities every day, but first you need to choose your game and learn to play the game."

"So that is why you chuckle when someone complains about missing out on a good deal or tells you that you must get into this deal or that deal?"

"Exactly. Again there are so many people who come from the mindset that there is scarcity, instead of abundance, in the world. They often cry about missing a deal and hang on to a deal too long thinking that it is the only deal, or they buy thinking that what they are looking at is the only deal. If you are good at the 'B' and 'I' side of the Quadrant, you have more time and more deals to look at, and your confidence is high because you know you can take a bad deal that most people would reject, and turn it into a good deal. That is what I mean about investing the time to be prepared. If you're prepared, there is a deal of a lifetime being presented to you every day of your life."

"And that is how you found that big piece of raw land—just walking down the street," I commented, recalling how rich dad found one of his best pieces of real estate. "You saw that the 'For Sale' sign had fallen down and had been trampled on so no one knew the land was for sale. You called the owner and offered him a low but fair price at your terms and he took it. He took your offer because no one else had made him an offer in over two years. That is what you mean, isn't it?"

"Yes, that is what I mean, and that piece of raw land was a better deal than most. That is what I mean about being prepared. I knew what the land was worth and I also knew what was going to happen in that neighborhood in a few months, so there was very low risk coupled with a very low price. I would love to find ten more pieces of land today in that same neighborhood."

"And what do you mean by 'Don't predict'?" I asked.

"Well have you ever heard someone say, 'What if the market crashes? What will happen to my investment then? That is why I am not going to buy. I am going to wait and see what happens'?"

"Many times," I said.

"I have heard many people, when presented with a good investment opportunity, back away from the investment because their core fears begin to predict the disasters that will occur. They sent out their negative vibes and never invest...or they sell when they shouldn't sell and they buy something they shouldn't buy based on either optimistic or pessimistic emotional predictions."

"And that would be handled if they were a little educated, had a little experience, and were prepared," I said.

"Exactly," said rich dad. "Besides, one of the basics of being a good investor is being prepared to profit when the market moves up or if it moves down. In fact, the best investors make more money in a down market move simply because the market falls faster than it rises. As they say, the bull comes up the stairs and the bear goes out the window. If you are not covered for either direction, you as the investor are too risky...not the investment."

"That means many people predict themselves right out of being rich investors."

Rich dad nodded. "I have heard so many people say, 'I don't buy real estate because I don't want calls at midnight to fix toilets.' Well I don't either. That is why I have property managers. But I do love the tax advantages that cash flow from real estate offers that stocks do not."

"So people often predict themselves right out of opportunities, instead of being prepared," I echoed, beginning to understand why being prepared was so important. "How do I learn to be prepared?"

"I'll teach you some basic trading techniques that all professional investors should know, techniques such as shorts, call options, put options, straddles, etc. But that will come later. Right now, that is enough about the advantages of preparation over prediction for you."

"But I have one more question about preparation."

"And what is that?" asked rich dad.

"What if I find a deal and I don't have any money?" I asked.

Basic Rule Number Six

"That is investment basic rule number six," said rich dad. "If you are prepared, which means you have education and experience, and you find a good deal, the money will find you or you will find the money. Good deals seem to bring out the greed in people. And I don't mean to use the world greed in a negative way. I speak of greed as a general human emotion, an emotion we all have. So when a person finds a good deal, the deal attracts the cash. If the deal is bad, then it is really hard to raise the cash."

"Have you ever seen a good deal that did not attract the money?" I asked.

"Many times, but it was not the deal that did not attract the cash. The person controlling the deal did not attract the cash. In other words, the deal would have been good if the guy in charge of the deal had stepped aside. It is like having a world-ranked racecar with an average driver. No matter how good the car is, no one would bet on it with an average driver at the wheel. In real estate, people often say the key to success is location, location, location. I think differently. In reality, in the world of investing—regardless of if it is real estate, business, or paper assets—the key is always people, people, people. I have seen the best real estate in the best location lose money because the wrong people were in charge."

"So, again, if I am prepared, I have done my homework, I have some experience and a track record, and I find something that is a good investment, then finding the money is not that hard."

"That has been my experience. Unfortunately, all too often, the worst deals, which are deals that investors like me would not invest in, are presented to unsophisticated investors, and the unsophisticated investors often lose their money."

"And that is why there is the Securities and Exchange Commission," I said. "Its job is to protect the average investor from these bad deals."

"Correct," said rich dad. "The primary job of investors is to make sure their money is secure. The next step is to do their best to convert that money into cash flow or capital gains. That is when you find out if you or the person to whom you entrusted your money can turn that security into an asset or if it will become a liability. Again, it is not the investment that is necessarily safe or risky, it is the investor."

"So is that the last investor basic rule?" I asked.

"No. Not by a long shot," said rich dad. "Investing is a subject you can learn the basics of for the rest of your life. The good news is that the better you are at the basics, the more money you make and the less risk you have. But there is one more investor basic rule I would like to leave you with. And that is investor basic rule number seven."

Basic Rule Number Seven

"And what is number seven?"

"It is the ability to evaluate risk and reward," said rich dad.

"Give me an example," I requested.

"Let's say your two basic investment plans are in place. Your nest egg is doing well and you happen to have, let's say, an extra $25,000 you can invest on something more speculative."

"I wish I had $25,000 right now," I commented dryly. "But tell me more about evaluating the risk and reward."

"So you have this $25,000 that you can more or less afford to lose—which means that if you lost it all, you would cry a little but you could still put food on the table and gas in the car and save another $25,000. Then you begin to evaluate risk and rewards of the more speculative investments."

"And how do I do that?"

"Let's say you have a nephew who has an idea for a hamburger stand. The nephew needs $25,000 to start. Would this be a good investment?"

"Emotionally, it could be, but financially it would not be," I replied.

"Why not?" asked rich dad.

"Too much risk and not enough reward," I replied. "On top of that, how would you get your money back? The most important thing here is not return on investment. The most important thing here is return of investment. As you said, security of capital is very important."

"Very good," said rich dad. "But what if I told you that this nephew has been working for a major burger chain for the past 15 years, has been a vice-president of every important aspect of the business, and is ready to go out on his own and build a worldwide burger chain? And what if for a mere $25,000 you could buy 5% of the entire company? Would that be of interest to you?"

"Yes," I said. "Definitely, because there is more reward for the same amount of risk. Yet it is still a high-risk deal."

"That is correct," said rich dad. "And that is an example of an investor basic, which is to evaluate risk and reward."

"So how does a person evaluate such speculative investments?" I asked.

"Good question," said rich dad. "That is the rich level of investing, the level of investing that follows the investment plans to be secure and comfortable. You're now talking about acquiring the skills to invest in investments that the rich invest in."

"So again, it is not the investment that is risky; it is the investor who doesn't have the adequate skills that makes the investment even higher risk."

The Three Es

"Correct," said rich dad. "At this level, the level at which the rich invest in, the investor should have the three Es. And the three Es are:

1. Education
2. Experience
3. Excessive cash

"Excessive cash?" I asked. "Not just extra cash?"

"No, I use the words 'excessive cash' for a reason: Investing in the investments of the rich takes excessive cash, which means you can truly afford to lose and still profit from the loss."

"Profit from the loss?" I asked. "What does that mean?"

"We will get into that," said rich dad. "In the rich level of investing, you will find out that things are different. At the rich level, you will find out that there are good losses and bad losses. Good debt and bad debt. Good expenses and bad expenses. At the rich level, your educational requirements and experience will need to go up dramatically. If not, you will not be there for long. Got it?"

"I'm getting it," I replied.

Rich dad went on to explain that if things do not follow the KISS (keep it simple, silly) formula, then the risk is probably high. He said, "If someone cannot explain the investment to you in less than two minutes, and you understand it, then either you don't understand, he doesn't understand, or you both don't understand. Whatever the case, it is best that you pass on the investment."

He also said, "All too often, people try to make investing sound complex, so they use intelligent-sounding jargon. If someone does that, ask him or her to use simple English. If he or she can't explain the investment so a 10-year-old can understand at least the overall concept, chances are he or she does not understand it either. After all, all p/e means is how expensive the stock is. And a cap rate, which is a term used in real estate, just measures how much money the property puts or does not put in your pocket."

"So if it is not simple, don't do it?" I asked.

"No, I'm not saying that either," said rich dad. "All too often, people who lack interest in investing or have a loser's attitude will say, 'Man if it's not easy, I won't do it.' I often say to that type of person, 'Well when you were born, your parents had to work hard and potty train you. So even going to the toilet was at one time difficult. Today, hopefully, you are potty trained, and going to the potty by yourself is just part of the basics.'"

Mental Attitude Quiz

I have found that too many people want to invest in the investments of the rich without first having a strong financial foundation under them. All too often, people want to invest at the rich person's level because they are hurting financially and often need money desperately. Obviously, I do not recommend investments at a rich person's level unless you are already rich. Neither did my rich dad.

Some people are fortunate enough that their financial plan to be "comfortable" creates enough excess cash to make them think they are rich. But unless they learn to think as rich people think, they will still be poor people. They will be just be poor people with money.

So the mental attitude question is:

1. If you are going to invest, or intend to invest, in what the rich invest in, are you willing to gain what rich dad called the 3-E's? They are:

   a. Education
   b. Experience
   c. Excessive cash

   Yes_____   No_____

If the answer is no, then the remainder of this book may not be of much value, nor could I in good conscience recommend any of the investments I will be writing about, which are the investments of the rich.

If you are uncertain or are curious about some of the requirements involved in the education and experience that can lead to acquiring excessive cash, then read on. At the end of this book, you can decide whether or not you want to go after the 3-Es, if you do not already have them.

Along the way, you may discover that your plans to be financially safe, and then financially comfortable, will allow you to "raise the bar." Just as a high jumper or pole-vaulter raises the bar after succeeding at each level, you can succeed financially at the safety and comfort levels. You can then "raise the bar"—and your goals—and focus more of your time on becoming rich.

As rich dad said, "Investing is a subject where you can study the basics for the rest of your life." What he meant was that it sounds complex at the start and then it gets simple. The more simple you can make this subject, or the more basics you learn, the richer you can become while reducing risk. But the challenge for most people is to invest the time.

Reduce Risk Through Financial Literacy

It was still early in the spring of 1974. I had but a couple of months to go before I was discharged from my military contract. I still did not know what I was going to do once I drove off the base for the last time. President Nixon was in trouble with Watergate and the trials were about to begin, so I realized that he had larger concerns than I did at that moment. We all knew the war in Vietnam was over and we had lost. I still had a very short military haircut and I stood out each time I went into the civilian world, where long hippie hair was the style. I began to wonder what I would look like in shoulder-length hair. I had worn a military hair cut since 1965, ever since I entered the military academy for college. It was the wrong period of time to have short hair.

The stock market had been going down for the past four days and people were nervous. Even in the pilots' ready room on base, the few pilots that did play the market were nervous and edgy. One had sold all his stock to stand aside with cash. I was not invested in the stock market at the time, so I could watch the effect of the ups and downs of the market had on people without emotion.

Rich dad and I met for lunch at his favorite beachside hotel. He was happy as ever. The market was falling and he was making even more money. I thought it strange that he would be calm and happy and everyone else, even the commentator on the radio, was nervous.

"How is it that you are happy and everyone else I meet who is in the stock market is nervous?"

"Well, we talked about it earlier," said rich dad. "We talked about one of the basics of being an investor is to be prepared for whatever happens, rather than attempt to predict what is about to happen. I doubt if anyone can predict the market, although there are many people who claim they can. A person can predict something happening maybe once, maybe even twice, but I have never seen anyone predict anything regarding the market, three times in a row. If there is such a person, he or she must have a high-powered crystal ball."

"But isn't investing risky?" I asked.

"No," said rich dad.

"Most people I talk to believe that investing is risky, so they keep their money in the bank, in money market funds or CDs."

"As they should," said rich dad, pausing for a moment and then continuing. "For most people, investing is risky, but always remember that it is not necessarily investing that is risky, it is the investor who is risky. Many people who think they are investors are not really investors. In reality, they are speculators, traders, or—even worse—gamblers. There are fine lines of distinction between those characters and a true investor. Don't get me wrong, there are speculators, traders, and gamblers who do very well financially. But they are not what I would categorize as investors."

"So how does an investor become less risky?" I asked.

"Good question," said rich dad. "Or maybe a better question might be, how do I become an investor who makes a lot of money with very little risk? And then hang on to the money I make?"

"Yes. That is definitely a more accurate question," I replied.

"My answer is the same. It is to keep things simple and understand the basics. Begin with having your investment plans for security and comfort in place. Those plans are often handled by someone else you hope is competent and following an automatic no-brainer formula. Then you have to pay the price to become an investor who wants to make more money with less risk."

"And what is that price?" I asked.

"Time," said rich dad. "Time is your most important asset. If you are not willing to invest your time, then leave your investment capital with people who are following the investment plan of your choice. Many people dream of getting rich but most will not pay the price of the investment of their time."

I could tell that rich dad was still very much into the mental preparation mode of our lessons. But by now, I was ready to go. I really wanted to learn to invest following his investment formula. Yet he was still testing my determination to invest my time and effort to learn what I needed to learn. I therefore raised my voice so the tables around me could hear and said, "I want to learn. I am willing to invest my time. I will study. I won't quit on you. You are not wasting your time teaching me. Just tell me what the basics are to becoming a successful investor with very low risk."

"Good," said rich dad. "I've been waiting for some fire. I got concerned this morning when you came in concerned about the market going down. If you let the ups and downs of the stock market run your life, you should not be an investor. The number one control you must have to be an investor is control over yourself. If you cannot control yourself, the highs and lows of the market will run you and you will lose during one of those ups or downs. The number one reason people are not good investors is that they lack control over themselves and their emotions. Their desire for security and comfort takes control of their heart, their soul, their mind, their view of the world, and their actions. As I said, a true investor does not care which direction the market goes. A true investor will make money in either direction. So 'control over yourself' is the first and most important control. Got it?"

"I got it," I said as I backed up in my chair a little. I had come in a little wimpy and concerned. Yet I had been studying with rich dad for years and I knew that his intensity was letting me know that the lessons on investing were just about to begin.

Rich dad continued at a rapid-fire pace. "So if you want to invest with very low risk and high returns, you have to pay the price. And the price involves study, lots of study. You need to study the basics of business. So to be a rich investor, you also have to either be a good business owner, or know what a business owner knows. In the stock market, investors want to invest in successful Bs. If you possess the skills of a B, you can either create your own business as a B or analyze other businesses as potential investments as an I. The problem is, most people are trained to be Es or Ss in school. They do not have the skills needed by a B. That is why so few people become very rich investors."

"And that is why so many people say or think that investing is risky."

"Exactly," said rich dad as he reached for his legal tablet. "This is what fundamental investing is. This is a simple diagram of the basic formula I follow as well as many ultra-rich investors."

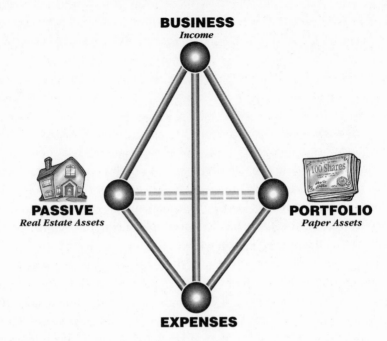

BUSINESS
Income

PASSIVE
Real Estate Assets

PORTFOLIO
Paper Assets

EXPENSES

"In the world of investing, there are three basic asset classes you can invest in. We already covered the idea of earned income, passive income, and portfolio income. Well, the big difference between the really rich and the average rich is the tetrahedron I drew here."

"You mean building a business is an investment?" I asked.

"Probably the best investment of all, if you want to become a rich investor. Roughly 80% of the very rich became rich through building a business. Most people work for people who build businesses or invest in businesses. Then they wonder why the person who built the business is so rich. The reason is that the builder of a business will always trade money for the asset."

"You mean the builder or owner of the business values the asset more than the money?" I asked.

"That is part of the picture because all an investor really does is trade time, expertise, or money for a security that they hope or intend will become an asset. So just as you trade money to buy an investment piece of real estate, like a rental house, or pay money for a share or stock, a business owner will pay people money to build a business asset. One of the main reasons the poor and middle class struggle is that they value money over true assets."

"So the poor and the middle class value money and the rich don't really value it. Is that what you're saying?"

"Partially," said rich dad. "Always remember Gresham's Law."

"Gresham's Law?" I replied. "I've never heard of Gresham's Law. What is that?"

"Gresham's Law is an economic law that states that bad money will always drive out good money."

"Good money, bad money?" I asked, shaking my head.

"Let me explain," said rich dad. "Gresham's Law has been in effect since humans began valuing money. Back in Roman times, people used to clip silver and gold coins. Clipping coins meant that people would shave a little bit off the coin before handing it to someone else. So the coin began to lose value. The Roman people were not stupid and soon noticed that the coins were lighter. Once the Roman people knew what was happening, they hoarded the coins with high silver and gold content and spent only the lighter coins. That is an example of bad money driving good money out of circulation.

"To combat this clipping of coins, the government began reeding coins, which is why coins of value have the tiny grooves on the edge. If a coin had the groves filed down, a person knew the coin had been tampered with. Ironically, it is the government that does the most clipping of the value of our money."

"But that was back in Roman times. How does that law apply today?" I asked.

"In 1965, less than ten years ago, Gresham's Law began working in the United States when the government stopped producing coins with silver in them. In other words, the government began producing bad coins, or coins without any real value to them. Immediately, people began hoarding the real silver coins and spending the debased or fake coins."

"In other words, people somehow intuitively know that government money is not worth much," I stated.

"It seems that way," said rich dad, "which may be why I think people save less and spend more. Unfortunately, the poor and middle class buy things that have even less value than their money. They turn cash into trash. Meanwhile, the rich buy things like businesses, stocks, and real estate with their money. They are looking for secure securities in a time when money has an ever-decreasing real value. That is why I've constantly said to you and Mike, 'The rich do not work for money.' If you want to be rich, you have to know the difference between good money and bad money...assets and liabilities."

"Good securities and bad securities," I added.

Rich dad nodded. "That is why I have always said to you, 'The rich don't work for money.' I say that because the rich are smart enough to know that money is worth less and less. If you work hard for bad money and do not know the difference between assets and liabilities, good securities, and bad securities, you may struggle financially all your life. It is truly a shame that those who work the hardest and are paid the least suffer the most from this constant erosion of money's value. People who do the hardest work have the hardest time getting ahead due to the effects of Gresham's Law. Since money has ever-declining value, a financially wise person must constantly seek things that do have value and can also produce more and more debased money. If you don't do that, you fall behind financially over time rather than get ahead."

Rich dad then pointed to the sketch on his legal tablet:

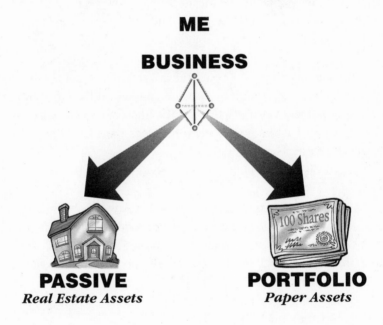

"I am more secure today than your dad because I worked hard to acquire all three of these basic assets or securities. Your dad has chosen to work hard for job security. So what he has worked hard for looks like this:"

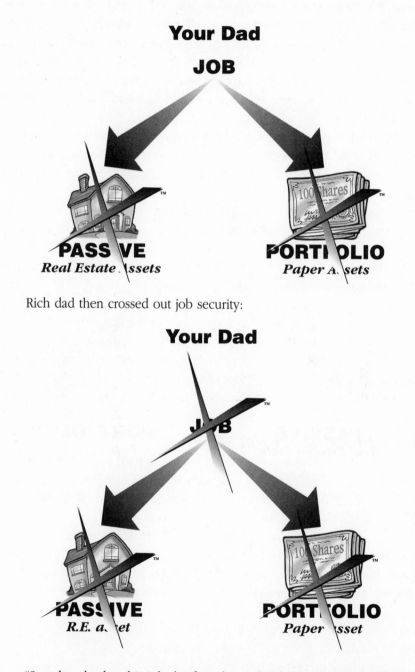

Rich dad then crossed out job security:

"So when he lost his job, he found out that he had worked hard for nothing. And worst of all, he was successful. He worked himself all the way to the top of the state education system but then he bucked the system. There goes his job security with the state government. I feel for your dad almost as much as you do. But you cannot talk to someone who has very set core values and is not willing to change. He is out looking for another job rather than asking himself if a job will get him what he really wants."

"So he clung to job security and false assets. However, he failed to convert his earned income into real assets so he could have a rich person's income, which is passive income or portfolio income," I said. "He should have done that, converting his paycheck into real securities, before taking on the system."

"Your dad is a brave man, highly educated, but not financially well educated. And that was his downfall. If he were rich, he could influence the system with campaign contributions, but since he had no money, all he could do was protest and defy the government. Protest is effective, but it takes a heck of a lot of people protesting to make any change in government. Just look at how many protesting people it is taking to stop this Vietnam War."

"The irony is that he was protesting against the power of the rich to influence government by campaign contributions," I said. "He saw the power that people with money had over politicians and the favors the rich receive or the laws that were passed in favor of the rich. My dad saw the money involved in politics and so he ran for lieutenant governor to try and stop that financial abuse. Now it has cost him his position in the government. He knows the laws are written in favor of the rich."

"Well, that is another subject on money. But not our subject today," said rich dad.

Why Investing Is Not Risky

"I've already made up my mind," I said. "I have not followed up on any of the jobs for pilots. I will soon begin looking for a job with a company that has sales training, so I can overcome my fear of rejection and learn to sell, or communicate, as you recommended."

"Good," said rich dad. "Both IBM and Xerox have excellent sales training programs. If you're going to be in the B quadrant, then you must know how to sell as well as market. You also have to have a very thick skin and not mind people saying 'No' to you. But you also have to be able to change their mind if it is appropriate to do so. Selling is a very necessary, basic skill for anyone who wants to become rich, especially in the B quadrant and very often in the I quadrant."

"But I have one burning question," I said.

"Ask it," said rich dad.

"How can you say investing is not risky when most people say investing is risky?"

"Easy," said rich dad. "I can read financial statements and most people cannot. Do you remember me saying to you years ago that your dad was word literate but not financially literate?"

I nodded, saying, "I remember you saying that very often."

"Financial literacy is one of the most important investor basics, especially if you want to be a safe investor, an inside investor, and a rich investor. Anyone who is not financially literate cannot see into an investment. Just as a doctor uses X-rays to look at your skeletal system, a financial statement allows you to look into an investment and see the truth, the facts, the fiction, the opportunities, and the risk. Reading a financial statement of a business or individual is like reading a biography or an autobiography."

"So one of the reasons many people say investing is risky is simply that they have never been taught to read financial statements?" I asked in surprise. "And that is why you began by teaching Mike and me to read financial statements starting when we were nine?"

"Well, if you remember, you told me when you were just 9 years old that you wanted to be rich. When you told me that, I began with the basics: never work for money, learn to spot opportunities not jobs, and learn to read financial statements. Most people leave school looking for jobs, not opportunities; they have been taught to work hard for earned income rather than passive income or portfolio income; and most have never been taught how to balance a checkbook, much less read and write a financial statement. Small wonder they say investing is risky."

Rich dad again took his legal tablet and drew the following diagram:

You

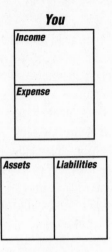

Your Business

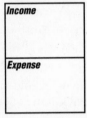
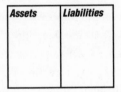

Real Estate

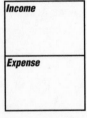
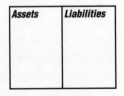

Stock

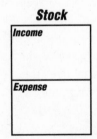

"A business has a financial statement, a stock certificate is a reflection of a financial statement, each piece of real estate has a financial statement, and each of us as an individual human being has a financial statement attached to us," said rich dad.

"Every security and human being?" I asked. "Even my dad? Even my mom?"

"Sure," said rich dad. "Everything—regardless of if it is a business, real estate, or human being—that transacts money has an income statement and balance sheet, whether or not they know it. People who are not aware of the power of a financial statement often have the least money and the biggest financial problems."

"You mean like my dad is having right now," I said.

"Unfortunately that is true," said rich dad. "Not knowing the simple difference between assets and liabilities, earned income from passive and portfolio income, and not knowing where they all appear and how they flow on a financial statement has been a costly oversight for your dad."

"So when you look at a business, you look at the financial statement, not the price of its stock that day?" I asked, doing my best to move the discussion away from my dad.

"That is correct," said rich dad. "That is called fundamental investing. Financial literacy is fundamental to fundamental investing. When I look at the financials of a business, I look at the guts of a business. When I look at the financials, I can tell if the business is fundamentally strong or weak, growing or declining. I can tell if the management is doing a good job or wasting a lot of the investors' money. The same is true with an apartment building or office building."

"So by reading the financials, you can tell for yourself if the investment is risky or safe," I added.

"Yes," said rich dad. A person's, a business's, or a piece of real estate's financials will tell me much more than that. But a cursory look at a financial does three more important things."

"And they are?"

"For one thing, being financially literate gives me a checklist of what is important. I can look at each line and determine what is not being done right, or what I can do to improve the business and make things right. Most investors look at the price and then the stock's p/e, or price earnings ratio. The p/e of a stock is an outsider's indicator of the business. An insider needs other indicators, and that is what I will teach you. Those indicators are part of a safety checklist to make sure all the parts of the business are functioning well. If you are not financially literate, you cannot tell the differences. Then, of course, investing is risky for that person."

"And the second thing?" I asked.

"The second thing is when I look at an investment, I also overlay it on my personal financial statement, and see where it fits. As I said, investing is a plan. I want to see how the business, the stock, mutual fund, bond, or real estate's financial statement impacts my personal financial statement. I want to know that this investment will get me to where I want to go. I can also analyze how I can afford the investment. By knowing my numbers, I know what will happen if I borrow money to buy an investment and the long-term impact balanced with income and outflow due to debt payments."

"And the third thing?"

"I want to know that this investment is safe and will make me money. I can tell if it is going to make money or lose money in a very short period of time. So if it does not make me money, or I cannot fix the reason why it will not make me money, why should I buy it? That would be risky."

"So if you do not make money, you don't invest?" I asked.

"In most instances," said rich dad. "Yet as simple as that sounds, it always amazes me when I meet people who are losing money or making no money and they think they are investors. Many people who invest in real estate lose money every month and then say, 'But the government gives me a tax break for my losses.' That is like saying, 'If you lose a dollar, the government will give you 30 cents back.' A few very sophisticated business people and investors know how to use that government ploy to their advantage, but very few people really do. Why not make a dollar and get an additional 30 cent bonus from the government? That is what a real investor does."

"People actually do that? They actually lose money and think it is investing?"

"On top of that, they think losing money for tax advantages is a good idea. Do you know how easy it is to find an investment that loses money?" asked rich dad.

"I imagine it would be pretty easy," I said. "The world is filled with stocks, mutual funds, real estate, and businesses that do not make any money."

"So a real investor first wants to make money, and then after making money, they want an additional bonus from the government. So a real investor will make a dollar as well as get a 30 cent bonus from the government. An unsophisticated investor will lose a dollar and be thrilled to get 30 cents from the government in the form of a tax write-off."

"Just because that person cannot read a financial statement?" I asked.

"That is one of the basics. Financial literacy is definitely an important investor basic at the rich investment level. The other basic is to invest to make money. Never invest with the intent to lose money and then be happy with a tax write-off. You invest for one reason only: to make money. Investing is risky enough without investing to lose money."

Your Report Card

As we ended the lesson for the day, rich dad said, "Now do you realize why I had you do your personal financial statements so often?"

I nodded and said, "As well as analyze the financial statements of businesses and real estate investments. You kept saying you wanted me to think in financial statements. Now I understand why."

"While you were in school, you got a report card once a quarter. A financial statement is your report card once you leave school. The problem is that since most people have not been trained to read financial statements or how to keep a personal financial statement, they have no idea how they are doing once they leave school. Many people have failing marks on their personal financial statements but think they are doing well because they have a high-paying job and a nice home. Unfortunately, if I were handing out the grades, anyone who was not financially independent by age 45 would receive a failing grade. It is not that I want to be cruel. I just want people to wake up and maybe do a few things differently...before they run out of their most important asset: time."

"So you reduce risk by being able to read financial statements," I replied. "A person needs to get his or her own personal financial statement under control before investing."

"Definitely," said rich dad. "This whole process I have been talking to you about is the process of taking control of yourself, which also means your financial statement. So many people want to invest because they are deep in debt. Investing in the hopes of making more money so you can pay bills or buy a bigger house or a new car is a fool's investment plan. You invest for one reason: to acquire an asset that converts earned income into passive income or portfolio income. That conversion of one form of income into another form of income is the primary objective of a true investor. And to do that requires a higher degree of financial literacy than simply balancing a checkbook."

"So you're not concerned about the price of a stock or piece of real estate. You're more concerned with the operating fundamentals, the fundamentals that you can see with a financial statement?"

"Right," said rich dad. "That is why I got upset with your being concerned about the prices on the stock market. While price is important, it is far from the most important thing in fundamental investing. Price is more relevant in technical investing, but technical investing is another lesson. Now do you understand why I had you do so many personal financial statements and analyze businesses and real estate investments?"

I nodded. "I hated it at the time, but now I'm glad you had me do so many of them. I realize now how much I think and analyze things using mental photos of my financial statement and how what I do with my money affects my financial statement. I did not realize that most people do not think with the same photo references."

The Magic Carpet

"You are far ahead of the game," said rich dad, "the game of getting rich. I have a term for the income statement and the balance sheet, the two primary reports that make up financial statements: the magic carpet."

"Why do you call them the magic carpet?" I asked.

"Because they seem to magically take you behind the scenes into any business, any piece of real estate, and any country in the world. It is much like taking a diving mask and suddenly looking below the surface of the water. The mask, symbolizing the financial statement, lets you see clearly what is going on beneath the surface. Alternatively, a financial statement is like having Superman's X-ray vision. Instead of trying to jump over the tall building, a financially literate person can see right through the building's concrete walls. Another reason I call them the magic carpet is because they free you to see and do so many things in so many parts of the world, all the while sitting at your desk. You can invest in so many parts of the world or just in your backyard with so much more knowledge and insight. Improving my financial literacy ultimately reduces my risk and improves my investment returns. A financial statement lets me see what the average investor cannot see. It also gives me control over my personal finances, and that allows me to go where I want to go in my life. Having control over financial statements also allows me to operate multiple businesses without being in the business physically. Truly understanding financial statements is one of the keys still necessary for an S quadrant person to move to the B quadrant. And that is why I call the income statement and balance sheet the magic carpet."

Mental Attitude Quiz

If we were going to buy a used car, we would probably want a mechanic to look it over and hook it up to an electronic analyzer before deciding if it was worth the asking price asked. If we were going to buy a house, we would ask a home inspector to go through a checklist and check out such things as the condition of the foundation, plumbing, electricity, roof, etc., before buying the house.

If we were going to marry someone, we would probably want to know what was really going on beneath the pretty face before deciding to spend a lifetime with that pretty face.

Yet, when it comes to investing, most investors never read the financial statements of the company they are investing in. Most investors would rather invest on a hot tip or a low price or high price, depending upon the momentum of the market. Most people get their cars tuned up and check out annually, or have an annual health physical, but most people have never have their financial statements analyzed for flaws or potential future problems. The reason is that most people leave school unaware of the importance of a financial statement, much less how to control one. Small wonder why so many people say investing is risky. Investing is not risky. But not being financially literate is.

How to See Investment Opportunities

If you have plans on becoming rich by being an investor, I would say that having a good working knowledge of a financial statement is a minimum requirement. Not only will it improve your safety factor, it will also allow you to make much more money in a shorter period of time. The reason I say this is because being able to read a financial statement will allow you to see investment opportunities that the average investor misses. The average investor looks primarily to price as the opportunity to buy or sell. The sophisticated investor has trained his or her brain to see opportunities other than price. The sophisticated investor knows that most of the best investment opportunities are not visible to the untrained eye.

Rich dad taught me that you make the most money as an investor by being financially literate as well as knowing internal strengths and weaknesses of the investment. He said, "Where you find the best investment opportunities is from understanding accounting, the tax code, business law, and corporate law. And it is in these invisible realms where the real investors shop for the biggest investment bargains. That is why I call the income statement and balance sheet the magic carpet."

So the mental attitude question is:

1. If you plan to become wealthy as an investor and invest in the investments of the rich, are you willing to keep an updated personal financial statement and practice reading other financial statements on a regular basis?

Yes _____ No _____

Financial Literacy Made Simple

"Your dad struggles financially because he is word literate, but not financially literate," rich dad often said to me. "If he just took the time to learn how to read numbers and the vocabulary of money, his life would change dramatically."

Financial literacy was one of rich dad's six lessons in *Rich Dad Poor Dad*. To rich dad, financial literacy was crucial for anyone who was sincere about being a business owner or a professional investor. In later sections of this book, Sharon and I will be going into greater detail on the importance of financial literacy as it pertains to business and investing, and how to find investment opportunities that the average investor misses. But for now, I think it best to quickly review financial literacy and how to make it simple and easier to understand.

The Basics

A sophisticated investor should be able to read many different financial documents. At the center of all the documents are the income statement and the balance sheet.

Income Statement

Income
Expense

Balance Sheet

Assets	Liabilities

I am not an accountant, yet I have attended several classes on accounting. In most of those classes, what struck me was how the instructors focused on one of the documents, but not the relationship between the two documents. In other words, the instructors never explained why one document was important to the other.

Rich dad thought the relationship between the income statement and the balance sheet was everything. He would say, "How can you understand one without the other?" or, "How can you tell what an asset or liability really is without the income column or the expense column?" He would go on and say, "Just because something is listed under the asset column does not make it an asset." I think that statement was the single most important point he made. He would say, "The reason most people suffer financially is because they purchase liabilities and list them under the asset column. That is why so many people call their home an asset when it is really a liability." If you understand Gresham's Law, you may know why such a seemingly minor oversight can cause a lifetime of financial struggle instead of financial freedom. He would also say, "If you want to be rich for generations, you and the ones you love must know the difference between an asset and a liability. You must know the difference between something of value and something of no value."

After *Rich Dad Poor Dad* was published, many people asked, "Is he saying that a person should not buy a house?" The answer to that question is "No, he was not saying do not buy a house." Rich dad was only emphasizing the importance of being financially literate. He was saying, "Don't call a liability an asset, even though it is your house." The next most asked question was, "If I pay off the mortgage on my house, will that make it an asset?" Again, the answer in most cases is "No, just because you have no debt on your home, it does not necessarily make it an asset." The reason for that answer is again found in the term "cash flow." For most personal residences, even if you have no debt, there still are expenses and property taxes. In fact, you never truly own your real estate. Real estate will always belong to the government. That is why the word is "real" (meaning "royal" in Spanish), not physical or tangible. Property has always belonged to the royals. Today it belongs to the government. If you doubt that statement, just stop paying your property taxes and you will find out who really owns your property, with a mortgage or without a mortgage. The non-payment of property taxes is where tax-lien certificates come from. In *Rich Dad Poor Dad*, I wrote about the high interest that investors obtained from tax liens. Tax liens are the government's way of saying, "You may control your real estate, but the government will always own it."

Rich dad was very much in favor of home ownership. He thought that a home was a secure place to put your money but it was not necessarily an asset. In fact, once he had acquired enough real assets, he lived in a big beautiful home. Those real assets generated the cash flow that allowed him to buy his big beautiful home. The point he was making was that a person should not call a liability an asset, or buy liabilities that he or she thinks are assets. He thought that was one of the biggest mistakes a person could make. He would say, "If something is a liability, you'd better call it a liability and watch it closely."

The Magic Words Are Cash Flow

To rich dad, the most important words in business and investing were cash flow. He would say, "Just as a fisherman must watch the ebb and flow of the tides, an investor and businessperson must be keenly aware of the subtle shifts in cash flow. People and businesses struggle financially because they are out of control of their cash flow."

Financial Literacy for a Child

Rich dad may not have been formally educated but he had a way of taking complex subjects and making them simple enough for a 9 year old child to understand, because that is how old I was when he began explaining these things to me, even though my wealth has increased. And I must confess that I have not progressed much beyond the simple line drawings rich dad drew for me. Yet rich dad's simple explanations allowed me to better understand money and its flow as well as guided me to a financially secure life.

Today, my accountants do the hard work and I continue to use rich dad's simple diagrams as my guides. So if you can understand the following diagrams, you have a better chance of acquiring great wealth. Leave the technical accounting work to the accountants who are trained to do such important work. Your job is to take control of your financial numbers and guide them to increasing your wealth.

Rich Dad's Basics of Financial Literacy

Literacy Lesson #1: It is the direction of cash flowing that determines if something is an asset or a liability, at that moment. In other words, just because your real estate broker calls your house an asset does not mean it is an asset.

This is the cash flow pattern of an asset. Rich dad's definition of an asset was: "An asset puts money in your pocket."

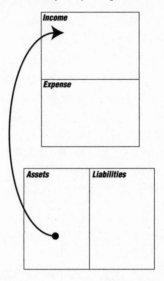

This is the cash flow pattern of a liability. Rich dad's definition of a liability was: "A liability takes money from your pocket."

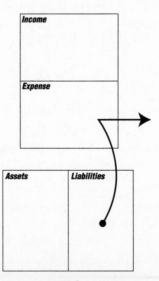

A Point of Confusion

Rich dad also said to me, "The confusion occurs because the accepted method of accounting allows us to list both assets and liabilities under the asset column." He would then draw a diagram to explain what he had just said and say, "This is why it is confusing."

He would say, "In this diagram, we have a $100,000 house that someone has put $20,000 cash down on and now has an $80,000 mortgage. How do you know if this house is an asset or a liability? Is the house an asset just because it is listed under the asset column?"

Income
Expense

Assets	Liabilities
$100,000	$80,000

The answer of course is "No." The real answer is: "You need to refer to the income statement to find out if it is an asset or a liability."

Rich dad then drew the following diagram, saying, "This is a house that is a liability. You can tell it is a liability because its only line items are under the expense column; nothing is in the income column."

Income	
Expense	
Mortgage	
Real estate taxes	
Insurance	
Utilities	
Maintenance	

Asset	Liability
$100,000	$80,000

Changing a Liability to an Asset

Rich dad then added to the diagram a line that read, "Rental Income and Net Rental Income," the key word being "net." "That change to the financial statement changed this house from a liability to an asset."

Income	
Rental Income	
Expense	
Mortgage Payment	
Real Estate Taxes	
Insurance	
Utilities	
Maintenance	

Net Rental Income

Asset	Liability
$100,000	$80,000

After understanding the concept, rich dad would add the numbers, just so I could understand the concept better. "Let's say all the expenses associated with this house add up to $1,000. That includes, the mortgage payment, real estate taxes, insurance, utilities, and maintenance. And you now have a tenant paying you $1,200 a month. You now have a net rental income of $200.00 a month, which makes it an asset because this house is now putting money in your pocket, as verified by the $200.00 income. If your expenses stayed the same, and you collected only $800.00 a month in rent, you would now be losing $200.00, and even though you had gross rental income of $800.00 a month, the property would become a liability. So even with rental income, the property could still be a liability instead of an asset. And then I hear people say, 'But if I sell it for more than I paid for it then it becomes an asset.' Yes that would be true but only when that event occurs sometime in the future. And contrary to popular belief, the price of real estate does go down on occasion. So the saying 'Don't count your chickens before they hatch,' is a wise bit of financial wisdom."

The Government Changed the Rules

Literally billions of dollars were lost on real estate after the 1986 Tax Reform Act. So many speculators lost money because they were willing to buy high-priced real estate and lose money on the assumption that the price of real estate would always go up and the government would give them a tax break for their passive real estate losses. In other words, the government would subsidize the difference between rental income and rental expenses, which were higher. As they say, "Someone changed the rules." After the tax law change, the stock market crashed, savings and loans went broke, and a huge transfer of wealth occurred between 1987 and 1995. Investment property flowed from primarily the S quadrant—the high-income professionals, such as doctors, lawyers, accountants, engineers, and architects—to the investors in the I quadrant. That single tax law change forced millions of people out of investing in real estate and into the paper asset market known as the stock market. Could another transfer of wealth from one side of the Quadrant to the other be ready to occur soon? This time, could it be paper assets instead of real estate? Only time will tell, and history does tend to repeat itself. When it does repeat itself, some people will lose, but many others will win.

In Australia today, the government still has laws that allow investors to "negatively gear" their investment real estate. In other words, you are encouraged to lose money on your rental real estate, with the idea of gaining a tax break from the government. We in the United States had the same tax rules until 1986. When I speak in Australia about investing, I often hear howls of protest about my warnings that the government could change the laws just as they did in the United States. I hear things such as "The government won't change the rules," and I just shake my head. They just don't realize how painful the law change was to millions of investors in the

United States. Several of my friends had to declare bankruptcy and lost everything they had worked years or decades to acquire.

The point I make is: Why subject yourself to the risk? Why not find a property that makes money? Any person can find a property or investment that loses money. You don't have to look too far to find an investment that loses money. You don't have to be smart or financially literate to find an investment that loses money. The problem I have and rich dad had with the idea that losing money was a good idea because of the tax breaks was that such ideas often caused people to be sloppy. I often hear people say even here in America, "It's OK that I am losing money. The government gives me a tax break for losing money." That means for every dollar you lose, the government gives you back approximately 30 cents (depending on your tax bracket). To me, there is something missing in that logic. Why not invest so you can have it all, which is security, income, appreciation, and tax breaks?

The idea behind investing is to make money, not to lose money. You can still gain many tax breaks and make money if you are a sophisticated investor. A friend of mine, Michael Tellarico, a real estate broker in Sydney, Australia, says, "People come into this real estate office every day and say, 'My accountant told me to come in here and look for property that I can negatively gear.'" In other words, my accountant told me to buy a property to lose money on. Michael then says, "You don't need my help to find a property that loses money. There are thousands of them all around you. What I can help you find is a property that will make you money and you will still get your tax breaks." The reply often is, "No. No. I want to find a property to lose money on." The same thing was going on in America just before 1986.

There are several important lessons from this example:

1. The idea that losing money is OK because of tax breaks often causes people to become sloppy in choosing investments.

2. These people do not look as hard for real investments. They do not look at the financials as closely when analyzing an investment.

3. Losing money destabilizes your financial position. In other words, there is enough risk involved with investing as it is. Why make it any more risky? Take the extra time and look for solid investments. You can find them if you can read the numbers.

4. The government does change the rules.

5. What might be an asset today could be a liability tomorrow.

6. While millions of investors lost money in 1986, there were other investors that were prepared for the change. Those who were prepared made the millions that the unprepared investors lost.

The Biggest Risk of All

Rich dad said, "The riskiest investor of all is a person who is out of control of his or her personal financial statement. The riskiest of all investors are those who have nothing but liabilities they think are assets, have as much in expenses as they have in income, and whose only source of income is their labor. They are risky because they are often desperate investors."

In my investment classes, I still have people come up to me and argue that their home is an asset. Recently one man said, "I bought my house for $500,000 and today it's worth $750,000." I then asked him, "How do you know that?" His reply was, "Because that is what my real estate broker said it was worth."

To which I asked, "Will your broker guarantee you that price for 20 years?"

"Why no," he said. "He just said that was the comparable average price of houses in the neighborhood being sold today."

And that is exactly why my rich dad said the average investor does not make much money in the market. Rich dad said, "The average investor has the count your chickens before they hatch mentality. They buy items that cost them money each month, yet call them assets based upon opinions. They count on their house going up in value in the future, or they act like their house can be sold immediately for what their real estate broker told them it is worth. Have you ever ended up selling your home for less than what your broker, or banker thought it was worth? I have. As a result of basing financial decisions on these opinions and expectations, people lose control over their personal finances. That to me is very risky. If you want to be rich, you must take control over your education as well as your personal cash flow. There is nothing wrong with hoping the price of something goes up in the future as long as you do not lose control of your finances today." He would also say, "If you're so certain the price is going up why not buy 10 of those houses?"

This mentality also applies to people who say, "My retirement account is worth $1 million dollars today. It will be worth $3 million when I retire." Again, I would ask, "How do you know that?" What I learned from my rich dad was that the average investor often "Counts their chickens before they hatch." Or they bet everything on one event which means they literally "Wait for their ship to come in," sometime in the future. In most cases, many eggs do hatch and most ships do eventually come in. Yet the professional investor does not want to take that chance. The sophisticated investor knows that being financially educated gives you more control today and if you keep studying, greater financial control tomorrow. The sophisticated investor knows that sometimes eggs get eaten or stepped on and sometimes the ship people are waiting for is the *Titanic*.

I meet many investors who are new to the world of investing. They have been investing for less than 20 years. Most have never been through a market crash or owned real estate worth much less than they paid for it where they still must make the monthly payments. These new investors come up to me and spout off industry averages such as, "The market on average has been going up since 1974." Or "Real estate over time has averaged over 4% per year for the last 20 years."

As rich dad said, "Averages are for average investors. A professional investor wants controls. And that control begins with yourself, your financial education, your sources of information, and your own cash flow." That is why rich dad's advice to the average investor was, "Don't be average." To him being an average investor was being a risky investor.

Why People Don't Have Control Over Their Personal Finances

People leave school not even knowing how to balance a checkbook much less how to prepare a financial statement. They never learned how to control their finances. And the only way you can tell if people are in control of themselves is by looking at their financial statements. Just because people have high-paying jobs, big houses, and nice cars does not necessarily mean they are in control financially. If people knew how a financial statement worked, they would be more financially literate and more in control of their money. By understanding financial statements, people can better see how their cash is flowing.

For example, this is the cash flow pattern of writing a check:

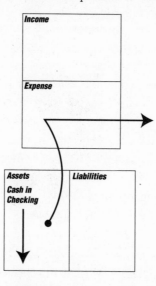

This is the cash flow pattern of using a credit card:

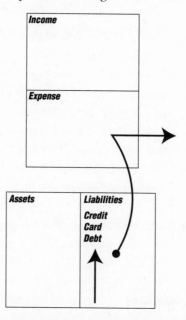

When people write checks, they are depleting an asset. And when people use their credit cards, they are increasing their liabilities. In other words, credit cards make it so much easier to get deeper and deeper into debt. Most people cannot see it happening to them simply because they have not been trained to fill out and analyze a personal financial statement.

Today, many individuals' financial statements look like this:

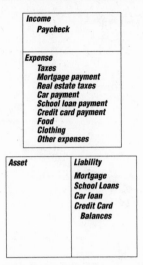

Unless something changes inside this person, chances are that this person will live a life of financial servitude. Why do I say financial servitude? Because each payment this person makes is making a rich person richer.

AUTHOR'S NOTE: Many people ask me: "What is my first step to financial freedom?" My response is, "Take control of your financial statement." I asked my tax strategist and accountant, Diane Kennedy, to put together an audiotape program and workbook to:

1. Learn how a personal financial statement works

2. Take control of your own financial statement

3. Get on track to become financially free

4. Learn how to manage money like the rich do by paying less in taxes

Diane and I produced these tapes, and we walk you through the process of getting out of debt. More importantly, however, you will learn how to manage your money like the rich do. This is important because most people think that making more money will solve their money problems. In most instances, it does not. Learning to manage the money you do have like a rich person does is how you can solve your short-term money problems. Doing so also gives you the opportunity to possibly become financially free. The audiotape set and workbook are contained in a program titled "Your First Step to Financial Freedom." The information found in this educational package is simple, easy to understand, and essential to start building a strong financial foundation. You can find out more information about this audiotape package in the back of this book or from our website at www.richdad.com.

Who Are You Making Rich?

Literacy Lesson #2: It takes at least two financial statements to see the entire picture.

Rich dad said, "Sophisticated investors must see at least two financial

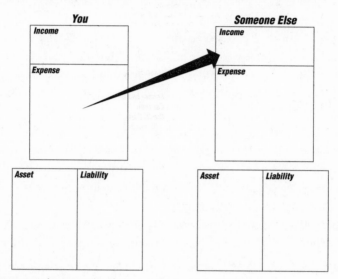

statements simultaneously if they want a true picture."

During one of my lessons, rich dad drew this diagram:

"Always remember that your expense is someone else's income. People who are out of control of their cash flow make the people who are in control of their cash flow rich."

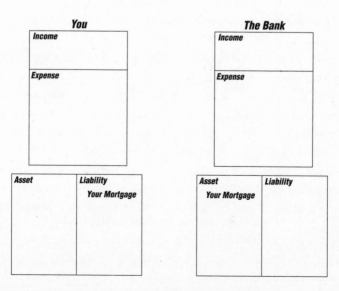

What an Investor Does

He then drew this diagram, saying, "Let me show you what an investor does, using a home owner and banker as an example":

I sat there looking at the diagram for a moment and then said, "The person's mortgage appears on two financial statements. The difference is that this same mortgage appears under two columns: the asset column and the liability column."

Rich dad nodded. "Now you are seeing a true financial statement."

"That is why you say it takes at least two different financial statements to see the entire picture," I added. "For every one of your expenses, it is someone else's income, and each one of your liabilities is someone else's asset."

Rich dad nodded, saying, "And that is why people leaving school who have not been trained to think in terms of financial statements often fall prey to those who do. That is why each time people use their credit card, they are actually adding to their own liability column and simultaneously adding to the bank's asset column."

"And when a banker says to you, 'Your home is an asset,' they are not really lying to you. They're just not saying whose asset it really is. Your mortgage is the bank's asset and your liability," I said, beginning to more fully understand the importance of financial statements and why it takes

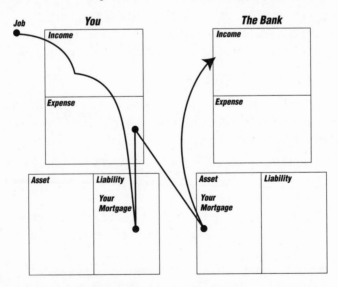

more than two statements to gain a more accurate picture.

Rich dad nodded and said, "Now let's add cash flow to this picture and we begin to see how an asset, in this example a mortgage, really works:

"In this example, the mortgage takes money from your pocket and puts it in the bank's pocket. That is why the mortgage is a liability to you and an asset to the bank. The point I am making is that it is the same legal document."

"So the bank has created an asset that for you is a liability," I added. "What an investor does is acquire an asset that someone else pays for. That is why investors own apartment houses. Every month, cash flows into the investors' income statements from the rent, just as their mortgage payments flow into the bank's income statement."

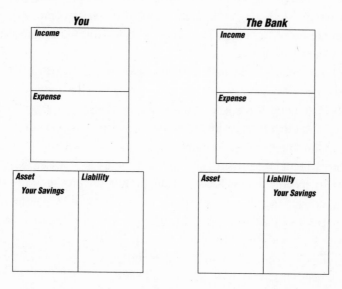

Rich dad nodded and grinned. "You're beginning to get it. You definitely want to be on one side of the equation more than the other. But it is a two-way street," he said as he drew the following diagram:

"Oh," I said. "My savings are my asset and the bank's liability. Again, it takes a minimum of two financial statements to see the complete picture."

"Yes," said rich dad. "And what else do you notice about these diagrams?"

I stared at the diagrams for a while, looking at the examples of the mortgage and the savings. "I don't know," I said slowly. "I just see what you have drawn there."

Rich dad smiled and said, "This is why you need to practice reading financial statements. Just as you learn more the second and third time you read or listen to someone, you learn more and more the more you practice being financially literate. More things come into your mind that your eyes often miss."

"So what have I missed? What have I not seen?" I asked.

"What is not visible from my diagrams is that the government gives you a tax incentive to acquire liabilities. That is why it gives you a tax break for buying a house."

"I forgot about that," I said.

"And it taxes you for your savings," said rich dad.

"The government gives me a tax break for having a liability and taxes me for having an asset?" I asked.

Rich dad nodded, saying, "Now think about what that does to a person's thinking and financial future. The average person gets excited about being in debt and not excited about acquiring assets."

"People get a tax break for losing money?" I asked in bewilderment. "Why do they do that?"

Rich dad chuckled, "As I said, the professional investor must think beyond the price of an investment going up or going down. A sophisticated investor reads the numbers to get the true story and begins to see things that the average investor does not see. A sophisticated investor must see the impact of government regulations, tax codes, corporate law, business law, and accounting law. One reason it is hard to find accurate investment information is that to gain a full picture requires financial literacy, an accountant, and an attorney. In other words, you needed two different professionals to get the real picture. The good news is that if you take your time and invest the time to learn the ins and outs of what goes on behind the scenes, you will find investment opportunities and great wealth, wealth that very few people ever find. You will find out the truth about why the rich get richer, and the poor and middle class work harder, pay more in taxes, and get deeper in debt. Once you know the truths, you can then decide which side of the Quadrant you want to operate from. It's not hard; it just takes some time...time that people who just want a hot investment tip do not want to invest."

I did not have to think about which side of the Quadrant I wanted to operate from. I knew I wanted to invest legally from the inside, not the outside. I wanted to know what the truths were, regardless of if I became rich or not. I now wanted to know how and why the rich got richer.

The Need for Financial Education

In the early 1980s, I began teaching entrepreneurship and investing to adults as a hobby. One of the problems I ran into immediately was that most people who wanted to start businesses or invest with greater confidence lacked the basics of financial literacy. I believe that this lack of financial education is why nine out of ten new businesses fail in the first five years, and why most investors think investing is risky and do not make or keep much money.

When I recommended that people take classes in accounting, finance, and investing before starting a business or investing, most groaned and did not want to go back to school. That is when I began to search for a way that individuals could gain the basic knowledge in an easy and fun way. In 1996, I created *CASHFLOW, Investing 101*, a game that teaches the basics of financial literacy, accounting, and investing.

Teaching Versus Learning

CASHFLOW is a board game because investing and financial analysis are subjects that you cannot learn by reading. My poor dad the school-teacher often said, "A teacher must know the difference between what can be taught and what must be learned." He would go on to say, "You can teach a child to memorize the word 'bicycle' but you cannot teach a child to ride one. A child needs to learn how to ride a bicycle by doing."

In the past three years, I have observed thousands of people learning to be investors by playing *CASHFLOW, Investing 101* and *202*. They learn by doing things I could never teach by writing or by lecturing, just as I could never teach you to ride a bicycle. The games teach in a few hours what my rich dad took 30 years guiding me to learn. And that is why this book is titled *Rich Dad's Guide to Investing* because that is what he did. He guided me because that was the best he could do. Investing and accounting are subjects that he could not teach me. I had to want to learn. The same is true for you.

Improving Your Results

The more you read financial statements, annual reports, and prospectuses, the more your financial intelligence, or financial vision, increases. Over time you will begin to see things that the average investor never sees.

We all know that repetition is how we really learn and retain what we learn. Recently, I was listening to an audiotape of an interview of Peter Lynch. I had listened to that audiotape a dozen times before. Each time I listen to it, I hear something new. For over 30 years, rich dad had me review financial statements. Today, I think automatically in financial statements.

When we learn to ride a bicycle, we train our subconscious mind to ride our bike. Once that is done, we don't have to think or remember how to ride a bike as we ride. When we learn to drive a car, we also train our subconscious mind. And that is why, once we have trained our subconscious mind to drive, we can drive and talk to someone else, eat a hamburger, think about problems at work, or listen to the radio and sing along. Driving is (hopefully) automatically handled. The same can happen with reading financial statements.

What takes the longest time in finding a good investment is analyzing the numbers. Learning to read financial statements is a tedious process, especially when you first begin to learn. The good news is that it gets easier and faster as you practice. Not only does it get easier, but you can also review many more investment opportunities almost automatically without thinking...just like riding a bike, or driving a car.

Mental Attitude Quiz

We as humans learn to do many things subconsciously. If you are serious about becoming a more successful investor, an investor who makes more money with less and less risk, I recommend training your brain to analyze financial statements. Analyzing financial statements is basic to the world's best fundamental investors, investors such as Warren Buffet.

The way this is done is by a term called "deal flow." Every professional investor has a continuous number of potential business or real estate investments that need investment capital. Rich dad had Mike and me read, study, and analyze these investments regardless of if we were interested in them or not. Even though it was slow and painful at first, over the years, the process became faster, easier, more fun, and more exciting. So we learned by repetition, and that repetition has paid off by allowing me to retire early, feel more financially secure, and make even more money.

So the mental attitude question is:

Are you willing to practice filling out your own financial statement and keep it up to date as well as read those of other businesses and real estate investment financial statements?

Yes_____ No_____

You will note that it is very similar to the question at the end of Chapter 15. It is repeated to emphasize the importance of financial literacy. This question is very important because one of the costs of becoming a rich investor and investing in investments of the rich is the price of investing time in continual improvement of your own financial literacy. If your answer is "No" to this question, then most of the investments that the rich invest in are far too risky for you. If you are financially literate, then you will be better prepared to find the very best investments in the world.

Chapter 17
Investor Lesson # 15

The Magic of Mistakes

My real dad came from the world of academics, a world where mistakes are perceived as bad and to be avoided. In the world of education, the more mistakes a person makes, the less intelligent that person is thought to be.

My rich dad came from the streets. He had a different view on mistakes. To him, mistakes were opportunities to learn something new, something he did not know before. To him, the more mistakes a person made, the more the person learned. He often said, "There is a bit of magic hidden in every mistake. So the more mistakes I make and I take the time to learn from, the more magic I have in my life."

My rich dad constantly used the example of learning to ride a bicycle to reinforce the idea of the magic found inside of mistakes. He would say, "Just remember the frustration you went through as you struggled to learn how to ride a bicycle. All your friends are riding but all you are doing is climbing on the bike and immediately falling off. You make mistake after mistake. Then suddenly, you stop falling off, you begin to peddle, the bike begins rolling, and then suddenly like magic, a whole new world opens to you. That is the magic found in mistakes."

Warren Buffet's Mistake

Warren Buffet, America's richest investor, is known and respected for his company Berkshire Hathaway. Today, Berkshire Hathaway's share price is one of the highest priced company shares in the world. While many investors value Berkshire Hathaway's stock, few people realize that acquiring Berkshire Hathaway was one of Warren Buffet's biggest investment mistakes.

When he acquired the company, Berkshire Hathaway was a shirt-manufacturing company that was slowly going out of business. Warren Buffet thought his team could turn the company around. Well as most of us know, textile manufacturing was dying in America and moving to other countries. It was a trend that even Warren Buffet could not go against, and the company eventually failed as a manufacturing company, even with Warren Buffet behind it. Yet, inside of this company failure, Warren Buffet found the gems that ultimately made him extremely rich. For those who are interested in this story, the book *The Warren Buffet Way*, by Robert Hagstrom, is most enlightening, giving the reader insights into one of the greatest investor minds in the world.

Other Mistakes

Another company, Diamond Fields, was formed to look for diamonds, which were never found. The company's head geologist had made a mistake. Yet, instead of finding diamonds, they struck one of the largest nickel deposits in the world. Their stock price soared upon the discovery. Today, although the name remains Diamond Fields, they make their money in nickel.

Levi Strauss headed for the gold fields of California to strike it rich in mining. However, he was not a good miner, so he instead began sewing pants out of canvas for the miners who were successful. Today, I think most of the world has heard of Levi's jeans.

It is said that Thomas Edison would never have invented the light bulb if he had been an employee for the company he ultimately founded—General Electric. It is said that Edison failed over 10,000 times before finally inventing the light bulb. If he had been an employee of a major corporation, he would most likely have been fired for making so many mistakes.

Christopher Columbus's big mistake was that he was looking for a trade route to China and accidentally bumped into America, the richest, most powerful country in the world.

Street Smarts Versus School Smarts

My rich dad was so very successful financially for many reasons. At the top of the list was his attitude towards making mistakes. Like most of us, he hated making them, yet he was not afraid of making them. He would take risks simply to make a mistake. He would say, "When you come to the boundaries of what you know, it's time to make some mistakes."

Several times, one of his businesses failed to get off the ground and he lost money. I have also seen him launch a new product only to have it be rejected by the marketplace. Yet each time he made a mistake, instead of being depressed, he often seemed happier, wiser, more determined, and even richer from the experience. He would say to his son and me, "Mistakes are how we learn. Every time I make a mistake, I always learn something about myself, I learn something new, and I often meet new people I would never have met."

In one of his failed ventures, a plumbing distribution company, he met one of his future business partners. And from that failed plumbing business, they formed a friendship and partnership that went on to make tens of millions of dollars. He said, "If I had not taken the risk to form that business, I would never have met Jerry. And meeting Jerry is one of the most important events in my life."

My poor dad was an excellent student in school. He rarely made mistakes, which was why he had such high grades. The problem was that at age 50, he seemed to have made one of the biggest mistakes in his life and he could not recover from it.

As I watched my real dad struggle financially and professionally, my rich dad said, "To be successful in the real world of business, you have to be school smart as well as street smart. Your dad entered school at the age of 5. Because he had good grades, he stayed in school, eventually becoming the top man in the school system. Now at age 50, he is hitting the streets...and the streets are a very tough teacher. In school, you're given the lesson first. On the street, you're given the mistake first and then it's up to you to find the lesson, if you ever find it. Since most people have not been taught how to make mistakes and learn from them, they either avoid mistakes altogether, which is a bigger mistake, or they make a mistake but fail to find the lesson from the mistake. That is why you see so many people making the same mistake over and over again. They make the same mistake over and over again because they have never been taught how to learn from their mistakes. In school, you are considered smart if you don't make mistakes. On the street, you're smart only if you make mistakes and learn from them."

The Biggest Failure I Know

Rich dad said to Mike and me, "I am so rich because I've made more financial mistakes than most people. Each time I made a mistake, I learned something new. In the business world, that something new is often called 'experience.' But experience is not enough. Many people say they have a lot of experience because they keep making the same mistake over and over again. If a person truly learns from a mistake, his or her life changes forever, and what that person gains instead of experience is 'wisdom.'" He went on to say, "People often avoid making financial mistakes, and that is a mistake. They keep saying to themselves, 'Play it safe. Don't take risks.' People may be struggling financially because they have already made mistakes and have not learned from the mistakes. So they get up every day, go to work, and repeat the mistake and avoid new mistakes, but they never find the lesson. These people often say to themselves, 'I'm doing everything right, but for some reason, I'm not getting ahead financially.'" Rich dad's comment to that statement was, "They may be doing all the right things but the problem is that they are avoiding the wrong things—wrong things such as taking more risks. They are avoiding their weaknesses instead of confronting them. They are not doing something they may be afraid of doing, and consciously choosing to avoid making a mistake rather than make one." He also said, "Some of the biggest failures I know are people who have never failed."

The Art of Making a Mistake

Instead of instructing his son and me to avoid mistakes, rich dad taught us the art of making a mistake and gaining wisdom from it.

During one of those lessons, rich dad said, "The first thing that happens after you make a mistake is that you become upset. Everyone I know gets upset. That is the first indication of a mistake," said rich dad. "At this point of upset, you find out who you really are."

What do you mean, "Who you really are?" asked Mike.

"Well at a moment of upset, we become one of these characters," rich dad said, going on to describe the cast of characters who are brought to center stage when upsets from mistakes occur:

1. **The Liar.** The liar will say such things as: "I didn't do that." Or "No, no, no. It wasn't me." Or "I don't know how that happened." Or "Prove it."

2. **The Blamer.** The blamer will say such things as: "It's your fault, not mine." Or "If my wife didn't spend so much money, I would be better off financially." Or "I would be rich if I didn't have you kids."

Or "The customers just don't care about my products." Or "Employees just aren't loyal anymore." Or "You weren't clear in your instructions." Or "It's my boss's fault."

3. The Justifier. The justifier says things such as: "Well, I don't have a good education so that is why I don't get ahead." Or "I would have made it if I had had more time." Or "Oh, I really didn't want to be rich anyway." Or "Well, everyone else was doing it."

4. The Quitter. The quitter says things such as: "I told you that it would never work." Or "This is too hard and it's not worth it. I'm going to do something else easier." Or "Why am I doing this? I don't need this hassle."

5. The Denier. Rich dad often called this person "the cat in the litter box," which means this person tends to bury his or her mistakes. The person who denies that he or she has made a mistake often says things such as: "No, there is nothing wrong. Things are fine." Or "Mistake? What mistake?" Or "Don't worry. Things will work out."

Rich dad said, "When people are upset due to a mistake or accident, one or more of these characters will take over their mind and body. If you want to learn and gain wisdom from this priceless mistake, you have to let The Responsible You eventually take control of your thinking. The Responsible You will eventually say, "What priceless lesson can I learn from this mistake?"

Rich dad went on to say, "If a person says, 'What I learned is that I'll never do this again,' he or she probably has not learned much. Too many people live in a diminishing world because they continue to say, 'I'll never do that again' instead of saying, 'I'm glad that happened because I learned this or that from the experience.' Besides people who avoid mistakes or waste mistakes never see the other side of the coin."

I Slept Like a Baby

For example, after I lost my nylon and Velcro wallet business, I was upset for about a year. I slept like a baby during that year, which meant I woke up crying every two hours. I could hear my mind saying, "I should never have started the business. I knew it would fail. I'll never start a business again." I also blamed a lot of people and found myself justifying my actions a lot, saying things such as, "It was Dan's fault" and "Well, I didn't really love the product."

Instead of run from my mistake and get a job, rich dad had me face the mess I had made and begin to work my way out from under the pile of rubble that was once my business. Today, I say to people, "I learned more about business by failing than I ever did by being successful. Working through the wreckage and rebuilding the company made me a much better businessman." Today, instead of saying, "I'll never do that again," I say, "I'm glad I did fail and learn because I am grateful for the wisdom I gained." And then I say, "Let's start another business." Instead of fear and resentment, there is excitement and fun. Instead of being afraid of failing, I now know that making mistakes is the way we were all designed to learn. If we fail to make mistakes, or make them and do not learn from them, the magic goes out of life. Life goes backward and gets smaller, instead of expansive and filled with magic.

I failed in high school twice because I could not write. To have my books on bestseller lists such as those of *The New York Times, Sydney Morning Herald,* and *The Wall Street Journal* is magical. It is ironic that I am well known for subjects I initially failed at: writing, business, selling, speaking, accounting, and investing. I am not known for the subjects that were easy and enjoyable for me: surfing, economics, rugby, and painting.

What Is the Lesson?

Whenever I hear people saying, "Investing is too risky" or "I don't like taking risks with my money" or "What if I fail?" or "What if I lose my money?" I am often reminded of my poor dad because what he was really saying was "I don't want to make a mistake." As I said, in his world, the world of academics, people who made mistakes were considered stupid.

In rich dad's world, he viewed risk, mistakes, and failure as an integral part of human development. So instead of avoiding risk and mistakes, he learned to manage risk and mistakes. His view on mistakes was that a mistake was simply a lesson with emotions attached to it. He said, "Whenever we make a mistake, we become upset. An upset is our maker's way of telling us that we need to learn something. It is a tap on our shoulder saying, 'Pay attention. You have something important to learn. If you lie, blame, justify, or deny the upset, you waste the upset and will waste a precious gem of wisdom.'"

Rich dad taught me to count to ten if I was angry or to a hundred if I was very angry. After cooling off, I simply say, "I apologize" and never blame the other person, no matter how angry I am. If I blame, I give power to the other person. If I take responsibility for whatever happened, I will learn a precious lesson that I obviously needed to learn. If I lie, blame, justify, or deny, I learn nothing.

Rich dad also said, "Unsuccessful people blame the other person. They often want the other person to change, and that is why they stay upset for so long. They are upset because they fail to learn their personal lesson.

Instead of being upset, such people should be grateful for the other person being there to teach them something they needed to learn.

"People come together to teach each other lessons. The problem is, we often do not know what lesson we are teaching. To be upset or hold a grudge against the other person is like being upset with your bicycle because you fell off once or twice while trying to learn something new," rich dad would say.

Mistakes Today

As I write, the stock market and real estate markets are climbing. Individuals who have never invested before are climbing into the market, most saying the same things. They say things like, "I have made so much money in the market." Or "I'm in early and the price has gone up 20%." Those are often enthusiastic words of new investors, investors who have never lost in a down market. I am afraid that in a short while, many of these new investors who are now winning will find out what it feels like to make a mistake in the market. At that moment, we will see who the real investors are. As rich dad said, "It's not how much your investment goes up that matters, it's how much it can come down that is most important. Real investors must be prepared to profit as well as learn when things do not go as they want them to in the market. The best thing a market can teach you is how to learn from your mistakes."

For me, learning to control my temper has been a lifelong process. So has the process of being willing to take risks, make mistakes, and be grateful for the other person—even though I may no longer speak to or do business with that person. When I reflect back on my life, I would say that it is this mental attitude that has made me the most money, has brought me the most success, and has ultimately allowed me to have the most magic in my life.

Mental Attitude Quiz

I learned from both dads that both school smarts and street smarts are important. Being intelligent is recognizing the differences between the two, or as rich dad said, "School smarts are important but street smarts make you rich."

So the mental attitude questions are:

1. What are your attitudes to risk, making mistakes, and learning?
2. What are the attitudes of the people around you to risk, making mistakes, and learning?
3. Are there still some financial, professional, or business upsets that remain unresolved?

4. Are you still angry with someone else in regards to money?
5. And if you are upset with someone else or yourself, what lesson can you learn and be grateful for because you were courageous enough to have taken a risk and maybe learned something?

I always remember my rich dad saying, "I have so much money because I was willing to make more mistakes than most people and learn from them. Most people have not made enough mistakes or continue to make the same mistakes over and over again. Without mistakes and learning, there is no magic in life."

ADDITIONAL NOTE:
This subject of the magic of mistakes is one of rich dad's most important lessons, especially in this brave new world we enter. It is the people who fear mistakes who will be left behind financially and professionally as the Information Age continues to pick up speed.

—I recently created an educational program on audiotape with Nightingale Conant titled "Rich Dad Secrets to Money, Business, and Investing," which covers this very important lesson from rich dad. In my opinion, this educational product is for anyone wanting to learn how to overcome the fear of failing, the fear of making mistakes, or the fear of taking risks.

If you are interested in this product, you may order it from us or directly from Nightingale Conant. As Winston Churchill said, "Success is the ability to go from one failure to another with no loss of enthusiasm."

What Is the Price of Becoming Rich?

Rich dad would tell me that there are many ways a person can become rich, and each one has a price.

1. **You can become rich by marrying someone for his or her money.** And we all know what that price is. Rich dad would scrunch up his face and say, "Both men and women marry for money, but can you imagine spending your life with someone you don't love? That is a very high price."

2. **You can become rich by being a crook, a cheat, or an outlaw.** He would say, "It is so easy to become rich legally. Why would people want to break the law and risk going to jail unless they really enjoyed the thrill of it all? To risk going to jail is much too high a price for me. I want to be rich for my freedom, so why risk going to jail? I would lose my self-respect. I could not face my family and friends if I were doing something illegal. Besides, I am a bad liar. I have a poor memory, and I could not keep track of all my lies, so it is best to just tell the truth. In my opinion, honesty is the best policy."

3. **You can become rich through inheritance.** Rich dad would say, "Mike often feels like he did not earn his keep. He wonders if he

could have become rich on his own. I have therefore given him very little. I have guided him as I guide you, but it is up to him to create his own wealth. It is important for him to feel he has earned it. Not everyone fortunate enough to inherit money feels that way."

As Mike and I had grown up together, both our families were relatively poor. By the time we were adults, however, Mike's dad had become very rich, while my real dad was still poor. Mike stood to inherit a fortune from his dad, the man I call my rich dad. I was starting with nothing.

4. **You can become rich by winning the lottery.** All rich dad could say to that was, "It's OK to buy a ticket now and then, but to bet your financial life on winning the lottery is a fool's plan on becoming rich."

Unfortunately, winning the lottery is how many Americans say they plan on becoming rich. Living your life with odds of one in a hundred million is a very high price to pay.

And if you do not have a plan on how to handle the problem of too much money, you will go back to being poor. Recently, there was a story in the paper of a man who won the lottery. He had a great time but was soon so deeply in debt that he considered filing bankruptcy. He was doing fine financially before he won the lottery. So to solve his problem, he went out and played the lottery again— and won. This time, he has financial advisors helping him with his money. So the moral of the story is: If you win the lottery once have a plan for the money. Not too many people win it twice.

5. **You can become rich by being a movie star, a rock star, a sports star, or someone outstanding in one field or another.** Rich dad would say, "I am not smart, talented, good looking, or entertaining. So becoming rich by being outstanding is not realistic for me."

Hollywood is filled with actors who are broke. Clubs are filled with rock bands dreaming of cutting a gold record. The golf courses are filled with golfers dreaming of becoming a pro like Tiger Woods. However, if you look closely at Tiger Woods, you will notice that he paid a high price to get to where he is today. Tiger started playing golf at the age of 3 and did not turn pro until he was 20. His price was 17 years of practice.

6. **You can become rich by being greedy.** The world is filled with people like this. Their favorite saying is: "I got mine and I am going

to keep it." Greedy with their money and assets usually means they are also tight with other things. When asked to help other people, or to teach other people, they often do not have the time.

The price for being greedy is that you have to work even harder to keep what you want. Newton's Law states, "For every action there is a reaction." If you're greedy, people will respond to you in kind.

When I meet people who are having a tough time with money, I ask them to start giving money away on a regular basis—to their church or favorite charity. Following the laws of economics and physics, give what you want. If you want a smile, first give a smile. If you want a punch, first throw a punch. If you want money, first give some money. For greedy people, opening up their fist or wallet can be very hard to do.

7. **You can become rich by being cheap.** This is the one that set rich dad's blood boiling. He said, "The problem with becoming rich by being cheap is that you are still cheap. The world hates rich people who are cheap. That is why people hated the character Scrooge in Charles Dickens' famous story, 'A Christmas Carol.'" Rich dad would say, "It is people who become rich like Scrooge that give the rich a bad name. To live poor and die poor is a tragedy. But to live poor and die rich is insanity."

After he calmed down, he would say, "I think money is meant to be enjoyed, so I work hard, my money works hard, and I enjoy the fruits of our labor."

Affording the Good Life

A recent article reinforces my rich dad's point of view. The article, "Affording the Good Life in an Age of Change," was in the *Strategic Investment Newsletter*, published by James Dale Davidson and Lord William Rees-Mogg. These two men have also co-authored several best-selling books: *Blood in the Streets*, *The Great Reckoning*, and *The Sovereign Individual*. These books have dramatically affected the way I invest and how I look to the future. Davidson is the founder of the National Taxpayers Union, and Rees-Mogg is a financial advisor to some of the world's wealthiest investors, a former editor of the *Times of London*, and vice-chairman of the British Broadcasting Corporation.

My rich dad would say, "There are two ways to become rich. One way is to earn more. The other way is to desire less. The problem is that most people are not good with either way." The article and this book are about how you can earn more so you can desire more. Here are excerpts from the article "Affording the Good Life in an Age of Change" as published in the *Strategic Investment Newsletter.*

"Being frugal is the cornerstone of wealth-building."
Thomas J. Stanley & William Danko
The Millionaire Next Door 1996

This reminds me of my complaint with the reasoning of the popular books, such as *The Millionaire Next Door,* by Stanley and Danko, and *Getting Rich In America: 8 Simple Rules for Building a Fortune and a Satisfying Life* by my friend Dwight Lee. Both books define success downward by suggesting that anyone who lives an abstemious lifestyle and pinches pennies will become "rich."...

Yes. If you never earn more than $50,000 a year, you may become a millionaire by pinching pennies. But there is a limit to the amount of wealth you can acquire by living as though you were poor. Even eating Spam or canned spaghetti from Chef Boyardee at every meal would not save enough money to make you a multimillionaire. This helps explain why only one-in-10 millionaires reaches a net worth of $5 million...Simply penny pinching, per se, is only a preliminary step that would permit someone without inherited capital or a significant annual cash flow to make the kind of investment that would lead to riches. For Americans, becoming a "millionaire" is a necessary step to allow you to participate as an "accredited investor" in private placements for private, high growth companies. This is the main route to riches. I was a millionaire in my early 20s. But I quickly recognized even then that a few millions did not amount to much. I could not afford my preferred lifestyle on such a small fortune.

...My conclusion is that the best way to make real money is to undertake private stage investments in private companies.

"Affording the Good Life in an Age of Change" discusses why being cheap is not a way to really become wealthy. Davidson's point is that while it is possible to become rich by being cheap, there is a huge price to pay. In fact, there are many prices to pay. One such price is that being cheap and scrimping money will get you only so far. Being cheap does not necessarily mean that you have the competence to become richer. All you know how to do is to be cheap, and that is an expensive price to pay.

Davidson disagrees and I disagree with the popularity of ideas such as cut up your credit cards and live below your means. That may be a good idea for some people, but it is not my idea of becoming rich and enjoying the bounties of the good life.

The Importance of Being Frugal

In contrast to Davidson's article, however, I did enjoy *The Millionaire Next Door*. It makes many fundamental points about frugality. There are differences between being cheap and frugal. Rich dad was more concerned with being frugal than being cheap. He said, "If you want to be really rich, you need to know when to be frugal and when to be a spendthrift. The problem is that too many people know how to be cheap only. That is like having only one leg to walk on."

A Million Dollars Is the Starting Point

Davidson also said it is best to acquire wealth with financial competence. Being a millionaire today does not mean that much. Today, $1 million is just the starting point to beginning to invest like the rich. So Davidson is in reality recommending choice #8 as the means to becoming rich. To rich dad, being financially smart included knowing when to be frugal and when not to be.

8. **You can become rich by being financially smart.** It was learning to be finanically smart where I began to harness the same investing power I had witnessed at the age of 12 standing on the beach looking at rich dad's new piece of ocean front land. Many people become rich by being very smart with knowledge from the B and I quadrants. Many of these individuals operate behind the scenes and manage, control, and manipulate the world's business and financial systems.

   Millions of people faithfully place their retirement savings and other monies into the market. However, the decision-makers of the marketing and distribution system of the underlying investments actually make the large sums of money, not necessarily the individual investor or retiree. As rich dad taught me years ago, "There are people who buy tickets to the game, and there are people who sell tickets to the game. You want to be on the side that is selling the tickets."

Why the Rich Get Richer

When I was younger, my rich dad said to me, "The rich get richer partly because they invest differently than others; they invest in investments that are not offered to the poor and the middle class. Most importantly, however, they have a different educational background. If you have the education, you will always have plenty of money."

Davidson points out that the dollar has lost 90% of its value in the last century. Being a cheap millionaire is therefore not enough. To qualify to invest in the investments of the rich, the price is at least $1 million of net worth. Even then, you may not be competent enough to safely invest in what the rich invest in.

Rich dad said, "If you want to invest in the same investments the rich invest in, you need:

1. Education,
2. Experience, and
3. Excessive cash."

At each level of what rich dad called the three Es, you find a different type of investor with a different level of education, experience, and excessive cash.

The price of being financially free requires time and dedication to gain the education, experience, and excessive cash to invest at those levels. You know you are financially smarter or increasing in sophistication when you can tell the differences between:

1. Good debt and bad debt
2. Good losses and bad losses
3. Good expenses and bad expenses
4. Tax payments versus tax incentives
5. Corporations you work for versus corporations you own
6. How to build a business, how to fix a business, and how to take a business public
7. The advantages and disadvantages of stocks, bonds, mutual funds, businesses, real estate, and insurance products as well as the different legal structures and when to use which product

Most average investors know only of:
1. Bad debt, which is why they try and pay it off
2. Bad losses, which is why they think losing money is bad
3. Bad expenses, which is why they hate paying bills
4. Taxes they pay, which is why they say that taxes are unfair

5. Job security and climbing the corporate ladder instead of owning the ladder
6. Investing from the outside, and buying shares of a company rather than selling shares of a company they own
7. Investing only in mutual funds, or picking only blue chip stocks

9. **You can become rich by being generous.** This was the way rich dad became rich. He often said, "The more people I serve, the richer I become." He also said, "The problem with being on the E and S side of the Quadrant is that you can serve only so many people. If

you build large operating systems in the B and I Quadrants, you can serve as many people as you want. And if you do that, you will become richer beyond your dreams."

Serving More and More People

Rich dad shared this example on how to become rich by serving more and more people, "If I am a doctor and I know how to work with one patient at a time only, there are just two ways for me to make more money. One is to work longer, and the other is to raise my rates. But if I keep my job and work in my spare time to find a drug that cures cancer, then I will become rich by serving many more people."

The Definition of Rich

Forbes magazine defines rich as $1 million in income and $10 million in net worth. Rich dad had a tougher definition: a consistent $1 million in passive income, which is income that comes in regardless of if you work or not, and $5,000,000 in assets, not net worth. Net worth can be an elusive and much-manipulated figure. He also felt that if you could not maintain a 20% return from capital invested, you were not really an investor.

The price to reach rich dad's goal, starting from nothing, is actually measured in rich dad's three E's: education, experience, and excessive cash.

When I returned from Vietnam in 1973, I had very little of all three. I had to make a choice: Was I willing to invest my time to attain all three of the Es? Rich dad did, his son Mike did, and many of my friends are still investing their time to gain the three Es. That is why they got richer and richer.

It Starts with a Plan

To be a rich investor, you must have a plan, be focused, and play to win. An average investor does not have a plan, invests in hot tips, and chases the hot investment products of the day, flitting from technology stocks to commodities to real estate to starting his or her own business. It's OK to invest on a hot tip now and then, but please do not delude yourself that one hot tip will make you rich forever.

In addition to the three Es, rich dad had a list of what he called the five Ds that were required to become very rich, especially when you start with nothing. They are:

1. Dream   4. Data
2. Dedication   5. Dollars
3. Drive

Most people focus on the last two, data and dollars. Many people go to school and think that the education or data they gain there will get them the dollars. Alternatively, if they don't have a formal education, they say, "I can't be rich because I don't have a college education" or "It takes money to make money" or "If I work harder and make more money, then I'll be rich." In other words, many people use the lack of education or money as their excuse for not being rich as investors.

Rich dad concluded his discussion on the five Ds by saying, "In reality, it is the focus on the first three Ds that ultimately gains you the data and dollars you need to become very, very rich." In other words, the data and the dollars are derived from having a dream, being dedicated, and having the drive to win. In my classes, I often find people who want more data before they begin doing anything, or think that first earning more money will make them rich. In most cases, exclusively trying to get more data or more dollars does not make a person rich. While data and dollars are important, it really takes just getting out there and doing it, especially if you are starting with nothing.

End of Phase One

This completes Phase One, which is, in my opinion, the most important phase. Money is just an idea. If you think money is hard to get and you'll never be rich, then it will be true for you. If you think that money is abundant, then that can be true.

The remaining four phases cover the specifics of rich dad's plan and how they were similar to the plans of some of the richest people in the world. As you read, consider how rich dad's plan conflicts, adds to, subtracts from, or agrees with your personal financial plan.

I caution you to use the information provided as a guide and not as hard data. Much of it is subject to legal interpretation and should be considered based on your individual circumstances. Its application is not always black and white and should be carefully reviewed. We advise you to consult with your legal and financial advisors to make sure you develop the plan most appropriate for your needs and goals.

Chapter 19

The 90/10 Riddle

In February of the year 2000, I was working with a group of very bright graduate students at Thunderbird University, The American School of International Management. During the three hour session I asked one of the young students, "What is your investment plan?"

Without hesitation he replied, "When I graduate I will find a job that pays me at least $150,000 a year and begin putting aside at least $20,000 a year to buy investments."

I thanked him for his willingness to share his plan with me. Then I said, "Do you remember me discussing my rich dad's 90/10 principle of money?"

"Yes," said the young man with a smile, knowing that I was about to challenge the way he was thinking. He was enrolled in the entrepreneurship program of this very prestigious school where I was a guest instructor. By now, he knew my style of teaching was not to give students answers. My style was to challenge core beliefs and ask students to evaluate old thought patterns. "What does the 90/10 principle of money have to do with my investment plan?" he asked cautiously.

"Everything," I replied. "Do you think your plan of finding a job and investing at least $20,000 a year will put you in the category of the 10% of investors that make 90% of the money?"

"I don't know," he replied. "I never really thought about my plan with that benchmark in mind."

"Most people don't," I replied. "Most people find an investment plan and think it is the only investment plan or the best investment plan, but few compare their plans to other plans. And the problem is, most people will not find out if their plan was the right plan until it's too late."

"You mean the average investor is investing for retirement and will not find out if their plan worked or not until they retire?" asked another student in the class. "They'll find out when it is too late."

"For many people my age that will be true," I replied. "Sad but true."

"But isn't the idea of finding a high paying job and putting $20,000 a year away a pretty good plan?" asked the student. "After all, I'm only 26 years old."

"A very good plan," I replied. "Definitely putting away more money than the average person and starting young with that much money will probably make you a very rich man. But my question is, 'Will your plan put you in the 90/10 league of investors?'"

"I don't know," said the young man. "What would you advise?"

"Do you remember me telling you the story of walking along the beach with my rich dad at the age of 12?" I asked.

"You mean the story of you wondering how he could afford such an expensive piece of real estate," another student replied. "Your rich dad's first big investment and his first move into the world of bigger investments?"

I nodded my head and replied, "That's the story."

"And that story has to do with the 90/10 rule of money?" asked the student.

"Yes it does. It applies because I always wondered how my rich dad could acquire an asset so big even though he had very little. So after asking him how he did it, he gave me what he called the 90/10 riddle."

"The 90/10 riddle?" replied one of the students. "What is the 90/10 riddle and what does it have to do with my investment plan?"

With that question, I turned, walked to the chalk board, and drew the following diagram. "This is the 90/10 riddle." I said.

Income
Expense

Assets	Liabilities

"That's the 90/10 riddle?" asked the student. "All it looks like is a financial statement without any assets in it."

"And it is. So this is the question that completes the riddle," I said with a grin, watching the students' faces to see if they were still with me.

After a long pause on my part, one of the students finally demanded, "So give us the question."

"The question is," I said slowly, "How do you fill your asset column without buying any assets?"

"Without buying any assets," replied the student. "You mean without any money?"

"More or less," I replied. "Your investment plan for putting $20,000 a year aside to invest with is a good idea. But my challenge to you is: Is the idea of buying assets with money a 90/10 idea, or is it an average investor idea?"

"So you're saying to create assets in the asset column instead of buying the assets with money, which is what most people do."

I nodded my head. "You see, this diagram, the diagram I call the 90/10 riddle is the riddle that my rich dad would challenge me with on a regular basis. He would ask me for my ideas on how I could create assets in the asset column without buying them with money."

The students were silent looking at the riddle on the chalk board. Finally one turned and said, "Is that why you often say, 'It doesn't take money to make money?'"

I nodded my head and replied, "You're catching on. Most people in the 90% who own the 10% often say, 'It takes money to make money.' Many often give up on investing if they do not have any money."

"So your rich dad's 90/10 riddle was to give you a blank asset column and ask you how you would fill it with assets without having to buy the assets."

"Constantly. After I came back from Vietnam, he would routinely have a lunch or dinner with me and ask me for new ideas on how to fill the asset column by creating assets instead of buying assets. He knew that is how many of the ultra-rich got rich in the first place. That is how Bill Gates, Michael Dell, Richard Branson all became billionaires. They did not become billionaires by looking for a job and putting a few dollars aside."

"So you're saying the way to become rich is by being an entrepreneur?"

"No, I am not saying that. I just use those examples because you are all in the entrepreneurship program at Thunderbird University. The Beatles became ultra-rich by creating a different kind of asset, none-the-less they created assets that still pay them money today. All I am saying is that rich dad put this financial statement with a blank asset column in front of me on a regular basis and asked me how I would create assets inside the asset column without having to spend money to acquire them. He began giving me this 90/10 quiz when I asked him how he found the power to acquire a piece of the most expensive beach front land without any money."

"So he said his business bought the land," another student chimed in.

"As I said, that is one way but there are many ways you can create assets inside an asset column without buying them. Inventors do it by inventing something of great value. Artists paint paintings that are priceless. Authors write books that pay them royalties for years. Creating a business is the way an entrepreneur does it, but you don't have to be an entrepreneur to create an asset inside the asset column. I've done it with real estate without using any money. All you have to do is be creative and you can be rich for life."

"You mean I can invent something with new technology and become rich?" asked one of the students.

"You could, but it does not have to be an invention or new technology," I said, pausing for awhile. "It is a way of thinking that creates assets and once you have that way of thinking you will be richer than you ever dreamed possible."

"What do you mean it doesn't have to be a new invention or technology? What else could it be?"

I said, doing my best to make my point, "Do you remember the story in my book, *Rich Dad Poor Dad*, the story of the comic books?"

"Yes," said one of the students. "The story of your rich dad taking away your 10 cents an hour and asking you to work for free after you asked for a raise? He took away the 10 cents because he did not want you to spend your life working for money."

"Yes, that story." I replied. "That is a story about filling the asset column with an asset without buying the asset."

The students stood quietly for awhile thinking about what I had just said. Finally one spoke up and said, "So you took old comic books and turned them into assets."

I nodded my head. "But were the comic books the asset?" I asked

"Not until you turned them into an asset," replied another student. "You took something that was being thrown out as trash and turned it into an asset."

"Yes but were the comic books the asset or were the comic books merely the part of the asset you could see?"

"Oh," another one of the students jumped in. "It was the invisible thought process that created the comic book into the asset that was the real asset."

"That is how my rich dad saw it. He later told me that the power he had was his thinking process. It was a thinking process that he often jokingly called, 'Turning trash into cash.' He also said, 'Most people do exactly the opposite and turn cash into trash. That is why the 90/10 rule holds true.'"

"He was like the ancient alchemists," said one of the students. "The alchemists who searched for the formula to turn lead into gold."

"Exactly," I said. "The people who are in the 90/10 grouping of money are modern day alchemists. The only difference is that they are able to turn nothing into assets. Their power is the ability to take ideas and turn them into assets."

"But as you say, many people have great ideas. They are just not able to turn them into assets," said a student.

I nodded my head. "And that was my rich dad's secret power I saw that day on the beach. It was that mental power or financial intelligence that allowed him to acquire such an expensive piece of real estate, while the average investor would walk away from it, saying 'I can't afford it,' or 'It takes money to make money.'"

"How often did he give you the 90/10 quiz?" asked a student.

"Very often," I replied. "It was his way of exercising my brain. Rich dad often said that our brains are our most powerful asset and, if used improperly, they can be our most powerful liability."

The students were silent, I assume contemplating and questioning their own thoughts. Finally the original student, the student who's plan it was to put the $20,000 dollars a year away, said, "So that is why in your book *Rich Dad Poor Dad*, one of rich dad's lessons was that the rich invent their own money."

I nodded my head and said, "'And lesson number one of the six lessons was 'the rich don't work for money.'"

Again there was silence from the young students before one then said, "So while we are planning on getting a job and saving money to buy assets, you were taught that your job was to create assets."

"Well said," I replied. "You see the idea of a 'job' was created in the Industrial Age and ever since 1989, we have been in the Information Age."

"What do you mean the idea of a job is an Industrial Age idea?" one student asked with a start. "Humans have always had jobs, haven't they?"

"No, at least not in the way we know of a job today. You see, in the Hunter-Gatherer period of humanity, humans lived in tribes and each person's job was to contribute to the communal survival of the tribe. In other words, it was all for one and one for all. Then came the Agrarian Age, the era when there were kings and queens. A person's job during that period was to be a serf or a peasant who paid the king to work the land the king owned. Then came the Industrial Age and serfdom or slavery was abolished and human beings began selling their labor on the open market. Most people became employees or self-employed, doing their best to sell their labor to the highest bidder. That is the modern concept of the word 'job.'"

"So the moment I said I'm going to get a job and put $20,000 away a year, you see that kind of thinking as Industrial Age thinking."

I nodded my head. "Just as today there are still Agrarian Age workers that are known as farmers and ranchers. Today there are still hunter gatherers, commercial fishermen for example. Most people are working with Industrial Age ideas and that is why so many people have jobs."

"So what would an Information Age idea of work be?" asked a student.

"People who do not work because their ideas are at work. Today, there are students who are much like my rich dad who are going from school to becoming rich without a job. Look at many of the Internet billionaires. Some of them dropped out of college to become billionaires without ever having a formal job."

"In other words, they started with an empty asset column and filled it with a very big asset, an Information Age asset," added one of the students.

"Many built multi-billion dollar assets," I said. "They went from students to billionaires and soon there will be high school students who will go from high school students to billionaires without ever applying for a job. I already know of one that is a millionaire without ever having a job. After reading my book and playing my games, he bought a large piece of real estate, sold off a section of vacant land, kept the apartment house, and paid off his loan with the money from the land. He now owns the apartment house which is worth a little over a million dollars and has cash flow of $4,000 a month income without working. He will graduate from high school in about a year."

The students stood silently again thinking about what I just said. Some had a hard time believing my story about the high school student, yet they knew the story of college drop outs becoming billionaires was true. Finally one spoke up, "So in the Information Age people are getting rich with information."

"Not just in the Information Age," I replied. "It has been this way throughout the ages. It is the people who do not have assets who work for, or are controlled by, those people who create, acquire, or control the assets."

"So you're saying a high school kid could beat me financially even though he does not have a great education from a prestigious school, or a high paying job," said the first student.

"That is exactly what I am saying. It's a matter of the way you think more than your education. Best selling author of *The Millionaire Next Door* Thomas Stanley in his latest book *The Millionaire Mind* states that his research found no correlation between high SAT scores, good grades and money."

The student with the $20,000 a year investment plan then said, "So if I want to join the 90/10 club I am better off to practice creating assets instead of buying assets. I should be creative rather than do what everyone else does, when it comes to acquiring assets."

"That is why billionaire Henry Ford said, 'Thinking is the hardest work there is. That is why so few people engage in it.'" I replied. "It also explains why if you do what the 90% of investors do you will join them in sharing only 10% of the wealth."

"Or why Einstein said, 'Imagination is more important than knowledge,'" added another student.

"Or why my rich dad gave me this tip when hiring an accountant. He said, when you're interviewing an accountant ask him or her, 'What is 1+1?' If the accountant answers '3' don't hire the person. They're not smart. If the accountant answers '2' you also don't hire them because they are not smart enough. But if the accountant answers, 'What do you want 1+1 to be?' You hire them immediately."

The students laughed as we began packing up our materials. "So you create assets that buy other assets and liabilities. Is that correct?" asked a student.

I nodded my head.

"Do you ever use money to buy other assets?" asked the same student.

"Yes, but I like to use money generated by the asset I create, to buy other assets," I replied, picking up my briefcase. "Remember that I don't like working for money. I'd rather create assets that buy other assets and liabilities."

A young student from China gave me a hand with my bags and said, "And is that why you recommend network marketing so much? For very little money and risk, a person can build an asset in their spare time."

I nodded my head, "A worldwide asset they can pass on to their kids if their kids want it. I don't know of too many companies that will let you pass on your job to your kids. That is one test of an asset, the test if you can hand it on down to the people you love. My dad, the man I call my poor dad, worked very hard to climb the government ladder. Even if he had not been fired, he would not have been able to pass on his years of hard work to his kids, not that any of us wanted the job or were qualified to take the job anyway."

The students gave me a hand out to my car. "So think about creating assets rather than working hard and buying assets," said the $20,000 dollar student.

"If you want to get into the 90/10 club," I replied. "That is why my rich dad constantly challenged my creativity to create different types of assets in the asset column without buying them. He said it was better to work years at creating an asset rather than to spend your life working hard for money to create someone else's asset."

The $20,000 dollar student then said as I climbed into my car, "So all I have to do is take an idea and create an asset, a big asset, that makes me rich. If I do that I will solve the 90/10 riddle and join the 10% of all investors that control 90% of the wealth."

Laughing, I pulled my door shut and replied to his last comment, "If you solve the 90/10 riddle in real life, you will have a good chance of joining the 10% that control 90% of the money. If you don't solve the 90/10 riddle in real life, you will probably join the 90% that control just 10% of the money." I thanked the students and drove away.

Mental Attitude Quiz

As Henry Ford said, "Thinking is the hardest work there is. That is why so few people engage in it." Or as my rich dad said, "Your brain can be your most powerful asset and if not used properly, it can be your most powerful liability."

My rich dad had me repeatedly create new assets in an empty asset column. He would sit down with his son and me and ask us how we could create a new and different asset. He really did not care if the idea was crazy and zany, he just wanted us to be able to substantiate how this idea could be turned into an asset. He would ask us to defend our thoughts and challenge his challenges. In the long run, it was a lot better than him telling us to work hard, save money, and live frugally, which is what my poor dad recommended.

So the mental attitude quiz question is:

"Are you willing to consider creating your own assets rather than buying them?"

Yes_____   No_____

There are many books and educational programs written on how to buy assets wisely. For most people, buying assets is the best plan for them. I would also recommend that for the secure and comfortable levels of your investment plan that those assets be assets you buy. Invest in such assets as blue chip stocks and well managed mutual funds for the secure and comfortable level. But if you have dreams of becoming a very rich investor, the question is "Are you willing to create your assets rather than buy someone else's assets?" If not, then as I said, there are many books and educational programs about how to purchase assets.

If you are willing to consider how to create assets, then the remainder of this book will be valuable, maybe priceless. It is about how to take an idea and turn it into an asset that will acquire other assets. It is not only about how to make a lot of money in the asset column, it is also about how to keep the money that asset makes and have it acquire even more assets as well as the luxuries of life. It reveals how many of the 10% came to acquire 90% of the money. So if this is of interest to you, then please read on.

Again, this is the 90/10 riddle:

The riddle is, "How do you create an asset in the asset column without spending money to acquire it?"

Robert's Note:

My first big business was the nylon and Velcro surfer wallet business in 1977. It was created as a very big asset in the asset column. The problem was, the size of the asset created was big, but my business skills were small. So while I was technically a millionaire in my twenties, I also lost it all in my twenties. I repeated the same process three years later in the rock and roll business. When MTV hit, our little company was in the perfect position to capitalize on the craze. Again, the asset created was bigger than the people that created it. We went up like a rocket ship and came down like a rocket ship without gas. The rest of this book is dedicated to creating big assets, having the professional talent to match the size of the asset, and how to keep the money made by investing in other, often more stable, assets. As my rich dad said, "What good is making a lot of money if you don't keep it?" Investing is the way smart people keep their money.

What Type of Investor Do You Want to Become?

Chapter 20

Solving the 90/10 Riddle

My rich dad said, "There are investors who buy assets and there are investors who create assets. If you want to solve the 90/10 riddle for yourself, you need to be both types of investors."

In the introduction, I told the story of rich dad, Mike and me walking along a beach looking at a very expensive piece of beach front real estate he had just purchased. You may recall me asking rich dad how he could afford such an expensive piece of real estate when my poor dad could not. Rich dad's reply was, "I can't afford this land either, but my business can." All I could see was a piece of land with old abandoned cars, a building half falling down, lots of brush and debris, and a large "For Sale" sign sticking up from the middle of the property. At the age of 12, I could not see any business on this land, but my rich dad could. The business was being created in his head and that ability to create businesses in his head was the reason he would go on to be one of the richest men in Hawaii. In other words, rich dad solved his 90/10 riddle by creating assets that in turn purchased other assets. That plan was not only rich dad's investment plan, it is the investment plan for most of the 10% who make 90% of the money, in the past, in the present, and into the future.

For those of you who read *Rich Dad Poor Dad*, you may recall the story of Ray Kroc saying to my friend's MBA class that McDonald's, the company he founded, was not in the business of hamburgers. Their business was the business of real estate. Again the formula is to create an asset that buys other assets and that formula is the reason why McDonald's owns the most expensive real estate in the world. It was all part of the plan. And that is why rich dad repeatedly said to me once he knew I was serious about becoming rich, "If you want to solve the 90/10 riddle for yourself, you need to be both types of investors. You need to be a person who knows how to create assets as well as a person who knows how to buy assets. The average investor is not generally aware of the different processes and is not good at either process of investing. The average investor usually does not even have a formally written plan."

Making Millions, Maybe Billions from Your Ideas

Much of the second half of this book is about how people create assets. Rich dad spent many hours with me teaching me the process on how a person takes an idea and turns it into a business that creates assets that buys assets. During one of these lessons with rich dad, he said, "Many people have ideas that could make them rich beyond their wildest dreams. The problem is, most people have never been taught how to put a business structure inside their ideas and so many of their ideas never take shape or stand on their own. If you want to be one of the 10% that makes 90% of the money, you will need to know how to build a business structure inside your creative ideas." Much of the second half of this book is about what rich dad called the "B-I Triangle" which is the mental structure that can give life to your financial ideas. It is the power of the B-I Triangle that takes an idea and turns it into an asset.

Rich dad often said, "More than just knowing how to create assets that buy assets, one of the main reasons the richest of investors are able to become richer is because they know how to turn their ideas into millions and maybe even billions of dollars. The average investor may have excellent ideas, but they often lack the skills to turn their ideas into assets that buy assets." The remainder of this book is dedicated to how ordinary people are able to turn their ideas into assets that buy assets.

"You Can't Do That"

While teaching me how to turn my ideas into assets, rich dad often said, "When you first set out to turn your ideas into your personal fortune, many people will say, 'You can't do that.' Always remember that nothing kills your great ideas more than people with small ideas and limited imaginations." Rich dad gave me two reasons he thought people tended to say, "You can't do that."

1. They say "You can't do that" even if you are doing what they say you cannot do, not because you can't do it but because they can't do it.
2. They say, "You can't do it" because they cannot see what you are doing.

Rich dad explained that the process of making a lot of money is a mental process more than a physical process.

One of rich dad's favorite quotes came from Einstein, which went, "Great spirits have often encountered violent opposition from mediocre minds." Commenting on Einstein's quote, rich dad said, "We all possess both a great spirit and a mediocre mind. The challenge in turning our ideas into a million dollar or even billion dollar asset is often the battle between our own great spirits and our own, often mediocre, minds.

When I explain the B-I Triangle, which is the business structure that gives life to business ideas and is explained in the second part of this book, some people become overwhelmed by the amount of knowledge required to make the B-I Triangle work for them. When that happens I often remind them of the battle between their great spirits and mediocre minds. Whenever a person's mediocre mind begins to oppose their own great spirits, I always remind them of what my rich dad said to me. He said, "There are many people with great ideas but very few people with great amounts of money. The reason the 90/10 rule holds true is because it does not take a great idea to become rich but it does take a great person behind the idea to become rich. You must be of strong spirit and strong in your convictions to turn your ideas into fortunes. Even if you understand the process via which your ideas can become millions even billions of dollars, always remember that great ideas only become great fortunes if the person behind the idea is also willing to be great. It is often difficult to keep going when everyone around you is saying, "You can't do it." You must have a very strong spirit to withstand the doubt of those around you. But your spirit must be even stronger when you are the person saying to yourself "You can't do that." This does not mean that you plough blindly on not listening to the good and bad ideas of your friends or yourself. Their thoughts and input should be listened to and often used when their ideas are better than yours. But at this moment, I am not talking to you about mere ideas or advice.

What I am talking to you about is more than just ideas. I am talking about your spirit and the will to go on even when filled with doubt and out of good ideas. No one can you tell you what you can or cannot do in your life. Only you can determine that. Your own greatness is often found at the end of the road, and when it comes to turning your ideas into money, there are many times when you come to the end of the road. The end of the road is when you are out of ideas, out of money, and filled with doubt. If you can find in yourself the spirit to go on, you will find out what it really takes to turn your ideas into great assets. Turning an idea into a great fortune is more a matter of human spirit rather than the power of the human mind. At the end of every road, the entrepreneur finds his or her spirit. Finding your entrepreneurial spirit and making it strong is more important than the idea or business you are developing. Once you find your entrepreneurial spirit, you will forever be able to take very ordinary ideas and turn them into extraordinary fortunes. Always remember the world is filled with people with great ideas and very few people with great fortunes.

The remainder of this book is dedicated to you finding your entrepreneurial spirit and developing your ability to turn ordinary ideas into extraordinary fortunes. Phase Two gives you insight into rich dad's different types of investors and allows you to choose the path that may be best for you. Phase Three analyzes rich dad's B-I Triangle and how it can provide the structure for you to make an asset out of your good idea.

Phase Four goes into the mind of the sophisticated investor and how he or she analyzes investments as well as the pathway of the ultimate investor who takes his or her idea and B-I Triangle and creates fortunes. The last phase is Phase Five, Giving It Back, the most important phase.

Chapter 21

Rich Dad's Categories of Investors

This book is an educational story about rich dad guiding me from having no money and no job when I left the Marines to well down my path to becoming the ultimate investor—a person who becomes a selling shareholder rather than a buying shareholder, a person who is on the inside of the investment rather than on the outside. Other investment vehicles in which the rich invest that the poor and middle class do not include initial public offerings of stock (IPOs), private placements, and other corporate securities. Whether you are on the inside of an investment or on the outside, it is important to understand the basics of the securities regulations.

By reading *Rich Dad Poor Dad*, you have learned about financial literacy, which is imperative for a successful investor. From reading *CASHFLOW Quadrant*, you have learned about the four different quadrants and the ways people make money as well as how the different tax laws affect the different quadrants. By just reading the first two books and possibly playing our educational board game *CASHFLOW*, you already know more about the fundamentals of investing than many people who actively invest.

Once you understand the fundamentals of investing, you can better understand rich dad's categories of investors and the ten investor controls he said were important to all investors:

The Ten Investor Controls

1. The control over yourself
2. The control over income/expense asset/liability ratios
3. The control over the management of the investment
4. The control over taxes
5. The control over when you buy and when you sell
6. The control over brokerage transactions
7. The control over the ETC (entity, timing, and characteristics)
8. The control over the terms and conditions of the agreements
9. The control over access to information
10. The control over giving it back, philanthropy, redistribution of wealth

Rich dad often said, "Investing is not risky, not being in control is risky." Many people find investing risky because they are not in control of one or more of these ten investor controls. This book will not go into all of these controls. As you read this book, however, you may gain some insights on how you can gain greater control as an investor—especially control number 7, the control over entity, timing, and characteristics. This is where many investors lack control, need more control, or simply lack any basic understanding about investing.

The first phase of this book was dedicated to rich dad's most important investor control—CONTROL OVER YOURSELF. If you are not mentally prepared and committed to becoming a successful investor, you should turn your money over to a professional financial advisor or team trained to help you choose your investments.

I Was More Than Ready

At this point in my financial education, rich dad knew I had made the choice:

> *I was mentally prepared to become an investor.*
> *I wanted to become a very successful investor.*

I knew I was mentally prepared and that I wanted to be rich. However, rich dad now asked me, "What kind of investor do you want to become?"

"A rich investor" was my answer. This is when rich dad brought out his yellow pad again and wrote down the following categories of investors:

1. The accredited investor
2. The qualified investor
3. The sophisticated investor
4. The inside investor

5. The ultimate investor

"What is the difference?" I asked.

Rich dad added a description to each type of investor:

1. The accredited investor earns a lot of money and/or has a high net worth.
2. The qualified investor knows fundamental and technical investing.
3. The sophisticated investor understands investing and the law.
4. The inside investor creates the investment.
5. The ultimate investor becomes the selling shareholder.

When I read the definition of the accredited investor, I felt pretty hopeless. I had no money and no job.

Rich dad saw my reaction, took the yellow pad back, and circled inside investor.

Start As an Insider

"This is where you'll start, Robert," rich dad said as he pointed to inside investor.

"Even if you have very little money and very little experience, it is possible to start at the inside level of investing," rich dad continued. "You need to start small and keep learning. It does not take money to make money."

At this point, he listed his three Es on the tablet:

1. Education
2. Experience
3. Excessive cash

"Once you have all three Es, you will have become a successful investor," rich dad said. "You've done well with your financial education, but now you need the experience. When you have the right experience combined with good financial literacy, the excessive cash will come."

"But you have inside investor listed fourth. How can I start as an inside investor?" I said, still confused.

Rich dad wanted me to start as an insider because he wanted me to be a person who created assets that eventually bought other assets.

Start by Building a Business

"I am going to teach you the fundamentals of building a successful business," rich dad continued. "If you can learn to build a successful B quadrant business, your business will generate excessive cash. Then you can use the skills you learned becoming a successful B to analyze investments as an I."

"It is like coming in through the back door, isn't it?" I asked.

"Well, I would rather say it is the opportunity of a lifetime!" rich dad replied. "Once you learn to make your first million, the next ten are easy!"

"OK, so how do I get started?" I asked impatiently.

"First let me tell you about the different categories of investors," rich dad answered, "so you can understand what I'm saying."

Overview—You Get to Choose

In this phase of *Rich Dad's Guide to Investing*, I share rich dad's descriptions of each one of his categories of investors. The following mini-chapters explain the distinctions (the advantages and disadvantages) of each category because the path I chose may not be the right path for you.

The Accredited Investor

The accredited investor is someone with high income or high net worth. I knew I could not qualify as an accredited investor.

A long-term investor who has chosen to invest for security and comfort may very well qualify as an accredited investor. There are many Es and Ss who are very content with their financial position. They recognized early on the need to provide for their financial future through the I quadrant and adopted a plan for investing with their income earned as Es and Ss. Their financial plans, whether to be secure or comfortable, have been met.

In *CASHFLOW Quadrant*, we discussed this "two-legged" approach to building financial security. I applaud these individuals for their foresight and discipline in developing a financial plan and providing for their financial future. For them, the path I took will sound like either an impossible mission or a lot of hard work.

There are also many highly paid Es and Ss who qualify as accredited investors based on their income alone.

If you can qualify as an accredited investor, you will have access to investments that most people do not. To be successful in choosing your investments, however, you still need financial education. If you choose not to invest your time in your financial education, you should turn your money over to competent financial advisors who can assist you with your investment decisions.

Aa a statistic of interest, in America today there are reportedly just 6 million people who meet the qualifications of an Accredited Investor. In a country of approximately 250 million people, and if this number is true, then there are only 2.4% of the population that meet this minimum requirement. If this statistic is true, then there are even fewer people who will meet the following levels of investors. This means there are many unqualified investors investing in high risk speculative investments they should not be investing in.

Again, the SEC definition of an Accredited Investor today is:

1. $200,000 or more annual income for an individual
2. $300,000 or more for a couple, or
3. 1 million dollars net worth.

Realizing that there are only 6 million people who qualify as Accredited Investors indicates to me that working hard for money is a very difficult way to qualify to invest in the investments of the rich. As I sit and ponder the idea of needing a $200,000 minimum income, I realize that my dad, the person I call my poor dad, would never have come close to qualifying, no matter how hard he worked and how many pay raises his government job provided.

If you have played *CASHFLOW 101*, you may note that the Fast Track of the game is the track that represents where the Accredited Investor meets the minimum requirements as an investor. In other words, technically, less than 2.4% of the U.S. population meets the requirements to invest in the investments found on the game's Fast Track. That means 97% of the population invests in the Rat Race.

The Qualified Investor

The qualified investor understands how to analyze publicly traded stock. This investor would be considered an "outside" investor as opposed to an "inside" investor. Generally, qualified investors include stock traders and analysts.

The Sophisticated Investor

The sophisticated investor typically has all three of rich dad's "three Es." In addition, the sophisticated investor understands the world of investing. He or she utilizes the tax, corporate, and securities laws to maximize both earnings and to protect the underlying capital.

If you want to become a successful investor but do not wish to build your own business to do so, your goal should be to become a sophisticated investor.

From the sophisticated investor on, these investors know that there are two sides of the coin. They know that on one side of the coin, the world is a world of black and white and they also know that the other side of the coin is a world of different shades of gray. It is a world where you definitely do not want to do things on your own. On the black and white side of the coin, some investors can invest on their own. On the gray side of the coin, an investor must enter with their team.

The Inside Investor

To build a successful business is the goal of the inside investor. The business may be a single piece of rental real estate or a multi-million-dollar retail company.

A successful B knows how to create and build assets. Rich dad would say, "The rich invent money. After you learn to make your first million, the next ten will be easy."

A successful B will also learn the skills needed to analyze companies for investment from the outside. Therefore, a successful inside investor can learn to become a successful sophisticated investor.

The Ultimate Investor

To become the selling shareholder is the goal of the ultimate investor. The ultimate investor owns a successful business in which he or she sells ownership interest to the public; hence, he or she is a selling shareholder. This is my goal. Although I have not achieved it yet, I continue to educate myself and learn from my experiences, and I have committed to doing so until I can become a selling shareholder.

Which Investor Are You?

The next few chapters will go into each type of investor in greater detail. After you have studied each type of investor, you may be better prepared to choose your own goal for investing.

Chapter 22

The Accredited
Investor

Who Is an Accredited Investor?

Most developed countries have laws written to protect the average person from bad and risky investments. The problem is that these very same laws can also prevent the masses from being able to invest in some of the best investments.

In America, we have the Securities Act of 1933, the Securities Exchange Act of 1934, SEC Regulations under these laws and the Securities and Exchange Commission (SEC). These laws and regulations were designed to protect the public from misrepresentations, manipulation, and other fraudulent practices in the buying and selling of securities. They limit certain investments only to accredited and sophisticated investors as well as require detailed disclosure of such investments. The SEC was created to be the watchdog for the laws.

In fulfilling its role as a watchdog over securities, the SEC defined the accredited investor as a person who has earned at least $200,000 or more as an individual (or $300,000 as a couple) in each of the last two years and who expects to earn the same amount in the current year. The individual or couple may also qualify with a net worth of at least $1 million.

Rich dad said, "An accredited investor is simply a person who earns significantly more money than the average person. It does not necessarily mean the person is rich or knows anything about investing."

The problem with this rule is that less than 3% of all Americans qualify under the $200,000 to $300,000 annual income requirement. This means that only this 3% can invest in these stock issues regulated by the SEC. The other 97% are not allowed to invest in the same investments because they are not accredited investors. The SEC's test for sophisticated investors has to do with the investor's level of financial intelligence.

I remember when rich dad was offered an opportunity to invest in a company called Texas Instruments before it went public. Not having the time to look into the company and do his analysis, he turned the opportunity down, a decision he regretted for years. Yet, he did not turn down other opportunities to invest in companies before they went public. He became even wealthier from those investments, investments not available to the general public. Rich dad qualified as an accredited investor.

When I asked to invest in the next pre-public offering of a company, rich dad informed me that I was not rich enough or wise enough to invest with him. I still remember him saying, "Wait until you're rich, and the best investments will come to you first. The rich always get first pick of the best investments. In addition, the rich can buy at very low prices as well as in volume. That is one of the reasons why the rich get richer."

My rich dad agreed with the SEC. He thought it a smart idea to protect the average investor from the risks of these types of investments although he had made a lot of money investing as an accredited investor himself.

However, rich dad cautioned me, "Even if you are an accredited investor, you still may not get the opportunity to invest in the best investments. To do that requires a completely different type of investor with the right knowledge and access to the information about new investment opportunities."

The Investor Controls of the Accredited Investor

None

Rich dad believed that an accredited investor, without financial education, had none of the ten investor controls. The accredited investor might have a lot of money but usually didn't know what to do with it.

The Three E's Possessed by the Accredited Investor

Excessive cash—maybe

Rich dad would clarify that although you might qualify as an accredited investor, you still needed the education and experience to progress to the qualified, sophisticated, inside, or ultimate investor. In fact, he knew many accredited investors who didn't actually have any excessive cash. They met the income thresholds but didn't know how to manage their cash very well.

Sharon's Notes

Just about anyone can open a brokerage account to buy and sell stocks of companies that are considered "public companies." The stock of a public company is traded freely as well as bought and sold by the public, usually through an exchange. The stock market is truly a free market in action. Without government or outside intervention, individuals can decide for themselves whether the price of a stock is fair or not. They can decide to buy it and therefore purchase an ownership interest in the company.

In the last decade, mutual funds have become increasingly popular. They are professionally managed portfolios in which each share of the mutual fund represents ownership of partial shares in many different individual securities. Many individuals invest in mutual funds because of the professional management as well as the appeal of owning a small piece of many different securities rather than stock in a single company. If you do not have the time to study investing (so you can make informed investment decisions), choosing a mutual fund or hiring an investment advisor to handle your investments may be wise.

One way to true wealth from securities comes from participating in the initial public offering (IPO) of a company's stock. Typically, the company's founders and initial investors already own blocks of stock. To attract additional funding the company can offer an IPO. This is when the Securities and Exchange Commission (SEC) steps in—with detailed filing and disclosure requirements—in its attempt to prevent fraud and protect the investor from misrepresentation. This does not mean, however, that the SEC prevents IPOs from being poor deals. An IPO can be legal and still be a poor investment or an outright liability (it goes down in value).

The Securities Act of 1933 and the Securities Exchange Act of 1934 were adopted to regulate this type of investment and to protect the investor from fraudulent or high-risk investments, as well as broker misman-agement. The SEC was formed to oversee the issuance of securities as well as the securities industry.

The regulations for stock issues apply to public issues as well as certain private issues of stock. There are certain exemptions from the regulations that we have not covered. For now, it is important to understand the definition of accredited investor. The accredited investor may invest in certain types of securities that a non-accredited, non-sophisticated investor cannot because the "accredited" status implies that the investor can withstand a higher level of monetary risk than the non-accredited investor.

Robert has discussed the accredited investor requirements of an individual or couple related to income or net worth. Any director, executive officer, or general partner of the issuer of the stock will also be considered an accredited investor even if that person does not meet the income or net worth requirements. This will become a very important distinction when we discuss the "inside investor." In fact, this is the path often taken by the inside and ultimate investor.

Chapter 23

The Qualified Investor

Rich dad defined the qualified investor as a person who has money as well as some knowledge about investing. A qualified investor is usually an accredited investor who has also invested in financial education. As it relates to the stock market, for example, he said qualified investors would include most professional stock traders. Through their education, they have learned and understand the difference between fundamental investing and technical investing..

1. **Fundamental investing:** Rich Dad said, "a fundamental investor reduces risk looking for value and growth by looking at the financials of the company." The most important consideration for selecting a good stock for investment is the future earnings potential of the company. A fundamental investor carefully reviews the financial statements of any company before investing in it. The fundamental investor also takes into account the outlook for the economy as a whole as well as the specific industry in which the company is involved. The direction of interest rates is a very important factor in fundamental analysis.

   Warren Buffet has been acknowledged as one of the best fundamental investors.

2. **Technical investing:** Rich Dad said, "a well-trained technical investor invests on the emotions of the market and invests with

insurance from catastrophic loss. The most important consideration for selecting a good stock for investment is based on the supply of and demand for the company's stock. The technical investor studies the patterns of the sales price of the company's stock. Will the supply of the shares of stock being offered for sale be sufficient based on the expected demand for those shares?

The technical investor tends to buy on price and market sentiment...just like a shopper shops for sales and discounted items. In fact, many technical investors are like my Aunt Doris. Aunt Doris goes shopping for bargains and sales with her lady friends, buying items because they are cheap, marked down, or because her friends are buying them. Then she gets home, wonders why she bought the item, tries it on and then takes it back for a refund so she can have money to go shopping again.

The technical investor studies the pattern of the history of the company's stock price. A true technical investor is not concerned with the internal operations of a company as a fundamental investor would be. The primary indicators the technical investor is concerned with are the mood of the market and the price of the stock.

One of the reasons so many people think the subject of investing is risky is because most people are technically operating as "technical investors" but don't know the difference between a technical investor and a fundamental investor. The reason investing seems risky from the technical side is because stock prices fluctuate with market emotions. Here are just a few examples of things that can cause fluctuations in stock prices:

one day a stock is popular and in the news, next week it isn't, or the company manipulates supply and demand by splitting the stock, diluting the pool with additional shares being created through such things as secondary offerings, or cutting back the number of shares by buying them back ; or

an institutional buyer (like a mutual fund or pension fund) buys or sells the shares of a certain company in such volume that it disturbs the market.

Investing seems risky to the average investor because they lack the basic financial education skills to be a fundamental investor and do not have adequate technical investor skills. If they are not on the board of the company changing the supply side of the shares they have no management control over the fluctuations of supply and demand of the stock's price on the open market. They remain at the whim of the market emotions.

Many times a fundamental investor will find an excellent company with great profits but, for some reason, the technical investors will not be interested in it so the price of the company's shares will not go up, even though it is a profitable well managed company. In today's market, many people are investing in IPO's of internet companies which have no sales or profits. That is a case of technical investors determining the value of a company's stock.

Since 1995, people operating strictly as fundamental investors have not done as well as investors who also consider the technical side of the market. In this wild market where the people who take the most risk win, people with more cautious and value oriented views lost out on this market mania. In fact, many of these risk takers frightened many technical investors as well with their high prices of stock without any value. But in a crash, it is those investors with the strong fundamental investments and technical trading skills who do well. The amateur speculators rushing into the market as well as all the new start up IPOs flush with money will be hurt in the down turn. Rich dad said, "The trouble with getting rich quickly without a parachute is that you fall farther and faster. Lots of easy money makes people think they are financial geniuses when in fact, they become financial fools." Rich dad believed that both technical as well as fundamental skills were important to survive the ups and downs of the world of investing.

Charles Dow of Dow-Jones fame was a technical investor. That is why The Wall Street Journal, the paper he helped found, is primarily a paper written for technical investors, and not necessarily for fundamental investors.

George Soros is often recognized as one of the best technical investors.

The difference between the two investment styles is dramatic. The fundamental investor analyzes the company from its financial statements to assess the company's strength and potential for future success. In addition, the fundamental investor tracks the economy and the industry of the company.

A technical investor invests from charts that track the price and volume trends and patterns of the company's stock. The technical investor may review the put/call ratio for the stock as well as the short positions taken in the stock. While both investors invest from the facts, they find their facts from different sources of data. Also, both types of investors require different skills and different vocabulary. The frightening thing is that most of today's investors are investing without technical or fundamental investor skills. In fact, I'll bet most new investors today do not know the difference between a fundamental and technical investor.

Rich dad used to say, "Qualified investors need to be well versed in both fundamental analysis as well as technical analysis. He would draw the following diagrams for me. These diagrams are why we developed our products the way we did. We want people to be able to learn to be financially literate and to teach their children to be financially literate at a young age, as rich dad taught me.

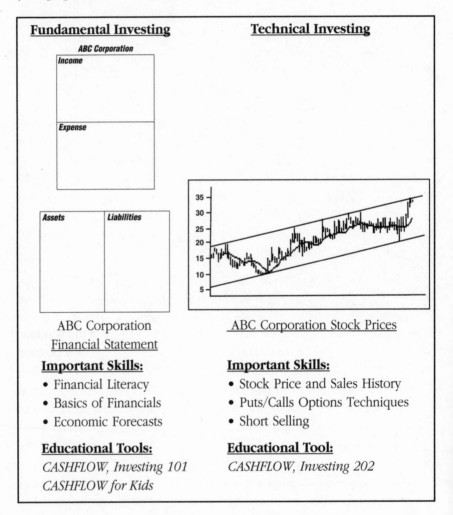

I am often asked, "Why does a qualified investor need to understand both fundamental investing as well technical investing?" My answer is found in one word: "confidence." Average investors feel that investing is risky because:

1. They are on the outside trying to look into the inside of the company or property they are investing in. If they do not know how to read financial statements, they are totally dependent on others' opinions. If only at an unconscious level, people know that insiders have better information and therefore lower risk.

2. If people cannot read financial statements, their personal financial statements are often a mess. And as rich dad said, "If a person's financial foundation is weak, his or her self-confidence is also weak." A friend of mine, Keith Cunningham, often says, "The main reason people do not want to look at their personal financial statements is that they might find out they have financial cancer." The good news is that once they cure the financial disease, the rest of their lives also improves—and sometimes even their physical health too.

3. Most people know how to make money only when the market is going up, and they live in terror of the market coming down. If a person understands technical investing, he or she has the skills to make money when the market goes down as well as when it goes up. The average investor without technical skills makes money only in a rising market, often losing all he or she has gained in a falling market. Rich Dad said, "a technical investor invests with insurance from huge losses. The average investor is like a person flying a plane without a parachute."

As rich dad often said about technical investors, "The bull comes up by the stairs and the bear goes out the window." A bull market will rise slowly, but when it crashes, the market is like a bear going out the window. Technical investors are excited about market crashes because they position themselves to make money quickly when average investors are losing their money, money that often increased very slowly.

So the chart of various investors and their returns often looks like this:

	Market	
	UP	DOWN
Losing investor	loses	loses
Average investor	wins	loses
Qualified investor	wins	wins

Many investors often lose because they wait too long to get into the market. They are so afraid of losing that they wait too long for proof that the market is going up. As soon as they enter, the market peaks and crashes and they end up losing on the way down.

Qualified investors are less concerned about the market going up or

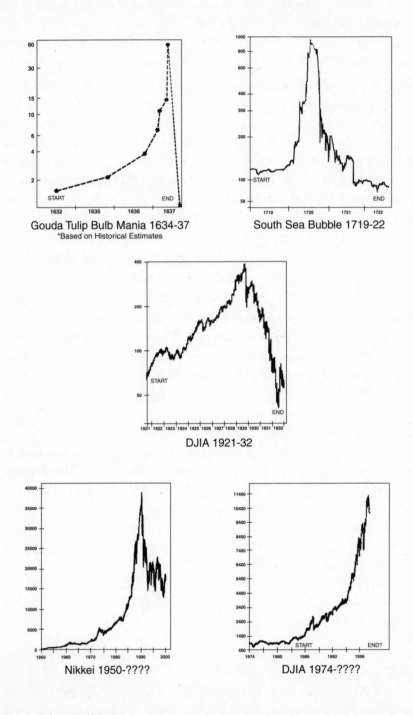

Gouda Tulip Bulb Mania 1634-37
*Based on Historical Estimates

South Sea Bubble 1719-22

DJIA 1921-32

Nikkei 1950-????

DJIA 1974-????

Source: Robert Prechter Jr.

going down. They enter confidently, with a trading system for an up-trending market. When the market reverses, they will often change trading systems, exiting their previous trades and using short selling, and put options to profit while the market comes down. Having multiple trading systems and strategies helps them have more confidence as investors.

Why You May Want to Be a Qualified Investor

The average investor lives in fear of the market crashing or prices coming down. You can often hear them say, "What if I buy a stock and the price comes down?" Hence many average investors fail to take advantage of profit opportunities in an up market and a down market. A qualified investor looks forward to the ups and downs of a market. When prices go up, they have the skills to minimize risk and earn a profit regardless if the price is going up or coming down. A qualified investor will often "hedge" their positions which means they are protected if the price goes down suddenly or goes up suddenly. In other words they have a good chance of making money in either direction while protecting themselves from losses.

The Problem with New Investors

Today, with such a hot market, I often hear new investors say with confidence, "I don't have to worry about a market crash because this time, things are different." A seasoned investor knows that all markets go up and all markets come down. Today as I write, we are in one of the biggest bull markets in the history of the world. Will this market come crashing down? If history holds any stories, then we should be in for one of the biggest crashes the world has ever seen. Today people are investing in companies without any profits...which means a mania is on. The diagrams on the previous page are diagrams of past bubbles, manias, or booms and busts the world has gone through.

Sir Issac Newton who lost most of his fortune in the South Sea Bubble is quoted as saying, "I can calculate the motions of heavenly bodies, but not the madness of people." Today, in my opinion, there is madness. Everyone is thinking about getting rich quick in the market. I am afraid that we may soon see millions of people lose everything simply because they invested in the market, some borrowed money to invest, instead of first investing in their education and experience. At the same time, I am excited because many people will soon be selling in a panic and that is when the qualified investor really becomes wealthy.

It is not the crash that is so bad but the emotional panic that occurs at the times of such financial disasters/opportunities. The problem with most new investors is that they have not yet been through a real bear market...since this current bull market started in 1974. Many mutual fund managers were not yet born or barely born in 1974 so how would they know what a market crash and bear market feels like, especially if it goes on for years, such as the Japanese market has done.

Rich dad simply said, "It is not possible to predict the market, but it is important that we be prepared for whichever direction it decides to go." He also said, "Bull markets seem to go on forever, which causes people to become sloppy, foolish, and complacent. Bear markets also seem to go on forever causing people to forget that bear markets are often the best times to become very, very rich. That is why you want to be a qualified investor."

Why Markets Will Crash Faster in the Information Age

In his book, *The Lexus and the Olive Tree*, a book I strongly recommend for anyone wanting to understand the new era of global business we are in, author Thomas L Friedman often makes reference to The Electronic Herd. The electronic herd is a group of several thousand, very often young, people who control great sums of electronic money. They are the individuals who work for large banks, mutual funds, hedge funds, insurance companies, and the like. They have the power with the click of their mouse to move literally trillions of dollars from one country to another country in a split second. That power gives the electronic herd more power than politicians.

I was in South East Asia in 1997 when the electronic herd moved their money out of countries like Thailand, Indonesia, Malaysia, and Korea, virtually sinking those countries' economies over night. It was not a pretty sight nor was it pleasant to be physically present in those countries.

For those of you who invest globally, you may recall how most of the world, even Wall Street was singing praises to the new Asian Tiger Economies. Everyone wanted to invest in these countries. Then suddenly, literally over night, their world changed. There were murders, suicides, riots, looting, and a general feeling of financial sickness everywhere. The electronic herd did not like what it saw in those countries and moved their money out in a matter of seconds.

Quoting from Thomas Friedman's book, he states:

"Think of the Electronic Herd as being like a herd of wildebeests grazing over a wide area of Africa. When a wildebeest on the edge of the herd sees something move in the tall, thick brush next to where it's feeding, that wildebeest doesn't say to the wildebeest next to it, 'Gosh, I wonder if that's a lion moving around there in the brush.' No way. That wildebeest just starts a stampede, and those wildebeests don't stampede for a mere hundred yards. They stampede to the next country and crush everything in their path."

That is what happened to the Asian Tigers in 1997. The Electronic Herd did not like what they saw going on in the area and moved out literally overnight. It went from high optimism to riots and murder in a matter of days.

That is why I predict that market crashes will come faster and more severely in the Information Age.

How Does One Protect Oneself from These Crashes?

The way some of these countries are protecting themselves from the power of the Electronic Herd is by cleaning up and tightening up their national financial statements and increasing their financial requirements and standards. In his book Thomas Friedman writes:

Standards: "If you were writing a history of the American capital markets," Deputy Treasury Secretary Larry Summers once observed, "I would suggest that the single most important innovation shaping that capital market was the idea of generally accepted accounting principles. We need that internationally. It is a minor, but not insignificant, triumph of the IMF that in Korea somebody who teaches a night school class in accounting told me that he normally has 22 students in his Winter term, and this year (1998) he has 385. We need that at the corporate level in Korea. We need that at the national level."

Years ago rich dad said a similar thing, but he was not referring to an entire country as Larry Summers is in this quote. Rich dad was referring to any individual who wanted to do well financially. Rich dad said, "The difference between a rich person and a poor person is much more than how much money they make. The difference is found in their financial literacy and the standards of importance they put on that literacy. Simply put, poor people have very low financial literacy standards, regardless of how much money they make." He also said, "People with low financial literacy standards are often unable to take their ideas and create assets out of them. Instead of creating assets, many people create liabilities with their ideas just because of low financial literacy standards."

Getting Out Is More Important than Getting In

Rich dad often said, "The reason most average investors lose money is because it is often easy to invest into an asset, but it is often difficult to get out. If you want to be a savvy investor you need to know how to exit an investment as well as how to get into the investment." Today when I invest, one of the most important strategies I must consider is what is called my "exit strategy." Rich dad put the importance of an exit strategy in these terms so I could understand it's importance. He said, "Buying an investment is often like getting married. In the beginning things are exciting and fun. But if things do not go well, then the divorce can be much more painful than all that initial excitement and fun. That is why you must really think about an investment almost like a marriage. Because getting in is often a lot easier than getting out."

Both my dads were very happily married men. So when rich dad talked about divorce, he was not encouraging people to get divorced he was just advising me to think long term. He said, "The odds are 50% of all marriages will end in divorce and the reality is nearly 100% of all marriages think they will beat those odds." And that may be why so many new investors are buying IPO's, buying shares from the more seasoned investors. Rich dad's best words on this subject were, "Always remember that when you are excitedly buying an asset there is often someone who knows more about the asset who is excitedly selling it to you!"

When people learn to invest by playing the *CASHFLOW* games, one of the technical skills they learn is when to buy and when to sell. Rich dad said, "When you buy an investment you should also have an idea of when to sell it, especially investments offered to Accredited Investors and above. In the more sophisticated types of investments, your exit is often more important than the entry strategy. When getting into such investments you should know what will happen if the investment goes well and what will happen if the investment goes bad."

The Financial Skills of a Qualified Investor

For people who want to learn the basic financial skills, we developed *CASHFLOW 101*. We recommend playing it at least six to twelve times. By playing *101* repeatedly, you begin to understand the basics of fundamental investment analysis. After playing *101* and gaining an understanding of the financial skills it teaches, you may want to move on to playing *CASHFLOW 202*. The advanced game uses the very same game board as *101*, but it goes to another level, using a different set of cards and scoring sheets. In *202*, you begin to learn the complex skills and vocabulary of technical trading. You learn to use trading techniques such as short selling, which is selling shares you do not own, in anticipation of the price coming down. You also learn to use call options, put options, and straddles. All of these are very sophisticated trading techniques, which all qualified investors need to know. The best thing about these games is that you learn by playing and using play money. That same education in the real world could be very expensive.

Why Games Are Better Teachers

In 1950 a nun, who was a history and geography teacher in Calcutta, was called on to help the poor and to live amongst them. Instead of just talking about caring for the poor she chose to say very little and helped the poor with her actions not her words. It was because of her actions that when she did speak, people listened. She had this to say about the difference between words and actions, "There should be less talk. A preaching point is not a meeting point. There should be more action on your part."

I chose to use games as the means of teaching the investment skills my rich dad taught me because games require more action than lecture in the teaching and learning process. As Mother Teresa said, "A preaching point is not a meeting point." Our games are meeting points. Games provide a social interaction for learning and helping someone else to learn. When it comes to investing, there are too many people trying to teach investing by preaching. We all know that there are certain things that are not best learned by simply reading and listening. Some things require action to be learned and games provide this elementary action step to learning.

There is an old aphorism that goes:

"I hear and I forget. I see and I remember. I do and I understand."

My purpose in going beyond just writing books about money and investing, and creating games as learning tools, is to create more understanding. The more understanding people have, the more they can see the other side of the coin. Instead of seeing fear and doubt, the players begin to see opportunties they never saw before because their understanding increases each time they play the game.

Our web site is filled with stories of people who have played our games and have had their lives suddenly changed. They have learned a new understanding about money and investing, an understanding that pushed out some old thoughts and gave them new possibilities for their lives.

At the back of this book is my edumercial about the games which gives you more information on how these educational tools can assist you in increasing your understanding of money, business, and investing.

Rich dad taught me to be a business owner and investor by playing the game of *Monopoly.* He was able to teach his son and me so much more after the game was over when we visited his businesses and real estate. I wanted to create educational games that taught the same fundamental and technical investing skills that rich dad taught me, far beyond what is taught in *Monopoly.* As rich dad said, "The ability to manage cash flow and to read financial statements is fundamental to success on the B and I side of the

CASHFLOW Quadrant."

The Investor Controls Possessed by the Qualified Investor

1. The control over yourself
2. The control over income/expense asset/liability ratios
5. The control over when you buy and when you sell

The Three Es Possessed by the Qualified Investor

1. Education
3. Excessive cash—maybe

Sharon's Notes

The qualified investors, both fundamental and technical, are analyzing a company from the outside. They are deciding whether to become "buying shareholders." Many very successful investors are happy operating as qualified investors. With the proper education and financial advice, many qualified investors can become millionaires. They are investing in businesses developed and run by others. Because they have studied and gained the financial education, they are able to analyze the company from its financial statements.

What Does p/e Mean?

The qualified investor understands the price earnings (p/e) ratio of a stock, which is also referred to as the market multiplier. The p/e ratio is calculated by dividing the current market price of a stock by the previous year's earnings per share. Generally, a low p/e would mean that a stock is selling at a relatively low price compared to its earnings; a high p/e would indicate that a stock's price is high and may not be much of a bargain.

$$\text{p/e Ratio} = \frac{\text{Market's Price (Per Share)}}{\text{Net Income (Per Share)}}$$

The p/e ratio of one successful company may be very different from that of another successful company if the two companies are in different industries. For example, high-tech companies with big growth and high earnings generally sell at much higher p/es than low-tech or mature companies where growth has stabilized. Just look at the stocks being sold in Internet companies today: Many of them are selling at very high prices even when the companies have no earnings. The high prices in these cases reflect the market's expectation for high earnings in the future.

The Future p/e Is the Key

A qualified investor recognizes that the current p/e is not as important as the future p/e. The investor wants to invest in a company where the company's financial future is strong. In order for the p/e ratio to be helpful to the investor, much more information about the company may be needed. Generally, the investor will compare a company's ratios for the current year with that of previous years to measure the growth of the company. The investor will also compare the company's ratios with those of other companies in the same industry.

Not All Day Traders Are Qualified

Many people today are participating in "day trading," which has become popular due to the convenience and availability of online trading. The day trader is hoping to earn profits through buying and selling securities within a single day. The day trader is very familiar with p/e ratios. What distinguishes a successful day trader from an unsuccessful day trader is often his or her ability to see behind the p/e ratio. For the most part, successful day traders have taken the time to learn the basics of technical or fundamental trading. Day traders without proper financial education and financial analysis skills are operating more like gamblers than traders. Only the most educated and successful day traders would be considered qualified investors.

In fact, it has been said that the majority of new day traders lose some or all of their capital and quit trading within two years. Day trading is an extremely competitive S quadrant activity in which the most knowledgeable and best prepared use everyone else's money.

Remember to get your free audio report "My Rich Dad said, 'Profit Don't Panic,'" available at www.richdadbook3.com. Learning how to keep a cool head and invest wisely during a crash is a very important qualified investor skill. Besides, it is during a crash that many people become very rich.

Chapter 24

The Sophisticated Investor

The sophisticated investor knows as much as the qualified investor but has also studied the advantages available through the legal system. Rich dad defined the sophisticated investor as an investor who knows what the qualified investor knows and who is familiar with the following specialties of law:

1. Tax law
2. Corporate law
3. Securities law

While not a lawyer, the sophisticated investor may base as much of his or her investment strategy on the law as well as the investment product and potential returns. The sophisticated investor often gains higher returns with very low risk by using the different disciplines of law.

Knowing the E-T-C

By knowing the basics of the law, the sophisticated investor is able to use the advantages of E-T-C, which stand for entity, timing, and characteristic:

Rich dad would describe the E-T-C as follows: "The E stands for control over the entity, which means the choice of business structure." If you are an employee, this is not usually in your control. A person from the S quadrant usually can choose from the following entities: a sole proprietorship, partnership (which is the worst structure because you are entitled to your share of income but are responsible for all the risk), an S Corporation, an LLC (limited liability corporation), an LLP (limited liability partnership), or a C-Corporation.

Today, if you are an attorney, doctor, architect, dentist, etc., and choose the C-Corporation as your entity of choice in the United States, your minimum tax rate is 35% versus 15% for someone like me because my business is a non-licensed professional services business.

That additional 20% tax rate differential adds up to a lot of money, especially when measured over years. It means a non-professional would have a 20% financial head start over a professional at the start of each year within a C-Corporation.

Rich dad would say to me, "But just think about people in the E quadrant who cannot elect their choice of entity. For them, regardless of how hard they work and how much they make, the government always gets paid first through income tax withholding. And the harder you work to make more money, the more the government takes. That's because the people in the E quadrant have virtually no control over entity, expenses, and taxes. Again, people in the E quadrant cannot pay themselves first because of the Current Tax Payment Act of 1943, which started withholding of income taxes from employees. After the passage of that act, the government always got paid first."

Sharon's Notes

In America, partnerships, S Corporations, LLPs, and LLCs are often called "pass-through" entities because the income passes through the entities' returns and shows up on the owner's return. Consult a tax advisor for applicability of which entity is appropriate for your situation.

C Corporations

"And you always try to operate via a C Corporate entity, don't you?" I would ask rich dad.

"In most cases," he replied. "Remember that it is the plan before the product or in this case the corporate entity. The point is that those who operate from the B quadrant tend to have more choices and hence more control over the best entity to best make their plan work. Again, those fine points should be discussed with both your tax attorney and your tax accountant."

"But why a C-Corporation?" I asked. "What is the difference that is so important to you?"

"This is the one big difference," he said, having waited a long time to explain it. "A sole proprietorship, a partnership, and an S-Corporation are all part of you. They are, in simple terms, an extension of you."

"And what is a C-Corporation?" I asked.

"A C-Corporation is another you. It is not just an extension of you. A C-Corporation has the ability to be a clone of you. If you are serious about doing business, then you do not want to do business as a private citizen. That is too risky, especially in this day and age of lawsuits. When you do business, you want a clone of you actually doing the business. You do not want to do business or own anything as a private citizen," rich dad guided me. "If you want to be a rich private citizen, you need be as poor and penniless as possible on paper." Rich dad also said, "The poor and the middle class, on the other hand, want to own everything in their name. 'Pride of ownership,' they call it. I call anything with your name on it 'a target for predators and lawyers.'"

The main point rich dad was trying to make was "The rich do not want to own anything but want to control everything. And they control via corporations and limited partnerships." That is why control of the E in E-T-C is so important to the rich.

Within the last two years, I have seen a devastating example of how the choice of entity could have helped prevent the financial destruction of a family.

A very successful local hardware store was owned as a family partnership. The family had been in town forever, knew everyone, had become wealthy, and was quite involved in civic and charitable organizations. You could not have asked for a more wonderful, caring, and giving couple. One night, their teenage daughter was drinking and driving, had an accident, and killed a passenger in the other car. Their lives were dramatically altered. Their 17-year-old daughter was sent to an adult prison for seven years and the family lost everything they owned, including the business. In sharing this example, I am not trying to make any moral or parenting statements; I'm simply pointing out that proper financial planning for both the family and the business might—through the use of insurance, trusts, limited partnerships, or corporations—have prevented this family from losing its livelihood.

What about Double Taxation?

I am often asked, "Why do you recommend C-Corporations instead of S-Corporations or LLC corporations? Why do you want to be subject to double taxation?"

Double taxation occurs when a corporation is taxed on its income and then when it declares a dividend to its shareholders they are taxed on the dividend. The same thing can occur when an improperly structured sale of a corporation occurs and a liquidity dividend is declared. The dividend is not deductible to the corporation but is taxable to the shareholder. Therefore, that income is taxed at both the corporate and individual level.

Business owners often increase their own salaries to reduce or wipe out corporate profits and thereby eliminate the possibility of having those profits taxed twice. Alternatively, as the corporation continues to grow, the retained profits are used to expand the business and help it grow. (In the United States, a C Corporation must justify this accumulation of earnings or it will become subject to the Accumulated Earnings Tax.) There is no double taxation unless dividends are declared.

I personally like C Corporations because I believe they provide the maximum flexibility. I always look at the big picture. When I start a business, I expect it to become a big business. Most big businesses today are C Corporations (or the equivalent in other countries). I grow businesses because I want to sell them or take them public, not receive dividends.

Sometimes, I choose a different entity for a business. For example, I just formed an LLC with partners so that I could buy a building.

You should consult with your financial and tax advisors to determine the appropriate structure for your situation.

Timing

Rich dad would describe the T as timing. "Timing is important because ultimately, we all need to pay taxes. Paying taxes is an expense of living in a civilized society. The rich want to control how much they pay in taxes as well as when they have to pay them."

Understanding the law helps in controlling the timing of paying taxes. For instance, Section 1031 of the U.S. Tax Code allows you to "roll over" your gain in investment real estate if you buy another property at a greater price. This allows you to defer paying taxes until the second property is sold (or you may choose to roll it over repeatedly—perhaps forever!).

Another important timing issue is provided by the C Corporation status. C Corporations can elect a different year-end for tax and accounting purposes (such as June 30, for instance) than December 31, which is required for most individuals, partnerships, S Corporations, and LLC Corporations. This allows for a certain amount of strategic tax planning as to the timing of distributions between corporations and to individuals.

Sharon's Notes

Although Robert discusses the entity and timing issues as simple tax planning vehicles, it is important to understand that all decisions related to entity selection as well as income timing issues should have legitimate business purposes and be thoroughly discussed with your legal and tax advisors. Although Robert uses these tax-planning opportunities personally, he does so with the careful guidance and planning of his legal and tax advisors.

The chart on the next page describes the various forms of business entities and related issues that you need to consider when choosing the entity right for your individual needs. It is imperative that you carefully review your individual financial and tax situation with your legal and tax advisors in choosing the right entity for your business.

Character of Income

As far as the third component of the E-T-C, rich dad would say, "Investors control. Everyone else gambles. The rich are rich because they have more control over their money than the poor and middle class. The moment you understand that the game of money is a game of control, you can focus on what is important in life, which is not making more money but gaining more financial control."

Reaching for his yellow pad, rich dad would write:

1. Earned income
2. Passive income
3. Portfolio income

"These are the three different kinds of income." Rich dad would stress that I should know the difference between these three different types of income. The C of the E-T-C stands for the character of the income.

"Is there a lot of difference?" I would ask.

"Very much so," he would reply. "Especially when combined with the E (entity) and T (timing) of the E-T-C. Controlling the characteristics of your income is the most important financial control of all. But you may first want to control the E and the T."

It took me awhile to fully appreciate and understand why controlling the characteristics of these three different types of income is so important.

"It's important because the characteristic of the income is what separates the rich from the working class," rich dad analyzed. "The poor and middle class focus on earned income, also called wages or paycheck income. The rich focus on passive income and portfolio income. That is the fundamental difference between the rich and the working class, which explains why control of the C (characteristic) is a fundamental control, especially if you plan on being rich."

"In America and other advanced economies, even the first dollar of earned income is taxed at higher rates than passive and portfolio income. The higher rates are necessary to provide various forms of 'social

LEGAL ENTITIES FOR BUSINESSES

ENTITY	CONTROL	LIABILITY	TAX	YEAR-END	CONTINUITY
SOLE PROPRIETORSHIP	You have complete control	You are completely liable	You report all income and expense on your personal tax return	Calendar year end	Business terminates with your death
GENERAL PARTNERSHIP	Each partner, including you, can enter into contracts and other business agreements	You are totally liable for all business debts including your partners' share.	You report your share of partnership income on your personal tax return	Must be same as the majority interest tax year, or principal partners. If neither, must be calendar.	Partnership terminates on death or withdrawal of any partner
LIMITED PARTNERSHIP	General Partners control the business	General partners are totally liable – Limited partners are liable for only the amount of their investment	Partnership files annual tax returns – General & Limited partners report their income or loss on their personal tax returns. Losses may be subject to limitations	Must be same as the majority interest tax year, or principal partners. If neither, must be calendar.	Partnership does not dissolve with death of a limited partner but may dissolve with death of a general partner unless the partnership agreement states otherwise
LIMITED LIABILITY COMPANY	Owners or members have the authority	Owners or members are not liable for business debts	Rules vary dependent on the State – "Check the box" allows election of treatment	Rules vary dependent on the State – "Check the box" allows election of treatment	Rules vary depending on the State – In some States the company will dissolve upon the death of a owner or member
CORPORATION C Corp	Shareholders appoint Board of Directors which appoints Officers who have the most authority	Shareholders risk only the amount of their investment in the corporation's stock	Corporation pays its own taxes – Shareholders pay tax on dividends received	Any month end. Personal service corp must use calendar.	The Corporation stands alone as a legal entity – It can survive the death of owner, officer or shareholder
SUBCHAPTER S	Shareholders appoint Board of Directors which appoints Officers who have the most authority	Shareholders risk only the amount of their investment in the corporation's stock	Shareholders report their share of the corporate profit or loss on their personal tax returns	Calendar Year	The Corporation stands alone as a legal entity – It can survive the death of owner, officer or shareholder

WARNING: Please consult your financial and tax advisors to determine the entity best suited for you.

insurance,'" rich dad would further explain. Social insurance stands for payments the government makes to various people. (In the United States, this would include Social Security, Medicare, and unemployment insurance, just to name a few.) Income taxes are then calculated on top of social insurance taxes. Passive and portfolio income are not subject to social insurance taxes.

"So every day that I get up and focus on working hard to earn money, I am focusing on earned income, which means I pay more in taxes," I would say. "That is why you have been encouraging me to change my focus on what kind of income I want to earn."

I realized rich dad was back to Lesson #1 of *Rich Dad Poor Dad.* "The rich don't work hard for money. They have their money work hard for them." It suddenly all made sense. I needed to learn how to convert earned income into passive and portfolio income so my money could start working for me.

The Investor Controls Possessed by the Sophisticated Investor

1. The control over yourself
2. The control over income/expense and asset/liability ratios
4. The control over taxes
5. The control over when you buy and when you sell
6. The control over brokerage transactions
7. The control over the E-T-C (entity, timing, characteristic)

The Three E's Possessed by the Sophisticated Investor

1. Education
2. Experience
3. Excessive cash

Sharon's Notes

The SEC test of a "sophisticated investor" is a non-accredited investor who either alone or with his purchasing representative has enough knowledge and experience in financial and business matters to be able to evaluate the merits and risks of the prospective investment. The SEC presumes that accredited investors (as defined earlier as the well-to-do, who can afford to hire advisors) are capable of watching out for their own interests.

In contrast, we believe many accredited and qualified investors are not sophisticated. Many wealthy individuals have not learned the basics of investing and the law. Many of them rely on investment advisors whom they hope are sophisticated investors to do the investing for them.

Our sophisticated investor understands the impact and advantages of the law and has structured his or her investment portfolio to take maximum advantage of entity selection, timing, and characteristic of income. In doing so, the sophisticated investor has sought the advice of his or her legal and tax counsel.

Many sophisticated investors are often content investing in other entities as outside investors. They may not possess control over the management of their investments, which distinguishes them from the inside investor. They may invest in management teams without possessing a controlling interest in the company. Alternatively, they may invest as partners in real estate syndications or as shareholders in large corporations. They study and invest prudently but lack control over the management of the underlying asset and therefore have access only to public information of the company's operations. This lack of management control is the defining difference between a sophisticated investor and an inside investor.

However, the sophisticated investor still uses the advantages provided by the E-T-C analysis for his or her own financial portfolio. In Phase Four, we will discuss how the sophisticated investor applies these principles to obtain the maximum advantage provided by the law.

Good Versus Bad

In addition to the three characteristics of income Robert discusses, three other general principles distinguish a sophisticated investor from an average investor. A sophisticated investor knows the difference between:

Good debt and bad debt
Good expenses and bad expenses
Good losses and bad losses

As a general rule, good debt, good expenses, and good losses all generate additional cash flow for you. For instance, debt taken to acquire a rental property, which has a positive cash flow each month, would be good debt. Likewise, paying for legal and tax advice are good expenses if they save you thousands of dollars in reduced taxes from tax planning. An example of a good loss is the loss generated by depreciation from real estate. This good loss is also called a phantom loss because it is a paper loss and does not require an actual outlay of cash. The end result is a savings in the amount of tax paid on the income offset by the loss.

Knowing the difference between good and bad debt, expenses, and losses is what distinguishes the sophisticated investor from the average investor. When average investors hear the words "debt, expense, and loss," they usually react negatively. Generally, their experiences with debt, expenses, and losses result in additional cash flowing "out of their pockets" instead of into their pockets.

The sophisticated investor enlists the advice of accountants, tax strategists, and financial advisors to structure the most beneficial financial organization for his or her investments. He or she looks for and invests in those deals that include the E-T-C features that support his or her personal financial plan—the map he or she is following to become rich.

How Can You Identify a Sophisticated Investor?

I remember a story my rich dad once told me about risk. While part of it has been covered in other parts of the book, it is worth repeating here. The average investor views risk from a completely different point of view than the sophisticated investor. And it is this view of risk that truly differentiates the sophisticated investor.

Why Being Secure Is Risky

One day, I went to my rich dad and said, "My dad thinks that what you do is far too risky. He thinks that one financial statement is secure but you think that controlling only one financial statement is risky. It seems like such a contradiction in points of view."

Rich dad just chuckled. "It is," said rich dad, continuing to chuckle. "Almost exactly opposite and contradictory." Rich dad paused for a moment to gather his thoughts. "If you want to become really rich," he said, "then one of the things you will have to change is your point of view on what you think is risky and what is secure. What the poor and middle class think is secure, I think is risky."

I thought about that statement for a brief moment, letting the idea that what my dad thought was secure, my rich dad thought was risky sink in. "I don't fully understand." I finally asked. "Can you give me an example?"

"Sure," said rich dad. "Just listen to our words. Your dad always says, 'Get a safe, secure job.' Is that correct?"

I nodded my head. "Yes, he thinks that is a secure way to run your life."
"But is it really secure?" asked rich dad.

"I guess for him it is." I replied. "But you see it differently?"

Rich dad nodded his head and then asked, "What often happens when a public company announces a large layoff of employees?"

"I don't know." I replied. "You mean what happens when a company fires a lot of employees?"

"Yes," said rich dad. "What often happens to the price of their stock?"

"I don't know," I replied. "Does the share price go down?"

Rich dad shook his head. Quietly he said, "No, unfortunately when a publicly listed company announces a large layoff of employees, the share price of that company often goes up."

I thought about that statement for a moment and then said, "And that is why you have often said there is a big difference between people on the left side of the CASHFLOW Quadrant and people on the right."

Rich dad nodded his head. "A big difference. What is secure for one side is risky to the other."

"And that is why so few people become really rich?" I asked.

Again rich dad nodded his head and repeated, "What seems secure to one side seems risky to the other side. If you want to be rich and keep your wealth for generations, you must be able to see both sides to risk and security. The average investor only sees one side."

What Seems Secure Is Really Risky

As an adult, I now see what my rich dad saw. Today, what I think is secure most people think is risky. The following are some of the differences.

AVERAGE INVESTOR	SOPHISTICATED INVESTOR
Only one financial statement.	Multiple financial statements.
Wants everything in their name.	Wants nothing in their name. Uses corporate entities. Often personal residence and automobile are not in their names.
Does not think of insurance as an investment. Uses words such as "diversify."	Uses insurance as an investment product to hedge against exposed risk. Uses words such as "covered," "exposure" and "hedge."
Holds only paper assets, which includes cash and savings.	Has both paper assets and hard assets such as real estate and precious metals. Precious metals are a hedge against government mismanagement of the money supply, also know as fiat money.
Focuses on job security.	Focuses on financial freedom.
Focuses on professional education Avoids making mistakes.	Focuses on financial education. Understands that mistakes are part of learning.
Does not seek financial information or wants it for free if sought.	Willing to pay for financial information.
Thinks in good or bad, black or white, right or wrong.	Thinks in financial gray.
Looks at past indicators – such as p/es and CAP rates.	Looks for future indicators – trends, proformas, changes in management & products.
Calls brokers 1st and asks for investment advice or invests alone, asking no one for advice.	Calls broker last...after consulting with plan and team of financial and legal advisors then calls appropriate broker. Their brokers are often part of team.
Seeks external security, such as job, company, government.	Values personal self-confidence and independence.

In conclusion, what looks secure to some investors seems risky to others.

Chapter 25

The Inside Investor

The inside investor is someone who is on the inside of the investment and has some degree of management control.

Although an important distinction of the inside investor is the aspect of control over management, the most important distinction rich dad pointed out was that you don't need to have a lot of income or net worth to be considered an inside investor. An officer, director, or owner of 10% or more of the outstanding shares of the corporation is an inside investor.

Most investment books are written for people who are on the outside of the world of investing. This book is written for people who want to invest from the inside.

In the real world, there is legal inside investment activity as well as illegal insider activity. Rich dad always wanted his son and me to be investors on the inside rather than the outside. It is one very important way to reduce risk and increase returns.

Someone with the financial education but not the financial resources of an accredited investor can still become an inside investor. This is where many people enter the world of investing today. By building their own companies, inside investors are building assets that they can run, sell, or take public.

In his book, *What Works on Wall Street*, James P. O'Shaughnessy analyzes the returns by market capitalization of various types of investments. It shows that the small stocks far outperform the other categories. A chart from his book is included for your reference on the next page.

Almost all of the high returns are found in the small microcap stocks with market capitalizations below $25 million. The down side is that these stocks are too small for mutual funds to invest in and hard to find for the average investor. As O'Shaughnessy states, "tantalizingly out of reach of nearly everyone." There is very little trading volume in these stocks so the ask price and bid price are usually far apart. This is an example of how 10% of the investors gain control of 90% of the shares.

If you can't find these stocks to invest in, then consider the next best thing. Build your own small cap stock company and enjoy the superior returns as the inside investor.

How I Did It

I found my financial freedom as an inside investor. Remember that I started small, buying real estate as a sophisticated investor. I learned how to use limited partnerships and corporations to maximize the tax savings and asset protection. I then started several companies to gain additional experience. With the financial education I learned from my rich dad, I built businesses as an inside investor. I did not become an accredited investor until I found success as a sophisticated investor. I have never considered myself a qualified investor. I do not know how to pick stocks and do not choose to buy stocks as an outsider. (Why would I? Being an insider is much lower risk as well as much more profitable!)

I share this with you to give you hope. If I can learn to become an inside investor through building a company, then so can you. Remember that the more controls you possess over your investment, the less risky it is.

The Investor Controls Possessed by the Inside Investor

1. The control over yourself
2. The control over income/expense and asset/liability ratios
3. The control over the management of the investment
4. The control over taxes
5. The control over when you buy and when you sell
6. The control over brokerage transactions
7. The control over the E-T-C (entity, timing, characteristic)
8. The control over the terms and conditions of the agreements
9. The control over access to information

Source: *What Works on Wall Street* by James P. O'Shaughnessy

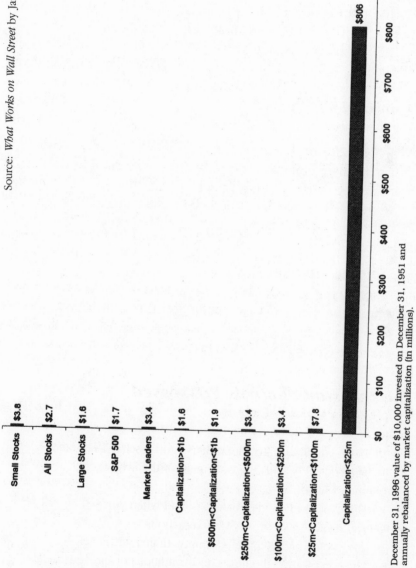

December 31, 1996 value of $10,000 invested on December 31, 1951 and annually rebalanced by market capitalization (in millions).

The Three E's Possessed by the Inside Investor

1. Education
2. Experience
3. Excessive cash

Sharon's Notes

The SEC defines an "insider" as anyone who has information about a company that has not yet been made publicly available. The Securities Exchange Act of 1934 made it illegal for anyone who had non-public information on a company to profit from that information. This includes the insider as well as anyone to whom he or she gives a "tip" who subsequently profits from the information.

Robert's use of the word "insider" defines investors who have management control over the operations of the business. The inside investor has control over the direction of the company. An outside investor does not. Robert distinguishes between legal and illegal insider trading, and strongly opposes illegal insider trading. It is too easy to make money legally.

Creating Control

The money you invest and risk as the owner of a private business is your own. If you have outside investors, you have a fiduciary responsibility to manage their investment well, but you are able to control the management of the investment as well as access to insider information.

Buying Control

In addition to building a business on your own, you may become an inside investor through buying a controlling interest in an existing company. Buying a majority of the stock in a company allows you to acquire the controlling interest. Remember that as you increase the number of investor controls you possess, you continue to reduce your risk in the investment—that is, of course, if you possess the skill to manage the investment properly.

If you already own a business and wish to expand, you may acquire another business through merger or acquisition. The important issues in mergers and acquisitions are far too numerous to explore here. However, it is very important to seek competent legal, tax, and accounting advice before any purchase, merger, or acquisition to make sure such transactions are done properly.

To move from being an inside investor to an ultimate investor, you must decide to sell a portion or all of your business. The following questions may help you in your decision process:

1. Are you still excited about the business?
2. Do you want to start another business?
3. Do you want to retire?
4. Is the business profitable?
5. Is the business growing too rapidly for you to handle it?
6. Does your company have large capital funding needs that can best be met through selling stock or through selling to another business?
7. Does your company have the money and time for a public offering?
8. Can your individual focus be diverted from the daily operations of the company to negotiate a sale or public offering without hurting the operations of the company?
9. Is the industry your business is in expanding or contracting?
10. What impact will your competitors have on a sale or public offering?
11. If your business is strong, can you pass it on to your children or other family members?
12. Are there well-trained and managerially strong family members (children) to pass it on to?
13. Does the business need managerial skills that you lack?

Many inside investors are extremely happy running their businesses and investment portfolios. They have no desire to sell a portion of their business through a public or private offering, nor do they want to sell the business outright. This is the type of investor that Robert's best friend Mike has become. He is very content running the financial empire that he and his father built.

Chapter 26

The Ultimate Investor

The ultimate investor is a person such as Bill Gates or Warren Buffet. These investors build giant companies that other investors want to invest in. The ultimate investor is a person who creates an asset that becomes so valuable that the asset they created is worth literally billions of dollars to millions of people.

Both Gates and Buffet became rich not because of their high salaries or their great products but because they built great companies and took the companies public.

While it is not likely that many of us will ever build a Microsoft or Berkshire Hathaway, we all have the possibility of building a smaller business and becoming wealthy by selling it privately or selling it publicly.

Rich dad used to say, "Some people build houses to sell; others build cars, but the ultimate is to build a business that millions of people want to own a share of."

The Investor Controls Possessed by the Ultimate Investor

1. The control over yourself
2. The control over income/expense and asset/liability ratios
3. The control over the management of the investment
4. The control over taxes
5. The control over when you buy and when you sell
6. The control over brokerage transactions
7. The control over the E-T-C (entity, timing, characteristic)
8. The control over the terms and conditions of the agreements

9. The control over access to information
10. The control over giving it back, philanthropy, redistribution of wealth

The Three E's Possessed by the Ultimate Investor

1. Education
2. Experience
3. Excessive cash

Sharon's Notes

There are advantages and disadvantages of "going public," which we will discuss in greater detail later. However, here are a few of the advantages and disadvantages of an initial public offering (IPO):

Advantages:

1. To allow business owners to "cash in" some of their equity in the business. For example, Gates's original partner, Paul Allen, sold some of his Microsoft shares in order to buy cable TV companies.
2. To raise expansion capital.
3. To pay off company debt.
4. To raise the company's net worth.
5. To allow the company to offer stock options as benefits to its employees.

Disadvantages:

1. Your operations become public. You are forced to disclose information to the public that had previously been private.
2. The IPO is very expensive.
3. Your focus is diverted from running the operations of the business to facilitating and meeting the requirements of being a public company.
4. Compliance with the IPO and ongoing quarterly and annual reporting requirements are extensive.
5. You risk losing control of your company.
6. If your stock does not perform well in the public market, you risk being sued by your shareholders.

For many investors the potential financial reward of taking their company public greatly overshadows any potential disadvantage of an IPO.

Starting on My Path

The rest of this book is about rich dad guiding me as an inside investor and sophisticated investor on my path to becoming the ultimate investor. He no longer had to guide his son Mike. Mike was content being an inside investor. You will gain some insights into what rich dad thought was important, what I needed to learn, and some of the mistakes I made along the way. It is my hope that you can learn from my successes as well as my mistakes on your own path to becoming the ultimate investor.

Chapter 27

How to Get Rich Quick

Rich dad would regularly review the various levels of investors with me. He wanted me to understand the various ways investors made their fortunes. My rich dad had become wealthy by first investing as an inside investor. He had started small and learned the tax advantages available to him. He quickly gained confidence and became a truly sophisticated investor at an early age. He had built an incredible financial empire. My real dad, on the other hand, had worked hard all his life as a government employee and had little to show for it.

As I got older, the gap between my rich dad and my poor dad was increasingly evident. I finally asked my rich dad why he was becoming wealthier while my real dad was working harder and harder.

In the introduction this book I related the story of walking along the beach with my rich dad looking at the large piece of ocean front property he had just purchased. During that walk on the beach, I realized that my rich dad had just purchased an investment that only a rich person could acquire. The problem was my rich dad was not really a rich man, yet. That is why I asked him how he could afford such an expensive investment when I knew my real dad, a man who made more money than my rich dad, could not.

It was during this walk on the beach that my rich dad shared the basis of his investment plan. He said, "I can't afford this land either, but my business can." As I stated in the introduction, this was when my curiosity about the power of investing began and when I became a student of the profession.   During that walk on the beach, at the age of 12, I was beginning to learn the secrets of how many of the very richest people in the world invest and why they are the 10% that control 90% of money.

Again, I refer to Ray Kroc, founder of McDonald's, saying virtually the same thing to my friend's MBA class.   Ray Kroc said to the class, "My business is not hamburgers.   My business is real estate."   That is why McDonald's owns the most valuable real estate in the world.   Ray Kroc and rich dad understood that the purpose of a business was to buy assets.

Rich Dad's Investment Plan

When I was a young boy still in elementary school, rich dad was already placing ideas in my head about the differences between being rich, poor, and middle class.   During one of our Saturday lessons, he said, "If you want job security, follow your dad's advice.   If you want to be rich, you need to follow my advice.   The chances of your dad having both job security and becoming rich are slim.   The laws are not written in his favor."

One of rich dad's six lessons as described in *Rich Dad Poor Dad* was a lesson about the power of corporations.   In *CASHFLOW Quadrant,* I wrote about how the different quadrants were governed by different tax laws. Rich dad used these lessons to show me the difference between his investment plan and my real dad's investment plan.   These differences greatly affected my life's path after my formal education was complete and my military duty was over.

"My business buys assets with pre-tax dollars," said rich dad as he drew the following diagram:

Income
Expense **Buy Assets**
Taxes

"Your dad tries to buy assets with after-tax dollars. His financial statement looks like this," said rich dad:

Income
Expense
Taxes
Buy Assets

As a young boy, I really did not fully comprehend what rich dad was trying to teach me, yet I recognized the difference. Because I was confused, I spent much time quizzing him on what it meant. To help me understand a little better, he drew the following diagram:

Income	
Expense	
Taxes	Your Dad
Buy Assets	
Taxes	Me

"Why?" I asked rich dad. "Why do you pay your taxes last and why does my dad pays his taxes first?"

"Because your dad is an employee and I am a business owner," said rich dad. "Always remember that we may live in a free country, but everybody does not live by the same laws. If you want to be rich, or get rich quickly, you had best follow the same laws the rich use."

"How much in taxes does my dad pay?" I asked.

"Well, your dad is a highly paid government employee, so I estimate that he pays at least 50% to 60% of his total income in taxes in one form or another," said rich dad.

"And how much do you pay in taxes?" I asked.

"Well, that is not really the correct question," said rich dad. "The real question is: 'How much is my taxable income?'"

I became confused and asked, "What is the difference?"

"Well," said rich dad. "I pay taxes on net income, and your dad's taxes are withheld from his total income. That is one of the biggest differences between your dad and me. I get ahead faster because I get to buy my assets with gross income and pay taxes on net income. Your dad pays taxes on gross income and then tries to buy assets with his net income. That is why it is very, very hard for him to achieve any kind of wealth. He gives a lot of his money to the government first, money that he could be using to buy assets. I pay my taxes on the net, or what is left over, after I buy my assets. I buy assets first and pay taxes last. Your dad pays taxes first and has very little money left over to buy assets with."

At the age of 10 or 11, I really did not understand exactly what rich dad was saying. I just knew it did not sound fair and I said so. "That is not fair," I protested.

"I agree," said rich dad, nodding. "It isn't fair, but that is the law."

The Laws Are the Same

When discussing this issue in my seminars, I often hear, "That may be a law in the United States but that is not the law in my country."

Since I teach in many English-speaking countries, I often reply with "How do you know? What makes you think the laws are different?" The fact is, most people do not know which laws are similar and which laws are different, so I offer a short lesson in economic history and laws.

I point out to my classes that most English-speaking countries' laws are based upon English common law, the law spread throughout the world by the British East India Company. I also point out to them the exact date the rich began to make the rules, "In 1215, the Magna Carta, the most famous document of British constitutional history, was signed. By signing the Magna Carta, King John yielded part of his power to the rich barons of England. It is now generally recognized that the Magna Carta showed the viability of opposition to the excessive use of royal power."

I then explain the importance of the Magna Carta just how my rich dad had explained it to me. "Ever since the signing of the Magna Carta, the rich have been making the rules." He also said, "The spiritual golden rule is: 'Do unto others as you would have them do unto you.' Other people say that the financial golden rule is: 'He who has the gold makes the rules.' However, I think the real financial golden rule is: 'He who makes the rules gets the gold.'"

The September 13, 1999, *The Wall Street Journal* discussed in the introduction article seems to back up rich dad's view of the real financial golden rule. The article said, "For all the talk of mutual funds for the masses, of barbers and shoeshine boys giving investment tips, the stock market has remained the privilege of a relatively elite group.

"Only 43.3% of all households owned any stock at all in 1997, the most recent year for which data is available, according to New York University economist, Edward Wolff. Of those, many portfolios were relatively small. Nearly 90% of all shares were held by the wealthiest 10% of households. The bottom line: That top 10% held 73% of the country's net worth in 1997, up from 68% in 1983."

Business Buys Your Assets

When I was 25 and almost out of the Marine Corps, rich dad reminded me of the difference in two life paths.

He said, "This is how your dad tries to invest and acquire assets":

He added, "This is how I invest":

"Always remember that the rules are different for the different quadrants. Therefore, make your next career decision carefully. While that job with the airlines might be fun in the short term, in the long run, you might not get to be as rich as you want to be."

How the Tax Laws Changed

Although rich dad did not finish school, he was an avid student of economics, world history, and laws. When I was attending the U.S. Merchant Marine Academy, at Kings Point, New York (1965 to 1969), studying world trade, rich dad was very excited that my studies included admiralty law, business law, economics, and corporate law. Because I had studied these subjects, it was much easier for me to decide to not take a job as an airline pilot.

The Reason Is Found in History

One of the differences between America and the rest of the world colonized by the English is that the colonists in America protested excess taxes by organizing the Boston Tea Party. America grew rapidly from the 1800s to the 1900s simply because we were a low-tax country. Being a low tax haven, the United States attracted entrepreneurs from all over the world who wanted to get rich quickly. In 1913, however, we passed the 16th Amendment, which made taxation of the rich possible, and that was the end of the low-tax state. Yet, the rich have always found a way out of the trap, which is why the laws are different for the different quadrants, especially favoring the B quadrant, the quadrant of the ultra-rich of America.

The rich have gotten even for the tax law change of 1913 by slowly changing laws and putting the pressure back on the other quadrants. So the slow creep of taxation has looked like this:

In 1943, the Current Tax Payment Act was passed. Now, instead of just taxing the rich, the federal government was allowed to tax everyone in the E quadrant. If you were an employee, in the E quadrant, you could no longer pay yourself first because the government got paid first. People are always shocked to see how much is taken out in both direct taxes as well as hidden taxes from their paycheck.

In 1986, the Tax Reform Act was passed. This law change dramatically affected anyone who was a professional worker—people such as doctors, lawyers, accountants, architects, engineers, etc. This law change prevented someone in the S quadrant from using the same tax laws used by the B quadrant. For example, if an S quadrant person has the same income as a B quadrant person, the S quadrant worker will have to pay a beginning tax rate of 35% (50% when you include social insurance taxes). On the other hand, the B quadrant person could possibly pay 0% on the same amount of income.

In other words, the golden rule—"He who makes the rules keeps the gold"—was once again true. The rules are made from the B quadrant and have been made from there ever since 1215, when the barons forced the king to sign the Magna Carta. Maybe the B in the B quadrant stands for baron.

Some of these laws and changes were explained in more detail in *Rich Dad Poor Dad* and in *CASHFLOW Quadrant.*

The Decision Is Made

Even after I had decided to follow rich dad's investment plan instead of my poor dad's plan, rich dad shared with me a simple analysis about my chances for success in life that reinforced my decision. Drawing the *CASHFLOW Quadrant,* he said, "Your first decision is to figure out in which quadrant you have the most chance of achieving long-term financial success."

Pointing to the E quadrant, he said: "You don't have the expertise that employers will pay the big money for, so you'll probably never make enough money as an employee to invest with. Besides, you're sloppy, you get bored easily, you don't have a very long attention span, you tend to argue, and you don't follow instructions well. Therefore, your chances for financial success in the E quadrant don't look very good."

Pointing to the S quadrant, he said, "S stands for smart. That is why so many doctors, lawyers, accountants, and engineers are in the S quadrant. You're bright, but you're not that smart. You were never much of a student. The S also stands for star. You'll probably never be a rock star, movie star, or sports star, so your chances of making the big money in the S quadrant are slim."

"That leaves the B quadrant," rich dad continued. "This quadrant is perfect for you. Since you lack any special talent or expertise, your chances

for attaining great wealth will be in this quadrant."

And with that comment, I was certain. I decided that my best chance for great wealth and financial success would be through building a business. The tax laws were in my favor, and my lack of stardom in the other quadrants just made my decision easier.

The Author's Lesson in Hindsight

I try to pass along the bits of wisdom I learned from my rich dad in the seminars I present today. When I am asked how I invest, I usually tell the group about investing through a business, or as rich dad said, "My business buys my assets."

Invariably, people raise their hands and say things as:

1. "But I am an employee and I do not own my own business."
2. "Not everyone can own a business."
3. "Starting a business is risky."
4. "I don't have any money to invest."

To these types of responses to rich dad's investment plan, I offer these ideas.

To the statement that not everyone can own a business, I remind people that less than 100 years ago, most people did own their own businesses. Just 100 years ago, approximately 85% of the U.S. population were either independent farmers or small shopkeepers. I know that both sets of my grandparents were small-business owners.

Only a small percentage of the population was comprised of employees. I then say, "It seems that the Industrial Age—with its promise of high-paying jobs, job security for life, and pension benefits—has bred that independence out of us." I also add that our educational system was designed to create employees and professional people, not entrepreneurs, so it would be only natural for people to feel that starting a business would be risky.

The points I make are:

1. Chances are that you all have the potential to be great business owners if you have the desire to develop the skills. Our ancestors developed and depended upon their entrepreneurial skills. If you do not have a business today, the question is: Do you want to go through the process of learning how to build a business? You are the only one who can answer that question.

2. When people say, "I have no money to invest," or "I need a real estate deal I can buy for no money down," I reply, "Maybe you should switch quadrants and invest from the quadrant that allows you to invest with pre-tax dollars. Then you might have a lot more money to invest."

One of the first considerations in your investment plan should be to decide in which quadrant lies the best opportunity for you to make the most money quickly. That way, you can begin investing for the highest returns, with the least risk, and you'll have the best chance of becoming very, very rich.

Chapter 28

Keep Your Day Job and Still Become Rich

Once I decided to build a business, the next problem facing me was that I had no money. First, I did not know how to build a business. Second, I had no money to build a business with, and third, I had no money to live on. Feeling weak in the stomach and lacking confidence in myself, I called rich dad and asked him what I should do.

He immediately said, "Go get a job."

His reply shocked me "I thought you were telling me to start my own business."

"Yes I did. But you still have to eat and put a roof over your head," he said.

What he said to me next I have passed on to countless people. Rich dad said, "Rule number one in becoming an entrepreneur is to never take a job for money. Take a job only for the long-term skills you will learn."

The first and only job I got after the Marine Corps was with the Xerox Corporation. I chose it because it had the best sales training program. Rich dad knew I was very shy and terrified of rejection. He recommended I learn to sell, not for the money but to learn to overcome my personal fears. Each day, I had to go from office building to office building knocking on doors trying to sell people a Xerox machine. It was a very painful learning process, yet this process has made me millions of dollars over the years.

Rich dad would say, "If you cannot sell, you cannot be an entrepreneur."

For two years, I was the worst salesperson in the Honolulu branch. I took extra classes on selling as well as bought tapes and listened to them. Finally, after nearly being fired several times, I began to make sales. Although I was still painfully shy, the sales training helped me to develop the skills I needed to acquire wealth.

The problem was that no matter how hard I worked and how many machines I sold, I was always short of cash. I had no money with which to invest or to start a business. One day, I told rich dad that I planned to take a part-time job to supplement my income so I could invest. That was the moment he had been waiting for.

Rich dad said, "The biggest mistake people make is that they work too hard for their money." He went on to say, "Most people do not get ahead financially because when they need more money, they take a part-time job. If they really want to get ahead, they need to keep their day job and start a part-time business."

Rich dad drew this diagram for me once he knew I was learning valuable skills and was serious about becoming a business owner and investor:

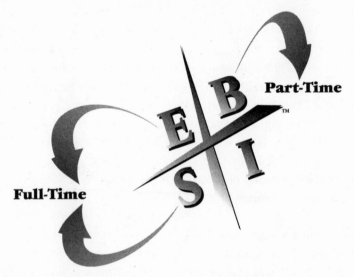

"It is time for you to start your business—part-time," he said. "Don't waste your time with a part-time job. A part-time job keeps you in the E quadrant, but a part-time business puts you in the B quadrant. Most big companies are started as part-time businesses."

In 1977, I started my nylon and Velcro wallet business part-time. Many of you are familiar with that product line today. From 1977 to 1978, I worked very hard at Xerox, eventually becoming one of the top sales representatives in the branch. In my spare time, I was also building a business that would soon become a worldwide, multi-million-dollar business.

When people ask me if I loved my product line—a line that consisted of colorful nylon wallets, nylon watchbands, and nylon shoe pockets that attached to the laces of a running shoe and held a key, money, and ID card—I answer, "No. I was not in love with the product line. But I did enjoy the challenge of building the business."

I mention this point specifically because so many people today say to me such things as:

1. "I have a great idea for a new product."
2. "You have to feel passionate about your product."
3. "I'm looking for the right product before I begin my business."

To these people, I generally say, "The world is filled with great ideas for new products. The world is also filled with great products. But the world is short of great businesspeople. The primary reason in starting a business part-time is not so much to make a product great. The real reason for start a part-time business is to make you a great businessperson. Great products are a dime a dozen. But great businesspeople are rare and rich."

If you look at Bill Gates, founder of Microsoft, he did not even invent his software product. He bought it from a group of computer programmers and then went on to build one of the most powerful and influential companies in world history. Gates did not build a great product, but he did build a great business that helped him become the richest man in the world. The message is, therefore, do not bother trying to make a great product. Focus more on starting a business so you can learn to become a great business owner.

Michael Dell of Dell Computers started his part-time business in his dormitory of the University of Texas. He had to quit school because his part-time business was making him far richer than any job he was studying for could.

Amazon.com was also started in a garage on a part-time basis. That young man is a billionaire today.

The Lesson in Hindsight

Many people dream of starting their own business but never do because they're afraid of failing. Many other people dream of becoming rich but don't become so because they lack the skills and experience. The business skill and experience is where money really comes from.

Rich dad said to me, "The education you receive in school is important, but the education you receive on the street is even better."

Starting a business at home, part-time, allows you to learn priceless business skills and subjects such as:

1. Communication skills
2. Leadership skills
3. Team-building skills
4. Tax law
5. Corporate law
6. Securities law

These skills or subjects cannot be learned in a weekend course or in a single book. I continue to study them today, and the more I study them, the more my businesses improve.

One reason people learn so much by starting a part-time business is that they start as insiders, insiders in their own business. If someone can learn to build businesses, a whole new world with virtually unlimited financial opportunity becomes available. One of the problems with being in the E quadrant or the S quadrant, however, is that the opportunities are often limited by how hard one person can work and how many hours there are in a day.

Chapter 29

The Entrepreneurial Spirit

People invest for two basic reasons:

1. To save for retirement
2. To make a lot of money

While most of us invest for both reasons—and both are important—it seems that the majority of people lean more toward the first reason. They put money away as savers do and hope it will increase in value over time. They invest but they are more concerned about losing than winning. I have met many people whose fear of losing prevents them from acting. People need to be true to their emotional senses when investing. If the pain and the fear of losing are too great, it is best for that investor to invest very conservatively.

Yet, if you look at the great wealth of this world, that wealth has not come from cautious investors. The great changes in this world have come from investors backing what my rich dad called the entrepreneurial spirit.

One of my favorite stories is that of Christopher Columbus, a brave explorer who believed the world was round and who had a bold plan to find a faster route to the riches of Asia. However, the popular belief of his day was that the world was flat. Everyone thought that Columbus would sail off the edge of the earth if he attempted his plan. In order to test his theory that the world was round, Columbus, an Italian, had to go to the royalty of Spain and convince them to invest in his business venture. King

Ferdinand and Queen Isabella put up what is called the "front money" and invested in his business venture.

My history teacher in school tried to tell me that the money was raised to further knowledge via exploration. My rich dad told me that it was purely a business venture that needed capital. The king and queen knew that if this entrepreneur named Columbus succeeded in sailing West to reach the East, they would earn a high return on their investment. Columbus and the king and queen who backed him all had the true spirit of the entrepreneur. The king and queen did not invest to lose money. They invested because they wanted to make more money. It was the spirit of venturing or risk with the possibility of great reward. They invested in that spirit.

Why Start a Business

As I began to formulate my plans to start my part-time business, rich dad was adamant about the spirit with which I undertook this new adventure, the adventure of building a worldwide business. He said, "You build a business because of the challenge. You build a business because it is exciting, it's challenging, and it will require all of you to make it successful."

Rich dad wanted me to start a business in order to find my entrepreneurial spirit. He often said, "The world is filled with people with great ideas but only a few people with great fortunes from their ideas." So he encouraged me to start a business, any business. He did not care about what the product was or how much I liked the product. He was not concerned about me failing. He just wanted me to start. Today I see so many people with great ideas who are afraid to start, or they start, fail and quit. That is why rich dad often quoted Einstein's saying of, "Great spirits have often encountered violent opposition from mediocre minds." He wanted me to simply start any business just so that I could challenge my own mediocre mind and, in the process, develop my entrepreneurial spirit. Rich dad would also say, "The main reason so many people buy assets rather than create them is because they have not called upon their own entrepreneurial spirit to take their ideas and turn those ideas into great fortunes."

Don't Do It for Only $200,000

In coming back to the definition of the accredited investor, rich dad said, "All a person needs to do to be an accredited investor is have a salary of $200,000. That is a lot of money to some people, but it is not enough of a reason to start building a business. If all you dream of is a salary of $200,000, then stay in the E or S quadrants. The risks are too great in the

B and I quadrants for such a small sum. If you decide to build a business, don't do it for a mere $200,000. The risks are too high for a payoff so low. Do it for a much bigger payday. Do it for millions, maybe billions, or don't do it at all. But if you decide to pursue building a business, you must call on your entrepreneurial spirit."

Rich dad also said, "There is no such thing as a successful poor entrepreneur or business owner. You can be a successful and poor doctor, or a successful and poor accountant. But you cannot be a successful and poor business owner. There is only one kind of successful business owner, and that is a rich one.'"

Lessons in Hindsight

I am often asked, "How much is too much?" or "How much is enough?" The person who asks that question is often someone who has never built a successful business that made a lot of money. I have also noticed that many of the people who ask that question are on the E and S side of the Quadrant. Another big difference between people on the left side of the Quadrant and people who operate on the right side is:

The people on the left side generally have only one financial statement because they often have only one source of income. Those on the right side have multiple financial statements and multiple sources of income. My wife and I are employees of several corporations in which we also have ownership interests. Therefore, we have financial statements as individuals and financial statements from our businesses. As our businesses become successful and generate cash flow for us, we need less income as employees. Many people on the left side do not know what it feels like to have more and more money coming in that requires less and less work.

While the money is important, it is not the primary motivating factor for building a business. I think the question can best be answered by asking the same question in another way. The question asked is similar to asking a golfer, "Why do you keep playing golf?" The answer is found in the spirit of the game.

Although it took me many years of occasional pain and misery, the challenge and the spirit were always the propelling factors for me wanting to build a business. Today, I have friends who have sold their businesses for millions of dollars. Many of them take a few months off, and then they are right back in the game. It is the excitement, the challenge, the spirit, and the potential for a big payoff at the end that keeps the entrepreneur going. Before I built my nylon and Velcro wallet business, my rich dad wanted me to make sure I was doing it with that spirit.

The entrepreneurial spirit is a valuable asset in building a successful B business. Many successful capitalists today are still entrepreneurs in their hearts.

How Do You Build a Strong Business?

Chapter 30

Why Build a Business?

Rich dad said, "There are three reasons for building a business more than to simply create an asset":

1. "To provide you with excessive cash flow." In his book *How to Be Rich*, J. Paul Getty states that his first rule is that you must be in business for yourself. He goes on to imply that you will never get rich working for someone else.

   One of the primary reasons rich dad started so many businesses was that he had excessive cash flow from his other businesses. He also had the time because his businesses required minimal effort on his part. This allowed him the free time and extra money to keep investing in more and more assets tax-free. That is why he became rich so quickly and why he said to "Mind your own business."

2. "To sell it." Rich dad went on to explain that the problem with having a job is that you cannot sell the job, regardless of how hard you work. The problem with building a business in the S quadrant is that there is usually a limited market that would want to buy it. For example, if a dentist builds a practice, generally the only other person who may want to buy it is another dentist. To rich dad, that was too narrow of a market. He said, "For something to be valuable, there must be many more people than you who want it. The problem with an S quadrant business is that you are often the only

person who wants it."

Rich dad said, "An asset is something that puts money in your pocket, or it can be sold to someone else for more than you have paid for or invested in it. If you can build a successful business, you will always have a lot of money. If you learn to build a successful business, you will have developed a profession that few people ever achieve."

In 1975, while I was learning to sell Xerox machines, I came across a young man who owned four quick-copy print shops in Honolulu. The reason he was in the business of making copies was interesting. While in school, he had run the university's copy shop and learned the business side of the operation. When he came out of school, there were no jobs, so he opened up a copy shop in downtown Honolulu doing what he knew best. Soon, he had four of these copy centers in four of the bigger downtown office buildings, all on long-term leases. A major copy shop chain came to town and made him an offer he could not refuse. He took their $750,000, a giant sum in those days, bought a boat, gave $500,000 to a professional money manager, and sailed around the world. When he returned a year and half later, the manager had grown his investment to nearly $900,000, so the young man just sailed off again, back to the islands of the South Pacific.

I was the guy who sold him the copy machines, and all I got was my small commission. He was the guy who built a business, sold it, and sailed away. I never saw him again after 1978, but I have heard that he pulls back into town every so often, checks his portfolio, and sails off again.

As my rich dad said, "As a business owner, you don't have to be right 51% of the time. You need to be right only once." He also said, "Building a business is the riskiest road for most people. But if you can survive and keep improving your skills, your potential for wealth is unlimited. If you avoid risk and play it safe on the E and S side, you may be safer, but you'll also limit what you can truly earn."

3. "To build a business and take it public." This was rich dad's idea of becoming what he called the ultimate investor. It was building a business and taking it public that made Bill Gates,

Henry Ford, Warren Buffet, Ted Turner, and Anita Roddick very, very wealthy. They were the selling shareholders, while we were all the buying shareholders. They were insiders, while we were outsiders trying to look in.

You're Never Too Old and You're Never Too Young

If anyone tells you that you can't build a business that others want to buy, use that small-minded thought to inspire you. It is true that Gates was very young when he started Microsoft but Colonel Sanders was 66 when he started Kentucky Fried Chicken.

In the next few chapters, I will be describing what rich dad called the B-I Triangle. I use this triangle as a guide to building a business. It outlines the primary technical skills that are required. Rich dad also felt certain personal traits were required to be a successful entrepreneur:

1. **Vision:** the ability to see what others could not see.
2. **Courage:** the ability to act despite tremendous doubt.
3. **Creativity:** the ability to think outside the box.
4. **The ability to withstand criticism:** There is not one successful person who has not been criticized.
5. **The ability to delay gratification:** It can be very difficult to learn to deny short-term immediate self-gratification in favor of a greater long-term reward.

Chapter 31

The B-I Triangle

The Key to Great Wealth

The following is a diagram rich dad called the B-I Triangle, the key to great wealth.

The B-I Triangle was very important to rich dad because it gave structure to his ideas. As he often said, "There are many people with great ideas but few people with great fortunes. The B-I Triangle has the power to turn ordinary ideas into great fortunes. The B-I Triangle is the guide to taking an idea and creating an asset." It represents the knowledge required to be successful on the B and I side of the CASHFLOW Quadrant. I have modified it a little over the years.

I was about 16 years old when I first saw this diagram. Rich dad drew it for me when I started asking him the following questions:

1. "How is it that you have so many businesses and other people can barely handle one?"
2. "Why do your businesses grow while other peoples' stay small?"
3. "How do you have free time when other business owners work constantly?"
4. "Why do so many businesses start and then fail so quickly?"

I did not ask him all these questions at the same time, yet they were questions that came to mind as I studied his businesses. Rich dad was about 40 years old, and I was amazed at how he could run several different companies all in different industries. For example, he had a restaurant business, a fast food business, a convenience store chain, a trucking company, a real estate construction business, and a property management business. I knew he was following his plan to have his businesses buy his true investments, which for him was real estate, but it was amazing how many businesses he could run all at the same time. When I asked him how he could start, own, and manage so many businesses, his response was to draw the B-I Triangle.

Today, I own interests in several different companies in completely different businesses because I use the B-I Triangle as a guide. I do not own as many companies as rich dad did, but by following the same formula outlined in the B-I Triangle, I could own more if I wanted.

Explaining the B-I Triangle

Obviously, the amount of material that could be written—and needs to be written—to cover the information represented by the B-I Triangle is more than this book could cover. However, we will review the basics.

The Mission

Rich dad said, "A business needs both a spiritual and a business mission to be successful, especially at the beginning." When he explained this diagram to his son and me, he always began with the mission since he thought it to be the most important aspect of the triangle and why it was at the base. "If the mission is clear and strong, the business will weather the trials every business goes through during its first ten years. When a business gets big and it forgets its mission, or the mission it was created for is no longer needed, the business begins to die."

Rich dad chose the words "spiritual" and "business." He said, "Many people start a business only to make money. Just to make money is not a strong enough mission. Money alone does not provide enough fire, drive, or desire. The mission of a business should fill a need that the customers want, and if it fills that need, and fills it well, the business will begin to make money."

When it came to a spiritual mission, rich dad said, "Henry Ford was a man driven by a spiritual mission first and a business mission second. He wanted to make the automobile available to the masses, not just the rich. That is why his mission statement was "Democratize the automobile." Rich dad went on to say, "When the spiritual mission and business mission are both strong and in line, the combined power builds huge businesses."

Rich dad's spiritual mission and business mission were closely in line. His spiritual mission was to provide jobs and opportunities for many of the poor people to whom he served food in his restaurants. Rich dad thought the mission of a business was very important although it was hard to see and to measure. He said, "Without a strong mission, a business is not likely to survive its first five to ten years." He also said, "At the start of a business, the mission and the entrepreneur's spirit are essential for the business to survive. The spirit and mission must be preserved long after the entrepreneur is gone, or the business dies." Rich dad would say, "The mission of a business is a reflection of the spirit of the entrepreneur. General Electric was a company founded from the brilliance of Thomas Edison, and it has grown by preserving the spirit of the great inventor by continuing to invent new and innovative products. Ford Motor Company has survived by continuing in the tradition of Ford."

Today, I believe that Bill Gates's spirit continues to drive Microsoft to dominate the world of software. By contrast, when Steven Jobs was pushed out of Apple and a management team from the traditional corporate world replaced him, the company went downhill rapidly. As soon as Jobs was brought back into Apple, the spirit of the company returned, new products came forth, profitability increased, and the share price went up.

Although the mission of a business is hard to measure, impossible to see, and for all practical purposes an intangible, most of us have experienced it. We can identify the mission of someone who is trying to sell us something for a commission as contrasted to someone trying to help answer our needs. As the world becomes crowded with more and more products, the businesses that survive and do well financially will be businesses that focus on serving and fulfilling the company's mission and their customers' needs, rather than just increasing the company's revenues.

CASHFLOW Technologies, Inc.—the company that Kim, Sharon, and I created to bring you this book as well as our other financial-education products—has the following mission: "To elevate the financial well-being of humanity." By being clear and true to the spiritual and business mission of this company, we have enjoyed success that goes beyond luck. By being clear on our mission, we attract individuals and other groups aligned with a similar mission. Some people call it luck... I call it being true to our mission. Over the years, I have come to believe that rich dad was right about the importance of having the spiritual mission and business mission be strong and in line.

In all truthfulness, not all of my businesses have as strong a dual mission as CASHFLOW Technologies, Inc. does. Other businesses in which I own interests have stronger business missions than spiritual missions.

I now realize that my nylon and Velcro wallet business had a very different mission than I first thought. The mission for building that business was to give me a fast education about building a worldwide business. That business fulfilled that mission rather painfully. In other words, I got what I wanted. The business grew very quickly, success was fast and furious, and so was the crash. Yet, as painful as the experience was, I realized that I had achieved my mission. After I dug myself out from under the rubble and rebuilt the business, I learned what I set out to learn. As rich dad said, "Many entrepreneurs don't really become businesspeople until after they lose their first business." In other words, I learned more by losing the business and rebuilding it than I did by being successful. As rich dad said, "School is important, but the street is a better teacher." So, my first big business venture after leaving the Marine Corps was expensive and painful, but the lessons I learned were priceless. And the business had fulfilled its mission.

Sharon's Note

A company's mission helps it maintain focus. In the early stages of development, many factors can cause distraction. The best way to get back on track is to revisit your mission. Does the distraction affect the achievement of your mission? If so, you must deal with the distraction as quickly as possible so that you can re-focus your efforts on the overall mission.

Today, I notice many people becoming instant millionaires, even billionaires, just by taking a company public through an IPO. I often wonder if the company's mission was just to make money for owners or investors or was the company really formed to fulfill a mission or some kind of service? I am afraid that many of these new IPOs will ultimately fail because their only mission was to make money quickly. Besides, it is in the mission of the company where the entrepreneur's spirit is found.

The Team

Rich dad always said, "Business is a team sport." He went on to say, "Investing is a team sport." He would also say, "The problem with being in the E and S quadrant is that you play the game as an individual, playing against a team."

Rich dad would draw the CASHFLOW Quadrant to illustrate his point:

One of rich dad's strongest criticisms of the educational system was: "In school, they train students to take tests on their own. If a child attempts to cooperate at test time, it is called 'cheating.'" Rich dad would also say, "In the real world of business, business owners cooperate at test time, and in the world of business, every day is test time."

A Very Important Lesson

For people considering building a powerful and successful business, I think this lesson on teamwork is crucial. It is one of the primary keys to my financial success. Business and investing are team sports, and remember that every day in business is test time. To be successful in school, you had to take tests alone. In business, success comes from taking tests as a team, not as an individual.

People in the E and S quadrant often make less money than they could or would like to because they attempt to do things on their own. If they work as a group, especially those in the E quadrant, they form a union instead of a team. And that is what is happening to medical doctors in America today. They are forming a professional union to combat the power of a team, the business team known as the health maintenance organizations (HMOs).

Many investors today are trying to invest as individuals. I see and read about thousands of people who are doing online day trading. This is a perfect example of an individual trying to trade against well-organized teams. That is why so few of them succeed as well as why many lose their money. I was taught that when it comes to investing, you should invest as a member of a team. Rich dad would say, "If people want to become sophisticated investors and above, they must invest as a team." On rich dad's team were his accountants, his attorneys, his brokers, his financial advisors, his insurance agents, and his bankers. I use the plurals here because he always had more than one advisor. When he made a decision, it was with input of the team. Today, I do the same.

Not a Big Boat...A Big Team

On television today, I see commercials of a rich couple, sailing their yacht in some warm tropical waters. The ad seems to draw in all the individuals who are trying to get rich on their own. Whenever I see that commercial, I often think of rich dad saying to me, "Most small-business people dream of someday owning a boat or a plane. That is why they will never own that boat or plane. When I was first starting out, I dreamed of having my own team of accountants and attorneys, not a boat."

Rich dad wanted me to aim to have a team of accountants and attorneys working only on my business—before I dreamed of a boat. To drive his point home, he had me go to an accountant in town with my meager little tax return. As I sat across the table from Ron, the CPA, the first thing I noticed was a stack of manila folders sitting on his desk. Immediately, I got rich dad's lesson. This CPA was minding about 30 other businesses on that day alone. How could he pay full attention to my business?

Returning to rich dad's office that afternoon, I saw something I had never noticed before. As I sat in the reception area waiting for rich dad's personal secretary to let me in, I could see a team of people working only on rich dad's business. In the working area of his office was a row of bookkeepers, about fourteen of them. There were also five full-time accountants, and a chief financial officer (CFO). He also had two full-time attorneys working in his main office. When I sat down in front of rich dad, all I said was, "They're all minding your businesses and no one else's."

Rich dad nodded. "As I said, most people work hard and dream of getting away on their own boat. I first dreamed of having a team of full-time accountants and attorneys. That is why I can now have the big boat and the free time. It is a matter of priorities."

How Do You Afford the Team?

In my seminars, I am often asked, "How can you afford to pay for this team?" That question usually comes from someone in the E or S quadrant. Again, the difference goes back to the different laws and rules for the different quadrants. For example, when a person in the E quadrant pays for professional services, the transaction looks like this:

Income
Expense
Taxes
Professional Services

For people in the B and S quadrants, the transaction looks like this:

Income
Expense **Professional Services** **Taxes**

There is also a difference between the B quadrant business owner and the S quadrant business owner. The B quadrant business owner does not hesitate to pay for these services because the business system, the entire B-I Triangle, is paying for the services. S quadrant business owners are often paying for the services out of their own sweat and blood, so most of them cannot afford to hire a full-time staff because they often do not earn enough to cover their own financial needs.

The Best Education

My answer is the same when I am asked questions such as:

1. "How did you learn so much about investing and business?"
2. "How do you get such high returns with such low risk?"
3. "What gives you the confidence to invest in what others see as risky?"
4. "How do you find the best deals?"

I answer, "My team." My team consists of my accountants, attorneys, bankers, brokers, etc.

When people say, "Building a business is risky," they often speak from a point of view of doing it alone, a habit they learned from school. In my opinion, not building a business is risky. By not building a business, you are failing to gain priceless real-world experience, and you are failing to get the best education in the world, the education that comes from your team of advisors. As rich dad would say, "People who play it safe lose out on the best education in the world and they waste a lot of precious time." He would also say, "Time is our most valuable asset, especially as you get older."

Tolstoy said it a little differently. He is quoted as saying, "The most unexpected thing that happens to us is old age."

Tetrahedrons and Teams

I am often asked, "What is the difference between a B quadrant business and an S quadrant business?" My reply is "The team."

Most S quadrant businesses are either structured as sole proprietorships or partnerships. They could be teams, but not the kind of team I think of. Just as people in the E quadrant often bind together as a union, people in the S quadrant often organize as a partnership. When I think of a team, I think of different types of people with different skills coming together to work together. In a union or partnership (e.g., the teachers' union or a law partnership), the same kinds of people and professions often come together.

One of my greatest teachers was Dr. R. Buckminster Fuller. Dr. Fuller set out years ago to find what he called "the building blocks of the universe." In his search, he found out that squares and cubes do not exist in nature. He would say, "Tetrahedrons are the basic building blocks of nature."

When I look at the great pyramids of Egypt, I understand a little more about what Dr. Fuller was talking about. While tall skyscrapers come and go, those pyramids have withstood the test of tens of centuries. While a skyscraper can come down with a few well-placed sticks of dynamite, the pyramids would not budge with the same blast.

Dr. Fuller was looking for a stable structure in the universe, and he found it in the tetrahedron.

The Different Models

The following are graphic portrayals of different business structures.

1. This is a sole proprietorship: ○

2. This is a partnership: ○——○

3. This is a B quadrant business:

The prefix "tetra" means four. In other words, it has four points. After studying with Dr. Fuller, I began to see the importance of having structures be in a minimum of fours. For example, when you look at the CASHFLOW Quadrant, it has four parts. Therefore, a stable business structure would look like the following diagram:

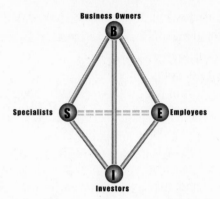

A well-managed business will have excellent employees. In this instance, I say the E stands for both "excellent" and "essential" because the employees are responsible for the day-to-day activities of the business. The E also stands for "extension" because the employees are the extension of the business owner and represent the business to the customer.

The specialists are typically from the S quadrant. The S stands for "specialized" because each specialist will guide you based on his or her trained area of expertise. While specialists may not participate daily, their guidance is invaluable to keep your business moving in the right direction.

The structure has a better chance of being stable and enduring if the four points are working in alignment. While the investors provide the funding, the business owners must work with the specialists and employees to develop the business and make it grow so there will be a return on the investors' original investment.

Another interesting tetra-relationship I came across is the four fundamental elements that make up this world we live in, which the ancients believed to be earth, air, fire, and rain (water). In a sole proprietorship as well as in a partnership, in order to be successful, the individual needs to be all four, which is difficult.

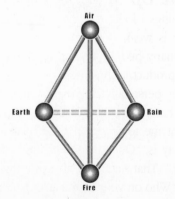

While most of us have all four elements in us, we each tend to be weighted predominantly to one of the elements. For example, I am fire, born under the sign of Aries and the planet Mars. That means I am good at starting things but not completing them. By having a tetrahedron, I am better able to be successful than if I were on my own. My wife, Kim, on the other hand, is earth. She and I have a good marriage because she has a grounding effect on me as well as on the people I upset around me. She often says, "Speaking to you is like speaking to a blowtorch." Without her, I would have nothing but angry and upset people around the company. Sharon, on the other hand, fulfills the role of air in this company. She feeds the fire, moves the company in the right direction, and keeps all systems running smoothly. As CEO of our company, Sharon ensures that all four of us stay in alignment and work toward our mission. When Mary, our operations manager, joined us, the company suddenly took off. Mary completed the company by making sure that we delivered what we promised. It's important to note that it took two years for this team to come together. People came and went until the right tetra-team finally locked in place. Once this model stabilized, the company began to radiate out, growing rapidly and with stability.

I am not saying this is a hard and fast rule for a successful business. However, all one needs to do is look at the pyramids of Egypt and a sense of strength, stability, and longevity comes to mind.

Only Two Elements

I often jokingly say that if you put only two elements together, as in a partnership, you get some strange phenomena. For example:

1. Air and Water = Spray
2. Air and Earth = Dust
3. Water and Earth = Mud
4. Earth and Fire = Lava or ashes
5. Fire and Water = Steam
6. Fire and Air = Flame

A Team Is Made Up of Different Levels

One of the first things I look at as an investor is the team behind the business. If the team is weak or lacks experience and a track record, I rarely invest. I meet many people who are running around trying to raise money for their new product or business. The biggest problems most of them have are that they personally lack experience and they have no team behind them, a team that inspires confidence.

Many people want me to invest in their business plan. One of the things most of them say is, "Once this company is up and running, we're going to take it public." That statement always intrigues me, so I ask what all of you should ask: "Who on your team has experience taking a company public, and how many companies has that person taken public?" If the answer to that question is weak, I know I am listening to a sales pitch more than to a business plan.

Another line I look at in the numbers of a business plan is the line item called "salaries." If the salaries are high, I know I am looking at people who are raising money in order to pay themselves fat salaries. I ask them if they are willing to work for free or to cut the salaries in half. If the answer is weak or a definite "No," I know the true mission of their business. The mission of the business is probably to provide them a job with a nice salary.

Investors invest in management. They look at the team within the proposed business and want to see experience, passion, and commitment. It is hard for me to believe there is a high level of commitment from people who are trying to raise money to pay their own salaries.

A Word on Our CASHFLOW Games

Many people have asked why we did not create our educational board games as electronic board games. One of the primary reasons is because we want to encourage cooperative learning. In the real world, being able to cooperate with as many people as possible and helping people without crippling them are very important human skills.

While we may release an electronic game of *CASHFLOW* in the future, for the moment, we are happy to encourage people to learn cooperatively —to teach each other—because the more we teach, the more we learn. Too much of our children's lives is already spent in isolation. They spend hours alone in front of a computer, alone watching TV, and alone taking tests. We then wonder why so many children are anti-social. To be successful, we all need to learn to get along with many different types of people. For this reason, *CASHFLOW* is still a board game that requires you play with other human beings. We need to learn to operate as individuals as well as members of a team—and we can always improve those skills.

Sharon's Notes

Robert has often mentioned that "money follows management" in the world of business capital. To succeed, a business must have the proper expertise in key areas.

When you do not have the money up front to hire the talent you need, consider attracting the talent as members of an advisory board with the understanding that once sufficient capital is raised, your team will come on board. Your chance of success is much stronger if your management team has a track record of success in the business or industry of your proposed business.

Your team also includes your outside advisors. Proper guidance from your accountants, tax advisors, financial advisors, and legal counsel is imperative for building a strong successful business. If your business is real estate, your real estate brokers become an important part of your team. Although these advisors can be "expensive," their advice can provide you with an incredible return on your investment by helping you structure a strong business while avoiding pitfalls along the way.

And that leads to the next part of the B-I Triangle: leadership, because every team needs a leader.

Leadership

One reason I attended a federal military academy rather than a normal university was that rich dad knew I needed to develop leadership skills if I wanted to become an entrepreneur. After graduation, I went into the U.S. Marine Corps and became a pilot to test my skills in the real world, in a place called Vietnam. As rich dad said, "School is important, but the street is a better teacher."

I still remember the commanding officer of my squadron saying, "Gentlemen, your most important job is to ask your troops to risk their lives for you, your team, and your country." He went on to say, "If you don't inspire them to do that, they will probably shoot you in the back. Troops do not follow a leader who does not lead." The same thing goes on in business today and every day. More businesses fail from the inside than from the outside.

In Vietnam, I learned that one of the most important qualities of a leader is trust. As a helicopter pilot with a crew of four, I had to trust my life to my team, and they had to entrust their lives with me. If that trust was ever broken, I knew that we would probably not come back alive. Rich dad would say, "A leader's job is to bring out the best in people, not to be the best person." He would also say, "If you are the smartest person on your business team, your business is in trouble."

When people ask how they can gain leadership skills, I always say the same thing: "Volunteer more." In most organizations, it is hard to find people who actually want to lead. Most people just hide in the corner hoping no one will call on them. I tell them, "At your church, volunteer to take on projects. At work, volunteer to lead projects." Now, volunteering alone will not necessarily make you a great leader, but if you accept the feedback and correct yourself well, you can grow into a great leader.

Through volunteering, you can get feedback on your real-life leadership skills. If you volunteer to lead and no one follows, you have some real-life learning and correcting to do. If you volunteer to lead and no one follows, ask for feedback and corrective support. Doing so is one of the greatest traits of a leader. I see many businesses that struggle or fail because the leader will not accept feedback from peers or the workers in the company. My squadron's commanding officer in the Marine Corps would often say, "True leaders are not born leaders. True leaders want to be leaders and are willing to be trained to be leaders, and training means being big enough to take corrective feedback."

A true leader also knows when to listen to others. I have said before I am not a good businessman or investor, I am average. I rely on the advice of my advisors and team members to help me be a better leader.

Sharon's Notes

A leader's roles are a combination of visionary, cheerleader, and pit boss.

As a visionary, the leader must keep his or her focus on the corporate mission. As a cheerleader, he or she must inspire the team as it works together towards that mission as well as herald the successes along the way. As the pit boss, he or she must be able to make the tough calls regarding issues that distract the team from achieving the mission. The unique ability to take decisive action while maintaining focus on the ultimate mission is what defines a true leader.

With the right mission, team, and leader you are well on your way to building a strong B business. As I said earlier, money follows management. It is at this point that you can start attracting money from outside investors. Five building blocks are essential to developing a strong business. Each will be discussed separately.

Chapter 32

Cash Flow Management

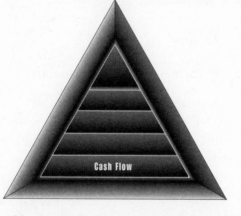

Rich dad would say, "Cash flow management is a fundamental and essential skill if a person truly wants to be successful in the B and I quadrant." That is why he insisted that Mike and I read financial statements of other companies so we could better understand cash flow management. In fact, he spent most of his time teaching us to be financially literate. He would say, "Financial literacy allows you to read the numbers, and the numbers tell you the story of the business, based on facts."

If you ask most bankers, accountants, or loan officers, they will tell you that many people are weak financially simply because they are not financially literate. I have a friend who is a respected accountant in Australia. He once said to me, "It is shocking to see a perfectly good business go down just because the owners are not financially literate." He went on to say, "Many small-business owners fail because they do not know the difference between profit and cash flow. As a result, many very profitable businesses go broke. They fail to realize that profit and cash flow are not the same things."

Rich dad would drum into my head the importance of cash flow management. He would say, "Business owners need to see the two types of cash flow if they want to be successful. There is actual cash flow and phantom cash flow. It is the awareness of these two cash flows that makes you rich or poor."

One of the skills the game *CASHFLOW, Investing 101,* teaches is how to recognize the differences between these two types of cash flow. Repeatedly playing the game helps many people begin to sense the differences. That is why the positioning statement of the game is "The more you play this game, the richer you become." You become richer because your mind begins to sense the often-invisible phantom cash flow.

Rich dad also said, "The ability to run a company from financial statements is one of the primary differences between a small-business owner and a big-business owner."

Sharon's Notes

Cash flow is to a business what blood is to the human body. Nothing can impact a business more dramatically than not being able to make payroll one Friday. Proper cash flow management starts on the first day you begin your business. When Robert, Kim, and I started CASHFLOW Technologies, Inc., we agreed that no purchase would be made if it were not justified by an increase in sales. In fact, we often chuckle about our strategy for increasing book sales early in 1998 so we could buy a $300 copy machine. Our strategy worked, and by December 1998 we were able to replace that $300 well-worn copy machine with a new $3,000 one. It is this attention to detail in the early stages of your business that will set the tone for your success.

A good cash flow manager reviews his or her cash position daily, looking at cash sources and needs for the next week, month, and quarter. This allows him or her to plan for any large cash need before it becomes a cash crisis. This type of review is imperative for a company that is growing quickly.

I have listed some cash flow tips that may help you in structuring your business. Each step applies to your business whether it is an international business, a single rental unit, or a hot dog stand.

Initial Corporate Startup Phase:

- Delay taking a salary until your business is generating cash flow from sales. In some cases, this may not be possible due to an extended development period. However, your investors will be much more supportive if they see that you are sharing in the development process by "investing your time." In fact, we advise keeping your full-time job and starting your business part-time. By delaying taking a salary, you can re-invest sales to help grow your business.

Sales and Accounts Receivable:

- Invoice your customers quickly upon shipment of goods or when services are provided.

- Require payment up front until credit has been established. Require that credit applications be completed before granting credit, and always check references. Standard credit forms are available at business supply stores.

- Establish a minimum dollar amount for orders before granting credit.

- Establish late-payment penalties as part of your terms and conditions—and enforce them.

- As your business grows, to speed up the receipt of cash, you may want to have your customers pay their bills directly to lockboxes or directly to your bank.

Expenses and Accounts Payable:

- Many businesses forget that a crucial part of cash flow is managing their own bill paying. Make sure you pay your bills promptly. Ask for extended payment terms up front. After you have paid timely for two to three months, ask for additional extensions on your payable terms. A supplier will usually extend credit for 30 to 90 days to a good customer.

- Keep your overhead to a minimum. Before purchasing something new, set a goal for increasing sales to justify the expense. Preserve your investors' funds for costs directly related to business operations, not overhead, if at all possible. As your sales increase, you can purchase the overhead-related items from the cash flow—but only if you have set and achieved new higher sales goals.

General Cash Management:

- Have an investment plan for your cash on hand to maximize its earning potential.

- Establish a line of credit with your bank before you need it.

- To make sure you can move quickly to borrow if needed, keep an eye on your current ratio (assets over liabilities—at least 2:1 is good) and quick ratios (liquid assets divided by current liabilities—should be over 1:1).

- Establish good internal controls over the handling of cash.
  - The people who record the cash receipts on the bank deposits are different from those who post it to the accounts receivable and general ledger.

  - Checks should be endorsed immediately "For Deposit Only."

  - The people authorized to sign checks should not prepare the vouchers or record the disbursements and post to the accounts payable and general ledger.

  - The person who reconciles the bank statement should have no regularly assigned functions related to cash receipts or cash disbursements. (Our outside accountant does this.)

While this may sound very complicated, each step of cash management is important. Call on your accountant, banker, and personal financial advisor for advice in structuring your cash management system. Once you establish a system for how to manage your cash, ongoing supervision is still essential. Review your cash position and funding needs daily, and prepare early for additional funding that may be required for your expanding business. Many people lose sight of cash management when their businesses become successful. This is a major cause of business failures. Proper cash management (and therefore expense management) is crucial to the on-going success of any business.

For those of you considering purchasing a franchise or joining a network marketing organization, you may find much of the cash management system will be provided for you. With a franchise, you will still need to implement the system and oversee it. Network marketing organizations often handle the cash management on your behalf. In these cases, the corporate headquarters performs the accounting functions for your organization and sends you a report of your earnings periodically with payment. In either case, it is still important to have your own advisors to help you structure your personal cash management.

Chapter 33

Communications Management

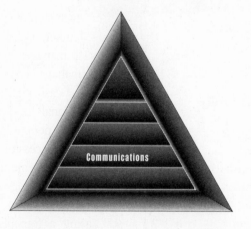

Rich dad would say, "The better at communicating you are, and the more people you communicate to, the better your cash flow will be." This is why communications management is the next level up on the B-I Triangle.

He would also say, "To be good at communications, you first need to be good at human psychology. You never know what motivates people. Just because something makes you excited does not mean it makes others excited. To be good at communications, you need to know what buttons to push. Different people have different buttons." He also said, "Many people are talking, but only a few are listening." He also said, "The world is filled with fabulous products, but the money goes to the best communicators."

I am always amazed at how little time businesspeople put into improving their overall communication skills. When I first balked in 1974 at the idea of learning to sell Xerox machines door to door, all rich dad said was, "Poor people are poor communicators." I repeat this negative statement with the intent of inspiring further study and practice of this vast subject.

Rich dad also said, "Cash flowing into your business is in direct proportion to communication flowing out." Whenever I find a business that is struggling, it is often a reflection of poor communications going out, not enough communications going out, or both. In general, I find a six week cycle between communication and cash flow. Stop communicating today and in six weeks you will see an impact on your cash flow.

However, external communications are not the only communications. Internal communications are also vital. By looking at the financial statements of a company, you can easily see which areas of a business are communicating and which are not.

A public company has increased communications problems. It is like two companies in one: one for the public and one for the shareholders. Communication to both groups is vitally important. When I hear people say, "I wish I had not taken my company public," it usually means that they are having shareholder communication problems.

As a general policy, rich dad attended one communications seminar a year. I continue in that tradition. I have always noticed that soon after I attend the seminar, my income increases. Over the years, I have attended courses on:

1. Sales
2. Marketing systems
3. Advertising, headlines, and copy writing
4. Negotiations
5. Public speaking
6. Direct-mail advertising
7. Running a seminar
8. Raising capital

Of all of these topics, raising capital interests budding entrepreneurs the most. When people ask me how to learn to raise capital, I refer them to numbers 1 through 7 above, explaining that raising capital requires each of them in one way or the other. Most businesses do not get off the ground because the entrepreneur does not know how to raise capital, and as rich dad said, "Raising capital is the entrepreneur's most important job." He did not mean that the entrepreneur was constantly asking for money from investors. What he meant was that an entrepreneur was always ensuring that capital was flowing in, either through sales, direct marketing, private sales, institutional sales, investors, etc. Rich dad would say, "Until the business system is built, the entrepreneur is the system to keep the money flowing in. At the start of any business, keeping the cash flowing in is the entrepreneur's most important job."

The other day, a young man came to me and asked, "I want to start my own business. What would you recommend I do before I start?" I answered with my usual response: "Get a job with a company that will train you in sales." He replied, "I hate sales. I don't like selling and I don't like salespeople. I just want to be the president and hire salespeople." Once he said that, I simply shook his hand and wished him luck. A priceless lesson that rich dad taught me was, "Don't argue with people who ask for advice but don't want the advice you're giving them. End the discussion immediately and go on minding your own business."

Being able to communicate effectively with as many people as possible is a very important life skill. It is a skill worthy of annual updating, which I do by attending seminars. As rich dad had already told me, "If you want to be a B quadrant person, your first skill is being able to communicate and speak the language of the other three quadrants. People in the other three quadrants can get away with speaking the language of only their quadrant, but those in the B quadrant cannot. Simply put, the primary—and possibly only—job of those in the B quadrant is to communicate with people in the other quadrants."

I have recommended that people join a network marketing company to gain sales experience. Some network marketing organizations have excellent communications and sales training programs. I have seen shy introverted individuals come out as powerful and effective communicators who are no longer afraid of rejection or ridicule. That thick-skin mind-set is vital for anyone in the B quadrant, especially when your personal communication skills are not yet polished.

My First Sales Call

I still remember my first sales call on the street along Waikiki Beach. After spending about an hour working up the nerve to knock on the door, I finally got in to see the owner of a small tourist trinket store. He was an older gentleman who had seen new salespeople like me for years. After stammering and sweating through my memorized sales pitch on the benefits of a Xerox copier, all he did was laugh. After he was through laughing, he said, "Son, you're the worst I have ever seen. But keep going because if you can get over your fears, your world will be very bright. If you quit, you may wind up like me sitting behind this counter fourteen hours a day, seven days a week, three hundred and sixty-five days a year waiting for tourists to come in. I wait here because I am too afraid to go out and do what you're doing. Get through your fears and the world will open up. Give in to your fears and your world will get smaller every year." To this day, I give thanks to that wise, older man.

After I began to overcome my fear of selling, rich dad had me join the Toastmasters organization to learn to overcome my fear of speaking in front of large groups. When I complained to rich dad, he would say, "All great leaders are great public speakers. Leaders of great businesses need to be great speakers. If you want to be a leader, you must be a speaker." Today, I can speak comfortably to tens of thousands of people in convention halls because of my training in sales and my early training from the Toastmasters organization.

If you are thinking about starting your own B quadrant business, I recommend those same two skills. First, develop the skill to overcome your fears, to overcome rejection, and to communicate the value of your product or service. Second, develop the skill of speaking to large groups of people and keeping them interested in what you have to say. As rich dad said to me, "There are speakers that no one listens to, there are salespeople that cannot sell, there are advertisers that no one watches, there are entrepreneurs that cannot raise capital, and there are business leaders that no one follows. If you want to be successful in the 'B' quadrant, don't be any of those people."

My first book in the Rich Dad series, *Rich Dad Poor Dad*, has been on the prestigious *Sydney Morning Herald* (Australia) best-selling booklist for well over two years. In the United States, it has been on *The Wall Street Journals'* bestseller list for nearly nine months, and it made *The New York Times* bestseller list in September 1999. When other authors ask me what my secret to getting on those lists is, I simply repeat a sentence from *Rich Dad Poor Dad*: "I am not a best-writing author. I am a best-selling author." I add that I flunked out of high school twice because I could not write and that I never even kissed a girl in high school because I was too shy. I end by saying the same thing my rich dad said to me: "Unsuccessful people find their strengths and spend their lives making their strengths stronger, often ignoring their weaknesses, until one day their weaknesses cannot be ignored any more. Successful people find their weaknesses and make them strengths."

A person's physical appearance often communicates far more than their words. Often, people who come to me with a business plan or to ask for money look like mice that have been chewed on by a cat. No matter how good their plan, their physical appearance is a limiting factor. In public speaking, it is said that body language accounts for approximately 55% of communication, voice tone 35%, and words 10%. If you remember President Keennedy, JFK, he had 100% working for him and it made him a very powerful communicator. While not all of us can be as physically attractive as he was, we can all do our best to dress and groom appropriately to make our points stronger.

An investigative TV program recently sent in very attractive job applicants and unattractive job applicants with exactly the same qualifications on their resumes to interview for the same jobs. It was interesting to note that the attractive applicants got more job offers than the unattractive ones.

A friend of mine sits on the board of a bank and shared with me that the president they had just hired was brought on board because of his appearance; he looks like a president. When I asked about his qualifications, all he said was, "His appearance was his qualification. He looks like a bank president should look and speaks in the way a bank president should speak. The board will run the business. We just want him to attract new customers." I use this example for anyone who says, "Oh, my appearance does not matter." In the world of business, appearance is a powerful communicator. Repeating an old cliché, "You have only one chance to make a first impression."

The Difference between Sales and Marketing

While still on the subject of communications, rich dad insisted that Mike and I know the difference between sales and marketing. He would say, "The big mistake that most people make when it comes to communication is that they say 'sales and marketing.' That is why they suffer with low sales or poor communications with staff and investors." Rich dad would go on to explain that the real statement looked like this:

SALES

MARKETING

He would add, "The real trick to communication is knowing that it is really 'sales over marketing,' not 'sales and marketing.'" He added, "If a business has strong and convincing marketing, the sales will come easily. If the business has weak marketing, the company must spend a lot of time and money and work very hard at gathering sales."

He also said to Mike and me, "Once you learn to sell, you need to learn how to market. An S quadrant business owner is often good at sales, but to be a successful B quadrant business owner, you must be good at marketing as well as sales."

He then drew the following diagram:

He said, "Sales is what you do in person, one on one. Marketing is sales done via a system." Most S quadrant businesspeople are very good at one-on-one sales. For them to make the transition to the B quadrant, they need to learn how to sell through a system, which is called marketing.

In conclusion, communications is a subject worthy of lifelong study because there is more to communication than just speaking, writing, dressing, or demonstrating. As rich dad said to me, "Just because you're speaking doesn't mean anyone is listening." When people ask where to start to build a strong communications foundation, I encourage them to begin with the two basic skills of selling one-on-one and public speaking to a group. I also advise them to carefully watch their results and listen for feedback. As you go through the process of transforming from a poor communicator to an excellent communicator with these two skills, you will find your fundamental everyday communication skills will also improve. When all three improve, you will see your cash flow increase as a result.

Sharon's Notes

Good first impressions are vital. Your marketing and sales efforts will often be the first impression your business makes on your potential customer. Whenever you are speaking, both your passion for your business and your appearance will have a lasting impact on your audience. Any published or printed material you produce or distribute is also important. It is a public representation of your business.

As Robert mentions, marketing is selling through a system. Always make sure you know your audience and that your marketing tool has been designed for that audience. In every marketing or sales effort, include these three key ingredients: identify a need, provide a solution, and answer your customers' question "What's in it for me?" with a special offer. It also helps if you can create a sense of urgency for your customers to respond to.

Most communication is directed towards external communication, but a business's internal communication is also vitally important. Some examples of each are:

External Communication
Sales
Marketing
Customer service
To investors
Public relations

Internal Communication
Sharing of wins and successes with your entire team
Regular meetings with employees
Regular communication with advisors
Human Resource policies

One of the most powerful forms of communication that affects a business is one over which you have little control: the communication from your existing customers to your potential customers. At CASHFLOW Technologies, Inc., we attribute a large part of our success to our customers telling other people about us. The power of this word-of-mouth advertising is immeasurable. This form of advertising can drive a company to success or failure very quickly. For this reason, customer service is a very vital communications function for any company.

When you buy a franchise or join a network marketing company, the communication systems are often provided for you. In addition, their communication materials have already been proven successful by other franchisees or members of your organization. You therefore have a tremendous head start over people trying to develop their own materials. These people won't know if their materials are successful until they use them and measure the results.

As Robert mentions, the ability to speak is vital to building a successful business. The personal development and mentoring programs offered by select franchises and network marketing organization provide wonderful opportunities for personal growth.

Chapter 34

Systems Management

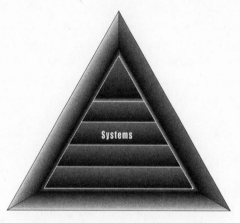

The human body is a system of systems. So is a business. The human body is made up of a blood system, oxygen system, food system, waste system, etc. If one of those systems stops, there is a good chance the body will be crippled or die. The same is true with a business. A business is a complex system of inter-operating systems. In fact, each item listed on the B-I Triangle is a separate system that is inter-linked into the overall business the triangle represents. It is difficult to separate the systems because they are interdependent. It is also difficult to say that one is more important than another.

For any business to grow, individuals must be accountable for each of the systems and a general overall director must be in charge of making sure all the systems operate to their highest capacity. When reading a financial statement, I am like a pilot sitting in the cockpit of the plane reading the gauges from all the operating systems. If one of the systems begins to malfunction, emergency procedures must be implemented. So many small startup businesses or S quadrant businesses fail because the operator of the system has too many systems to monitor and take care of. When one system fails, such as when cash flow dries up, all the other systems begin to fail almost simultaneously. It is like when a person gets a cold and fails to take care of him- or herself. Pneumonia soon sets in and if it's not treated, the person's immune system begins to break down.

I believe real estate is a great investment to start with because the average investor gets to tinker with all the systems. A building on a piece of land is the business—the system for which a tenant pays you rent. Real estate is fairly stable and inert, so it gives the new businessperson more time to correct things if something begins to go wrong. Learning to manage property for a year or two teaches you excellent business management skills. When people ask me where to find the best real estate investments, I say, "Just find someone who is a poor business manager and you will find a real estate bargain." But never buy a property just because it is a bargain because some bargains are cleverly disguised nightmares.

Banks like to lend money on real estate because it is generally a stable system that retains its value. Other businesses are often hard to finance because they may not be considered stable systems. I have often heard the following: "The only time a bank will loan you money is when you don't need it." I see it differently. I have always found that the bank will loan you money when you have a stable system that has value and when you can demonstrate that the money will be paid back.

A good businessperson can manage multiple systems effectively without becoming part of the system. A true business system is much like a car. The car does not depend upon only one person to drive it. Anyone who knows how to drive it can do so. The same is true for a B quadrant business but not necessarily for an S quadrant business. In most cases, the person in the S quadrant is the system.

One day, I was considering starting a small coin shop that specialized in rare collectable coins, and rich dad said to me, "Always remember that the B quadrant gets more money from investors because investors invest in good systems and people who can build good systems. Investors do not like to invest in businesses where the system goes home at night."

Sharon's Notes

Every business, whether large or small, needs to have systems in place to enable it to conduct its day-to-day activities. Even a sole proprietor has to wear different hats to conduct his or her business. In essence, the sole proprietor is all systems in one.

The better the system, the less dependent you become on others. Robert described McDonald's in this way: "It's the same everywhere in the world—and is run by teenagers." This is possible because of the excellent systems in place. McDonald's depends on systems, not people.

The Role of a CEO

A CEO's job is to supervise all systems and identify weaknesses before the weaknesses turn into system failures. This can happen in many different ways, but it is exceptionally disconcerting when your company is growing rapidly. Your sales are increasing, your product or service is getting attention from the media, and suddenly you can't deliver. Why? Usually, it's because your systems imploded from the increased demand. You didn't have enough phone lines, or operators answering the phones; you didn't have enough production capacity or enough hours in the week to meet the demand; or you didn't have the money to build the product or hire additional help. Whatever the reason, you missed the opportunity to move your business to the next level of success due to a failure of one of your systems.

At each new level of growth, the CEO must start planning the systems needed to support the next level of growth, from phone lines to lines of credit for production needs. Systems drive both cash flow management and communication. As your systems get better, you or your employees will have to exert less and less effort. Without well-designed and successful operating systems, your business will be labor intensive. Once you have well-designed and successful operating systems, you will have a saleable business asset.

Typical Systems

In the next section is a list of typical systems that successful businesses must have. In some instances, the system required might be defined differently from the way it is listed, but it is still necessary to the business operations. (For instance, "Product Development Systems" might be "Procedures for Providing Services" in a service organization. While the specifics may differ, the basic elements are the same. Both of these require the business to develop the product [or service] that it will ultimately offer to its customers.)

In the case of franchises and network marketing organizations, many of these systems are automatically provided. For the cost of the franchise or membership fee of the network marketing organization, you will be given an operations manual that describes the systems provided for your business. This is what makes these "ready-made" businesses so attractive to many people.

If you want to build your own business, review the list of systems. Although you are already performing many of these functions, you may not have defined them as separate systems. The more you can formalize your operations, the more efficient your business will become.

Systems Required by Every Business for Optimal Efficiency

Daily Office Operations Systems:

- Answering the telephone and 800 line system
- Receiving and opening the mail
- Purchasing and maintaining office supplies and equipment
- Faxing and e-mailing
- Dealing with incoming/outgoing delivery needs
- Backing up and archiving data

Product Development Systems:

- Developing product and protecting it legally
- Developing packaging and collateral material (e.g., catalogs, etc.)
- Developing manufacturing method and process
- Developing manufacturing costing and bidding process

Manufacturing and Inventory Systems:

- Selecting vendors
- Determining product or service warranties offered
- Establishing product or service pricing (retail and wholesale)
- Establishing reorder process for inventory production
- Receiving and storing product as inventory
- Reconciling physical inventory with accounting records

Order Processing Systems:

- Taking orders and recording the orders—by mail, fax, phone, or online
- Fulfilling and packaging the orders
- Sending the orders

Billing and Accounts Receivable Systems:

- Billing customers for the orders
- Receiving payments for the orders and crediting customers for payment (whether cash, check, or credit card)

- Starting the collection process for delinquent receivables

Customer Service Systems:
- Returns procedure for inventory receiving and customer payment return
- Responding to customer complaints
- Replacing defective product or performing other warranty service

Accounts Payable Systems:
- Purchasing procedures and approvals required
- Payment process for supplies and inventory
- Petty cash

Marketing Systems:
- Creating an overall marketing plan
- Designing and producing promotional materials
- Developing general leads and prospects
- Creating an advertising plan
- Creating a public relations plan
- Creating a direct mail plan
- Developing and maintaining a database
- Developing and maintaining a website
- Analyzing and tracking sales statistics

Human Resources Systems:
- Hiring procedures and employee agreements
- Training employees
- Payroll process and benefit plans

General Accounting Systems:
- Managing the accounting process with daily, weekly, monthly, quarterly, and annual reports
- Managing cash with future borrowing needs secured and available
- Budgeting and forecasting
- Reporting payroll taxes and withholding payments

General Corporate Systems:
- Negotiating, drafting, and executing contracts
- Developing and protecting intellectual property
- Managing insurance needs and coverage
- Reporting and paying federal and state or other jurisdictional taxes
- Planning for federal and state or other jurisdictional taxes
- Managing and storing records

- Maintaining investor/shareholder relations
- Ensuring legal security
- Planning and managing growth

Physical Space Management Systems:
- Maintaining and designing telephone and electrical systems
- Planning permits and fees
- Licensing
- Ensuring physical security

You may want to record your operations in a policies and procedures manual. Such a manual can become an invaluable reference to your staff. In creating the manual, you will find ways to streamline your operations and improve your profitability. You will also be a step closer to owning a B quadrant business.

Chapter 35

Legal Management

This level of the B-I Triangle, legal management, was one of the most painful lessons I ever had to learn. My rich dad identified a serious flaw in my business: I had failed to secure the legal rights to the nylon and Velcro products I had designed before I started producing them. More specifically, I failed to patent some of my products (I failed to do so because I believed the $10,000 in patent attorney fees was too expensive and not important enough to spend that much money on). Another company quickly came along and copied my idea, and I could do nothing about it.

Today, I am now an evangelist for the other side. Today, especially in the Information Age, your intellectual property attorney and your contract attorney are some of your most important advisors because they help create your most important assets. These attorneys, if they are good, will protect your ideas and your agreements from intellectual bandits, people who steal your ideas and therefore your profits.

The world of business is filled with stories of smart entrepreneurs with great ideas who begin selling their products or ideas before protecting them. In the world of intellectual property, once your idea is exposed, it is almost impossible to protect. Not too long ago, a company came out with a spreadsheet program for small businesses. I bought this brilliant product for my company. A few years later, the company was out of business. Why? Because it had failed to patent its idea and another company, which I will not mention, came along, took its idea, and put it out of business. Today, the company that took the idea is a prominent leader in the software business.

It is said that Bill Gates became the richest man in the world with only an idea. In other words, he did not get rich by investing in real estate or factories. He simply took information, protected the information, and became the richest man in the world while still in his thirties. The irony of it all is that he didn't even create the Microsoft operating system. He bought it from other programmers, sold it to IBM, and the rest is history.

Aristotle Onassis became a shipping giant with a simple legal document. It was a contract from a large manufacturing company guaranteeing him the exclusive rights to transport its cargo all over the world. All he had was this document. He owned no ships. Yet with this legal document, he was able to convince the banks to lend him the money to buy the ships. Where did he get the ships? He got them from the U.S. government after W.W. II. The U.S. government had a surplus of Liberty and Victory class ships used to haul war materials from America to Europe. There was one catch. In order to buy the ships, the person needed to be a U.S. citizen and Onassis was a Greek citizen. Did that stop him? Of course it didn't. By understanding the laws of the B quadrant, Onassis purchased the ships using a U.S. corporation he controlled. This is another example of the laws being different for different quadrants.

Protect Your Ideas

My intellectual property attorney is Michael Lechter, one of the leading IP attorneys today. He is responsible for securing worldwide patents and trademarks for CASHFLOW Technologies, Inc. He is also the husband of my business partner and co-author, Sharon Lechter. Although he is married to Sharon, we still pay the same hourly rate as any other of Michael's clients. No matter what we pay him, the value he returns to our company is priceless. He has made us so much money and protected our rights to continue making money by protecting what we do and guiding us through some delicate negotiations. Michael has written a book, *The Intellectual Property Handbook*, which is a wonderful explanation of the various protection mechanisms available. He discusses each individually (patents, trademarks, copyrights, and mask works) as well as how they can be used in combinations to give you the broadest protection. It is available through our website.

In Summary

Many a business has been started and has survived by a simple piece of paper. One legal document can be the seed of a worldwide business.

Sharon's Notes

Some of the most valuable assets you can own are the intangible assets called patents, trademarks, and copyrights. These legal documents grant you specific protection and ownership to your intellectual property. As Robert found out with his Velcro wallet business, without this type of protection, you risk losing everything. Once you have protected your rights, not only can you keep others from using your property, but you can also sell or license those rights and receive royalty income when doing so. Licensing your rights to a third party is a perfect example of your assets working for you!

However, legal issues can also surface in almost every facet of a business. Obtaining competent legal counsel is very important not only as you are forming your business but as an ongoing part of your advisory team. Legal fees may seem expensive at first. However, when you compare them to the cost of legal fees from lost rights or subsequent litigation, it is much less expensive to set out your agreements properly in the beginning. In addition to the monetary expense, you must also factor in the cost of lost time. Instead of focusing on your business, you may be forced to focus on legal matters.

This is another area where franchising and network marketing can help you jumpstart your business. Typically, when you purchase a franchise or join a network marketing organization, most of the necessary legal documents to start and grow your business will be provided for your use. This saves you not only a lot of money but also a tremendous amount of time, and it allows you to focus your efforts on the business development. It is still advisable to have your own counsel review the documents on your behalf.

Some specific areas where proper legal counsel can help you avoid potential problems in legal aspects of a business are:

General Corporate:
- Choice of business entity
- Buy-sell agreements
- Business licenses
- Regulatory compliance
- Office lease or purchase contracts

Consumer Laws:
- Terms and conditions of sales
- Direct mail
- Product liability laws
- Truth in advertising laws
- Environmental laws

Contracts:
- With suppliers
- With wholesale customers
- With employees
- Uniform commercial code
- Warranties
- Jurisdiction

Intellectual Property:
- Work-for-hire agreements
- Nondisclosure agreements
- Copyrights
- Mask works
- Patents
- Trademarks
- Licensing of intellectual property

Labor Laws:
- Human Resource issues
- Employee agreements
- Employee disputes
- OSHA
- Workers' compensation

Securities and Debt Instruments:
- Equipment leasing or purchase
- Loan documents
- Private placements
- IPOs

Shareholder Issues:
- Corporate bylaws
- Board authority
- Stock issuance
- Mergers and acquisitions
- Spin-offs

Chapter 36

Product Management

The company's product, which the customer ultimately buys from the business, is the last important aspect of the B-I Triangle. It could be a tangible item such as a hamburger or an intangible item such as consulting services. It is interesting to note that when evaluating a business, many average investors focus on the product rather than the rest of the business. Rich dad thought that the product was the least important piece to inspect when evaluating a business.

Many people come to me with ideas for new innovative products. My response is that the world is full of great products. People also say to me that their new idea or product is better than an existing product. Thinking that a better product or better service is most important is usually the domain of the E and S quadrant, where being the best or highest quality is important for success. In the B and I quadrants, however, the most important part of a new business is the system behind the product or idea, or the rest of the B-I Triangle. I then point out that most of us can cook a better hamburger than McDonald's but few of us can build a better business system than McDonald's.

Rich Dad's Guidance

In 1974, I decided I was going to learn to build a business following the model of the B-I Triangle. Rich dad warned me by saying, "Learning to build a business according to this model is high risk. Many people attempt it, and few accomplish it. However, although there is high risk at the start, if you learn how to build businesses, your earning potential is unlimited. For the people who are not willing to take the risk, those who don't wish to undertake such a steep learning curve, their risk may be lower but so will their lifetime returns."

I still recall experiencing the highest of highs and lowest of lows as I learned to build a solid business. I remember some of the advertising copy I wrote that never sold anything. I remember some of the brochures I wrote where no one could understand what I was trying to say. And I remember the struggle of learning to raise capital and learning to spend the investors' money wisely in the hopes of building a powerful business. I also remember going back to my investors and telling them that I had lost their money. I am forever grateful for the investors who understood and told me to come back when I had another venture for them to invest in. However, through it all, each mistake was a priceless learning experience as well as character-building experience. As rich dad said, the risk at the start was very high, yet if I could stick it out and continue to learn, the rewards were unlimited.

In 1974, I was very weak at every level of the B-I Triangle. I think I was weakest in cash flow management and communications management. Today, although I am still not great on any one sector of the triangle, I would say I am the strongest in cash flow management and communications management. Because I can create synergies among all the levels, my companies are successful. The point I make here is that even though I was not strong at the start, and am still not great at this stage of my development, I continue with my learning process. For anyone who wants to acquire great wealth in this manner, I offer encouragement to start, to practice, make mistakes, correct, learn, and improve.

When I look at the 10% of Americans who control 90% of all the shares in America and 73% of the wealth, I understand exactly where their wealth was derived. Many acquired that wealth in much the same way as Henry Ford and Thomas Edison (who was worth far more than Bill Gates at his day and age). The list includes Bill Gates, Michael Dell, Warren Buffet, Rupert Murdock, Anita Roddick, Richard Branson, and others who all acquired their wealth the same way. They found their spirit and their mission; built a business; and allowed others to share in the dreams, the risks, as well as the rewards. You can do the same thing if you want. Just follow the same diagram rich dad guided me with: the B-I Triangle.

Helen Keller said, "True happiness is not attained through self-gratification but through fidelity to a worthy purpose."

Sharon's Notes

The product is at the top of the B-I Triangle because it is the expression of the business's mission. It is what you are offering to your customer. The rest of the B-I Triangle lays the foundation for long-term success of your business. If your communication to the marketplace is strong, your systems are set up to facilitate production, ordering, and fulfillment. If your cash is managed properly, you will be able to sell your product successfully and support a strong growth curve for your business.

The B-I Triangle and Your Ideas

Rich dad said, "It is the B-I Triangle that gives shape to your ideas. It is knowledge of the B-I Triangle that allows a person to create an asset that buys other assets." Rich dad guided me in learning how to create and build many B-I Triangles. Many of these businesses failed because I was not able to put all the pieces together harmoniously. When people ask me what caused some of my businesses to fail, it was very often the failure of one or more of the sectors of the B-I Triangle. Rather than become permanently discouraged as many people who fail become, rich dad encouraged me to keep practicing, building these triangles. Instead of calling me a failure when my first big venture failed, rich dad encouraged me to continue on and learn how to build new triangles. He said, "The more you practice building these B-I Triangles, the easier it will be for you to create assets that buy other assets. If you diligently practice, it will become easier and easier for you to make more and more money. Once you are good at taking ideas, building a B-I triangle around the idea, people will come to you and invest money with you and then it will be true for you that it does not take money to make money. People will be giving you their money to make more money for yourself and for them. Instead of spending your life working for money, you will be getting better at creating assets that make more and more money."

The B-I Triangle and the 90/10 Rule Go Hand in Hand

One day while rich dad was teaching me more about the B-I Triangle, he made a comment I found interesting. He said, "There is a B-I Triangle inside each of us." Not understanding what he meant, I inquired further. Even though his explanation was a good one, it took me awhile to realize how true his statement was. Today whenever I find a person, a family, a business, a city, or a country that is having financial difficulties, to me that means one or more segments of the B-I Triangle are missing or out of synchronicity with the other parts. When one or more parts of the B-I Triangle are not functioning, the chances are the individual or family, or country, will be in the 90% that are sharing in 10% of the money available. So if you, your family or your business is struggling today, look at the model of the B-I Triangle and do an analysis of what can be changed or improved.

Solving the B-I Triangle Riddle

Rich dad gave me another reason to begin mastering the B-I Triangle that I thought was unique. He said, "Your dad believes in hard work as the means of making money. Once you master the art of building B-I Triangles, you will find that the less you work the more money you will make and the more valuable what you are building becomes." At first I did not understand what rich dad was saying, but after a number of years of practice, I understand more fully. Today I meet people who work hard building a career, working their way up the corporate ladder, or building a practice based upon their reputation. These people generally come from the E and S quadrants. In order for me to become rich, I needed to learn to build and put together systems that could work without me. After my first B-I Triangle was built and I sold it, I realized what rich dad meant by the less I work the more money I will make. He called that thinking "solving the B-I Triangle riddle." If you are a person who is addicted to hard work, or what rich dad calls "staying busy in your busyness and not building anything," then I would suggest sitting down with other people who are busy in busyness and discuss how working less can make you more money. I have found that the difference between people in the E and S quadrants and the people in the B and I quadrants is that the E and S side are often too "hands-on." Rich dad used to say, "The key to success is laziness. The more hands-on you are, the less money you can make." One of the reasons so many people do not join the 90/10 club is because they are too "hands on," when they should be seeking new ways of doing more with less and less. If you are going to become the kind of person who creates assets that buy other assets, you will need to find ways of doing less and less so you can make more and more. As rich dad said, "The key to success is laziness." That is why he could create so many assets that bought other assets. He could not have done it if he were like my real dad who was a very hard working man.

A *Summary* of the B-I Triangle

The B-I Triangle as a whole represents a strong system of systems— supported by a team with a leader—all working toward a common mission. If one member of the team is weak, or falters, the overall success of the business can be jeopardized. I would like to highlight three important points in summarizing the B-I Triangle:

1. Money always follows management. If any of the management functions of the five individual levels are weak, the company will be weak. If you are personally having financial difficulty, or not having the excessive cash flow that you desire, you can often find the weak spot(s) by analyzing each level. Once you identify your weakness, you may then want to consider turning it into your strength, or hiring someone with that strength.

2. Some of the best investments and businesses are the ones you walk away from. If any of the five levels are weak and the management is not prepared to strengthen them, it is best to walk away from the investment. Too many times, I have discussed the five levels of the B-I Triangle with a management team with which I am considering investing and I hear arguments instead of discussion. When business owners or business teams are weak in any of the five levels, they will become defensive rather than receptive to questioning. If they do become defensive rather than excited to identify and correct a weakness, I usually walk away from the investment. I have on a wall in my house a photo of a pig I took on Fiji. Under it is printed: "Don't teach pigs to sing. It wastes your time and it annoys the pigs." There are too many excellent investments out there to waste your time trying to teach pigs to sing.

3. The personal computer and the Internet make the B-I Triangle more available, affordable, and manageable for everyone. In my talks, I say that it has never been easier to access great wealth. In the Industrial Age, you needed millions of dollars to build a car factory. Today, with a $1,000 used computer, some brainpower, a telephone line, and a little education in each of the five aspects of the B-I Triangle, the world can be yours.

If you still desire to build a business on your own, there has never been greater opportunity for success. I recently met a young man who sold his small Internet company to a major computer software company for $28 million. All he said to me was, "I made $28 million at the age of 28. How much will I make when I am 48?"

Sharon's Notes

If you want to be an entrepreneur who builds successful businesses or invests in businesses, the entire B-I Triangle must be strong and interdependent. If it is, the business will grow and flourish. The good news is that if you are a team player, you don't have to be an expert at every level of the B-I Triangle. Just become part of a team with a clear vision, a strong mission, and an iron stomach.

B-I Triangle

From B-I Triangle to Business Tetrahedron

A business with a defined mission, a determined leader, and a qualified and unified team begins to take shape as the sections of the B-I Triangle come together. This is when the B-I Triangle becomes three-dimensional and turns into a tetrahedron.

The point of completion is the introduction of integrity. The definition of integrity is wholeness, entirety, as well as perfect condition and soundness. The more common definition of integrity is honesty or sincerity. While the definitions may sound different, they are in fact the same.

A business run with honesty and sincerity when built on the principles of the B-I Triangle will become complete, whole, and sound.

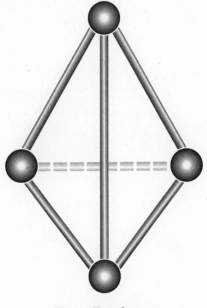

Your Business

Phase Four

Who Is a Sophisticated Investor?

Chapter 37

How a Sophisticated Investor Thinks

"Now that you understand the B-I Triangle, are you ready to build a business?" rich dad asked me.

"Yes, absolutely. Even though it is a little intimidating," I replied. "There is so much to remember."

"That's the point, Robert. Once you build a successful business, you will have the skills to build as many as you want. You will also have the skills to analyze other businesses from the outside before you invest in them."

"It still seems like an impossible mission," I replied.

"Maybe it is because you're thinking of building huge businesses," rich dad continued.

"Of course I am. I am going to be rich," I answered vehemently.

"To learn the skills needed for the B-I Triangle, you need to start small. Even a hot dog cart or a small rental home needs its own B-I Triangle. Every component of the B-I Triangle applies to even the smallest business. You will make mistakes. If you learn from those mistakes, you can build bigger and bigger businesses. In the process, you will become a sophisticated investor."

"So learning to build a business will make me a sophisticated investor?" I asked. "Is that all it takes?"

"If you learn the lessons along the way and build a successful business, you can become a sophisticated investor," rich dad continued, as he brought out his infamous yellow pad. "It's making the first million dollars that's difficult. After you've made the first million, the next ten million are easy. Let's discuss what makes a successful businessperson and investor a sophisticated investor."

Who Is a Sophisticated Investor?

"A sophisticated investor is an investor who understands each of the ten investor controls. The sophisticated investor understands and benefits from the advantages of the right side of the Quadrant. Let's go through each investor control so you get a better understanding of how a sophisticated investor thinks," rich dad explained.

The Ten Investor Controls

1. The control over yourself
2. The control over income/expense and asset/liability ratios
3. The control over the management of the investment
4. The control over taxes
5. The control over when you buy and when you sell
6. The control over brokerage transactions
7. The control over the E-T-C (entity, timing, characteristics)
8. The control over the terms and conditions of the agreements
9. The control over access to information
10. The control over giving it back, philanthropy, redistribution of wealth

"It is important to understand that a sophisticated investor may choose not to become an inside investor or ultimate investor; rather, he or she understands the benefits of each control," rich dad continued. "The more controls these investors possess, the less risk they have in the investment."

Investor Control # 1:

The Control over Yourself

"The most important control you must have as an investor is control over yourself." It can determine your success as an investor and is why the entire first phase of the book is dedicated to getting control over yourself. Rich dad often also said, "It isn't the investment that is risky, it is the investor who is risky!"

Most of us were taught in school to become employees. There was only one right answer, and making mistakes was horrible. We were not taught financial literacy in school. It takes a lot of work and time to change your thinking and to become financially literate.

A sophisticated investor knows that there are multiple right answers, that the best learning comes through making mistakes, and that financial literacy is essential to be successful. They know their own financial statement, and they understand how each financial decision they make will ultimately impact their financial statement.

To become rich, you must teach yourself to think like a rich person.

Investor Control #2:

The Control over Income/Expense and Asset/Liability Ratios

This control is developed through financial literacy. My rich dad taught me the three cash flow patterns of the poor, middle class, and the rich. I decided at an early age that I wanted to have the cash flow pattern of a rich person.

The cash flow pattern of the poor:

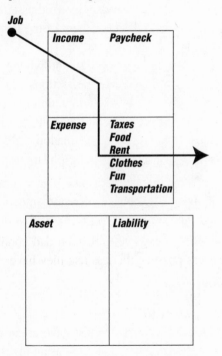

The poor spend every penny they make—they have no assets and no debt.

The cash flow pattern of the middle class:

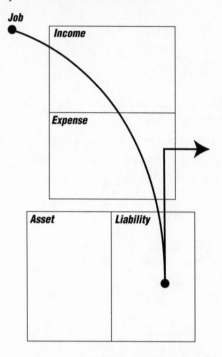

Individuals in the middle class accumulate more debt as they become more successful. A pay raise qualifies them to borrow more money from the bank so they can buy personal items like bigger cars, vacation homes, boats, and motor homes. Their wage income comes in and is spent on current expenses and then on paying off this personal debt.

As their income increases, so does their personal debt. This is what we call the "Rat Race."

The cash flow pattern of the rich:

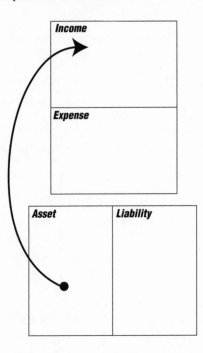

The rich have their assets work for them. They have gained control over their expenses and focus on acquiring or building assets. Their businesses pay most of their expenses, and they have few, if any, personal liabilities.

You may have a cash flow pattern that is a combination of these three types. What story does your financial statement tell? Are you in control of your expenses?

Buy Assets Not Liabilities

Sophisticated investors buy assets that put money in their pockets. It is just that simple.

Turning Personal Expenses into Business Expenses

Sophisticated investors understand that businesses are allowed to deduct all the ordinary and necessary expenses paid or incurred for the business. They analyze their expenses and convert non-deductible personal expenses into deductible business expenses whenever possible. Not every expense will be an allowable deduction.

Review your business and personal expenses with your financial and tax advisors so that you can maximize the deductions available to you through your business. Some examples of personal expenses that could be legitimate business expenses are:

Personal Expense	Business Expense	Justification
Computer	Business equipment	Business use
Cellular phone	Business equipment	Use your phone to call clients
Meals out	Business meals	Note business purpose and with whom
Medical expense	Medical reimbursement	Adopt medical reimbursement plan.
Tuition	Education	Authorize and document applicability for business
Home costs	Home office	Follow guidelines—track all home expenses and reimburse based on square footage

These are just a few examples of the types of business expenses that are deductible expenses for business owners. The same expenses are not usually deductible for employees. Your expenses must be properly documented and have a legitimate business purpose. Can you think of expenses you are paying personally today that could be deductible business expenses if you owned a business?

Investor Control #3:

The Control over the Management of the Investment

An inside investor who owns enough of an interest in the investment whereby he or she can control the management decisions has this investor control. It can be as a sole owner or where the investor owns enough of an interest that he or she is involved in the decision-making process.

The skills learned through building a successful business using the B-I Triangle are essential to this investor.

Once the investor possesses these skills, he or she is better able to analyze the effectiveness of the management of other potential investments. If the management appears competent and successful, the investor is more comfortable investing funds.

Investor Control #4:

The Control over Taxes

The sophisticated investor has learned about the tax laws, either through formal study or by asking questions and listening to good advisors. The right side of the CASHFLOW Quadrant provides certain tax advantages, which the sophisticated investor uses thoughtfully to minimize his or her taxes paid as well as to increase tax deferrals wherever possible.

In the United States, those on the right side of the Quadrant enjoy many tax advantages that are not available to those on the left side. Three specific advantages are:

1. "Social insurance" taxes (Social Security in the United States, Medicare tax, unemployment tax, and disability income, to name just a few) do NOT apply to passive and portfolio income (right side of the Cashflow Quadrant) but do apply to earned income (left side of the Cashflow Quadrant).

2. It may be possible to defer payment of taxes, perhaps indefinitely, by using the laws available to you related to real estate and owning a company (an example would be a profit-sharing plan sponsored by your business corporation).

3. C Corporations may pay for a number of expenditures with pre-tax dollars that E income recipients must pay for with after-tax dollars. Some examples are included under Investor Control #2.

Sophisticated investors recognize that each country, state, and province has difference tax laws, and they are prepared to move their business affairs to the place best suited for what they are doing.

Recognizing that taxes are the largest expense in the E and S quadrants, sophisticated investors may well seek to reduce their income in order to reduce income taxes while increasing funds for investment simultaneously. See the example under Investor Control #7.

Investor Control #5:

The Control over When You Buy and When You Sell

The sophisticated investor knows how to make money in an up market as well as in a down market.

In building a business, the sophisticated investor has great patience. I sometimes refer to this patience as "delayed gratification." A sophisticated investor understands that the true financial reward is after the investment, or business, becomes profitable and can be sold or taken public.

Investor Control #6:

The Control over Brokerage Transactions

The sophisticated investor operating as an inside investor can direct how the investment is sold or expanded.

As an outside investor in other companies, the sophisticated investor carefully tracks the performance of his or her investments and directs his or her broker to buy or sell.

Many investors today rely on their brokers to know when to buy and sell. These investors are not sophisticated.

Investor Control #7:

The Control over the E-T-C (Entity, Timing, Characteristics)

"Next to control over yourself, the control over the E-T-C is the most important control," rich dad would repeat often. To have control over the entity, timing, and characteristics of your income, you need to understand corporate, security, and tax law.

Rich dad truly understood the benefits offered through choosing the right entity, with the right year-end, and converting as much earned income into passive and portfolio income as possible. This, combined with the ability to read financial statements and "think in terms of financial statements," helped rich dad build his financial empire more quickly.

To illustrate what proper E-T-C planning can do, let's review the following case studies about James and Cathy.

CASE #1

James and Cathy are the absentee owners of a restaurant.

The restaurant is operated as a sole proprietorship.

They have two children.

Their net income from the restaurant is $60,000.

James and Cathy have one financial statement.

James and Cathy's Financial Statement

Income

Business net income		$60,000
(after restaurant mortgage payments and depreciation of $120,000)		

Expense

Social Insurance Taxes	$9,200	
Income Taxes	$5,000	
Total Taxes		$14,200
Home Mortgage	$10,200	
Living Expenses:		
Utilities	$3,000	
Auto	$3,000	
Food	$12,000	
Health Insurance	$8,000	
Legal & Accounting	$2,000	
Education	$1,000	
Charity	$1,000	
Total Living Expenses		$40,200

Net Cash Flow	$5,600

Assets	Liabilities
Restaurant Building	Home Mortgage
Restaurant Fixtures	Restaurant Mortgage

CASE #2

James and Cathy met with their financial and tax advisors to structure their businesses to maximize their cash flow and minimize the amount they must pay in taxes.

James and Cathy own two corporations; one owns the restaurant, and the other owns the building where the restaurant is located.

James is the general manager for both corporations.

James and Cathy have two children.

James and Cathy have three sets of financial statements that impact their financial position.

How Did James and Cathy Benefit from the Advice of Their Financial and Tax Advisors?

By setting up this two-corporation structure:

1. James and Cathy can convert certain personal expenses into legitimate business expenses (health insurance, legal and accounting expenses, education expenses, and a home office and auto deduction).
2. They were able to reduce the total amount paid in taxes by $7,885.
3. They were able to put $12,000 into a retirement fund.
4. Both #2 and #3 were made possible although they reduced their personal income to zero.
5. They have protected their personal assets by putting their business operations into corporations, one owned 100% by James and the other owned 100% by Cathy.

Let's see how they were able to accomplish all of this:

James and Cathy's Financial Statement

Income

General Manager Salary

Restaurant	$20,000	
Real Estate Company	$10,000	
Office Reimbursement	$ 1,000	
Auto travel Reimbursement	$ 1,000	
Total Income		$32,000

Expense

Social Insurance Taxes	$ 2,300	
Income Taxes	$ 1,500	
Total Taxes		$ 3,800*
Home Mortgage	$10,200	
Living Expenses		
Utilities	$ 3,000	
Auto	$ 3,000	
Food	$12,000	
Total Living Expenses		$28,200
Net Cash Flow		$ 0

Assets	Liabilities
Restaurant Company	Home Mortgage
Real Estate Company	

Restaurant's Financial Statement

Income

Food Service	$180,000

Expense

General Manager	$20,000
Social Ins Taxes	$1,500*
Rent Expense	$155,000
Reimbursement	$1,000
Legal & Acct	$1,000
Income Taxes	$225*
Net Income	$1,275

Assets	Liabilities

Real Estate Co's Financial Statement

Income

Rental Income	155,000

Expense

General Manager	$10,000
Social Ins Taxes	$750*
Mortgage + Depreciation	$120,000
Reimbursement	$1,000
Legal & Acct	$1,000
Retirement Plan	$12,000
Health Plan	$8,000
Education Reim	$1,000
Charity	$1,000
Income Taxes	$40*
Net Income	$210

Assets	Liabilities
Building	Building Mortgage
Fixtures	

* Total Taxes = $6,315

309

Now let's compare CASE #1 to CASE #2

	CASE #1 Sole Proprietorship	CASE #2 Individual + Two Corporations	Difference
Taxes Paid	($ 14,200)	($ 6,315)	$ 7,885
Income:			
Retirement funds	0	$ 12,000	
Profit			
Personal	$ 5,600	$ 0	
Corp #1		$ 1,275	
Corp #2		$ 210	
Total Cash Flow	$ 5,600	$ 13,485	$ 7,885

The end result of this financial plan for James and Cathy is that they have added $7,885 to their personal wealth by saving $7,885 in taxes. More importantly, however, they have protected their personal assets by moving their businesses into corporations. By having validly established corporations, their personal assets should be safe even if a judgment is awarded against one of the corporations. For instance, if a customer becomes ill in the restaurant, he or she can sue the corporation that owns the restaurant. Any judgment against the restaurant corporation would be paid out of the assets of that corporation. The corporation that owns the building, and the personal assets of James and Cathy, should be protected.

James and Cathy's example is very simplified and provided for illustration purposes only. It is extremely important that you seek professional legal and tax advice before structuring your own financial plan. You must consider many complex issues to ensure you comply with all laws.

All of these numbers look very complicated to me so I have also included the simple diagram rich dad showed me when he described his restaurant and real estate corporations. I learn better with pictures than numbers, so maybe it will help you too.

More Control, Not Less

Rich dad would say, "Once you can think automatically in financial statements, you can then operate multiple businesses as well as evaluate other investments quickly. However, most importantly, once you can think in financial statements, you will gain even greater control over your financial life and make even more money, money that the average person doesn't realize can be made."

He then drew the following diagram:

My Personal

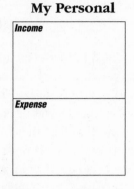

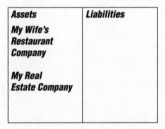

My Wife's Restaurant   My Real Estate Company

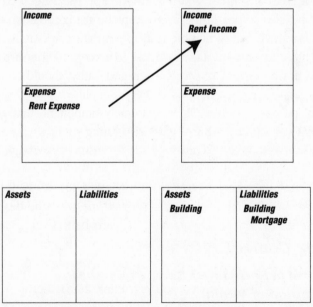

I looked at the diagram and said, "Your expenses go to what you have control of. In this case, your restaurant business pays its rent to your real estate investment company."

Rich dad nodded, saying, "And technically, what am I doing?"

"You are taking earned income from your restaurant business and converting it into passive income for your real estate company. In other words, you are paying yourself."

"And that is just the beginning," said rich dad. "Yet, I want to caution you that from here on in, you will need the best accounting and legal advice possible. This is where unsophisticated investors begin to get into trouble. They get into trouble because the diagram I showed you can be done legally and it can be done illegally. There must always be a business purpose for the transactions between the corporations, and certain control group ownership issues must be considered when you own stock in multiple corporations. It is too easy to make money legally, so hire the best advisors, and you will learn even more about how the rich get richer, legally.

Investor Control #8:

The Control over the Terms and Conditions of the Agreements

The sophisticated investor is in control over the terms and conditions of agreements when he or she is on the inside of the investment. For instance, when I rolled over the sale of several of my small houses into a small apartment building, I used a Section 1031 exchange (U.S. law), which allowed me to roll over the gain. I did not have to pay any taxes on the sale because I controlled the terms and conditions of the agreements.

Investor Control #9:

The Control over Access to Information

As an inside investor, the sophisticated investor again has control over access to information. This is where the investor needs to understand the legal requirements of insiders imposed by the SEC in the United States (other countries have similar oversight organizations).

Investor Control #10:

The Control over Giving It Back, Philanthropy, Redistribution of Wealth

The sophisticated investor recognizes the social responsibility that comes with wealth and gives back to society. This may be through charitable giving, philanthropy. Some of it will be through capitalism, by creating jobs and expanding the economy.

Chapter 38

Analyzing Investments

"The numbers tell a story," my rich dad would say. "If you can learn to read financial statements you can see what is happening within any company or investment."

My rich dad taught me how he used financial ratios to manage his businesses. Whether it is an investment in the stock of a company or purchase of real estate I always analyze the financial statements. I can determine how profitable a business is, or how highly leveraged a business is, just by looking at its financial statements and calculating financial ratios.

For a real estate investment, I calculate what the cash on cash return will be based on the amount of cash I need to spend for the down payment.

But the bottom line always came back to financial literacy. This chapter will cover some of the important thought processes every sophisticated investor goes through in choosing investments for their financial plan:

Financial Ratios of a Company

Financial Ratios of Real Estate

Natural Resources

Is It Good Debt or Bad Debt?

Saving Is Not Investing

Financial Ratios of a Company

Gross Margin Percentage = $\dfrac{\text{Sales - Cost of Goods Sold}}{\text{Sales}}$

The Gross Margin Percentage is the Gross Margin divided by Sales, which tells you what percentage of sales is left after deducting the cost of goods sold. Sales minus the cost of the things sold {"Cost of Goods Sold"} is called the Gross Margin. I remember rich dad saying, "if the gross isn't there, there'll be no net (income)."

How high the Gross Margin Percentage needs to be depends on how a business is organized and the other costs it has to support. After calculating the gross margin percentage, rich dad's convenience stores still had to rent the building, pay the clerks, the utilities, the taxes and government permit fees, pay for wasted or damaged goods, and a long list of other expenses, plus have enough left over to give rich dad a good return on his original investment.

For Internet e-commerce sites today, these additional costs are usually much lower, so these businesses can afford to sell and make a profit with a lower Gross Margin Percentage.

The higher the gross margin the better.

Net Operating Margin Percentage = $\dfrac{\text{EBIT}}{\text{Sales}}$

The Net Operating Margin Percentage tells you the net profitability of the operations of the business before you factor in your taxes and cost of money. EBIT stands for Earnings Before Interest and Taxes, or Sales minus all costs of being in that business, not including capital costs (Interest, Taxes, Dividends).

The ratio of EBIT to Sales is called the Net Operating Margin Percentage. Businesses with high Net Operating Margin Percentages are typically stronger than those with low percentages.

The higher the net operating margin the better.

Operating Leverage = $\dfrac{\text{Contribution}}{\text{Fixed Costs}}$

Contribution is the name for Gross Margin (Sales less Cost of Goods Sold) minus Variable Costs (all costs that are not Fixed Costs are Variable and will fluctuate with sales). Fixed costs include all sales, general, and administrative costs that are fixed and do not fluctuate based on sales volume. For instance, the labor costs related to full-time employees, and most costs related to your facilities, are generally considered fixed costs.

Some people refer to this as "overhead."

A business that has an operating leverage of 1 means that the business is generating just enough revenue to pay for its fixed costs. This would mean that there is no return for the owners.

The higher the operating leverage the better.

$$\text{Financial Leverage} = \frac{\text{Total Capital Employed (Debt \& Equity)}}{\text{Shareholders' Equity}}$$

Total Capital Employed is the book or accounting value of all interest bearing debt (leave out payables for goods to be resold and liabilities due to wages, expenses and taxes owed but not yet paid), plus all owners equity. So if you have $50,000 of debt and $50,000 of shareholder's equity, your financial leverage would be 2 (or $100,000 divided by $50,000).

$$\text{Total Leverage} = \text{Operating} \times \text{Financial Leverages}$$

The total risk that a company carries in its present business is the multiple of its Operating Leverage and its Financial Leverage. Total Leverage tells you what total effect a given change in the business should have on the equity owners (common shares or General Partner). If you are the business owner, and therefore on the inside, your company's Total Leverage is at least partly under your control.

If you are looking at the stock market, Total Leverage will help you decide whether you want to invest. Well run, conservatively managed (publicly traded) American companies usually keep the Total Leverage figure under 5.

$$\text{Debt to Equity Ratio} = \frac{\text{Total Liabilities}}{\text{Total Equity}}$$

The Debt to Equity Ratio measures just that, the portion of the whole enterprise [Total Liabilities] financed by outsiders in proportion to the part financed by insiders [Total Equity]. Most businesses try to stay at a ratio of one-to-one or below. Generally speaking, the lower the debt-to-equity ratio the more conservative the financial structure of the company.

$$\text{Quick Ratio} = \frac{\text{Liquid Assets}}{\text{Current Liabilities}}$$

$$\text{Current Ratio} = \frac{\text{Current Assets}}{\text{Current Liabilities}}$$

The significance of the quick and current ratios is that they tell you whether or not the company has enough liquid assets to pay its liabilities for the coming year. If a company doesn't have enough current assets to cover its current liabilities, it is usually a sign of impending trouble. On the other hand a current ratio and quick ratio of 2 to 1 is more than appropriate.

$$\text{Return on Equity} = \frac{\text{Net Income}}{\text{Average Shareholders' Equity}}$$

The Return on Equity is often considered one of the most important ratios. It allows you to compare the return this company is making on its shareholder's investment compared to alternative investments.

What Do the Ratios Tell Me?

My rich dad taught me to always consider at least 3 years of these figures. The direction and trend of Margin Percentages, Contribution Margin, Leverages and Returns on Equity tell me a lot about a company and its management and even its competitors.

Many published company reports do not include these ratios and indicators. A sophisticated investor learns to calculate these ratios (or hires someone knowledgeable to do so) when they aren't provided.

A sophisticated investor understands the terminology of the ratios and can use the ratios in evaluating the investment. However, the ratios cannot be used in a vacuum. They are indicators of a company's performance. They must be considered in conjunction with analysis of the overall business and industry. By comparing the ratios over at least a three-year period as well as with other companies in the same industry, you can quickly determine the relative strength of the company.

For example, a company with excellent ratios over the last three years and strong profits could appear to be a sound investment. However, after reviewing the industry you find out that the company's main product has just been rendered obsolete by a new product introduced by the company's main competitor. In this instance, a company with a history of strong performance may not be a wise investment due to its potential loss in market share.

While the ratios may appear complicated at first, you will be amazed at how quickly you can learn to analyze a company. Remember these ratios are the language of a sophisticated investor. Through educating yourself on financial literacy, you too can learn to "speak in ratios."

While the ratios may appear complicated at first, you will be amazed at how quickly you learn to analyze a company.

Investing in Real Estate:
Financial Ratios for a Piece of Real Estate

When it came to real estate, rich dad had two questions.

1. Does the property generate a positive cash flow?
2. If yes, have you done your due diligence?

The most important financial ratio of a piece of real estate to rich dad was his cash on cash return.

$$\text{CASH on CASH Return} = \frac{\text{Positive Net Cash Flow}}{\text{Down Payment}}$$

Let's say you buy an apartment building for $500,000. You put $100,000 down and secure a mortgage for the $400,000 balance. You have a monthly cash flow of $2,000 after all expenses and mortgage payment are paid. Your cash on cash return is 24% or $24,000 ($2,000 x 12 months) divided by $100,000.

Before buying the apartment building, you must decide how you will purchase it. Will you buy it through a C-corporation, an LLC Corporation, or a limited partnership? Consult with your legal and tax advisors to make sure that you choose the entity that will provide the most legal protection and tax advantages to you.

Due Diligence

In my opinion, the words due diligence are some of the most important words in the world of financial literacy. It is through the process of due diligence that a sophisticated investor sees the other side of the coin. When people ask me how I find good investments I simply reply, "I find them through the process of due diligence." Rich dad said, "The faster you are able to do your due diligence on any investment, regardless if it is a business, real estate, a stock, mutual fund or bond, the better able you will be to find the safest investments with the greatest possibility for cash flow or capital gains.

In the audio cassette learning program entitled *Financial Literacy: How Sophisticated Investors Find the Investments That Average Investors Miss* is a workbook filled with very sophisticated due diligence forms that can be adapted to evaluate many investments quickly. If you would like to find out more about this audio educational program and work book, please refer to our website, www.richdad.com. Not only will you listen to very sophisticated investors share their investment secrets, you will learn how to use these due diligence forms. These rarely publicized due diligence forms have the power to not only make you a more sophisticated investor, the forms can save you a lot of time analyzing investments, and they may also help you find the high yielding investments you have been looking for.

For example, once you have determined that a piece of real estate will generate a positive cash flow for you, you still need to perform due diligence on the property.

Rich dad had a checklist that he always used. I use a due diligence checklist created by Cindy Shopoff. It is very thorough and includes items that did not exist 30 years ago (eg. Phase I Environmental Audit). I have included Cindy's checklist as a reference for you.

If I have questions about the property, I often bring in the experts and have my attorneys and accountants review the deal.

Due Diligence Checklist

_____ 1. Current rent roster with paid to dates

_____ 2. List of security deposits

_____ 3. Mortgage payment information

_____ 4. Personal property list

_____ 5. Floor plans

_____ 6. Insurance policy, agent

_____ 7. Maintenance, service agreement

_____ 8. Tenant information: leases, ledger cards, applications, smoke detector forms

_____ 9. List of vendors and utility companies, including account number

_____ 10. A statement of structural alterations made to the premises

_____ 11. Surveys and engineering documents

_____ 12. Commission agreements

_____ 13. Rental or listing agreements

_____ 14. Easement agreements

_____ 15. Development plans, including plans and specifications and as-built architectural, structural, mechanical, electrical and civil drawings

_____ 16. Governmental permits or zoning restrictions affecting development of the property

_____ 17. Management contracts

_____ 18. Tax bills and property tax statements

_____ 19. Utility bills

_____ 20. Cash receipts and disbursements journals pertaining to the property

_____ 21. Capital expenditure disbursement records pertaining to the property for the past five years

_____ 22. Income and expense statements pertaining to the property for two years prior to the submission date

_____23. Financial statements and state and federal tax returns for the property

_____24. A termite inspection in form and content reasonably satisfactory to the buyer

_____25. All other records and documents in Seller's possession or under Seller's control which would be necessary or helpful to the ownership, operation or maintenance of the property

_____26. Market surveys or studies of the area

_____27. Construction budget or actuals

_____28. Tenant profiles or surveys

_____29. Work-order files

_____30. Bank statements for 2 years showing operating account for property

_____31. Certificates of occupancy

_____32. Title abstract

_____33. Copies of all surviving guarantees and warranties

_____34. Phase I Environmental Audit (if exists) For Every Investment

Natural Resources

Many sophisticated investors include investments in the earth's natural resources as part of their portfolio. They invest in oil, gas, coal and precious metals, just to name a few.

My rich dad strongly believed in the power of gold. As a natural resource, gold has a limited supply. As rich dad told me, people throughout the centuries have cherished gold. Rich dad also believed that owning gold attracted other wealth to you.

To read more about my rich dad's lesson about investing in gold, please visit *www.richdadgold.com*

Is It Good Debt or Bad Debt?

A sophisticated investor recognizes good debt, good expenses and good liabilities. I remember rich dad asking me, "How many rental houses can you afford to own where you lose $100 per month?" I, of course answered, "Not too many." Then he asked me, "How many rental houses can you afford to own where you earn $100 per month?" The answer to that question is, "as many as I can find!"

Analyze each of your expenses, liabilities and debts. Does each particular expense, liability or debt apply to a corresponding income or an asset? If so, is the resulting cash flow in from the income and/or asset greater than the cash flow out for the expense/liability/debt?

For example, a friend of mine, Jim, has a mortgage on an apartment building for $600,000, for which he pays out $5,500 each month in mortgage and interest payments. He receives rental income from his tenants of $8,000 each month. After all other expenses he has a net positive cash flow of $1,500 each month from that apartment building. I would consider Jim's mortgage a GOOD DEBT.

Saving Is Not Investing

A sophisticated investor understands the difference between saving and investing. Let's look at the case of two friends, John and Terry, both of whom believe themselves to be sophisticated investors.

John is a highly paid professional and invests the maximum in his 401(k) retirement plan at work. John is 42 and has $250,000 in his 401(k) plan already because he has been adding to it for 11 years. There is no return, or cash flow, from it until he retires and then it will be fully taxable at his regular earned income rates.

John's details : Earning $100,000 salary

Taxes - assume average rate of 25% (low)

Investment - Pension Plan - 401(k)

Maximum 15% contribution or $15,000 ⁻

Pension Plan - earns 8% per year

Current Cash Flow from investments - none

Terry is the same age as John and makes a similar salary. She has invested in a series of real estate deals over the past 11 years and just put $250,000 down on a $1,000,000 property. Terry is earning a cash on cash return of 10% and expects a conservative appreciation of her property of 4% per year. When she retires, Terry expects to 1031 Exchange into another property to take advantage of the high equity and cash flow. Terry has never contributed to the 401(k) plan and the income from her property is taxed currently.

Terry's details : Earning $100,000 salary

Taxes - assume average rate of 25% (low)

Investment - Buy Real Estate at $1,000,000

with 25% or $250,000 down

Property - earns 10% cash on cash return

Appreciates 4% per year

Current Cash Flow - $25,000 per year from

Real Estate investment

The following chart shows the asset accumulation, annual after taxes cash flow available for spending, and the annual retirement cash flow (also after taxes) for both John and Terry. I thank my tax advisor, Diane Kennedy, CPA for preparing this analysis so I could share it with you.

	Beginning		yrs 1 - 19		At 20 years		Annual Retired
	Assets	Cash Flow	Invests	Cash Flow	Assets	Cash Flow	Net Cashflow
John	$250,000	$63,750	$15,000	$63,750	$1,968,000	$63,750	$118,100
Terry	$250,000	$73,560	0	$73,560	$2,223,000	$73,560	$342,700

As you see, Terry's family will be able to spend almost $10,000 more per year than John's family, each and every year for the next 20 years. After which, they both retire at age 62, having worked 31 years.

At retirement, John begins drawing out 8% of his accumulated 401(k) plan, receiving $118,100 per year ($157,400 before taxes). He plans to withdraw none of the principal amount. He succeeded, after 31 total years of investing $15,000 in his plan each year, in replacing 150% of his work income.

Even though Terry had only put $250,000 down on the property, she benefited from the 4% appreciation on the total $1,000,000 value of the property. During the 20 years, the rental income from the property paid off the mortgage of $750,000, so when Terry retires she can roll over the complete equity of $1,000,000 into a much larger property (worth $8,892,000 according to these calculations). This new property will generate a cash flow of $342,700 per year for Terry.

While John's retirement will be comfortable, Terry's will be rich.

If, for some reason, John needs more income in retirement, he must start drawing out the principal from his retirement plan. Terry would only need to do another tax-free exchange into other buildings to capture the mortgage principal paid down by her tenants, leveraging that into higher income.

John's example will have taught his children to go to school, get good grades, get a good job, work hard, "invest" in the retirement plan regularly; and as a result, be comfortable in retirement.

Terry's example will have taught her children that if they learn how to invest by starting small, to mind their own business, and to keep their money working hard for them, they'll be rich.

It is easy to see that investing in a building generated much more cash flow and income for Terry than saving in his 401(k) did for John. I would categorize Terry as an investor and John as a saver.

A sophisticated investor understands the difference between investing and saving and generally has both as part of his or her financial plan.

Chapter 39

The Ultimate Investor

So the question remains, how does a person like Bill Gates become the richest businessperson in the world in his thirties? Or how does Warren Buffet become the richest investor in America? Both men came from middle-class families so they were not handed the keys to the family vault. Yet, without great family wealth behind them, they rocketed to the apex of wealth within a span of a few years. How? They did it how many of the ultra-rich have done so in the past and will be doing so in the future. They became ultimate investors by creating an asset that is worth billions of dollars.

The September 27, 1999, issue of *Fortune* ran a cover story titled "Young and Rich, the 40 wealthiest Americans under 40." Some of these young billionaires are:

Position	Name	Age	Wealth	Business
#1	Michael Dell	34	$21.5 billion	Dell Computer
#2	Jeff Bezos	35	$5.7 billion	Amazon.com
#3	Ted Waitt	36	$5.4 billion	Gateway Computer
#4	Pierre Omidyar	32	$3.7 billion	eBay
#5	David Filo	33	$3.1 billion	Yahoo!
#6	David Yang	30	$3.0 billion	Yahoo!
#7	Henry Nicholas	39	$2.4 billion	Broadcom
#8	Rob Glaser	37	$2.3 billion	RealNetworks

| #9 | Scott Blum | 35 | $1.7 billion | Buy.com |
| #10 | Jeff Skoll | 33 | $1.4 billion | eBay |

You may notice that the top 10 of the top 40 young rich are from computer or Internet companies. Yet there were other types of businesses listed as well:

#26	John Schattner	37	$403 million	Papa John's Pizza
#28	Master P	29	$361 million	Recording star
#29	Michael Jordan	36	$357 million	Sports star

I find it interesting to note that the non-Internet-related rich people came from businesses such as a pizza company, the rap music business, and sports. Everyone else was in computers or the Internet.

Bill Gates and Warren Buffet did not make the list because they were over 40. In 1999, Bill Gates was 43 and worth $85 billion. Warren Buffet was 69 and worth $31 billion, according to *Forbes.*

They Made It the Old-Fashioned Way

So how did most of these people join the ranks of the ultra-rich so early in life? They made it the old-fashioned way: the same way that Rockefeller, Carnegie, and Ford became yesterday's ultra-rich and the same way that tomorrow's ultra-rich will do it. They built companies and sold shares in their company to the public. They worked hard to become selling shareholders rather than buying shareholders. In other words, it could be said that by being selling shareholders, they printed their own money— legally. They created valuable business and then sold shares of ownership in the business to others, buying shareholder.

In *Rich Dad Poor Dad,* I wrote about how at the age of 9, I began making my own money by melting down lead toothpaste tubes and forging lead coins in Plaster of Paris molds. My poor dad told me what the word "counterfeiting" meant. My first business opened and closed on the same day.

My rich dad, on the other hand, told me that I was very close to the ultimate formula for wealth: to print or invent your own money—legally. And that is what the ultimate investor does. In other words, why work hard for money when you can print your own? In *Rich Dad Poor Dad,* rich dad's lesson #5 is "the rich invent their own money." Rich dad taught me to invent my own money with real estate or with small companies. That technical skill is the domain of the inside and ultimate investors.

How 10% Own 90% of the Shares

One reason the wealthiest 10% own 90% of all the shares, as reported in *The Wall Street Journal,* is that the wealthiest 10% include the ultimate investors, the people who created the shares. Another reason is that only this 10% are eligible (per SEC rules) to invest in a company at the early stages before it becomes available to the public through an IPO. In this elite group are founders of companies (a.k.a. founding shareholders), friends of the founders, or a select list of investors. These are the people who become richer and richer, while the rest of the population often struggles to make ends meet, investing the few dollars they may have left over as buying shareholders, if they have any dollars left at all.

The Difference between Selling and Buying

In other words, the ultimate investor is someone who builds a company and sells shares in his or her company. When you read an IPO prospectus, ultimate investors are the ones listed as the selling shareholders; they are not buying shareholders. And as you can tell by the net worth of these individuals, there seems to be a tremendous difference in wealth between those who sell and those who buy shares.

The Last Leg

By 1994, I felt I had successfully completed much of the plan rich dad and I had created back in 1974. I felt relatively comfortable with my abilities to manage most of the components of the B-I Triangle. I understood corporate law well enough to talk to an attorney and/or accountant. I knew the differences among the entity types (S-Corporation, an LLC, an LLP, and a C-Corporation, a limited partnership), and when to use one versus the other. I felt fairly comfortable with my ability to successfully buy and manage real estate investments. By 1994, our expenses were under control with as much as possible becoming pre-tax business expenses. We paid little in regular income tax simply because we did not have jobs in the normal sense. Most of our income was in the form of passive income with a little from portfolio income, primarily from mutual funds. We had some income from investments in other peoples' businesses.

But one day, while I was evaluating my tetrahedron, it was glaringly obvious that one leg of my tetrahedron was really weak: the leg dedicated to paper assets.

My tetrahedron looked like this:

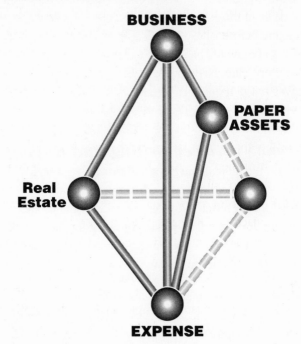

BUSINESS

PAPER ASSETS

Real Estate

EXPENSE

In 1994, I felt good about my success. Kim and I were financially free and could afford not to work for the rest of our lives, barring financial disaster. However, it was obvious that one leg of my tetrahedron was weaker. My financial empire looked out of balance.

I took a year off in the mountains between 1994 and 1995 and spent a lot of time contemplating the idea of strengthening the last leg, paper assets. I had to decide if I really wanted to do all the work needed to strengthen it. I was doing OK financially, and in my mind, I really did not need much more in the way of paper assets to be financially secure. I was fine exactly the way I was, and I could have gotten richer and richer without paper assets.

After a year of mental turmoil and vacillation, I decided that the paper asset leg of my portfolio needed to be strengthened. If I did not do so, I would be quitting on myself. That was a disturbing thought.

I also had to decide if I wanted to invest from the outside, as most people did when it came to buying stocks in companies. In other words, I needed to decide if I wanted to be a buying shareholder and invest from the outside or learn to invest from the inside. Either would be a learning experience, almost like starting over.

It is relatively easy to get into the inside of a real estate deal or the acquisition of a small business. That is why I recommend to individuals who are serious about gaining experience of the ten investor controls to start with small deals in those types of investments. However, to get to the inside of a company before it went public, through a pre-IPO, was another story. Generally, to be invited to invest in a company before it goes public is reserved for a very elite group of people, and I did not belong to that elite group. I was not rich enough, and my money was too new for me to belong to the elite group. In addition, I do not come from the right family or university. My blood is red, not blue; my skin is not White; and Harvard has no record of me applying to its prestigious institution. I had to learn how to become part of the elite group that is invited to invest in the best companies before they go public.

I felt sorry for myself for a few moments, enjoying a brief moment of self-discrimination, a lack of self-confidence, and a strong dose of self-pity. Rich dad had already passed on, and I had no one to turn to for advice. After my few moments of misery were over, I realized that this is a free country. If Bill Gates can drop out of college, build a company, and take it public, why can't I? Isn't this why we want to live in a free country? Can't we be as rich or poor as we want? Isn't this why the barons in 1215 forced King John to sign the Magna Carta? In late 1994, I decided that since no one was going to ask me to join the insiders' club, I might have to find one and ask to be invited to join—or start my own club. The problem was that I did not know where to start, especially in Phoenix, Arizona, two thousand miles from Wall Street.

On New Year's Day 1995, my best friend Larry Clark and I hiked up to a mountaintop near our home. We went through our annual New Year's Day ritual of discussing our past year, planning for the next year, and writing down our goals for the coming year. We spent about three hours up on the rocky peak discussing our lives; the past year; and our hopes, dreams, and goals for the future. Larry and I have been best friends for over 25 years (we started at Xerox together in Honolulu in 1974). He had become my new best friend because he and I had more in common than Mike and I did at that stage of my life. Mike was already very, very rich, and Larry and I were just starting out with virtually nothing but a strong desire to become very, very rich.

Larry and I spent years together as partners, starting several businesses. Many of those businesses failed even before they got off the drawing board. When he and I reflect back on some of those businesses, we laugh at how naive we were back then. Yet, some of those businesses did very well. We were partners in starting the nylon and Velcro wallet business in 1977 and developing it into a worldwide business. We became best friends through starting businesses together and have remained best friends ever since.

After the nylon and Velcro wallet business began to fail in 1979, Larry moved back to Arizona and began to build his fame and fortune as a real estate developer. In 1995, *Inc.* Magazine named him America's fastest-growing homebuilder and he joined its prestigious list of fast-growing entrepreneurs. In 1991, Kim and I moved to Phoenix for the weather and golf, but more importantly for the millions of dollars of real estate the federal government was giving away for pennies on the dollar. Today, Kim and I are neighbors of Larry and his wife Lisa.

On that bright New Year's Day in 1995, I showed Larry the diagram of my tetrahedron and my need to increase my paper assets leg. I shared my desire to either invest in a company before it went public, or maybe even build a company and take it public. At the end of my explanation, all Larry said was "Good luck." We ended that day by writing our goals on a 3x5 card and shaking hands. We wrote down our goals because rich dad had always said, "Goals have to be clear, simple, and in writing. If they are not in writing and reviewed daily, they are not really goals. They are wishes." Sitting on the chilly mountain peak, we then went over Larry's goal of selling his business and retiring. At the end of his explanation, I shook his hand and said, "Good luck" and we hiked back down the mountain.

Periodically, I would review what I had written on that 3x5 card. My goal was simple. It was stated as, "To invest in a company before it goes public and acquire 100,000 shares or more for less than $1.00 a share." At the end of 1995, nothing had happened. I had not achieved my goal.

On New Year's Day 1996, Larry and I sat on the same mountain peak and discussed our results for the year. Larry's company was on the verge of being sold, but it had not yet happened. So we had not accomplished our goals for 1995. Larry was close to achieving his goal, but I seemed far away from achieving mine. Larry asked if I wanted to drop the goal or choose something new. As we discussed the goal, I began to realize that although I had written the goal, I did not believe that it was possible for me. In my soul, I did not really believe that I was smart enough, qualified enough, or that anyone wanted me to belong to that elite group. The more we talked about my goal, the angrier I got at myself for doubting myself and putting myself down so much. "After all," Larry said, "you have paid your dues. You know how to build and run a profitable private company. Why shouldn't you be a valuable asset to a team that takes a company public?" After rewriting our goals and shaking hands, I walked down the mountain with a lot of nervousness and self-doubt because I now wanted my goal more than ever. I also walked down with more determination to have my goal become reality.

Nothing happened for about six months. I would read my goal in the morning and then go about my daily activities, which at that time was to produce my board game *CASHFLOW.* One day, my neighbor Mary knocked on my door and said, "I have a friend I think you should meet." I asked her why. All she said was, "I don't know. I just think the two of you would get along. He's an investor like you." I trusted Mary so I agreed to meet her friend for lunch.

A week or two later, I met her friend Peter for lunch at a golf club in Scottsdale, Arizona. Peter is a tall, distinguished man who is well spoken and about the same age my own dad would have been if he were still alive. As lunch went on, I found out that Peter had spent much of his adult life on Wall Street, owning his own brokerage firm, occasionally forming companies and taking them public. He has had his own companies listed on the American Exchange, the Canadian exchanges, NASDAQ, and on the big board of The New York Stock Exchange. Not only was he a person who created assets, he was a person who invested from the other side of the coin of the public stock markets. I knew he could guide me into a world very few investors ever see. He could guide me through the looking glass, get me behind the scenes and increase my understanding of the greatest capital markets of the world.

After retiring, he had moved to Arizona with his wife and lives in relative seclusion on his own desert estate, far away from the hustle and bustle of the growing city of Scottsdale. When Peter told me that he had been involved in taking nearly 100 companies public during his career, I knew why I was having lunch with him.

Not wanting to appear too excited or overly aggressive, I did my best to control myself. Peter is a very private individual and grants time to very few people. (That is why I use the name Peter instead of his real name. He continues to prefer his anonymity.) Lunch ended pleasantly without me discussing what I wanted to discuss. As I said, I did not want to appear too eager and naive.

For the next two months, I called asking for another meeting. Always the gentleman, Peter would politely say "No," or avoid setting a time to get together. Finally, he said "Yes," and gave me directions to his home way out in the desert. We set a date, and I began rehearsing what I wanted to say.

After a week of waiting, I found myself driving up to his home. The first thing that greeted me was a "Beware of dog" sign. My heart raced as I drove up his long driveway and when I saw this large black lump lying in the middle of the road. It was the dog I was supposed to be wary of, and it was a very big dog. I parked the car just in front of the dog because the dog would not move out of the way. About twenty feet separated my truck and the front door of the house, and this big dog was in between. I opened the door of my truck slowly until I realized the dog was sound asleep. I slowly stepped down from the cab of the truck, but as soon as my foot hit the gravel, the dog suddenly came to life. This big black dog stood to full height, it looked at me, and I looked at it. My heart raced as I prepared to jump back into the cab of the truck. Suddenly, the dog began wagging its stubby tail as well as its whole back end and walked forward to greet me. I spent five minutes petting and being licked to death by this large black guard dog.

My wife Kim and I have a personality rule when it comes to business: "Never do business with pets you don't trust." Over the years, we have discovered that people and their pets are very similar. Once, we did a real estate transaction with a husband and wife who had many pets. He loved small dogs known as "pugs," and she loved colorful exotic birds. When Kim and I went to their house, their small cute dogs and birds appeared friendly, but once you got close to them, they were vicious. As soon as we approached them, they would snap at us and start to bark or squawk loudly and aggressively. A week after the deal was closed, Kim and I found out that the owners were just like their pets—cute on the outside but vicious on the inside. In the fine print of the contract, we had been bitten badly. Even our attorney at the time had missed the subtle bite. The investment came out all right, but since then, Kim and I have developed this new policy: If we are having any doubts about whom we are doing business with and they have pets, find a way to check out their pets. Humans are able to put forth a pleasant front and say things they really don't mean with a smile, but their pets don't lie. Over the years, we have found this simple guideline to be fairly accurate. We have found that a person's insides are reflected on his or her pet's outside. My meeting with Peter was therefore off to a good start. Besides, his big black dog's name was "Candy."

The meeting with Peter did not go so well at first. I asked Peter if I could apprentice with him and be an inside investor with him. I told him that I would work for free if he would teach me what he knew about the process of taking a company public. I explained to him that I was financially free and that I did not need money to work with him. Peter was skeptical for about an hour. He and I went back and forth discussing the value of his time and questioning my ability to learn quickly and willingness to stick with the process. He was afraid that I would quit once I found out how hard it was, since my background was weak when it came to finance and the capital markets such as Wall Street. He also said, "I've never had anyone offer to work for free just so they could learn from me. The only times people have ever asked me for anything is when they wanted to borrow money or they wanted a job." I reassured him that all I wanted was the opportunity to work with him and to learn. I told him about my rich dad guiding me for years and my working for free much of the time. Finally, he asked, "How badly do you want to learn this business?" I looked him squarely in the eye and said, "I want to learn it very badly."

"Good," he said. "I am currently looking at a bankrupt gold mine located in the Andes Mountains of Peru. If you really want to learn from me, then fly to Lima this Thursday, inspect the mine with my team, meet with the bank, find out what it wants for it, return, and give me a report on your findings. And by the way, this entire trip is at your own expense."

I sat there with a stunned look on my face. "Fly to Peru this Thursday?" I restated.

Peter smiled, "Still want to join my team and learn the business of taking a company public?" My stomach turned into a knot and I broke out in a mild cold sweat. I knew my sincerity was being tested. This was a Tuesday and I had appointments already scheduled for Thursday. Peter sat patiently as I thought over my options. Finally, he asked quietly with a very pleasant tone and smile, "Well, still want to learn my business?"

I knew I was at a defining moment. I knew it was time to put up or shut up. I was now testing myself. My choice had nothing to do with Peter. It had everything to do with the next evolution of my personal development. At times like this, I recall the wisdom of the great philosopher Johann Wolfgang Von Goethe:

"Until one is committed there is hesitancy,
a chance to draw back, always ineffectiveness.
Concerning all acts of initiative and creation,
There is one elementary truth,
the ignorance of which
kills countless dreams and splendid plans.
That the moment one definitely commits oneself,
then Providence moves too."

It is the line "then Providence moves too" that has kept me from taking a step forward when the rest of me wanted to step backwards over the years. Webster defines "providence" as "Divine guidance or care. God conceived as the power sustaining and guiding human destiny." Now I am not intending to preach or say that God is on my side. All I am saying is that whenever I come to the edge of my world, or when I am about to take a step into the unknown, all I have at that moment is my trust in a power much larger than myself. It is at such moments—moments when I know I must step over the edge—that I take a deep breath and take the step. It can be called a leap of faith. I call it a test of my trust in a power much bigger than I am. In my opinion, it is those first steps that have made all the difference in my life. The initial results have not always been as I would have liked them to be, but my life has always changed for the better in the long run.

"I have learned a deep respect for one of Goethe's couplets:
Whatever you can do or dream you can, begin it.
Boldness has genius, power, and magic in it."

As the words of the poem faded, I looked up and said, "I'll be in Peru this weekend."

Peter smiled a wide quiet smile. "Here is a list of people you are to meet and where to meet them. Call me when you get back."

This Is Not a Recommendation

This is definitely not the path I would recommend for anyone wanting to learn to take a company public. There are smarter and easier paths. Yet this was the path that was laid forth for me. Therefore, I faithfully describe to you the process via which I came to achieve my goal. In my opinion, everyone must be true to his or her own mental and emotional strengths and weaknesses. I am simply relating the process I went through once I knew the next direction in my life. It was not mentally hard but emotionally challenging, as most significant changes in life tend to be.

Rich dad often said, "An individual's reality is the boundary between faith and self-confidence." He would draw a diagram that looked like this:

```
                        r
                        e
                        a
   self-confidence      l        faith
                        i
                        t
                        y
```

He would then say, "The boundaries of a person's reality often do not change until that person forsakes what he or she feels confident in and then goes blindly with faith. So many people do not become rich because they are limited by their self-confidence rather than the limitlessness of faith."

On that Thursday, in the summer of 1996, I was on my way to the Andes Mountains to inspect a gold mine that was once mined by the Incas and then the Spaniards. I was taking a bold step of faith into a world I knew nothing about. Yet, because of that step, a whole new world of investing opened to me. My life has not been the same since I decided to take that step. My reality on what is possible financially has not been the same. My reality on how rich a person can become has expanded. The more I continue working with Peter and his team, the further those limits to wealth expand.

Today, I continue to expand my limits, and I can hear my rich dad say, "A person is limited only to his or her reality of what is possible financially. Nothing changes until that person's reality changes. And a person's financial reality will not change until he or she is willing to go beyond the fears and doubts of his or her own self-imposed limits."

Peter Kept His Word

Upon returning from the trip, I reported back to Peter. The mine was a great mine with strong and proven veins of gold, but it had financial problems as well as many operational challenges. I recommended against acquiring it because the mine had severe social problems and had severe environmental problems that would have cost millions to clean up. In order to make the mine operate efficiently, any new owners would have to downsize the workforce by at least 40%. It would destroy the town's economy. I said to Peter, "For centuries, these people have lived there at 16,000 feet above sea level. Generations of their families are buried here. I do not think it is wise for us to be the ones to force them to leave the home of their ancestors to seek work in the cities at the base of the mountain. I think we would have more problems than we want to deal with."

Peter agreed with my findings and—more importantly—agreed to teach me. We were soon looking at mines and oil fields in other parts of the world, and a new chapter in my educational process began.

From the summer of 1996 to the fall of 1997, I worked as an apprentice to Peter. He was busy working on developing his company, EZ Energy Corporation (not the real name), which was just about to go public on the Alberta Stock Exchange when I joined him. Since I was late joining his team, I was not able to acquire any of the pre-IPO shares at the insider's price. It would not have been appropriate for me to invest with the founders since I was still new and untested. Yet, I was able to acquire a sizeable block of stock at the IPO price of $.50 (Canadian) a share.

After striking oil in Colombia, and possibly finding what appears to be a large oil and gas field in Portugal, EZ Energy's stock is trading at around $2.00 to $2.35 (Canadian) a share. If the find in Portugal is proven to be as big as the tests indicate, the price per share of the stock may be as high as $5.00 (Canadian) a share sometime in 2000. If, and that is a qualified if, the field in Portugal proves to be as big as we hope it is, the price per share of EZ Energy could climb from $15.00 (Canadian) to $25.00 (Canadian) in the next two to three years. That is the upside. There is also a downside with these micro-cap stocks. The shares could also go to $.00 a share in the next two to three years. A lot of things are possible when companies are at this stage of development.

Although EZ Energy is a very small company, the increase in value for what Peter calls the "front money investors" is pretty good to date. If things go as hoped, these investors will make a lot of money. The front money investors (pre-IPO accredited investors) put up $25,000 (U.S.) for 100,000 shares of stock, or 25 cents per share. They invested this money on the reputation of Peter, the strength of the board of directors, and the business expertise of the oil-exploration team. At the time of the private offering, and even the public offering, there were no guarantees or certain value to invest in. In other words, in the beginning, this investment was all "P" (price) and no "E" (earnings). It was initially offered only to Peter's friends and his circle of investors.

At this stage of the investment cycle, investors invest in the people on the team. The people—much more than the product, be it oil, gold, an Internet product, or widgets—are far more important than any other part of the equation. The golden rule of "Money follows management" is extremely important at this stage of a company's development.

The management of EZ Energy has done extremely well. But rather than go into the hype, hopes, and dreams of this company, I think it best to quote you just the facts of this publicly traded company.

The founders of the company put up their time and expertise in exchange for shares in the company. In other words, most of the founders work for free, investing their time and expertise in return for blocks of shares of stock. The value of their stock when issued is very small, so they have very little, if any, earned income. They work without pay, intending to increase the value of their stock, which will generate portfolio income rather than earned income. A few of the founders are paid a small salary for their services. They work for the bigger payoff, which comes if they do a good job of growing the company and making it more valuable.

Since most of the directors are not drawing a salary, it is in their best interest to increase and keep increasing the company's value. Their personal interest is the same as the shareholders', which is an ever-increasing price per share. The same is true for many of the company's officers. They may draw a small salary but are really more interested in the price per share going up.

The founders are very, very important to the success of a startup because their reputation and expertise give credibility, confidence, momentum, and legitimacy to a project that often exists only on paper. Once the company is public and successful, some of the founders may resign, taking their stock with them. A new management team replaces them, and the founders move on to another startup, repeating the process.

History of EZ Energy

The following is a sequence of events that occurred after the company was founded:

1. Front money investors put up $25,000 (U.S.) for 100,000 shares, or 25 cents per share. At this stage, the company had a tentative plan but owned no exploration leases. There were no assets. Front money investors invested in management.

2. The shares currently trade in range between $2.00 and $2.35 (Canadian) per share.

3. Therefore, the front money investors' block of 100,000 shares is currently worth $200,000 to $235,000 (Canadian)—$160,000 to $170,000 (U.S.). The directors' job now is to keep increasing the value of the company and its share price by bringing to market the oil it has found, drilling more wells, and finding more oil reserves. On paper, the front money investors have made about $140,000 on their $25,000 investment. They have been in the deal for five years, so their annual rate of return would be 45% if they could sell their shares.

4. The problem for the investors is that the company is small and the shares are very thinly traded. An investor with 100,000 shares would be hard pressed to sell 100,000 shares all at once without seriously depressing the price of the stock. So, the valuation of the entire block of stock is in many ways a paper valuation at this time.

If things go as planned, the company will grow and more people will begin to follow the company and the stock. Buying and selling larger blocks of these shares should then become easier. It is safe to say that due to the good news of the discoveries, most large-block investors are holding on to their shares rather than selling.

Why a Canadian Exchange?

When I first began working with Peter, I asked him why he used the Canadian exchanges rather than the more well-known NASDAQ or Wall Street. In America, the Canadian exchanges are often treated as the Rodney Dangerfields of the North American Securities industry. Yet, Peter uses the Canadian exchanges because:

1. The Canadian exchanges are the world leaders for financing small natural-resource companies. Peter uses them because he primarily develops these types of companies. Peter is like Warren Buffet, who tends to stay with businesses he understands. "I understand oil and gas, silver and gold," Peter says. "I understand natural resources and precious metals." If Peter were to develop a technology company, he would probably list it on an American exchange.

2. NASDAQ and Wall Street have gotten too big for a small company to gain any attention there. Peter said, "When I started in this business in the 1950s, a small company could gain some attention from the brokers on the major exchanges. Today, Internet companies, many without any earnings, are commanding more money than many larger well-known Industrial Age companies. Hence, most larger brokerage houses are not very interested in small companies that need to raise only a few million dollars. Brokerage houses in America are interested primarily in offerings of $100 million or more.

3. The Canadian exchanges let the small entrepreneurs stay in the business. I think Peter uses Canadian exchanges mainly because he is retired. He often says, "I don't need the money, so I don't need to build a big company to make a big score. I just enjoy the game; it keeps me active, and where else can my friends get into an IPO play for only $25,000 for 100,000 shares of stock? I do this because it's still fun, I love the challenges, and the money can be rewarding. I love starting companies, taking them public, and watching them grow. I also love having my friends and their families become rich."

4. Peter offers a word of caution. "Just because the Canadian exchanges are small does not mean that anyone can play their game. Some of the Canadian exchanges have gained a shaky reputation due to past transactions. To work with these exchanges, a person

should be very familiar with the ins and outs of taking a company public."

The good news is that the Canadian system of stock exchanges appears to be tightening up on regulations, which are being enforced more closely. In a few years, I think the Canadian exchanges will grow as more and more small companies from all over the world look to the smaller exchanges to raise the capital they need.

Beware of the stock promoter: In the few years I have been actively involved in this business, I have come across three individuals who had the right credentials as well as the right alphabets after their name, told a great story, raised tens of millions of dollars, and had absolutely no idea how to start a business and build one from scratch. For several years, such people fly around in first class or on private jets, stay at the best hotels, put on lavish dinner parties, drink the best wines, and live high on the hog on their investors' money. The company soon dies because there is no actual development. The cash flow has all been going out. These people then go on to start another company and do it all over again. How do you spot a sincere entrepreneur from a big-spending dreamer? That I do not know. Two of the three sure had me fooled until their companies folded. The best advice I can give is to ask for a past track record, check references, and let your sixth sense or intuition be your guide.

5. If a small company grows and prospers, it can later move from a small exchange to a bigger exchange such as NASDAQ or NYSE due to its success. Companies that make the move from a Canadian exchange to an American exchange average a substantial increase in the valuation of the company (sometimes over 200%).

Most of today's big name companies started out as small companies that were unknown. In 1989, Microsoft was a small company whose stock sold for $6 a share. That same stock has since split eight times. In 1991, Cisco stock was just $3 a share, which was eight splits ago. These companies used their investors' money wisely and grew into major powerhouses in the world economy.

Sharon's Notes

The entry requirements of the major stock markets in the United States have made the IPO a difficult process for most businesses. As described in the *Ernst & Young Guide to Taking Your Company Public*, The New York Stock Exchange requires a company to have net tangible assets of $18 million and pre-tax income of $2,500,000. The

American Stock Exchange requires a stockholders' equity of $4 million and a market value of the IPO to be a minimum of $3 million. And the NASDAQ National Market requires net tangible assets of at least $4 million and a market value of the IPO to be a minimum of $3 million.

In addition, it has been estimated that the IPO process can cost $400,000 to $500,000 for one of these major exchanges. These costs include the registration fees as well as the fees paid to legal counsel, accountants and underwriters.

Many small to medium companies that cannot meet these qualifications look for "reverse merger" opportunities, which allow them to merge with an existing public company. Through that process, the company can become a publicly traded company by taking control of the newly combined public company.

Companies may also look to other foreign exchanges, like the Canadian exchange, where the entry requirements are not as severe.

Who Buys Canadian?

During one of my talks on investing in Australia two years ago, a member of the audience questioned my sanity at investing in precious metals and oil. He asked, "If everyone else is in high-tech and Internet stocks, why are you working on the dogs of the economy?"

I explained that it is always less expensive to be a contrarian investor, which is an investor who seeks out-of-favor or out-of-cycle stocks. "A few years ago," I said, "when everyone was into gold, silver, and oil, the prices of the exploration leases that make up these startups were very high. It was very difficult to find a deal at a good price. Now that the prices of oil, gold, and silver are down, finding good properties is easy and people are more willing to negotiate because these commodities are out of favor."

The price of oil has begun to rise, making the shares in our oil company much more valuable. Also, during this period, Buffet announced that he was taking a sizeable position in silver. In February 1998, the billionaire investor disclosed that he had acquired 130 million ounces of silver and stored it in a warehouse in London. On September 30, 1999, *Canadian Business* ran an article indicating that the world's richest man, Gates, had made a buy in silver, acquiring a 10.3% stake for $12 million (U.S.) of a Canadian silver company listed on the Vancouver Stock Exchange. Gates had been quietly acquiring shares in the company since February 1999. When this announcement went out to our investors, the news was welcome relief for their years of trust and confidence.

You Don't Always Hit Homeruns

Not all startup companies do as well as EZ Energy. Some never get off the ground even after going public, and the investors lose most if not all of their front money. Investors therefore need to be accredited, and they are warned about the "all or nothing" type of investments we bring to market.

As one of Peter's partners, I now speak to potential investors about becoming front money investors in new companies. I explain the risks to potential investors before I discuss the business, the people involved, or the rewards. I often start my presentation by saying, "The investment I am about to talk about is a very high-risk speculative investment, offered primarily to individuals who meet the requirements of an accredited investor." If a person does not know the requirements for being an accredited investor, I explain the guidelines as laid out by the SEC. I also stress the possibility that they can lose all of their invested money, repeating that statement several times. If they are still interested, I go on to explain that any money placed with us should never be more than 10% of their total investment capital. Then and only then, if they are still interested, do I go on to explain the investment, the risks, the team, and the possible rewards.

At the end of my presentation, I ask for questions. After all the questions have been answered, I again reiterate the risks. I end by saying, "If your money is lost, all I can offer you is the first opportunity to invest in our next business." By this time, most people are fully aware of the risks, and I would say that 90% decide not to invest with us. We give the 10% that are still interested more information as well as more time to think things over and to back out if they desire.

I suspect that many of today's high-flying Internet IPOs will come crashing down in the next few years and investors will lose millions, if not billions, of dollars. Although the Internet does provide a tremendous new frontier, the forces of economics allow only a few of the pioneering companies to be winners. So regardless of if the company going public is a gold-mining company, a plumbing-supply company, or an Internet company, the forces of the public market still have much of the control.

A Great Education

Deciding to fly to Peru has turned out to be a great decision for me. I have learned as much from being Peter's student and partner as I did from my rich dad. After I put in about a year and a half as an apprentice to Peter and his team, he offered me a partnership in his private venture-capital company.

Since 1996, I have gained the experience of a lifetime watching EZ

Energy Company go public and develop into a viable company that someday may become a major oil company. I have not only become a wiser businessperson because of my association, but I have also learned much about how stock markets work. One of my policies is to invest five years in the learning process—and so far I have spent four in this phase. At this time, I have still not made any real money—at least not money I can put in my pocket. My gains have been all paper gains, yet the business and investment education has been priceless. Maybe someday in the future I will build a company to take public on an American exchange.

Future IPOs

Currently, Peter and his private venture-capital team in which I am a partner are developing three other companies to bring to the public market: a precious-metals company that secures leases in China, an oil company that secures oil and gas leases in Argentina, and a silver company that acquires leases in Argentina.

The company that has taken the longest to develop is the Chinese precious-metals company. We were doing fine with our negotiations with the Chinese government, and then suddenly, in 1999, a U.S. warplane bombed the Chinese Embassy in Kosovo. They say the maps were not updated. Whatever the reason for the bombing, the incident set our relations back two years. Yet we continue to make steady but slow progress.

When people ask why we take such great risks working in China, we reply, "It will soon be the largest economy in the world. Although the risks are huge, the potential payoff could be staggering."

Investing in China today is like the English investing in America in the 1800s. We are investing in contacts and goodwill. We are well aware of the political differences and the human-rights issues. As a company, we do our best to develop strong relationships and open communications with our contacts in China in the hope that we can be part of the transformation of the American/Chinese relationship. The educational experience has been priceless for me. It is like being a part of history. Sometimes, it almost feels like being on the same boat with Columbus as he set sail for the New World.

It usually takes three to five years to bring a company to the public market. If things go well, we may bring two of the three companies to the public market within the next year. When that happens, I will have achieved my goal of becoming an ultimate investor. It will be my first public company but Peter's number ninety something. So although I have not yet qualified as an ultimate investor, I am closing in on that goal, a goal

I set for myself in 1995.

Given the risk involved, every one of these projects I am currently working on could fail and never go public. And if that happens, the pieces will be picked up and new projects will be started. Our investors know the risks involved and also know that their investment plan is to put a little money in several of these smaller ventures. They also know that they will be called and asked to invest in any new start up we have. All it takes is one project to hit a home run. In investments such as these it is definitely not wise to put all your eggs in one basket. It is because of such risks that the SEC has the minimum requirements for investors in such speculative investments.

The next chapter briefly outlines the basic steps of starting with an idea, building a company, and perhaps eventually taking that company public. Although it has not been an easy process for me, it has been a very exciting one.

The Right of Passage

Taking a company public is the rite of passage for any entrepreneur. It would be like a college sports star being selected to play for a professional team. According to the September 27, 1999 issue of *Fortune*, "If you're acquired, a company validates you. If you go public, the market—the world—validates you."

That is why rich dad called a person who could build a company from scratch, and take it public, an ultimate investor. That title eluded him. Although he invested in several businesses that ultimately did go public, none of the companies he actually started ever did go public. His son Mike took over his business and continued to grow it, but he has never built a company to take public. So to become an ultimate investor will mean that I will have completed rich dad's training process.

Chapter 40

Are You the Next Billionaire?

The 1999 edition of *Forbes'*, richest 400 people states on the cover, "The Billionaire Next Door." That issue has an article titled "A Century of Wealth" and a subtitle that reads, "Where does great wealth come from?" Years ago, oil and steel were the foundations of many American fortunes. Today, it's more a matter of how many eyeballs you command.

According to the article: "If you want to talk about super-rich, you have to set your sights higher: to billionaires, who are being minted faster than ever, using ever more ephemeral products to make their money. It took Rockefeller 25 years of finding, drilling and distributing oil to make his first billion. Last year, Garry Winnick joined the billionaires' club just 18 months after putting his money into Global Crossing, a company that intends to, but has yet to, develop a global fiber optic telecommunications network."

So how long does it take to become super-rich these days? The answer is "not long." That reality becomes even more apparent for someone like me, a member of the Baby Boomer generation, when I look at the ages of the new billionaires. For example, billionaire Jerry Yang was born in 1968—a year before I finished college—and David Filo, his partner, was born in 1966—a year after I entered college. Together, they founded Yahoo! and are now worth over $3 billion each and climbing. At the same time these young people are super-rich, I meet individuals who are wondering if they will have enough money in their retirement plans when they retire in ten years. Talk about a gap between the haves and future have-nots.

I'm Taking My Company Public

In 1999, all I hear and read about are IPOs. There is definitely a mania. As someone who is often asked to invest in other people's businesses, I often hear sales pitches like this: "Invest in my company, and in two years we'll be going public." The other day, a budding future billionaire CEO called me and asked for an opportunity to show me his business plan and offer me the opportunity to invest in his future Internet company. After the presentation, he nodded slowly with a sly cockiness as he said, "And of course you know what will happen to the price of your shares after the IPO." I felt like I was talking to a new car salesman who had just informed me that the car I wanted was the last one of its kind and he was doing me a special favor by letting me have it for the list price.

The IPO mania, also called the "new issues" mania, is back on. Just a little while ago, even Martha Stewart took her company public and became a billionaire. She became a billionaire because she teaches civilized and common-sense social graces to the masses, people who feel the need to be more civilized and more gracious. I think her service is valuable, but I wonder about the billion dollars of value. Yet if you follow the *Forbes* 400 definition (wealth is dictated by how many eyeballs you command), Martha Stewart qualifies to be a billionaire. She definitely commands many eyeballs.

My concern about all these new tech stock IPOs and internet IPOs is that the 90/10 rule of money is still in control. Too many of these new start ups are started by individuals with very little business experience. I predict that when we look back upon this time in history, we will find that 90% of the new IPOs will have failed and only 10% have survived. Statistics for small business show that in 5 years, 9 out of 10 small businesses have failed. If this statistic holds true for these new IPOs, this mania could put us into the next recession and possible depression. Why? Because millions of average investors will be depressed. Not only will millions lose their investment money, the ripple effect could spread to them not being able to afford their new homes, cars, boats, and planes. This could take down the rest of the economy. There was a joke going around Wall Street after the 1987 crash that went like this. "What is the difference between a seagull and a stock broker?" Answer: "The seagull can still leave a deposit on a BMW."

The Flavor of the Month

I first began working on an IPO back in 1978 in Hawaii. Rich dad wanted me to learn the process of building a company to sell to the public while I was building my nylon and Velcro wallet company. He said, "I've never taken a company public, but I have invested in several businesses that have gone public. I'd like you to learn the process from the gentleman I invest with." The person he introduced me to was Mark, a man similar to my partner Peter. The difference was that Mark was a venture capitalist, or VC, as they say in the trade. I am a Vietnam veteran, so the letters have a different initial meaning to me.

Small businesses came to Mark when they needed venture capital, or money to expand their businesses. Since I needed lots of money to expand, rich dad encouraged me to meet with him and learn from his point of view. It was not a pleasant meeting. Mark was far tougher than my rich dad. He looked at my business plan and my actual financial statements, and listened for about 23 seconds to my glorious plans for the future. Then he began to tear me apart. He told me why I was an idiot, a fool, and completely out of my league. He told me that I should never have quit my daytime job and that I was lucky my rich dad was his client. Otherwise, he would never have wasted any time on someone as incompetent as me. He then told me how much he thought my business was worth, how much money he could raise for it, his terms and conditions for the money, and that he would become my new partner with a controlling interest in the company. As I said, the term VC had a very familiar ring to it.

In the business of IPOs, investment bankers, and VCs, there is a sheet of paper known as the "term sheet." It is similar to the sheet of paper that real estate agents call the listing agreement. Simply, a term sheet states the terms and conditions of the sale of your business, just as a listing agreement states the terms and conditions for the sale of your house.

Just as in listing agreements with real estate, a term sheet is different for different people. In real estate, if you're selling just one little house in a bad neighborhood and you want a high price, the terms on the listing agreement will be tough and inflexible. However, if you are a real estate developer with thousands of homes to sell, and the houses are nice, easy to sell, and priced low, the real estate agent is more likely to soften his or her terms in order to get your business. The same is true in the world of the VC. The more successful you are, the better terms you get and vice-versa.

Well, after looking at Mark's term sheet, I felt his terms were too severe. I definitely did not want to give him 52% of my company to end up working for him in the company I started. Those were his terms. I am not blaming Mark and, in retrospect, maybe I should have taken those terms. Given what I know today, and how little I knew back then, if I had been in Mark's position, I would have offered the same terms. I think the only reason he offered me anything was out of respect for my rich dad. I was a new businessperson, and I was successfully incompetent. I say successfully incompetent because I had a growing company but I was not able to manage its growth.

Although Mark was tough, I liked him and he seemed to like me. We agreed to meet regularly, and he agreed to give me free advice as I grew. His advice might have been free but it was always tough. He eventually began to trust me more as my knowledge and understanding of business grew. I even worked with him briefly on an oil company he was bringing to the public market. It was similar to the oil company I am working on today. Working with him on that oil company in 1978, I got my first taste of the excitement that comes from working on an IPO.

During one of my lunches with him, he said something about the IPO business that I never forgot. He said, "The new issues and IPO market is just like any other business. The market is always looking for the flavor of the month."

Mark was saying that, at certain times, the stock market favors certain businesses more than others. He went on to say, "If you want to become very rich, part of your strategy as a business owner is to be building the company the market wants, before the market wants it."

Mark went on to explain that history makes famous the pioneer who has the business that is the flavor of the month. He said that inventions such as television created new millionaires just as oil and cars made billionaires at the start of this century. Mark's concept of the progression of wealth is in line with that seen in this abbreviated list from *Forbes* magazine:

1. 1900—Andrew Carnegie made his fortunes in steel—$475 million
2. 1910—John D. Rockefeller became a billionaire in oil—$1.4 billion
3. 1920—Henry Ford became a billionaire in the auto industry—
   $1 billion
4. 1930—John Dorrance became a millionaire condensing
   soup into a can (Campbell's Soup)—$115 million
5. 1940—Howard Hughes became a billionaire with military aircraft
   contracts, tools, and movies—$1.5 billion
6. 1950—Arthur Davis became a millionaire in aluminum—
   $400 million
7. 1960—H. Ross Perot founded EDS (1962)—$3.8 billion
8. 1970—Sam Walton took retailing giant Wal-Mart
   public (1970)—$22 billion

9. 1980—Ron Perelman made his fortune as a Wall Street deal
maker—$3.8 billion

10. 1990—Jerry Yang co-founded Yahoo!—$3.7 billion

Obsolete at 35

I did not work with Mark after 1978. As he predicted, my business
success had begun to sour and I had massive internal problems in my
company. I therefore had to put all my attention into my business rather
than spend time trying to take someone else's business public. However, I
never forgot his lesson on businesses being the flavor of the month. As I
plod along continuing to gain my fundamental business experience, I often
wonder what the next business flavor of the month will be.

In 1985, I stopped by the Marine Base at Camp Pendelton, California,
where I had been stationed in 1971 just before going to Vietnam. My friend
and fellow pilot, James Treadwell was now the commanding officer of the
squadron on the base. Kim and I were shown around the squadron where
Jim and I had been new pilots 14 years earlier. Walking on to the flight
line, Jim showed Kim an aircraft that looked like the ones he and I flew in
Vietnam. Opening up the cockpit, he said, "You and I are now obsolete.
We are not able to fly these aircraft."

He said that because the instruments and controls were now fully
electronic and video oriented. Jim continued, saying, "These new pilots
grew up in video arcades. You and I grew up on pinball machines and
pool tables. Our brains are not the same as theirs. That is why they fly
and I sit behind a desk. I am obsolete as a pilot."

I remember that day clearly because I too felt obsolete then. I felt old
and out of date at age 37. I remember thinking that my own dad was
obsolete by age 50 and here I was obsolete by age 37. On that day, I fully
realized how fast things were changing. I also realized that if I did not
change myself as rapidly, I would be left further and further behind.

Today, I work with Peter, continuing my education in the IPO and VC
business. I am making paper money because I am acquiring paper assets.
However, the most important thing I am gaining is experience in capital
markets. Even though I work on oil, gas, and precious-metal companies—
industries that were the flavor of the month 20 to 30 years ago—my mind
continues to race ahead and wonder what the next frontier in business will
become. I wonder what the next flavor of the month will be and if I will
be part of that next explosion of wealth. Who knows? I am 52 today;
Colonel Sanders was 66 when he started. My goal is still to become a
billionaire in my lifetime. Maybe I'll get there and maybe I won't, but I am
working every day towards that goal. Becoming a billionaire is quite

possible today—if you have the right plan. So I'm not giving up, and I have no plans on becoming poor or becoming more obsolete. As rich dad said, "It's the first million that was the hardest." If that is the case, then the first billion could be the second hardest task I take on.

Are You the Next Billionaire?

For those of you who may have similar ambitions and aspirations, I offer the following guidelines on taking your company public. The information comes generously from my partner Peter, a person who has taken almost a hundred companies public.

Although there is a tremendous amount to learn, these guidelines will help you get started.

Why Take a Company Public?

Peter lists six primary reasons to do so:

1. You need more money. This is one of the main reasons you take a company public. In this case, you might have an established profitable company and need capital to grow. You have already been to your banker and have raised some funds through private placements and your VC, but now you need really big money from an investment banker.

2. Your company—an Internet company, for example—is new, and you need massive amounts of money to gain market share. The market gives you the money, although your company is unprofitable today because the market is investing in your future earnings.

3. Many times, a company will use its own company stock to acquire other companies. It is what rich dad called "printing your own money." In the corporate world, it is called "mergers and acquisitions."

4. You want to sell your company without giving up control. In a private company, the owner all too often gives up control or gains a new partner who wants to tell him how to run the business when raising capital. By getting the money from the public market, the owner gains cash by selling yet maintains control of the business. Most shareholders have very little power to influence the operations of the company they are invested in.

5. Estate reasons. Ford Motor Company went public because the family had many heirs but no liquidity. By selling a part of the company to the public, it raised the cash the family needed for the heirs. It is interesting how often a private company will use this strategy.

6. To get rich and have cash to invest elsewhere. Building a business

is much like building an apartment house and selling it. When you are building a business for sale through a public offering, however, only a part of the asset is broken off; it is broken into millions of pieces and sold to millions of people. The builder may therefore still own most of the asset, may still maintain control, and may generate a lot of cash by selling it to millions of buyers (instead of just one buyer). Talk about good things coming in small packages.

Sharon's Note

There are restrictions that apply to the major shareholders and officers in a company issuing an IPO. While their holdings in the company may increase dramatically in value as a result of the IPO they are severely regulated when selling any of their shares. Their stock is usually called "restricted" which means they have agreed not to sell it for a pre-determined amount of time.

A shareholder wanting to "cash out" might be better served selling the company, or merging into another company with free-trading shares as opposed to using an IPO.

Additional Points to Consider

Peter offers these additional considerations to keep in mind before you go public:

1. Who on the team has run a business? There is a big difference between running a business and dreaming of a new product or a new business. Has the person handled payroll, employees, tax issues, legal issues, contracts, negotiations, product development, cash flow management, raising capital, etc.?
   You may notice that much of what Peter thinks is important is found on rich dad's B-I Triangle. Therefore, the core of the question is: Are you (or someone on the team) successful at managing the entire B-I Triangle?
2. How much of the company do you want to sell? This is where term sheets come in.
   Another point I brought up with Peter is that in my three years of working with him, I noticed that he always knows his goal for a company before he starts the company. He knows before he starts that his goal is to sell the company on the public market. He may not know how he is going to achieve his goal, but the goal is set. I mention this because so many business owners start a business without a concrete goal in mind for the end of the business. Many business owners start a business because they think the business is

a good idea, but they have no plan on how to get out of the business. Fundamental to any good investor is an exit strategy. The same is true for an entrepreneur who is considering building a business. Before you build it, have a solid plan on how you're going to get out of it.

Before you build a business, you might want to consider some of these issues:

    a. Are you going to sell it, keep it, or pass it on to heirs?

    b. If you are going to sell it, are you going to sell it privately or publicly?

        i. Selling a company privately can be as difficult as selling it publicly.

        ii. Finding a qualified buyer can be difficult.

        iii. Financing for the business may be difficult to come by.

        iv. You may get it back if the new owner cannot pay you or mismanages it.

3. Does the prospective public company have a well-written and well-thought-through business plan? This plan should include descriptions of:

    a. The team and team's experience

    b. Financial statements

        i. The standard is three years of audited financials.

    c. Cash flow projections

        i. I recommend three years of very conservative cash flow projections.

Peter states that investment bankers dislike CEOs and entrepreneurs who puff up their projections for future earnings. Peter also states that Bill Gates of Microsoft often understates its earning projections. That is an excellent strategy for keeping the price of the stock strong. When CEOs exaggerate and earnings expectations are not met, the price of their stock often falls and investors lose confidence in the company.

4. Who is the market, how big is the market, and how much growth is possible for the company's products into the market?

While there is a market for your products, there is another market for the shares in your business. At different times, certain types of companies are more attractive to stock buyers than other companies. As I write, technology and Internet companies are the flavors of the month.

When a person has a public company, it is often said that it is like having two companies instead of one. One company is for your regular customers, and one is for your investors.

5. Who is on your board of directors or advisory board? The market runs on confidence. If the company has a strong and respected board of directors or advisors, the market has more confidence in the future success of the business.

Peter advises, "If someone comes to you and says, 'I'm going to take my company public,' ask that person, 'Who on your team has taken a company public and how many companies has he or she taken public?' If that person cannot answer that question, ask him or her to come back with the answer. Most never come back."

6. Does the company own something proprietary? A business should own or control something that another company does not. It could be a patent on a new product or drug, a lease of ground in an oil field, or a trademark such as Starbucks or McDonald's. Even people who are owners and respected experts in their field can be considered assets. Examples of people being assets are Martha Stewart, Steven Jobs when he started his new company (Apple Computer), and Steven Spielberg when he formed his new production company. People invested in these people because of their past success and future potential.

7. Does the company have a great story to tell? I am sure Christopher Columbus must have told a great story to his underwriters, the king and queen of Spain, before they raised the capital for him to sail off to the ends of the earth. A great story must interest, excite, and cause people to look into the future and dream a little. There should also be integrity behind the story, because our jails are filled with great storytellers who have no integrity.

8. Do those involved with the company have passion? This is the most important thing that Peter looks for. He says that the first and last thing he looks for in any business is the passion of the owner, the leaders, and the team. Peter says, "Without passion, the best business, the best plan, and the best people will not become successful."

Here is an excerpt from *Fortune* magazine's article on the 40 richest people under 40:

The MBAs don't fit into the (Silicon) Valley scene. MBAs are traditionally risk-averse. The reason most people go to business school is to ensure getting a six-figure job after graduation. Valley veterans look at B-school people and don't see the fire in the belly they themselves had when they were romantic renegades. MBAs look at Silicon Valley and see something far different from what they were taught in business school. Michael Levine joined eBay after graduating from Berkeley's Haas School. The former investment banker does not speak with the same passion displayed by hard-core entrepreneurs. He also works shorter hours than most—60 per week instead of the customary 80. "I'd love it if in ten to 15 years I had $10 million to $15 million, well invested," he told me. "But I'd like to have a life. I don't know. Maybe I'm not there yet."

Rich dad would say that he was definitely not there yet. Rich dad often cautioned me to be aware of the difference between successful corporate people and successful entrepreneurs. He would say, "There is a difference between a person who climbs the corporate ladder and someone who is building his own corporate ladder. The difference is in the view when you look up the ladder. One sees the big blue sky and the other sees—well, you know that saying: 'If you're not the lead dog, the view is always the same.'"

How Do You Raise Money?

Peter discusses four sources of money:

1. **Friends and family.** These people love you and will often give you money blindly. He does not recommend this method of raising money. Both Peter and my rich dad have often said, "Don't give your children money. It keeps them weak and needy. Teach them how to raise money instead."

Rich dad took the issue of money one step further. As you may recall, he did not pay his son and me a salary for working for him. He said, "Paying people to do work is training them to think like employees." Instead, he trained us to look for business opportunities and to create a business out of that opportunity. You may recall the comic book story in *Rich Dad Poor Dad*. I continue to do the same thing today. I look around for opportunities to build a business, while others look for high-paying jobs.

Rich dad did not make being an employee wrong. He loved his employees. He was just training his son and me to think differently and to be aware of the differences between a business owner and other positions. He wanted us to have more choices as we grew older rather than fewer.

We created the educational board game *CASHFLOW for Kids* for parents who want to give their kids more financial choices and keep them from being trapped in debt as soon as they leave home. In addition, it was created for parents who may suspect that their children could be the next Bill Gates of Microsoft or the next Anita Roddick of the Body Shop. The game provides an early financial education on cash flow management that every entrepreneur needs. Most small businesses fail because of poor cash flow management. *CASHFLOW for Kids* will teach your children the skill of cash flow management before they leave home.

2. **Angels.** Angels are rich individuals who have a passion to help new entrepreneurs. Most major cities have angel groups that support budding new entrepreneurs financially as well as provide advice on how to become rich, young entrepreneurs.

Angels realize that a city with growing young businesses is a growing city. Thriving entrepreneurial spirit in a city will keep the city thriving as well. These angels provide a vital service for any city of any size. It is now possible with computers and the Internet for even the most remote towns to bring the entrepreneur's spirit to life.

Many young people leave small towns to look for great job opportunities in a bigger city. I think that this loss of smart young talent is caused by our schools teaching young people to look for jobs. If our young people were taught to create businesses, many small towns could continue to thrive because they could electronically hook into the rest of the world. Groups of private citizens operating as angel groups could do wonders to revitalize small towns everywhere.

When you look at what Bill Gates did for Seattle; what Michael Dell did for Austin, Texas; and what Alan Bond did for Freemantle, Western Australia, you can see the power of entrepreneurial spirit. Entrepreneurs and angels both play important roles in the vitality of a city.

3. **Private investors.** People who invest in private companies are called private investors. These accredited investors are hopefully more sophisticated than the average investor. They stand to gain—

as well as lose—the most. Therefore, it is recommended to get both financial education and business experience before investing large sums of money into private companies.

4. **Public investors.** People who invest through publicly traded shares of public companies are called public investors. This is the mass market for securities. Because these investments are marketed to the masses, they generally come under great scrutiny from agencies such as the Securities and Exchange Commission (SEC). Securities traded here are generally less risky than investments done privately. Yet, when it comes to investing, there is always risk. This may seem to contradict what I said earlier about having more control, and therefore less risk, as an insider. Please remember, however, that a private investor is not always in control. The SEC requires strict compliance with reporting and disclosure requirements to reduce the risk to a public investor who is definitely not in control of the investment.

Peter's Recommendations

As I was interviewing Peter on the main points of taking a company public, I asked him what he would recommend for a person who wanted to learn to raise substantial sums of capital. He said: "I recommend that a person become familiar with the following sources of funding if they want to take a company public," he said. They are:

1. **Private placement memorandums (PPMs).** These should be the start of your formal capital-raising activities. They are sort of a do-it-yourself way of raising money. A PPM is a way for you to dictate the terms you want, and hopefully the investor will be interested.

Peter strongly recommends that you begin this process by hiring a corporate attorney who specializes in securities. This is where your formal education begins if you are serious about starting small and getting big. It begins with paying for advice from the attorney and hopefully following that advice. If you do not like the advice, it is best to find a new attorney.

Most attorneys will give you a free consultation, or you can invite them to lunch. This type of professional advisor is vital to your team at the beginning and as you get bigger. I personally have learned the hard way by trying to do such things on my own to save a few dollars. Those few dollars saved have cost me fortunes in the long run.

2. **Venture Capitalists (VCs).** They, like my friend Mark, are in the business of providing capital. People usually go to VCs after they have exhausted personal funds, the money of family and friends, and their banker's money. Peter says, "VCs often cut a tough deal, yet if they are good, they will earn their money."

A VC will often become a partner and help you get your company into shape to move to the next level of financing. In other words, just as a person may go to a gym and hire a personal trainer to get his or her body into shape and become more attractive, a VC may act as a personal trainer who gets your business into financial shape so that it will be attractive to other investors.

3. **Investment bankers.** They are generally where you go when you are ready to sell your company to the public market. Investment bankers often raise money for IPOs and for secondary offerings. A secondary offering is a public offering of shares of a company that has already raised capital through an initial offering to the public. When you look in financial papers such as *The Wall Street Journal*, many of the large ads are from investment bankers informing the market about offerings they have sponsored.

Sharon's Notes

There is another type of funding called mezzanine financing, sometimes referred to as bridge funding. A company usually looks for this kind of funding when it is past its early stages of development but not quite ready for an IPO.

An Important First Step

If you are ready to try your hand at raising capital for your business, you may want to start with a PPM. Peter recommends starting with this for these reasons:

1. You begin to interview and talk to corporate lawyers who specialize in this area. Interview several of them. Your education and knowledge will increase with each interview. Ask them about some of their failures as well as their successes.

2. You begin to learn about the different kinds of offerings you can make and how to structure them legally. In other words, not all offerings are equal. Different offerings are designed to fill different needs.

3. You begin to place a value on your business and develop the terms you want when you sell the business.

4. You begin formally talking to potential investors as well as get to practice the art and science of raising capital. First, you may need to overcome your fear of asking. Second, you may need to get over your fear of criticism. Third, you get to learn how to handle rejection or phone calls that are not returned.

Peter offers this advice: "I have seen individuals give the best presentation on their investment but fail to pick up the check at the end. The one thing an entrepreneur needs to do is learn how to pick up the check. If you cannot do that, then take along a partner who can."

Peter also says the same thing my rich dad said: "If you want to be in this business, you must know how to sell. Selling is the most important skill you can learn and continue to improve. Raising capital is selling a different product to a different audience."

People are not successful financially mainly because they cannot sell. They cannot sell because they lack self-confidence, they are afraid of rejection, and they cannot ask for the order. If you are serious about being an entrepreneur and need more sales and confidence development, I strongly recommend finding a network marketing company with a good training program, stick with it for at least five years, and learn to be a confident salesperson. A successful salesperson is not afraid of approaching people, not afraid of being criticized or rejected, and not afraid of asking for the check.

Even today, I continue to work on overcoming my fear of rejection, improving my ability to handle disappointment, and finding ways of improving my bouts with low self-esteem. I have noticed a direct correlation between my ability to handle those obstacles in my life and my wealth. In other words, if those obstacles appear overwhelming, my income goes down. If I overcome those obstacles, which is a constant process, my income goes up.

How to Find Someone Like Peter or Mark to Advise You

After you have gained some fundamental business experience and have achieved a degree of success—and you think you are ready to bring your business to market—you will need specialized advice. The advice and guidance I received from Peter, an investment banker, and Mark, a VC, has been priceless. That advice has created worlds of possibilities that did not exist for me before.

When you are ready, get *Standard & Poor's Security Dealers*, published by McGraw Hill. You can find it in most bookstores or your local library. This book lists security dealers by state. Get the book and find a person who would be willing to listen to your ideas and your business. Not all are willing to give free advice, but some are. Most are busy and do not have time for hand holding if you are not ready. I therefore suggest getting some real-life business experience and having success under your belt before finding one who would be willing to be part of your team.

So Are You the Next Billionaire?

Only one person can answer this question: you. With the right team, the right leader, and a bold and innovative new product, anything is possible. The technology is already in place, or about to be developed soon.

Right after I knew that achieving my goal of making my first $1 million was possible, I began thinking about setting the next goal. I knew I could go on to make $10 million doing things much the same way. However, $1 billion would require new skills and a whole new way of thinking. That is why I set the goal despite continuing to come up against much personal self-doubt. Once I had the nerve to set the goal, I began to learn how others had made it. If I had not set the goal, I would not have thought it a remote possibility, and I would not have come across books and articles about how so many people are achieving that goal.

Several years ago, when I was deeply in debt, I thought becoming a millionaire was impossible. Therefore, in retrospect, I do not think actually achieving the goal is as important as writing down the goal and then going for it. Once I committed to the goal, my mind seemed to find the ways my goal could be possible. If I had said the goal of becoming a millionaire was impossible, I believe it would have become a self-fulfilling prophecy.

After I set the goal to become a billionaire, I was plagued with self-doubt. However, my mind began to show me ways it was possible. As I focus on the goal, I continue to see how becoming a billionaire could be possible for me. I often repeat this saying to myself: "If you think you can, you can; if you think you can't, you can't. Either way you're right." I don't know who the author is, but I thank that person for thinking it.

Why It Is Possible to Be a Billionaire?

Once I set my goal to become a billionaire, I began to find reasons you can become a billionaire today more easily than ever before. They are:

1. With just a telephone line, the Internet is making a world of

customers available to most of us.

2. The Internet is creating more business beyond the Internet. Just as Henry Ford created more business as a ripple effect of mass producing cars, the Internet will magnify its effect. The Internet makes it possible for 6 billion of us to each become a Henry Ford or Bill Gates.

3. In the past, the rich and the powerful controlled the media. With technological changes yet to come, the Internet is almost like each of us having the power of owning our own radio and television stations.

4. New inventions breed more new inventions. An explosion of new technology will make other areas of our lives better. Each new technological change will allow more people to develop more new and innovative products.

5. As more people become more prosperous, they will want to invest more and more money into new startup businesses, not only to help the new business but also to share in the profits. Today, it is hard for most people to grasp the reality that there are literally tens of billions of dollars looking for new innovative companies to invest in every year.

6. It does not have to be high tech to be a new product. Starbucks made a lot of people rich with just a cup of coffee, and McDonald's became the largest holder of real estate with just a hamburger and fries.

7. The key word is "ephemeral." In my opinion, that word is one of the most important words for anyone who desires to become rich or super-rich. Webster's defines the word as meaning lasting only a day, or lasting only a short time.

One of my teachers, Dr. R. Buckminster Fuller, often used the word "ephemeralization." I understood him to use the word in the context of "the ability to do so much more with so much less." A more common term is the word "leverage," or the ability to do a lot with just a little. Dr. Fuller said that humans were able to provide more and more wealth for more and more people, while using less and less.

In other words, with all these new technological inventions—inventions that actually use very little raw material—each of us can now make a lot of money with very little time and effort.

On the flip side of ephemeral, the people who will make less and less in the future are those who use the most in raw materials and physically work the hardest in the process of earning their money. In other words, the financial future belongs to those who do the most with the least effort.

So What Is My Plan to Become a Billionaire?

The answer is found in the word "ephemeral." To become a billionaire, I need to provide a lot for many, for very little. I need to find an area of business that today is fat, bloated, and inefficient, an area where people are dissatisfied with the current system and whose products need improving. The industry I have the most opportunity in is the biggest industry of all: education. If you take a moment and think about all the money that is spent on education and training, the dollar amount will stagger you. This goes beyond counting the money for public schools, colleges, etc. When you look at the amount of education that goes on in business, the military, homes, and professional seminars, the dollar amount is the biggest of all. Yet, education is the one industry that has remained the most mired in the past. Education as we know it is obsolete, expensive, and ready for change.

Earlier this year, a friend of mine, Dan Osborne, an international foreign exchange trader, sent me an article from *The Economists'* website. The following are excerpts from that article:

> Michael Milken, the junk-bond king who once earned $500 million in a single year, is now building one of the world's biggest education companies, Knowledge Universe. Kohlberg, Kravis and Roberts, a buyout firm that strikes fear into managers the world over, also owns an education company called Kindercare. In Wall Street firms, analysts have taken to issuing breathless reports making such assertions as the education industry is undergoing a paradigm shift toward privatization and rationalization.
>
> Why is everyone suddenly so excited? Because of the parallels they see between education and healthcare. Twenty-five years ago, healthcare was mostly stuck in the public and voluntary sectors. Today it is a multi-billion-dollar, largely private industry. A lot of rich people, not just Mr. Milken and Henry Kravis, but also Warren Buffett, Paul Allen, John Doerr, and Sam Zell, are all betting that education is moving in the same direction. Companies from a range of conventional industries are investing in the business, including Sun, Microsoft, Oracle, Apple, Sony, Harcourt General, and the Washington Post Group.
>
> The U.S. government says that the country spends a total of $635 billion a year on education, more than it devotes to pensions

or defense, and predicts that spending per pupil will rise by 40% over the next decade. Private companies currently have only 13% of the market, mostly in the area of training, and most of them are mom-and-pop companies, ripe for consolidation. International Data Corporation, a trends consultancy, reckons that this share will expand to 25% over the next two decades.

The article continues by saying:
America's public schools are increasingly frustrating parents and falling behind international standards. America spends more of its GDP on education than most countries, yet it gets mediocre results. Children in Asia and Europe often trounce their American counterparts in standardized scholastic tests. More than 40% of American ten-year-olds cannot pass a basic reading test; as many as 42 million adults are functionally illiterate. Part of the reason for this dismal performance is that close to half of the $6,500 spent on each child is eaten up by non-instructional services, mostly administration.

Now the barriers between public and private sectors are eroding, allowing entrepreneurs into the state system. The 1,128 (and growing) charter schools are free to experiment with private management without losing public money.

The article also points out:
Not surprisingly, there is plenty of opposition to creeping privatization. The teachers' unions have an impressive record of crushing the challenges to their power...

Don't Go Where You Are Not Wanted

In 1996, my educational board game *CASHFLOW* was submitted to a group of instructors at a prominent university for their feedback. Their verbal reply was, "We do not play games in school, and we are not interested in teaching young people about money. They have more important subjects to learn."

So there is a rule of thumb in business: "Don't go where you're not wanted." In other words, it is easier to make money where you and your products are wanted.

The good news is that more and more schools have been using our games as teaching products in their classrooms. However, the best news was that the public likes our products. Our board games are selling well to private individuals who want to improve their business and financial education.

We knew we had come full circle when in January 2000, Thunderbird, The American Graduate School of International Management, utilized *Rich Dad Poor Dad, CASHFLOW Quadrant,* and the *CASHFLOW* games in its curriculum for the Entrepreneurship Program. This very prestigious university is internationally recognized for its educational programs.

Back to the Plan

I see a great need in the area of money management, business, and investing—subjects that are not taught in school. I predict that in the next few years, there will be a major stock market crash, and the grim reality that many people will not have enough money to retire on and get old with will emerge. I suspect that there will be a tremendous outcry in about ten years for more relevant financial education. Recently, the federal government let the American people know that they should not count solely on Social Security or Medicare when they retire. Unfortunately, that word is too late for millions of people, especially since the school system has never taught them how to manage their money. Sharon, Kim, and I intend to provide that education—both with our current products as well as over the Internet—for a much lower cost than the current school system could deliver it.

Once we have those educational programs ready for delivery over the Internet, we will become a technology and Internet company rather than just the publishing company we are today. Once we can deliver our products in that ephemeral way, the value and multipliers on the value of our company will go up because we will be able to deliver a better product to our international market, more conveniently, and for much less money. In other words, we will be able to do more and more with less and less, which is the key to becoming very, very rich.

So will I ever become a billionaire? I don't know. I am continuing to go for the goal. How will I do it if I do it? I don't know that either. It has yet to be figured out. But I do know this: For years, I grumbled and complained that school never taught me anything about money, business, or becoming rich. I often wondered why they did not teach subjects I could use once I left school rather than teach subjects I knew I would never use. Then one day, someone said to me, "Quit your complaining and do something about it." And today I am. I figured that if I was unhappy about not learning much about money, business, and becoming rich, other people probably had the same complaint.

In closing, Kim, Sharon, and I do not want to compete with the school system. The current school system is designed to teach people to be employees or professionals. We can sell our ephemeral products to those who want what we offer, which is education for people who want to be entrepreneurs and own businesses or invest in business, rather than work in someone else's business. That is our target market, and we see the Internet as the perfect system to reach it without going through the antiquated school system. That is our plan; only time will tell if the three of us will reach our goal.

If you want to be financially free, a multi-millionaire, or maybe even the next billionaire, we want to be your financial-education company.

Chapter 41

Why Do Rich People Go Bankrupt?

I often hear people say, "When I make a lot of money, my money problems will be over." In reality, their new money problems are just beginning. One of the reasons so many newly rich people suddenly go broke is because they use their old money habits to handle new money problems.

In 1977, I started my first big business, which was my nylon and Velcro surfer wallet business. As I said in a previous chapter, the asset created was bigger than the people who created it. A few years later I created another asset that grew rapidly and again the asset got bigger than the people who created it. Again I lost the asset. It took the third business for me to learn what my rich dad had been guiding me to learn.

My poor dad was shocked at my financial ups and downs. He was a loving father but it pained him to see me on top of the world one minute and in the gutter the next. But my rich dad was actually happy for me. He said after my two big creations and disasters, "Most millionaires lose three companies before they win big. It took you only two companies. The average person has never lost a business and that is why 10% of the people control 90% of money."

After my stories about making millions and losing millions, I am often asked an important question, "Why do rich people go bankrupt?" I offer some of the following possibilities, all from personal experience.

Reason #1: People who have grown up without money have no idea how to handle a lot of money. As stated earlier, too much money is often as big a problem as not enough money. If a person is not trained to handle large sums of money or does not have proper financial advisors, then the chances are very strong that they will either stash the money away in the bank or just lose it. As my rich dad said, "Money does not make you rich. In fact, money has the power to make you both rich and poor. There are billions of people each day who prove that fact. Most have some money but they spend it only to get poorer or greater in debt. That is why today there are so many bankruptcies being reported in the best economy in history. The problem again stems from people receiving money and then buying liabilities they think are assets. In the next few years, I am certain that many of today's young or instant millionaires will be in financial struggle because of their lack of money management skills.

Reason #2: When people come into money, the emotional euphoria is like a drug that boosts your spirits. My rich dad said, "When the 'money high' hits, people feel more intelligent, when in fact they are becoming more stupid. They think they own the world and immediately go out and start spending money like King Tut with tombs of gold."

My tax strategist and CPA, Diane Kennedy once said to me, "I have been an advisor to many rich men. Just before they go broke after making a ton of money, they tend to do three things. One, they buy a jet or big boat. Two, they go on safari. And three, they divorce their wife and marry a much younger woman. When I see that happening I begin preparing for the crash." Again, much like reason number one, they buy liabilities or divorce an asset, which then creates a liability, and then they marry a new liability. They now have two or more liabilities.

Reason #3: When you have money certain friends and relatives tend to become closer. The hardest thing for many people is to say "no" to people they love when they ask to borrow money. This has not happened to me, but I have seen many families and friendships break up when one person suddenly becomes rich. As rich dad said, "A very important skill in becoming rich is to develop the ability to say 'no' to yourself and the people you love." The people who come into money and begin buying boats and big houses are not able to say "no" to themselves, let alone their family members. They end up further in debt, just because they suddenly had a lot of money.

Not only do people want to borrow money from you when you have money, banks want to lend you more money. Which is why people say, "Banks lend you money when you don't need it." If things go bad, not only do you have trouble collecting the loans you made to friends and relatives, the banks then have trouble collecting from you.

Reason #4: The person with money suddenly becomes an "investor" with money, but without education and experience. Again, this goes back to rich dad's statement that when people suddenly have money they think their financial IQ went up also, when in fact it has gone down. When a person has money, they suddenly begin receiving phone calls from stockbrokers, real estate brokers, and investment brokers. Rich dad also had a joke about brokers, "The reason they are called 'brokers' is because they are broker than you." My apologies to any "brokers" who are offended, but I think my rich dad's stockbroker is the one who told the joke to him originally.

I had a friend of my family who came into a $350,000 inheritance. In less than 6 months all that money was lost in the stock market, not to the market but to the broker that "churned" the suddenly rich person who thought that money made him more intelligent. For those who do not know what churning means, it is when the broker advises the person to buy and sell regularly, so the broker makes the commission on each buy and sell. This practice is frowned upon and severe fines are levied if brokerage houses find their brokers involved in this practice...yet it does happen.

As stated at the start of this book just because you meet the qualifications of an Accredited Investor, simply a person with money, does not mean you know anything about investing.

In today's heated stock market, many companies are investing as foolishly as individuals are. With so much money in the market, many companies are running around buying other companies they hope are assets. In the industry it is often called M&As, or mergers and acquisitions. The problem is, many of these new acquisitions can become liabilities. Often the big company that bought a small company ends up in financial trouble.

Reason #5: The fear of losing increases. Many times a person with a poor person's outlook on money has lived a life being terrified of being poor. So when the sudden wealth hits, the fear of being poor does not diminish, in fact it increases. As my friend who is a psychologist for professional day traders says, "You get what you fear." That is why so many professional investors have psychologists as part of their team, at least that is why I have one. I have fears like everyone else. As stated earlier, there are many ways to lose money other than through the investment markets.

Reason #6: The person does not know the difference between good expenses and bad expenses. I often receive a phone call from my accountant or tax strategist saying, "You have to buy another piece of real estate." In other words, I have the problem of making too much money and I need to invest more money in something like real estate because my retirement plan cannot take any more money. One of the reasons the rich get richer is because they buy more investments by taking advantage of the tax laws. In essence, money that would have been paid in taxes is used to buy additional assets, which provide a deduction against income, reducing the taxes due, legally.

The tetrahedron illustrated earlier is to me one of the most important diagrams for wealth creation as well as keeping and increasing the wealth created. When I show people the diagram, I am often asked why expenses are part of the structure. The reason is because it is through our expenses that we become richer or poorer, regardless of how much money we make. Rich dad often said, "If you want to know if a person is going to be richer or poorer in the future just look at the expense column of their financial statement." Expenses were very important to, rich dad. He often said, "There are expenses that make you rich and expenses that make your poor. A smart business owner and investor knows which kind of expenses they want and controls those expenses."

"The main reason I create assets is because I can increase my good expenses," rich dad said to me one day. "The average person has mainly bad expenses." This difference in good expenses and bad expenses was one of rich dad's most important reasons for creating assets. He did so because his created assets could buy other assets. As he said to me when I was just a kid walking along the beach looking at the very expensive piece of real estate he had just purchased, "I can't afford this land either. But my business can."

If you understand the tax laws available to the B quadrant, you soon realize that one of the reasons the rich get richer is because the tax laws allow the B quadrant, more than other quadrants, to spend pre-tax dollars, to build, create, or buy other assets. In fact, the tax laws almost require you to buy more investments with pre-tax dollars, which is why I receive those phone calls telling me to buy more real estate or buy another company. The E quadrant on the other hand, must often use after-tax dollars to build, create, or buy other assets.

What to Do with Too Much Money

"If you want to be rich, you must have a plan on how to make a lot of money and you must also have a plan on what to do with that money before you make it. If you do not have a plan on what to do with it before you make it, you will often lose it faster than you made it." One of the reasons he had me study real estate investing was so that I would understand how to invest in real estate before I had a lot of money. Today when my accountant calls and says, "You have too much money. You need to buy more investments," I already know where to move my money, the corporate structures to use, and what to buy with that money. I call my broker and buy more real estate. If I buy paper assets, I often call my financial planner and buy an insurance product, which then buys my stocks, bonds, or mutual funds. In other words, the insurance industry produces special insurance products for rich people who are business owners. When a business buys insurance, it is an expense to the company and it often becomes an asset to the owner with many tax advantages. In other words, when my accountant calls, much of the money is already spent according to a predetermined plan. It is spent as expenses that make the person richer and more secure. That is why a financial advisor and an insurance agent for the rich are very important members of the team.

Over the years, I have seen many people start very profitable businesses and still end up broke. Why, because they did not control their expenses. Instead of spending money to acquire other assets, assets such as real estate or paper assets, they expensed it through frivolous business expenses, or bought bigger homes, nice boats, fast cars, and new friends. Instead of getting financially stronger, they became financially weaker with every dollar they made and then spent.

The Other Side of the Coin

Rich dad often said, "It is through the expense column that the rich person sees the other side of the coin. Most people only see expenses as bad, events that make you poor. When you can see that expenses can make you richer, the other side of the coin begins to appear to you." He also said, "Seeing through the expense column is like going through the looking glass as Alice did in *Alice in Wonderland.* Once Alice went through the looking glass, she saw this bizarre world that in many ways reflected the other side of the looking glass." Both sides of the coin really did not make much sense to me but rich dad said, "If you wanted to be rich, you had to know the hopes, the fears, and the illusions on both sides of the coin."

During one of my meetings with rich dad, he said something that changed my thinking from a poor person to a rich person. Rich dad said to me, "By having a plan to be rich, understanding the tax laws and corporate laws, I can use my expense column to get rich. The average person uses their expense column to become poor. That is one of the biggest and most important reasons why some people get rich and others become poor. If you want to become rich and stay rich, you must have control of your expenses." If you understand this statement you will

RICH DAD'S GUIDE TO INVESTING

understand why rich dad wanted low income and high expenses. That was his way of getting rich. He said, "most people eventually lose their money and go broke because they continue to think like a poor person and poor people want high income and low expenses. If you don't make this switch in your head, you will always live in fear of losing money, trying to be cheap, trying to be frugal, rather than being financially intelligent and becoming richer and richer. Once you can understand why a rich person would want high expenses and low income, you will begin to see the other side of the coin."

A Very Important Point

This last paragraph is one of the most important paragraphs in this book. In fact, this book has been written around this one paragraph. If you do not understand it, I suggest sitting down with a friend who has also read this book and begin a discussion to deepen your understanding of what it says. I do not expect you to necessarily agree with it. It would be good just to begin to understand it. You may begin to understand that there is a world of too much money and you may understand how you can become a part of that world. Rich dad said, "People who do not change their point of view about money in their head, will see only one side of the coin. They will see the side of the coin that only knows a world of not enough money. They may never see the other side of the coin, the side where the world is a world of too much money, even if they do make a lot of money."

By understanding that a world of too much money can exist, understanding a little of the tax laws and corporate laws, and why control of your expenses is so important, you can begin to see an entirely different world, a world very few people ever see. And seeing that world begins in your head. If your mental view can change, then you will begin to understand why rich dad always said, "I use my expenses to get richer and richer and the average person uses their expenses to become poorer and poorer." If you understand that statement you may understand why I think the teaching of financial literacy is important for our school system. It is also why my educational games *CASHFLOW* can help you see a world of money that few people ever see. The financial state is much like the looking glass in *Alice in Wonderland*. In the game *CASHFLOW*, it is via the mastery of the financial statement that the player moves from the Rat Race of life onto the Fast Track of the investment world, the world that begins with the Accredited Investor.

How Can Low Income and High Expenses Be Good?

So as rich dad said, "Money is just an idea." And these last few paragraphs contain some very important ideas. If you understand fully why low income and high expenses is good then move on. If not, please invest some time in discussing this point with someone who has also read this book. This idea is the pivotal point of this book. It also explains why many rich people go broke. So please do your best to understand this point because it makes not much sense to be creative, build an asset, and make a lot of money—only to lose it all. When I studied the 90/10 rule the one thing I discovered is that the 90% who earn the 10% are people who want high income and low expenses. That is why they stay where they are.

A Guide Line

So the question is, "How can low income and high expenses make you rich?" And the answer is found in how the sophisticated investor utilizes the tax laws and corporate laws to bring those expenses back to the income column.

For example:

This is a diagram of what a sophisticated investor is working to do.

This is the Diagram of the 10% Who Make 90%

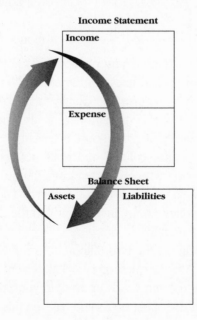

Again the question is, "How can low income and high expenses make you rich?"

If you can begin to understand how and why this is done, then you will begin to see a world of greater and greater financial abundance.

Compare the previous diagram with the following diagram:

This is the Diagram of the 90% Who Make 10%

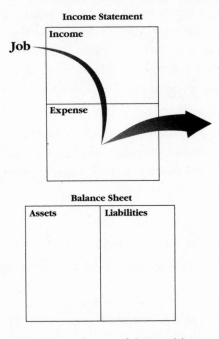

This is the financial diagram of most of the world's population. In other words, the money comes in and goes out the expense column and never comes back in. That is why so many people try to save money, be frugal, and cut back on expenses. This diagram here is also the diagram of the person who will emphatically say, "My house is an asset." Even though the money goes out the expense column and does not return at least not immediately. Or the person who says, "I'm losing money each month but the government gives me a tax break to lose money." They say that rather than say "I'm making money on my investment and the government gives me a tax break to make money."

My rich dad said, "One of the most important controls you can have is found in this question. And the question is, 'What percentage of the money going out your expense column winds up back in your income column in the same month?'" Rich dad spent hours and days on this subject with me. By understanding his point of view I saw a completely different world that most people do not see. I could see a world of ever increasing wealth, unlike people who work hard, earn a lot of money and keep their expenses down. So ask yourself the same question. "What percentage of the money going out your expense column comes back in your income column in the same month?" If you can understand how this is done you should be able to see and create a world of ever increasing wealth. If you are having difficulty understanding this idea, find someone else and discuss how it might be done. If you can begin to understand it, you will begin to understand what a sophisticated investor is doing. I would say it's worth the discussion and why you may want to read and discuss this book often. It really was written to change a person's point of view from the view of not enough money to the view of creating a world of too much money.

What Is the Value of a Network Marketing Business?

When I speak to network marketing companies, I often say to them, "You don't know the value of your network marketing business." I say that because many network marketing businesses only focus on how much money such a business can generate. I often warn them that it's not how much money they make, but much money they can invest with pre-tax dollars that is important. This is what the E quadrant cannot do. To me, that advantage is one of the biggest advantages of a network marketing business. If used properly a network marketing business can make you far richer than merely the residual income the business generates. I have several friends who have made tens of millions of dollars in network marketing and are still broke today. When I speak to the industry, I often remind the leaders of network marketing that a vital part of their job is to not only educate people on how to make a lot of money, it is as important to educate them on how to keep the money they make and it is through their expenses that they will ultimately become rich or poor.

Why Are More Businesses Better than One?

It is not only network marketing people who fail to realize the true value of their business. I have seen entrepreneurs who are good at building a business yet do not realize the true value of that business. The reason this happens is because there is a popular idea going around today that you only build a business to sell it. That is the idea of a business owner who does not know what a sophisticated investor knows about the tax laws and corporate laws. So instead of building a business to buy assets, they often just build the business, sell it, pay the taxes, put the cash in the bank, and start all over again,

I have had several friends who have built businesses just to sell them. Two friends of mine have sold their companies for cash and then lost all that cash in their next business venture. They lost because the 90/10 rule for business survival is still in effect. These two were individuals from the S quadrant who built B quadrant business. They then sold those businesses to people from the B quadrant. The buyers recognized the often-unseen value of a B quadrant business. So the friends who sold their businesses ultimately went broke, even though they had collected several million dollars. The businesses they sold went on to make the new owners even richer.

A sophisticated business owner and investor would do their best to keep the business as long as possible, have it acquire as many stable assets as possible and then trade the business with as small a tax consequence as possible, while keeping as many of the assets as possible. As my rich dad said, "The main reason I build a business is for the assets the business buys me." For many entrepreneurs, the business they build is their only asset because they utilize a single corporation strategy and fail to harness the power of a multi-corporation investment strategy. (Again, to utilize such a strategy requires a team of professional advisors.) This points out that the big advantage the B quadrant has is that the tax laws for that quadrant allow you to spend pre-tax dollars to make you financially richer and in fact, the laws reward you for investing as much money as possible. After all, it is the rich who write the rules.

The Power of Expenses

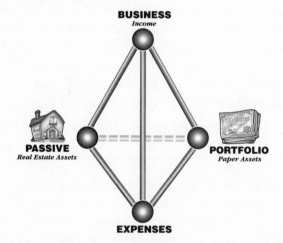

So this is why expenses can be an asset or liability, regardless of how much money you make. One of the reasons 90% of the people only have 10% of the money is because they do not know how to spend the money they make. As rich dad said, "A rich person can take trash and turn it to cash. The rest of the people take cash and turn it to trash."

So what is the answer to the question, "Why do rich people go bankrupt?" "The same reason poor people remain poor and the middle class struggles financially." The reason the rich, the poor, and middle class go broke is because they lose control of their expenses. Instead of using their expenses to make them rich, they use their expenses to make them poor.

Phase Five

Giving It Back

Chapter 42

Are You Prepared to Give Back?

The Tenth Investor Control:
The Control of Giving It Back

Recently a high school classmate of mine, Dan, was passing through town and asked if we could play golf. Dan was always a great golfer and I had not played in months, so I hesitated at first. Realizing that the purpose of the game was to spend time together to renew an old friendship, rather than compete in a round of golf, I agreed to play.

While riding around on the golf cart, being humiliated by Dan's golf game, the conversation turned to what we were doing at this stage of our lives. When I told Dan that I had retired and was building businesses, one to take public and one to be held privately, he became very angry. His anger caused him to accuse me of being greedy, thinking only of myself, and exploiting the poor. After about an hour of trying to keep my cool, I could take no more. Finally I said, "What causes you to think that the rich are greedy."

His reply was, "Because all I see are poor people all day long. I never see rich people doing anything for them." Dan is a legal aid attorney for people who cannot afford an attorney. "The gap between the haves and have nots is bigger than ever and it is not improving. We now have families who have no hope of ever getting out of poverty. They have lost sight of the dream that America was founded on. And guys like you make more and more money. Is that all you can think about? Build businesses and get rich? You've become just as bad as Mike's dad...a greedy rich man who only got richer."

Dan's temper began to calm down as the game continued. Finally at the end of the game we agreed to meet the next day at the hotel's restaurant and I would show him something I was working on.

The next day I showed Dan the game. "What is the game board for?" asked Dan after we were seated at the table.

Showing him the game, I explained my theory that poverty is caused by lack of education. "It is a learned condition," I said. "It is taught at home. Since school doesn't teach you about money, you learn about it at home."

"So what does this game teach?" Dan asked.

"It teaches the vocabulary of financial literacy," I said. "Words are, in my opinion, the most powerful tools or assets we as humans have, because words affect our brain, and our brains create our reality on the world. The problem many people have is that they leave home and school and never learn or understand the vocabulary associated with money...resulting in a lifetime of financial struggle."

Dan studied the colorful game board while the waitress brought us more coffee. "So you plan to end poverty with a board game?" he asked sarcastically.

"No," I chuckled. "I'm not that naive or optimistic. I created this game primarily for people who want to become business owners and investors. Cash flow management is a basic skill necessary for anyone who wants to be rich."

"So you created this game for people who want to be rich, not for the poor?" Dan said, his anger rising again.

Again I chuckled at his emotional reaction. "No, no, no," I said. "I did not create this product to exclude the poor. I'll say it again. I created this game for people who want to be rich, regardless if you are rich or poor today."

The look on Dan's face softened, if only a little.

"Exactly," I said softly. "My products are designed for people who want to be rich," I repeated again. "My products cannot help anyone, regardless of who or what their financial station in life, unless they first want to be rich. My products will not help a rich person or a middle class person unless they too want to become richer."

Dan sat there shaking his head. His anger was getting higher. Finally he said, "You mean I've spent all my life trying to help people and you're saying I can't help them?"

"No. I am not saying that," I said. "I cannot comment on what you do or how effective you are. Besides that is not for me to judge."

"So what are you saying?" Dan asked.

"I'm saying you can't help people unless they truly want to help themselves," I said. "If a person is not interested in becoming rich, my products are worthless."

Dan sat there quietly absorbing the distinction I was attempting to make. "In my world of law and legal aid, I often give advice to people. Many people don't take it," said Dan. "I see them again after a year or two and their situation is the same. They're back in jail or they're brought up again on charges for domestic violence or whatever. Is that what you're getting at? Advice alone does no good unless the people truly want to change the situations in their lives?"

"That is what I am saying," I said. "That is why the best diet and exercise plan will not work unless the person really and truly wants to lose weight. Or why it is often a waste of time and a disturbance to the rest of the class to have a student in the room that is not interested in learning a subject. It is tough to teach anyone who is not interested in learning. And that includes me. For example, I have no interest in learning to wrestle sharks. So you cannot force me to learn. But my golf game is different. I will study hard, practice for hours, and pay big money for lessons, because I want to learn."

Dan sat there nodding his head. "I understand," he said.

"But I did not show you this game for the getting rich aspect," I said. "I want to show you what rich dad taught Mike and me about being generous. About giving money back."

For the next ten minutes I explained Phase 5 of rich dad's plan, pointing out to Dan that it was a big part of rich dad's plan to be generous, to be charitable. I said to Dan as I pointed to the game board, "Mike's dad taught us five distinct phases of wealth and money. Phase five was the responsibility of giving money back, after you made it. Mike's dad strongly believed that to make money and hoard it was a misuse of the power of money."

"So you put Phase 5 of Mike's dad's plan on your game board?" Dan asked a little suspiciously. "Your game board not only teaches people to be rich, but it also teaches people to be generous?"

I nodded my head, "It was part of the plan. A very important part."

Having grown up with Mike and me, Dan knew who rich dad was. He had heard about the investment plan rich dad and I had drawn up after I returned from Vietnam. Dan was aware of what I had gone through to learn to be a business owner and an investor. He had lost his temper when

I spoke of Phases 3 and 4, where I was investing in other business and getting richer. He was now learning about Phase 5.

"As I said, Phase 5 is probably the most important phase of rich dad's plan and I purposely built it into this game," I said.

"So what is Phase 5?" asked Dan. "Show it to me on the game board."

I then pointed to the pinkish colored squares on the "Fast Track" of the board game. The board game consists of two different tracks. One circular track on the inside, known as the "Rat Race" and the outer more rectangular track known as the "Fast Track," which is where the rich invest. "These pink squares are Phase 5," I said, pointing to one of the squares.

"A kids library," Dan read out loud as he read the corner square where my finger was pointing.

I then pointed at another square.

"A research center for cancer," Dan read aloud.

"And so is this square," I said moving my finger and pointing to another square.

"A gift of faith," Dan said reading the line just below where my finger was pointing.

"You mean you built charitable squares into the Fast Track?" asked Dan. "The investment track of the very rich."

Nodding my head I said, "Yes. There are two kinds of dreams on the Fast Track. Dreams for personal indulgence and dreams for creating a better world with your excessive wealth."

Dan shook his head slowly, saying, "You mean Mike's dad taught you and Mike to be charitable as well as rich?"

I nodded my head as I quickly pointed to all the different charitable dreams found on the Fast Track of the game board. "Rich dad said one of the most important controls an investor had was the control over returning most of the money back to society."

"He had a reputation as a rich greedy man," said Dan. "Many people said terrible things about him, about how greedy he was."

"That is what most people thought," I replied. "Yet Mike and I knew differently. The more money he made, the more money he gave away. But he gave it away quietly."

"I did not know that," said Dan. "So his later years were dedicated to giving all the money he amassed back to society."

"Well not all of it," I said. "He wanted to leave some for his children. The point I want to make is that many people have this belief that the rich are greedy. That belief blinds them to the truth or the reality that not all the rich are greedy. If you open your eyes, you will see that many of the very rich have made tremendous financial contributions to society. Look at what

Andrew Carnegie has given back through libraries, Henry Ford through his Ford Foundation and the Rockefellers through the Rockefeller Foundation. My hero, George Soros, the founder of The Quantum Fund, is today dedicating massive amounts of money in the hopes of creating a global society and promoting greater financial understanding amongst nations. But often all we hear about are the nasty things political leaders say about him and his hedge fund.

"John D. Rockefeller not only created his charitable foundation to give away his money, he donated extensively to the University of Chicago, as many rich alumni donate to their schools. Many other ultra rich have founded their own institutions of higher learning just as Stanford founded Stanford University and Duke founded Duke University. The rich have always been very generous to higher education."

"Vanderbilt University was founded by a very rich entrepreneur," added Dan.

"I realize that the rich create jobs and provide goods and services to make life a little better. So now you're telling me that they often give the money back to the society," said Dan.

"That is exactly what I am saying," I replied. "And yet many people can only see what they think is the greedy side of the rich. I know that there are greedy rich people, but so are there greedy poor people."

"So your rich dad gave it back?" Dan repeated.

"Yes," I replied. "Phase 5 made him the happiest of all the phases. Besides being charitable increased his expenses, reduced his income, and took him through the looking glass."

"What?" stammered Dan in confusion. "What looking glass?"

"Never mind," I said. "Just know that being generous made him happy in more ways than one."

"What did he give to?" asked Dan.

"Since his own father died of cancer, rich dad's foundation gave tremendous amounts of money to cancer research. He also built a cancer ward on a small country hospital, so the country people could be closer to their loved ones when they were hospitalized. Being a very religious man, he also built a classroom building for his church so the church could have a larger Sunday school for kids. And he was a patron of the arts, acquiring artwork from many talented artists as well as donating money to the museums. The best thing is that his foundation is so well directed, that even after his death, it will continue to earn and donate money. Even in death he will still do a lot of good for society. The trusts and foundations he set up will be providing money for many worthy causes for years to come."

"He planned to have too much money in life and he planned on having too much money in death," said Dan.

"He definitely had a plan," I replied.

"So your game *CASHFLOW* really does include everything your rich dad taught you. He taught you how to make the money and how to give the money back," said Dan.

"I did my best to include the important things rich dad taught me about money in the game. And the importance of giving back was one of the things he taught me," I replied. "He taught me to control the acquisition of wealth and he taught me how to control the giving it back."

"I wish more people did that," said Dan.

"Oh there will be more people giving more money back," I said. "Just look at this Baby-boomer generation. Many were hippies in the sixties and they are fast becoming multi-millionaires today. In a few years, the revolution they were a part of will be in full force with cash flow. Many of these one-time hippies and others of that generation are very socially responsible people. What they learned from the sixties, their poor college days, will be brought to fruition in the next few years. Their ideals coupled with their wealth will be a powerful financial, political, and social force in the world. I think that they will do the charitable deeds that our government cannot afford to do today. Many rich boomers will be completing socially-responsible deeds they wanted to perform when they were poor...but now they're rich."

"What makes you think they will be generous?" asked Dan.

"Because it is already happening," I replied. "Ted Turner pledged a billion dollars to the U.N. and chided people like Bill Gates and others for not being generous enough. In less than three years, after that challenge, Bill Gates alone has pledged $4 billion to various causes...and Gates is still a young man. Can you imagine how much he will be donating in his later years?"

"But wasn't that because he was on trial with the federal government?" asked Dan. "He's just giving money so he can look good?"

"Well, many of the reporters like to point that out in the articles they write about his generosity. But let me ask you this. How many reporters are giving away $4 billion dollars?" I asked quietly. "The facts are, in 1999 alone, Bill Gates has a full time staff to give away $325 million. How many reporters are giving away $325 million in 1999? So even if it took an encouraging nudge from Ted Turner, the fact remains that he is giving money away. And the fact remains that this baby-boomer generation of wealthy entrepreneurs will be pressuring each other to be generous. It will be very socially un-cool to be rich and not be generous."

"So Mike's dad was a generous man and he taught you and Mike to be generous."

I nodded my head. "And even though many people in town criticized him for being rich, he continued to give quietly. Being generous made financial sense to him as well as giving him pleasure."

"I really did not know that," Dan said quietly and almost reverently, having perceived him differently. "And giving money away made him happy?"

I nodded my head. "In the later years of his life, I saw a peace come over him that I had never seen before. He had done a lot of good during life and he would continue to do good when his life was over. His life was complete."

"He was very proud of both Mike and me," I replied. "He also said he knew I was more like my real dad. He knew I was a teacher and he hoped I would go on to teach others as he had taught me. He wanted me to be both dads...a rich man as well as a teacher."

"And was that it?" asked Dan.

"No," I replied. "He couldn't leave it at that. He was always afraid that I would give up along the way. He was afraid that I would not have the persistence to make my investment plan come true, which would mean my financial dreams would not come true. He was always afraid that I would join the quitters of the world, doing what was easy, rather than doing what was necessary.

"Keep going, keep minding your own business, keep being true to your dreams and all your dreams will come true," I said quietly. "That was the last advice he gave me."

Bringing me back to the present, Dan asked, "So have all your dreams come true?"

"Almost," I replied. "I still want to become the ultimate investor and we have just started our Foundation."

"What Foundation?" he asked.

"When Kim, Sharon and I started CASHFLOW Technologies, Inc., our mission was to 'Elevate the financial well-being of humanity.'"

"That's a pretty aggressive mission," Dan said with his eyebrows raised.

"I can see how you would say that but we accomplish our mission every day. We receive calls, letters, e-mails every day from people who have taken action to improve their financial lives. We have been overwhelmed by the response we have from the people using our products. Every time we hear from someone who has improved their financial well-being, we have accomplished our mission."

"So what about the Foundation?" Dan persisted.

"We created the Foundation for Financial Literacy so we would have a not for profit entity with which to give back. We have been so blessed by our students and customers that we wanted to give back. The Foundation will support other organizations in their efforts to teach financial literacy.

"For example, we have a high school teacher in Indiana teaching *CASHFLOW 101* and *202* to his students. He has been helping us develop a curriculum that other teachers can use in the classroom. This spring he is going to send his high school students into the elementary schools to teach elementary school students using *CASHFLOW for Kids.* In fact, we also have the older kids teaching the younger kids in the Boys and Girls Club in Tucson, Arizona. We are so excited by the concept of 'kids teaching other kids' that we hope to expand the program worldwide. The Foundation can help make that happen."

"That sounds great, Robert. It's nice to see you so energized by giving," Dan said.

"We are still developing the Foundation and its programs. The important thing is to support learning wherever we can. Kim, Sharon and I have been very blessed with success and we want to continue to look for ways to give back through helping others teach financial literacy."

The Foundation for Financial Literacy was organized and will be operated as a nonprofit corporation for charitable and educational purposes within the meaning of Section 501(c)(3) of the Internal Revenue Code of 1986, as amended, to support needy, educational, charitable, religious, and scientific programs and organizations that support financial education. The Foundation welcomes inquiries at:

The Foundation for Financial Literacy
P.O. Box 5870
Scottsdale, AZ 85261-5870
www.richdad.com

CASHFLOW® Technologies, Inc. supports the Foundation, in part, by donating the time of its staff members and providing office space and services to the Foundation, in addition to financial support.

Why It Does Not Take Money to Make Money...Anymore

Recently, while teaching an investment class, I was asked, "What Internet company would you recommend I invest in?"

I replied, "Why invest in someone else's Internet company? Why don't you start your own Internet company and ask people to invest in it?"

As stated earlier in the book, there are many investment books written on how to buy assets. This book has been dedicated to learning how to create assets that buy assets. So why not take the time to consider creating an asset, rather than simply buying an asset? I say this because it has never been easier to create your own asset.

The World Is 10 Years Old

On October 11, 1998, Merrill Lynch ran a full-page ad in several of the larger American newspapers, announcing that the world was just 10 years old. Why just 10 years old? Because it had been approximately ten years since the Berlin Wall had come down. Tearing down the Berlin Wall is the event some economic historians use to mark the end of the Industrial Age and the beginning of the Information Age.

Until the Information Age, most people had to be investors from the outside. Now that the world is just over ten years old, more and more people can invest from the inside, rather than from the outside. When I answered, "Why invest in someone else's Internet company? Why not start your own Internet company?" I meant, "It is now the Information Age, so why not become an insider instead of an outsider?"

Three Ages

In the Agrarian Age, the rich were those who owned a castle that overlooked large tracks of fertile agricultural land. These people were known as the monarchs and the nobles. If you were not born into this group, you were an outsider with very little chance of becoming an insider. The 90/10 rule controlled life. Therefore, the 10% who were in power were there because of marriage, birth, or conquest; the other 90% were serfs or peasants who worked the land but owned nothing.

During the Agrarian Age, if you were a good, hardworking person, you were respected; the idea of being diligent was handed down from parent to child. It was also when the idle rich began to be loathed—90% of the people worked to support the other 10%, who appeared not to be working; that idea was also handed down from parent to child. These ideas continue to be popular and are still handed down from generation to generation.

Then came the Industrial Age and wealth shifted from agricultural land to real estate. Improvements such as buildings, factories, warehouses, mines, and residential homes for the workers were placed on top of the land...improvements. Suddenly, rich fertile agricultural land dropped in value because the wealth shifted to the owners of the buildings upon the land. In fact, an interesting thing happened. Suddenly, rich fertile land became less valuable than rocky land, where farming was difficult. Rocky land suddenly became more valuable because it was cheaper than fertile land. It could also hold taller building such as skyscrapers, or factories, and it often contained resources such as oil, iron, and copper that fueled the Industrial Age. When the shift in ages occurred, many farmers' net worth went down; to maintain their standard of living, they had to work harder and farm more land than before.

It was during the Industrial Age that the "Go to school so you can find a job" idea became popular. In the Agrarian Age, a formal education was not necessary since professions were handed down from parent to child; bakers taught their children to be bakers, and so on. Near the end of this era, the idea of "a" job, or the idea of one job for life, became popularized. You went to school, got that one job for life, worked your way up the corporate ladder or up the union ladder, and when you retired, the company and the government took care of your needs.

In the Industrial Age, those not of noble birth could become rich and powerful. Rags-to-riches stories spurred on the ambitious. Entrepreneurs started with nothing and became billionaires. When Henry Ford decided to mass-produce the automobile, he found some cheap rocky land that farmers did not want near a small town known as Detroit, and an industry was born. The Ford family became, in essence, the new nobility, and anyone around them who did business with them also became the new, rich nobility. New names became as prestigious as those of kings and queens—names such as Rockefeller, Stanford, and Carnegie. People often respected as well as despised them for their great wealth and power.

In the Industrial Age, as during the Agrarian Age, however, only a few controlled most of the wealth. The 90/10 rule still held true, although this time, the 10% was not determined by birth but by determination itself. The 90/10 rule held true simply because it took great effort and coordination as well as a lot of money, people, land, and power to build and control the wealth. For example, to start an automobile company or an oil or mining company is still capital intensive; it takes massive amounts of money, lots of land, and many smart formally educated people to build that type of company. On top of that, you often must get through years of bureaucratic red tape—such as environmental studies, trade agreements, labor laws, and so on—to get such a business off the ground. In the Industrial Age, the standard of living went up for most people, but the control of real wealth continued to remain in the hands of a few. The rules have changed.

The 90/10 Rule Has Changed

When the Berlin Wall came down and the World Wide Web went up, many of the rules changed. One of the most important rules that changed was the 90/10 rule. Although it's likely that only 10% of the population will always control 90% of the money, the access or the opportunity to join that 10% has changed. The World Wide Web has changed what it costs to join the 10%. Today, it does not take being born into a royal family as it did in the Agrarian Age. It does not require massive sums of money, land, and people to join the 10%. The price of admission today is an idea, and ideas are free.

In the Information Age, all it takes is information or ideas to become very, very, wealthy. It is therefore possible for individuals who are financially obscure one year to be on the list of the richest people in the world the next. Such people often fly past individuals who made their money in the ages gone by. College students who have never had a job become billionaires. High school students will surpass their college student counterparts.

In the early 1990's, I remember reading a newspaper article that said, "Many Russian citizens complained that under the Communist rule their creativity was stifled. Now that Communist rule is over, many Russians citizens are finding out that they had no creativity." Personally, I think all of us have a brilliant creative idea that is unique to us, an idea that could be turned into an asset. The problem for the Russians, as it is with many citizens all over the world, is they did not have the advantage of my rich dad's guidance in teaching them to understand the power of the B-I Triangle. I think it is very important that we teach more individuals to be entrepreneurs and how to take their unique ideas and turn them into businesses that create wealth. If we do so, our prosperity will only increase as the Information Age expands around the world.

For the very first time in world history, the 90/10 rule to wealth may no longer apply. No longer does it take money to make money. No longer does it take vast tracts of land or resources to become rich. No longer does it take friends in high places to become rich. No longer does it matter if your relatives came over on the *Mayflower*, it does not matter what university you went to, or what sex, race, or religion you are a part of. Nowadays, all it takes is an idea, and as rich dad has always said, "Money is an idea." For some people, however, the hardest thing to change is an old idea. There is an old truth to the saying "You can't teach an old dog new tricks." I think a more accurate saying is: "You can't teach someone who clings to old ideas new tricks, regardless of if they are young or old."

So when I am asked, "What Internet company would you invest in?" I still reply, "Why not invest in your own Internet company?" I am not necessarily suggesting the askers start an Internet company; all I am doing is asking them to consider the idea, the possibility of starting their own company. In fact, many franchise and network marketing opportunities are now available on the internet. When people simply consider the idea of starting their own B quadrant business, their minds shift from hard work and physical limits to the possibility of unlimited wealth. All it takes is the idea—and we are in the Age of Ideas. I am not suggesting that such people quit their job and leap into starting a company. But I do suggest that they keep their full-time job and consider starting a business part-time.

The Challenge of Old Ideas

In the stock market today you often hear announcers say, "Old economy versus new economy." In many ways, the people being left behind are often people who continue to think in old economy ideas versus new economy ideas.

Rich dad constantly reminded his son and me that money was just an idea. He also warned us to be ever vigilant, to watch our ideas and challenge them when they needed to be challenged. Being young and lacking experience at the time, I never fully realized what he meant. Today, older and wiser, I have tremendous respect for his warning to challenge our old ideas. As rich dad said, "What is right for you today could be wrong for you tomorrow."

I have watched Amazon.com, a company without any profits or any real estate, grow faster and become more valuable in the stock market than established retailers such as Wal-Mart, Sears, J.C. Penny, and K-Mart. A new not-profitable Web retailer is perceived more valuable than Industrial Age retailers with solid profits, years of experience, massive real estate holdings, and more assets than any monarch of old. But the new web retailer is more valuable just because it does not require massive amounts of real estate, money, and people in order to do business. The very things that made Industrial Age retailers valuable in the Industrial Age are making them less valuable in the Information Age. You often hear people say, "The rules have changed." I often wonder what the future holds for these older retailers and their investors as more and more Internet companies slice into profit margins, selling the same products for a lower price. In other words, although Amazon.com is not profitable today, it is cutting into the profit margins of companies that are profitable today. What will that mean to job security, pay raises, and benefits for employees and investor loyalty in the future? And what will happen to the value of real estate? Only time will tell.

I believe that many of the new Internet companies will fold and investors will lose literally billions. They will fold because ultimately, profits and positive cash flow are how a business survives. But many Industrial Age companies will also fold because of price competition from these on-line retailers with no real estate. I recently heard an old-school retailer saying, "We will make shopping an entertaining experience." The problem with such thinking is that making shopping an entertaining experience is expensive, and many shoppers will come to enjoy the experience but will still buy on line for a better price.

I have a dear friend who has been my travel agent for years. However, she has to charge me a service fee to write my tickets these days because the airlines have stopped paying her a commission on ticket sales. She has had to release several of her loyal staff and now worries that I will shift to buying my tickets for a lower price on line. During this same period, a person who is not a travel agent and not regulated by the rules of the travel industry started an online company called Priceline.com. Suddenly, with the idea of auctioning off a perishable product known as an empty airline seat, Priceline.com's founder Jay Walker joins the *Forbes* 400 list of the richest people in the world. He does this in just a few years. So he becomes wealthy, and my dear friend lays off staff and counts on her loyal customers to stay with her because she will work harder and provide better service. I am sure she will do OK, but the business she started years ago as her retirement safety net has now become a full-time job with no assurance that it will be of any value whatever when she's ready to retire.

Things Have Changed

Since it does not take money to make money, then why not go out and make a lot of money? Why not find investors to invest in your idea so you can all become rich? The answer is because often, old ideas are in the way.

As Merrill Lynch announced, "The World Is 10 Years Old." The good news is that it is not too late to change your thinking and begin to catch up if you already have not started. The bad news is that sometimes, the hardest things to change are old ideas. Some of the old ideas that may need to be challenged are the following ideas that have been handed down for generations:

1. "Good, hard-working person." The reality today is that the people who physically work the hardest are paid the least and taxed the most. I am not saying not to work hard. All I am saying is that we need to constantly challenge our older thoughts and maybe rethink new ones. Consider working hard in a part-time business for yourself.

   Today, instead of being in just one quadrant, we need to be very familiar with all four quadrants of the CASHFLOW Quadrant. After all, we're in the Information Age, and working hard at one job for life is an old idea.

2. "The idle rich are lazy." The reality is that the less you are involved physically in your work, the more your chances are of becoming very rich. Again, I am not saying to not work hard. I am suggesting that today, we all need to learn to make money mentally, not just physically. Those who make the most money work the least physically. They work the least because they work for passive income and portfolio income rather than earned income. And as you know by now, all a true investor does is turn earned income into passive and portfolio income.

   In my mind, today's idle rich are therefore not lazy. It is just that their money is working harder than they are. If you want to join the 90/10 crowd, you must learn to make money mentally more than physically.

3. "Go to school and get a job." In the Industrial Age, people retired at age 65 because they were often too worn out to lift tires and put engines into a car on the assembly line. Today, you are technically obsolete and ready for retirement every eighteen months, which is how fast information and technology are doubling. Many people say a student today is technically obsolete immediately upon graduation from school. Now more than ever, my rich dad's advice of "School smarts are important but so are street smarts" is even more relevant. We are a self-learning society, not a society that learns from its parents (as in the Agrarian Age) or from its schools (as in the Industrial Age). Kids are teaching their parents how to use computers, and companies are looking for high-tech kids more than college-degreed middle-aged executives.

To stay ahead of the obsolescence curve, continual learning from school as well as the street is vitally important. When I speak to young people, I advise them to think like professional athletes as well as college professors. Professional athletes know their careers will be over as soon as younger athletes can beat them. College professors know that they will become more valuable the older they get if they continue to study. Both points of view are important today.

Rich Dad's Advice Is Even More True Today

For those of you who have read our first two books, you know the difficulty I went through listening to two different dads and their ideas about money, business, and investing. In 1955, my poor dad kept saying, "Go to school, get good grades, and find a safe and secure job." On the other hand, my rich dad kept saying, "Mind your own business." My poor dad did not think investing was important because he believed "The business and the government are responsible for your retirement and medical needs. A retirement plan is part of your benefit package, and you are entitled to it." My rich would say, "Mind your own business." My poor dad believed in being a good, hard-working man. He would say, "Find a job and work your way up the ladder. Remember that companies do not like people who move around a lot. Companies reward people for seniority and loyalty." My rich dad said, "Mind your own business."

My rich dad believed that you must constantly challenge your ideas. My poor dad believed strongly that his education was valuable and most important. He believed in the idea of right answers and wrong answers. My rich dad believed that the world was changing and we needed to continually keep learning. Rich dad did not believe in right answers or wrong answers. He believed instead in old answers and new answers. He would say, "You cannot help but get older physically, but that does not mean you have to get older mentally. If you want to stay younger longer, just adopt younger ideas. People get old or obsolete because they cling to right answers that are old answers."

Here are some examples of right answers that are old answers:

1. Can humans fly? The correct answer prior to 1900 was "No." Today, it is obvious that humans are flying everywhere, even in space.

2. Is the earth flat? The correct answer in 1492 was "Yes." After Columbus sailed to the New World, the old right answer was obsolete.

3. Is land the basis of all wealth? The answer before the Industrial Age was "Yes." Today, the answer is a resounding "No." It takes an idea and knowledge from the B and I side of the Quadrant to make that idea real. Once you prove you know what to do, the world is full of rich investors looking to give their money to you.

4. Doesn't it take money to make money?" I am most frequently asked this question. The answer is "No." In my opinion, it has always been "No." My answer has always been "It does not take money to make money. It takes information to make as well as to keep money." The difference is that it has become much more obvious that it does not take money or hard labor to make a lot of money.

I don't know what tomorrow will bring; no one does. That is why rich dad's idea of constantly challenging and updating ideas was one the most important ideas he passed on to me.

Today, I see so many of my friends falling behind professionally as well as financially simply because they fail to challenge their own ideas. Their ideas are often right answers that are very very old answers handed down for generations, from one economic era to another. Some high school kids plan on never having jobs. Their plan is to bypass the whole Industrial Age idea of job security and become financially free billionaires instead. This is why I ask people to think about building their own Internet business— either on their own or through a franchise or network marketing company—instead of just looking for one to invest in. Today's thinking process is very different, and it may challenge some very, very, old right ideas. Those old ideas often make the process of change so difficult.

Ideas Do Not Need to Be New, They Just Need to Be Better

Always remember that once you have mastered the guidelines found in the B-I Triangle, you can virtually take nothing and turn it into an asset. When I am asked what my first successful investment was I simply reply, "My comic book business." In other words, I took comic books that were going to be thrown away and created an asset around them, using the principles found in the B-I Triangle. Starbucks did the same thing with a cup of coffee. So ideas do not have to be new and unique, they just have to be better. This has been going on for centuries. In other words, things do not have to be high-tech to be better. In fact, many things that we take for granted today, were very high-tech yesterday.

There are many individuals who spend their lives copying other people's ideas rather than creating their own. I have two acquaintances that make it a practice of taking other people's ideas. Although they may make a lot of money there is a price for taking other people's ideas without their permission or giving credit where credit is due for those ideas. The price these people pay, although they may make a lot of money, is the respect of the people that know they take other people's ideas without permission. There are two people I used to be associated with that I do not associate with today because they make it a practice to take other people's ideas without permission and claim them as their own.

As my rich dad often said, "There is a fine line between copying and stealing. If you are creative, you have to be careful of thieves who steal ideas. They are just as bad as people who burglarize your home." Because there are more people stealing than creating, it becomes ever more important to have an intellectual property attorney on your team protecting your creations.

One of the most important technological changes in the history of the Western World took place during the Crusades, when Christian soldiers came across the Hindu-Arab system of numbers. The Hindu-Arabic system of numbers, so named because the Arabs found this numbering system during their invasion of India, replaced what we call Roman numerals. Few people appreciate the difference this new system of numbers has made upon our lives. The Hindu-Arabic system of numbers allowed people to sail further out to sea with greater accuracy; architecture could be more ambitious; time keeping could more accurate; and the human mind sharpened, and people thought more accurately, abstractly, and critically. It was a major technological change that had a tremendous effect on all of our lives.

The Hindu-Arabic numbering system was not a new idea; it was simply a better idea—and on top of that, it was someone else's idea. Many of the most financially successful people are not necessarily people who have creative ideas; many of them often just copy other people's ideas and turn the idea into millions or even billions of dollars. Fashion designers watch young kids to see what new fashions they are wearing, and then they simply mass-produce those fashions. Bill Gates did not invent the operating system that made him the richest man in the world. He simply bought the system from the computer programmers who did invent it and then licensed their product to IBM. The rest is history. Amazon.com simply took Sam Walton's idea for Wal-Mart and put it on the Internet; Jeff Bezos became rich much more quickly than Sam Walton. In other words, who says you need to have creative ideas to be rich? You just need to be better at the B-I Triangle and at taking ideas and turning them into riches.

Following in Your Parents' Footsteps

Tom Peters, author of *In Search of Excellence* has been saying over and over again, "Job security is dead." Yet, many people continue saying to their children, "Go to school so you can find a secure job." Many people struggle financially simply because they have their parents' ideas about money. Instead of creating assets that bought assets, most of our parents worked for money and then bought liabilities with that money, innocently thinking they were assets. That is why many people go to school and get good jobs because that is what their parents did or advised them to do. Many struggle financially, or live paycheck to paycheck because that is what their parents did. When I teach my investment classes, a very important exercise is for students to compare what they are doing today to what their parents did or advised them to do. Many times, students realize that they are either following closely in their parents' footsteps or are following their parents' advice. At that point, they have the power to question these old ideas that have been running their lives.

If a person truly wants to change, adopting a better idea is often a good idea. My rich dad always said, "If you want to get richer faster, simply look for ideas that are better than the ones you are using today." That is why, to this day, I read biographies of rich entrepreneurs, listen to audiotapes of their lives, and listen to their ideas. As rich dad said, "Ideas need not be new; they just need to be better—and a rich person is always looking for better ideas. Poor people often defend their old ideas or criticize new ones."

Only the Paranoid Survive

Andy Grove, the chairman of Intel, titled his book *Only the Paranoid Survive.* He got that title from Dr. Joseph A. Schumpeter, a former Austrian minister of Finance and Harvard Business School professor. Dr. Schumpeter expressed this idea of only the paranoid surviving in his book *Capitalism, Socialism, and Democracy.* (Dr Schumpeter was the "father" of the modern study of growth and change in economics—dynamics—just as Lord Keynes was the "father" of the study of static economics—statics.) It is Dr. Schumpeter's idea that capitalism is creative destruction; a perpetual cycle of destroying the old, less-efficient product or service and replacing it with new, more-efficient ones. Dr. Schumpeter believed that governments that allow the existence of capitalism, which tears down weaker and less efficient businesses, will survive and thrive. Governments that put up walls to protect the less efficient will fall behind.

My rich dad agreed with Dr. Schumpeter, which is why he was a capitalist. Rich dad challenged Mike and me to constantly challenge our ideas because if we didn't, someone else would. Today, people with old ideas are those who are falling behind the fastest, even though the world is only a little more than ten years old. The world we face today reminds me of the song "The Times They Are A'Changin'." A line from that song goes, "For you'd better start swimming or you'll sink like a stone." Although that song was written approximately 40 years ago, it will reflect the next 40 years more and more. In other words, just because you're rich or poor today does not mean you will be in the near future.

Your Past Success Means Nothing

In the near future, those who do not risk failing will ultimately fail. My poor dad looked upon failure as a noun, and my rich dad looked upon failure as a verb—and that difference made a big difference over a lifetime. In *Future Edge,* Joel Barker wrote, "When a paradigm shifts, everyone goes back to zero. Your past success means nothing." In this fast-changing world, paradigms will be changing faster and faster, and your past successes could mean nothing. In other words, just because you work for a good company today does not ensure that it will be a good company tomorrow. For this reason, Grove chose the title of his book: *Only the Paranoid Survive.*

Even employee benefits are changing. Not only has the Information Age changed the rules of retirement plans, the change from Defined Benefit Pension Plans to Defined Contribution Pension Plans, the change has also affected some employee benefits. Recently a friend who works for an airline said, "It used to be easy to get free flights on airlines, which is one of the benefits of being an airline employee. But today, with airlines auctioning off empty seats on line, the planes are flying full and I find it harder to use a benefit I love."

A Tale of Two Texans

Most of us have heard of Ross Perot and Michael Dell. Both are Texans, and both made their money in the Information Age economy. Yet recently, an article in a financial magazine stated that Perot's wealth has actually gone down substantially while Dell's wealth continues to skyrocket. So what is the difference? It's not the industry, since both are in the Information Industry. I'll let you come to your own conclusions.

The Rules Have Changed

As this book draws to a close, I will leave you with some ideas about the changes that we all face today, changes that were brought on once the Berlin Wall went down and the World Wide Web went up. In his book, *The Lexus and the Olive Tree*, *New York Times* foreign affairs columnist Thomas L. Friedman describes several changes between the Industrial Age and the Information Age. Some of the changes are:

Cold War	Globalization
1. Einstein's E=mc2	Moore's Law

During the Cold War, Einstein's theory of relativity—E=mc2—ruled. In 1945, when the United States dropped the atomic bomb on Japan, America became the economic power of the world and took military dominance away from England. During the 1980s, everyone thought Japan was about to beat the United States economically, and the Nikkei stock market surged. But Japan's period of economic dominance was short lived because the United States redefined itself. The United States redefined itself because it shifted from E=mc2 to Moore's Law. Moore's Law says that the power of the microchip will double every 18 months. Today, America is the leading world power because it leads in technology as well as weaponry.

If America had remained in the weapons race only, we might be a bankrupt nation like the former Soviet Union. When the Berlin Wall came down in 1989, America's capital markets shifted quickly into the Information Age. That freedom to change quickly is the financial power provided by a free capitalistic society. Japan as well as England cannot change that quickly because both countries have too many ties to the days of the feudal system—otherwise known as the monarchy, an Agrarian Age institution. Unconsciously, those countries are waiting for the monarch to lead them. In other words, innovation is often hampered by traditions. That idea is true for individuals as well as nations. As rich dad said,

"Old ideas get in the way of new ideas." I am not suggesting getting rid of old traditions, but rather that we are in the Information Age and so we need expanded ideas as well as old ideas.

Cold War	Globalization
2. Weight of missiles	Speed of modems

When the Berlin Wall came down, E=mc2 changed to Moore's Law. The power in the world shifted from the weight of nuclear warheads to how fast your modem is. The good news is that a fast modem costs a lot less than big missiles; speed matters more than weight.

Cold War	Globalization
3. Two world powers in charge	No one in charge

During the Cold War, there were two superpowers: the United States and the Soviet Union. Today, the web makes the idea of a borderless world and a global economy a reality.

Today, the electronic herd, which is the thousands of fund managers who control great sums of money, have the power to affect world politics more than politicians. If the electronic herd does not like the way a country is managing their financial affairs, they will move their money elsewhere at the speed of light. That is what happened in Malaysia, Thailand, Indonesia, and Korea just a few years ago. The same thing could happen to any country. It is not the politicians that have the power today, as they did in the Industrial Age. In the Information Age, it is the power of global electronic money that often dictates a country's affairs.

Bill Gates crossed the border from the United States to Canada. When the customs agent asked him if he had anything of value to declare, he pulled out a stack of floppy disks wrapped in rubber bands. "This is worth at least $50 billion." The customs agent shrugged, thinking he was talking to a nut and let the richest man in the world pass through the border without paying anything in taxes. The point is that the bundle of floppy disks wrapped in rubber bands was worth at least $50 billion. That bundle of floppy disks was the prototype of Microsoft's Windows 95.

Today, super-rich individuals like Gates often have more money and more influence over the world than many large nations. Such power caused the U.S. government, the strongest government in the world, to take Gates to court for monopolistic practices. When that case started, a friend of mine said, "The frightening thing is that Gates can afford to hire better attorneys than the U.S. government can." That is because the U.S. government is an Industrial Age institution and Gates is an Information Age individual.

Following in this line of thinking, George Soros wrote in *The Crisis of Global Capitalism* that many corporations had much more money and power than many Western nations. That means there are corporations today that could damage the economy of an entire nation just to benefit a few shareholders. That is how much power many corporations have.

In the next few years, many changes, both good and bad, will occur. I believe that capitalism will be unleashed to its fullest extent. Old and obsolete businesses will be wiped out. Competition as well as the need to be cooperative will increase (e.g., there will be mega-mergers such as the one of AOL with Time Warner). Notice that the younger company buys the older one. These changes are all happening because the genie known as technology has been released from the bottle, and information and technology are now cheap enough for everyone to afford.

The Good News

The good news is that for the very first time, the 90/10 rule of the rich no longer needs to apply. It is now possible for more and more people to gain access to the great world of infinite wealth, the wealth found in information—and information is infinite, not restricted as land and resources were in ages gone by. The bad news is that the people who cling to old ideas may be brutalized by the changes upon us as well as by the changes yet to come.

If rich dad were alive, he might say, "This Internet craze is much like the California Gold Rush of the 1850s. The only difference is that you do not need to leave your home to participate in it, so why not participate in it?" He would probably go on to say, "During any economic bonanza, there are only three kinds of people: those who make things happen, those who watch things happen, and those who say, 'What happened?'"

Although I started with Einstein's Theory of Relativity as an obsolete idea from the Cold War, I also think of Einstein as a true visionary. Even then, he recognized an idea that is even truer today—"Imagination is more important than knowledge."

The really good news is that for the first time in history, the Internet gives more and more people the ability to see the other side of the coin if they go there with open eyes.

Taking my ideas and creating an asset with those ideas was one of the best challenges I have undertaken. Although not always successful, with each new venture my skills increased and I could see a world of possibilities that few people see. So the good news is that the Internet makes it easier for more people to access a world of abundance that for centuries has been available to just a few. The internet makes it possible for more people to take their ideas, create assets that buy other assets, and have their financial dreams come true.

We've Only Just Begun

Karen and Richard Carpenter sung a great song titled "We've Only Just Begun." For those of you who think you may be too old to start over again, always remember that Colonel Sanders started all over again at 66. The advantage we have over the Colonel is that we are all now in the Information Age, where how young we are mentally matters, not how old we are physically. After all, Merrill Lynch reported, "The world is 10 years old."

Your Most Important Investment

You are making an important investment by reading this book, regardless of if you agree with it or not, regardless of if you understood it or not, and regardless of if you ever use any of the information or not. In today's ever-changing world, the most important investment you can make is an investment in on-going education and searching for new ideas. So keep searching, keep challenging your old ideas.

One of the main points of this book is that you have the power to create a world of not enough money as well as a world of an abundance of money. In order to create a world of an abundance of money it does require a degree of creativity, a high standard of financial and business literacy, seeking opportunities rather than seeking more security, and to be more cooperative instead of competitive. Rich dad guided me in shaping my thoughts by saying, "You can choose to live in a world of not enough money or too much money. That choice is up to you."

A Final Word

Rich dad's advice to the average investor at the beginning of the book was, "Don't be average." Regardless if you invest to be secure, comfortable, or rich, please have a plan for each level. In the Information Age, an age with faster changes, fewer guarantees, and more opportunities, your financial education and investor knowledge is vitally important. And that is why rich dad's advice of "Don't be average" is vitally important today.

Robert T. Kiyosaki

Robert Kiyosaki, author of *Rich Dad Poor Dad* — *USA Today's* #1 Money Book for two years running and the international runaway best seller — is an investor, entrepreneur and educator whose perspectives on money and investing fly in the face of conventional wisdom.

He has, virtually single-handedly, challenged and changed the way tens of millions, around the world, think about money.

In communicating his point of view on why 'old' advice – get a good job, work hard, save money, get out of debt, invest for the long term, and diversify – is 'bad' (both obsolete and flawed) advice, Robert has earned a reputation for straight talk, irreverence and courage.

Rich Dad Poor Dad ranks as the longest-running best seller on all four of the lists that report to *Publisher's Weekly* – *The New York Times, Business Week, The Wall Street Journal* and *USA Today* – and has held a top spot on the famed *New York Times* list for over five years.

Translated into 51 languages and available in 109 countries, the Rich Dad series has sold over 28 million copies worldwide and has dominated best sellers lists across Asia, Australia, South America, Mexico and Europe. In 2005, Robert was inducted into the Amazon.com Hall of Fame as one of that bookseller's Top 25 Authors. There are currently 13 books in the Rich Dad series.

Robert writes a monthly column – 'Why the Rich Are Getting Richer' – for *Yahoo! Finance* and a monthly column titled 'Rich Returns' for *Entrepreneur* magazine.

Prior to writing *Rich Dad Poor Dad*, Robert created the educational board game *CASHFLOW*® *101* to teach individuals the financial and investment strategies that his rich dad spent years teaching him. It was those same strategies that allowed Robert to retire at age 47.

Today there are more than 3,300 CASHFLOW Clubs – game groups independent of The Rich Dad Company – in cities throughout the world.

Born and raised in Hawaii, Robert Kiyosaki is a fourth-generation Japanese-American. After graduating from college in New York, Robert joined the Marine Corps and served in Vietnam as an officer and helicopter gunship pilot. Following the war, Robert went to work in sales for the Xerox Corporation and, in 1977, started a company that brought the first nylon and Velcro 'surfer wallets' to market. He founded an international education company in 1985 that taught business and investing to tens of thousands of students throughout the world. In 1994 Robert sold his business and, through his investments, was able to retire at the age of 47. During his short-lived retirement he wrote *Rich Dad Poor Dad*. In Robert's words, "We go to school to learn to work hard for money. I write books and create products that teach people how to have money work hard for them."

Sharon L. Lechter

Sharon Lechter has dedicated her professional efforts to the field of education. She is a C.P.A., publishing executive, wife and mother of three.

Sharon graduated Summa Cum Laude with a degree in accounting from Florida State University. She went on to be one of the first women to join the ranks of what was then one of the big eight accounting firms, the CFO of a turn-around company in the computer industry, tax director for a national insurance company and founder and Associate Publisher of the first regional woman's magazine in Wisconsin, all the while maintaining her professional credentials as a CPA.

Her focus quickly changed to education as she watched her own three children grow. It was a struggle to get them to read. They would rather watch TV.

So she joined forces with the inventor of the first electronic "talking book" and helped expand the electronic book industry to the multi-million dollar international market it is today. She remains a pioneer in developing new technologies to bring the book back into children's lives.

"Our current educational system has not been able to keep pace with the global and technological changes in the world today. We must teach our young people the skills, both scholastic and financial, that they will need not only to survive, but to flourish, in the world they face."

As co-author of both *Rich Dad, Poor Dad* and *The CASHFLOW Quadrant* she turns her attention to another failing of the educational system, the total omission of even the fundamentals of finance. *Rich Dad Poor Dad* and *The CASHFLOW Quadrant* are educational tools for anyone interested in bettering their own education and financial position.

CASHFLOW Technologies, Inc.

Robert Kiyosaki, Kim Kiyosaki and Sharon Lechter have joined forces as principals of *CASHFLOW Technologies, Inc.* to produce innovative financial education products.

The Company's mission statement reads:
"To elevate the financial well-being of humanity."

CASHFLOW Technologies, Inc. presents Robert's teaching through products such as *Rich Dad Poor Dad, The CASHFLOW Quadrant* and the patented game board *CASHFLOW* (Patent Number 5,826,878). Additional products are available and under development for people searching for financial education to guide them on their path to financial freedom.

Spiritual Money

Rich Dad said, "Spiritual Money is not about money. It is about doing something that must be done and it disturbs you that no one else is doing it."

Money is a life skill – but we don't teach our children about money in school. We are asking for your help in getting financial education into the hands of interested teachers and school administrators.

RichKidSmartKid.com was created by The Rich Dad Company as a free, innovative and interactive Web site designed to convey key concepts about money and finance in ways that are fun and challenging... and educational for young people in grades K through 12.

Schools around the world can register at www.richkidsmartkid.com to receive a FREE download of our electronic version of CASHFLOW for Kids at School ™.

By taking financial education to our schools we can better prepare our children for the world they will face.

www.richkidsmartkid.com

CASHFLOW Clubs

The Benefits of Joining
a CASHFLOW Club

Invest Time Before You Invest Money

The philosophy of The Rich Dad Company is that there are only two things you can invest: time and money. We recommend you invest some time studying and learning before you invest your money. The CASHFLOW games offer the opportunity to learn and 'invest' with 'play money' – before you invest real money.

Meet New Friends from Around the World

When you visit or join a CASHFLOW Club (or play the CASHFLOW games on line) you'll meet like-minded people – from all over the world. The world is filled with people with negative attitudes, know-it-all attitudes and loser attitudes. The type of person a CASHFLOW Club attracts is a person who is open minded, wants to learn and wants to develop his or her potential.

Have Fun Learning

Learning should be fun! Too often financial education is dull, boring and fear-based. Many financial experts want to educate you on how risky investing is and why you should trust them. That is not the Rich Dad philosophy on learning. We believe that learning should be fun and cooperative and lead you toward becoming smarter about money so you can tell the difference between good and bad financial advice.

Find a CASHFLOW Club near you:
www.richdad.com

Rich Dad's Wisdom:

The Power of Words

Words are gasoline for your brain. If you improve your financial vocabulary, you will become richer and richer. The good news is: words are free. Which proves, once more, that it does not take money to make money. To expand your vocabulary beyond the financial terms in the glossary you'll find on the Rich Dad web site you might consider acquiring a dictionary of financial terms. When you look up financial words on a regular basis (or look the definition of a term you hear but do not understand) you may find yourself becoming richer and richer.

An example of the power of words: When people advise you to get out of debt, do they know what they are talking about?

> *When you buy a bond, you are buying debt. For example, a U.S. T-bill is a bond – an IOU from the U.S. government. So when you buy a bond you are buying debt... debt that is an asset to you and a liability to the government. So debt can be good. Some of the richest people in the world (as well as financial institutions) get richer because they invest in debt.*

When a banker says your house is an asset... ask yourself: Whose asset is it? By definition, assets put money in your pocket and liabilities take money from your pocket. When you look at your bank's financial statement, you can better see whose asset your home really is...

To improve your brain's financial power... improve your financial vocabulary. Words are fuel for your brain!

To learn more about...
Rich Dad's Coaching • Rich Dad's Franchise
Rich Dad Education

Visit: www.richdad.com

FREE AUDIO DOWNLOAD
from Robert Kiyosaki

Visit
www. richdad.com/FIQ
to access your free download

The Rich Dad Company
www.richdad.com
or call 1-800-308-3585